Online Business All-in- For Dummies®

Online Business Models

Goal	Type of Web Site	What to Do
Make big bucks	Sales	Sell items or get lots of paying advertisers
Gain credibility and attention	Marketing	Put your CV and samples of your work online
Turn an interest into a source of income	Hobby/special interest	Invite like-minded people to share your passion, participate in your site, and generate traffic so that you can gain advertisers or customers.

Opening Your Own Online Business in Ten Easy Steps

Step 1: Identify a need

Step 2: Know what you're offering

Step 3: Come up with a virtual business plan

Step 4: Get your act together and set up shop

Step 5: Get help

Step 6: Construct a Web site

Step 7: Process your sales

Step 8: Provide personal service

Step 9: Alert the media and everyone else

Step 10: Review, revise, and improve

Making Your Mark

- Do something you know all about.
- Make a statement.
- Include contact details.
- Give something away for free.
- Be obvious.
- Find your niche.
- Do something you love.

What to Look for In a Web Host

- E-mail addresses
- Domain names
- Web page software
- Multimedia/CGI scripts
- Shopping trolley software
- Automatic data backups
- Site statistics
- Shopping and electronic commerce features

For Dummies: Bestselling Book Series for Beginners

Online Business All-in-One For Dummies®

Cheat Sheet

Finding the Right Computer for Your Online Business

Here are some general terms you need to understand:

- **Gigahertz (GHz) and megahertz (MHz):** This unit of measure indicates how quickly a computer's processor can perform functions. The central processing unit (CPU) of a computer is where the computing work gets done. In general, the higher the processor's internal clock rate, the faster the computer.

- **Random access memory (RAM):** This is the memory that your computer uses to temporarily store information needed to operate programs. RAM is usually expressed in millions of bytes, or megabytes (MB). The more RAM you have, the more programs you can run simultaneously.

- **Synchronous dynamic RAM (SDRAM):** Many ultra-fast computers use some form of SDRAM synchronised with a particular clock rate of a CPU so that a processor can perform more instructions in a given time.

- **Double data rate SDRAM (DDR SDRAM):** This type of SDRAM can dramatically improve the clock rate of a CPU.

- **Auxiliary storage:** This term refers to physical data-storage space on a hard drive, tape, CD-RW, or other device.

- **Virtual memory:** This is a type of memory on your hard drive that your computer can 'borrow' to serve as extra RAM.

- **Network interface card (NIC):** You need this hardware add-on if you have a cable or DSL modem or if you expect to connect your computer to others on a network. Having a NIC usually provides you with Ethernet data transfer to the other computers. (*Ethernet* is a network technology that permits you to send and receive data at very fast speeds.)

Top-Level Domain Names

Domain Name	Primary Use	In Original Six Domains?	Good for Online Businesses?
.biz	Businesses	No	Yes
.com	Companies or individuals involved in commerce	Yes	Yes
.co.uk	Same as above, but for business located in the UK	No	Yes
.gov.uk	Government agencies	Yes	No
.info	Sites that provide information about you, your ideas, or your organisation	No	Yes
.name	Any individual	No	No
.net	Network providers	Yes	Potentially
.org	Not-for-profit organisations	Yes	No
.pro	Licensed professionals	No	Potentially

Online Business

ALL-IN-ONE

FOR

DUMMIES®

Online Business

ALL-IN-ONE

FOR

DUMMIES®

By Colin Barrow, Paul Barrow, Gregory Brooks,
Ben Carter, Frank Catalano, Marsha Collier,
Peter Economy, Lita Epstein, Alexander Hiam,
Greg Holden, Jane Hoskyn, Bob Nelson,
Steven D. Peterson, Richard Pettinger,
Bud E. Smith, Craig Smith, and Paul Tiffany

Edited by Dan Matthews

BICENTENNIAL
1807
WILEY
2007
BICENTENNIAL

John Wiley & Sons, Ltd

Online Business All-in-One For Dummies®

Published by
John Wiley & Sons, Ltd
The Atrium
Southern Gate
Chichester
West Sussex
PO19 8SQ
England

E-mail (for orders and customer service enquires): cs-books@wiley.co.uk

Visit our Home Page on www.wiley.com

For general information on our other products and services, please contact our Customer Care Department within the U.S. at 800-762-2974, outside the U.S. at 317-572-3993, or fax 317-572-4002.

For technical support, please visit www.wiley.com/techsupport.

Wiley also publishes its books in a variety of electronic formats. Some content that appears in print may not be available in electronic books.

British Library Cataloguing in Publication Data: A catalogue record for this book is available from the British Library.

ISBN: 978-0-470-51646-1

Printed and bound in Great Britain by Bell & Bain Ltd, Glasgow

10 9 8 7 6 5 4 3 2 1

WILEY

About the Authors

Dan Matthews is Online Publisher of Caspian Publishing, which produces magazines, Web sites, and events for an audience of UK entrepreneurs. Primarily working on realbusiness.co.uk, Dan writes about stellar business success stories as well as up-and-coming start-ups. He was previously Group Online Editor of Crimson Business Publishing, with responsibility for sites such as startups.co.uk and growingbusiness.co.uk. He has contributed to a range of business magazines, including being contributing editor of *Real Business Magazine* and *Growing Business Magazine*.

Colin Barrow is Head of the Enterprise Group at Cranfield School of Management, where he teaches entrepreneurship on the MBA and other programmes. He is also a visiting professor at business schools in the US, Asia, France, and Austria. His books on entrepreneurship and small business have been translated into fifteen languages including Russian and Chinese. He worked with Microsoft to incorporate the business planning model used in his teaching programmes into the software programme, Microsoft Business Planner, now bundled with Office. He is a regular contributor to newspapers, periodicals and academic journals such as the *Financial Times*, *The Guardian*, *Management Today*, and the *International Small Business Journal*. Thousands of students have passed through Colin's start-up and business growth programmes, raising millions in new capital and going on to run successful and thriving enterprises. He is a non-executive director of two venture capital funds, on the board of several small businesses, and serves on a number of Government Task Forces.

Paul Barrow trained and qualified as a Chartered Accountant with Deloitte & Touche before obtaining his MBA at Bradford University. As a senior consultant with Ernst & Young he was responsible for managing and delivering quality consulting assignments. During the mid-1980s, he was Investment Review Director for a UK venture capital business. In 1998, as Group Finance Director of Adval Group plc, he was part of the team which took their software company on to the Alternative Investment Market. Adval specialises in providing multimedia training – both bespoke and generic. Paul has also been a director of several owner-managed businesses, and has started up and sold other businesses. He currently works with businesses as diverse as software, turkey farming, and food retailing. Paul is a Visiting Fellow at Cranfield University where he teaches on the Business Growth Programme. This programme is designed specifically for owner managers who want to grow and improve their businesses. He also teaches at Warwick University and Oxford Brookes on similar programmes. Paul has written several other business books: *The Business Plan Workbook* and *Raising Finance* (both Kogan Page/Sunday Times); *The Best Laid Business Plans* and *The Bottom Line* (both Virgin Books). All these books are aimed at owner managers trying to grow and improve their businesses.

Greg Brooks is a freelance journalist who has written for a number of broadcasters, newspapers, and magazines including Channel 4, *The Guardian*, *Marketing*, *New Media Age* and *Marketing Direct*. He has also carried out corporate ghostwriting and consultancy duties for a number of blue-chip clients around the globe. As part of his role as an industry commentator, he has spoken to organisations such as the BBC about how to communicate with consumers and journalists using interactive channels.

Ben Carter runs his own digital agency helping famous and not so famous brands launch marketing initiatives to capitalise on the changing media landscape and ever-changing consumer behaviour. Current clients of Ben Carter & Associates include npower and AOL, and the company has also provided consultancy services for several major UK-based blue-chip companies. Before setting up BCA, Ben worked as a business journalist for eight years, covering the UK's media and marketing sectors and most recently was News Editor of *Marketing* magazine. He has also freelanced for a number of national newspapers including *The Times* and *The Guardian* and is used regularly as a commentator on the booming digital economy by different media, including the BBC, *The Independent*, and CNN.

Frank Catalano is a veteran marketing consultant and analyst. He's the principal of Catalano Consulting, a strategic marketing firm advising Internet and technology companies. His consulting assignments include stints as Managing Director for PC Data's Internet Monitoring Division, VP Marketing for McGraw-Hill Home Interactive, VP Marketing for iCopyright, and VP Marketing for Apex Computer. He also was a marketing manager for Egghead Software and for the Apple Programmers and Developers Association. When not consulting, Frank provides tech industry analysis and commentary for KCPQ-TV Fox Seattle and is the author of the long-running Byte Me columns for *Seattle Weekly* and others. His essays and short fiction about technology have appeared in a wide variety of print and broadcast media, including ClickZ, Omni, Inside Multimedia, and Analog.

Marsha Collier spends most of her time on eBay. She loves buying and selling – she's a PowerSeller – as well as meeting eBay users from around the world. As a columnist, and author of several best-selling books on eBay, a television and radio expert, and a lecturer, she shares her knowledge of eBay with millions of online shoppers. Thousands of eBay fans also read her monthly newsletter, *Cool eBay Tools*, to keep up with changes on the site. Out of college, Marsha worked in fashion advertising for the *Miami Herald* and then as special projects manager for the *Los Angeles Daily News*. She also founded a home-based advertising and marketing business. Her successful business, the Collier Company, Inc., was featured in *Entrepreneur* magazine in 1985, and in 1990, Marsha's company received the Small Business of the Year award from her California State Assemblyman and the Northridge Chamber of Commerce. More than anything, Marsha loves a great deal. That's what drew her to eBay in 1996, and that's what keeps her busy on the site now. She buys everything from light bulbs to parts for her vintage Corvette to designer dresses.

Peter Economy is associate editor of *Leader to Leader*, the award-winning magazine of the Peter F. Drucker Foundation for Nonprofit Leadership, and author of numerous books. Peter combines his writing expertise with more than 15 years of management experience to provide his readers with solid, hands-on information and advice. He received his bachelor's degree (with majors in economics and human biology) from Stanford University and his MBA at the Edinburgh Business School. Visit Peter at his Web site: www.petereconomy.com.

Lita Epstein, who earned her MBA from Emory University's Goizueta Business School, enjoys helping people develop good financial, investing, and tax planning skills. While getting her MBS, Lita worked as a teaching assistant for the financial accounting department and ran the accounting lab. After completing her MBA, she managed finances for a small nonprofit organization and for the facilities management section of a large medical clinic. She designs and teaches online courses on topics such as investing for retirement, getting ready for tax time, and finance and investing for women. She's written more than ten books, including *Trading For Dummies* (Wiley) and *Streetwise Retirement Planning*. Lita was the content director for a financial services Web site, MostChoice.com, and managed the Web site Investing for Women. As a Congressional press secretary, Lita gained firsthand knowledge about how to work within and around the Federal bureaucracy, which gives her great insight into how government programmes work. In the past, Lita has been a daily newspaper reporter, magazine editor, and fundraiser for the international activities of former US President Jimmy Carter through The Carter Center.

Alex Hiam is a consultant, corporate trainer, and public speaker with 20 years of experience in marketing, sales, and corporate communications. He is the director of Insights, which includes a division called Insights for Marketing that offers a wide range of services for supporting and training in sales, customer service, planning, and management. His firm is also active in developing the next generation of leaders in the workplace through its Insights for Training & Development. Alex has an MBA in marketing and strategic planning from the Haas School at U.C. Berkeley and an undergraduate degree from Harvard. He has worked as marketing manager for both smaller high-tech firms and a *Fortune* 100 company, and did a stint as a professor of marketing at the business school at U. Mass. Amherst. Alex is the co-author of the best-seller, *The Portable MBA in Marketing* (Wiley) as well as *The Vest-Pocket CEO* and numerous other books and training programs. He has consulted to a wide range of companies and not-for-profit and government agencies, from General Motors and Volvo to HeathEast and the U.S. Army (a fuller list of clients is posted at www.insightsformarketing.com). Alex is also the author of a companion volume to this book, the *Marketing Kit For Dummies* (Wiley), which includes more detailed coverage of many of the hands-on topics involved in creating great advertising, direct mail letters, Web sites, publicity campaigns, and marketing plans. On the CD that comes with the *Marketing Kit For Dummies*, you'll find forms, checklists, and templates that may be of use to you. Also, Alex maintains an extensive Web site of resources that he organised to support the chapters in the book.

Greg Holden started a small business called Stylus Media, which is a group of editorial, design, and computer professionals who produce both print and electronic publications. The company gets its name from a recording stylus that reads the traces left on a disk by voices or instruments and translates those signals into electronic data that can be amplified and enjoyed by many. He has been self-employed for the past ten years. He is an avid user of eBay, both as a buyer and seller, and he recently started his own blog. One of the ways Greg enjoys communicating is through explaining technical subjects in nontechnical language. The first edition of *Starting an Online Business For Dummies* was the ninth of his more than 30 computer books. He also authored *eBay PowerUser's Bible* for Wiley Publishing. Over the years, Greg has been a contributing editor of *Computer Currents* magazine, where he writes a monthly column. He also contributes to *PC World* and the University of Illinois at Chicago alumni magazine. Other projects have included preparing documentation for an electronics catalogue company in Chicago and creating online courses on Windows 2000 and Microsoft Word 2000. Greg balances his technical expertise and his entrepreneurial experience with his love of literature. He received an MA in English from the University of Illinois at Chicago and also writes general interest books, short stories, and poetry. Among his editing assignments is the monthly newsletter for his daughters' grade school. After graduating from college, Greg became a reporter for his hometown newspaper. Working at the publications office at the University of Chicago was his next job, and it was there that he started to use computers. He discovered, as the technology became available, that he loved desktop publishing (with the Macintosh and LaserWriter) and, later on, the World Wide Web. Greg loves to travel, but since his two daughters were born, he hasn't been able to get around much. He was able to translate his experiences into a book called *Karma Kids: Answering Everyday Parenting Questions with Buddhist Wisdom.* However, through the Web, he enjoys traveling vicariously and meeting people online. He lives with his family in an old house in Chicago that he has been rehabbing for – well, for many years now. He is a collector of objects such as pens, cameras, radios, and hats. He is always looking for things to take apart so that he can see how they work and fix them up. Many of the same skills prove useful in creating and maintaining Web pages. He is an active member of Jewel Heart, a Tibetan Buddhist meditation and study group based in Ann Arbor, Michigan.

Jane Hoskyn has been a journalist for 15 years. After a number of years writing features for leading UK lifestyle magazines including *FHM* and *Cosmopolitan*, she joined IPC Media's *Web User* magazine as Features Editor. In 2003 Jane was named IPC Commissioning Editor of the Year, and a year later she returned to the successful freelance writing and editing career that spans publications from *Woman & Home* to *Loaded.*

Bob Nelson, PhD, is founder and president of Nelson Motivation, Inc., a management training and products firm headquartered in San Diego, California. As a practising manager, researcher, and best-selling author, Bob is an internationally recognised expert in the areas of employee motivation, recognition and rewards, productivity and performance improvement, and leadership. Bob has published 20 books and sold more than 2.5 million books on management, which have been translated into some 20 languages. He earned his BA in communications from Macalester College, his MBA in organisational behavior from UC Berkeley, and his PhD in management from the Peter F. Drucker Graduate Management Center of the Claremont Graduate University. Visit his Web site at www.nelson-motivation.com or contact Bob directly at BobRewards@aol.com.

Steven Peterson is a senior partner and founder of Home Planet Technologies, a management training company specializing in hands-on software tools designed to enhance business strategy, business planning, and general management skills. He is the creator and designer of The Protean Strategist, a state of the art computer-based business simulation. The simulation creates a dynamic business environment where participants run companies and compete against each other in a fast-changing marketplace. Each management team in the simulation is responsible for developing its own strategy, business plan, and program to make the plan work. Steven has used The Protean Strategist to add excitement, hands-on experience, teamwork, and a competitive challenge to corporate training programs around the world. He has worked with both large and small companies on products and services in industries ranging from telecommunications to financial services and from high technology to consumer goods and industrial equipment. He can be reached by e-mail at peterson@HomePlanetTech.com. When he's not planning his own business, Steven is planning to remodel his 80-year old house or to redesign the garden. And he confesses that of the three, the garden proves to be the most difficult. Steven holds advanced degrees in mathematics and physics, receiving his doctorate from Cornell University. He teaches part-time at the Haas School of Business, University of California at Berkeley, and lives in the Bay Area with his long-time companion, Peter, and their long-lived canine, Jake.

Richard Pettinger (BA, MBA, DipMktg) has taught at University College London since 1989, where he is senior lecturer in management. He teaches on the foundation courses, organisational change, and construction marketing courses. He has also taught strategic and operations management; the management of change; human resource management; and leadership to a wide range of undergraduate, postgraduate, professional, and international students. Richard is also enhancing and developing Management Studies Centre activities and courses, including the directorship of the new Information Management for Business course. Since 2005, Richard has been a visiting professor at the Jagiellonian Business School, Krakow, teaching strategic management and developing a common UCL/Jagiellonian syllabus in strategic management and organisational change. Richard is the author of over thirty business and management books and textbooks, and also writes journal, conference, and study papers.

Bud Smith's experience is split between the technical and marketing sides of the computer and Internet industries. Bud was a short-order cook before starting in the computer industry at the age of 21. He was a data entry supervisor, programmer, and technical writer before working as a competitive analyst and QuickTime marketing manager at Apple Computer. He has been a full-time writer and has joined Frank in several consulting projects. Bud is currently Director of Marketing at AllPublish, a venture-funded Silicon Valley startup. Bud's writing experience is all on the nonfiction side and includes computer and medical articles as well as a dozen computer books.

Craig Smith is the editor of *Marketing*, the UK's highest circulation weekly magazine, and PPA Weekly Business Magazine of the Year, serving the marketing and advertising industries. He has worked as a business journalist for 18 years and is a regular commentator on marketing issues to the national press and broadcast media. Craig works closely with industry trade bodies the Association of Publishing Agencies and Business in the Community to promote best practice in the areas of customer magazines and cause related marketing.

Paul Tiffany is the managing director of Paul Tiffany & Associates, a Santa Rosa, California-based firm that has offered management training and consulting services to organizations throughout the world for the past fifteen years. In addition, he has taught business planning courses at some of the top business schools in the country, including Stanford, Wharton, and The Haas School of Business at the University of California, Berkeley, where he currently serves as adjunct professor. He holds an MBA from Harvard University and a PhD from Berkeley. He can be reached by e-mail at tiffany@haas.berkeley.edu.

Publisher's Acknowledgements

We're proud of this book; please send us your comments through our Dummies online registration form located at www.dummies.com/register/.

Some of the people who helped bring this book to market include the following:

Media Development

Project Editor: Daniel Mersey

Content Editor: Steve Edwards

Commissioning Editor: Samantha Clapp

Executive Editor: Jason Dunne

Executive Project Editor: Martin Tribe

Art Consultant: Steve Hill

Screenshots: These materials have been reproduced with the permission of eBay Inc. Copyright © eBay Inc. All Rights Reserved.

Cover Photos: © Getty Images/Ciaran Griffin

Cartoons: Ed McLachlan

Composition Services

Project Coordinator: Erin Smith

Layout and Graphics: Claudia Bell, Stacie Brooks, Carl Byers, Stephanie D. Jumper

Proofreaders: John Greenough, Todd Lothery

Indexer: Galen Schroeder

Publishing and Editorial for Consumer Dummies

Diane Graves Steele, Vice President and Publisher, Consumer Dummies

Joyce Pepple, Acquisitions Director, Consumer Dummies

Kristin A. Cocks, Product Development Director, Consumer Dummies

Michael Spring, Vice President and Publisher, Travel

Kelly Regan, Editorial Director, Travel

Publishing for Technology Dummies

Andy Cummings, Vice President and Publisher, Dummies Technology/General User

Composition Services

Gerry Fahey, Vice President of Production Services

Debbie Stailey, Director of Composition Services

Contents at a Glance

Table of Contents

Introduction

● ●

*W*elcome to *Online Business All-in-One For Dummies*, your launch pad to understanding the fundamentals of setting up, establishing, running, and growing a successful business on the Internet.

This book draws together information on the key areas of successful business – planning, funding, researching customers, competitors and the industry, setting up, structuring and designing a Web site, financial implications and considerations involved in setting up a Web site, consulting expert advice and services, establishing an online presence, secure online trading, using new business tools and technology, understanding and taking advantage of Web 2.0, online advertising and promotion, using eBay as a business tool, handling customers and staff, bookkeeping, accounting and tax, and planning for growth– all in one bumper guide. Phew!

With help from this book, you can transform a simple idea into your very own online business empire.

About This Book

This book is aimed at those considering, interested in or aspiring to start up a business or expand an existing one online. It brings together the essential elements of knowledge that are a prerequisite to understanding the online business world.

Online Business All-In-One For Dummies draws on advice from several other For Dummies books, which you may wish to check out for more in-depth coverage of certain topics (all published by Wiley):

- ✔ *Bookkeeping For Dummies* (Paul Barrow and Lita Epstein)
- ✔ *Business Plans For Dummies* (Paul Tiffany and Steven D. Peterson, adapted by Colin Barrow)
- ✔ *Digital Marketing For Dummies* (Ben Carter, Gregory Brooks, Frank Catalano, Bud E. Smith)
- ✔ *eBay.co.uk For Dummies* (Jane Hoskyn and Marsha Collier)
- ✔ *Managing For Dummies* (Richard Pettinger, Bob Nelson, Peter Economy)

✔ *Marketing For Dummies* (Craig Smith and Alexander Hiam)

✔ *Starting A Business For Dummies* (Colin Barrow)

✔ *Starting A Business on eBay.co.uk For Dummies* (Dan Matthews and Marsha Collier)

✔ *Starting And Running An Online Business For Dummies* (Dan Matthews and Greg Holden)

Conventions Used in This Book

To make your reading experience easier and to alert you to key words or points, we use certain conventions in this book:

✔ **In This Chapter lists:** Chapters start with a list of the topics that we cover in that chapter. This list represents a kind of table of contents in miniature.

✔ **Numbered lists:** When you see a numbered list, follow the steps in a specific order to accomplish the task.

✔ **Bulleted lists:** Bulleted lists (like this one) indicate things that you can do in any order or list related bits of information.

✔ **Italics:** *Italics* are used to introduce new terms and explain what they mean.

✔ **Web addresses:** When we describe activities or sites of interest on the World Wide Web, we include the address, or Uniform Resource Locator (URL), in a special typeface like this: http://www.wiley.com/. Because popular Web browsers such as Microsoft Internet Explorer and Mozilla Firefox don't require you to enter the entire URL, this book uses the shortened addresses. For example, if you want to connect to the Wiley site, you can get there by simply entering the following in your browser's Go To or Address bar: www.wiley.co.uk.

Don't be surprised if your browser can't find an Internet address you type or if a Web page that's depicted in this book no longer looks the same. Although the sites were current when the book was written, Web addresses (and sites themselves) can be pretty fickle. Try looking for a missing site by using an Internet search engine. Or try shortening the address by deleting everything after the .co.uk (or .com or .org.uk).

Foolish Assumptions

This book brings together the essential elements of knowledge that are essential for understanding the world of online business. As a consequence, to keep the book down to a reasonable number of pages, we've made a few assumptions about you (we hope you don't mind!). Maybe you're:

✔ A budding online entrepreneur with a great idea for a world-beating product that no one has ever thought of but everyone will need desperately once you hang out your e-sign.

✔ A small business owner seeking a comprehensive reference guide to making your business work on the Internet.

✔ An aspiring business owner who's read the stories about everyone else earning a fortune online and recognised the benefits of an online presence, but you're not sure where to start.

How This Book Is Organized

We've divided _Online Business All-in-One For Dummies_ into seven separate books. This section explains what you'll find out about in each one of these books. Each book is broken into chapters tackling key aspects of that part of the online business world.

Book 1: E-Business 101

This book is the place to look if you're trying to work out what it takes to set up an online business. Providing tips for setting up a business and preparing a business plan, this book also shows you how to set up your business in ten easy steps.

Book 11: Setting Up Your Web Site

This book is your guide to the technical side of running an online business. Talking you through the right equipment and finding the best Web host, to structuring your Web site and keeping it secure, in this book you should find answers to all of your basic computer and Web-based queries.

Book III: Getting Known E-asily

Having a great business idea and snazzy Web site is one thing, getting customers and making money is another! This book helps you to market your wares, scope out the opposition, make the most of search engines, and use online PR to your advantage. This is the book showing you how to get known about!

Book IV: Keeping Business Ticking Over

An online business needs to function in the same way as any other business in terms of operational management and staying on the right side of the law. This book gives you the lowdown on looking after your accounts, your sales, and other facts and figures. Staying on top of these gives your business a greater chance of success and longevity.

Book V: Handling Customers and Staff

This book is the 'People Book'! Any business needs people to survive and flourish – certainly in terms of customers, but (as you grow) in terms of staff, too. The chapters in this book show you how to keep your staff happy and your customers coming back.

Book VI: Using eBay.co.uk

Using eBay.co.uk is one of the easiest ways to start up an online business, so we've dedicated this whole book to showing you how to get the best from this Web site.

Book VII: Understanding Web 2.0

Web 2.0 offers the online business owner exciting new opportunities, so we wrap up with a look at how new technology can help now or in the future.

Icons Used in This Book

When you flick through this book, you'll notice some snazzy little icons in the margin. These pick out key aspects of starting and running a business, and present you with important nuggets of information:

Want to get ahead in online business? Check out the text highlighted by this icon to pick up some sage advice.

They say elephants never forget, and nor should good online business owners. This icon focuses on key information you should never be without.

Running an online business isn't without its dangers – be they security, financial, or legal – and the text beside this icon points out common pitfalls to avoid like the plague.

This icon calls your attention to interviews we conducted with online entrepreneurs who provide tips and instructions for running an online business.

Where to Go from Here

We've made this book into an easy-to-use reference tool that you should be comfortable with, no matter what your level of experience. You can use this book in a couple of ways: as a cover-to-cover read or as a reference for when you run into problems or need inspiration. Feel free to skip straight to the chapters that interest you. You don't have to scour each chapter methodically from beginning to end to find what you want. The Web doesn't work that way, and neither does this book!

If you're just starting out and need to do some essential business planning, see Part I. Want to find out how to accept online payments? Check out Part V. If you're not yet sure where to start, check out the table of contents to get an idea of what you'll read about where in the book. Start where it suits you and come back later for more.

Book I
E-Business 101

'You may have spotted a gap in the market, but . . .'

In this book . . .

This book walks you through the basics of setting up an online business. From working out if you've got what it takes to start up and run a successful online business, and walking through the basics of setting yourself up in business online, we conclude this book with a guide to opening your own business in ten simple steps. What are you waiting for?

Here are the contents of Book I at a glance:

Chapter 1

Can You Do the Business?

In This Chapter

▶ Understanding if being your own boss is right for you

▶ Taking a skills inventory to identify any gaps

*I*t's fairly clear why governments are so keen to foster entrepreneurship. New businesses create jobs for individuals and increased prosperity for nations, which are both primary goals for any government. If those new firms don't throw people out of work when recessions start to bite, supporting them becomes doubly attractive.

But people, you included, don't start businesses or grow existing ones simply to please politicians or to give their neighbours employment. There are many reasons for considering self-employment. Most people are attracted by the idea of escaping the daily grind of working for someone else and being in charge of their own destiny. But despite the many potential benefits there are real challenges and problems, and self-employment is not a realistic career option for everyone.

The questions you need to ask yourself are: – Can I do it? Am I really the entrepreneurial type? What are my motivations and aims? How do I find the right business for me? This chapter can help you discover the answers to these questions.

Deciding What You Want from a Business

See whether you relate to any of the following most common reasons people give for starting up in business.

- ✔ Being able to make your own decisions
- ✔ Having a business to leave to your children
- ✔ Creating employment for the family

- ✔ Being able to capitalise on specialist skills
- ✔ Earning your own money when you want
- ✔ Having flexible working hours
- ✔ Wanting to take a calculated risk
- ✔ Reducing stress and worry
- ✔ Having satisfaction of creating something truly of your own
- ✔ Being your own boss
- ✔ Working without having to rely on others

The two central themes connecting all these reasons seem to revolve around gaining personal satisfaction, which can be seen as making work as much fun as any other aspect of life, and creating wealth, which is essential if an enterprise is going to last any length of time.

Even when your personality fits and your goals are realistic, you have to make sure that the business you're starting is a good fit for your abilities.

The following sections explore each of these reasons in more detail.

Gaining personal satisfaction (or, entrepreneurs just wanna have fun)

No one particularly enjoys being told what to do and where and when to do it. Working for someone else's organisation brings all those disadvantages.

The only person to blame if your job is boring, repetitive, or takes up time that should perhaps be spent with family and friends is yourself.

Another source of personal satisfaction comes from the ability to 'do things my way'. Employees are constantly puzzled and often irritated by the decisions their bosses impose on them. All too often managers in big firms say that they would never spend their own money in the manner they are encouraged or instructed to by the powers that be. Managers and subordinates alike feel constrained by company policy, which seems to set out arbitrary standards for dealing with customers and employees in the same way.

The high failure rate for new businesses would suggest that some people are seduced by the glamour of starting up on their own, when they might be more successful and more contented in some other line of endeavour.

Running your own firm allows you to do things in a way that you think the market, and your employees, believe to be right for the time. Until, of course, you become big and successful yourself!

Making money

Apart from winning the lottery, starting your own business is the only possible way to achieve full financial independence. That is not to say it is not without risks. In truth most people who work for themselves do not become mega rich. But many do and many more become far wealthier than they would probably have become working for someone else.

You can also earn money working at your own pace when you want to and even help your family to make some money too.

Running your own business means taking more risks than you do if you're working for someone else. If the business fails, you could stand to lose far more than your job. If, like most owner managers, you opt for *sole trader status*, that is someone working usually on their own without forming a limited company, you could end up personally liable for any business debts incurred. This could mean having to sell up your home and other assets to meet your obligations. In these circumstances, not only will all your hard work have been to no avail, you could end up worse off than when you started. Also winding up a business is far from fun or personally satisfying.

Running a business is never easy and on an hourly wage basis is often less well paid than working for someone else. So why do people set up their own business, and do your aims seem realistic in that context?

If you want to strike out on your own because you think you'll make millions, consider this: on an hourly wage basis, you'll probably make less than you do now. And, if you think, 'well, at least I'll be working for myself', consider for how long. The harsh reality is that most start-ups fail.

We don't want to discourage you, just to apply a reality check. The truth is that running your own business is hard work that often doesn't pay well at first. You have to be OK with those facts in order to have a chance of success.

Assessing Yourself

Business is not just about ideas or about market opportunities. Business is about people too, and at the outset it is mostly about you. You need to make really sure that you have the temperament to run your own business and the expertise and understanding required for the type of business you have in mind to start.

The test at the end of this section requires no revision or preparation. You will find out the truth about yourself and whether or not running a business is a great career option or a potential disaster.

Discovering your entrepreneurial attributes

The business founder is frequently seen as someone who is bursting with new ideas, highly enthusiastic, hyperactive, and insatiably curious. But the more you try to create a clear picture of the typical small business founder, the fuzzier that picture becomes. Many efforts have been made to define the characteristics of people who are best suited to becoming small business founders with limited success. In fact, the most reliable indicator that a person is likely to start a business is whether he or she has a parent or sibling who runs a business – such people are highly likely to start businesses themselves.

That being said, some fairly broad characteristics are generally accepted as being desirable, if not mandatory. Check whether you recognise yourself in the following list of entrepreneurial traits:

- ✔ **Totally committed:** You must have complete faith in your business idea. That's the only way that you can convince all the doubters that you are bound to meet on the way. But blind faith is not enough. That commitment has to be backed up with a sound business strategy.

- ✔ **Hard working:** Hard work should not be confused with long hours. There will be times when an owner-manager has to put in 18-hour days, but that should not be the norm. But even if you do work long hours and enjoy them, that's fine. Enthusiasts can be very productive. Workaholics, on the other hand, have a negative kind of black, addictive driven quality where outputs (results) become less important than inputs. This type of hard work is counterproductive. Hard work means sticking at a task however difficult until it is completed. It means hitting deadlines even when you are dead-beat. It means doing some things you don't enjoy much to work your way through to the activities that are really what you enjoy most.

- ✔ **Accepting of uncertainty:** An essential characteristic of someone starting a business is a willingness to make decisions and to take risks. This does not mean gambling on hunches. It means carefully calculating the odds and deciding which risks to take and when to take them.

  Managers in big business tend to seek to minimise risk by delaying decisions until every possible fact is known. There is a feeling that to work without all the facts is not prudent or desirable. Entrepreneurs, on the other hand, know that by the time the fog of uncertainty has been completely lifted too many people will be able to spot the opportunity clearly. In point of fact an entrepreneur would usually only be interested in a decision that involved accepting a degree of uncertainty and would welcome, and on occasion even relish, that position.

✔ **Healthy:** Apart from being able to put in long days, the successful small business owner needs to be on-the-spot to manage the firm every day. Owners are the essential lubricant that keeps the wheels of the small business turning. They have to plug any gaps caused either by other people's sickness or because they just can't afford to employ anyone else for that particular job. They themselves cannot afford the luxury of sick leave. Even a week or so's holiday would be viewed as something of a luxury in the early years of a business life.

✔ **Self-disciplined:** The owner manager needs strong personal discipline to keep him or her and the business on the schedule the plan calls for. This is the drumbeat that sets the timing for everything in the firm. Get that wrong and wrong signals are sent to every part of the business, both inside and out.

One of the most common pitfalls for the novice business man or woman is failing to recognise the difference between cash and profit. Cash can make people feel wealthy and if it results in a relaxed attitude to corporate status symbols such as cars and luxury office fittings, then failure is just around the corner.

✔ **Innovative:** Most people recognise innovation as the most distinctive trait of business founders. They tend to tackle the unknown; they do things in new and difficult ways; they weave old ideas into new patterns. But they go beyond innovation itself and carry their concept to market rather than remain in an ivory tower.

✔ **Well-rounded:** Small business founders are rarely geniuses. There are nearly always people in their business who have more competence, in one field, than they could ever aspire to. But they have a wide range of ability and a willingness to turn their hands to anything that has to be done to make the venture succeed. They can usually make the product, market it, and count the money, but above all they have the self-confidence that lets them move comfortably through uncharted waters.

✔ **Driven to succeed:** Business founders need to be results-oriented. Successful people set themselves goals and get pleasure out of trying to achieve them as quickly as possible and then move on to the next goal. This restlessness is very characteristic.

Taking a skills and knowledge inventory

The self-evaluation questions in this section probe only those areas that you can control or affect. Do the evaluation and get one or two people who know you well to rate you too.

A high score is not a guarantee of success and a poor score does not necessarily bode failure. But the combination of answers should throw up some things to consider carefully before taking the plunge.

If the statement is rarely true, score 1; if usually true, score 2; and if nearly always true, score 3.

1. I know my personal and business objectives.
2. I get tasks accomplished quickly.
3. I can change direction quickly if market conditions alter.
4. I enjoy being responsible for getting things done.
5. I like working alone and making my own decisions.
6. Risky situations don't alarm me.
7. I can face uncertainty easily.
8. I can sell my business ideas and myself.
9. I haven't had a day off sick for years.
10. I can set my own goals and targets and then get on with achieving them.
11. My family is right behind me in this venture – and they know it will mean long hours and hard work.
12. I welcome criticism – there is always something useful to learn from others.
13. I can pick the right people to work for me.
14. I am energetic and enthusiastic.
15. I don't waste time.

A score of 30 plus is good; 20–30 is fair; below 20 is poor. A high score won't guarantee success but a low one should cause a major re-think.

Working out a business idea that's right for you

Take some time to do a simple exercise that can help you decide what type of business is a good match with your abilities. Take a sheet of paper and draw up two columns. In the left-hand column, list all your hobbies, interests, and skills. In the right-hand column, translate those interests into possible business ideas. Table 1-1 shows an example of such a list.

Table 1-1	Matching a Business Idea to Your Skills
Interest/skills	*Business Ideas*
Cars	car dealer/repair garage/home tuning service
Cooking	restaurant/home catering service/bakery shop providing produce for freezer outlets
Gardening	supplier of produce to flower or vegetable shop/running a nursery/running a garden centre/landscape design
Using a computer	typing authors' manuscripts from home/typing back-up service for busy local companies/running a secretarial agency/Web design/book-keeping service

Having done this exercise, balance the possibilities against the criteria important to you in starting a business.

Figuring out what you're willing to invest

I'm not just talking about money here. How much are you willing to invest of your time, your interest, and your education, as well as your (and your investors') money?

Spending time

How much time are you willing to devote to your business? That may sound a basic enough question, but different business done in different ways can have quite different time profiles. One business starter we know started a French bakery in London. He was determined to make his own croissants and did so for the first three months. But making his own bread meant starting work at 4 a.m. As he didn't close until city workers passed his door on their way home, by the time he cleaned up and took stock, he had worked a fifteen-hour day. But he still had the books to do, orders to place and plans to prepare. He eventually settled for a ten-hour day, which meant he had to buy in croissants already baked.

Furthering your education

You may have identified a market opportunity that requires skills over and above those that you currently have. There may, for example, be a gap in the market for Teaching English as a Foreign Language (TEFL), but to do so requires a month of intensive study plus a £1,000 course fee.

Doing the TEFL certificate may involve you in more skill upgrading than you want to commit to, at the outset at least. So either you need to find customers who don't require you to have that qualification, or you need to think about a less educationally challenging business.

Keeping things interesting

If you want to start a restaurant, and have never worked in one, get a job in one. That's the best way to find out if you would like a particular type of work. You may find that a restaurant looks very different from behind the chair as opposed to on it. Some businesses are inherently repetitive, with activities that follow a predictable pattern. If that suits you fine, but if not then perhaps you need to consider a business venture with a shifting range of tasks.

Weighting your preferences

After you have an idea of some of the businesses you may want to start, you can rank those businesses according to how closely they match what you want from starting a business.

Go through the standards you want your business to meet and assign a weight between 1 and 5 to each on a range from not important at all to absolutely must have. Next, list your possible business opportunities and measure them against the graded criteria.

Table 1-2 shows a sample ranking for Jane Clark, an imaginary ex-secretary with school-aged children, who needs work because her husband has been made redundant and is busy looking for another job. Jane isn't in a position to raise much capital, and she wants her hours to coincide with those of her children. She wants to run her own show and she wants to enjoy what she does. The criteria she selected are shown in the table.

Table 1-2	Weighing Up the Factors
Criteria	*Weighting factor*
Minimal capital required	5
Possibility to work hours that suit lifestyle	5
No need to learn new skills	4
Minimal paperwork	3

Criteria	Weighting factor
Work satisfaction	2
Opportunity to meet interesting people	1

Since minimal capital was a very important criterion for Jane she gave it a weight of five, whereas the opportunity to meet interesting people, being far less important to her, was only weighted one.

Jane then gave each of her three business ideas a rating, in points (out of five) against these criteria. A secretarial agency needed capital to start so was given only one point. Back-up typing needed hardly any money and was allocated five points.

Her worked-out chart is shown in Table 1-3.

Table 1-3		Scoring Alternatives					
		Secretarial agency		Back-up typing		Authors' manuscripts	
	Weighting factor	Score	Points	Points	Score	Points	Score
Criteria							
Minimal capital	5 x	1 =	5	5	25	4	20
Flexible hours	5 x	1 =	5	3	15	5	25
No new skills	4 x	2 =	8	5	20	5	20
Work satisfaction	3 x	4 =	12	1	3	3	9
Minimal paperwork	2 x	0 =	0	4	8	5	10
Meeting people	1 x	4 =	4	3	3	4	4
Total score			34		74		88

The weighting factor and the rating point multiplied together give a score for each business idea. The highest score indicates the business that best meets Jane's criteria. In this case, typing authors' manuscripts scored over back-up typing since Jane could do it exactly when it suited her.

Chapter 2

Testing Feasibility

. . . .

In This Chapter

▶ Making sure you can find the product and people

▶ Doing market research

▶ Seeing if you can make a profit

. . . .

*Y*ou need to decide whether or not starting up your own business is for you. Maybe you have reached some tentative decision on whether to go it alone or to join forces with others with valuable resources or ideas to add to your own and now have the bones of an idea of what type of business you will start, buy into, franchise or in some other way get into.

So all you have to do now is wait for the customers to turn up and the cash to roll in. Right? Wrong, regrettably. Although you are beyond square one, there are still a good few miles to cover before you can be confident your big business idea will actually work and make money. This chapter gives you the right questions to ask to make you as sure as you can be that you have the best shot at success.

Finding Enough Product or People

The first test of feasibility is whether you can get enough goods to sell or enough people to provide the service you're offering. You need to be sure that you can get your product manufactured at the rate and quantity to meet your needs. Likewise, if you're starting a service business, you need to be sure that you can hire the people with the skills you need, whether you need housecleaners or Web page designers.

Of course, if you're buying into a franchise or joining an existing business or co-operative, these issues are already addressed for the most part. Still, it never hurts to do your own assessment of the supply chain if only to familiarise yourself with the process.

How much is enough?

The amount of goods or services you need depends in part on the scale of your ambitions and also on what you believe the market will bear. If the restaurant you plan to open has a total population of 100 people within a fifty mile radius, that fact alone will limit the scale of your venture.

It makes sense to work backwards to answer this question. For example if you want to make at least as much money from your business as you have in wages in your job, then that figure can be used to work out the initial scale of your level of output. As a rough rule of thumb if you want to make £10,000 profit before tax, a business involved in manufacturing or processing materials will need to generate between £80,000 and £100,000 worth of orders. Taking away your anticipated profit from the sales target leaves you with the value of the goods and services you need to buy in.

Buying in equipment and supplies

In this area there are four main areas to check out:

- **Premises:** Finding the right premises can be the limiting factor for some businesses. If, for example you need to be in a particular type of area, as with restaurants, coffee shops, and night clubs, it could take months for the right place to come on the market and even longer to get planning or change of use consent if those are required. Once you have a clear idea of the type of premises you want, check out all the commercial estate agents in the area. It will make sense to have a few alternative locations in your plans too.

- **Equipment:** If you are going to make any or all of your products yourself then you need to check out suppliers, delivery times, payment terms and so forth for the equipment needed for the production processes. You will first need to check out the output levels and quality standards of any equipment you want, to make sure it will meet your needs. You can find equipment suppliers in either *Kelly's Directories* (www.kellys.co.uk) or *Kompass* (www.kompass.com). Between these two directories there is information on hundreds of thousands of branded products and services from suppliers in over 70 countries. These directories are available both in your local business library or, to a limited extent, online.

- **Finished goods:** It is usually a better use of scarce cash for a new business to buy in product in as close to finished state as possible, leaving you to complete only the high value-added tasks to complete. Few niche mail-order catalogue businesses make any of their own product; their key skills lie in merchandise selection, advertising copy, Web design or buying in the right mailing lists. Kelly's and Kompass directories list almost every finished good supplier.

✓ **Consumable materials:** If you are making things yourself then you will need to check out suppliers of raw materials. Even if, like mail-order firms, you are buying in finished product you will need to check that out too. You can search in Google, Ask Jeeves, or any of the major search engines for almost any product or service. However unless the quantities are large and significantly better terms can be had elsewhere it is better to stick to local suppliers for consumables. This is an inexpensive way to build up goodwill in the local community and may even create business for you. See *Kelly's* and *Kompass* directories for details of suppliers of consumables.

Hiring in help

Unless you plan to do everything yourself on day one, you will need to check out that people with the skills you need are available at wage rates you can afford in your area. Start by looking in the situations vacant section of your local newspaper under the appropriate headings. If you need kitchen staff for your new restaurant and the paper has 20 pages of advertisers desperately looking for staff, then you could well have a problem on your hands. In Book III we look at finding employees for your business.

Sizing Up the Market

You need to ensure that there are enough customers out there, with sufficient money to spend, to create a viable marketplace for your products or services. You must also see who will be competing against you for their business. In other words, you need to research your market.

Market research is something that potential financial backers – be they banks or other institutions – will insist on. And in this they are doing you a favour. Many businesses started with private money fail because the founders don't thoroughly research the market at the outset.

Whatever your business idea, you must undertake some well thought out market research before you invest any money or approach anyone else to invest in your venture.

You don't have to pay professional companies to do your research, although sometimes it may make good sense to do so. You can often gather information effectively (and cheaply) yourself.

Market research has three main purposes:

- ✔ **To build credibility for your business idea:** You must prove, first to your own satisfaction and later to outside financiers, that you thoroughly understand the marketplace for your product or service. This proof is vital to attracting resources to build the new venture.

- ✔ **To develop a realistic market entry strategy:** A successful marketing strategy is based on a clear understanding of genuine customer needs and on the assurance that product quality, price, promotional and distribution methods are mutually supportive and clearly focused on target customers.

- ✔ **To gain understanding of the total market, both customers and competition:** You need sufficient information on your potential customers, competitors, and market to ensure that your market strategy is at least on the target, if not on the bull's-eye itself. If you miss the target altogether, which you could well do without research, you may not have the necessary cash resources for a second shot.

The military motto 'Time spent in reconnaissance is rarely time wasted' holds true for business as well.

Researching the market need not be a complex process, nor need it be very expensive. The amount of effort and expenditure needs to be related in some way to the costs and risks associated with the business. If all that is involved with your business is simply getting a handful of customers for products and services that cost little to put together, then you may spend less effort on market research than you would for, say, launching a completely new product or service into an unproven market that requires a large sum of money to be spent up front. However much or little market research you plan to carry out the process needs to be conducted systematically.

Before you start your research:

- ✔ **Define your objectives:** Figure out what you vitally need to know. For example, how often do people buy and how much?

- ✔ **Identify the customers to sample for this information:** Decide who you want to sample and how you can best reach them. For example, for DIY products, an Ideal Home Exhibition crowd might be best.

- ✔ **Decide how best to undertake the research:** Choose the research method best suited to getting the results you need. For example, face-to-face interviews in the street may allow you direct access to potential customers.

- ✔ **Think about how you will analyse the data:** If your research involves complex multi-choice questions, or a large sample size, you may need to plan in advance to use a computer and the appropriate software to help you process the data, which in turn means coding the questions. An even better idea is to keep it so simple you don't need a computer!

The raw market research data can be analysed and turned into information to guide your decisions on price, promotion, location, and the shape, design, and scope of the product or service itself.

The following sections cover the areas you need to consider to make sure you have properly sized up your business sector.

Figuring out what you need to know

Before embarking on your market research, set clear and precise objectives. You don't want just to find out interesting information about the market in general, and you don't want to spend the time and money to explore the whole market when your target is just a segment of that market. (We talk about segmenting the market in the 'Finding your segment of the market' section coming up in a bit.)

You have to figure out who your target customer is and what you need to know about him or her. For example, if you are planning to open a shop selling to young fashion-conscious women, your research objective could be to find out how many women between the ages of 18 and 28, who make at least £25,000 p.a., live or work within two miles of your chosen shop position. That would give you some idea if the market could support a venture such as this.

You also want to know what the existing market is for your product and how much money your potential customers spend on similar products. You can get a measure of such spending from Mintel reports (www.mintel.com). Mintel publishes over 400 reports every year examining nearly every consumer market from baby foods to youth holidays.

Figuring out the size of the market may require several different pieces of information. You may want to know the resident population of a given area, which may be fairly easy to find out, and also something about the type of people who come into your area for work, for leisure, on holiday, or for any other purpose. A nearby hospital, library, railway station, or school, for example, may pull potential customers into your particular area.

You also want to know as much as you can about your competitors – their share of the market, their marketing strategy, their customer profile, product pricing schemes, and so on.

You need to research in particular:

✔ **Your customers:** Who will buy your goods and services? What particular customer needs will your business meet? How many of them are there, are their numbers growing or contracting, how much do they spend and how often do they buy?

✔ **Your competitors:** Which established businesses are already meeting the needs of your potential customers? What are their strengths and weaknesses? Are they currently failing their customers in some way that you can improve on?

✔ **Your product or service:** Could, or should, it be tailored to meet the needs of particular groups of customers? For example if you are starting up a delivery business, professional clients may require a 'same day service', whilst members of the public at large would be happy to get goods in a day or two, provided it was less costly.

✔ **The price you should charge:** All too often small firms confine their research on pricing to seeing what the competition charges and either matching it or beating it. That may be a way to get business, but it is not the best route to profitable business. You need to know what price would be perceived as being too cheap, what would represent good 'value for money' and what would be seen as a rip off, so you can pitch in at the right price for your offering.

✔ **Which promotional material will reach your customers:** What newspapers and journals do they read and which of these is most likely to influence their buying decision?

✔ **Your location:** From where could you reach your customers most easily and at minimum cost?

✔ **Most effective sales method:** Can you use telesales, the Internet, or a catalogue, or will customers only buy face to face either from a salesperson or from a retail outlet?

Research is not just essential in starting a business but should become an integral part in the on-going life of the business. Customers and competitors change; products and services don't last forever. Once started, however, ongoing market research becomes easier, as you will have existing customers (and staff) to question. It is important that you regularly monitor their views on your business (as the sign in the barber shop stated: 'We need your head to run our business') and develop simple techniques for this purpose (for example, questionnaires for customers beside the till, suggestion boxes with rewards for employees).

Finding your segment of the market

Market segmentation is the process whereby customers and potential customers are organised into clusters of similar types, such as age, sex, education level or location.

The starting point for your business may be to sell clothes, but every person who buys clothes is too large and diverse a market to get a handle on. So you divide that market into different segments – clothes for men, women, and children, for example – and then further divide those segments into clothes for work, leisure, sports, and social occasions. You just segmented your market.

Most businesses end up selling to several different market segments, but when it comes to detailed market research you need to examine each of your main segments separately.

Above all it is customers who increasingly want products and services tailored to their needs and will pay for the privilege.

Grouping market segments

Some of the tried-and-tested ways by which markets can be segmented follow:

- **Demographic segmentation** groups customers together by such variables as age, sex, interest, education, and income. Some companies have made their whole proposition age focused. Live4now.com was only interested in those aged between 18 and 35, for example.

- **Psychographic segmentation** divides individual consumers into social groups such as Yuppie (young, upwardly mobile, professional), Bumps (borrowed-to-the-hilt upwardly mobile professional show off) and Jollies (jet-setting oldies with lots of loot). These categories try to explain how social behaviour influences buyer behaviour.

- **Benefit segmentation** recognises that different people get different benefits from the same product or service. The Lastminute.com bargain travel site claims two quite distinctive benefits for its users. Initially it aims to offer people bargains, which appeals because of price and value. But lately the company has been laying more emphasis on the benefit of immediacy. The theory is rather akin to the impulse buy products placed at checkout tills that you never thought of buying until you bumped into them on your way out. Whether ten days on a beach in Goa, or a trip to Istanbul, is the type of thing people pop in their baskets before turning off their computer screens, time will tell.

- **Geographic segmentation** recognises that people in different locations have different needs. For example, an inner city store might sell potatoes in 1kg bags, recognising its customers are likely to be on foot. An out of town shopping centre sells the same product in 20kg sacks, knowing their customers have cars.

- **Industrial segmentation** groups together commercial customers according to a combination of their geographic location, principal business activity, relative size, frequency of product use, urgency of need, loyalty, order size and buying policies. Using this approach a courier service would price its overnight delivery service higher than its 48 hour service.

- **Multivariant segmentation** uses a combination of segments to get a more precise picture of a market than using just one factor.

Use the following guidelines to help determine whether a market segment is worth trying to sell into:

- **Measurability:** Can you estimate how many customers are in the segment? Are there enough to make it worth offering something different for?

- **Accessibility:** Can you communicate with these customers, preferably in a way that reaches them alone? For example you could reach the over 50s through advertising in a specialist magazine, with reasonable confidence that young people will not read it. So if you are trying to promote a large-print edition of a game, you might prefer young people did not hear about it, so that they don't think of the game as strictly for old folks.

- **Open to profitable development:** The customers must have money to spend on the benefits you propose offering. Once upon a time oldies were poor, so that market wasn't a good target for upscale, expensive products. Then they became rich and everyone had products aimed at older markets.

Seeing natural market subsegments

Even after you determine your target market segments, your growth may not come through as fast as you were hoping. You have to realise that every market segment is itself made up of subsegments. Everett M Rogers, in his book *Diffusion of Innovations* (New York Free Press, 1962) broke markets into the following sub-segments:

- Innovators, the adventurous types who try out new things early on represent 2.5 per cent of the average market.

- The Early Adopters make up 13.5 per cent of the average market. This type of customer only starts buying when the service has the seal of approval from the Innovators.

- Early Majority and Late Majority buyers, each 34 per cent of the market, follow on, after the Early Adopters have shown the way.

- Laggards, 16 per cent of the average market, follow well behind, perhaps taking years and some significant price drops before they can be tempted to put down their cash.

One further issue that has a profound effect on marketing strategy is that Innovators, Early Adopters, and all the other sub-segments don't necessarily read the same magazines or respond to the same images and messages. So they need to be marketed to in very different ways. This makes the blitz approach to market penetration taken by some new ventures look a bit suspect. Blitz marketing with a single message may work in stimulating a mature market, but how much use is it in a market that is still looking for the signal of approval from further up the chain?

You need to identify the innovators who will buy from you first. Whilst your product or service may not be earth shatteringly new, you and your business may well present a mature market with established competitors with a situation that looks much similar to a new innovation.

Budgeting for your research

Market research isn't free even if you do it yourself. At the very least, you have to consider your time. You may also spend money on journals, phone calls, letters, and field visits. And, if you employ a professional market research firm, your budgeting needs shoot to the top of the scale.

For example, a survey of 200 executives responsible for office equipment purchasing decisions cost one company £12,000. In-depth interviews with 20 banking consumers cost £8,000.

Doing the research in-house may save costs but limit the objectivity of the research. If time is your most valuable commodity, it may make sense to get an outside agency to do the work. Another argument for getting professional research is that it may carry more clout with investors.

Whatever the cost of research, you need to assess its value to you when you are setting your budget. So if getting it wrong will cost £100,000, then £5,000 spent on market research may be a good investment.

Doing the preliminary research

Research methods range from doing it all from your desk to getting out in the field yourself and asking questions – or hiring someone to do it for you. The following sections explore the various methods you can use to find out what you need to know.

If you are a member of a chamber of commerce, a trade association, small business association, or are or have taken a small business course, the chances are you can access some market data for free.

Even if it does cost something in time and money, getting the data you need helps you make better decisions. If you think knowledge is expensive, you should try ignorance!

Doing research behind your desk

Once you know the questions you want answers to, the next step is finding out if someone else has the answers already. Much of the information you need may well be published, so you can do at least some of your market research in a comfortable chair either in your home or in a good library. Even if you use other research methods, it is well worth doing a little desk research first.

Gathering information at the library

There are thousands of libraries in the UK and tens of thousands elsewhere in the world that between them contain more desk research data than any entrepreneur could ever require. Libraries offer any number of excellent information sources. You can either take yourself to your local library or bring the library's information to you via the Internet if you're dealing with one of the reference libraries in a larger city or town.

As well as the fairly conventional business books, libraries contain many hundreds of reference and research databases. For example, the official Census of Population supplies demographic data on size, age, and sex of the local populace. You can also find a wealth of governmental and other statistics that enable you to work out the size and shape of the market nationwide and how much each person spends.

Details of every journal, paper, and magazines readership are to be found in *BRAD* (British Rate and Data) and every company has to file details of its profits, assets, liabilities, and directors at Companies House, the place where all business details and accounts are kept (www.companies-house.org.uk).

Sources of Unofficial UK Statistics published by Gower (www.gowerpub.com) gives details of almost 900 publications (including electronic publications) and services produced by trade associations, professional bodies, banks, consultants, employers' federations, forecasting organisations and others, together with statistics appearing in trade journals and periodicals. Titles and services are listed alphabetically by publisher and each entry contains information, where available, on subject, content, and source of statistics, together with frequency, availability and cost, and address, telephone, and fax details for further information.

Some market information data costs hundreds of pounds and some is available only to subscribers who pay thousands of pounds to have it on tap. Fortunately for you, your library (or an Internet link to a library) may have the relevant directory, publication, or research study on its shelves.

Librarians are trained, amongst other things, to archive and retrieve information and data from their own libraries and increasingly from Internet data sources as well. Thus, they represent an invaluable resource that you should tap into early in the research process. You can benefit many times from their knowledge at no cost, or you may want to make use of the research service some libraries offer to business users at fairly modest rates.

Connecting to the world's libraries

The 123 World.com Web site (www.123world.com/libraries) claims to be the ultimate source of authentic and reliable information about the library resources of the world on the net. Their list of libraries includes public and state libraries, national archives, research, university, and other educational libraries, agricultural, science, and technical libraries, business libraries, and many other specialist libraries. The links in this directory guide you to the official sites of the libraries you choose. Using 123 World.com you can find out about all the libraries in your vicinity and anywhere else in the world.

Apart from public libraries, there are hundreds of university libraries, specialist science and technology libraries, and government collections of data that can be accessed with little difficulty.

Using the Internet

The Internet can be a powerful research tool. However, it has some particular strengths and weaknesses that you need to keep in mind when using it.

Strengths of the Internet include:

- ✔ Access is cheap and information is often free
- ✔ Provides good background information
- ✔ Information is produced quickly
- ✔ Covers a wide geographic scope

Weaknesses of the Internet include:

- ✔ The bias is strongly toward the US
- ✔ Coverage of any given subject may be patchy
- ✔ Authority and credentials are often lacking

It would be a brave or foolhardy entrepreneur who started up in business or set out to launch new products or services without at least spending a day or two surfing the Internet. At the very least this will let you know if anyone else has taken your business idea to market. At best it might save you lots of legwork around libraries, if the information you want is available online.

You can gather market research information on the Internet two main ways:

- Use directories, search engines, or telephone directories to research your market or product.
- Use bulletin or message boards, newsgroups, and chat rooms to elicit the data you require.

These three useful search engines can help get you started:

- **Business.com** (www.business.com) contains some 400,000 listings in 25,000 industry, product, and service sub-categories. Useful for general industry background or details about a particular product line.
- **Easy Searcher 2** (www.easysearcher.com) is a collection of 400 search engines, both general and specialist, available on drop down menus, listed by category.
- **The Small Business Research portal** (www.smallbusinessportal.co.uk/index.php) links Internet sites of interest to small business researchers, policy-makers, and support agencies. The site is a valuable portal for small business research.

Getting to the grass roots

If the market information you need is not already available, and the chances are that it won't be, then you need to find the answers yourself. Going out into the marketplace to do market research is known as *field research*, or sometimes *primary research*, by marketing professionals.

Field research allows you to gather information directly related to your venture and to fine-tune results you get from other sources. For example, entrepreneurs interested in opening a classical music shop in Exeter aimed at young people were encouraged when desk research showed that of a total population of 250,000, 25 per cent were under 30. However, it did not tell them what percentage of this 25 per cent was interested in classical music nor how much money each potential customer might spend. Field research showed that 1 per cent was interested in classical music and would spend £2 a week, suggesting a potential market of only £65,000 a year (250,000 × 25% × 1% × £2 × 52)! The entrepreneurs sensibly decided to investigate Birmingham and London instead. But at least the cost had been only two damp afternoons spent in Exeter, rather than the horror of having to dispose of a lease of an unsuccessful shop.

Most field research consists of an interviewer putting questions to a respondent. No doubt you've become accustomed to being interviewed while travelling or resisting the attempts of an enthusiastic salesperson on your doorstep posing as a market researcher (*slugging* as this is known has been illegal since 1986).

The more popular forms of interviews are:

✔ Personal (face-to-face) interview (especially for consumer markets)

✔ Telephone (especially for surveying businesses)

✔ Postal survey (especially for industrial markets)

✔ Test and discussion groups

✔ Internet surveys

Personal interviews and postal surveys are clearly less expensive than getting together panels of interested parties or using expensive telephone time. Telephone interviewing requires a very positive attitude, courtesy, an ability not to talk too quickly and listening while sticking to a rigid questionnaire. Low response rates on postal surveys (normally less than 10 per cent) can be improved by including a letter explaining the purpose of the survey and why respondents should reply; by offering rewards for completed questionnaires (small gift); by associating the survey with a charity donation based on the number of respondents; by sending reminder letters and, of course, by providing pre-paid reply envelopes.

Internet surveys using questionnaires similar to those conducted by post or on the telephone are growing in popularity. On the plus side, while the other survey methods involve having the data entered or transcribed at your expense, with an Internet survey, the respondent enters the data. Internet survey software also comes with the means to readily analyse the data turning it into useful tables and charts. Such software may also have a statistical package to check out the validity of the data itself and so give you some idea how much reliance to place on it.

Whilst buying the software to carry out Internet surveys may be expensive, you can rent it and pay per respondent for each survey you do.

Another negative aspect of using the Internet is that, at present at any rate, the sample of users is heavily biased. Students, big companies, and university academics would be well represented in any sample you chose, but other sectors, for example the over 70s (up to a fifth of the population), may not.

Conducting the research

Field research means that you have to do the work yourself. Decide the questions, select the right people to ask those questions and then interpret the data once you have it. This is completely different from desk research where all that work has been done for you. But field research can be worth every ounce of sweat that goes into it. You get information that no one else is likely to have at their finger tips, and knowledge in the business start-up arena is definitely power. When you come to writing up your business plan (see Chapter 6) you will have the evidence to support your belief in your business.

Setting up a sample

It is rarely possible or even desirable to include every potential customer or competitor in your research. Imagine trying to talk to all pet owners before launching petfeed.com! Instead you select a sample group to represent the whole population.

Sampling saves time and money and can be more accurate than surveying an entire population. Talking to every pet owner may take months. By the time you complete your survey, the first people questioned may have changed their opinions, or the whole environment may have changed in some way.

You need to take care and ensure you have included all the important customer segments that you have targeted as potential users or buyers of your products or services in your research sample.

The main sampling issue is how big a sample you need to give you a reliable indication as to how the whole population will behave. The accuracy of your survey increases with the sample size, as Table 2-1 shows. You need to ensure that each of your main customer segments, for example, the over 50s, people earning between £20,000 and £30,000 a year or those without university degrees, if those are groups of people whose views are important to your strategy, are included in sample in numbers sufficient to make your sample reasonably reliable.

Table 2-1	Sample Size and Accuracy
Number in Sample	*Percentage accuracy of 95% of Surveys*
250	6.2
500	4.4
750	3.6
1000	3.1
2000	2.2
6000	1.2

For most basic research a small business will find the lower sample sizes accurate enough given the uncertainty surrounding the whole area of entering new markets and launching new products.

Asking the right questions

To make your field research pay off you have to ask the questions whose responses tell you what you need to know. Writing those questions is both an art and a science – both aspects of which you can master by using the following tips:

- Keep the number of questions to a minimum. A dozen or so should be enough – 25 is getting ridiculous.

- Keep the questions simple. Answers should be either Yes/No/Don't Know or somewhere on a scale such as Never/Once a Month/Three or Four Times a Month/Always.

- Avoid ambiguity. Make sure the respondent really understands the question by avoiding vague words such as 'generally', 'usually', 'regularly'. Seek factual answers; avoid opinions.

- Make sure you have a cut-out question at the beginning to eliminate unsuitable respondents. You don't want to waste time questioning people who would never use your product or service.

- Put an identifying question at the end so that you can make sure you get a suitable cross-section of respondents. For example, you may want to identify men from women, people living alone from those with children, or certain age groups.

The introduction to a face-to-face interview is important; make sure you are prepared, either carrying an identifying card (maybe a student card or watchdog card) or with rehearsed introduction (such as 'Good morning, I'm from Cranfield University [show card] and we are conducting a survey and would be grateful for your help'). You may also need visuals of the product you are investigating (samples, photographs), to ensure the respondent understands. Make sure these are neat and accessible.

Try out the questionnaire and your technique on your friends prior to using them in the street. You may be surprised to find that questions that seem simple to you are incomprehensible at first to respondents!

Remember, above all, however, that questioning is by no means the only or most important form of fieldwork. Another form of fieldwork market research you should undertake is to get out and look at your competitors' premises, get their catalogues and price lists, go to exhibitions and trade fairs relevant to your chosen business sector, and get information on competitors' accounts and financial data. One would-be business starter found out from the company's accounts, obtained from Companies House (www.companies-house.org.uk) that the 'small' competitor near to where he planned to locate was in fact owned by a giant public company that was testing out the market prior to a major launch themselves.

All methods can be equally valid depending only on the type of market data you need to gather. The results of each piece of market research should be carefully recorded for subsequent use in presentations and business plans.

Once the primary market research (desk and field research) and market testing (stalls and exhibitions) are complete, if you are investing a substantial amount of money up front in your venture, then pilot testing of the business should take place in one location or customer segment before launching fully into business. Only then can you make a reasonably accurate prediction of sales and the cash flow implications for your business.

Finding test subjects

Now you need someone to ask your questions to. If you're doing a street survey then you will have to make do with whoever comes along. Otherwise to carry out a survey, your best bet is to buy or rent a mailing list. Typically, you'll pay a fee to the list owner, such as a magazine with its list of subscribers. You'll negotiate a fee for how many times you are allowed to use the list. Note that you are not the owner of the list.

There are several individual freelancers who specialise in brokering lists and building lists You may want to consider hiring an individual for a consultation or to manage the entire process. Marketing professionals claim there's a science to buying lists, but it's quite possible to master this science on your own, especially if you are trying to reach a local or regional market. Think of publications, organisations, and businesses whose lists would most likely contain people who could buy your product or service. Don't overlook trade magazines, regional magazines, or non-competing businesses with a similar customer base. You can then select and narrow your lists by looking at nearly any demographic variable to arrive at as close to your description of your target market as possible. Listbroker.com (www.listbroker.com) and List-Link International Limited (www.list-link.com) between them can provide lists of all types.

Determining whether you have enough information

Use Table 2-2 to check out whether you know enough about your market yet. Complete the questionnaire by entering the score in the box that most closely describes your knowledge. For example in the first question below if you don't know the likely age, sex or income group of your prospective or actual customers, put a zero in the left-hand column. Try to be honest and perhaps get someone else who knows your business area well to answer the questions also.

Table 2-2	Evaluating Your Results		
	No (0)	*Have some idea (1)*	*Yes, have detailed information (2)*
Do you know the likely age, sex, or income group of your prospective (or actual) customers?			
Do you know your customers' buying habits and preferences?			
Do know what other related products and services your customers buy?			
Do you know which of your competitors they also use?			
Do you know how much of your competitors' business you want or have?			
Do you know who else operates in this marketplace?			
Do you know how successful they are in terms of sales and profits?			
Do you know how they promote their goods and services?			
Do you know how satisfied their customers are with their service?			
Do you know how much your competitors charge?			
Do you know the overall size of your market?			
Do you know if your market is growing or contracting, and by how much?			

(continued)

Table 2-2 *(continued)*			
	No (0)	*Have some idea (1)*	*Yes, have detailed information (2)*
Do you know what papers, journals, and magazines your customers read?			
Do you know which other Web sites your customers are most likely to visit?			
Do you know how your competitors recruit their best staff?			

Add up all your scores and rate whether or not you know enough about your market yet:

- ✔ Less than 10: It seems unlikely that you know enough to start up yet.

- ✔ 10–15: You still have a lot more to find out, but at least you have made a start.

- ✔ 15–25: You have got a handle on the basic information, but there are still a few more important bits of data to research.

- ✔ Over 25: A high score is no guarantee of success, but you seem to have the right level of sector knowledge to start a business. Superior information can in itself be a source of competitive advantage, so keep up the good work.

Working Out Whether You Can Make Money

There isn't much point in trying to get a new business off the ground if it is going to take more money than you can raise or take longer to reach break-even and turn in a profit than you can possibly survive unaided. For more detail on financial matters such as profits and margins check out *Starting a Business For Dummies* (Wiley), but you can't start looking at the figures soon enough. Doing some rough figures at the outset can save you a lot of time pursuing unrealistic or unprofitable business opportunities.

Estimating start-up costs

Setting up a business requires money – there is no getting away from that. You have rent to pay, materials and equipment to purchase, and all before any income is received. Starting a business on the road to success involves ensuring that you have sufficient money to survive until the point where income continually exceeds expenditure.

Raising this initial money and the subsequent financial management of the business is therefore vital, and great care should be taken over it. Unfortunately, more businesses fail due to lack of sufficient day-to-day cash and financial management than for any other reason.

The first big question is to establish how much money you need. Look at every possible cost and divide them into one-off, fixed, or variable categories.

The *fixed costs* are those that you have to pay even if you make no sales (rent, rates, possibly some staff costs, repayments on any loans, and so on) as well as some *one-off costs,* or one-time purchases such as buying a vehicle or computer, which will not be repeated once the business is up and running. *Variable costs* are those that vary dependent on the level of your sales (raw materials, production and distribution costs, and so on).

Your finance requirements will be shown very clearly on your cash flow forecast, which is a table showing, usually on a monthly basis, the amount of money actually received into the business, and the amount of money paid out.

Six out of every ten people starting up a businesses use personal funds as their initial source of finance. Naturally, using your own money, your savings, your un-mortgaged property, your life insurance, and your other assets, is a logical starting point. You may not feel you can put all of your worth behind a business because of the risks involved, but whichever route you go down you will normally be expected to invest some of your own assets. Banks seek personal guarantees; venture capitalists like to see owners taking risks with their own money – why should they risk their clients' money if you will not risk yours?

If you can fund the project from your own resources there are attractions to doing so. Only in this way do all of the rewards of success flow to you. As soon as you bring in other sources of finance they slice off some of the reward, be it interest, share of the value on the sale of the business, or dividends. They may also constrain the business through the use of covenants, borrowing limits, and the placement of financial obligations on the business – potentially not only carving off part of your rewards but also capping them by restricting your operation. But if not at the outset, at some stage in their growth, most firms require outside finance to realise their full potential.

Forecasting sales

While all forecasts may turn out to be wrong, it is important to demonstrate in your strategy that you have thought through the factors that will impact on performance. You should also show how you could deliver satisfactory results even when many of these factors work against you. Backers and employees alike will be measuring the downside risk, to evaluate the worst scenario and its likely effects, as well as looking towards an ultimate exit route.

Here are some guidelines to help you make an initial sales forecast:

- **Credible projections:** Your overall projections have to be believable. Most lenders and investors have an extensive experience of similar business proposals. Unlike you they have the benefit of hindsight, being able to look back several years at other ventures they have backed, and see how they fared in practice as compared with their initial forecasts.

  You could gather some useful knowledge on similar businesses yourself by researching company records (at Companies House, where the accounts of most UK companies are kept), or by talking with the founders of similar ventures, who will not be your direct competitors.

- **Market share:** How big is the market for your product or service? Is it growing or contracting and at what rate, percentage per annum? What is the economic and competitive position? These are all factors that can provide a market share basis for your forecasts. An entry market share of more than a few percent would be most unusual. But beware of turning this argument on its head. Unsubstantiated statements such as 'In a market of £1 billion per annum we can easily capture 1 per cent, which is £1 million a year', will impress no investor.

- **Customers:** How many customers and potential customers do you know who are likely to buy from you, and how much might they buy? Here you can use many types of data on which to base reasonable sales projections. You can interview a sample of prospective customers, issue a press release or advertisement to gauge response, and exhibit at trade shows to obtain customer reactions. If your product or service needs to be on an approved list before it can be bought, then your business plan should confirm that you have that approval, or less desirably, show how you will get it.

  You should also look at seasonal factors that might cause sales to be high or low at certain periods in the year. This will be particularly significant for cash flow projections. You should then relate your seasonal, customer-based, forecast to your capacity to make or sell at this rate. Sometimes your inability to recruit or increase capacity may limit your sales forecasts.

- **Market guidelines:** Some businesses have accepted formulas you can use to estimate sales. This is particularly true in retailing where location studies, traffic counts, and population density are known factors.

✔ **Desired income:** This approach to estimating sales embraces the concept that forecasts may also accommodate the realistic aims of the proprietor. Indeed, you could go further and state that the whole purpose of strategy is to ensure that certain forecasts are achieved. In a mature company with proven products and markets, this is more likely to be the case than with a start-up.

Nevertheless, an element of 'How much do we need to earn?' must play a part in forecasting, if only to signal when a business idea is not worth pursuing.

One extreme of the 'desired income' approach to forecasting comes from those entrepreneurs who think that the forecasts are the business plan. Such people cover the business plan with a mass of largely unconnected numbers. With reams of computer printout covering every variation possible in business, complete with sensitivity analysis, these people are invariably a big turn-off with financiers.

Calculating break-even

So far we've taken certain decisions for granted and ignored how to cost the product or service you're marketing, and indeed, how to set the selling price. These decisions are clearly very important if you want to be sure of making a profit.

At first glance the problem is simple. You just add up all the costs and charge a bit more. The more you charge above your costs, provided the customers will keep on buying, the more profit you make. Unfortunately as soon as you start to do the sums the problem gets a little more complex. For a start, not all costs have the same characteristics. Some costs, for example, do not change however much you sell. If you are running a shop, the rent and rates are relatively constant figures, completely independent of the volume of your sales. On the other hand, the cost of the products sold from the shop is completely dependent on volume. The more you sell, the more it costs you to buy in stock. You can't really add up those two types of costs until you have made an assumption about how much you plan to sell. You can find out more detail about this subject in Book III.

Becoming lean and mean

Paradoxically, one of the main reasons small businesses fail in the early stages is that too much start-up capital is raised and used to buy fixed assets. While clearly some equipment is essential at the start, other purchases can be postponed until later in the day. This may mean that you rent or borrow desirable and labour-saving devices for a while. This is not quite as convenient but may mean the difference between surviving in business and going bust.

Suppose you are producing widgets and decide to rent bigger premises from the outset, with room to store your widgets, rather than keeping them in your spare garage space. The rent and business rates on these larger premises are set at £3,500, which becomes your new fixed cost. Your break-even sales figure now becomes 1,000 (£3,500 fixed cost divided by £3.50 contribution per widget sold). In other words, you have to sell an extra 285 widgets, or 60 per cent more, just to cover the cost of having the extra storage space, which you had for free in your garage. Only you will know if the benefit of having the extra space is worth the cost.

One other very good reason for keeping fixed costs as low as possible is that you may not know what you really need until you actually start trading. You may find that your suppliers are so reliable that you need only carry a couple of days' stock in hand rather than the month you anticipated that called for the extra space. In which case you will have spent the extra money for no gain whatsoever.

In any event, you need to keep your fixed costs low enough to break-even within six to nine months of starting up.

Chapter 3

Preparing the Business Plan

· ·

In This Chapter

▶ Turning your ideas into plans

▶ Satisfying financiers' concerns

▶ Making your plan stand out

▶ Using software

▶ Preparing for an elevator pitch

· ·

*P*erhaps the most important step in launching any new venture or expanding an existing one is the construction of a *business plan*. Such a plan must include your goals for the enterprise, both short and long term; a description of the products or services you offer and the market opportunities you anticipate; finally, an explanation of the resources and means you need to achieve your goals in the face of likely competition.

Preparing a comprehensive business plan along these lines takes time and effort – The Cranfield School of Management estimates anywhere between 200 and 400 hours, depending on the nature of your business and how much data you have already gathered. Nevertheless, such an effort is essential if you are both to crystallise and focus your ideas, and test your resolve about starting or expanding your business.

The core thinking behind business plans and their eventual implementation is strategic analysis. The strategic analysis refines or confirms your view of what is really unique about your proposition. Or to put it another way, 'why on earth would anyone want to pay enough for this to make me rich'.

Once completed, your business plan will serve as a blueprint to follow which, like any map, improves the user's chances of reaching their destination.

Finding a Reason to Write a Business Plan

There are a number of other important benefits you can anticipate arising from preparing a business plan. All these benefits add up to one compelling reason. Businesses that plan make more money than those that don't and they survive longer too.

The research on planning generally shows a positive relationship between planning and business performance. Businesses that follow a well thought out plan generally out perform businesses with no plans or informal plans in every relevant category. Businesses that continue to update their plans throughout the life of the business enjoy significantly more success than businesses that don't.

Key reasons for writing up your business plan are covered in the following sections.

Building confidence

Completing a business plan makes you feel confident in your ability to set up and operate the venture because you put together a plan to make it happen. It may even compensate for lack of capital and experience, provided of course you have other factors in your favour, such as a sound idea and a size-able market opportunity for your product or service.

Testing your ideas

A systematic approach to planning enables you to make your mistakes on paper, rather than in the marketplace. One potential entrepreneur made the discovery while gathering data for his business plan that the local competitor he thought was a one-man band was in fact the pilot operation for a proposed national chain of franchised outlets. This had a profound effect on his market entry strategy!

Another entrepreneur found out that, at the price he proposed charging, he would never recover his overheads or break even. Indeed 'overheads' and 'break even' were themselves alien terms before he embarked on preparing a business plan. This naive perspective on costs is by no means unusual.

Showing how much money you need

Your business plan details how much money you need, what you need it for, and when and for how long you need it.

As under-capitalisation and early cash flow problems are two important reasons why new business activities fail, it follows that if you have a soundly prepared business plan, you can reduce these risks of failure. You can also experiment with a range of alternative viable strategies and so concentrate on options that make the most economic use of scarce financial resources.

It would be an exaggeration to say that your business plan is the passport to sources of finance. It will, however, help you to display your entrepreneurial flair and managerial talent to the full and to communicate your ideas to others in a way that will be easier for them to understand and to appreciate the reasoning behind your ideas. These outside parties could be bankers, potential investors, partners, or advisory agencies. Once they know what you are trying to do they will be better able to help you.

Providing planning experience

Preparing a business plan gives you an insight into the planning process. It is this process itself that is important to the long-term health of a business, and not simply the plan that comes out of it. Businesses are dynamic, as are the commercial and competitive environments in which they operate. No-one expects every event as recorded on a business plan to occur as predicted, but the understanding and knowledge created by the process of business planning helps prepare the business for any changes that it may face, and so enables it to adjust quickly.

Satisfying financiers' concerns

If you need finance, it is important to examine what financiers expect from you if you are to succeed in raising those funds.

It is often said that there is no shortage of money for new and growing businesses, the only scarce commodities are good ideas and people with the ability to exploit them. From the potential entrepreneur's position this is often hard to believe. One major venture capital firm alone receives several thousand business plans a year. Only 500 or so are examined in any detail, less than 25 are pursued to the negotiating stage, and only six of those are invested in.

To a great extent the decision whether to proceed beyond an initial reading of the plan depends on the quality of the business plan used in supporting the investment proposal. The business plan is your ticket of admission, giving you your first and often only chance to impress prospective sources of finance with the quality of your proposal.

It follows from this that to have any chance at all of getting financial support, your business plan must be the best that can be written and it must be professionally packaged. The plans that succeed meet all of the following requirements.

Presenting evidence of market orientation and focus

You need to demonstrate that you recognise the needs of potential customers, rather than simply being infatuated with an innovative idea. Business plans that occupy more space with product descriptions and technical explanations than with explaining how products will be sold and to whom usually get cold-shouldered by financiers. They rightly suspect that these companies are more of an ego trip than an enterprise.

But market orientation is not in itself enough. Financiers want to sense that the entrepreneur knows the one or two things their business can do best and that they are prepared to concentrate on exploiting these opportunities.

Demonstrating customer acceptance

Financiers like to know that your new product or service will sell and is being used, even if only on a trial or demonstration basis.

The founder of Solicitec, a company selling software to solicitors to enable them to process relatively standard documents such as wills, had little trouble getting support for his house conveyancing package once his product had been tried and approved by a leading building society for their panel of solicitors.

If you are only at the prototype stage, financiers have no immediate indication that, once made, your product will appeal to the market. They have to assess your chances of succeeding without any concrete evidence that you will. Under these circumstances you have to show that the problem your innovation seeks to solve is a substantial one that a large number of people will pay for.

As well as evidence of customer acceptance, you need to demonstrate that you know how and to whom your new product or service must be sold, and that you have a financially viable means of doing so.

Owning proprietary position

Exclusive rights to a product through patents, copyright, trade mark protection, or a licence helps to reduce the apparent riskiness of a venture in the financiers' eyes, as these can limit competition, for a while at least.

However well-protected legally a product is, marketability and marketing know-how generally outweigh 'patentability' in the success equation. A salutary observation made by an American Professor of Entrepreneurship revealed that less than 0.5 per cent of the best ideas contained in the *US Patent Gazette* in the last five years have returned a dime to the inventors.

Making believable forecasts

Entrepreneurs are naturally ebullient when explaining the future prospects for their businesses. They frequently believe that the sky's the limit when it comes to growth, and money (or rather the lack of it) is the only thing that stands between them and their success.

It is true that if you are looking for venture capital, then the providers are also looking for rapid growth. However, it is as well to remember that financiers are dealing with thousands of investment proposals each year, and already have money tied up in hundreds of business sectors. It follows, therefore, that they already have a perception of what the accepted financial results and marketing approaches currently are for any sector. Any new company's business plan showing projections that are outside the ranges perceived as acceptable within an industry will raise questions in the investor's mind.

Make your growth forecasts believable; support them with hard facts where possible. If they are on the low side, then approach the more cautious lending banker, rather than venture capitalists. The former often see a modest forecast as a virtue, lending credibility to the business proposal as a whole.

Benefiting your business

Despite many valuable benefits, thousands of would-be entrepreneurs still attempt to start without a business plan. The most common among these are entrepreneurs who think that they need little or no capital at the outset, or those who have funds of their own. Both types of entrepreneurs may believe that they don't need a business plan because they don't need to expose their project to harsh financial appraisal.

The former type may believe the easily exploded myth that customers will all pay cash on the nail and suppliers will wait for months to be paid. In the meantime, the proprietor has the use of these funds to finance the business. Such model customers and suppliers are thinner on the ground than optimistic entrepreneurs think. In any event, two important market rules still apply: either the product or service on offer fails to sell like hot cakes and mountains of unpaid stocks build up, or the product or service does sell like hot cakes and more financially robust entrepreneurs are attracted into the market. Without the staying power that adequate financing provides these new competitors will rapidly kill the business off.

Those would-be entrepreneurs with funds of their own, or worse still borrowed from friends and relatives, tend to think that the time spent in preparing a business plan could be more usefully (and enjoyably) spent looking for premises, buying a new car, or installing a computer. In short, anything that inhibits them from immediate action is viewed as time wasting.

As most people's initial perception of their business venture is flawed in some important respect, it follows that jumping in at the deep end is risky, and unnecessarily so. Flaws can often be discovered cheaply and in advance as, when preparing a business plan, they are almost always discovered.

Writing Up Your Business Plan

In these sections, we give you some guidelines to make sure your plan attracts attention and succeeds in the face of some fierce competition. More than a thousand businesses start up in the UK each day, and many of those are looking for money or other resources that they are hoping their business plan will secure for them. Making your business plan the best it can be gives it a chance to stand out.

Defining your readership

Clearly a business plan will be more effective if it is written with the reader in mind. This will involve some research into the particular interests, foibles, and idiosyncrasies of those readers. Bankers are more interested in hearing about certainties and steady growth, whilst *venture capitalists*, who put up risk capital on behalf of institutions such as pension funds, are also interested in dreams of great things to come. *Business angels*, who put their own money at risk, like to know how their particular skills and talents can be deployed in the business.

It is a good idea to carry out your reader research before the final editing of your business plan, as you should incorporate something of this knowledge into the way it is presented. You may find that slightly different versions of the business plan have to be made for different audiences. This makes the reader feel the proposal has been addressed to them rather than just being the recipient of a 'Dear Sir or Madam' type of missive. However the fundamentals of the plan remain constant.

Choosing the right packaging

Appropriate packaging enhances every product and a business plan is no exception. Most experts prefer a simple spiral binding with a clear plastic cover front and back. This makes it easy for the reader to move from section to section, and it ensures the document will survive the frequent handling that every successful business plan is likely to get.

A letter quality printer, using size 12 typeface, double-spacing and wide margins, will result in a pleasing and easy to read plan.

Deciding on layout and content

There is no such thing as a universal business plan format. That being said, experience has taught us that certain styles have been more successful than others. Following these guidelines will result in an effective business plan, which covers most requirements. Not every sub-heading will be relevant, but the general format is robust.

The following list contains the elements of an effective business plan, one that covers most requirements. You may not need all of these sections, and you may need others to cover special requirements.

- ✔ The **cover** should show the name of your business, its address, phone and fax numbers, e-mail address, website, contact name, and the date on which this version of the plan was prepared. It should confirm that this is the current view on the business's position and financing needs.

- ✔ The **title page,** immediately behind the front cover, should repeat the above information and also give the founder's name, address, and phone number. A home phone number can be helpful, particularly for investors, who often work irregular hours too.

- ✔ The **executive summary** is ideally one page, but certainly no longer than two, and contains the highlights of your plan.

  Writing this summary is a difficult task but it is the single most important part of your business plan. Done well it can favourably dispose the reader from the outset. Done badly, or not at all, then the plan may not get beyond the mail-room. This one page (or two pages) must explain:

  - The current position of the company, including a summary of past trading results.

  - A description of the products or services, together with details on any rights or patents and details on competitive advantage.

  - The reasons why customers need this product or service, together with some indication of market size and growth.

  - A summary of forecasts of sales and profits, together with short- and long-term aims and the strategies to be employed.

  - How much money is needed to fund the growth and how and when the provider will benefit.

Write the executive summary only after you complete the business plan itself. Read the real-life example executive summary to get a feel for how this vital task can be successfully carried out.

- ✔ The **table of contents,** with page numbers, is the map that guides readers through the business plan. If that map is obscure, muddled, or even missing, then you are likely to end up with lost or irritated readers who are in no mind to back your proposal. Each main section should be listed, numbered, and given a page identity. Elements within each section should also be numbered: 1, 1.1, 1.2, and so on.

- ✔ Details of the **business and its management** should include a brief history of the business and its performance to date and details on key staff, current mission, legal entity, capital structure, and professional advisers.

- ✔ A description of **products and services,** their applications, competitive advantage, and proprietary position. Include details on state of readiness of new products and services and development cost estimates.

- ✔ The **marketing** section should provide a brief overview of the market by major segment showing size and growth. Explain the current and proposed marketing strategy for each major segment, covering price, promotion, distribution channels, selling methods, location requirements, and the need for acquisitions, mergers, or joint ventures, if any.

- ✔ Information on **management and staffing** should give details on current key staff and on any recruitment needs. Include information on staff retention strategies, reward systems, and training plans.

- ✔ The **operations** section describes how your products and services are made, how quality standards are assured, and how output can be met.

- ✔ A summary of the key **financial data,** including ratios together with a description of the key controls used to monitor and review performance.

- ✔ **Financing requirements** needed to achieve the planned goals, together with how long you will need the money for. You should also demonstrate how the business would proceed using only internal funding. The difference between these two positions is what the extra money will help to deliver.

- ✔ **E-commerce** isn't just about selling goods and services online, though that is important. It covers a range of activities that can be carried out online to make your business more efficient. These solutions extend across the supply chain from ordering your raw materials right through to after-sales service. It can incorporate market intelligence gathering, customer relationship management, and a whole range of back office procedures. Your business plan should show how you plan to tackle this area.

- ✔ Include **major milestones** with dates. For example: get prototype for testing by 20 December, file patents by 10 January, or locate suitable premises by such and such a date.

✔ **Risk assessment** features high on your reader's list of concerns, so it's best to anticipate as many as you can, together with your solution. For example: Our strategy is highly dependent on finding a warehouse with a cold store for stock. But if we can't find one by start date we will use space in the public cold store 10 miles away. Not as convenient but it will do.

✔ Detail an **exit route** for venture capitalists and business angels. Typically, they are looking to liquidate their investments within three to seven years, so your business plan should show them how much money they can make and how quickly.

If you think you need long-term investment then you need to say something about who might buy the business and when you might be able to launch it on a stock market.

✔ **Appendixes** include CVs of the key team members, technical data, patents, copyrights and designs, details on professional advisers, audited accounts, consultants' reports, abstracts of market surveys, details of orders on hand, and so on.

Writing and editing

The first draft of the business plan may have several authors and it can be written ignoring the niceties of grammar and style. The first draft is a good one to talk over the proposal with your legal adviser to keep you on the straight and narrow, and with a friendly banker or venture capitalist. This can give you an insider's view as to the strengths and weaknesses of your proposal.

When the first draft has been revised, then comes the task of editing. Here grammar, spelling, and a consistent style do matter. The end result must be a crisp, correct, clear, complete plan no more than 20 pages long. If you are not an expert writer you may need help with editing. Your local library or college may be able to help here.

Maintaining confidentiality

Finding an investor or a bank to lend to your business may take weeks or months. During that time, potential investors diligently gather information about the business so that they won't have surprises later about income, expenses, or undisclosed liabilities. The business plan is only the starting point for their investigations.

If you and the prospective financiers are strangers to one another, you may be reluctant to turn over sensitive business information until you are confident that they are serious. (This is not so sensitive an issue with banks as it is with business angels and venture capital providers.) To allay these fears, consider asking for a confidentiality letter, or agreement.

A confidentiality letter will suffice in most circumstances. But if substantial amounts of intellectual property are involved you may prefer a longer, more formal confidentiality agreement drafted by a lawyer. That's OK, but you (and perhaps your lawyer as well) should make sure that the proposed document contains no binding commitment on you. The confidentiality letter should be limited to their agreement to treat the information as strictly confidential and to use the information only to investigate lending or investing in the business, and to the other terms set out in the letter. Figure 3-1 shows a sample confidentiality agreement.

Doing due diligence

Don't be surprised if the investor wants to learn about your personal financial status, job, or business history. They are interested in your financial stability, your reputation for integrity, and your general business savvy because they will, in effect, extend credit to you until you deliver them the interest or return they are expecting on their money. That is what the *due diligence* process is all about.

Usually the due diligence process, which involves a thorough examination of both the business and its owners, takes several weeks, if not longer. But that depends on how much money your plan calls for and from whom you are trying to raise it.

Accountants and lawyers will usually subject your track record and the business plan to detailed scrutiny. You will then be required to warrant that you have provided *all* relevant information, under pain of financial penalties. The cost of this due diligence process, rarely less than a big five-figure sum and often running into six, will have to be borne by the firm raising the money, but will be paid out of the money raised, if that is any consolation.

Using Business Planning Software

You may consider taking some of the sweat out of writing your business plan by using one of the myriad of software programmes on the market. You need to take some care in using such systems as the end result can be a bland plan that pleases no one and achieves nothing worthwhile.

WHEREAS

1. The purpose of communication between the Parties to this Agreement is for the investor/lender to evaluate the suitability as an investment or lending proposition, the business proposition as set out in the business plan

2. The information to be communicated in strict confidence between the Parties to this Agreement includes the business plan, demonstrations, commercial and technical information, all forms of intellectual property and includes material for which patent or similar registration may have been filed.

THEREFORE THE PARTIES HEREBY UNDERTAKE AS FOLLOWS:

FIRST: Each Party hereto agrees to maintain as confidential and not to use any of the information directly or indirectly disclosed by the other Party until or unless such information becomes public knowledge through no fault of the recipient Party, or unless the Parties to the Agreement complete a further Agreement making provision for utilisation of information disclosed. Each Party undertakes to prevent the information disclosed from passing to other than those representatives who must be involved for the purpose of this Agreement.

SECOND: In the event that no further Agreement on utilisation or publication of information is concluded each Party hereto undertakes to return to the other all confidential items submitted and to furnish certification that no copies or other records of those items have been retained.

THIRD: In the event that either Party requires the assistance of a further party in pursuing the purposes of the Agreement the approval of the other Party to this Agreement shall be secured.

FOURTH: Any information which either Party can prove was in his possession prior to disclosure hereunder and was not acquired from the other Party or his representatives is excepted from this Agreement.

FIFTH: The construction, validity and performance of this Agreement shall be governed in all respects by Law and the Parties hereto submit to the jurisdiction of the Courts.

SIGNED for
First Party...

Position:..

For and on behalf of:

....

In the presence of:

....

SIGNED for
Second Party...

Position:..

For and on behalf of:

....

In the presence of:

....

Figure 3-1:
A confi-
dentiality
agreement.

Don't buy a package with several hundred business plans covering every type of business imaginable. The chances are that the person who wrote the plans knows far less than you do about your business sector and will add little or no value to your proposition. Worse still there is at least an even chance that the reader of your plan will have seen the fruits of these packaged plans before and may be less than enthusiastic to see yet another one.

You may well find it useful to use the test shown in Figure 3-2 as an uncomplicated form of self-assessment, before becoming bogged down in number-crunching software.

Recognising the limits of software

Good business planning software provides a useful structure to drop your plan in to and may provide a few helpful spreadsheets and templates for financial projections and market analysis. It also provides a valuable repository for your work-in-progress as you assemble the evidence to convince yourself and others that your business will succeed.

What software does not do is write a convincing business proposition by itself. The maxim, 'garbage in garbage out' applies to business planning software just as it does to everything to do with computers.

The other danger is that you end up with spreadsheet solutions – numbers just pumped into the financials – without any evidence of the underlying logic to support them.

Use business planning software as an aid and not a crutch. Go beyond that and you may end up worse than if you had started with a blank sheet of paper.

Reviewing systems

This section provides reviews of some business planning software packages that have been used to good effect.

- American Express (home3.americanexpress.com/smallbusiness/tool/biz_plan/index.asp): American Express run something they call the Small Business Exchange Business Plan Workshop. This workshop will help you write a business plan using their 'Toolboxes' of samples, worksheets, and glossaries. You can experiment on someone else's business in the 'Try It Yourself' section by testing your skills on a fictional business plan and be rated on how prepared you are to create your own.

Book I

E-Business
101

By answering the questions below you will get some idea of how well your business plan is progressing. Score 1, 2, or 3 following the key below for each of the questions. Mark the options closest to your instincts, and be honest. Then add up your scores and refer to the results at the end of the questionnaire to see how you scored and to check the potential of your plan.

Whatever your score, remember that this type of self-assessment test is broad brush. It is designed only to give an indication of whether you have the basic attitude, instincts, and capabilities to make a success of launching a home-based business.

If your score is low, the chances are that you do not. If it is high, the opposite is true.

1 = Made a start   2 = Some data only   3 = Comprehensive

Title page   ☐1 ☐2 ☐3

Name of business contact details, date of business plan, contents

Executive summary   ☐1 ☐2 ☐3

Your details; summary of key strategies; why you are better or different; summary of profit projections; summary of financial needs

The business and its management ☐1 ☐2 ☐3

You and your team's relevant experience; business goals and objectives; legal structure of the business

The marketing strategy   ☐1 ☐2 ☐3

Market segment analysis; pricing strategy; promotion plans; product mix and range; e-commerce strategy; location; selling strategy

Management and staffing   ☐1 ☐2 ☐3

Staff numbers; roles and responsibilities; recruitment needs

Operations   ☐1 ☐2 ☐3

What facilities and equipment are needed; what services will be brought in?

Legal issues   ☐1 ☐2 ☐3

What intellectual protection do you have as a barrier to entry; what other legal issues affect your business?

Financial forecasts   ☐1 ☐2 ☐3

Summary of financial projections; monthly cash flows; profit and loss accounts; balance sheets; break-even analysis

Financing requirements   ☐1 ☐2 ☐3

How much money do you need; what is it needed for; how much money can you provide; how much do you need to raise from outside; what security is available?

Figure 3-2:
Assessing
the Content
of Your
Business
Plan.

Results:

9 points or less
You still have a lot more information to gather or decisions to make. No serious plan can be drawn up at this stage.
Between 10 and 20 points:
You have made progress, but still have a few gaps to fill. Concentrate your efforts on completing your plan.
More than 20 points:
Your plan is now complete and ready for final editing.

✔ BizPlanit.Com (website:www.bizplanit.com; e-mail: biz@bizplanit.com): BizPlanIt.Com's website has free resources offering information, advice, articled links to other useful sites and a free monthly newsletter, the *Virtual Business Plan* to pinpoint information. They also have an email service, providing answers to business plan questions within 24 hours.

✔ Royal Bank of Canada (www.royalbank.com): This site has a wide range of useful help for entrepreneurs. At www.royalbank.com/sme/index.html you can have access to their business plan writer package and three sample business plans.

✔ National Federation of Enterprise Agencies (NFEA) (www.smallbusinessadvice.org.uk): The Website of NFEA has a step-by-step business planning guide with free downloads to help with the financial calculations.

Presenting Your Plan

Anyone backing a business does so primarily because they believe in the management. They know from experience that things rarely go according to plan so they must be confident that the team involved can respond effectively to changing conditions. You can be sure that any financier you are presenting to will have read dozens of similar plans, and will be well rehearsed. They may even have taken the trouble to find out something of your business and financial history.

Starring in show time

When you present your business plan to financial backers, your goal is to create empathy between yourself and your listeners. Whilst you may not be able to change your personality you could take a few tips on presentation skills. Eye contact, tone of speech, enthusiasm, and body language all have a part to play in making a presentation go well.

Wearing a suit is never likely to upset anyone. Shorts and sandals could just set the wrong tone! Serious money calls for serious people and even the Internet world is growing up.

Rehearse your presentation beforehand, having found out how much time you have. Explain your strategy in a business-like manner, demonstrating your grasp of the competitive market forces at work. Listen to comments and criticisms carefully, avoiding a defensive attitude when you respond.

Use visual aids and if possible bring and demonstrate your product or service. A video or computer-generated model is better than nothing.

Allow at least as much time for questions as you take in your talk. Make your replies to questions brief and to the point. If they want more information, they can ask. This approach allows time for the many different questions that must be asked either now or later, before an investment can proceed.

Making an 'elevator pitch'

You never know when the chance to present your business plan may occur – maybe even in a lift between floors (hence the term *elevator pitch*). You need to have every aspect of your business plan in your head and know your way around the plan backwards, forwards, and sideways. It's as well to have a five-, ten- and 20-minute presentation ready to run at a moment's notice.

One entrepreneur was given a chance to make a presentation of her business plan to the most powerful and influential person in her industry. This person could make or break new businesses and frequently did. The opportunity was a ten-minute ride in a chauffeur-driven car between the Dorchester hotel and Harrods. She had no room to demonstrate the product, set up flip charts or PowerPoint presentations or to involve the team. That was just enough space and time for a handful of powerful facts to be conveyed with passion, conviction, and authority. Fortunately the entrepreneur concerned had rehearsed her impromptu presentation and was completely prepared to seize the opportunity presented. She now has a £10 million business, eight years after taking that fateful car ride.

Stuff for Other Places?

Two friends, who eventually made it to an enterprise programme, and to founding a successful company, had great difficulty in getting backing at first. They were exceptionally talented designers and makers of clothes. They started out making ball-gowns, wedding dresses, and children's clothes – anything the market wanted. Only when they focused on designing and marketing clothes for the mother-to-be that allowed them still to feel fashionably dressed, was it obvious that they had a winning concept. That strategy built on their strength as designers and their experiences as former mothers-to-be, and exploited a clear market opportunity neglected at that time by the main player in the marketplace.

From that point their company made a quantum leap forward from turning over a couple of hundred thousand pounds a year into the several million pound league within a few years.

Chapter 4

Setting Off in the Right Direction

· ·

In This Chapter

▶ Understanding why a set of values is so important

▶ Figuring out who your stakeholders are

▶ Identifying your company's current beliefs and principles

▶ Putting together your company values statement

▶ Creating a vision statement for your company

· ·

*Y*ou may ask yourself why on earth you're reading a chapter on values and vision in a book on business planning. We can hear what you're thinking: Hey, it's the twenty-first century. Today's business ethics revolve around survival in the marketplace: Cater to your customers, beat the competition (hey, demolish them!), make 'loadsamoney', and run.

Yet even in a business world dominated by market economies, global competition, and the laws of the jungle, values still matter. In fact, we're convinced that successful business plans must start with a statement of company values.

Now, don't get us wrong here – we have no quarrel with profits. We absolutely love them, and we expect to earn lots for ourselves over time. But short-term profits don't go far over the long haul. Values and a vision keep everybody in your company – even if there are only two of you – on course and heading in the same direction. What if you're a company of one? Taking time to establish your values and vision will still keep you on track as your business grows.

In this chapter, we point out why values are so important in the first place. We help you identify your company's values by noting who has a stake in your business and discovering the beliefs and business principles that you already hold. Then we show you how to put together a values statement and create a vision statement for your company.

Why Values Matter

Your company faces all sorts of options, alternatives, and decisions every day that you're in business. If you take the time to define your company's values, these principles and beliefs can guide your managers, employees, or just you (if you're in business for yourself) as you face complicated issues that don't have easy answers. When the unexpected happens, you'll be able to react quickly and decisively, based on a clear sense of what's important.

Tough choices

Consider a scenario. Frank Little is an independent consultant working for a large UK-based petrochemical firm that we'll call Bigg Oil. He's conducting market analysis for one of the company's largest divisions and is involved in an important project concerning the development of new overseas business.

Frank's good at what he does, and he sketches out several options for the production, distribution, and pricing of petrochemicals in three countries. In one of his most promising scenarios, the numbers for a country that we'll call Friedonia yield substantially higher short-term profits than the other two – primarily because that nation doesn't yet have expensive pollution-control procedures in place. The other two nations have environmental laws similar to those in the UK.

Here's Frank's dilemma: By introducing its product line into Friedonia, Frank's client can make huge profits. Sure, the resulting pollution may cause ecological damage that could possibly be traced back to Bigg Oil. But there is nothing illegal in the company's activities, according to Friedonia's current laws, and Frank stands to get a lot more business from Bigg Oil if the project goes ahead.

He agonises over the situation and his report. What should Frank recommend to senior management?

- Go for the short-term bucks.
- Voluntarily enact procedures to control pollution, even though the company is not legally required to do so.
- Forget Friedonia until the country has stronger environmental laws.

Maybe you can relate to our friend Frank's quandary, having faced similar kinds of ethical questions and trade-offs in your own business.

If Frank had a set of values written down, those values could help him out of his quandary. Values provide a framework to guide people who are confronted with difficult choices.

Having no fundamental guidelines to follow – or, worse yet, being told to play it safe or 'don't rock the boat' – businesspeople in Frank's position are forced to choose the safest path, and that path is often determined by profits alone. But the easiest path is not always the best.

Lost and unprepared

What happens when disaster strikes? We all remember headline-grabbing stories in which unexpected troubles tarnished the images of all sorts of companies, such as the following:

- ✔ **Exxon (oil manufacturer and exporter):** The infamous oil tanker *Valdez* spilled millions of gallons of crude oil into a pristine Alaskan bay, causing incalculable environmental damage.

- ✔ **Perrier (natural carbonated water bottler):** In 1989, French-based Perrier was the market leader in bottled mineral water, its name synonymous with purity and quality. Perrier water was on the tables of virtually every high-class restaurant around the world. Sales peaked at 1.2 billion bottles a year. The plant at Vergèze, near Nimes, was tooled up for 1.5 billion, with capital investment and personnel to match. The Perrier water benzene contamination incident in 1990 wiped out a lifetime investment in promoting the images of purity and quality.

- ✔ **Intel (computer chip manufacturer):** A flaw in its Pentium chip (which was or wasn't really significant, depending on who you talked to) led to corporate apologies and product replacement.

These companies all stumbled over so-called externalities (to use economics doublespeak). *Externalities* refer to those circumstances that extend beyond a firm's immediate control to issues that are deeper than simply making a mint. Over time, the failure to see the power of these outside forces – and to account for social and ethical values when you make decisions – can result in serious or even disastrous consequences for your company. As the examples illustrate, we're not talking about one unhappy customer, folks; we're talking about big-time trouble.

Our list of examples could include episodes involving companies of every size in all industries. Faced with unexpected events, unprepared companies often react as though they are in total disarray. When a company lacks a set of stated values that everybody subscribes to, the interpretation of important issues is left up to anyone and everyone in the company. Then the company is likely to find itself speaking with many voices and going in several directions, resulting in confused employees, unhappy customers, an angry public, and maybe, disappointed investors.

The value of having values

A *values statement* is a set of beliefs and principles that guides the activities and operations of a company, no matter what its size. The people at the top of your company must exemplify your stated values, and your company's incentive and reward systems should lead all employees to act in ways that support your company's values.

The Johnson & Johnson Credo

'We believe our first responsibility is to the doctors, nurses, and patients, to mothers and all others who use our products and services. In meeting their needs, everything we do must be of high quality. We must constantly strive to reduce our costs in order to maintain reasonable prices. Customers' orders must be serviced promptly and accurately. Our suppliers and distributors must have an opportunity to make a fair profit.

We are responsible to our employees, the men and women who work with us throughout the world. Everyone must be considered as an individual. We must respect their dignity and recognize their merit. They must have a sense of security in their jobs. Compensation must be fair and adequate, and working conditions clean, orderly, and safe. Employees must feel free to make suggestions and complaints. There must be equal opportunity for employment, development, and advancement for those qualified. We must provide competent management, and their actions must be just and ethical.

We are responsible to the communities in which we live and work and to the world community as well. We must be good citizens – support good works and charities and bear our fair share of taxes. We must encourage civic improvements and better health and education. We must maintain in good order the property we are privileged to use, protecting the environment and natural resources.

Our final responsibility is to our stockholders. Business must make a sound profit. We must experiment with new ideas. Research must be carried on, innovative programs developed and mistakes paid for. New equipment must be purchased, new facilities provided and new products launched. Reserves must be created to provide for adverse times. When we operate according to these principles, the stockholders should realise a fair return.'

Here's an example of just how important a values statement can be. In the summer of 1985, the United States experienced what was described by many people as a terrorist attack. Someone in the Chicago area tampered with bottles of Tylenol, the best-selling pain reliever from McNeil Laboratories, a subsidiary of the health care giant Johnson & Johnson. An unknown number of Tylenol capsules were laced with cyanide, and eight people died. The tragedy created a business crisis for Johnson & Johnson.

Johnson & Johnson reacted quickly and decisively to the threat against its customers. The company pulled every bottle of Tylenol from retail shelves throughout America – a massive undertaking that ultimately cost the company more than $100 million – and it did so immediately upon learning of the problem.

When the crisis was finally over, Johnson & Johnson became a corporate role model. The company's lightning-fast response to the Tylenol incident earned it a reputation as one of the most responsible companies in the world, one that takes its civic duties seriously and is willing to put the public good ahead of its own profits. Johnson & Johnson's many businesses benefited accordingly.

Why did Johnson & Johnson behave so well when so many other companies find themselves paralysed in similar situations? The reasons are summed up in the company's statement of values, an extraordinary document called the Johnson & Johnson Credo (see the 'The Johnson & Johnson Credo' sidebar).

For more than half a century, the credo has successfully guided behaviour and actions across the sprawling Johnson & Johnson empire, currently a £17 billion worldwide corporation employing more than 109,500 people.

The Johnson & Johnson Credo works so well because each employee takes it seriously. With the active encouragement and involvement of top management, from the chairperson on down, the credo is invoked, praised, and communicated throughout the company. Old-timers and new employees alike are continually reminded of the importance of the message. Promotions depend, in part, on how well managers live up to and disseminate the values of the credo within their areas of responsibility. The credo is a significant factor in Johnson & Johnson's continued performance near the top of its industry – and an indication of why the company is so well regarded by so many people.

Identifying Your Company's Values

Values statements often address several audiences. The Johnson & Johnson Credo (refer to the preceding section), for example, speaks to doctors, patients, customers, suppliers, distributors, employees, stockholders, and the community at large. As you begin to work on your own company's values, you should think about different groups, each of which has some relationship with your company.

Stakeholders are groups of people who have some claim or interest in how you operate your business. The stakes involved can be tangible and legally binding, or they may be informal arrangements or expectations that have developed over time. Although all of these interested parties have a stake in what you do, stakeholders may have different ideas and rather strong feelings about what values your company should embrace.

You're going to put together a values statement primarily for the benefit of employees, of course (or just for yourself, if you operate a business alone). But your company's values are going to have an obvious impact on all your stakeholders, including owners, shareholders, customers, suppliers, regulators – and even your mother, if she loaned you £10,000 to start your business. As you start to identify the values that are most important to your company, you're going to have to consider different viewpoints, including the following:

✔ The demands of your shareholders (if you have any)

✔ The interests and expectations of all your stakeholders

✔ The beliefs and principles that you and your company already hold

In the following sections, we take a closer look at each of these factors. When you come up with a preliminary list of company values that you feel are most important, you'll be in a good position to go on and create a values statement.

Investors

Economists argue that when it comes to company values, you really have to worry about only one significant group: the shareholders. On paper, at least, the shareholders are the true owners of the firm, and they deserve your undivided attention. In this view of the world, managers are simply paid agents of those who own the company, no matter how far removed those owners may be, and you don't need to know much more about values except to carry out your shareholders' wishes.

Now, we can't really argue with this picture, as far as it goes, but it doesn't square with the intentions of many shareholders out there today. For starters, your company may not have any investors, unless you count yourself and the bank account that you wiped out to start your company. In addition, pension and mutual funds now control the majority of publicly-held stocks, and the investors who buy these funds are mainly interested in making their own personal nest eggs grow. These shareholders are absentee owners. They seldom demand a serious say in management decision making. When something goes wrong with the company or with their fund, they simply sell the shares and get on with their next investment.

So what's our point? Although shareholders obviously are an important bunch, deserving the attention of companies that have shareholders, their demands shouldn't necessarily crowd out all other voices. Remember – your shareholders have the luxury of selling off shares and moving on to other choices when things go wrong. As a manager or owner, you don't have that option.

Your company will be much better off in the long run if you take a broader view, acknowledging not just the shareholders, but also all the stakeholders, giving each group the attention that it deserves.

The rest of the crew

If you think about it, you may be surprised at how many types of people are involved in what your company does – everyone from suppliers to distributors and from bankers to customers. Each group has its own set of interests and looks to your company to fulfil a series of promises. The explicit promises that you make may take the form of legal agreements, licences, freelance agreements, or purchase orders. Your implicit promises represent the unwritten expectations of the various groups that have dealings with your company.

For each group of stakeholders that you identify, you should ask two basic questions:

- ✔ What are these people most interested in?
- ✔ What do these people expect from my company?

In other words, what is their stake in the activities and behaviour of your company? At first glance, it may seem that your interests conflict with your stakeholders' interests. *You* may want to maximise profits over time as one of your company's key values, for example. You may decide that serving customers is important as well. But what do your *customers* want? They certainly have a stake in your business, and it's probably safe to say that they are looking for quality products and services at reasonable prices.

Do these two values conflict with each other? Not necessarily. Wouldn't most customers rather buy from companies that they trust, companies that they feel comfortable with, companies that have served them well in the past? In addition, customers don't really like the uncertainty and time wasted in trying new products or services, and they won't make a change unless they're really pushed to do so. In other words, most of your customers don't want to deny you profits, because they realise that your business – and their favourite goods and services – won't be around for long if you can't make any money.

At the same time, customers aren't stupid and certainly don't want to be taken advantage of. We've all heard stories about food and hardware stores that try to make a quick buck after floods, hurricanes, or earthquakes. Although competition usually keeps prices in check, scarcity creates opportunity and the temptation to overcharge customers. But again, customers are stakeholders in the business, with interests and expectations. After a disaster is over and the clean-up is behind them, those same customers often take their cash elsewhere, rewarding stores that may have behaved more responsibly in the crisis.

It's time to bring together all your information on the people who have a stake in your company and to create a stakeholder profile. Follow these steps:

1. **List all interest groups that have a relationship with your company.**

   Don't forget to include the less-obvious candidates. Your list may include customers, owners, shareholders, banks, creditors, suppliers, distributors, business partners, industry associates, regulatory agencies, advocacy groups, and so on.

2. **Rank the stakeholders by importance to the business.**

   How does each group affect your business goals?

3. **Record what you think are the interests of each group.**

4. **Record what you think are the expectations of each group.**

Do your company's actions fit with what you have identified as being your key stakeholders' expectations? You should always be aware of how your business decisions are perceived by the general public. How do those decisions look from the other side? Do you see satisfied customers, contented employees, helpful creditors, responsive suppliers, and eager distributors? If not, how is your company going to respond to those stakeholders who feel that you are letting them down?

Ideally, of course, you want to plan ahead when it comes to your dealings with all stakeholders. The secret to responding before molehills become mountains lies in having a clear understanding of each group's expectations and a set of values that acknowledges each group's interests.

Book I

E-Business
101

Existing beliefs and principles

Drawing up a list of abstract beliefs and principles is one thing, putting those beliefs to the test is another. Tough choices come along, forcing you to examine your beliefs closely. If you run a one-person company, you already know something about what you stand for. If you're part of a bigger company, chances are that certain beliefs and values are inherent in the way in which your company does business. The best way to get to the heart of those beliefs and principles is to imagine how youd respond to tough dilemmas.

Think about the situations described in the Beliefs and Principles Questionnaire (see Figure 4-1). Ask other people in your company, or trusted colleagues from outside your business, how they'd react to these situations. Chances are you'll wish that the questionnaire included a box marked *Other* or *Don't know*. But the whole point of situations that put your values to the test is that they're not always easy.

Beliefs and Principles Questionnaire

Situation	*Possible response*
A disgruntled customer demands a full sales refund on a product. The product isn't defective but can't be resold. The customer insists that it just doesn't work correctly. Would you be more inclined to:	❏ Send the customer away, keeping the sale on the books ❏ Refund the customer's money, absorbing the loss but betting on repeat business and loyal customers
You are faced with filling a key position in your company. Would you be more inclined to:	❏ Recruit a person from the outside who has the necessary job skills but little experience in your industry ❏ Promote an experienced and loyal employee, providing job-skills training
You are forced to let one of your employees go. Would you tend to dismiss:	❏ The young, recently hired university graduate, inexperienced but energetic ❏ The 55-year-old manager with 20 years at the company, solid and hard-working but somewhat set in his or her ways
You find out that a long-term supplier has been routinely undercharging you for services, increasing your own profit margins. Would you be inclined to:	❏ Let the matter pass, assuming that it's ultimately the supplier's mistake and responsibility ❏ Take the initiative to correct the invoice error in the future ❏ Offer to not only correct the mistake, but also pay back the accumulated difference

(continued)

Figure 4-1:
Beliefs and Principles Questionnaire.

Beliefs and Principles Questionnaire *Continued*

Situation	Possible response
You have a brilliant and creative employee. Unfortunately, this employee continually flouts the rules and disrupts the entire company. Would you tend to:	❏ Tolerate the behaviour ❏ Work on ways to correct the situation ❏ Sack the employee
An employee is faced with a personal dilemma. To meet a deadline on an important project, the employee must work overtime and miss a child's birthday celebration. Which do you tend to think of as the "better" employee:	❏ The one who willingly agrees to work overtime ❏ The one who declines to come in and instead attends the birthday party
To meet your profit target for the coming quarter, you are faced with reducing costs. Would you lean toward:	❏ Cutting back on customer-service expenses ❏ Reducing current investment in new product development ❏ Missing the quarterly target, concluding that the long-term investments are both necessary and justified
When developing the compensation packages for managers in your company, would you support:	❏ Incentives based primarily on rewarding individual effort ❏ Compensation systems that promote attainment of group or team-based goals
You discover that one of your products doesn't quite meet its published specifications. Would your likely response be to:	❏ Immediately alert your customers to the discrepancy ❏ Invest some time and effort in understanding the problem before informing customers ❏ Quietly correct the error, assuming that if customers were having problems, they would have already come to you
Rank the following in terms of their importance to you in your business:	❏ Maximize profits ❏ Satisfy customers ❏ Create jobs ❏ Promote new technologies ❏ Win product-quality awards ❏ Beat the competition ❏ Maintain long-term growth ❏ Dominate markets

Answers to the questionnaire point to the beliefs and principles that your company's managers and employees already hold.

Keep in mind that there are no right or wrong answers; no one's going to send a note home or give anyone a bad mark. You're simply trying to identify the basic values that your company already feels comfortable with. Completed questionnaires give insights into the general beliefs and principles that your company considers to be important.

Putting Together the Values Statement

When you have a good idea of just who your company's stakeholders are, and when you have got to grips with the general beliefs and principles that your company already holds, you have to bring these two worlds together. But how do you create a written statement of values based on those general beliefs and principles that will also guide your company toward doing the right thing in the eyes of all your stakeholders?

First, keep in mind that your company's values statement represents more than a quick to-do list. Your values reach beyond quarterly goals or even yearly targets. They're meant to guide you through those tough decisions as you build a sustainable business that will last and grow over years and decades.

Maybe your company already has some sort of values credo in place. If so, you're a step ahead of the game. (You lose points, however, if you have to glance at the dusty plaque on the office wall to read it.) If you can't dig up a ready-made values statement to start with, begin putting together your own. You have two options.

The quick way to develop a values statement

You may not have the luxury of spending weeks or months to develop a values statement, so we'll show you a quick way to create one that will set your company on the right track. If your company is small, you can follow the steps yourself or with one or two of your colleagues – no need for long meetings and careful review. If you're part of a larger company, however, you're going to have to go through a bit more rigmarole to get a consensus. Sorry.

1. **Meet with your company's chief decision-makers to talk about the general company values that should guide employee behaviour.**

2. **Prepare a first-draft list of all the values discussed in the meeting and circulate copies for review.**

3. **Schedule one or two follow-up meetings with senior managers to clarify and confirm a final set of values.**

4. **Create a values statement that captures the agreed-upon values clearly and concisely, and get it approved.**

5. **Meet with managers at all levels to make sure that they understand the importance of, and reasoning behind, the company values statement.**

6. **See that every employee gets a copy of the statement.**

The values statement that you come up with here may serve you well for a long time. At the very least, it should meet your needs while you work on a more complete and permanent version.

Make sure that every employee receives a copy of your company's values statement, along with an explanation of its purpose. If you're in business for yourself, place a framed copy of the values statement near your desk or (if you work from home) stick it on the fridge. Don't let it gather dust. For a bigger company, print the values statement on wallet-sized cards, and don't forget to include it in the annual report. It's important that your company's values are referred to, relied on, and understood to be a guiding force in the actions and activities of every person who represents your company.

The long way to develop a values statement

Why is the quick way to create a values statement not always good enough? If you're part of a large firm, the quick way relies heavily on the ideas and suggestions of people at the top of the organisation. Yet the best insights on company values often come from employees themselves – people from different backgrounds and various levels in the company who can draw on a range of business experiences.

The long way to create a values statement takes a little more effort, but getting these employees involved usually is worth it. Follow these steps:

1. **Select three or four representative groups of employees, including a mix of people from all levels and functions in your company.**

2. **Have the groups meet on a rather formal basis over a two- to three-month period to come up with values that should guide the behaviour of every employee in the firm.**

   You have to point the groups in the right direction at the beginning. Start by asking everyone to fill out the questionnaire shown in Figure 3-1 earlier in this chapter.

3. **Ask group members to create a short list of the values that they think are most important.**

   Encourage them to back up this list with their reasons, reminding them that values are often the tiebreakers when it comes to tough management decisions and difficult choices.

4. **Bring the lists together and create a priority ranking of all the values suggested.**

5. **Compose a statement, motto, or credo that includes the most significant and widely held values, along with compelling reasons for those values.**

6. **Have the groups review and ratify your values statement.**

When it's time to conduct those annual employee performance reviews (you know, the ones that everyone loves to hate), use them as an opportunity to promote your company's values. Bring out a copy of the values statement and ask each employee how well his or her individual activities reflect the company's values. At the same time, ask yourself whether the incentive and reward systems in your company work toward supporting those values.

Creating Your Company's Vision Statement

After you identify the stakeholders in your company and create your company's values statement, it's time to come up with a *vision statement* – a precise, well-crafted set of words announcing where your company wants to go or painting a picture of what your company wants to become. To people inside and outside your company, your vision statement is your compass, showing the whole world the direction in which your company is headed.

A vision statement not only points the way to the future, but also makes you want to get up and go there. It represents your company's best hopes and brightest dreams. Now, we know that Karl Marx and his crew seldom come up in conversation at cocktail parties any longer, even in Moscow. But when you hear his message

> *Workers of the world, unite! You have nothing to lose but your chains!*

it's hard not to be roused, even today. Effective vision statements are, in part, inspirational calls to action. What if Marx had come up with something like this:

> *Hey, guys, let's all get together over here! Maybe we can figure out how to make you more dosh!*

Karl who? Forget that place in history.

Don't panic if you don't have the makings of a dynamic, charismatic leader in your back pocket. An insightful corporate vision is much more likely to develop out of a diverse team of hard-working folks than to spring mysteriously from an inspired moment in the life of a leader. And if you wait around for the person at the top to produce something, you may never see a vision statement. Tackle the task on your own, before it's requested from above, and you just may jump-start a process that's long overdue.

It shouldn't surprise you to learn that the best way to create a meaningful vision statement looks a lot like the best way to create a values statement. Just follow these steps:

1. **Select a small group of dedicated employees from various levels across your company.**

   If your company is small, get the whole gang together. If you're the chief cook and bottle washer all in one, you can represent yourself. Remember – the more people you involve, the broader the perspective and the better the chance you'll get a vision statement that truly reflects your company's future.

2. **Have the group reread your company's values statement and review the list of stakeholders who have an interest in your company.**

3. **Begin a verbal free-for-all.**

   Allow everybody to add his or her own two pennies' worth and to volunteer personal opinions and ideas about the company's future form and direction.

4. **After the vision team feels comfortable with its work, add the finishing touches and send the draft upstairs.**

   If it's to take on its rightful role, a vision statement must be embraced and promoted by managers at the top.

Keep these tips in mind when you create your vision statement:

- ✔ Make sure that no one dominates the discussion as the team begins to toss around ideas and the phrases that will form your company's vision. There's no faster way to kill off creativity than having every idea come from one person.

- ✔ Allow sufficient time for the words to grow on the group, permitting the deeper meanings to sink in. You can't accomplish the vision statement process in one quick take. Good vision statements have a tendency to evolve over time – and several meetings.

- ✔ Make sure that your company's vision statement is tied to your company's reality. Nothing is worse than creating a vision that has more to do with fantasy than with the future. Fantasy visions generate nothing but a sense of confusion and alienation among everyone involved.

Although your vision statement may be only a couple of sentences or even just a phrase, the vision statement is the compass that provides your company's direction into the future. Spend enough time with your statement to make sure that the north on your compass truly is north – that it does indeed point in the direction in which you want to go.

As a rule of thumb, you should assume that your vision statement will serve the company for the next decade. Does this mean that you can never change the statement? No – but you should change a vision statement only if business conditions truly warrant a new course of action. Keep in mind that the ideas you captured in your company's vision statement aren't meant to be crossed out or rewritten on a whim; they represent the lasting themes that guide your company at any time and under any circumstance.

But only diamonds are forever. If a changing environment throws you an unexpected curve, by all means alter your vision to reflect the new reality. If the words on paper no longer have meaning for your company, they are wasted on everyone. Again, the company's vision statement is useful only to the extent that it has the power to move your people forward into the future.

Book I

E-Business 101

Chapter 5

Harnessing Creativity in Your Business

*O*kay, time to be creative. Ready, set, go. Come up with any good ideas yet? No? Then try again. Now do you have some good ideas? What? No?

If you can't be creative at will, don't be alarmed. Most people face this problem. When there's a need to be creative in marketing, many people find that they require some help. This chapter helps you put the processes in place to generate some unusually creative – and hopefully profitable – ideas.

The Creative Process at a Glance

If you think of creativity as generating wild and crazy ideas, you're right – but only partly right. You have to do some open-minded thinking to come up with creative concepts (We tell you how in the following sections). But to actually make any money from your creativity, you need to have a mix of activities that includes exploring for new ideas and developing the best of them into practical applications in your ads, products, sales presentations, or other marketing activities. Here is a simple four-step process for turning ideas into action:

1. **Initiate.**

   In this step, you recognise a need or opportunity and ask questions that begin the creative process. For example, you may take a look at your delivery vehicle(s) and ask yourself if there isn't some way to make them stand out and communicate what your business is all about. The creative brief that we discuss later on in this chapter is useful at the initiate stage.

2. **Imagine.**

In this stage of the creative process, you engage in the imaginative, uninhibited thinking that taps into your artistic side. The techniques that we cover in the 'Brainstorming' section later in this chapter are good for this stage; your goal is to see how many wild ideas you can generate.

3. **Invent.**

Now you need to get more practical. Take a critical look at all those wild ideas and choose one or a few that seem most promising. Work on these ideas to see how to make them more practical and feasible. You can't put flashing lights all over your company vans to catch attention – it's certainly creative but falls foul of road traffic law. Is there another fun, engaging but workable idea from stage 2? Innocent Drinks, which makes fresh fruit and yoghurt smoothies, covered its vans in artificial grass and flowers – an eye-catching solution that said a lot about what the company made and even more about its fun approach to business.

4. **Implement.**

Finally, you need to complete the creative process by pursuing successful adoption or implementation of your new idea or design. You may have a great design for a new company vehicle, but is there a company that can actually transfer your ideas onto the real thing – how, for instance, do you get a phone number and Web address onto fake grass?

Finding Out What You Need to Change

The smartest thing to do when you have a stunning, timeless, classic success in marketing is to leave it alone. But how many of those kinds of concepts can you think of? A tin of Heinz Baked Beans. The Apple computer logo. A Porsche sports car. A Swiss army knife. The Michelin Man. The truth is that even these marketing icons have made many changes over the years – but they're careful to protect the brand heritage they have got. So if you're not changing many of the aspects of your marketing, you should ask yourself why not?

Harnessing creativity in your business allows you to do things differently – differently from before, and differently from your competition. Once you start thinking about creativity and change, you might find yourself surprised by how much of what you do has remained the same. You don't want to allow others to catch up, or for your marketing to become stale, so it's time you started a creative overhaul of your business.

The marketing audit: More fun than it sounds

To find out what your next marketing project should be, do a quick marketing creativity audit right now. Respond to each of the situations in Table 5-1 as honestly as you can, circling 1 if your answer is 'rarely', 5 if your answer is 'frequently', and the numbers in between if your answer is somewhere between 'rarely' and 'frequently'.

Table 5-1	Marketing Creativity Audit
Marketing Creativity Actions	*Rating (1 = rarely; 5 = frequently)*
We make improvements to the selection, design, packaging, or appearance of our product(s).	1 2 3 4 5
We experiment with prices, discounts, and special offers to achieve our marketing goals.	1 2 3 4 5
We find new ways to bring our product(s) to customers, making buying or using the product(s) more convenient or easier for them.	1 2 3 4 5
We update and improve our brand image or the ways we communicate that brand image.	1 2 3 4 5
We try creative new ways of communicating with customers and prospects.	1 2 3 4 5
We improve the look and feel of our sales or marketing materials.	1 2 3 4 5
We listen to customer complaints or objections, and we find creative ways to turn those complaints into our next business opportunities.	1 2 3 4 5
We change our marketing message.	1 2 3 4 5
We reach out to new types of customers to try to expand or improve our customer base.	1 2 3 4 5
We share creative ideas and have freewheeling discussions with all those people who are involved in marketing our product(s).	1 2 3 4 5

Add up all the numbers you circled to get a score between 10 and 50. See where your score falls in the range following this paragraph to find out what your Marketing Creativity Score means. Depending on your answers, you can rate your marketing creativity as very low, low, medium, or high. You need to be at least in the medium range, if not at the high end, to gain any benefits from creativity.

- 10–19 = very low
- 20–29 = low
- 30–39 = medium
- 40–50 = high

You can't leave anything alone in marketing. This audit reveals aspects of your marketing that nobody has looked at or tried to improve for the past few years. If you can identify any unchanging elements of your sales, service, advertising, mailings, or anything else that touches the customer, you have just found your next marketing project. So jot down three to six things that you tend to take for granted. You've just made your creative to-do list.

Picking your creative role

In marketing (and in business, in general) you have to actually do something with your creative ideas, and make those ideas work, to profit from your imagination. You must make a focused effort to invent practical ways to implement what you imagine.

The creative process includes four steps (see the preceding section) that rely on different types of behaviours. You may be especially suited to one or two of the steps, but probably not to all of them. We recommend you work out which steps you are best and worst at, and then find people to help you fill your creative gaps. Read the following list of styles to see which suits your temperament best:

- **Entrepreneur:** The entrepreneur senses a need or problem and asks tough questions to initiate the creative process. ('Why do we do it this way? It seems so inefficient.') This style proves valuable in Step 1 of the creative process, Initiate.

- **Artist:** The artist is highly imaginative and a free thinker. When given a focus by the entrepreneur's initiating question, the artist can easily dream up many alternatives and fresh approaches from which to choose. ('We could do this, or this, or this, or . . . ') The artist comes to the fore in Step 2 of the creative process, Imagine.

✔ **Inventor:** The inventor has a more practical sort of imagination and loves to develop and refine a single good idea until he makes it work. ('Let's see. If we adjust this, and add that, it will work much better.') The inventor is most productive in Step 3 of the creative process, Invent.

✔ **Engineer:** The engineer's style is practical and businesslike, and engineers are particularly good at getting closure by taking an untested or rough invention the rest of the way and making it work smoothly and well. ('Great ideas, but let's come up with a firm plan and budget so we can get this thing started.') Engineers make sure the process reaches its essential Step 4, Implement.

Whichever one of these creative roles most closely represents your approach to work, recognise that one role alone can't make good, creative marketing happen. Be prepared to adjust your style by wearing some of the other creative hats at times, or team up with others whose styles differ from your own. That way, you have the range of approaches that you need to combine in order to harness the power of creativity for all your marketing efforts.

Generating Great Ideas

Creativity is the most fundamental and powerful of all the marketing skills. There's always a better way. And if things aren't going your way – sales are slow, the boss rejects your proposals, customers complain about service, or your mailings don't get a good response – then remember to take some time out for creativity. The right creative idea at the right moment can turn the marketing tide your way. But generating that creative spark takes a little time, a little work, and a few strategies.

Finding the time to think

To be creative, you first must give yourself permission to be creative in your work. Creativity requires you to let the mind's engine sit in idle. You can't be creative if you're busy returning e-mails or phone calls, or rushing to finish your paperwork for the day. If the hands are busy, the mind is distracted from creativity, and your imagination may not be able to work. So, for starters, we must ask you to budget time for creativity.

How much time? Well, if creativity is the most powerful and profitable of the marketing skills, how often do you think you should use it? One hour a month? One hour a week? One hour a day? One day a week? You have to decide exactly how much creativity time you need based on what your product or company demands. We don't know how much creativity your business needs or how many opportunities you may capture by being innovative, but we do know that you need to commit some time and effort to using your imagination when you're at work.

We urge you not to think about creativity as something you wheel out from time to time as it's needed, but to make it something you do all the time.

Becoming an ideas factory

Once you've found the time, what do you do with it? You can profitably apply creativity in every aspect of marketing, from finding new customers to developing new products. The important thing is that you have a purpose, but after that the only rule is that there are no rules.

Try soaking up information, questioning the problem, tossing ideas back and forth with an associate, and then setting the whole thing aside to incubate in the back of your mind while you do something else. Plan to work in different ways when you're doing your creativity. Set up a large flip chart and start listing crazy ideas for your next mailing. Ask someone to help you find 20 words that rhyme with your company or brand's name in the hope that this list may lead you to a clever idea for print or radio advertising. Cut out faces from magazines to try to find one that expresses an appealing new personality that can represent your product, and then see how that face might influence everything you then do.

Open yourself up through new and different ways of working, asking questions, and exploring your marketing problems and opportunities.

You can start coming up with more ideas almost straight away, simply by changing the way you approach your work. Here's a list of fundamentals to think about; obsessing about just a few of them will make you a more creative marketer:

- ✔ **Seek ways to simplify.** Can you come up with a simpler way to explain your product or your business and its mission? Life is complicated enough for your customers. Most marketing and advertising is, too. Simplify everything to attract attention and zap the key idea into the customer's mind.

- ✔ **Think like a customer.** This should be easy, shouldn't it – after all, you are a consumer. So why do you change when you go to work? You stop thinking about what you want (like a customer) and start thinking about what you do (like a businessperson). You need to think about what your customers like and might dislike about your business – constantly.

- ✔ **Tinker with everything.** Look at every aspect of what your company does and find a way to change it – for the better, obviously. We explore the idea of change later in this chapter, because it's so important and because so few marketers truly embrace the idea of disrupting what their company does in order to make it do it better.

- ✔ **Try to cut your prices.** If you can't, then it's already the right price – so congratulate yourself and change something else. If you can cut prices, then why haven't you – or put another way, how long will it be before someone else does? You may not think of pricing as creative but, as with all other aspects of your marketing, thinking about how to do it differently can yield startling results – especially if you haven't thought about it at all for a while.

- ✔ **Separate yourself from the competition.** If you are doing things the same as your competitors, why will customers come to you? You need to offer something different, something you will be remembered for. You don't need to spend a lot – what about striking outfits for your customer-facing staff (as long as your staff like the idea, too).

- ✔ **Borrow great ideas from other businesses.** You should show an interest in what other businesses, totally outside your field, do and say. If you can find an idea that is working in another market, but no one is doing in yours, ask yourself how you can apply it to your business.

- ✔ **Find new places to advertise.** Can you think of places to put messages to your customers that nobody in your industry has used before?

- ✔ **Get other people to put the word out for you.** Some people call this public relations and that's what it amounts to. Good marketers are natural publicists – always finding ways to get their business written or talked about by others.

These activities spur you to engage your imagination in new and unusual ways – it's surprising how often a useful insight comes out of half an hour spent on one of these approaches.

Group creativity

Being creative on your own is hard enough. But often in marketing, and work in general, you have to get a group or team of people to come up with some creative concepts.

Most groups of people, when confined to a conference room for a morning, do little more than argue about stale old ideas. Or even worse, somebody suggests an absolutely terrible new idea, and the rest of the group jumps on it and insists the suggestion is great . . . thus eliminating the need for *them* to think. If you hope to get a group to actually be creative, you need to use structured group processes. That means you have to talk the group into going along with an activity such as brainstorming. Sometimes the group resists at first, but be persistent – ask them what they have to lose by generating ideas for half an hour. We bet that after they try one brainstorming technique, they see how productive the group becomes and want to try more techniques.

We've included some of the best group creativity techniques later in this section. We know that all these techniques work – as editor of *Marketing* magazine, Craig used them to generate new content and product ideas, and seen other companies use them profitably as well.

Note that these techniques generally produce a list of ideas. Hopefully a long and varied list. But still, just a list. So be sure to schedule some time for analysing the list in order to identify the most promising ideas, and then develop those ideas into full-blown action plans.

Brainstorming

Brainstorming is a great way to increase the number and variety of ideas. The goal of brainstorming is to get people to generate a very long list of unusual ideas beyond their normal thought patterns – if you push them to use brainstorming this way. To brainstorm, you first state the problem and then ask participants to offer solutions – any solution that comes to mind, the more creative the better. Each solution is written or recorded.

You may need to encourage your group by example. If you've stated the problem as 'Think of new ideas for our exhibition stand', you can brainstorm half a dozen ideas to start with, just to illustrate what you're asking the group to do: A stand shaped like a giant cave, in the form of one of your products, decorated to look like an outdoor space complete with blue sky and white clouds overhead, a stand that revolves slowly, or where you offer tea and strawberries to visitors.

These ideas aren't likely to be adopted by the average company, but they do illustrate the spirit of brainstorming, which is to set aside your criticisms and have some fun generating ideas. The rules (which you must tell the group beforehand) are as follows:

- **Quantity, not quality, is what matters.** Generate as many ideas as possible.
- **No member of the group can criticise another member's suggestion.** No idea is too wild to not write down, and you can even go as far as keeping a water gun on hand and squirting the naysayer.
- **No one person 'owns' any of the ideas.** Everyone builds off of each other's ideas.

Don't let your group just go through the motions of brainstorming. To really get in the spirit of it, they have to *free associate* – to allow their minds to wander from current ideas to whatever new ideas first pop up, no matter what the association between the old and new idea may be.

Question brainstorming

Question brainstorming is another way to generate novel questions that can provoke your group into thinking more creatively. This technique follows the same rules as brainstorming, but you instruct the group to think of questions rather than ideas.

For example, if you need to develop an exhibition stand that draws more prospects, then the group may think of the following kinds of questions:

Book I

E-Business 101

- ✔ Do bigger stands draw much better than smaller ones?
- ✔ Which stands drew the most people at the last trade show?
- ✔ Are all visitors equal, or do we want to draw only certain types of visitors?
- ✔ Will the offer of a resting place and free coffee do the trick?

After getting these questions from the group, you get the job of answering them and seeing how those answers can help you create a new and successful exhibition stand.

Wishful thinking

Wishful thinking is a technique suggested by Hanley Norins, of ad agency Young and Rubicam, and follows the basic rules of brainstorming, but with the requirement that all statements start with the words *I wish*.

The sort of statements you get from this activity often prove useful for developing advertising or other marketing communications.

If you need to bring some focus to the list to make it more relevant to your marketing, just state a topic for people to make wishes about. For example, you can say, 'Imagine that the Exhibition Fairy told you that all your wishes can come true – as long as they have to do with the company's stand.'

Analogies

Analogies are a great creativity device. You don't think we're serious, we know, because the idea sounds so trivial. But we define creativity as making unobvious combinations of ideas. A good analogy is just that.

To put analogies to work for you, ask your group to think of things similar to the subject or problem you're thinking about. For example, you may ask a group to brainstorm analogies for your product as a source of inspiration for creating new advertisements about that product. At first, group members come up with conventional ideas – but they soon run out of these obvious answers, and they must create fresh analogies to continue.

Analogies are everywhere in advertising. One of the best examples we've seen is a press ad for the haemorrhoids treatment cream Preparation H. The ad was simply a picture of a bicycle saddle, except it wasn't a saddle, it was a jagged saw blade. The image was so striking, you could almost feel it. Although the ad was from Japan, it could have worked equally well anywhere. That's the trick of a good visual analogy like this – you can communicate your message quickly, cleverly, and effectively. So what is your product or service similar to, or what is the customer need it meets?

Pass-along

Pass-along is a simple party game that can also help a business group break through its mental barriers to reach free association and collaborative thinking.

Say a team of marketing and salespeople meets to generate new product concepts for the product development department of a bank. Now, that sounds like a tough assignment – what can be new under the sun in banking? You may be surprised by what you come up with if you play pass-along:

1. **You, the creative marketer, pick a subject and pass the paper to the first person.**

   Say your subject is how to make your customers' personal finances run better.

2. **This person writes something about the topic in question on the top line of a sheet of paper and passes it to the next person.**

3. **The next person writes a second line beneath the first.**

4. **Go around the table or group as many times as you think necessary. In general, try to fill up a full page of lined paper.**

If people get into the spirit of the game, a line of thought emerges and dances on the page. Each previous phrase suggests something new until you have a lot of good ideas and many ways of thinking about your problem. Players keep revealing new aspects of the subject as they build on or add new dimensions to the lines above. You may end up with a list of ideas similar to those in Figure 5-1.

One idea leads to another. So even if the first idea isn't helpful, associating new ideas from the first one can produce useful thoughts. A bank probably can't get into the lottery business (there must be a law against that). But after the members of this group thought along those lines, they came up with some practical ways of increasing their customers' wealth, like plans that can help them transfer money to savings automatically each month.

As this simple example illustrates, generating novel ideas doesn't take long, even in a mature industry like banking – as long as you use creativity techniques.

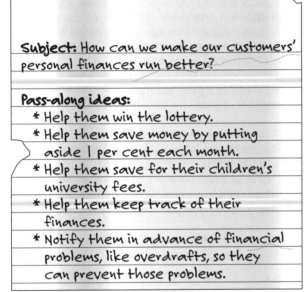

Figure 5-1:
A list generated by a game of pass-along.

> **Subject:** How can we make our customers' personal finances run better?
>
> **Pass-along ideas:**
>   * Help them win the lottery.
>   * Help them save money by putting aside 1 per cent each month.
>   * Help them save for their children's university fees.
>   * Help them keep track of their finances.
>   * Notify them in advance of financial problems, like overdrafts, so they can prevent those problems.

Applying Your Creativity

Advertising – whether in print, TV, radio, outdoors, at point of purchase, or elsewhere – is a key area of application for creativity. If you work in the advertising industry, or use advertising in your marketing, you're dependent on creativity for your success. Why? Because if your ads just say what you want people to remember, people won't pay any attention to those ads. Too many other ads compete for consumers' attention. Only the most creative ads cut through the clutter, attract attention, and make a permanent mark on consumer attitudes.

Think of the role of creativity in advertising as a vehicle for building relationships between your brand and your prospects. We find this a particularly powerful way to think about advertising's role in marketing – and you can make this role possible with the addition of creativity to your ads. Marketers use creativity to add something special and unique, to accentuate a brand's differences in order to help that brand stand out in the consumers' eyes.

We know you will have seen the advertising for Halifax bank – but have you ever thought about how they applied creativity to make their ads stand out from the crowd. Halifax works hard to produce some unique banking products, such as high interest current accounts, but so does every other major bank on the high street – and no one gets ahead of the rest for long. So how did Halifax make its products and services stand out? It thought creatively. First, the bank decided to sing about what it did, so it came up with new words promoting its products, set to well-known tunes. But Halifax didn't stop there. Instead of hiring a professional singer, the bank ran a competition among its own staff to find a star for its ads – and it found Howard.

Even a few years on, Halifax advertising stands out from the rest of the banking crowd, and Howard has become a celebrity (he's even been animated for one TV ad). The ads have attracted a lot more customers because Howard, as a former bank teller, is a real person and the tunes he sings to are catchy. Mainly, though, the ads work because they are so different and can't be easily copied. Halifax's advertising is judged a success because it

- ✔ Attracted attention to itself.
- ✔ Was memorable.
- ✔ Helped convey a positive perception of the product.

Writing a creative brief

Advertising benefits from the use of a *creative brief,* an information platform on which to do your creative thinking. A creative brief lays out the basic purpose and focus of the ad, and provides some supporting information that provides helpful grist for your creative mill.

Leading advertising agencies design the creative brief with three key components:

- ✔ **Objective statement:** What the advertising is supposed to accomplish. Make the goals or objectives clear and specific – and one objective is easier to accomplish than many. The objective statement also includes a brief description of who the ad is aimed at because this target group's actions determine if you accomplish an objective.

Think about the task of designing a new pack for one of your product lines. If you write a creative brief first, you have to define what the packaging should accomplish and what sort of customers you want to aim the pack design at. The objective statement demands that you make these decisions.

✔ **Support statement:** The product's promise and the supporting evidence to back up that promise. You use this point to build the underlying argument for the persuasive part of your ad. The support statement can be based on logic and fact, or on an intuitive, emotional appeal – either way, you need to include a basis of solid support.

You have to review (and maybe do some creative thinking about) the evidence available to support your product's claims to fame. What may make you stand out from rival products on the shelves? If you aren't sure, then use the demands of the support statement to do some research and creative thinking. Make sure that you have your evidence at hand so that your ideas for packaging design can communicate this evidence effectively.

✔ **Tone or character statement:** A distinct character, feel, or personality for the ad. You choose whether the statement should accentuate the brand's long-term identity or put forth a unique tone for the ad itself that dominates the brand's image. The choice generally flows from your objectives. A local retailer's objective may be to pull in a lot of shoppers for a special Bank Holiday sale. The retailer should give their event a strong identity, so would want to define an appropriate tone for the ad. In contrast, a national marketer of a new health-food line of soft drinks should build brand identity, so the creative brief should focus on defining that brand identity in words (or verbal images).

Here, you have to define the tone of your packaging, or think about your product's overall image and how the pack can reflect that image in its tone. The tone or character statement requires this step.

The creative brief is useful for any marketing communication, or for any situation in which you must design something creative to communicate and persuade. Figure 5-2 shows an example of a creative brief for a new coffee shop's local advertising.

After you fill in the three sections of the creative brief to your satisfaction, you're ready to start brainstorming or using any other creativity tools you care to try. The creative brief gives you a clear focus and some good working materials as you apply your creativity to developing a great ad or other promotional piece.

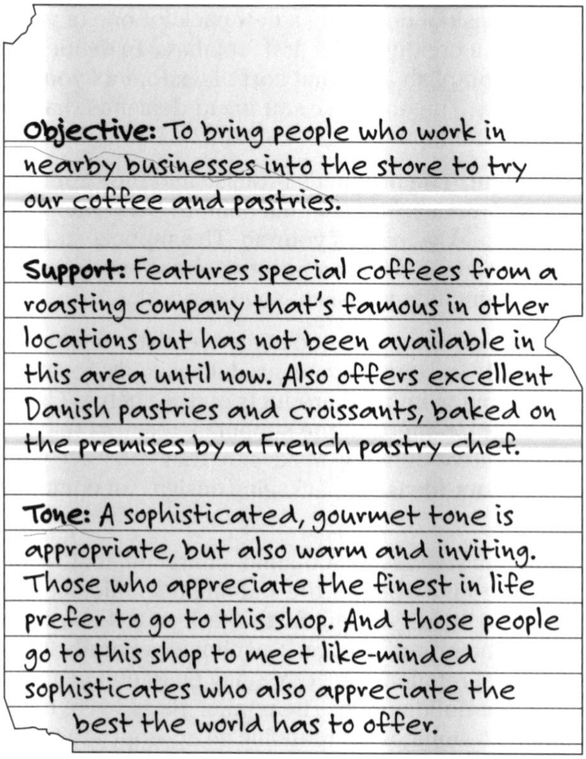

Objective: To bring people who work in nearby businesses into the store to try our coffee and pastries.

Support: Features special coffees from a roasting company that's famous in other locations but has not been available in this area until now. Also offers excellent Danish pastries and croissants, baked on the premises by a French pastry chef.

Tone: A sophisticated, gourmet tone is appropriate, but also warm and inviting. Those who appreciate the finest in life prefer to go to this shop. And those people go to this shop to meet like-minded sophisticates who also appreciate the best the world has to offer.

Figure 5-2: A sample creative brief.

Creativity and brand image

One of the most important things you can do in marketing is create a strong, appealing brand image. Creativity is the key to doing just that. As you saw in the section 'Writing a creative brief' earlier in this chapter, advertising communicates the all-important brand image or personality to the consumer. Sometimes advertising focuses on that image – and, by doing so, provides a common focus for all other design decisions, from product design to packaging to special events and other marketing communications. A strong brand identity, or personality, can become a living entity, something that the marketer creates and gives to the world. Brand development takes creativity to its farthest extreme by creating new forms of life.

Chapter 6

Opening Your Own Online Business in Ten Easy Steps

....

In This Chapter

▶ Finding a unique niche for your business

▶ Identifying a need and targeting your customers

▶ Turning your Web site into an indispensable resource

▶ Finding more than one way to market your business

▶ Evaluating your success and revising your site

....

Starting an online business is no longer a novelty. It's a fact of life for individuals and established companies alike. The good news is that *e-commerce* – the practice of selling goods and services through a Web site – is not only here to stay, but it's thriving. More good news is that the steps required to conduct commerce online are well within the reach of ordinary people like you and me, even if you have no business experience. Constantly updated software and services make creating Web pages and transacting online business easier. All you need is a good idea, a bit of startup cash, computer equipment, and a little help from your friends.

One of our goals in this book is to be friends who provide you with the right advice and support to get your business off the ground and turn it into a big success. In this chapter, we give you a step-by-step overview of the entire process of coming up with and launching your business.

The Time Is Now

Now is the perfect time to start your online business. More and more people are shopping online and a growing number of businesses are seeing the unique value of advertising on the Web. We're happy to tell you that business opportunities are springing up all over the place and that the fragile dotcom bubble of 1998–2001 has been replaced by a stable – and sustainable – business medium. eBay is booming. Other well-known Web-based service providers like Yahoo!, PayPal, and Amazon are helping small entrepreneurs to energise their businesses. Bloggers are taking the Internet by storm, and some are making tidy sums from their online diaries. Google and Overture are making it easier than ever to build up advertising revenue.

The immense popularity of the Web and the wildfire spread of broadband Internet connections means you can offer more to your customers online. Once upon a time, jazzy Web sites took ages to upload and people got tired of them quickly; nowadays ultra-speedy connections mean that anything is possible. Still, you may have concerns about the future of e-commerce. We promise your fears will quickly evaporate when you read this book's case studies of our friends and colleagues who do business online. They're either thriving or at least treading water, and they enthusiastically encourage others to take the plunge.

Step 1: Identify a Need

The fact is, no matter how good you are, you always have room for improvement. Even those at the top of their business game, like Tesco, Topshop, and Innocent Smoothies, are always looking over their shoulder at the competition. But the chances are that someday someone else will come along and do it either cheaper or better or both. The same goes for the Web, and it's this fact that you should keep in mind when you're coming up with your business ideas.

From an everyday point of view, e-commerce and the Web have been around for more than a decade now. But new products and ways to sell them are being identified all the time. Think of the things that didn't exist when the first Web sites were created: MP3s, wireless modems, DVDs, eBay. Consider Dan's fledgling Web site InfoZoo.co.uk. He had the idea for a search engine that would allow small businesses to advertise their products and services cheaply and to a wide audience. Like many people in business, Dan's first thought was that the specific product didn't exist and that it may do a lot of good if it did. Will Dan succeed because he has the benefit of both business and online experience? Success is never guaranteed. It depends on you – your energy, dedication, and enthusiasm; as well as your initial business idea.

Your first job is to identify your market (the people who'll be buying your stuff or using your service) and determine how you can best meet its needs. After all, you can't expect Web surfers to flock to your online business unless you identify services or items that they really need. Who are you targeting and why? Is your market likely to splash out on what you're promoting? Is there a genuine need for your product? Ask around and gauge the reaction of your friends and family. Ask them to be honest (you can waste a lot of money if they're not) and listen out for any constructive feedback that may help develop your site into a better offering.

Getting to know the marketplace

The Internet is a perfect venue for individuals who want to start their own business, who can cope with using computers, and who believe that 'cyberspace' is the place to do it. You don't need much money to get started, after all. If you already have a computer and an Internet connection and can create your own Web pages, making the move to your own business Web site may cost as little as a few hundred pounds. After you're online, the overheads are pretty reasonable, too: You can get your Web site hosted online for as little as £5 a month.

With each month that goes by, the number of Internet users increases exponentially. In turn, this creates a vibrant money-making marketplace for the savviest Internet businesses. To illustrate, figures from the Internet Media Retail Group (IMRG) show that more than £5 billion was spent online in the 10 weeks before Christmas 2005; £1.7 billion more than the same period the previous year. Not convinced? Well how about the fact that around half the UK population shopped online last year, spending around £800 each on average? The Internet has become fertile ground for innovative businesses. Just look at Google; it has become one of the world's largest media companies and with a value of tens of billions of pounds.

Many people decide to start an online business with little more than a casual knowledge of the Internet. But when you decide to get serious about going online, it pays to know how the land lies and who's walking on it with you.

One of your first steps should be to find out what it means to do business online and figure out whether your idea fits in the market. For example, you need to realise that customers are active, not passive, in the way that they absorb information; and that the Net was established within a culture of people sharing information freely and helping one another.

Some of the best places to find out about the culture of the Internet are the blogs (or *Web logs:* they're online diaries usually written by people who aren't qualified writers), forums, newsgroups, chat rooms, and bulletin boards where individuals exchange ideas and messages online. Visiting Web sites devoted to topics that interest you personally can be especially helpful, and you may even end up participating! Also visit some leading commerce Web sites (in other words, where people buy and sell items online), such as eBay.co.uk, Amazon.co.uk, ASOS.com, and Play.com, and take note of ideas you like. Pay special attention to the design and the way you *drill down* through the Web site. Remember that appearance and function are as important as the stuff you're selling.

'Cee-ing' what's out there

The more information you have about the 'three Cs' of the online world, the more likely you are to succeed in doing business online:

- ✔ **Competitors:** Familiarise yourself with who's already out there. Work out whether there's space for you and how you plan to fill that space. Don't be intimidated by their existence – you're going to do it a lot better!

- ✔ **Customers:** Who's gonna visit your Web site, and how will you get them there? Just like with any business, you must encourage demand for your products and make potential customers aware that you exist.

- ✔ **Culture:** Every demographic has its own culture. If you're selling clothes to teenagers then your online business will look and feel very different than the site of someone selling stair lifts to the elderly. What's their style? How do they talk? What will they expect to see when they arrive at your site?

As you take a look around the Internet, notice the kinds of goods and services that tend to sell, as well as who's doing the selling. You have to be either different, better, or, at least, more talked about than these guys. Keep the four Cs in mind if you want achieve this goal:

- ✔ **Cheapness:** Items tend to be sold at a discount compared with high street shops in the real world – at least, that's what shoppers expect.

- ✔ **Customise:** Anything that's hard-to-find, personalised or, better yet, unique, sells well online.

- ✔ **Convenience:** Shoppers are looking for items that are easier to buy online than at a bricks-and-mortar shop – a rare book that you can order in minutes from Amazon.co.uk (www.amazon.co.uk) or an electronic greeting card that you can send online in seconds (www.free-greetingcards.co.uk).

- ✔ **Content:** Consumers go online to breeze through news and features available free or through a subscription, such as newspapers and TV channels, or that exist online only, such as blogs and online magazines (sometimes called *ezines*).

Visit one of the tried-and-tested indexes to the Internet, such as Yahoo! (www.yahoo.co.uk), or the top search service Google (www.google.co.uk). Enter a word or phrase in the site's home page search box that describes the kinds of goods or services you want to provide online. Find out how many existing businesses already do what you want to do. Better yet, determine what they *don't* do and set a goal of meeting that need yourself.

Working out how to do it better

The next step is to find ways to make your business stand out from the crowd. Direct your energies toward making your site unique in some way. Can you provide things that others don't offer? The things that set your online business apart from the rest can be as tangible as half-price sales, contests, seasonal sales, or freebies. Or they can be features of your site that make it higher quality or make it a better user experience than your competitors. Maybe you want to concentrate on making your customer service better than anyone else.

What if you can't find other online businesses doing what you want to do? In this case, you've either struck gold (you've come up with an idea that no one else has thought of) or struck out (it doesn't exist because it's a bad idea). In e-commerce, being first often means getting a head start and being more successful than latecomers, even if they have more resources than you do. The Internet is getting more and more crowded, however, and genuinely new ideas are getting harder to come by. But don't let that put you off trying something new and outlandish. It just might work!

Step 2: Know What You're Offering

Business is all about identifying customers' needs and figuring out exactly what goods or services you're going to provide to meet those needs. It's the same both online and off.

To determine what you have to offer, make a list of the items you plan to sell or the services that you plan to provide to your customers. Next, you need to decide where you're going to obtain them. Are you going to create sale items yourself? Are you going to purchase them from a supplier? Jot down your ideas on paper and keep them close at hand as you develop your business plan.

The Internet is a personal, highly interactive medium. Be as specific as possible with what you plan to do online. Don't try to do everything; the medium favours businesses that do one thing well. The more specific your business, the more personal the level of service you can provide to your customers.

Step 3: Come Up with a Virtual Business Plan

The process of setting goals and objectives and then working out how you'll attain them is essential when starting a new business. What you end up with is a *business plan*. A good business plan should be your guide not only in the startup phase, but also as your business grows. It should provide a blueprint for how you run your business on a day-to-day basis and can also be instrumental in helping you obtain a bank loan or any other type of funding.

To set specific goals for your new business, ask yourself these questions:

✔ Why do you want to start a business?

✔ Why do you want to start it online?

✔ What would attract you to a Web site (regardless of what it's selling)?

✔ Why do you enjoy using some Web sites and not others?

✔ Why are you loyal to some Web sites and not others?

These questions may seem simple, but many businesspeople never take the time to answer them. Make sure that you have a clear game plan for your business so that your venture has a good chance of success over the long haul.

You can link your plan to your everyday tasks by taking the following steps:

1. **Write a brief description of your business and what you hope to accomplish with it.**

2. **Draw up a marketing strategy.**

3. **Anticipate financial incomings and outgoings. (See Chapter 15 for specifics.)**

Consider using specialised software to help you prepare your business plan. Programs such as Business Plan Pro by Palo Alto Software (www.paloalto. co.uk) lead you through the process by making you consider every aspect of how your business will work. If you don't want to splash out on software, take a look at one of the many free guides to business plans out there. Business Link (www.businesslink.gov.uk), the government network supporting small businesses, is one of the best places to start.

Step 4: Get Your Act Together and Set Up Shop

One of the great advantages of opening a shop on the Internet rather than on the high street is the savings you should be able to make. Showcasing your products online instead of in a real life shop means that you won't have to pay rent, decorate, or worry about lighting and heating the place. Instead of renting a space and putting up furniture and fixtures, you can buy a domain name, sign up with a hosting service, create some Web pages, and get started with an investment of only a few hundred pounds, or maybe even less.

In addition to your virtual showroom, you also have to find a real place to conduct the operations and logistics of your business. You don't necessarily have to rent a warehouse or other large space. Many online entrepreneurs use a home office or even just a corner in a room where computers, books, and other business-related equipment sit.

Finding a host for your Web site

Although doing business online means that you don't have to rent space in a shopping centre or open a real, physical shop, you do have to set up a virtual space for your online business. You do so by creating a Web site and finding a company to host it. In cyberspace, your landlord is called a Web hosting service. A Web *host* is a company that, for a fee, makes your site available 24 hours a day by maintaining it on a special computer called a Web *server*.

A Web host can be as large and well known as America Online (AOL), which gives all its customers a place to create and publish their own Web pages. Some Web sites, such as Yahoo! GeoCities (`uk.geocities.yahoo.com`) or Tripod (`www.tripod.lycos.co.uk`), act as hosting services and provide easy-to-use Web site creation tools as well.

When Greg's brother decided to create his Web site, he signed up with a company called Webmasters.com, a US-based company, which charged him about $15 per month and offers many features. For example, the form shown in Figure 6-1 enables you to create a simple Web page without typing any HTML.

Figure 6-1:
Take the
time to
choose an
affordable
Web host
that makes
it easy for
you to
create and
maintain
your site.

www.Webmasters.com

The company that gives you access to the Internet – your Internet Service Provider (ISP) – may also offer to publish your Web pages. Make sure that your host has a fast connection to the Internet and can handle the large numbers of simultaneous visits, or *page impressions,* that your Web site is sure to get eventually.

Assembling the equipment you need

Think of all the equipment you *don't* need when you set up shop online: You don't need shelving, a cash register, a car park, fancy displays, or lighting . . . the list goes on and on. You may need some of those for your home, but you don't need to purchase them especially for your online business itself.

For doing business online, your most important piece of equipment is your computer. Other hardware, such as scanners, printers, cameras, modems, and monitors, are also essential. You need to make sure that your computer equipment is up to scratch because you're going to be spending a lot of time online: answering e-mails, checking orders, revising your Web site, and marketing your product. Expect to spend anywhere between $500 and $5,000 for equipment, if you don't have any to begin with.

It's a good idea to buy second-hand equipment, especially if items are unopened and still come under a guarantee. It saves you money, and as long as you're careful with what you buy and who you buy it from, you can get as much use as from a product bought new. Remember that your business is likely to grow, so choose equipment that can accommodate the extra use you'll get out of it as you move forward.

Choosing business software

You can build a Web site by either doing it yourself or paying someone else to do it for you. The first option is cheaper, but nine times out of ten, the latter produces something a lot more sophisticated. Try searching for *Web design,* and you'll be confronted with a long list of businesses that offer design skills. Pick one that is reputable, has good references, and allows you to contact current customers for their views on the service. However, if you're confident about your ability to learn fast and are determined to create your Web site by yourself, then you'll need to buy in some funky software.

For the most part, the programs you need in order to operate an online business are the same as the software you use to surf the Internet. But you may need a wider variety of tools than you would use for simple information gathering.

Because you're going to be in the business of information *providing* now, as well as information gathering, you need programs such as the following:

- ✔ **A Web page editor:** These programs, which you may also hear called *Web page creation tools* or *Web page authoring tools,* make it easy for you to format text, add images, and design Web pages without mastering HTML.

- ✔ **Graphics software:** If you decide to create your business Web site yourself instead of finding someone to do it for you, you need a program that can help you draw or edit images that you want to include on your site, such as Microsoft FrontPage or Adobe Dreamweaver.

- ✔ **Shop-front software:** You can purchase software that leads you through the process of creating a fully fledged online business and getting your pages on the Web.

- ✔ **Accounting programs:** You can write your expenses and income on a sheet of paper. But it's far more efficient to use software that acts as a spreadsheet, helps you with billing, and even calculates VAT.

Step 5: Get Help

Conducting online business does involve relatively new technologies, but they aren't impossible to figure out. In fact, the technology is becoming more accessible all the time. Many people who start online businesses find out how to create Web pages and promote their companies by reading books, attending classes, or networking with friends and colleagues. Of course, just because you *can* do it all doesn't mean that you have to. You may be better off hiring help, either to advise you in areas where you aren't as strong or simply to help you tackle the growing workload – and help your business grow at the same time.

Hiring technical bods

Spending money up front to hire professionals who can point you in the right direction can help you maintain an effective Web presence for years to come. Many businesspeople who usually work alone (us included) hire knowledgeable individuals to do design or programming work that they would find impossible to tackle otherwise.

Don't be reluctant to hire professional help in order to get your business off the ground. The Web is full of developers that can provide customers with Web access, help create Web sites, and host sites on their servers. The expense for such services may be relatively high at first – probably several thousand pounds – but it'll pay off in the long term. Choose a designer carefully and check out the sites he's designed by getting in contact with customers and asking whether they're satisfied. Don't just tell a designer your business plan; send them the document (omitting your projected finances), explaining in fine detail exactly what you want each page to do.

If you do find a business partner, make sure that the person's abilities balance your own. If you're great at sales and public relations, for example, find a writer, Web page designer, or someone who is good with the accounts to partner with.

Gathering your team

Many fast growing businesses are family affairs. For example, a husband-and-wife team started Scaife's Butcher Shop in England, which has a simple Web site (www.jackscaife.co.uk). A successful eBay business, Maxwell Street Market is run by a husband-and-wife team, as well as family members and neighbours. The husband does the buying; the wife prepares sales descriptions; and the others help with packing and shipping.

Early on, when you have plenty of time for planning, you probably won't feel a pressing need to hire others to help you. Many people wait to seek help when they have a deadline to meet or are in a financial crunch. Waiting to seek help is okay – as long as you realise that you probably *will* need help, sooner or later.

Of course, you don't have to hire family and friends, it's just that they'll probably be more sympathetic to your startup worries. They'll probably work harder for you and may even lend a hand for free.

If you feel you have to hire someone from the outside world, you must find people who are reliable and can make a long-term commitment to your project. Keep these things in mind:

✔ Because the person you hire will probably work online quite a bit, pick someone who already has experience with computers and the Internet.

✔ Online hiring works the same as hiring offline: You should always review a *CV* (or work history) get a couple of references, and ask for samples of the candidate's work.

✔ Choose someone who responds promptly and in a friendly manner and who demonstrates the talents you need.

Step 6: Construct a Web Site

Even the most prolific eBay.co.uk sellers usually complement their shop with their own Web site. Luckily, Web sites are becoming easier to create. You don't have to know a line of HTML in order to create an okay-looking Web page yourself.

Make your business easy to find online. Pick an easy-to-remember Web address (otherwise known as a *domain name* or a *URL*). If the ideal .com or .co.uk name isn't available, you can try one of the newer domain suffixes, such as .biz.

Making your site content-rich

The words and pictures of a Web site (as well as the products) are what attract visitors and keep them coming back on a regular basis. The more useful information and compelling content you provide, the more visits your site will receive. By compelling content, we're talking about words, headings, or images that make visitors want to continue reading. You can make your content compelling in a number of ways:

✔ Provide a call to action, such as 'Click Here!' or 'Buy Now!'

✔ Explain how the reader will benefit by clicking a link and exploring your site. ('Visit our News and Offers page to find out how to win double discounts this month.')

✔ Briefly and concisely summarise your business and its mission. Make it sound important.

✔ Use a digital camera to capture images of your sale items (or of the services you provide) and post them on a Web page.

Don't forget the personal touch when it comes to connecting with your customers' needs. People who shop online don't get to meet the shop owner in person, so anything you can tell them about yourself helps make the process more personal and puts your visitors at ease. For example, one of Lucky Boyd's primary goals for his MyTexasMusic.com site is to encourage people to become members so that they're more likely to visit on a regular basis. His photos of music fans (see Figure 6-2) personalise the site and remind visitors that they are members of a community of music lovers. Let your visitors know that they're dealing with real people, not remote machines and computer programs.

Figure 6-2: Personalise your business to connect with customers online.

Sneaking a peek on other businesses' Web sites – to pick up ideas and see how they handle similar issues to your own – is a common and perfectly legitimate practice. In cyberspace, you can visit plenty of businesses that are comparable to yours from the comfort of your home office, and the trip takes mere minutes.

Copying other Web sites will land you in legal trouble, although there's no harm in gaining inspiration from what other people do well.

Establishing a visual identity

When you start your first business on the Web, you have to do a certain amount of convincing. You need to show customers that you're competent and professional. One factor that helps build trust is a visual identity. A site with an identity has a consistent look and feel no matter what part of the Web site you access. For example, take a look at Figure 6-3, as well as Figure 6-4 later in this chapter. Both pages are from the Graphic Maps Web site. Notice how each has the same white background, the same distinctive and simple logo, and similar heading styles. Using these standard elements from page to page creates a brand identity that gives your business credibility and helps users find what they're looking for.

Figure 6-3:
Through careful planning and design, the Graphic Maps site maintains a consistent look and feel, or visual identity, on each page.

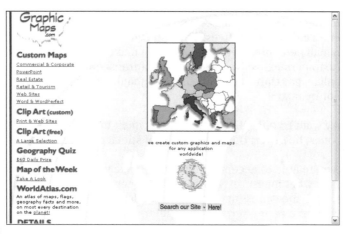

Step 7: Process Your Sales

Many businesses go online and then are surprised by their own success. They don't have systems in place for completing sales, shipping goods in a timely manner, and tracking finances and stock.

An excellent way to plan for success is to set up ways to track your business finances and to create a secure online purchasing environment for your customers. That way, you can build on your success rather than be surprised by it.

Providing a means for secure transactions

Getting paid is the key to survival, let alone success. When your business exists online only, the payment process is not always straightforward. Make your Web site a safe and easy place for customers to pay you. Provide different payment options and build customers' level of trust any way you can.

Although the level of trust among people who shop online is increasing steadily, a few Web surfers are still squeamish about submitting credit-card numbers online. And fresh-faced businesspeople are understandably intimidated by the requirements of processing credit-card transactions. In the past, many businesses used simple forms that customers had to print and mail along with a cheque. This arrangement is a pretty rare practice nowadays, because it slows down what should be a lightening quick transaction. Handling transactions in this manner today will raise some eyebrows among your customers and many will go elsewhere.

You can use numerous types of transaction software. PayPal and Google both operate their own, for example, and a host of independent businesses have also set up cheap alternatives. These services are often free to use, but do take a small percentage of the money you make every time you complete a sale. Customers expect to see this kind of transaction software when they shop online; gone are the days when the majority of e-shoppers paid over the phone or by post.

You may want to offer these low-tech payment methods as an option to newer ones, however; there are plenty of sticklers for tradition out there!

When you're able to accept credit cards, make your customers feel at ease by explaining what measures you're taking to ensure that their information is secure. Such measures include signing up for an account with a Web host that provides a *secure server,* a computer that uses software to encrypt data and uses digital documents called certificates to ensure its identity.

Safeguarding your customers' personal information is important, but you also need to safeguard your business. Many online businesses get burned by bad guys who submit fraudulent credit-card information. If you don't verify the information and submit it to your bank for processing, you're liable for the cost. Strongly consider signing up with a service that handles credit-card verification for you in order to cut down on lost revenue.

How not to cook your books

What does *keeping your books* mean, anyway? In the simplest sense, it means recording all your business's financial activities – in other words, your incomings and outgoings, including any expenses you incur, all the income you receive, as well as your equipment and tax deductions. The financial side of running a business also means creating reports, such as profit-and-loss statements, that banks require if you apply for a loan. Such reports also give you good information about how well business is going, and where (if it all) things need to improve.

You can record all this information the old-fashioned way by writing it in ledgers and journals, or you can use a spreadsheet (like Microsoft Excel), or you can use accounting software. (See Book IV for some suggestions of easy-to-use accounting packages that are great for financial novices.) Because you're making a commitment to using computers on a regular basis by starting an online business, it's only natural for you to use computers to keep your books, too. Accounting software can help you keep track of expenses and provide information that may save you a headache when the taxman comes knocking.

After you've saved your financial data on your hard drive, make backups so that you don't lose information you need to do business. See Book II for ways to back up and protect your files.

Step 8: Provide Personal Service

The Internet, which runs on cables, networks, and computer chips, may not seem like a place for the personal touch. But technology didn't actually create the Internet and all its content; *people* did that. In fact, the Internet is a great place to provide your clients and customers with outstanding, personal customer service.

In many cases, customer service on the Internet is a matter of being available and responding quickly to all enquiries. You check your e-mail regularly; you make sure you respond within a day; you cheerfully solve problems and hand out refunds if needed.

By helping your customers, you help yourself, too. You build loyalty as well as credibility among your clientele. For many small businesses, the key to competing effectively with larger competitors is to provide superior customer service.

Sharing your expertise

Your knowledge and experience are among your most valuable commodities. So you may be surprised when we suggest that you give them away for free. Why? It's a *try-before-you-buy* concept. Helping people for free builds your credibility and makes them more likely to pay for your services down the road.

Back when Dan was editor of Startups.co.uk, he regularly saw lawyers and accountants give away free advice on the Web site's forum. One accountant in particular, James Smith, has posted well over a thousand pieces of advice to fledgling entrepreneurs. Why? Because they'll remember his sound advice down the line when they need to pay for financial expertise. You should be thinking along the same lines.

When your business is online, you can easily communicate what you know about your field and make your knowledge readily available. One way is to set up a Web page that presents the basics about your company and your field of interest in the form of Frequently Asked Questions (FAQs). Another technique is to create your own newsletter in which you write about what's new with your company and about topics related to your work.

Making your site appealing

Many *ontrepreneurs* (online entrepreneurs) succeed by making their Web sites not only a place for sales and promotion but also an indispensable resource, full of useful hyperlinks and other information, that customers want to visit again and again. For example, the World Atlas Web site, acts as a resource for anyone who has a question about geography. To promote the site, John Moen gives away free maps for not-for-profit organisations, operates a daily geography contest with a £50 prize to the first person with the correct answer (shown in Figure 6-4), and answers e-mail promptly. 'I feel strongly that the secret on the Web is to provide a solution to a problem and, for the most part, to do it for free,' he suggests.

Figure 6-4:
This site uses free art, a mailing list, and daily prizes to drum up business.

MySpace (www.myspace.com) uses its 'community' ethic to strengthen connections with users and to build its brand – something it has achieved with extraordinary success. The main purpose of the site is to let people interact with each other. You can share photos, music files, blogs, the works. It means someone living in the United States can share all kinds of information with someone in the UK. And best of all, it's completely free. The site makes its money through advertising.

The site ties musicians with music lovers, artists, photographers, and people who just want to chat. Its members provide information about who they are and where they live, and they create their own username and password so that they can access special content and perform special functions on the site.

For any online business, knowing the names and addresses of people who visit and who don't necessarily make purchases is a gold mine of information. The business can use the contact information to send members special offers and news releases; the more frequently contact is maintained, the more likely casual shoppers or members will eventually turn into paying customers.

The concept of membership also builds a feeling of community among customers. By turning the e-commerce site into a meeting place for members who love Texas musicians, MyTexasMusic.com helps those members make new friends and have a reason to visit the site on a regular basis. Community building is one way in which commerce on the Web differs from traditional brick-and-mortar selling, and it's something you should consider, too.

Another way to encourage customers to congregate at your site on a regular basis is to create a dedicated discussion area.

E-mailing your way to the top

E-mail is, in our humble opinion, the single most important marketing tool that you can use to boost your online business. Becoming an expert e-mail user increases your contacts and provides you with new sources of support, too.

The two best and easiest e-mail strategies are the following:

- ✔ Check your e-mail as often as possible.
- ✔ Respond to e-mail enquiries immediately.

Additionally, you can e-mail enquiries about co-operative marketing opportunities to other Web sites similar to your own. Ask other online business owners if they'll provide links to your site in exchange for you providing links to theirs. And always include a signature file with your message that includes the name of your business and a link to your business site.

We're encouraging you to use e-mail primarily for one-to-one communication. The Internet excels at bringing individuals together. Mailing lists, desktop alerts, and newsletters can use e-mail effectively for marketing, too. However, we're *not* encouraging you to send out mass quantities of unsolicited commercial e-mail, a practice that turns off almost all consumers and that can get you in trouble with the law, too.

Step 9: Alert the Media and Everyone Else

In order to be successful, small businesses need to get the word out to the people who are likely to purchase what they have to offer. If this group turns out to be a narrow demographic, so much the better; the Internet is great for connecting to niche markets that share a common interest.

The Internet provides many unique and effective ways for small businesses to advertise, including search services, e-mail, blogs, forums, electronic mailing lists, and more.

Listing your site with Internet search services

How, exactly, do you get listed on the search engines such as Yahoo! and Google? Frankly, it's getting more difficult. While you can almost always get listed for free, your chances of getting noticed next to search-dominating mega-brands is pretty slim in many cases. It was this problem that inspired Dan to create InfoZoo.co.uk.

However, you can increase the chances that search services will list your site by including special keywords and site descriptions in the HTML commands for your Web pages. You place these keywords after a special HTML command (the <META> tag), making them invisible to the casual viewer of your site.

Reaching the whole Internet

Your Web site may be the cornerstone of your business, but if nobody knows it's out there, it can't help you generate sales. Perhaps the most familiar form of online advertising are *banner ads* (which run across the top of Web sites) and *skyscrapers* (which run vertically down the side of pages), those little electronic billboards that appear at the top and down the side (respectively) of high traffic Web sites.

But banner advertising can be expensive and may not be the best way for a small business to advertise online. In fact, the most effective marketing for some businesses hasn't been traditional banner advertising or newspaper/magazine placements. Rather, the e-marketers target electronic bulletin boards and mailing lists where people already discuss the products being sold. You can post notices on the bulletin boards where your potential customers congregate, notifying them that your services are now available. (Make sure that the board in question permits such solicitation before you do so, or you'll chase away the very customers you want.)

This sort of direct, one-to-one marketing may seem tedious, but it's often the best way to develop a business on the Internet. Reach out to your potential customers and strike up an individual, personal relationship with each one.

Step 10: Review, Revise, and Improve

For any long-term endeavour, you need to establish standards by which you can judge its success or failure. You must decide for yourself what you consider success to be. After a period of time, take stock of where your business is and then take steps to do even better.

Taking stock

When all is said and done, your business may do so well that you can reinvest in it by buying new equipment or increasing your services. You may even be in a position to give something back to not-for-profits and those in need. The young founders of The Chocolate Farm (www.thechocolate-farm.com) set up a scholarship fund designed to bring young people from other countries to the United States to help them find out about free enterprise. Perhaps you'll have enough money left over to reward yourself, too – as if being able to tell everyone 'I own my own online business' isn't reward enough!

The truth is, plenty of entrepreneurs are online for reasons other than making money. That said, it *is* important from time to time to evaluate how well you're doing financially. Accounting software makes it easy to check your revenues on a daily or weekly basis. The key is to establish the goals you want to reach and develop measurements so that you know when and if you reach those goals.

Updating your data

Getting your business online and then updating your site regularly is better than waiting to unveil the perfect Web site all at once. In fact, seeing your site improve and grow is one of the best things about going online. Over time, you can create contests, strike up relationships with other businesses, and add more background information about your products and services.

Book II
Setting Up Your Web Site

'Still no luck with the bank loan, Mr Blenkinsop?'

In this book . . .

If you've decided that an online business could work for you, this book helps you to set that business up by acquainting you with the technical expertise and software know-how you're going to need. From choosing the best Web host for your business needs to making sure your e-business is more secure than the Tower of London, all of your basic computing and Internet queries should be answered in these pages.

Here are the contents of Book II at a glance:

Chapter 1

Finding the Money

· ·

In This Chapter

▶ Working out how much outside money you need

▶ Looking at the different types of money available to you

▶ Choosing the best source of money for you

▶ Finding money to work with

· ·

Setting up a business requires money – there is no getting away from that. You have bills such as rent to pay, materials and equipment to purchase, and all before any income is received. Starting a business on the road to success involves ensuring that you have sufficient money to survive until the point where income continually exceeds expenditure.

Raising this initial money and the subsequent financial management of the business is therefore vital, and great care should be taken over it. Unfortunately, more businesses fail due to lack of sufficient day-to-day cash and financial management than for any other reason. This chapter helps you avoid common pitfalls and helps you find the right type of money for your business.

Assessing How Much Money You Need

You should work out from the outset how much money you will need to get your business off the ground. If your proposed venture needs more cash than you feel comfortable either putting up yourself or raising from others, then the sooner you know the better. Then you can start to revise your plans. The steps that lead to an accurate estimate of your financial needs start with the sales forecast, which you do as part of feasibility testing, which we cover in Book I, along with advice on estimating costs for initial expenditures such as retail or production space, equipment, staff, and so on.

Forecasting cash flow is the most reliable way to estimate the amount of money a business needs on a day-to-day basis.

Do's and don'ts for making a cash flow forecast:

- ✔ Do ensure your projections are believable. This means you need to show how your sales will be achieved.

- ✔ Do base projections on facts not conjecture.

- ✔ Do describe the main assumptions that underpin your projections.

- ✔ Do explain what the effect of these assumptions not happening to plan could be. For example, if your projections are based on recruiting three sales people by month three, what would happen if you could only find two suitable people by that date?

- ✔ Don't use data to support projections without saying where it came from.

- ✔ Don't forget to allow for seasonal factors. At certain times of the year most business are influenced by regular events. Sales of ice-cream are lower in winter than in summer, sales of toys peak in the lead up to Christmas and business-to-business sales dip in the summer and Christmas holiday periods. So rather than taking your projected annual sales figure and dividing by twelve to get a monthly figure, you need to consider what effect seasonal factors might have.

- ✔ Don't ignore economic factors such as an expanding (or shrinking) economy, rising (or falling) interest rates and an unemployment rate that is so low that it may influence your ability to recruit at the wage rate you would like to pay.

- ✔ Don't make projections without showing the specific actions that will get those results.

- ✔ Don't forget to get someone else to check your figures out – you may be blind to your own mistakes but someone else is more likely to spot the mistakes/flaws in your projections.

Projecting receipts

Receipts from sales come in different ways, depending on the range of products and services on offer. And aside from money coming in from paying customers, the business owner may, and in many cases almost certainly will, put in cash of their own. However not all the money will necessarily go in at the outset; you could budget so that £10,000 goes in at the start, followed by sums of £5,000 in months four, seven, and ten respectively.

There could be other sources of outside finance, say from a bank or investor, but these are best left out at this stage. In fact the point of the cash flow projection, as well as showing how much money the business needs, is to reveal the likely shortfall after the owner has put in what they can to the business and the customers have paid up.

You should total up the projected receipts for each month and for the year as a whole. You would be well advised to carry out this process using a spreadsheet program, which will save you the problems caused by faulty maths.

A sale made in one month may not result in any cash coming into the business bank account until the following month, if you are reasonably lucky, or much later if you are not.

Estimating expenses

Some expenses, such as rent, rates, and vehicle and equipment leases, you pay monthly. Others bills such as telephone, utilities, and bank charges come in quarterly.

If you haven't yet had to pay utilities, for example, you put in your best guesstimate of how much you'll spend and when. Marketing, promotion, travel, subsistence, and stationery are good examples of expenses you may have to estimate. You know you will have costs in these areas, but they may not be all that accurate as projections.

After you've been trading for a while, you can get a much better handle on the true costs likely to be incurred. Total up the payments for each month and for the year as a whole.

Working out the closing cash balances

This is crunch time, when the real sums reveal the amount of money your great new business needs to get it off the ground. Working through the cash flow projections allows you to see exactly how much cash you have in hand, or in the bank, at the end of each month, or how much cash you need to raise. This is the closing cash balance for the month. It is also the opening cash balance for the following month as that is the position you are carrying forward.

Testing your assumptions

There is little that disturbs a financier more than a firm that has to go back cap-in-hand for more finance too soon after raising money, especially if the reason should have been seen and allowed for at the outset.

So in making projections you have to be ready for likely pitfalls and be prepared for the unexpected events that will knock your cash flow off target. Forecasts and projections rarely go to plan, but the most common pitfalls can be anticipated and to some extent allowed for.

You can't really protect yourself against freak disasters or unforeseen delays, which can hit large and small businesses alike. But some events are more likely than others to affect your cash flow, and it is against these that you need to guard by careful planning. Not all of the events listed here may be relevant to your business, but some, perhaps many, will at some stage be factors that could push you off course.

Getting the numbers wrong

It's called estimating for a reason. You can't know ahead of time how the future will pan out, so you have to guess, and sometimes you guess wrong. Some of the wrong guesses you can make about stock and costs are:

- ✔ **A flawed estimate:** There is no doubt that forecasting sales is difficult. The numbers of things that can and will go awry are many and varied. In the first place the entire premise on which the forecast is based may be flawed. Estimating the number of people who may come into a restaurant as passing trade, who will order from a catalogue mailing, or what proportion of Internet site hits will turn into paying customers, depends on performance ratios. For example a direct mail shot to a well-targeted list could produce anything from 0.5–3 per cent response. If you build your sales forecast using the higher figure and actually achieve the lower figure then your sales income could be barely a sixth of the figure in your cash flow projection. You can't avoid this problem, but you can allow for it by testing to destruction (see later in this checklist).

- ✔ **Carrying too much stock:** If your sales projections are too high, you will experience the double whammy of having less cash coming in and more going out than shown in your forecast. That is because in all probability you will have bought in supplies to meet anticipated demand. Your suppliers offering discounts for bulk purchases may have exacerbated the situation if you took up their offers.

- ✔ **Missed or wrong cost:** You may underestimate or completely leave out certain costs due to your inexperience. Business insurance and legal expenses are two often missed items. Even where a cost is not missed altogether it may be understated. So, for example, if you are including the cost of taking out a patent in your financing plan, it is safer to take it from the supplier's Web site rather than from a friend who took out a patent a few years ago.

✔ **Testing to destruction:** Even events that have not been anticipated can be allowed for when estimating financing needs. 'What if' analysis using a cash flow spreadsheet will allow you to identify worst-case scenarios that could knock you off-course. After this you will end up with a realistic estimate of the financing requirements of the business or project.

✔ **Late deliveries:** If your suppliers deliver late, you may in turn find you have nothing to sell. Apart from causing ill will with your customers, you may have to wait weeks or months for another opportunity to supply. This problem can be minimised using online order tracking systems, if your suppliers have them, but some late deliveries will occur. Increasing your stocks is one way to insure against deficiencies in the supply chain, but that strategy too has an adverse impact on cash flow.

Settling on sales

Sales may be slow, pricing may be high – just two of the ways sales can make your projections look silly. More ways follow:

✔ **Slower than expected sales:** Even if your forecasting premise is right, or nearly so, customers may take longer to make up their minds than you expect. A forecast may include an assumption that people will order within two weeks of receiving your mail-order catalogue. But until you start trading you will not know how accurate that assumption is likely to be. Even if you have been in business for years, buying patterns may change.

✔ **Not being able to sell at list price:** Selling price is an important factor in estimating the amount of cash coming into a business and hence the amount of finance needed.

Often the only way a new or small business can win certain customers is by matching a competitor's price. This may not be the price in your list, but it is the one you have to sell at.

Also the mix of products or services you actually sell may be very different from your projection and this can affect average prices. For example a restaurant owner has to forecast what wines his or her customers will buy. If the house wine is too good, then more customers might go for that rather than the more expensive and more profitable wines on the list.

✔ **Suppliers won't give credit:** Few suppliers are keen to give small and particularly new businesses any credit. So before you build in 30, 60, or even 90 days' credit into your financial projections, you need to confirm that normal terms of trade will apply to what a supplier may view as an abnormal customer.

You need to remember that whilst taking extended credit may help your cash flow in the short term, it could sour relationships in the long term. So in circumstances where a product is in short supply poor payers will be last on the list to get deliveries and the problems identified above may be further exacerbated.

Miscounting customers

Customers can confound your most well thought out projections. They pay late, they may rip you off, and they may not buy your goods as quickly as you'd like. Some of the ways customers can be to blame for throwing your estimates off are:

- **Paying slowly:** Whilst you set the terms and conditions under which you plan to do business, customers are a law unto themselves. If they can take extra credit they will. Unless you are in a cash-only business, you can expect a proportion of your customers to be late payers. Whilst with good systems you will keep this to an acceptable figure, you will never get every bill paid on time. You need to allow for this lag in your cash flow projections.

- **Bad debts:** Unfortunately late payers are not the only problem. Some customers never pay. Businesses fail each year and individuals go bankrupt, each leaving behind a trail of unpaid bills. You can take some steps to minimise this risk, but you can't eliminate the risk. You can try to get a feel for the rate of non-payment in your sector and allow for it in your plans. For example, the building and restaurant industries have a relatively high incidence of bad debts, whilst business services have a lower rate.

- **Fraud and theft:** Retailers claim they could knock 5 per cent off everything they sell if they could eliminate theft. But despite their best endeavours with security guards and cameras, theft continues.

- **Repeat orders take longer to come in than expected:** It is hard to know exactly what a customer's demand for your product or service is. The initial order may last them months, weeks, or days. For strategic reasons they may want to divide up their business between a number of suppliers. If, for example, they have three suppliers and they order a month's worth at a time, it may be some time before they order from you again. If your customer sales are sluggish or seasonal, then that timeframe could extend further still. So even delighted customers may not come back for quite some time.

Reviewing Your Financing Options

Knowing how much money you need to get your business successfully started is an important first step, but it is only that: a first step. There are many sources of funds available to small firms. However not all are equally appropriate to all firms at all times. These different sources of finance carry very different obligations, responsibilities, and opportunities. The differences have to be understood to allow an informed choice.

Most small firms confine their financial strategy to long-term or short-term bank loans, viewing other financing methods as either too complex or too risky. In many respects the reverse is true. Almost every finance source other than banks shares some of the risks of doing business with you to a greater or lesser extent.

The great attraction of borrowing from a bank lies in the speed of the transaction. Most small businesses operate without a business plan so most events that require additional funds, such as sudden expansion or contraction, come as a surprise, either welcome or unwelcome, and with a sense of urgency. Basing financing choices on the fact that you need the money quickly may lead to more difficulties in the long run.

Deciding between debt capital and equity capital

At one end of the financing spectrum lie shareholders – either individual *business angels* who put their own money into a business, or corporate organisations such as *venture capital providers* – who provide equity capital which is used to buy a stake in a business. These investors share all the risks and vagaries of the business alongside you and expect a proportionate share in the rewards if things go well. They are less concerned with a stream of dividends, which is just as well as few small companies ever pay them, and instead hope for a radical increase in the value of their investment. They expect to realise this value from other investors who want to take their places for the next stage in the firm's growth cycle, rather than from any repayment by the founder. Investors in new or small businesses don't look for the security of buildings or other assets to underpin their investment. Rather they look to the founder's vision and the core management team's ability to deliver results.

At the other end of the financing spectrum are debt financiers – banks that try hard to take no risk and expect some return on their money irrespective of your business's performance. They want interest payments on money lent, usually from day one. Whilst they too hope the management is competent, they are more interested in making sure either you or the business has some type of asset such as a house that they can grab if things go wrong. At the end of the day, and that day can be sooner than the borrower expects, a bank wants all its money back, with interest. Think of bankers as people who help you turn part of an illiquid asset such as property into a more liquid asset such as cash – for a price.

Understanding the differences between lenders, who provide debt capital, and investors, who provide equity, or share, capital is central to a sound grasp of financial management.

In between the extremes of shareholders and the banks lie a myriad of other financing vehicles, which have a mixture of lending or investing criteria. You need to keep your business finances under constant review, choosing the most appropriate mix of funds for the risks you plan to take and the economic climate ahead. The more risky and volatile the road ahead, the more likely it is that taking a higher proportion of equity capital will be appropriate. In times of stability and low interest, higher borrowings may be more acceptable.

As a rule of thumb debt and equity should be used in equal amounts to finance a business. If the road ahead looks more risky than usual go for £2 of equity to every £1 of debt. Table 1-1 illustrates some of the differences between risk-averse lenders and risk-taking investors.

Table 1-1	Comparing Benefits of Lenders and Investors	
Category	*Lenders*	*Investors*
Interest	Paid on outstanding loan	None, though dividends sometimes paid if profits warrant it
Capital	Repaid at end of term or sooner if lender has concerns	Returned with substantial growth through new shareholders
Security	Either from assets or personal guarantees	From belief in founders and their business vision

If your business sector is generally viewed as very risky, and perhaps the most reliable measure of that risk is the proportion of firms that go bust, then financing the business almost exclusively with borrowings is tantamount to gambling.

Debt has to be serviced whatever your business performance, so it follows that, in any risky, volatile marketplace, you stand a good chance of being caught out one day.

If your business risks are low, the chances are that profits are relatively low too. High profits and low risks always attract a flood of competitors, reducing your profits to levels that ultimately reflect the riskiness of your business sector. As venture capitalists and shareholders generally are looking for much better returns than they could get by lending the money, it follows they will be disappointed in their investment on low-risk, low-return business. So if they are wise they will not get involved in the first place, or if they do they will not put any more money in later.

Book II

Setting Up Your Web Site

Examining your own finances

Obviously the first place to start looking for money to finance your business is in your own pockets. Whilst you may not have much in ready cash you may have assets that can be turned into cash or used to support borrowing.

Start by totalling your assets and liabilities. The chances are that your most valuable assets are your house, your car, and any life assurance or pension policies you may have. Your liabilities are the debts you owe. The difference between your assets and liabilities, assuming you have more of the former than the latter, is your 'net worth'. That in effect is the maximum security you can offer anyone outside the business that you want to raise money from.

Now the big questions are: what is your appetite for risk and how certain are you your business will be successful? The more of your own money you can put into your business at the outset, the more you will be truly running your own business in your own way. The more outside money you have to raise, the more power and perhaps value you have to share with others.

Now you have a simple piece of arithmetic to do. How much money do you need to finance your business start-up, as shown in your worst-case scenario cash flow forecast? How much of your own money are you willing and able to put into your business? The difference is the sum you are looking to outside financiers to back you with.

If that sum is more than your net worth, then you will be looking for investors. If it is less then bankers may be the right people to approach.

If you do have free cash or assets that you could but won't put into your business, then you should ask yourself if the proposition is worth pursuing. You can be absolutely certain that any outsider you approach for money will ask you to put up or shut up.

Another factor to consider in reviewing your own finances is your ongoing expenses. You have to live whilst getting your business up and running. So food, heat, and a roof over your head are essential expenses. But perhaps a two-week long-haul summer holiday, the second car, and membership of a health club are not essentials. Great whilst you were a hired hand and had a pay cheque each month, but an expendable luxury once you are working for yourself.

Determining the Best Source of Finance for You

Choosing which external source of finance to use is to some extent a matter of personal preference. One of your tasks in managing your business's financial affairs is to keep good lines of communication open with as many sources as possible.

The other key task is to consider which is the most appropriate source for your particular requirement at any one time. The main issues you need to consider are explored in the following sections.

Considering the costs

Clearly if a large proportion of the funds you need to start your business are going to be consumed in actually raising the money itself, then your set-up costs are going to be very high. Raising capital, especially if the amounts are relatively small (under £500,000) is generally quite expensive. You have to pay your lawyers and accountants, and those of your investor or lender, to prepare the agreements and to conduct the due diligence examination (the business appraisal). It is not unusual to spend between 10 and 15 per cent of the first £500,000 you raise on set-up costs.

An overdraft or factoring agreement is relatively cheap to set up, usually a couple of per cent or so. However, long-term loans, leasing, and hire-purchase agreements could involve some legal costs.

Sharing ownership and control

The source of your money helps determine how much ownership and control you have to give up in return. Venture capitalists generally want a large share of stock and often a large say in how the business is run. At the other end of the spectrum are providers of long-term loans who generally leave you alone so long as you service the interest and repay the capital as agreed. You have to strike the balance that works best for you and your business.

If you do not want to share the ownership of your business with outsiders then clearly raising equity capital is not a good idea. Even if you recognise that owning 100 per cent of a small venture is not as attractive as owning 40 per cent of a business ten times as large it may not be the right moment to sell any of your shares. Particularly if, in common with many business founders, long-term capital gain is one of your principal goals. If you can hold onto your shares until profits are reasonably high you will realise more gain for every share sold than if you sell out in the early years or whilst profits are low.

Book II

**Setting
Up Your
Web Site**

Parting with shares inevitably involves some loss of control. Letting 5 per cent go may just be a mild irritation from time to time. However once 25 per cent has gone, outsiders could have a fair amount of say in how things are run. At that point, even relatively small groups of shareholders could find it easy to call an Extraordinary General Meeting and put it to a vote to remove you from the board. Nevertheless, whilst you have over 51 per cent you are in control, if only just. Once past the 51 per cent things could get a little dangerous. Theoretically you could be out voted at any stage.

Some capital providers take a hands-on approach and will have a view on how you should run the business.

Beating the clock

Overdrafts can be arranged in days, raising venture capital can take months. Very different amounts of scarce management time are needed, dependent on the financing route taken. So if speed matters, your funding options may be limited.

Venture capital providers (also called Venture Capitalists or VCs) have been known to string out negotiations long enough to see if the bullish forecasts made in the business plan come to pass. After all, venture capital is there to help businesses to grow faster than they might otherwise do not just to keep them afloat. Don't expect a decision from a venture capital firm in under three months whatever their brochure says. Four to six months is a more realistic timescale and nine months is not too unusual.

Business Angels can usually make investment decisions much more quickly than VCs, after all it's their money they are risking. Weeks rather than months, is the timescale here.

Banks finance is usually a fairly speedy process. Even large loans of £100,000 and upwards can be arranged in a few weeks. But the speed depends more on how much collateral you have to give the bank manager comfort that his money is safe.

Staying flexible

As your plans change, the amount of money you actually need may alter during negotiations. Some sources of funds such as leasing, hire-purchase agreements, and long-term loans dictate the amount that has to be agreed at the outset. If you're selling shares in the company, you have some fluidity during negotiations, and if you're arranging overdrafts it is possible to draw down only what you need at any one time, with the upper limit negotiated usually each year.

Once you have investigated and used a source of funds you may want to be able to use that source again as your plans unfold. Loans and hire purchase/ leasing agreements are for a specific sum and it can be difficult and expensive going back to the same source for more. Many venture capitalists, for example, already have a full weighting of investments in your business sector and so may not be anxious to invest more, however successful your firm. So that might mean starting all over again with another venture capital firm.

It may pay to make sure that at least some of your financing comes from a source such as factoring, which gives you total flexibility to change the amount of money drawn down to mirror the amount needed at any one time – both upwards and downwards.

Adding value to the business

With some sources of finance you can get useful expertise as well as money. For example, with factoring you could get expertise in managing your home and overseas credit, which could result in better credit control, fewer bad debts, and less capital tied up in debtors. You could even close or reduce your credit control department. With new share capital you may get a director with relevant experience in the industry. While the director's principal task is to ensure the capital provides interest, you also get the benefit of his or her knowledge.

Gaining security and certainty

For most sources of money, if you comply with the agreed-upon terms, the future is reasonably predictable – in so far as that money is concerned. The exception to this rule is an overdraft. An overdraft is technically, and often actually, repayable on demand. Overdrafts are sometimes called in at the moment you need them most.

Limiting personal liability

As a general rule most providers of long-term loans and overdrafts look to you and other owners to provide additional security if the business assets are in any way inadequate. You may be asked to provide a personal guarantee – an asset such as your house. Only when you raise new share capital, by selling more stock in your company, do you escape increasing your personal liability. Even with the new share capital you may be asked to provide warranties to assure new investors that everything in the company's past history has been declared.

Book II

Setting
Up Your
Web Site

Going for Debt

You can explore borrowing from a number of possible sources in your search for outside finance. It is worth giving them all the once over, but it has to be said that most people start and stop at a bank. The other major first source of money is family and friends, but many business starters feel nervous about putting family money at risk and in any event would rather deal with professional financiers. *Credit Unions* and *mezzanine finance* are relatively unusual sources of finance for a start-up, but finding any money to start a business is a tough task, so no source should be completely overlooked. (These terms are explained later in this chapter.)

Borrowing from banks

Banks are the principal, and frequently the only, source of finance for nine out of every ten new and small businesses.

Banks are usually a good starting point for almost any type of debt financing. They are also able to provide many other cash flow and asset backed financing products, although they are often not the only or the most appropriate provider. As well as the main clearing banks, a number of the former building societies and smaller regional banks are competing hard for small firm lending.

All the major clearing banks offer telephone banking and Internet services to their small business customers or are in the process of doing so. Branch location seems less likely to be a significant factor to bank customers in the future, so you no longer have to confine your search for a bank to those with a branch nearby.

Bankers, and indeed any other sources of debt capital, are looking for property, land, insurance policies, or any other investments you may have to back their loan and the near certainty of getting their money back. They also charge an interest rate that reflects current market conditions and their view of the risk level of the proposal.

If you import raw materials, the bank can provide you with Letters of Credit, which guarantees your suppliers payment from the bank when they present proof of satisfactory delivery. If you have a number of overseas suppliers who prefer settlement in their own currency for which you will need foreign currency, cheque facilities or buying forward, banks can make the necessary arrangements.

Running an overdraft

The principal form of short-term bank funding is an *overdraft*. An overdraft is permission for you to use some of the bank's money when you don't have enough of your own. The permission is usually agreed annually, but can be withdrawn at anytime. A little over a quarter of all bank finance for small firms is in the form of an overdraft. The overdraft was originally designed to cover the time between having to pay for raw materials to manufacture finished goods and selling those goods. The size of an overdraft will usually be limited to a modest proportion of the amount of money owed to you by your customers and the value of your finished goods stock. The bank will see those items as assets, which in the last resort can be used to get their money back.

Starting out in a cleaning business, for example, you need sufficient funds initially to buy the mop and bucket. Three months into the contract they will have been paid for and so there is no point in getting a five-year bank loan to cover this, as within a year you will have cash in the bank.

However if your overdraft does not get out of the red at any stage during the year then you need to re-examine your financing. All too often companies utilise an overdraft to acquire long-term assets, and that overdraft never seems to disappear, eventually constraining the business.

The attraction of overdrafts is that they are very easy to arrange and take little time to set up. That is also their inherent weakness. The keywords in the arrangement document are 'repayable on demand', which leaves the bank free to make and change the rules as they see fit. (This term is under review and some banks may remove this term from the arrangement.) With other forms of borrowing, as long as you stick to the terms and conditions, the loan is yours for the duration. Not so with overdrafts.

Taking on a term loan

If you are starting up a manufacturing business, you will be buying machinery to last probably five years, designing your logo and buying stationery, paying the deposit on leasehold premises, buying a vehicle, and investing funds in winning a long-term contract. As the profits on this are expected to flow over a number of years, then they need to be financed over a similarly long period of time, either through a bank loan or inviting someone to invest in shares in the company – in other words a long-term commitment.

Term loans, as these long-term borrowings are generally known, are funds provided by a bank for a number of years. The interest can be either variable – changing with general interest rates – or it can be fixed for a number of years ahead. In some cases it may be possible to move between having a fixed interest rate and a variable one at certain intervals. It may even be possible to have a moratorium on interest payments for a short period, to give the business some breathing space. Provided the conditions of the loan are met in such matters as repayment, interest and security cover, the money is available for the period of the loan. Unlike having an overdraft, the bank cannot pull the rug from under you if their circumstances (or the local manager) change.

Going with a loan guarantee

These are operated by banks at the instigation of governments in the UK, and in Australia, the US, and elsewhere. These schemes guarantee loans from banks and other financial institutions for small businesses with viable business proposals, which have tried and failed to obtain a conventional loan because of a lack of security.

Loans are available for periods of between two and ten years on sums from £5,000 to £250,000 .The government guarantees 70–90 per cent of the loan. In return for the guarantee the borrower pays a premium of 1–2 per cent per year on the outstanding amount of the loan. The commercial aspects of the loan are matters between the borrower and the lender.

Book II

Setting Up Your Web Site

Uniting with a credit union

If you don't like the terms on offer from the *high street banks,* as the major banks are often known, you may consider forming your own bank. It's not as crazy an idea as it sounds. Credit unions formed by groups of small business people, both in business and aspiring to start up, have been around for decades in the US, UK, and elsewhere. They have been an attractive option for people on low incomes, providing a cheap and convenient alternative to banks. Some self-employed people such as taxi drivers have also formed credit unions. They can then apply for loans to meet unexpected capital expenditure either for repairs, refurbishments, or technical upgrading.

Established credit unions will usually require you to be in a particular trade, have paid money in for a number of months or perhaps years and have a maximum loan amount limited to the types of assets people in their trade are most likely to need.

Certainly, few could argue about the attractiveness of an annual interest rate 30 per cent below that of the high-street lenders, which is what credit unions aim for. Members have to save regularly to qualify for a loan, though there is no minimum deposit and, after ten weeks, members with a good track record can borrow up to five times their savings, though they must continue to save while repaying the loan. There is no set interest rate, but dividends are distributed to members from any surplus, usually about 5 per cent a year. This too compares favourably with bank interest on deposit accounts.

Borrowing from family and friends

Those close to you are often willing to lend you money or invest in your business. This helps you avoid the problem of pleading your case to outsiders and enduring extra paperwork and bureaucratic delays. Help from friends, relatives, and business associates can be especially valuable if you've been through bankruptcy or had other credit problems that make borrowing from a commercial lender difficult or impossible.

Involving friends and family in your business brings a range of extra potential benefits, costs, and risks that are not a feature of most other types of finance. You need to decide if these are acceptable.

Some advantages of borrowing money from people you know well are that you may be charged a lower interest rate, may be able to delay paying back money until you're more established, and may be given more flexibility if you get into a jam. But once the loan terms are agreed to, you have the same legal obligations as you would with a bank or any other source of finance.

Borrowing money from relatives and friends can have a major disadvantage. If your business does poorly and those close to you end up losing money, you may well damage your personal relationships. So in dealing with friends, relatives, and business associates be extra careful not only to establish clearly the terms of the deal and put them in writing but also to make an extra effort to explain the risks. In short, it's your job to make sure your helpful friend or relative won't suffer true hardship if you're unable to meet your financial commitments.

Many types of business have loyal and devoted followers, people who care as much about the business as the owners do. A health food restaurant, a specialist bookstore, or an art gallery, for example, may attract people who are enthusiastic about lending money to, or investing in, the business because it fits in with their lifestyle or philosophy. Their decision to participate is driven to some extent by their feelings and is not strictly a business proposition. The rules for borrowing from friends and relatives apply here as well. Put repayment terms in writing, and don't accept money from people who can't afford to risk it.

When raising money from family and friends, follow these guidelines.

1. Do agree proper terms for the loan or investment.

2. Do put the agreement in writing and if it involves a limited partnership, share transaction, or guarantee have a legal agreement drawn up.

3. Do make an extra effort to explain the risks of the business and the possible downside implications to their money.

4. Do make sure when raising money from parents that other siblings are compensated in some way, perhaps via a will.

5. Do make sure you want to run a family business before raising money from them. It will not be the same as running your own business.

6. Don't borrow from people on fixed incomes.

7. Don't borrow from people who can't afford to lose their investment.

8. Don't make the possible rewards sound more attractive than you would say to a bank.

9. Don't offer jobs in your business to anyone providing money unless they are the best person for the job.

10. Don't change the normal pattern of social contact with family and friends after they have put up the money.

Book II

Setting
Up Your
Web Site

Managing mezzanine money

Mezzanine finance (also known as subordinated debt) is a form of debt where the lender takes on more risk than a bank would normally be up for. Mezzanine finance providers accept the fact that they will only get their money back after bank overdraft and loans and the like have been paid back. But in return they expect a higher rate of interest and they may ask for an option to convert some of that debt into shares in the company at a certain point. By doing that they can get a slice of the upside if your business is a roaring success.

The benefit of mezzanine finance is that it often bridges the gap between the funds provided by a bank and the high-risk investment by you, a venture capitalist, and business angels.

Mezzanine finance can now also be considered a stand-alone funding solution, often as an alternative to more expensive equity finance. Mezzanine is now commonly used to provide acquisition finance, development capital, and replacement capital, as well as finance for the more traditional management buy-out, buy-in scenarios.

Sources of mezzanine finance include many of the clearing banks and insurance companies, as well as specialist finance boutiques. With larger transactions it is possible to access the capital markets using an investment bank to achieve public offerings of high yield or 'junk' bonds. These are typically sold to institutional investors such as insurance companies and pension funds.

The amount and cost of funds under a mezzanine arrangement will depend on many factors including industry sector, historic performance, credit ratings, seasonality, and predictability of revenues and forecasts for future cash flow and profitability, as well as the strength of management, the nature of a company's financial backers and the structure of the overall financing package.

It is usual for mezzanine finance to be provided on an interest-only basis until some or all of general bank debt has been repaid, typically after four to five years, with typical loan terms ranging up to ten years. Loans are usually secured with a second charge on a company's assets such as property, plant, and equipment.

Sharing out the Spoils

If your business is particularly risky, requires a lot of up-front finance, or involves new technology, then you usually have to consider selling a portion of your business's shares to outside investors.

However, if your business plan does not show profit returns in excess of 30 per cent compound and you are not prepared to part with upwards of 15 per cent of your business, then equity finance is probably not for you.

A number of different types of investor could be prepared to put up the funds if the returns are mouth-watering enough. we talk about each type in the following sections.

Going for venture capital

Venture capital is a means of financing the start-up, development, expansion, or the purchase of a company. The venture capitalist acquires a share of the company in return for providing the requisite funding. Venture capital firms often work in conjunction with other providers of finance in putting together a total funding package for a business.

Venture capital providers (*VCs*) invest other people's money, often from pension funds. They are likely to be interested in investing a large sum of money for a large stake in the company.

Venture capital is a medium- to long-term investment, of not just money, but of time and effort. The venture capital firm's aim is to enable growth companies to develop into the major businesses of tomorrow. Before investing, a venture capital provider goes through *due diligence*, a process that involves a thorough examination of both the business and its owners. Accountants and lawyers subject you and your business plan to detailed scrutiny. You and your directors are required to warrant that you have provided *all* relevant information, under pain of financial penalties.

In general VCs expect their investment to pay off within seven years. But they are hardened realists. Two in every ten investments they make are total write offs, and six perform averagely well at best. So the one star in every ten investments they make has to cover a lot of duds. VCs have a target rate of return of 30 per cent plus, to cover this poor success rate.

Raising venture capital is not a cheap option. The arrangement costs will almost always run to six figures. The cost of the due diligence process is borne by the firm raising the money, but will be paid out of the money raised, if that's any consolation. Raising venture capital is not quick either. Six months is not unusual and over a year has been known. Every VC has a deal done in six weeks in their portfolio, but that truly is the exception.

Venture capital providers want to exit from their investment at some stage. Their preferred route is via a public offering, taking your company onto the

Book II

Setting Up Your Web Site

stock market, but a trade sale to another, usually larger business in a related line of work, is more usual.

New venture capital funds are coming on stream all the time and they too are looking for a gap in the market.

The British Venture Capital Association (www.bvca.co.uk) and the European Venture Capital Association (www.evca.com) both have online directories giving details of hundreds of venture capital providers.

Benefiting by business angels

One source of equity or risk capital is a private individual, with their own funds, and perhaps some knowledge of your type of business, who is willing to invest in your company in return for a share in the business.

Such investors have been christened *business angels,* a term first coined to describe private wealthy individuals who backed theatrical productions, usually a play on Broadway or in London's West End.

By their very nature such investments are highly speculative in nature. The angel typically has a personal interest in the venture and may want to play some role in the company – often an angel is determined upon some involvement beyond merely signing a cheque.

Business angels are informal suppliers of risk capital to new and growing businesses, often taking a hand at the stage when no one else will take the chance; a sort of investor of last resort. But whilst they often lose their shirts, they sometimes make serious money. One angel who backed Sage with £10,000 in their first round of £250,000 financing, saw his stake rise to £40 million.

These angels often have their own agenda and frequently operate through managed networks. Angel networks operate throughout the world, in some cases on the Internet. In the UK and the US there are hundreds of networks with tens of thousands of business angels prepared to put up several billion pounds each year into new or small businesses.

One estimate is that the UK has approximately 18,000 business angels and that they annually invest in the region of £500 million.

Business Direct in Association with *The Daily Telegraph* (www.business-direct.uk.com), Business Link for London (www.bl4london.com), and National Business Angels Network (www.nationalbusangels.co.uk) all have online directories of business angels.

Research has unravelled these sketchy facts about business angels as a breed. Knowing them may help you find the right one for your business.

- Business angels are generally self-made, high net-worth individuals, with entrepreneurial backgrounds. Most are in the 45–65 year age group; 19 per cent are millionaires; and only 1 per cent are women.

- Fifty per cent of angels conduct minimal or no research on the business in question, meet their entrepreneur an average of 5.4 times before investing (compared with venture capitalists who meet on average 9.5 times), and 54 per cent neglected to take up independent personal references compared to only 6 per cent of venture capitalists. Angels fundamentally back people rather than propositions and venture capitalists do the reverse.

- Typically business angels invest 5–15 per cent of their investment portfolio in start-up business ventures and their motivation is, first and foremost, financial gain through capital appreciation, with the fun and enjoyment of being involved with an entrepreneurial business an important secondary motive. A minority are motivated in part by altruistic considerations, such as helping the next generation of entrepreneurs to get started, and supporting their country or state.

- Business angels invest in only a very small proportion of investments that they see: typically at least seven out of eight opportunities are rejected. More than 90 per cent of investment opportunities are rejected at the initial screening stage.

- Around 30 per cent of investments by business angels are in technology-based businesses. Most will tell you that they vigorously avoid investing in industries they know nothing about.

- The majority of business angels invest in businesses located in close proximity to where they live – two-thirds of investments are made in businesses located within 100 miles of their home or office. They are, however, prepared to look further afield if they have specific sector-related investment preferences or if they are technology investors.

- Ninety-two per cent of angels had worked in a small firm compared, for example, with only 52 per cent of venture capitalists who had similar experience.

- On average, business angels sell their shareholding in the most successful investments after four years (and 75 per cent after seven years). Conversely, half of the investments in which business angels lost money had failed within two years of the investment being made.

- Business angels are up to five times more likely to invest in start-ups and early stage investments than venture capital providers in general.

Book II

Setting Up Your Web Site

Looking to corporate venturing

Alongside the venture capital firms are 200 or so other businesses who have a hand in the risk capital business, without it necessarily being their main line of business. For the most part these are firms with an interest in the Internet or high technology that want an inside track to new developments. Their own research and development operations have slowed down and become less and less entrepreneurial as they have gotten bigger. So they need to look outside for new inspiration.

Even successful firms invest hundreds of millions of dollars each year in scores of other small businesses. Sometimes, if the company looks a particularly good fit, they buy the whole business.

Apple, for example, whilst keeping its management team focused on the core business, has a $12 million stake in Akamai Technologies, the firm whose software tries to keep the Web running smoothly even under unusual traffic demands.

It's not only high-tech firms that go in for corporate venturing. Any firm whose arteries are hardening a bit is on the look out for new blood. McDonald's, for example, hardly a business in the forefront of the technological revolution, has stakes in over a dozen ventures including a 35 per cent stake in Prêt-à-Manger. Table 1-2 lists the top corporate venturers.

Table 1-2	The World's Top Corporate Venturers
Company	*$ millions*
Electronic Data Systems	1,500
Accenture Consulting	1,000
PriceWaterhouseCoopers	500
Time Warner Inc	500
Intel Corporation	450
Cisco Systems	450
Microsoft	450
Softbank	350
News Corporation	300

Company	$ millions
Comcast Corporation	250
Unilever	200
Sun Microsystems	200
Novell Inc.	170

Finding Free Money

Sometimes, if you're very lucky or very smart – or both – you can get at least some of the money you need for free. The following sections tell you how to cash in on government grants and how winning a contest can earn you lots of lovely loot.

Getting help from the government

Unlike debt, which has to be repaid, or equity, which has to earn a return for the investors, grants and awards from the government or the European Union are often not refundable. So, although they are frequently hard to get, they can be particularly valuable.

Almost every country has incentives to encourage entrepreneurs to invest in particular locations or industries. The US, for example, has an allowance of Green Cards (work and residence permits) for up to several hundred immigrants each year prepared to put up sufficient funds to start-up in a substantial business in the country.

In the UK, if you are involved in the development of a new technology then you may be eligible for a grant for Research and Development that is now available. Under the new grant scheme, 60 per cent of eligible project costs up to a maximum grant of £75,000 can be claimed on research projects (previously called 'feasibility studies'); 35 per cent of costs up to £200,000 on development projects; 35 per cent of costs up to £500,000 on exceptional development projects; and 50 per cent of costs up to a maximum grant of £20,000 on micro projects. Business Links can give full details of the new grants.

Support for business comes in a very wide variety of forms. The most obvious is the direct (cash) grant but other forms of assistance are also numerous. The main types of grant also include *soft loans* – money lent on terms more advantageous than would usually be available from a bank – additional share capital, free or subsidised consultancy, which could help you with market research, staff development or identifying business opportunities, or with access to valuable resources such as research facilities.

Though several grant schemes operate across the whole of the UK and are available to all businesses that satisfy the outline criteria, there are a myriad of schemes that are administered locally. Thus the location of your business can be absolutely crucial, and funding may be strongly dependent on the area into which you intend to grow or develop. Additionally, there may well be additional grants available to a business investing in or into an area of social deprivation, particularly if it involves sustainable job creation.

The assistance provided for enterprise is limited so you will be competing for grants against other applicants. You can enhance your chances of success by following these seven rules:

1. **Keep yourself informed about which grants are available.**

   Grants are constantly being introduced (and withdrawn), but there is no system that lets you know automatically. You have to keep yourself informed.

   Business Link (www.businesslink.org), the Department of Trade and Industry (www.dti.gov.uk), Funders online (www.fundersonline.org), and Grants On-line (www.co-financing.co.uk) are all websites that can help you find out about grants.

2. **Do not start the project for which you want a grant before you make the application.**

   The awarding body will almost certainly take the view that if you can start the project without a grant you must have sufficient funds to complete it without assistance. Much better to show that your project is dependent on the grant being made.

3. **Talk to the awarding body before you apply.**

   Make contact with an individual responsible for administering the scheme. You will be given advice on whether it is worthwhile your applying before you start spending time and effort on making the application; you may get some help and advice on completing the application form; you may get an insight into how you should shape your application.

4. **Make sure your application is in respect of a project.**

Usually, grants are given for specific projects, not for the normal organic growth of a business. If, for example, you need new equipment to launch a product, make sure your application emphasises the project, not the equipment. State the advantages of the project's success (for example, it will safeguard or create jobs) and explain that the purchase of the equipment is a prerequisite for that success.

5. **Get your application in early.**

   The chances of a successful application are always highest just after a scheme is launched. That is when there is the most money in the pot, and it's also the time when those administering the scheme are keenest to get applications in and grants awarded. Competition is likely to be less fierce.

6. **Make your application match the awarding body's objectives.**

   The benefits of your project should fit in with the objectives of the awarding body and the grant scheme itself. So if the grant is intended to help the country in the form of potential exports, for example, make sure your application details your exports.

   Most grant applications require the submission of a business plan, so make sure you have an up to date one.

7. **Make sure you have matching funds available.**

   It is unusual for a grant to finance 100 per cent of the costs of any project. Typically nowadays a grant will contribute 15–50 per cent of the total finance required. Those making the decision about the grant are spending public money. They have a duty to ensure it is spent wisely and they will need to be absolutely convinced that you have, or can raise from other sources, the balance required.

Winning money

If you enjoy publicity and like a challenge then you could look out for a business competition to enter. Like government grants, business competitions are ubiquitous and, like national lotteries, they are something of a hit or miss affair. But one thing is certain. If you don't enter you can't win.

There are more than 100 annual awards in the UK alone, aimed at new or small businesses. For the most part, these are sponsored by banks, the major accountancy bodies, chambers of commerce, local or national newspapers, business magazines, and the trade press. Government departments may also have their own competitions as a means of promoting their initiatives for exporting, innovation, job creation, and so forth.

Book II

Setting
Up Your
Web Site

The nature and the amount of the awards change from year to year, as do the sponsors. But looking out in the national and local press, particularly the small business sections of *The Times*, *Daily Telegraph*, *Daily Mail*, and *The Guardian*, should put you in touch with a competition organiser quickly, as will an Internet search. Money awards constitute 40 per cent of the main competition prizes. For the most part, these cash sums are less than £5,000. However, a few do exceed £10,000 and one UK award is for £50,000. Other awards are for equally valuable goods and services, such as consultancy or accountancy advice, training, and computer hardware and software.

Chapter 2

Choosing and Equipping
Your New E-Business

- -

In This Chapter

▶ Picturing your successful online business

▶ Understanding your options: sales, services, and auctions

▶ Making your e-shop stand out from the crowd

▶ Buying or upgrading your computer hardware

▶ Assembling a business software suite

- -

Starting your online business is like refurbishing an old house. Both projects involve a series of recognisable phases:

✔ **The idea phase:** First, you tell people about your great idea. They hear the enthusiasm in your voice, nod their heads, and say something like, 'Good luck.' They've seen you in this condition before and know how it usually turns out.

✔ **The decision phase:** Undaunted, you begin honing your plan. You read books (like this one), ask questions, and shop around until you find just the right tools and materials to get you on your way. Of course, when you're up to your neck in work, you may start to panic, asking yourself whether you're really up for the task.

✔ **The assembly phase:** Undeterred, you forge ahead. You plug in your tools and go to work. Drills spin, and sparks fly, as your idea becomes reality.

✔ **The test-drive phase:** One fine day, out of the dust and fumes, your masterpiece emerges. You invite everyone over to enjoy the fruits of your labour. All those who were sceptical before are now awe-struck and full of admiration. Satisfied with the result, you enjoy your project for years to come.

If refurbishing a house doesn't work for you, think about restoring an antique car, planning an anniversary party, or devising a mountain-climbing excursion in Tibet. The point is that starting an online business is a project like any other – one that you can construct and accomplish in stages. Right now, you're at the first stage of launching your new business. Your creativity is working overtime. You may even have some rough sketches that only a mother could love.

This chapter helps you get from concept to reality. Your first step is to imagine how you want your business to look and feel. Then you can begin to develop and implement strategies for achieving your dream. You've got a big advantage over those who started new businesses a few years ago: You've got thousands of predecessors to show you what works and what doesn't.

Starting Off on the Right Foot

As you travel along the path from idea to reality, you must also consider equipping your online business properly – just like you would have to equip a traditional, bricks-and-mortar business. One of the many exciting aspects of launching a business online, however, is the absence of many *overheads* (that is, operating expenses). Many real world businesses resort to taking out loans to pay the rent and design their shop fronts, pay fees, and purchase shop furniture. In contrast, the primary overhead for an online business is computer gadgetry. It's great if you can afford top-of-the-line equipment, but you'll be happy to know that the latest bells and whistles aren't absolutely necessary in order to build a business online and maintain it effectively. But in order to streamline the technical aspects of connecting to the Internet and creating a business Web site, some investment is always necessary.

Mapping Out Your Online Business

How do you get off square one? Start by imagining the kind of business that is your ultimate goal. This step is the time to indulge in some brainstorming. Envisioning your business is a creative way of asking yourself the all-important questions: Why do I want to go into business online? What are my goals? Table 2-1 illustrates possible objectives and suggests how to achieve them. By envisioning the final result you want to achieve, you can determine the steps you need to take to get there.

Table 2-1	Online Business Models	
Goal	*Type of Web Site*	*What to Do*
Make big bucks	Sales	Sell items or get lots of paying advertisers
Gain credibility and attention	Marketing your work online	Put your CV and samples of
Turn an interest into a source of income	Hobby/special interest	Invite like-minded people to share your passion, participate in your site, and generate traffic so that you can gain advertisers or customers.

Book II

Setting Up Your Web Site

Looking around

You don't need to feel like you have to reinvent the wheel. A great idea doesn't necessarily mean something completely fresh that has never been done before (although if you have a great, new idea, then good for you!). Sometimes, spending just half an hour surfing the Net can stimulate your mental network. Find sites with qualities you want to emulate. Throughout this book, we suggest good business sites you can visit to find good models to follow.

Many people start up online selling to people just like themselves. For example, a motorbike enthusiast may start up a parts business or an informative site about the best bikes and where to buy them. If you're a hobby geek, then your own likes and dislikes have a lot of value. As you search the Web for inspiration, make a list as you go of what you find appealing and jot down notes on logos, designs, text, and *functionality* (how the site lets you access its features). That way, you'll have plenty of data to draw upon as you begin to refine what you yourself want to do.

Making your mark

The online world has undergone a population explosion. According to Internet Systems Consortium's Domain Survey (www.isc.org), in 2006, 439.2 million computers that hosted Web sites were connected to the Internet, compared with 171.6 million in 2002. As an *ontrepreneur* (online entrepreneur), your goal is to stand out from the crowd – or to 'position yourself in the marketplace', as business consultants like to say. Consider the following tried-and-tested suggestions if you want your Web site to be a popular corner of the Internet:

✔ **Do something you know all about.** Experience adds value to the information you provide. Doing something that you have experience of also keeps you interested throughout the roller-coaster ride that is starting a business. Most importantly, in the online world, expertise sells.

✔ **Make a statement.** On your Web site, include a mission statement that clearly identifies what you do, the customers you hope to reach, and how you're different from your competitors. Depending on what you plan to set up, this statement may be on the home page (in the form of a concise About Us statement) or in an FAQ section of the site.

✔ **Include contact details.** We may be in a digital age, but people still crave the personal touch. You must prove that you're not a machine by keeping the language you use friendly, and by including a phone number. People are also very suspicious of Web sites that don't declare their address.

✔ **Give something away for free.** This tip really can't be said enough. Giveaways and promotions are proven ways to gain attention and develop a loyal customer base. In fact, entire Web sites are devoted to providing free stuff online, such as `www.freestuffjunction.co.uk` or `www.thefreesite.com`. You don't have to give away an actual product; it can be words of wisdom based on your training and experience.

✔ **Be obvious.** The domain names listed in the preceding bullet all do free stuff. What do they have in common? The word 'free'. It helps if your Web site tells people what is does before they even get to the home page. Dan's Web site, InfoZoo.co.uk, is called such because it lets users access a *zoo* (in other words, a diverse selection) of different types of information.

✔ **Find your niche.** Web space is a great place to pursue *niche marketing*. In fact, it often seems that the quirkier the item, the better it sells. Don't be afraid to target a narrow audience and direct all your sales efforts to a small group of devoted followers.

✔ **Do something you love.** The more you love your business, the more time and effort you're apt to put into it and, therefore, the more likely it is to be successful. Such businesses take advantage of the Internet's worldwide reach, which makes it easy for people with the same interests to gather at the same virtual location.

Evaluating commercial Web sites

Is your Web site similar to others? How does it differ? (Or to put it another way: How is it better?) Your customers will be asking these questions, so you may as well start out by asking them as well.

Commercial Web sites – those whose Internet addresses usually end with `.co.uk`, `.com`, or `.biz` – are the fastest-growing segment of the Net and is the area you'll be entering. The trick is to be comfortable with the size and level of complexity of a business that's right for you. In general, your options are

✔ **A big commercial Web site:** The Web means big business, and plenty of big companies create Web sites with the primary goal of supplementing a product or service that's already well known and well established. Just a few examples are the Ribena Web site (`www.ribena.co.uk`), the Pepsi World Web site (`www.pepsiworld.com`), and the Toyota Web site (`www.toyota.com`). True, these commercial Web sites were created by corporations with many millions of pounds to throw around, but you can still look at them to get ideas for your own site.

✔ **A mid-size site:** You can look at mid-sized companies, too, who use the Web as an extension of their brand. Brilliant examples of mid-sized companies are Ben & Jerry's ice cream (`www.benjerry.co.uk`) and Innocent Smoothies (`www.innocentsmoothies.co.uk`). John Cleese has a simply awesome Web site (`www.thejohncleese.com` – note that `www.johncleese.com` was pinched by a look-alike before the real one could get in there, which businesses can learn a lot from). Sites such as CD Wow (`www.cdwow.co.uk`) and Play.com (`www.play.com`) are mid-sized companies, but their Web sites are as good as any blue chip you're likely to come across.

✔ **A site that's just right:** No prerequisites for prior business experience guarantee success on the Web. It's also fine to start out as a single person, couple, or family. In fact, the rest of this book is devoted to helping you produce a top-notch, home-grown entrepreneurial business with the minimum of assistance. This chapter gets you off to a good start by examining the different kinds of business you can launch online and some business goals you should be setting yourself.

Book II

Setting Up Your Web Site

Flavours of Online Businesses You Can Taste Test

If you're an excitable character, you may have to curb your enthusiasm as you comb the Internet for ideas. Use the following examples to create a picture of your business and then zero in on the kind of sites that can help you formulate its look and feel.

Selling consumer products

The Web has always attracted those looking for unique items or something customised just for them. Consider taking your wares online if one or both of the following applies to you:

- ✔ You're a creative person who creates as a hobby the type of stuff people may want to buy (think artists, designers, model makers, and so on). For example, Dan's mum is great at calligraphy, and he thinks she'd make a packet by selling her writing online.

- ✔ You have access to the sort of products or services that big companies simply can't replicate. Those items may mean regional foods, hand-made souvenirs, or items for car enthusiasts; the list is truly endless – you just have to find your niche.

Sorry to bang on about Ben & Jerry's (we're big fans), but we sometimes go to their Web site (www.benjerry.com or www.benjerrys.co.uk) just to drool. These guys should be your role models. The motivation for starting their business was that they just couldn't get enough of ice cream and loved creating bizarre flavours. They're entrepreneurs just like you, and we think their Web site is nearly as tasty as their products. It focuses on the unique flavours and high quality of their ice cream, as well as their personalities and business standards.

Innocent Smoothies (www.innocentdrinks.co.uk) are the same. They build on that 'community' feel by offering you fun things to do when you're bored. They even suggest popping over to Fruit Towers (their headquarters) for a visit. Their branding is brilliant and rare – try to match it (without copying), but remember that you must reflect your own business-style and the people you want to sell to.

Punting what you're good at

Either through a Web site or through listings in indexes and directories, offering your professional services online can expand your client base dramatically. It also gives existing clients a new way to contact you or just see what's new with your business. Here are just a few examples of professionals who are offering their services online:

- ✔ **Solicitors:** John Pickering and Partners are personal injury solicitors (aren't they all nowadays) who specialise in severe diseases and critical injuries sustained at work. The firm is based in Manchester, but its Web site gives it a national and even global reach (www.johnpickering.co.uk). To give it a professional feel, something which is vital in this profession, the Web site features relevant news updates, information about claims, and even information on how to choose a solicitor.

- ✔ **Psychotherapists:** Dr. Thomas Kraft, a Harley Street practitioner, has a nice, easy-to-understand Web site at www.londonpsychotherapy.co.uk (see Figure 2-1). The format is simple, yet a good amount of important information appears on the home page. Without clicking, we know his name, fields of expertise, and phone number. On top of this easy navigation there are chunky buttons providing a visible route to other facts you may need to know.

- ✔ **Architects:** At the time of writing, the Web site of Robertson Francis Partnership, a chartered architect based in Cardiff, was under construction (www.rfparchitects.co.uk). Plenty of professional Web sites take an age to get up and running because people are too busy running their businesses. If this sounds like you, do what these guys did and at least get something up there – even if it's just your name and contact details.

- ✔ **Music teachers:** Do a search on Gumtree (www.gumtree.com) or Google local (local.google.co.uk) and you'll see just how many music teachers are plying their wares online. Many don't have a Web site themselves, but are savvy enough to know that people will be searching for their services online.

Book II

Setting
Up Your
Web Site

Figure 2-1:
A London psycho-therapist provides his contact information and fields of expertise on this simple, yet informative, Web page.

www.londonpsychotherapy.co.uk

We're busy people who don't always have the time to pore over the small print. Short and snappy nuggets of information draw customers to your site and make them feel as though they're getting 'something for free'. One way you can put forth this professional expertise is by starting your own online newsletter. You get to be editor, writer, and mailing-list manager. Plus, you get to talk as much as you want, network with tons of people who subscribe to your publication, and put your name and your business before lots of people.

Making money from your expertise

The original purpose of the Internet was to share knowledge via computers, and information is the commodity that has fuelled cyberspace's rapid growth. As the Internet and commercial online networks continue to expand, information remains key.

Collecting and disseminating data can be a profitable pastime. Think of all the Web sites where information is the chief commodity rather than clothes or music. The fact is, people love to get knowledge they trust from the comfort of their own homes.

Here are just a few examples of the types of business that feed on our love of knowledge:

- ✔ **Search engines:** Some businesses succeed by connecting Web surfers with companies, organisations, and individuals that specialise in a given area. Yahoo! (www.yahoo.co.uk) is the most obvious example. Originally started by two college students, Yahoo! has become an Internet behemoth by gathering information in one index so that people can easily find things online.

- ✔ **Links pages:** On her 'Grandma Jam's I Love to Win' sweepstakes site (www.grandmajam.com), Janet Marchbanks-Aulenta gathers links to current contests along with short descriptions of each one. Janet says her site receives as many as 22,000 visits per month and generates income through advertising and affiliate links to other contest Web sites. She says she loves running her own business despite the hard work involved with keeping it updated. 'The key to succeeding at this type of site is to build up a regular base of users that return each day to find new contests – the daily upkeep is very important,' she says.

- ✔ **Personal recommendations:** The personal touch sells. Just look at Web 2.0 site Digg.com (more about Web 2.0 appears in Book VII). This guide to the online world provides Web surfers with a central location where they can track down popular news stories. It works because real people submit the stories, and only the most popular stories make it to the top of page one. The users themselves are who 'digg' stories – the most popular ones rise up the rankings. Just listen to Digg's description of itself:

Digg is all about user powered content. Every article on digg is submitted and voted on by the digg community. Share, discover, bookmark, and promote the news that's important to you!

Note that the emphasis is on *the user* and that it's written for *you*. Describing your services in this way makes people feel at home.

Resource sites can transform information into money in several ways. In some cases, individuals pay to become members. Sometimes, businesses pay to be listed on a site. Other times, a site attracts so many visitors on a regular basis that other companies pay to post advertising on the site. Big successes – such as MySpace (www.myspace.com) and Digg (www.digg.com) – carry a healthy share of ads and strike lucrative partnerships with big companies as well.

Book II

Setting Up Your Web Site

Creating opportunities with technology

What could be more natural than using the Web to sell what you need to get and stay online? The online world itself, by the very fact that it exists, has spawned all kinds of business opportunities for entrepreneurs:

- **Computers:** Some discount computer houses have made a killing by going online and offering equipment for less than conventional high street shops. Being on the Internet means that they save on overheads and then pass on those savings to their customers.

- **Internet Service Providers:** These businesses connect you to the Internet. Many ISPs, such as AOL or BT Retail, are big concerns. But smaller companies, such as Eclipse Internet, offer home-based broadband, similar levels of service, and sometimes discounts, too.

- **Software:** Matt Wright is well known on the Web for providing free computer scripts that add important functionality to Web sites, such as processing information that visitors submit via online forms. Matt's Script Archive site (www.worldwidemart.com/scripts) now includes an ad for a book on scripting that he co-authored, as well as an invitation to businesses to take out advertisements on his site.

Being a starving artist without starving

Being creative no longer means you have to live out of your flower-covered VW van, driving from art fairs to craft shows (unless you want to, of course).

If you're simply looking for exposure and feedback on your creations, you can put samples of your work online. Consider the following suggestions for virtual creative venues (and revenues):

- ✔ **Host art galleries.** Thanks to online galleries, artists whose sales were previously limited to one region can get enquiries from all over the world. Artists Online (www.artistsonline.org.uk) is a new Web site dedicated to promoting artists who are not yet well known. It showcases and sells artwork and lets users know about upcoming events and exhibitions. The personal Web site (see Figure 2-2) created by artist Marques Vickers (www.marquesv.com) has received worldwide attention. (The upcoming sidebar, 'Painting a new business scenario', profiles Vickers's site.)

- ✔ **Publish your writing.** *Blogs* (Web logs, or online diaries) are all the rage these days. The problem is that absolutely millions exist, and most aren't worth your time. However, the most successful are generating ad revenue. To find out how to create one yourself, check out Blogger (www.blogger.com). For inspiration, check out a successful independent blog, such as Seth Godin's (sethgodin.typepad.com) or a blog attached to an online newspaper. *The Times*'s Web site has a whole host of them.

Figure 2-2: A Californian artist created this Web site to gain recognition and sell his creative work. It's very basic – but seems all the more artistic for that fact.

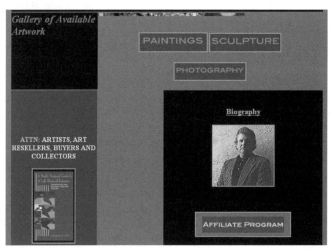

> ✔ **Sell your music.** Singer-songwriter Sam Roberts sells his own CDs, videos, and posters through his online shop (www.samrobertsband.com).

You can, of course, also sell all that junk that's been accumulating in your loft, as well as anything else you no longer want, on eBay.co.uk.

Marketing One-to-One with Your Customers

After you've reviewed Web sites that conduct the sorts of business ventures that interest you, you can put your goals into action. First you develop a marketing strategy that expresses your unique talents and services. People need encouragement if they're going to flock to your Web site, so try to come up with a cunning plan. One marketing ploy may be enough; we suggest coming up with five individual means to bring the customers in. For example, you can blog about your Web site, answer questions in forums, do a competition, go to networking events, and so on.

The fact is that online communities are often close-knit, long-standing groups of people who are good friends. The Web, newsgroups, and e-mail allow you to communicate with these communities in ways that other media can't match.

Focus on a customer segment

Old-fashioned business practices, such as getting to know your customers as individuals and providing personal service, are alive and well in cyberspace. Your No. 1 business strategy when it comes to starting your business online sounds simple: Know your market.

What's not so simple about this little maxim is that, in cyberspace, it takes some work to get to know exactly who your customers are. Web surfers don't leave their names, addresses, or even e-mail addresses when they visit your site. Instead, when you check the raw, unformatted records (or *logs*) of the visitors who have connected to you, you see pages and pages of what appears to be computer gobbledygook. You need special software, such as the program WebTrends, to interpret the information.

Painting a new business scenario

Marques Vickers is an artist based in Vallejo, California. Through his self-named Web site (www.marquesv.com), as well as 15 to 20 'mini-sites', he markets his own painting, sculpture, and photography, as well as his books on marketing and buying fine art online. He first went online in November 1999 and spends about 20 hours a week working on his various Web sites. His sites receive anywhere from 25,000 to 40,000 visits per month.

Q. What are the costs of running all your Web sites and doing the associated marketing?

A. It costs approximately £18 a month for a Web site hosting and Internet access package. New domain name registrations and renewals probably add another £140 as I own more than 20 domain names.

Q. What would you describe as the primary goals of your online business?

A. My initial objective was to develop a personalised round-the-clock global presence in order to recruit sales outlets, sell directly to the public, and create a reference point for people to access and view my work. A Web presence will be a marketing necessity for any future visual artist and a lifelong outlet for their work. Having an online presence builds my credibility as a fine artist and helps me to take advantage of the evolution of the fine arts industry, too.

Q. Has your online business been profitable financially?

A. Absolutely – but make no mistake, achieving sales volume and revenue is a trial-and-error process and involves a significant time commitment. I'm still perfecting the business model, and it may require years to achieve the optimum marketing plan.

Q. How do you promote your site?

A. With the Internet, you can take advantage of multiple promotional sources. Experimenting is

essential because you never know who's going to pick up your Web site. Postings in cyberspace are often stumbled across by sources that you never knew existed, let alone planned for. I try multiple marketing outlets, including paid ad-positioning services such as Yahoo! Search Marketing (formerly called Overture) and Google, bartered advertising space, and reciprocal links. Some have had moderate success, some unforeseen and remarkable exposure. Unlike traditional advertising media that have immediate response times, the Internet may lag in its response. It is a long-term commitment and one that cannot be developed by short-term tactics or media blitzes.

Q. Do you create your Web pages yourself, or do you work with someone to do that?

A. I'm too particular about the quality of content to subcontract the work out. Besides, I know what I want to say, how, and am capable of fashioning the design concepts I want. The rectangular limitations of HTML design make colour a very important component, and the very minimal attention span of most Web viewers means that you'd better get to the point quickly and concisely. The more personalised, timely, and focused your content, the more reason an individual has to return to your Web site.

Q. What advice would you give to someone starting an online business?

A. Don't hesitate one minute longer than necessary. Read a diverse selection of sources on the subject. Subscribe to ezines on related subject matter and query the webmasters of sites that impress you with their content. Go to informational seminars; ask questions. Experiment with marketing ideas and by all means, consider it a lifelong project. The Internet is continuing to evolve and the opportunities have never been more prevalent.

How do you develop relationships with your customers?

✔ **Get your visitors to identify themselves.** Encourage them to send you e-mail messages, place orders, enter contests, or provide you with feedback.

✔ **Become an online researcher.** Find existing users who already purchase goods and services online that are similar to what you offer. Visit newsgroups that are relevant to what you sell, search for mailing lists, and participate in discussions so that people can find out more about you.

✔ **Keep track of your visitors.** Count the visitors who come to your site and, more importantly, the ones who make purchases or seek out your services. Manage your customer profiles so that you can sell your existing clientele the items they're likely to buy.

✔ **Help your visitors get to know you.** Web space is virtually unlimited. Feel free to tell people about aspects of your life that don't relate directly to your business or to how you plan to make money. Consider Judy Vorfeld, who does Internet research, Web design, and office support. Her Web site (www.ossweb.com), shown in Figure 2-3, includes the usual lists of clients and services; however, it also includes a link to her personal home page and a page that describes her community service work.

Figure 2-3:
Telling
potential
customers
about
yourself
makes them
more
comfortable
telling you
about
themselves.

After you get to know your audience, job No. 2 in your marketing strategy is to catch their attention. You have two ways to do this:

- ✔ **Make yourself visible.** In Web-space, your primary task is simply making people aware that your site exists at all. You do so by getting yourself included in as many indexes, search sites, and business listings as possible.

- ✔ **Make your site an eye-catcher.** Getting people to come to you is only half the battle. The other half is getting them to shop when they get there. Combine striking images with promotions, offering useful information, and providing ways for customers to interact with you.

Boost your credibility

Marketing task No. 3 is to transfer your confidence and sense of authority about what you do to anyone who visits you online. Convince people that you're an expert and a trustworthy person with whom they can do business.

Customers may have fewer reasons to be wary about using the Internet nowadays. But remember that the Web as we know it has been around only a short time, and a large minority of people are still wary of surfing online, let alone shopping. Here, too, you can do a quick two-step in order to market your expertise.

Document your credentials

Feature any honours, awards, or professional affiliations you have that relate to your online work. If you're providing professional or consulting services online, you may even make a link to your online CV. If you feel it's relevant, give details about how long you've been in your field and how you got to know what you know about your business.

If these forms of verification don't apply to you, all is not lost. Just move to the all-important technique that we describe in the next section.

Convince with must-have information

Providing useful, practical information about a topic is one of the best ways to market yourself online. One of the great things about starting an online business is that you don't have to incur the design and printing charges to get a brochure or flyer printed. You have plenty of space on your online business site to talk about your sales items or services in as much detail as you want.

What, exactly, can you talk about on your site? Here are some ideas:

- ✔ Provide detailed descriptions and photos of your sale items.
- ✔ Include a full list of clients you have worked for previously.
- ✔ Publish a page of testimonials from satisfied customers.
- ✔ Give your visitors a list of links to Web pages and other sites where people can find out more about your area of business.
- ✔ Toot your own horn: Explain why you love what you do and why you're so good at it.

Ask satisfied customers to give you a good testimonial. All you need is a sentence or two that you can use on your Web site.

A site that contains compelling, entertaining content will become a resource that online visitors bookmark and return to on a regular basis. Be sure to update it regularly, and you'll have fulfilled the dream of any online business owner.

Book II

Setting
Up Your
Web Site

Create customer-to-customer contact: Everybody wins

A 16-year-old cartoonist named Gabe Martin put his cartoons on his Web site, called The Borderline. Virtually nothing happened. But when his dad put up some money for a contest, young Gabe started getting hundreds of visits and enquiries. He went on to create 11 mirror sites around the world, develop a base of devoted fans, and sell his own cartoon book.

People regularly take advantage of freebies online by, for example, downloading *shareware* or *freeware* programs (programs that are developed and distributed for free). They get free advice from newsgroups, and they find free companionship from chat rooms and online forums. Having already paid for network access and computer equipment, they actually *expect* to get something for free.

Your customers will keep coming back if you devise as many promotions, giveaways, or sales as possible.

In online business terms, anything that gets your visitors to click links and enter your site is good. Provide as many links to the rest of your site as you can on your home page. Many interactions that don't seem like sales do lead to sales, and it's always your goal to keep people on your site as long as possible.

For more about creating Web sites, check out *Creating Web Pages For Dummies,* 7th Edition, by Bud E. Smith and Arthur Bebak (Wiley).

Be a player in online communities

You may wait until the kids go off to school to tap away at your keyboard in your home office, but that doesn't mean that you're alone. Thousands of home-office workers and entrepreneurs just like you connect to the Net every day and share many of the same concerns, challenges, and ups and downs as you.

Starting an online business isn't only a matter of creating Web pages, scanning photos, and taking orders. Marketing and networking are essential to making sure that you meet your goals. Participate in groups that are related either to your particular business or to online business in general. Here are some ways that you can make the right connections and get support and encouragement at the same time.

Be a newsgroupie

Businesspeople tend to overlook newsgroups or forums because of admonitions about *spam* (pesky e-mails sent without permission by people trying to make money dishonestly) and other violations of *Netiquette* (the set of rules that govern newsgroup communications). However, when you approach newsgroup participants on their own terms (not by spamming them but by answering questions and participating in discussions), newsgroups can be a wonderful resource for businesspeople. They attract knowledgeable consumers who are strongly interested in a topic – just the sort of people who make great customers.

A few newsgroups (in particular, the ones with `biz` at the beginning of their names) are especially intended to discuss small business issues and sales. Here are a few suggestions:

- `www.realbusiness.co.uk/Forums.aspx`
- `www.startups.co.uk/Forums/ShowForum.aspx?ForumID=223`
- `www.ukbusinessforums.co.uk/forums`

The easiest way to access newsgroups is to use Google's Web-based directory (`www.google.co.uk/grphp?hl=en`). You can also use the newsgroup software that comes built into the most popular Web browser packages. Each browser or newsgroup program has its own set of steps for enabling you to access Usenet. *Usenet* is an Internet discussion system that has existed since the earliest days of the Web; users post messages to distributed newsgroups in a kind of bulletin board system. Use your browser's online help system to find out how you can access newsgroups in this way.

Be sure to read the group's FAQ (frequently asked questions) page before you start posting. It's a good idea to *lurk before you post* – that is, simply read messages being posted to the group in order to find out about members' concerns. Stay away from groups that seem to consist only of get-rich-quick schemes or other scams. When you do post a message, be sure to keep your comments relevant to the conversation and give as much helpful advice as you can.

The most important business technique in communicating by either e-mail or newsgroup postings is to include a signature file at the end of your message. A *signature file* is a simple message that newsgroup and mail software programs automatically add to your messages (just like corporate e-mails). A typical one includes your name, title, and the name of your company. You can also include a link to your business's home page. A good example is Judy Vorfeld's signature file, shown in Figure 2-4.

Book II

Setting Up Your Web Site

Figure 2-4: A descriptive signature file on your messages serves as an instant business advertise- ment.

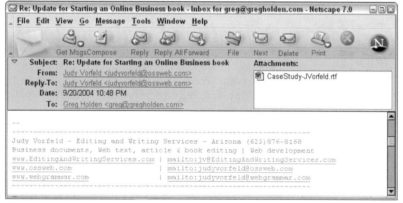

Be a mailing list-ener

A *mailing list* is a discussion group that communicates by exchanging e-mail messages between members who share a common interest. Each e-mail message sent to the list is distributed to all the list's members. Any of those members can, in turn, respond by sending e-mail replies. The series of back-and-forth messages develops into discussions.

The nice thing about a mailing list is that it consists only of people who have subscribed to the list, which means that they really want to be involved and participate.

An excellent mailing list to check out is the Small and Home-Based Business Discussion List (www.talkbiz.com/bizlist/index.html). This list is *moderated,* meaning that someone reads through all postings before they go online and filters out any comments that are inappropriate or off-topic. Also, try searching the Topica directory of discussion groups (lists.topica.com). Click Small Business (under Choose From Thousands Of Newsletters And Discussions) to view a page full of discussion groups and other resources for entrepreneurs.

The number of groups you join and how often you participate in them is up to you. The important thing is to regard every one-to-one-personal contact as a seed that may sprout into a sale, a referral, an order, a contract, a bit of useful advice, or another profitable business blossom.

It's not a newsgroup or a mailing list, but a Web site called iVillage.com (www.ivillage.com) brings women together by providing chat rooms where they can type messages to one another in real time, as well as message boards where they can post messages. (Men, of course, can participate, too.) Experts (and some who just claim to be experts) often participate in these forums.

Add ways to sell and multiply your profits

Many successful online businesses combine more than one concept of what constitutes electronic commerce. Book IV discusses ways to sell your goods and services on your Web site, but the Internet offers other venues for promoting and selling your wares.

Selling through online classifieds

If you're looking for a quick and simple way to sell products or promote your services online without having to pay high overhead costs, consider taking out a classified ad in an online publication or a popular site like Craigslist (www.craigslist.org) or InfoZoo (www.infozoo.co.uk).

The classifieds work the same way online as they do in print publications: You pay a fee and write a short description along with contact information, and the publisher makes the ad available to potential customers. However, online classifieds have a number of big advantages over their print equivalents:

✔ **Audience:** Rather than hundreds or thousands who may view your ad in print, tens of thousands, or perhaps even millions, can see it online.

✔ **Searchability:** Online classifieds are often indexed so that customers can search for particular items with their Web browser. This index makes it easier for shoppers to find exactly what they want, whether it's a Precious Moment figurine or a Martin guitar.

✔ **Time:** On the Net, ads are often online for a month or more.

✔ **Cost:** Some sites, such as Commerce Corner (`www.comcorner.com`), let you post classified ads for free.

On the downside, classifieds are often buried at the back of online magazines or Web sites, just as they are in print, so they're hardly well-travelled areas. Also, most classifieds don't make use of the graphics that help sell and promote goods and services so effectively throughout the Web.

Dan's site InfoZoo.co.uk gets around this obstacle by letting customers upload their own logo and by including a search mechanism that prevents adverts from becoming buried. It's aimed at small UK-based businesses, too – so you're in good company.

Classifieds are an option if you're short on time or money. But don't forget that on your own online business site you can provide more details and not have to spend a penny.

Selling via online auctions

Many small businesses, such as antique dealerships or jewellery shops, sell individual merchandise through online auctions. eBay.co.uk and other popular auction sites provide effective ways to target sales items at collectors who are likely to pay top dollar for desirable goodies. If you come up with a system for finding things to sell and for turning around a large number of transactions on a regular basis, you can even turn selling on eBay into a full-time source of income. See Book VI for more information about starting a business on eBay.co.uk.

Easyware (Not Hardware) for Your Business

Becoming an information provider on the Internet places an additional burden on your computer and peripheral equipment, such as your phone, printer, scanner, and so on. When you're 'in it for the money', you may very well start to go online every day, perhaps for hours at a time, especially if you buy and sell on eBay.co.uk. The better your computer setup, the more e-mail messages you can download, the more catalogue items you can store, and so on. In this section, we introduce you to many upgrades you may need to make to your existing technology.

Some general principles apply when assembling equipment (discussed in this section) and programs (discussed in a subsequent section, 'Software Solutions for Online Business') for an online business:

- ✔ **Look on the Internet for what you need.** You can find just about everything you want to get you started.

- ✔ **Be sure to pry before you buy!** Don't pull out that credit card until you get the facts on what warranty and technical support your hardware or software vendor provides. Make sure that your vendor provides phone support 24 hours a day, 7 days a week. Also ask how long the typical turnaround time is in case your equipment needs to be serviced.

If you purchase lots of new hardware and software, remember to update your insurance by sending your insurer a list of your new equipment. Also consider purchasing insurance specifically for your computer-related items from a company such as Insure and Go (www.insureandgo.com) or Hiscox (business.hiscox.co.uk).

The right computer for your online business

You very well may already have an existing computer setup that's adequate to get your business online and start the ball rolling. Or you may be starting from scratch and looking to purchase a computer for personal and/or business use. In either case, it pays to know what all the technical terms and specifications mean. Here are some general terms you need to understand:

- ✔ **Gigahertz (GHz) and megahertz (MHz):** This unit of measure indicates how quickly a computer's processor can perform functions. The central processing unit (CPU) of a computer is where the computing work gets done. In general, the higher the processor's internal clock rate, the faster the computer.

- ✔ **Random access memory (RAM):** This is the memory that your computer uses to temporarily store information needed to operate programs. RAM is usually expressed in millions of bytes, or megabytes (MB). The more RAM you have, the more programs you can run simultaneously.

- ✔ **Synchronous dynamic RAM (SDRAM):** Many ultra-fast computers use some form of SDRAM synchronised with a particular clock rate of a CPU so that a processor can perform more instructions in a given time.

- ✔ **Double data rate SDRAM (DDR SDRAM):** This type of SDRAM can dramatically improve the clock rate of a CPU.

✔ **Auxiliary storage:** This term refers to physical data-storage space on a hard drive, tape, CD-RW, or other device.

✔ **Virtual memory:** This is a type of memory on your hard drive that your computer can 'borrow' to serve as extra RAM.

✔ **Network interface card (NIC):** You need this hardware add-on if you have a cable or DSL modem or if you expect to connect your computer to others on a network. Having a NIC usually provides you with Ethernet data transfer to the other computers. (*Ethernet* is a network technology that permits you to send and receive data at very fast speeds.)

The Internet is teeming with places where you can find good deals on hardware. A great place to start is a review site, such as Ciao (www.ciao.co.uk) or Review Centre (www.reviewcentre.com), which allows customers to express their views about the equipment they have bought. Visit a few of these sites and select the most popular items.

Book II

**Setting
Up Your
Web Site**

Processor speed

Computer processors are getting faster all the time. Don't be overly impressed by a computer's clock speed (measured in megahertz or even gigahertz). By the time you get your computer home, another, faster chip will already have hit the streets. Just make sure that you have enough memory to run the types of applications shown in Table 2-2. (Note that these numbers are only estimates, based on the Windows versions of these products that were available at the time of writing.)

Table 2-2	Memory Requirements	
Type of Application	*Example*	*Amount of RAM Recommended*
Web browser	Internet Explorer	32MB
Web page editor	Macromedia Dreamweaver	128MB
Word processor	Microsoft Word	136MB (on Windows XP)
Graphics program	Paint Shop Pro	256MB
Accounting software	Microsoft Excel	8MB (if you are already running an Office application)
Animation/Presentation	Macromedia Flash	128MB

The RAM recommended for the sample applications in Table 2-2 adds up to a whopping 688MB. If you plan to work, be sure to get at least 512MB of RAM – more if you can swing it. Memory is cheap nowadays, and the newer PCs allow you to install several GB (that's gigabytes) of RAM.

Hard drive storage

Random access memory is only one type of memory your computer uses; the other kind, *hard drive,* stores information, such as text files, audio files, programs, and the many essential files that your computer's operating system needs. Most of the new computers on the market come with hard drives that store many gigabytes of data. Any hard drive with a few gigabytes of storage space should be adequate for your business needs if you don't do a lot of graphics work. But most new computers come with hard drives that are 60GB or larger in size.

CD-RW/DVD±RW drive

Although a DVD and/or CD recordable drive may not be the most important part of your computer for business use, it can perform essential installation, storage, and data communications functions, such as installing software and saving and sharing data. A large number of machines are now available with a *digital versatile disc* (DVD) drive. You can fit 4.7GB or more of data on a DVD±RW, compared with the 700MB or so that a conventional CD-RW can handle.

Be sure to protect your equipment against electrical problems that can result in loss of data or substantial repair bills. You can limit the damage caused by power outages or surges, or just by glitches in your computer programs, simply by saving your data. You can buy separate hard drives, as well as disks and data sticks on which you can store your most precious data. Keep this away from your workstation so that in the event of a fire or flood you'll still have a surviving copy.

Monitor

In terms of your online business, the quality or thinness of your monitor doesn't affect the quality of your Web site directly. Even if you have a poor-quality monitor, you can create a Web site that looks great to those who visit you. The problem is that you won't know how good your site really looks to customers who have high-quality monitors.

Flat-panel LCD (liquid crystal display) monitors continue to be a hot item, and they're becoming more affordable, too. You've got a real choice between a traditional CRT (cathode-ray tube) monitor and a flat LCD. Whether you choose flat or traditional, the quality of a monitor depends on a few factors:

- **Resolution:** The resolution of a computer monitor refers to the number of pixels it can display horizontally and vertically. A resolution of 640 x 480 means that the monitor can display 640 pixels across the screen and 480 pixels down the screen. Higher resolutions, such as 800 x 600 or 1,024 x 768, make images look sharper but require more RAM in your computer. Anything less than 640 x 480 is unusable these days.

- **Size:** Monitor size is measured diagonally, as with TVs. Sizes such as 14 inches, 15 inches, and up to 21 inches are available. (Look for a 17-inch CRT monitor, which can display most Web pages fully, and which is now available for less than £100.)

- **Refresh rate:** This is the number of times per second that a video card redraws an image on-screen (at least 60 Hz [hertz] is preferable).

Book II

Setting Up Your Web Site

Keep in mind that lots of Web pages seem to have been designed with 17-inch or 21-inch monitors in mind. The problem isn't just that some users (especially those with laptops) have 15-inch monitors, but you can never control how wide the viewer's browser window will be.

Fax equipment

A fax machine is no longer an essential item for a small business. E-mail and scanners have made faxes nearly obsolete, but if you simply can't do without one, you can install software that helps your computer send and receive faxes. You have three options:

- You can install a fax modem, a hardware device that usually works with fax software. The fax modem can be an internal or external device.

- You can use your regular modem but install software that enables your computer to exchange faxes with another computer or fax machine.

- You can sign up for a service that receives your faxes and sends them to your computer in the body of an e-mail message.

We also recommend that you look into WinFax PRO by Symantec, Inc. (www.symantec.co.uk). Your Windows computer needs to be equipped with a modem in order to send or receive faxes with WinFax.

If you plan to fax and access the Internet from your home office, you should get a second phone line or a direct connection, such as DSL or cable modem. The last thing a potential customer wants to hear is a busy signal.

Image capture devices

When you're ready to move beyond the basic hardware and on to some jazzy value-adding add-ons, think about obtaining a tool for capturing photographic images. (By *capturing,* we mean *digitising* an image or, in other words, saving it in digital format.) Photos are often essential elements of business Web pages: They attract a customer's attention, they illustrate items for sale in a catalogue, and they can provide before-and-after samples of your work. If you're an artist or designer, having photographic representations of your work is vital.

Including a clear, sharp image on your Web site greatly increases your chances of selling your product or service. You have two choices for digitising: a scanner or digital camera.

Digital camera

Not so long ago, digital cameras cost thousands of pounds. These days, you can find a good digital camera made by a reputable manufacturer, such as Nikon, Fuji, Canon, Olympus, or Kodak, for £150 to £300. You have to make an investment up front, but this particular tool can pay off for you in the long run. With the addition of a photo printer, you can even print your own photos, which can save you a pile in photo lab costs.

Don't hesitate to fork over the extra dough to get a camera that gives you good resolution. Cutting corners doesn't pay when you end up with images that look fuzzy, but you can find many low-cost devices with good features. For example, the Fujifilm FinePix S 5600, which Dan spotted online for £180, has a resolution of more than 5 megapixels – fine enough to print on a colour printer and to enlarge. *Megapixels* are calculated by multiplying the number of pixels in an image – for example, when actually multiplied, 1,984 x 1,488 = 2,952,192 pixels or 2.9 megapixels. The higher the resolution, the fewer photos your camera can store at any one time because each image file requires more memory. Getting a bigger memory card with more storage potential solves this problem.

Online material is primarily intended to be displayed on computer monitors (which have limited resolution), so having super-high resolution images isn't critical for Web pages. Before being displayed by Web browsers, images must be compressed by using the GIF or JPEG formats. Also, smaller and simpler images (as opposed to large, high-resolution graphics) generally appear more quickly on the viewer's screen. If you make your customers wait too long to see an image, they're well within their rights to go to someone else's online shop.

When shopping for a digital camera, look for the following features:

- ✔ The ability to download images to your computer via a FireWire or USB connection
- ✔ Bundled image-processing software
- ✔ The ability to download image files directly to a memory card that you can easily transport to a computer's memory card reader
- ✔ An included LCD screen that lets you see your images immediately

On the downside, because of optical filtering that's intended to reduce *colour artefacts* – distortions of an image caused by limitations in hardware – photos taken with digital cameras tend to be less sharp than conventional 35mm photos. Correcting this problem in a graphics program can be time consuming. For high-quality close-ups on the cheap, try a scanner instead.

Digital photography is a fascinating and technical process, and you'll do well to read more about it in other books, such as *Digital Photography All-in-One Desk Reference For Dummies*, 2nd Edition, by David Busch or *Digital Photography For Dummies,* 4th Edition, by Julie Adair King (both by Wiley).

Scanners

Scanning is the process of turning the colours and shapes contained in a photographic print or slide into digital information (that is, bytes of data) that a computer can understand. You place the image in a position where the scanner's camera can pass over it, and the scanner turns the image into a computer document that consists of tiny bits of information called *pixels*. The type that we find easiest to use is a flatbed scanner. You place the photo or other image on a flat glass bed, just like what you find on a photocopier. An optical device moves under the glass and scans the photo.

The best news about scanners is that they've been around for a while, which, in the world of computing, means that prices are going down at the same time that quality is on the rise. The bargain models are well under £50, and you can pick one up for around £30 if you use cost comparison Web sites, such as Pricerunner (www.pricerunner.co.uk) or Kelkoo (www.kelkoo.co.uk).

A type of scanner that has lots of benefits for small or home-based businesses is a multifunction device. You can find these units, along with conventional printers and scanners, at computer outlets or at the online search engines mentioned in the preceding paragraph.

Book II

Setting Up Your Web Site

Getting Online: Connection Options

In the past, the monthly cost of Internet access would be up there among your biggest online business expense. Thankfully, *metered Internet access,* where you pay for the amount of time you spend on line, is practically extinct. Now you can get a broadband connection from a reputable company for £15 a month. You can also bundle Internet access up with your phone connection and even digital TV to save a bit more cash.

No one uses dialup any more; there's simply no point. It's only marginally cheaper than broadband, and the frustration caused by painfully slow surfing will leave you wishing you'd spent the extra cash. This frustration is especially true for a small business, because being able to upload Web pages quickly can help you improve your productivity. A broadband connection can save you an hour a day, which you can spend on planning, on stock checks, or taking well-earned rests.

Broadband, also known as a Digital Subscriber Line (DSL), is a generic term describing the bandwidth of your Internet connection. It's broad, so more information can pass through it in a shorter space of time. DSL comes in different varieties. *Asymmetrical Digital Subscriber Line* (ADSL) transmits information at different speeds depending on whether you're sending or receiving data. *Symmetrical Digital Subscriber Line* (SDSL) transmits information at the same speed in both directions. As DSL gets more popular, it becomes more widely available, and the pricing drops. In no time at all, we should be seeing light-speed Internet access for less than ten quid a month.

Software Solutions for Online Business

One of the great things about starting an Internet business is that you get to use Internet software. As you probably know, the programs you use online are inexpensive (sometimes free), easy to use and install, and continually updated.

Although you probably already have a basic selection of software to help you find information and communicate with others in cyberspace, the following sections describe some programs you may not have as yet and that will come in handy when you create your online business.

Don't forget to update your insurance by sending your insurer a list of new software (and hardware) or even by purchasing insurance specifically for your computer-related items.

Anyone who uses firewall or antivirus software will tell you how essential these pieces of software are, for home or business use. Find out more about such software in Greg's book *Norton Internet Security For Dummies* (Wiley).

Web browser

A *Web browser* is software that serves as a visual interface to the images, colours, links, and other content contained on the Web. The most popular such program is Microsoft Internet Explorer, which powers 90 per cent of UK Web browsers (that's why Bill Gates has so much dosh). However, new and increasingly popular browsers such as Mozilla Firefox and Opera are gaining new fans every day. See which one you like the best.

Your Web browser is your primary tool for conducting business online, just as it is for everyday personal use. When it comes to running a virtual shop or consulting business, though, you have to run your software through a few more paces than usual. You need your browser to

- Preview the Web pages you create
- Display frames, animations, movie clips, and other goodies you plan to add online
- Support some level of Internet security, such as Secure Sockets Layer (SSL), if you plan to conduct secure transactions on your site

In addition to having an up-to-date browser with the latest features, installing more than one kind of browser on your computer is a good idea. For example, if you use Microsoft Internet Explorer because that's what came with your operating system, be sure to download the latest copy of Firefox as well. That way, you can test your site to make sure that it looks good to all your visitors. Remember, too, that people use Apple Macs as well as PCs, laptops, palmtops, and, increasingly, 4G mobile phones. Your Web site has to look good on all of them.

Book II

Setting Up Your Web Site

Web page editor

HyperText Markup Language (HTML) is a set of instructions used to format text, images, and other Web page elements so that Web browsers can correctly display them. But you don't have to master HTML in order to create your own Web pages. Plenty of programs, called *Web page editors,* are available to help you format text, add images, make hyperlinks, and do all the fun assembly steps necessary to make your Web site a winner.

In many cases, Web page editors come with electronic shop-front packages. QuickSite comes with Microsoft FrontPage Express. Sometimes, programs that you use for one purpose can also help you create Web documents: Microsoft Word has an add-on called Internet Assistant that enables you to save text documents as HTML Web pages, and Microsoft Office 98 and later (for the Mac) or Office 2000 or later (for Windows) enable you to export files in Web page format automatically.

Taking e-mail a step higher

You're probably very familiar with sending and receiving e-mail messages. But when you start an online business, you should make sure that e-mail software has some advanced features:

- **Autoresponders:** Some programs automatically respond to e-mail requests with a form letter or document of your choice.

- **Mailing lists:** With a well-organised address book (a feature that comes with some e-mail programs), you can collect the e-mail addresses of visitors or subscribers and send them a regular update of your business activities or, better yet, an e-mail newsletter.

- **Quoting:** Almost all e-mail programs let you quote from a message to which you're replying, so you can respond easily to a series of questions.

- **Attaching:** Attaching a file to an e-mail message is a quick and convenient way to transmit information from one person to another.

- **Signature files:** Make sure that your e-mail software automatically includes a simple electronic signature at the end. Use this space to list your company name, your title, and your Web site URL.

Both Outlook Express, the e-mail component of Microsoft Internet Explorer, and Netscape Messenger, which is part of the Netscape Communicator suite of programs, include most or all these features. Because these functions are all essential aspects of providing good customer service, we discuss them in more detail in Book V.

Discussion group software

When your business site is up and running, consider taking it a step farther by creating your own discussion area right on your Web site. This sort of discussion area isn't a newsgroup as such; it doesn't exist in Usenet, and you don't need newsgroup software to read and post messages. Rather, it's a Web-based discussion area where your visitors can compare notes and share their passion for the products you sell or the area of service you provide. Programs such as Microsoft FrontPage enable you to set up a discussion area on your Web site.

FTP software

FTP (File Transfer Protocol) is one of those acronyms you see time and time again as you move around the Internet. You may even have an FTP program that your ISP gave you when you obtained your Internet account. But chances are you don't use it that often.

In case you haven't used FTP yet, start dusting it off. When you create your own Web pages, a simple, no-nonsense FTP program is the easiest way to transfer them from your computer at home to your Web host. If you need to correct and update your Web pages quickly (and you will), you'll benefit by having your FTP software ready and set up with your Web site address, user-name, and password so that you can transfer files right away.

Image editors

You need a graphics-editing program either to create original artwork for your Web pages or to crop and adjust your scanned images and digital photographs. In the case of adjusting or cropping photographic image files, the software you need almost always comes bundled with the scanner or digital camera, so you don't need to buy separate software for that.

In the case of graphic images, the first question to ask yourself is, 'Am I really qualified to draw and make my own graphics?' If the answer is yes, think shareware first. Two programs we like are Adobe Photoshop Elements (www. adobe.co.uk) and Paint Shop Pro by Jasc, Inc. You can download both these programs from the Web to use on a trial basis. After the trial period is over, you'll need to pay a small fee to the developer in order to register and keep the program.

The ability to download and use free (and almost free) software from shareware archives and many other sites is one of the nicest things about the Internet. Keep the system working by remembering to pay the shareware fees to the nice folks who make their software available to individuals like you and me.

Instant messaging

You may think that MSN Messenger, AOL Instant Messenger, Google Talk, and Yahoo Messenger are just for chatting online, but instant messaging has its business applications, too. Here are a few suggestions:

✔ If individuals you work with all the time are hard to reach, you can use a messaging program to tell you whether those people are logged on to their computers. The program allows you to contact them the moment they sit down to work (provided they don't mind your greeting them so quickly, of course).

✔ You can cut down on long-distance phone charges by exchanging instant messages with far-flung colleagues.

✔ With a microphone, sound card, and speakers, you can carry on voice conversations through your messaging software.

MSN Messenger enables users to do file transfers without having to use FTP software or attaching files to e-mail messages.

Backup software

Losing copies of your personal documents is one thing, but losing files related to your business can hit you hard in the pocket. That makes it even more important to make backups of your online business computer files. Iomega Zip or Jaz drives (www.iomega.com) come with software that lets you automatically make backups of your files. If you don't own one of these programs, we recommend you get really familiar with the backup program included with Windows XP, or you can check out backup software on the Review Centre Web site (www.reviewcentre.co.uk).

Chapter 3

Selecting the Right Web Host and Design Tools

. . . .

In This Chapter

▶ Developing compelling content that attracts customers

▶ Selecting a hosting service for your Web site

▶ Transferring your Web site files to your hosting service

▶ Choosing software to create and edit your Web pages

. . . .

*Y*ou *can* sell items online without having a Web site. But do you really want to? Doing real online business without some sort of online 'home base' is simply inefficient. The vast majority of online commercial concerns use their Web sites as the primary way to attract customers, convey their message, and make sales. A huge number of micro-entrepreneurs use online auction sites such as eBay (www.ebay.co.uk) to make money, but the auctioneers who depend on eBay for a regular income often have their own Web pages, too.

The success of a commercial Web site depends in large measure on two important factors: where it's hosted and how it's designed. These factors affect how easily you can create and update your Web pages, what special features such as multimedia or interactive forms you can have on your site, and how your site appears to your users. Some hosting services provide Web page creation tools that are easy to use but that limit the level of sophistication you can apply to the page's design. Other services leave the creation and design up to you. In this chapter, we provide an overview of your Web hosting options as well as different design approaches that you can implement.

Plenty of Web sites and CD-ROMs claim that they can have your Web site up and running online 'in a matter of minutes' using a 'seamless' process. The actual construction may indeed be quick and smooth – as long as you've done all your preparation work. This preparation work includes identifying your goals for going online, deciding what market you want to reach, deciding what products you want to sell, writing descriptions and capturing images of those products, and so on. Before you jump over to Yahoo! Small Business or Microsoft Small Business Centre and start assembling your site, be sure that you've done all the groundwork that we discuss in Chapter 2, such as identifying your audience and setting up your hardware.

Getting the Most from Your Web Host

An Internet connection and a Web browser are all you need if you're just interested in surfing through the Web, consuming information, and shopping for online goodies. But when you're starting an online business, you're no longer just a consumer; you're becoming a provider of information and consumable goods. In addition to a means to connect to the Internet, you need to find a hosting service that will make your online business available to your prospective customers.

A *Web hosting service* is the online world's equivalent of a landlord. Just as the owner of a building gives you office space or room for a shop front where you can hang your shingle, a hosting service provides you with space online where you can set up shop.

A Web host provides space on special computers called *Web servers* that are connected to the Internet all the time. Web servers are equipped with software that makes your Web pages visible to people who connect to them by using a Web browser. The process of using a Web hosting service for your online business works roughly like this:

1. **You decide where you want your site to appear on the Internet.**

   Do you want it to be part of a virtual shopping centre that includes many other businesses? Or do you want a standalone site that has its own Web address and doesn't appear to be affiliated with any other organisation?

2. **You sign up with a Web host.**

   Sometimes you pay a fee. In some cases, no fee is required. In all cases, you're assigned space on a server. Your Web site gets an address – or *URL* – that people can enter in their browsers to view your pages.

3. **You create your Web pages.**

   Usually, you use a Web page editor to do this.

4. **After creating content, adding images, and making your site look just right, you transfer your Web page files (HTML documents, images, and so on) from your computer to the host's Web server.**

   You generally need special File Transfer Protocol (FTP) software to do the transferring. But many Web hosts help you through the process by providing their own user-friendly software. (The most popular Web editors, such as Macromedia Dreamweaver, let you transfer, too.)

5. **You access your own site with your Web browser and check the contents to make sure that all the images appear and that any hypertext links you created go to the intended destinations.**

   At this point, you're open for business – visitors can view your Web pages by entering your Web address in their Web browser's Go To or Address box.

6. **You market and promote your site to attract potential clients or customers.**

REMEMBER

Carefully choose a Web host because the host will affect which software you'll use to create your Web pages and get them online. The Web host also affects the way your site looks, and it may determine the complexity of your Web address.

Finding a Web Server to Call Home

Hi! We're your friendly World Wide Web real estate agents. You say you're not sure exactly what kind of Web site is right for you, and you want to see all the options, from a tiny shop front in a shopping centre to your own landscaped corporate complex? Your wish is our command. Just hop into our 2007-model Internet Explorer, buckle your seat belt, and we'll show you around the many different business properties available in cyberspace.

Here's a road map of our tour:

 ✔ **Online Web-host-and-design-kit combos:** Fasthosts, Yahoo!, GeoCities, and Blogger, among others.

 ✔ **eBay:** A site that lets its users create their own About Me Web pages and their own shops.

 ✔ **An online shopping centre:** You can rent a space in these virtual malls.

✔ **Your current Internet Service Provider (ISP):** Many ISPs are only too happy to host your e-commerce site – for an extra monthly fee in addition to your access fee.

✔ **Companies devoted to hosting Web sites full time:** Businesses whose primary function is hosting e-commerce Web sites and providing their clients with associated software, such as Web page building tools, shopping trolleys, catalogue builders, and the like.

Some of these options combine Web hosting with Web page creation kits. Whether you buy these services or use them on the Web for free, you simply follow the manufacturer's instructions. Most of these hosting services enable you to create your Web pages by filling forms; you never have to see a line of HTML code if you don't want to. Depending on which service you choose, you have varying degrees of control over how your site ultimately looks.

Others tend to be do-it-yourself projects. You sign up with the host, you choose the software, and you create your own site. However, the distinction between this category and the others is blurring. As competition between Web hosts grows keener, more and more companies are providing ready-made solutions that streamline the process of Web site creation for their customers. For you, the end user, this streamlining is a good thing: You have plenty of control over how your site comes into being and how it grows over time.

If you simply need a basic Web site and don't want a lot of choices, go with one of the kits. Your site may seem a little generic and basic, but setup is easy, and you can concentrate on marketing and running your business.

However, if you're the independent type who wants to control your site and have lots of room to grow, consider taking on a do-it-yourself project. The sky's the limit as far as the degree of creativity you can exercise and the amount of blood, sweat, and tears you can put in (as long as you don't make your site so large and complex that customers have a hard time finding anything, of course). The more work you do, the greater your chances of seeing your business prosper.

Housing your Web site for free

Free Web hosting is still possible for small businesses. If you're on a tight budget and looking for space on a Web server for free, turn first to your ISP, which probably gives you server space to set up a Web site. You can also check out one of a handful of sites that provide customers with hosting space for no money down and no monthly payments, either. They may make you advertise their products or use their Internet connection to design your site, but if you're happy with this tradeoff, then you can get a basic Web site up and running fairly easily.

- ✔ **Freeola** (www.freeola.co.uk)**:** For no charge, Freeola gives you unlimited (or unmetered) Web space and free use of a big stock of Freeola domain names, as well as optional database software. Freeola rewards the best sites built using its design tools by promoting them on its Web site. Customer reviews of Freeola say that it's easy to use and you can achieve decent results.

- ✔ **Lycos Tripod** (www.tripod.lycos.co.uk)**:** Like Freeola, Lycos doesn't make you share its ads and allows to create a simply Web site without too much fuss. In fact, you can publish a site with your CV, contact details, and pictures in a matter of moments. Lycos also lets you create more sophisticated Web sites using Microsoft's Frontpage, or you can transfer an existing Web site to its hosting platform in seconds.

- ✔ **Yahoo! GeoCities** (geocities.yahoo.com)**:** Yahoo! GeoCities is a popular spot for individuals who want to create home pages and fully fledged personal and business Web sites at a low cost. The site provides a free hosting option that requires users to display ads on the sites they create.

Most importantly, be sure that the site you choose lets you set up for-profit business sites for free.

Investigating electronic shop-front software

Another option for creating a business site and publishing it online is to buy an application that carries you through the entire process of creating an electronic shop front. The advantage is control: You own and operate the software and are in charge of the entire process (at least until the files get to the remote Web servers). The speed with which you develop a site depends on how quickly you master the process, not on the speed of your Internet connection.

Like hosting services such as Yahoo! Store, Tripod, and Freeola, electronic shop-front software lets you create Web pages while shielding you from having to master HTML. Most shop-front software provides you with pre-designed Web pages, called *templates,* which you customise for your particular business. Some types of electronic shop-front options go a step or two beyond the other options by providing you with shopping trolley systems that enable customers to select items and tally the cost at the checkout. They should also provide some sort of electronic payment option, such as credit-card purchases.

Usually, you sign up to transaction software online and tie it to your Web site in a few simple steps. Plenty of options are out there, so do some research and weigh up the pros and cons of each. Try these sites for a start: ekmPowershop (www.ekmpowershop.com), Storefront.net (www.storefront.net), or Lynx Internet (www.lynxinternet.co.uk).

You should consider the following features when selecting your checkout software:

- ✔ **The shop front:** The shop front contains the Web pages that you create. Some packages include predesigned Web pages that you can copy and customise with your own content.

- ✔ **The inventory:** You can stock your virtual shop-front shelves by presenting your wares in the form of an online catalogue or product list.

- ✔ **The delivery van:** Some shop-front packages streamline the process of transferring your files from your computer to the server. Instead of using FTP software, you publish information simply by clicking a button in your Web editor or Web browser.

- ✔ **The checkout counter:** Most electronic shop-front packages give you the option to accept orders online with a credit card, but you may want to consider taking them by phone or fax, too.

Besides providing you with all the software that you need to create Web pages and get them online, electronic shop fronts instruct you on how to market your site and present your goods and services in a positive way. In addition, some programs provide you with a back room for your business, where you can record customer information, orders, and fulfilment.

The problem with many electronic shop-front packages is that they can be very expensive – some cost thousands of pounds. Watch out for the ones that aren't intended for individuals starting a small businesses, but for large corporations that want to branch out to the Web. A few packages provide a Ford-type alternative to the Rolls-Royce shop fronts.

Moving into an online shopping centre

In addition to Web site kits, Internet service providers, and businesses that specialise in Web hosting, online 'shopping centres' – or directories – provide another way to show off your Web site. After you've set up your site, possibly using one of the methods listed in the preceding sections, you should sign up to one of the many directories out there. eDirectory.co.uk (`www.edirectory.co.uk`), Yahoo! Business Finder (`uk.search.yahoo.com/yp`), Google Local (`www.google.co.uk/lochp?hl=en`), and InfoZoo (`www.infozoo.co.uk`) all offer a home for your business.

Some are free, and some are paid for. Some are the Web site's core business, and some are mere offshoots of the Web site's main business. But the good news is that you don't have to restrict yourself to just one directory. Each has its own audience of potential customers and can offer you increased exposure, so sign up to as many as you can.

The directory may be a simple list of shops on a single Web page. For larger centres with a thousand shops or more, the online businesses are arranged by category and can be found in a searchable index.

In theory, an online shopping centre gives small businesses additional exposure in more than one way. A customer who shops at one of the directory's outlets may notice other businesses on the same site and visit them, too. A few function as Web hosts that enable their customers to transfer Web page files and present their shops online, using one of their Web servers. Most, however, let people list their business in the shopping centre with a hyperlink.

Amazon.co.uk doesn't look like an online shopping centre, but it has instituted some opportunities for entrepreneurs to sell items on its site. Unlike eBay.co.uk, you can't create your own shop front, but you have the option of selling items individually on the Amazon.co.uk site. You pay fees to list items for sale and for completed sales as well. Find out more by going to the Amazon.co.uk home page (`www.amazon.co.uk`) and clicking the Sell Your Stuff link near the top of the page.

Turning to your ISP for Web hosting

People sometimes talk about Internet Service Providers (ISPs) and Web hosts as two separate types of Internet businesses, but that's not necessarily the case. Providing users with access to the Internet and hosting Web sites are two different functions, to be sure, but they may well be performed by the same organisation.

In fact, it's only natural to turn to your own ISP first to ask about its Web hosting policies for its customers. If you already go online with Pipex, using sister business 123-Reg (`www.123-reg.co.uk`) for your hosting makes sense.

Likewise, if you have a broadband Internet account with the ISP Fasthosts (www.fasthosts.co.uk), by all means, consider Fasthosts as a Web host for your business site.

Fasthosts comes highly recommended by individuals and small businesses alike. In fact, Andrew Michael started the company while still in his teens because he couldn't find anyone who'd host a small business Web site cost-effectively. That was back in the dotcom boom, when Web sites commanded silly money. Now, companies like Fasthosts encourage small and micro-sized businesses, too.

Fasthosts offers three types of hosting packages (home, developer, and business), each with increasingly sophisticated tools to create and run a Web site. The main differences are to do with the amount of Web space available to you, the number of subdomains you can use, and how many e-mail accounts you can have. Prices range from £3.99 for the starter package to £15.99 for the most sophisticated one. However, all the packages have certain things in common:

- ✔ **Visitor statistics:** Shows you who's looking where on your Web site.
- ✔ **Search engine optimisation:** Fasthosts' own TrafficDriver helps to boost your search engine rankings.
- ✔ **SSL secure Web space:** Gives you secure ecommerce capabilities and data transactions.
- ✔ **Password protected Web site folders:** Are available to restrict access to specific areas of your site.
- ✔ **MS SQL and MySQL databases plus open database connectivity:** Are all available.

What should you look for in an ISP Web hosting account, and what constitutes a good deal? For one thing, price: Expect to pay no more than £5 a month for a small amount of Web space, say 500 to 750MB. Look for a host that doesn't limit the number of Web pages that you can create. Also find one that gives you at least a couple of e-mail addresses with your account and that lets you add extra addresses for a nominal fee. Finally, look for a host that gives you the ability to include Web page forms on your site so that visitors can send you feedback.

What to expect from an ISP Web hosting service

The process of setting up a Web site varies from ISP to ISP. Here are some general features that you should look for, based on Greg's experience with his own ISP:

✓ **Web page editor:** You don't necessarily need to choose a provider that gives you a free Web page editor. You can easily download and install the editor of your choice. Greg tends to use one of two programs, either Microsoft FrontPage or Macromedia Dreamweaver, to create Web pages. (We describe both programs later in this chapter – see 'Fun with Tools: Choosing a Web Site Editor'.)

✓ **Password and username:** When Greg's Web pages are ready to go online, he can use the same username and password to access his Web site space that he uses when he dials up to connect to the Internet. Although you don't need to enter a password to view a Web site through a browser (well, at least at most sites), you do need a password to protect your site from being accessed with an FTP program. Otherwise, anyone can enter your Web space and tamper with your files.

✓ **FTP software:** When Greg signed up for a hosting account, he received a CD-ROM containing a basic set of software programs, including a Web browser and an FTP program. FTP is the simplest and easiest-to-use software to transfer files from one location to another on the Internet. When he accesses his Web site space from his Macintosh, he uses an FTP program called Fetch. (Check out this link to find out how to use it: `www.elated.com/tutorials/management/ftp/fetch`). From his PC, he uses a program called WS-FTP. Cute FTP (`www.cuteftp.com`) is another program that many Web site owners use, which costs $39.95 (around £20). Many FTP programs are available for free on the Internet or can be purchased cheaply.

Check out some other programs on the market:

- Coffee Cup FTP (`www.coffeecup.com`)
- FTP Client (`www.ftpclient.com`)
- Smart FTP (`www.smartftp.com`)

✓ **URL:** When you set up a Web site using your ISP, you're assigned a directory on a Web server. The convention for naming this directory is ~username. The ~username designation goes at the end of your URL for your Web site's home page. However, you can (and should) register a shorter URL with a domain name registrar, such as Nominet. You can then 'point' the domain name to your ISP's server so that it can serve as an 'alias' URL for your site.

After you have your software tools together and have a user directory on your ISP's Web server, it's time to put your Web site together. Basically, when Greg wants to create or revise content for his Web site, he opens the page in his Web page editor, makes the changes, saves the changes, and then transfers the files to his ISP's directory with his FTP program. Finally, he reviews the changes in his browser.

What's the ISP difference?

What's the big difference between using a kit, such as Lycos Tripod, to create your site, and using your own inexpensive or free software to create a site from scratch and post it on your ISP's server? It's the difference between putting together a model airplane from a kit and designing the airplane yourself. If you use a kit, you save time and trouble; your plane ends up looking pretty much like everyone else's, but you get the job done faster. If you design it yourself, you have absolute control. Your plane can look just the way you want. It takes longer to get to the end product, but you can be sure you get what you wanted.

On the other hand, three differences lie between an ISP-hosted site and a site that resides with a company that does *only* Web hosting, rather than providing Internet dialup access and other services:

- ✔ A business that does only Web hosting charges you for hosting services, whereas your ISP may not.

- ✔ A Web hosting service lets you have your own domain name (www.company.co.uk), whereas an ISP may not. (Some ISPs require that you upgrade to a business hosting account in order to obtain the vanity address. See the 'What's in a name?' sidebar, earlier in this chapter, for more about how Web hosting services offer an advantage in the domain-name game.)

- ✔ A Web hosting service often provides lots of frills, such as super-fast connections, one-button file transfers with Web editors such as Microsoft FrontPage, and tons of site statistics, as well as automatic backups of your Web page files.

To find out more about using a real, full-time Web hosting service, see the section, 'Going for the works with a Web hosting service', later in this chapter.

Where to find an ISP

What if you don't already have an Internet service provider, or you're not happy with the one you have? On today's Internet, you can't swing a mouse without hitting an ISP. How do you find the one that's right for you? In general, you want to look for the provider that offers you the least expensive service with the fastest connection and the best options available for your Web site.

Bigger doesn't necessarily mean cheaper or better; many smaller ISPs provide good service at rates that are comparable to the giants such as Tiscali, Pipex, or NTL. When you're shopping around for an ISP, be sure to ask the following types of questions:

✔ What types of connections do you offer?

✔ What type of tech support do you offer? Do you accept phone calls or e-mail enquiries around the clock or only during certain hours?

✔ Are real human beings always available on call, or are clients sent to a phone message system?

✔ Are there any hidden costs?

✔ What other services do you offer?

✔ Can I speak to existing customers?

Some Web sites are well known for listing ISPs by the services they offer. Here are a few good starting points in your search for the ideal ISP:

Book II

Setting Up Your Web Site

✔ **ADSL Guide:** This great Web site (www.adslguide.org.uk) gives you the low-down on a big range of ISPs in an accessible format. You can search for specific services or by price. It's well worth a look.

✔ **ISP Review:** This site (www.ispreview.co.uk) provides authoritative articles, news, and reviews dedicated to ISPs in the UK. It's a very useful site if you really want to know your ISP inside-out.

Going for the works with a Web hosting service

After you've had your site online for a while with a free Web host, such as Freeola (www.freeola.co.uk) or Heart Internet (www.heartinternet.co.uk), you may well decide that you need more room, more services (such as Web site statistics), and a faster connection that can handle many visitors at one time. In that case, you want to locate your online business with a full-time Web hosting service.

As the preceding sections attest, many kinds of businesses now host Web sites. But in this case, I'm defining *Web hosting service* as a company whose primary mission is to provide space on Web servers for individual, nonprofit, and commercial Web sites.

What to look for in a Web host

Along with providing lots of space for your HTML, image, and other files (typically, you get anywhere from 100MBs to a few GBs of space), Web hosting services offer a variety of related services, including some or all the following:

✔ **E-mail addresses:** You're likely to be able to get several e-mail addresses for your own or your family members' personal use. Besides that, many Web hosts give you special e-mail addresses called *auto-responders*. These are e-mail addresses, such as info@yourcompany.com, that you can set up to automatically return a text message or a file to anyone looking for information.

✔ **Domain names:** Virtually all the hosting options that we mention in this chapter give customers the option of obtaining a short domain name, such as www.infozoo.co.uk (in Dan's case). But some Web hosts simplify the process by providing domain-name registration in their flat monthly rates.

✔ **Web page software:** Some hosting services include Web page authoring/editing software, such as Microsoft FrontPage. Some Web hosting services even offer Web page forms that you can fill out online in order to create your own online shopping catalogue. All you have to provide is a scanned image of the item you want to sell, along with a price and a description. You submit the information to the Web host, who then adds the item to an online catalogue that's part of your site.

✔ **Multimedia/CGI scripts:** One big thing that sets Web hosting services apart from part-time hosts is the ability to serve complex and memory-intensive content, such as RealAudio sound files or RealVideo video clips. They also let you process Web page forms that you include on your site by executing computer programs called *CGI scripts*. These programs receive the data that someone sends you (such as a customer service request or an order form) and present the data in readable form, such as a text file, e-mail message, or an entry in a database.

✔ **Shopping trolley software:** If part of your reason for going online is to sell items, look for a Web host that can streamline the process for you. Most organisations provide you with Web page forms that you can fill out to create sale items and offer them in an online shopping trolley, for example.

✔ **Automatic data backups:** Some hosting services automatically back up your Web site data to protect you against data loss – an especially useful feature because, in extreme cases, major data losses have been known to sink businesses. The automatic nature of the backups frees you from the worry and trouble of doing it manually.

✔ **Site statistics:** Virtually all Web hosting services also provide you with site statistics that give you an idea (perhaps not a precisely accurate count, but a good estimate) of how many visitors you've received. Even better is access to software reports that analyse and graphically report where your visitors are from, how they found you, which pages on your site are the most frequently viewed, and so on.

✔ **Shopping and electronic commerce features:** If you plan to give your customers the ability to order and purchase your goods or services online by using their credit cards, be sure to look for a Web host that provides you with secure commerce options. A *secure server* is a computer that can encrypt sensitive data (such as credit-card numbers) that the customer sends to your site.

Having so many hosting options available is the proverbial blessing and curse. It's good that you have so many possibilities and that the competition is so fierce because that can keep prices down. On the other hand, deciding which host is best for you can be difficult. In addition to asking about the preceding list of features, here are a few more questions to ask prospective Web hosts to help narrow the field:

✔ **Do you limit file transfers?** Many services charge a monthly rate for a specific amount of electronic data that is transferred to and from your site. Each time a visitor views a page, that user is actually downloading a few kilobytes of data in order to view it. If your Web pages contain, say, 1MB of text and images and you get 1,000 visitors per month, your site accounts for 1GB of data transfer per month. If your host allocates you less than 1GB per month, it will probably charge you extra for the amount you go over the limit.

✔ **What kind of connection do you have?** Your site's Web page content appears more quickly in Web browser windows if your server has a super-fast T1 or T3 connection. Ask your ISP what kind of connection *it* has to the Internet. If you have a DSL line, speeds differ depending on the ISP: You may get a fast 1.5MBps connection or a more common 684Kbps connection. Make sure that you're getting the fastest connection you can afford.

✔ **Will you promote my site?** Some hosting services (particularly online shopping centres) help publicise your site by listing you with Internet search indexes and search services so that visitors are more likely to find you.

Besides these questions, the other obvious ones to ask any contractor apply to Web hosting services as well. These include questions like 'How long have you been in business?' and 'Can you suggest customers who will give me a reference?'

The fact that we include a screen shot of a particular Web hosting service's site in this chapter or elsewhere in this book doesn't mean that we're endorsing or recommending that particular organisation alone. A number of companies can offer your business a good deal, so shop around carefully and find the one that's best for you. Check out the hosts with the best rates and most

Book II

Setting
Up Your
Web Site

reliable service. Visit some other sites that they host and e-mail the owners of those sites for their opinion of their hosting service.

Competition is tough among hosting services, which means that prices are going down. But it also means that hosting services may seem to promise the moon in order to get your business. Be sure to read the small print and talk to the host before you sign a contract, and always get statements about technical support and backups in writing.

What's it gonna cost?

Because of the ongoing competition in the industry, prices for Web hosting services vary widely. If you look in the classified sections in the back of magazines that cover the Web or search on the Internet itself, you'll see ads for hosting services costing next to nothing. Chances are, these prices are for a basic level of service – Web space, e-mail addresses, domain name, and software – which may be all you need.

The second level of service provides CGI script processing, the ability to serve audio and video files on your site, regular backups, and extensive site statistics, as well as consultants who can help you design and configure your site. This more sophisticated range of features costs more and may set you back £20 to £50 a month, depending on the service level you require. At Easyspace.com, for example, you can conduct secure electronic commerce on your site as part of hosting packages that cost between £70 and £160 a year. MySQL database support starts at £70 a year.

Fun with Tools: Choosing a Web Page Editor

A carpenter has his or her favourite hammer and saw. A chef has an array of utensils and pots and pans. Likewise, a Web site creator has software programs that facilitate the presentation of words, colours, images, and multimedia in Web browsers.

Knowing HTML comes in handy when you need to add elements that Web page editors don't handle. Some programs, for example, don't provide you with easy buttons or menu options for adding <META> tags, which enable you to add keywords or descriptions to a site so that search engines can find them and describe your site correctly.

If you really want to get into HTML or find out more about creating Web pages, read *HTML 4 For Dummies,* 4th Edition, by Ed Tittel and Natanya Pitts, or *Creating Web Pages For Dummies,* 6th Edition, by Bud Smith and Arthur Bebak (both by Wiley).

It pays to spend time choosing a Web page editor that has the right qualities. What qualities should you look for in a Web page tool, and how do you know which tool is right for you? To help narrow the field, we've divided this class of software into different levels of sophistication. Pick the type of program that best fits your technical skills.

For the novice: Use your existing programs

A growing number of word-processing, graphics, and business programs are adding HTML to their list of capabilities. You may already have one of these programs at your disposal. By using a program with which you're already comfortable, you can avoid installing a Web page editor.

Here are some programs that enable you to generate one type of content and then give you the option of outputting that content in HTML, which means that your words or figures can appear on a Web page:

- ✔ **Microsoft Word:** The most recent versions of the venerable word processing standby work pretty much seamlessly with Web page content. You can open Web pages from within Word and save Word files in Web page format.

- ✔ **Adobe PageMaker/Quark Xpress:** The most recent versions of these two popular page layout programs let you save the contents of a document as HTML – only the words and images are transferred to the Web, however; any special typefaces become generic Web standard headings.

- ✔ **Microsoft Office XP, 2003, or 2007:** Word, Excel, and PowerPoint all give users the option of exporting content to Web pages.

- ✔ **WordPerfect and Presentations 12:** These two component programs within Corel's suite of tools let you save files as an HTML page or a PDF file that you can present on the Web. If you have chosen to present one slide per Web page, the program adds clickable arrows to each slide in your presentation so that viewers can skip from one slide to another.

Although these solutions are convenient, they probably won't completely eliminate the need to use a Web page editor. Odds are, you'll still need to make corrections and do special formatting after you convert your text to HTML.

For intermediate needs: User-friendly Web editors

If you're an experienced Web surfer and eager to try out a simple Web editor, try a program that lets you focus on your site's HTML and textual content, provides you with plenty of functionality, and is still easy to use. Here are some user-friendly programs that are inexpensive (or, better yet, free), yet allow you to create a functional Web site.

The following programs don't include some of the bells and whistles you need to create complex, interactive forms, format a page using frames, or access a database of information from one of your Web pages. These goodies are served up by Web page editors that have a higher level of functionality, which we describe in the upcoming section for advanced commerce sites.

BBEdit

If you work on a Macintosh and you're primarily concerned with textual content, BBEdit is one of the best choices you can make for a Web page tool. It lives up to its motto: 'It doesn't suck.' BBEdit is tailored to use the Mac's highly visual interface, and Version 8 will run on the Mac OS 10.3.5 or later. You can use Macintosh drag-and-drop to add an image file to a Web page in progress by dragging the image's icon into the main BBEdit window, for example. Find out more about BBEdit at the Bare Bones Software, Inc. Web site (www.barebones.com/products/bbedit/index.html).

Good choices of Web editors for the Macintosh are Taco HTML Edit by Taco Software (www.tacosw.com) or PageSpinner by Optima System (www.optima-system.com).

Macromedia HomeSite

HomeSite is an affordable tool for Web site designers who feel at ease working with HTML code. However, HomeSite isn't just an HTML code editor. It provides a visual interface so that you can work with graphics and preview your page layout. HomeSite also provides you with step-by-step utilities called *wizards* to quickly create pages, tables, frames, and JavaScript elements. A version of HomeSite is bundled with Macromedia Dreamweaver MX 2004, the latest version of the Dreamweaver Web site editor. HomeSite is also available as a standalone program that works with Windows 98 or later; find out more about it at www.macromedia.com/uk/software/homesite.

Microsoft FrontPage Express

Microsoft doesn't support FrontPage Express any more, but if you still use Windows 98 and you're on a tight budget, give it a try. The software comes bundled with Windows 98, and you don't have to do a thing to install it. Just choose Start⇨Programs⇨Internet Explorer⇨FrontPage Express to open FrontPage Express.

Book II

Setting Up Your Web Site

CoffeeCup HTML Editor

CoffeeCup HTML Editor, by CoffeeCup Software (www.coffeecup.com), is a popular Windows Web site editor that contains a lot of features for a low price of about £26). You can begin typing and formatting text by using the CoffeeCup HTML Editor menu options. You can add an image by clicking the Insert Image toolbar button, or use the Forms toolbar to create the text boxes and radio buttons that make up an interactive Web page form. You can even add JavaScript effects and choose from a selection of clip art images that come with the software.

CoffeeCup HTML Editor doesn't let you explore database connectivity, add Web components, or other bonuses that come with a program like FrontPage or Dreamweaver. But it does have everything you need to create a basic Web page.

Netscape Composer

When we read reviews of Web page software, we don't often see Netscape Composer included in the list. But to us, it's an ideal program for an entrepreneur on a budget. Why? Let us spell it out for you: F-R-E-E.

Netscape Composer is the Web page editing and authoring tool that comes with Netscape 7.2 as well as earlier versions. It's not available through the UK Web site, but all you have to do is download one of these packages from the US Netscape Browser Central page (channels.netscape.com/ns/browsers/default.jsp) and Composer is automatically installed on your computer along with Navigator (the Netscape Web browser) and several other Internet programs.

With Composer, you can create sophisticated layout elements, such as tables, with an easy-to-use graphical interface. After you edit a page, you can preview it in Navigator with the click of a button. Plus, you can publish all your files by choosing a single menu item.

For advanced commerce sites: Programs that do it all

If you plan to do a great deal of business online, or even want to add the title of Web designer to your list of talents (as some of the entrepreneurs profiled in this book have done), it makes sense to spend some money up front and use a Web page tool that can do everything you want – today and for years to come.

The advanced programs that we describe here go beyond the simple designation of Web page editors. They not only let you edit Web pages but also help you add interactivity to your site, link dynamically updated databases to your site, and keep track of how your site is organised and updated. Some programs (notably, FrontPage) can even transfer your Web documents to your Web host with a single menu option. This way, you get to concentrate on the fun part of running an online business – meeting people, taking orders, processing payments, and the like.

Macromedia Dreamweaver

What's that you say? You can never have enough bells and whistles? The cutting edge is where you love to walk? Then Dreamweaver, a Web authoring tool by Adobe (formerly Macromedia), is for you. Dreamweaver is a feature-rich, professional piece of software.

Dreamweaver's strengths aren't so much in the basic features such as making selected text bold, italic, or a different size; rather, Dreamweaver excels in producing *Dynamic HTML* (which makes Web pages more interactive through scripts) and HTML style sheets. Dreamweaver has ample FTP settings, and it gives you the option of seeing the HTML codes you're working within one window and the formatting of your Web page within a second, WYSIWYG window. The latest version, Dreamweaver 8, is a complex and powerful piece of software. It lets you create Active Server pages, connect to the ColdFusion database, and contains lots of templates and wizards. Dreamweaver is available for both Windows and Macintosh computers; find out more at the Adobe Web site (www.adobe.com/uk/products/dreamweaver).

Microsoft FrontPage

FrontPage (www.microsoft.com/uk/frontpage) is a powerful Web authoring tool that has some unique e-commerce capabilities. For one thing, it provides you with a way to organise a Web site visually. The main FrontPage window is divided into two sections. On the left, you see the Web page on which you're currently working. On the right, you see a treelike map of all the pages on your site, arranged visually to show which pages are connected to each other by hyperlinks.

Another nice thing about FrontPage – something that you're sure to find helpful if you haven't been surfing the Web or working with Web pages for very long – is the addition of wizards and templates. The FrontPage wizards enable you to create a discussion area on your site where your visitors can post messages to one another. The wizards also help you connect to a database or design a page with frames.

Book II

Setting Up Your Web Site

Chapter 4

Giving Your E-Business Site Structure and Style

*N*ot so long ago, a business that was on the World Wide Web was distinctive by definition. Nowadays, it seems that every business – from your local newsagent to international conglomerates – is on the Web. As cyberspace fills up with small businesses trying to find their niches, standing out from the crowd and attracting attention on the Internet becomes increasingly difficult.

But the same tried and tested principles apply, even though Web surfers are increasingly mobile and increasingly accustomed to sophisticated content. You don't have to load your site with scripts, animations, and flashy gimmicks. Often, the trick is to have no trick: Keep your site simple, well organised, and content rich.

In this chapter, we present one of the best ways for a new business to attract attention online: through a clearly organised and eye-catching Web site.

Feng Shui Your Web Site

According to the Web site The Geomancer (`thegeomancer.netfirms.com/fengshui.htm`), *Feng Shui* is the art of arranging objects in an environment to achieve (among other things) success in your career, wealth, and happiness. If that's true, you should try to practise some Feng Shui with your online business environment, too.

You may be tempted to rush into the process of designing and building your Web site, but while enthusiasm is always a good thing, you should try to think with a clear head and take time to plan what you're going to do. Whether you're setting off on a road trip across the country or building a new extension on your house, you'll progress more smoothly by drawing a blueprint of how you want to progress. Do you remember when you were a tiny little nipper and did your homework with a pencil and paper? Dig 'em out again and make a list of the elements you want to have on your site.

Look over the items on your list and break them into two or three main categories. These main categories will branch off your *home page,* which functions as the grand entrance for your online business site. You can then draw a map of your site that assumes the shape of a triangle, as shown in Figure 4-1.

Figure 4-1: A home page is the point from which your site branches into more specific levels of information.

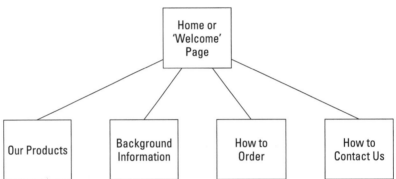

Note: The page heading 'Background Information' is a placeholder for detailed information about some aspect of your online business. For Greg's brother's audio restoration business, he suggested including a page of technical information listing the equipment he uses and describing the steps he takes to process audio. You can write about your experience with and love for what you buy and sell, or anything else that will personalise your site and build trust.

The preceding example results in a very simple Web site. But there's nothing wrong with starting out simple. For Greg's brother, who is creating his first Web site and is intimidated by getting started, this simple model is working well. Many other businesses start with a three-layered organisation for their Web sites. This arrangement divides the site into two sections, one about the company and one about the products or services for sale (see Figure 4-2).

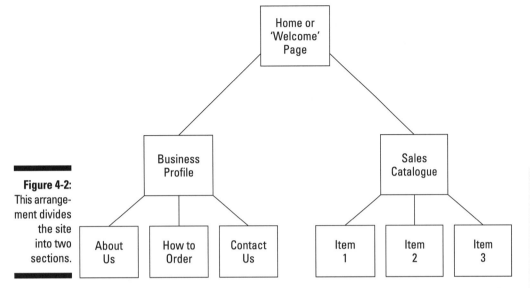

Figure 4-2:
This arrange-
ment divides
the site
into two
sections.

Think of your home page as the lobby of a museum where you get the help of
the friendly person at the information desk who hands you a list of the special exhibits you can visit that day and shows you a map so that you can
begin to figure out how you're going to get from here to there. Remember to
include the following items on your home page:

✔ The name of the shop or business

✔ Your logo, if you have one

✔ Links to the main areas of your site or, if your site isn't overly extensive,
to every page

✔ Contact information, such as your e-mail address, phone/fax numbers,
and (optionally) your business address so that people know where to
find you in the Land Beyond Cyberspace

Nip and Tuck: Establishing
a Visual Identity

The prospect of designing a Web site may be intimidating if you haven't tried
it before. But just remember that it really boils down to a simple principle:

effective visual communication that conveys a particular message. The first step in creating graphics is not to open a painting program and start drawing, but rather to plan your page's message. Next, determine the audience you want to reach with that message and think about how your graphics can best communicate what you want to say. Some ways to do this follow:

- Gather ideas from Web sites that use graphics well – both award-winning sites and sites created by designers who are using graphics in new or unusual ways. To find some award winners, check out The Webby Awards (www.webbyawards.com), The International Web Page Awards (www.websiteawards.com), and the Interactive Media Awards (www.interactivemediaawards.com).

- Use graphics consistently from page to page to create an identity and convey a consistent message.

- Create graphics that meet visitors' needs and expectations. If you're selling fashions to teenagers, go for out-there graphics. If you're selling financial advice to OAPs, choose a distinguished and sophisticated typeface.

How do you become acquainted with your customers when it is likely that you will never meet them face to face? Find newsgroups and mailing lists in which potential visitors to your site are discussing subjects related to what you plan to publish on the Web. You'd be amazing what people are blogging about these days. Don't believe us? Go to www.blogger.com and type *sandwich* or some other obscure subject matter into the search bar. We guarantee you'll be met with a string of blog posts. Now try again with a term relevant to your business. Read the posted messages to get a sense of the concerns and vocabulary of your intended audience.

Wallpaper that will wow

The proper term for the wallpaper behind the contents of a Web page is its *background*. Most Web browsers display the background of a page as light grey or blue unless you specify something different. In this case, leaving it alone isn't good enough. If you don't choose a different colour, viewers are likely to get the impression that the page is poorly designed or that the author of the page hasn't put a great deal of thought into the project. So even a neutral colour, such as white, is better than grey.

You can change the background of your Web page by tinkering with the HTML source code, but why would you want to? Most Web page creation programs offer a simple way to specify a colour or an image file to serve as the background of a Web page. For example, in an HTML editor called Netscape Composer, a free and easily overlooked Web page design tool that comes with the Netscape Communicator Web browser package, you use the Page Colours and Background dialog box (see Figure 4-3) to set your Web page wallpaper.

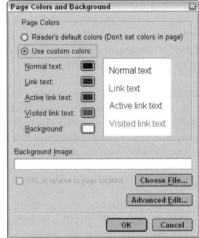

Figure 4-3:
Most
Web page
editors let
you specify
background
image/colour
options in a
dialog box
like this.

Colour your Web site effective

You can use colours to elicit a particular mood or emotion and also to convey your organisation's identity on the Web. The right choice of colour can create impressions ranging from elegant to funky.

The basic colour scheme chosen by the phone group T-Mobile (www. t-mobile.co.uk) conveys to customers its professionalism, yet also gives an impression of being with it – cool if you will. Compare that to Dan's favourite Web site, brought to you by John Cleese (www.thejohncleese. com), which is a riot of colour and movement. Remember that while it's a personal Web site, a huge business operation is behind it. Note how many items on the Web site are for sale, as well as the fact that you can pay to become a member.

When selecting colours for your own Web pages, consider the demographics of your target audience. Do some research on what emotions or impressions are conveyed by different colours and which colours best match the remit or identity of your business. Refer to resources such as the online essay by Noble Image Web Design (www.nobleimage.com/no_flash/articles/color_ choices.htm), which examines in some detail the subject of how colour choices make Web surfers react differently.

Even if you have the taste of a professional designer, you need to be aware of what happens to colour on the Web. The best colour choices for Web backgrounds are ones that don't shift dramatically from browser to browser or platform to platform. The best palette for use on the Web is a set of 216 colours that is common to all browsers. These are called *browser-safe colours* because they appear pretty much the same from browser to browser and on different monitors. The palette itself appears on Victor Engel's Web site (the-light. com/netcol.html).

Keep in mind that the colours you use must have contrast so that they don't blend into one another. For example, you don't want to put purple type on a brown or blue background, or yellow type on a white background. Remember to use light type against a dark background, and dark type against a light background. That way, all your page's contents will show up.

Sometimes your own instincts are the best way to decide what colours to use. Do you need to attract kids with wild designs? Or would that put off your older, more discerning customers? Pay attention to your gut reactions, then get feedback from your colleagues, and test your choice on a few sample members of your audience before you make your final decision.

Tiling images in the background

You can use an image rather than a solid colour to serve as the background of a page. You specify an image in the HTML code of your Web page (or in your Web page editor), and browsers automatically *tile* the image, reproducing it over and over to fill up the current width and height of the browser window.

Background images only work when they're subtle and don't interfere with the page contents. Be careful to choose an image that doesn't have any obvious lines that will create a distracting pattern when tiled. The effect you're trying to create should literally resemble wallpaper.

What you absolutely don't want to have happen is that the background image makes the page unreadable. Visit the Maine Solar House home page (www.solarhouse.com), shown later in Figure 4-8, for a rare example of a background image that is faint enough to not interfere with foreground images and that actually adds something to the page's design.

Using Web typefaces like a pro

If you create a Web page and don't specify that the text be displayed in a particular font, the browser that displays the page will use its default font – which is usually Times or Helvetica (although individual users can customise their browsers by picking a different default font).

However, you don't have to limit yourself to the same-old, same-old. As a Web page designer, you can exercise a degree of control over the appearance of your Web page by specifying that the body type and headings be displayed in a particular nonstandard font. A few of the choices available to you have names such as Arial, Courier, Century Schoolbook, and so on.

But just because you fall in love with a particular typeface doesn't mean your audience will be able to admire it in all its beauty. The problem is that you don't have ultimate control over whether a given browser will display the specified typeface because you don't know for sure whether the individual user's system has access to your preferred typefaces. If the particular font you specified is not available, the browser will fall back on its default font (which, again, is probably Helvetica or Times).

That's why, generally speaking, when you design Web pages, you're better off picking a generic typeface that is built into virtually every computer's operating system. This convention ensures that your Web pages look more or less the same no matter what Web browser or what type of computer displays them.

Where, exactly, do you specify type fonts, colours, and sizes for the text on a Web page? Again, special HTML tags tell Web browsers what fonts to display, but you don't need to mess with these tags yourself if you're using a Web page creation tool. The specific steps you take depend on what Web design tool you're using. In Dreamweaver, you have the option of specifying a group of preferred typefaces rather than a single font in the Property Inspector (see Figure 4-4). If the viewer doesn't have one font in the group, another font is displayed. Check the Help files with your own program to find out exactly how to format text and what typeface options you have.

Book II

Setting Up Your Web Site

Figure 4-4:
Most Web page design tools let you specify a preferred font or fonts for your Web page in a dialog box like this.

Not all typefaces are equal in the eye of the user. Serif typefaces, such as Times Roman, are considered to be more readable (at least, for printed materials) than sans-serif fonts, such as Helvetica. However, an article on the Web Marketing Today Web site (www.wilsonweb.com/wmt6/html-email-fonts.htm) found that by a whopping two-to-one margin, the sans-serif font Arial is considered more readable on a Web page than Times Roman.

If you want to make sure that a heading or block of type appears in a specific typeface (especially a nonstandard one that isn't displayed as body text by

Web browsers), scan it or create the heading in an image-editing program and insert it into the page as a graphic image. But make sure that it doesn't clash with the generic typefaces that appear on the rest of your page.

Clip art is free and fun

Not everyone has the time or resources to scan or download photos, or create their own original graphics. But that doesn't mean you can't add graphic interest to your Web page. Many Web page designers use clip-art bullets, diamonds, or other small images next to list items or major Web page headings to which they want to call special attention. Clip art can also provide a background pattern for a Web page or highlight sales headings such as Free!, New!, or Special!

When Greg first started out in the print publications business, he bought catalogues of illustrations, literally clipped out the art, and pasted it down. It's still called clip art, but now the process is different. In keeping with the spirit of exchange that has been a part of the Internet since its inception, some talented and generous artists have created icons, buttons, and other illustrations in electronic form and offered them free for downloading.

Here are some suggestions for sources of clip art on the Web:

- Clip Art Warehouse (www.clipart.co.uk)
- Cool Clips (www.coolclips.com)
- ZeroWeb (www.zeroweb.org)

If you use Microsoft Office, you have access to plenty of clip art images that come with the software. If you're using Word, just choose Insert⇨Picture⇨ Clip Art to view clip art images as displayed in the Insert Picture dialog box. If these built-in images aren't sufficient, you can also connect to a special Microsoft Office online by clicking the Clip Art On Office Online toolbar button in the Insert Clip Art dialog box. Web page editors – such as Microsoft FrontPage and CoffeeCup HTML Editor – come with their own clip art libraries, too.

Be sure to read the copyright fine print *before* you copy graphics. All artists own the copyright to their work. It's up to them to determine how they want to give someone else the right to copy their work. Sometimes, the authors require you to pay a small fee if you want to copy their work, or they may restrict use of their work to not-for-profit organisations.

A picture is worth a thousand words

Some customers know exactly what they want from the get-go and don't need any help from you. But most customers love to shop around or could use some encouragement to move from one item or catalogue page to another. This is where images can play an important role.

Even if you use only basic clip art, such as placing spheres or arrows next to sale items, your customer is likely to thank you by buying more. A much better approach, though, is to scan or take digital images of your sale items and provide compact, clear images of them on your site. Here's a quick step-by-step guide to get you started:

1. **Choose the right image to scan.**

   After you purchase a scanner or digital camera (see the suggestions in Chapter 2), the next step is to select images (if you're going to scan) or take images (if you're using a camera) that are well illuminated, have good contrast, and are relatively small in size.

   The original quality of an image is just as important as how you scan or retouch it. Images that are murky or fuzzy in print will be even worse when viewed on a computer screen.

2. **Preview the image.**

   Most digital cameras let you preview images so that you can decide whether to keep or delete individual pictures before downloading to your computer. If you're working with a scanner, scanning programs let you make a quick *preview scan* of an image so that you can get an idea of what it looks like before you do the actual scan. When you press the Preview button, you hear a whirring sound as the optical device in the scanner captures the image. A preview image appears on-screen, surrounded by a rectangle made up of dashes, as shown in Figure 4-5.

Figure 4-5: The software lets you crop a preview image to make it smaller and reduce the file size.

3. **Crop the image.**

   Cropping an image is a good idea because it highlights the most important contents and reduces the file size. Reducing the file size of an image should always be a primary goal – the smaller the image, the quicker it appears in someone's browser window. *Cropping* means that you resize the box around the image in order to select the portion of the image that you want to keep and leave out the parts of the image that aren't essential.

4. Select an input mode.

Tell the scanner or graphics program how you want it to save the visual data – as colour, line art (used for black-and-white drawings), or greyscale (used for black-and-white photos).

5. Set the resolution.

In Chapter 2, we note that digital images are made up of little bits (dots) of computerised information called *pixels*. The more pixels per inch, the higher the level of detail. When you scan an image, you can tell the scanner to make the dots smaller (creating a smoother image) or larger (resulting in a more jagged image). This adjustment is called *setting the resolution* of the image. (When you take a digital photo, the resolution of the image depends on your camera's settings.)

How many dots per inch (dpi) do you want your image to be? When you're scanning for the Web, you expect your images to appear primarily on computer screens. Because many computer monitors can display resolutions only up to 72 dpi, 72 dpi – a relatively rough resolution – is an adequate resolution for a Web image. (By contrast, many laser printers print at a resolution of 600 dpi.) But using this coarse resolution has the advantage of keeping the image's file size small. Remember, the smaller the file size, the more quickly an image appears when your customers load your page in their Web browsers.

6. Adjust contrast and brightness.

Virtually all scanning programs and graphics editing programs provide brightness and contrast controls that you can adjust with your mouse to improve the image. If you're happy with the image as is, leave the brightness and contrast set where they are. (You can also leave the image as is and adjust brightness and contrast later in a separate graphics program, such as Paint Shop Pro, which you can try out by downloading it from the Corel Web site (www.corel.co.uk).)

7. Reduce the image size.

The old phrase 'good things come in small packages' is never more true than when you're improving your digital image. If you're scanning an image that is 8" x 10" and you're sure that it needs to be about 4" x 5" when it appears on your Web page, scan it at 50 per cent of the original size. This step reduces the file size right away and makes the file easier to transport. That's really important if you have to put it on a floppy disk to move it from one computer to another.

8. Scan away!

Your scanner makes a beautiful whirring sound as it turns those colours into pixels. Because you're scanning only at 72 dpi, the process shouldn't take too long.

9. Save the file.

Now you can save your image to disk. Most programs let you do so by choosing File⇨Save. In the dialog box that appears, enter a name for your file and select a file format. (Because you're working with images to be published on the Web, remember to save either in GIF or JPEG format.)

When you give your image a name, be sure to add the correct filename extension. Web browsers recognise only image files with extensions such as `.gif`, `.jpg`, or `.jpeg`. If you name your image product and save it in GIF format, call it `product.gif`. If you save it in JPEG format and you're using a PC, call it `product.jpg`. On a Macintosh, call it `product.jpeg`.

For more details on scanning images, check out *Scanning For Dummies,* 2nd Edition, by Mark Chambers (Wiley).

Book II

Setting Up Your Web Site

Creating a logo

An effective logo establishes your online business's graphic identity in no uncertain terms. A logo can be as simple as a rendering of the company name that imparts an official typeface or colour. Whatever text it includes, a logo is a small, self-contained graphic object that conveys the group's identity and purpose. Figure 4-6 shows an example of a logo.

Figure 4-6: A good logo effectively combines colour, type, and graphics to convey an organisation's identity or mission.

A logo doesn't have to be a fabulously complex drawing with drop-shadows and gradations of colour. A simple, type-only logo can be as good work as well. Pick a typeface you want, choose your graphic's outline version, and fill the letters with colour.

Extreme Web Pages: Advanced Layouts

People who have some experience creating Web sites typically use frames and tables. On the other hand, they may be right up the street of an adventurous type who wants to start an online business. So this section includes some quick explanations of what tables and frames are so that you know where to start when, and if, you decide you do want to use them.

We should point out that learning HTML is almost like learning a foreign language. Of course, you don't to speak HTML, but you do have to know it well if you want to get by. If you're taking the HTML route, as opposed to paying a designer or using standard WISYWIG software, then you must spend at least a few weeks getting to know it well before you have a crack at creating your Web site. Remember: People are put off easily by poor design and functionality, so yours has to work perfectly when you launch it.

Setting the tables for your customers

Tables are to designers what statistics are to sports fans. In the case of a Web page, they provide another means to present information in a graphically interesting way. Tables were originally intended to present tabular data in columns and rows, much like a spreadsheet. But by using advanced HTML techniques, you can make tables a much more integrated and subtle part of your Web page.

Because you can easily create a basic table by using Web page editors, such as Dreamweaver and FrontPage, starting with one of these tools makes sense. Some adjustments with HTML are probably unavoidable, however, especially if you want to use tables to create blank columns on a Web page (as we explain later in this section). Here is a quick rundown of the main HTML tags used for tables:

- <TABLE> </TABLE> encloses the entire table. The BORDER attribute sets the width of the line around the cells.
- <TR> </TR> encloses a table row, a horizontal set of cells.

✔ <TD> </TD> defines the contents of an individual cell. The HEIGHT and WIDTH attributes control the size of each cell. For example, the following code tells a browser that the table cell is 120 pixels wide:

```
<TD WIDTH=120> Contents of cell </TD>
```

Don't forget that the cells in a table can contain images as well as text. Also, individual cells can have different colours from the cells around them. You can add a background colour to a table cell by adding the BGCOLOR attribute to the <TD> table cell tag.

The clever designer can use tables in a hidden way to arrange an entire page, or a large portion of a page, by doing two things:

✔ Set the table border to 0. Doing so makes the table outline invisible, so the viewer sees only the contents of each cell, not the lines bordering the cell.

✔ Fill some table cells with blank space so that they act as empty columns that add more white space to a page.

An example of the first approach, that of making the table borders invisible, appears in Figure 4-7, David Nishimura's Vintage Pens Web site (www.vintagepens.com), where he sells vintage writing instruments.

Book II

Setting
Up Your
Web Site

Figure 4-7:
This page is divided into table cells, which give the designer a high level of control over the layout.

Framing your subject

Frames are subdivisions of a Web page, each consisting of its own separate Web document. Depending on how the designer sets up the Web page, visitors may be able to scroll through one frame independently of the other frames on the same page. A mouse click on a hypertext link contained in one frame may cause a new document to appear in an adjacent frame.

Simple two-frame layouts such as the one used by one of Greg's personal favourite Web sites, Maine Solar House (see Figure 4-8), can be very effective. A page can be broken into as many frames as the designer wants, but you typically want to stick with only two to four frames because they make the page considerably more complex and slower to appear in its entirety.

Frames fit within the BODY section of an HTML document. In fact, the <FRAMESET> </FRAMESET> tags actually take the place of the <BODY> </BODY> tags and are used to enclose the rest of the frame-specific elements. Each of the frames on the page is then described by <FRAME> </FRAME> tags.

Figure 4-8:
This site uses a classic two-frame layout: A column of links in the narrow frame on the left changes the content in the frame on the right.

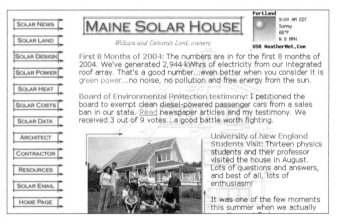

Only the more advanced Web page creation programs provide you with menu options and toolbar buttons that enable you to create frames without having to enter the HTML manually. Most of the popular Web page editors do this, including Adobe Dreamweaver and HotDog Professional by Sausage Software. See each program's Help topics for specific instructions on how to implement framing tools.

Breaking the grid with layers

Tables and frames bring organisation and interactivity to Web pages, but they confine your content to rows and columns. If you feel confined by the old up-down, left-right routine, explore layers for arranging your Web page content.

Layers, like table cells and frames, act as containers for text and images on a Web page. Layers are unique because you can move them around freely on the page – they can overlap one another, and they can 'bleed' right to the page margin.

Layers carry some big downsides: You can't create them with just any Web editor. Macromedia Dreamweaver is the Web editor of choice, and it's not free. (At time of writing, Dreamweaver Version 8 costs around £280–£300.) Layers are supported only by Versions 4.0 or later of Microsoft Internet Explorer or Netscape Navigator. However, Dreamweaver lets you create a layout in layers and then convert it to tables, which are supported by almost all browsers.

With Dreamweaver, you can draw a layer directly on the Web page you're creating. You add text or images to the layer and then resize or relocate it on the page by clicking and dragging it freely. The result is some innovative page designs that don't conform to the usual grid.

Hiring a Professional Web Designer

Part of the fun of running your own business is doing things yourself. So it comes as no surprise that many of the entrepreneurs we interviewed in the course of writing this book do their own Web page design, despite the extra time requirement and the fact that designers generally do it better! They discovered how to create Web sites by reading books or taking classes on the subject. But in many cases, the initial cost of hiring someone to help you design your online business can be a good investment in the long run. Dan, whose HTML is about as good as his Swahili, employed a Web design company to construct his Web site (www.infozoo.co.uk). The results are very professional and would take the average person a lot of time and expense to mimic. Keep in mind that after you pay someone to help you develop a look, you may be able to implement it in the future more easily yourself. For example:

- ✔ If you need business cards, stationery, brochures, or other printed material in addition to a Web site, hiring someone to develop a consistent look for everything at the beginning is worth the money.

- ✔ You can pay a designer to get you started with a logo, colour selections, and page layouts. Then you can save money by adding text yourself.

- ✔ If you're artistically impaired, consider the benefits of having your logo or other artwork drawn by a real artist.

Professional designers charge up to £100 per hour for their work (which is less than the average plumber). You can expect a designer to spend five or six hours to create a logo or template. But if your company uses that initial design for the foreseeable future, you're not really paying that much per year.

Chapter 5

Building in Security Up Front

*W*hether the perceived threat is from terrorists or roving gangs of teenage hoodlums, everyone seems to be on heightened security alert these days. And when you're an online businessperson, you face some real concerns that involve your own equipment and data, as well as the welfare of your customers.

The whole idea of security can seem intimidating. After all, you need to protect your business from the viruses and other hack attacks that are proliferating at a rate of knots. Ironically, always-on broadband Internet connections are partly to blame, because they're especially vulnerable to these intrusions. Fortunately, you can take some down-to-earth measures, most of which involve nothing more than good old common sense. You don't need to spend lots of money to make your information and that of your all-important customers secure.

Some measures are easy to put into practice and are especially important for home-based businesspeople. Others are technically challenging to implement on your own. But even if you have your Web host or a consultant do the work, you need to familiarise yourself with Internet security schemes. Doing so gives you the ability to make informed decisions about how to protect your online data. You can then take steps to lock your virtual doors so that you don't have to worry that your cyberstock is easy pickings for hackers and other bogeymen.

Practising Safe Business

If you work from home, you'd be forgiven for thinking that your safety concerns are the same as when you're watching TV on a Saturday afternoon. Unfortunately, this isn't the case. In law, you now have greater responsibility for yourself and the people you employ. You've got equipment to take care of, possibly stock, as well as lots of precious data to keep safe. Luckily, it doesn't take a brain surgeon to stay on the right side of employment law and keep your business interests secure.

We all know what a drag commuting can be, and working from your home-based business sounds like an ideal solution. But beware, distractions are everywhere. When Dan started work on InfoZoo.co.uk he made an agreement with his former managing director to keep using his old desk space, just so he could concentrate on getting the job done. When Greg works from home he's pestered by all manner of interruptions, mainly phone calls from relatives who assume that he isn't busy. So, knowing all too well that it's easier said than done, here are some simple steps that can help you set more clearly defined boundaries between work and domestic life, even when it all happens under the same roof.

When the computer is a group sport

Even if you're of a certain age, it's probably hard to comprehend that not so very long ago, there was one telephone per household and even that was connected to a party line shared by a number of other families. Now it seems everyone thinks they're entitled to their own computers. We haven't reached that level of paradise yet, but there is a lot to be said for having at least two separate machines in your home – one for personal use and one for business use. The idea is that you set up your system so that you have to log on to your business computer with a username and password. (For suggestions on how to devise a good password that's difficult to crack, see the section 'Picking passwords that are hard to guess', later in this chapter.)

If you have only one computer, passwords can still provide a measure of protection. Windows gives you the ability to set up different user profiles, each associated with its own password. You can assign a different profile to each member of your family. You can even make a game out of selecting profiles: Each person can pick his or her own background colour and desktop arrangement for Windows. User profiles and passwords don't necessarily protect your business files, but they convey to your family members that they should use their own software, stick to their own directories, and not try to explore your company data.

You can also set up different user profiles for your copy of Netscape Communicator. That way, your kids won't receive your business e-mail while they're surfing the Internet because you'll have different e-mail inboxes. If you're on Windows, choose Start⇨Programs⇨Netscape Communicator⇨Utilities⇨User Profile Manager. If you use Outlook Express for e-mail, choose File⇨Identities⇨Add New Identity to create an identity and assign a password to it.

Folder Guard, a program by WinAbility Corporation (`www.winability.com/folderguard`), enables you to hide or password-protect files or folders on your computer. The software works with Windows 95/98/Me/2000/XP. You can choose from the Standard version, which is intended for home users, or the Professional version, which is designed for business customers. A 14-day trial version is available for download from the WinAbility Web site; if you want to keep the Standard version of Folder Guard, you have to pay about £22.

Book II

Setting Up Your Web Site

Your call centre

Even thrifty guys like us consider it a necessity, not a luxury, to get a separate phone line for business use (even if it's your mobile phone rather than a land line). Having a devoted phone line not only makes your business seem more serious, but also separates your business calls from your personal ones. Additionally, if you need a phone line to connect to the Net, you then have a choice of which line to use for your modem.

The next step is to set up your business phone with its own answering machine or voice mail. On your business voice mail, identify yourself with your business's name. This arrangement builds credibility and makes you feel like a real business owner. You can then install privacy features, such as caller ID, on your business line as needed.

Even though we've resigned ourselves to paying for multiple phone lines, we're still constantly on the lookout for the best deal possible. One place Dan goes to for tips and news on telephone service, not only for small businesses but also for personal use, is SimplySwitch.com. This Web site offers price comparisons of landlines, mobile phone networks, and while you're at it, gas, electricity, credit cards, and even mortgages. SimplySwitch also offers a call centre service so that you can talk to a real person.

Preparing for the worst

When you're lying awake at night, you can be anxious about all sorts of grim disasters: flood, fire, theft, computer virus, you name it. Prevention is always better than cure, so the following sections outline steps you can take to prevent problems. But, should a problem arise, you also find ways to recover more easily.

Insurance . . . the least you can do

We can think of ways to spend money that are a whole lot more fun than paying insurance premiums. But there we are every month, writing cheques to protect ourselves in case something goes wrong with our houses, cars, even ourselves. And yes, there's another item to add to the list: protecting our business investment by obtaining insurance that specifically covers us against hardware damage, theft, and loss of data. You can also go a step farther and obtain a policy that covers the cost of data entry or equipment rental that would be necessary to recover your business information.

It is important that you take stock of everything that you consider an asset for your business and make sure that it's all covered by your policy. This will probably add to your standard home insurance, but it's worth it if the worst happens. Here are some specific strategies:

- Make a list of all your hardware and software and how much each item cost and store a copy of it in a place such as a fireproof safe or safety-deposit box, preferably in a different building to where your business is located.

- Take photos of your computer setup in case you need to make an insurance claim and put them in the same safe place.

- Save your electronic files on CD-ROM or DVD and place the disc in a safe storage location, such as a safety-deposit box.

Investigate the many options available to you for insuring your computer hardware and software. Your current homeowner's or renter's insurance may offer coverage, but make sure that the money amount is sufficient for replacement. You may also want to take a look at a business insurance search engines and brokers that can give you some ideas of which provider best suits your needs. Try www.thebroker.co.uk or www.insurancewide.com.

Consider the unthinkable

The Gartner Group estimates that two out of five businesses that experience a major disaster will go out of business within five years. We'd guess that the three that get back up on their feet and running quickly are those that already had recovery plans in place. Even if your company is small, you need to be prepared for big trouble – not only for terrorist attacks, but natural disasters such as floods, hurricanes, or tornadoes. A recovery effort may include the following strategies:

✔ **Backup power systems:** What will you do if the power goes out and you can't access the Web? Consider a battery backup system such as APC Back-UPS Office (`www.apcc.co.uk`). It instantly switches your computers to battery power when the electricity goes out so that you can save your data and switch to laptops. Even more important, make sure that your ISP or Web host has a backup power supply so that your store can remain online in case of a power outage. Having a laptop, as well as a PC, can help, too. Simply switch to your laptop in the event of a power cut, and you'll get an extra couple of hours (depending on the machine's battery life) to bridge the power gap.

✔ **Data storage:** This is probably the most practical and essential disaster recovery step for small or home-based businesses. Back up your files on a computer that's not located in the place where you physically work. At the very least, upload your files periodically to the Web space that your hosting service gives you. Also consider storing your files with an online storage service. (See the section on online storage space in this book's Internet Directory for suggestions, including one free storage option.)

✔ **Telecommunications:** Having some alternate method of communication available in case your phone system goes down ensures that you're always in touch. The obvious choice is a mobile phone. Also set up a voice mailbox so that customers and vendors can leave messages for you, even if you can't answer the phone.

Book II

Setting Up Your Web Site

Creating a plan is a waste of time if you don't regularly set aside time to keep it up to date. Back up your data on a regular basis, purchase additional equipment if you need it, and make arrangements to use other computers and offices if you need to – in other words, *implement* your plan. You owe it not only to yourself but also to your customers to be prepared in case of disaster.

Antivirus protection without a needle

Antivirus group Sophos says only 0.4 per cent of e-mails are infected with viruses, well down on just a year ago. But it identified 2,000 new threats in August 2006 alone, bringing the total number of recognised malware programs to more than 186,000. As an online businessperson, you're going to be downloading files, receiving disks from customers and vendors, and exchanging e-mail with all sorts of people you've never met. Surf safely by installing antivirus programs such as:

✔ **Norton Internet Security 2006 by Symantec Corporation (go to** `www.symantecstore.com` **and select UK site):** This application, which includes an antivirus program and a firewall and lists for £49.99, automates many security functions and is especially good for beginners. A standalone version, Norton Anti-Virus, is available for £39.99, but we recommend the full-featured package, which includes a firewall that will block many other dangerous types of intrusions, such as Trojan horses.

- ✔ **AVG AntiVirus by GriSoft** (www.grisoft.com): Many users who find Norton Internet Security too intrusive (it leaves lots of files on your computer and consumes a great deal of memory) turn to this product, which comes in a free version as well as a more full-featured version for just under £20.

- ✔ **Sophos Anti-Virus Small Business Edition** (www.sophos.com): Another popular free program, Sophos is a British-based company with a global reach. You can't buy its products through its Web site, but it gives you a directory of shops where you can.

- ✔ **Internet Security Suite by McAfee (go to** www.mcafeestore.com **and select the United Kingdom store):** This is the leading competitor to Norton Anti-Virus. This is its most comprehensive program and costs £49.99. You can get lesser packages for between £20 and £45. Check out the Web site and assess what they've got on offer.

This is another area that demands your attention on a regular basis. Viruses change all the time, and new ones appear regularly. The antivirus program you install one day may not be able to handle the viruses that appear just a month later. You may want to pick an antivirus program that gives free regular updates. Also check out www.reviewcentre.com and take a look at the antivirus software reviews. People seem to feel quite passionate about this and they don't hold back in their opinions!

Greg loves gadgets, and few things get him more excited than hand-held devices, laptops, and other portable computing devices. Yet those are the items that he seems to have the most trouble keeping track of, literally and figuratively. At the very least, you should make the device's storage area accessible with a password. You can also install protection software designed especially for mobile devices, such as VirusScan PDA by McAfee (www.mcafee.com/uk/smb/products/mobile_security/mobile_security_smb.html).

Installing Firewalls and Other Safeguards

You probably know how important a firewall is in a personal sense. It filters out unwanted intrusions such as executable programs that hackers seek to plant on your file system so they can use your computer for their own purposes. When you're starting an online business, the objectives of a firewall become different: You're protecting not just your own information but also that of your customers. In other words, you're quite possibly relying on the firewall to protect your source of income as well as the data on your computers.

Just what is a firewall, exactly? A *firewall* is an application or hardware device that monitors the data flowing into or out of a computer network and that filters the data based on criteria that the owner sets up. Like a porter in the reception of a block of flats, a firewall scans the packets (small, uniform data segments) of digital information that traverse the Internet, making sure that the data is headed for the right destination and that it doesn't match known characteristics of viruses or attacks. Authorised traffic is allowed into your network. Attack attempts or viruses are either automatically deleted or cause an alert message to appear to which you must respond with a decision to block or allow the incoming or outgoing packets.

Keeping out Trojan horses and other unwanted visitors

Book II

Setting
Up Your
Web Site

A *Trojan horse* is a program that enters your computer surreptitiously and then attempts to do something without your knowledge. Some people say that such programs enter your system through a 'back door' because you don't immediately know that they've entered your system. Trojan horses may come in the form of an e-mail attachment with the filename extension .exe (which stands for *executable*). For example, Dan recently received an e-mail that purported to be from a US-based company and that claimed it contained a security update. The attachment looked innocent enough, but had he saved the attachment to his computer, it would have used it as a staging area for distributing itself to many other e-mail addresses.

He didn't run into trouble, however. A special firewall program we installed, called Norton Internet Security, recognised the attachment and alerted him to the danger. We highly recommend that anyone who, like us, has a cable modem, DSL, or other direct connection to the Internet install one right away. Take a look at PC Advisor Magazine's Web site (www.pcadvisor.co.uk/ downloads), which lists antiviral software (free and not so free) that you may like to try out.

Cleaning out spyware

You've also got to watch out for software that 'spies' on your Web surfing and other activities and that reports them back to advertisers, potentially invading your privacy. Ad-Aware isn't a firewall exactly, but it's a useful program that detects and erases any advertising programs you may have downloaded from the Internet without knowing it. Such advertising programs may be running on your computer, consuming your processing resources and slowing down operations. Some *spyware programs* track your activities as you surf the Web; others simply report that they've been installed. Many users regard these spyware programs as invasions of privacy because they install themselves and do their reporting without your asking for it or even knowing they're active.

When Greg ran Ad-Aware the first time, he detected a whopping 57 programs he didn't know about that were running on his computer and that had installed themselves when he connected to various Web sites or downloaded software. As you can see in Figure 5-1, when he ran Ad-Aware while he was working on this chapter, sure enough, it found four suspicious software components running.

Figure 5-1:
Ad-Aware,
produced by
Swedish
company
Lavasoft,
deletes
advertising
software
that, many
users
believe, can
violate your
privacy.

We recommend Ad-Aware; you can download a version at `www.lavasoft.de/purchase/business`, the cheapest version is about £15.

Positioning the firewall

These days, most home networks are configured so that the computers on the network can share information, as well as the same Internet connection. Whether you run a home-based business or a business in a discrete location, you almost certainly have a network of multiple computers. A network is far more vulnerable than a single computer connected to the Internet: A network has more entry points than a single computer, and more reliance is placed on each of the operators of those computers to observe good safety practices.

And if one computer on the network is attacked, there is the real potential for the others to be attacked as well.

You are probably acquainted with software firewalls, such as Norton Personal Firewall or McAfee Firewall (www.mcafee-uk.co.uk/mcafee). Software firewalls protect one computer at a time. In a typical business scenario, however, multiple computers share a single Internet connection through a router that functions as a gateway. Many network administrators prefer a *hardware firewall* – a device that functions as a filter for traffic both entering and leaving it. A hardware firewall may also function as a router, but it can also be separate from the router. The device is positioned at the perimeter of the network where it can protect all the company's computers at once. Examples of hardware are the Symantec Gateway Security 1600 Series (one example is at enterprisesecurity.symantec.com/landingpages/YB/1600_mini_uk.cfm), and the SonicWall TZ170 (www.sonicwallonline.co.uk).

Book II

**Setting
Up Your
Web Site**

Companies that want to provide a Web site that the public can visit as well as secure e-mail and other communications services create a secure sub-network of one or more specially hardened (in other words, secured because all unnecessary services have been removed from them) computers. This kind of network is sometimes called a *Demilitarised Zone* or DMZ.

Keeping your firewall up to date

Firewalls work by means of attack *signatures* (also called *definitions*), which are sets of data that identify a connection attempt as a potential attack. Some attacks are easy to stop: They've been attempted for years, and the amateur hackers who attempt intrusions don't give much thought to them. The more dangerous attacks are new ones. They have signatures that have emerged since you installed your firewall.

You quickly get a dose of reality and find just how serious the problem is by visiting one of the Web sites that keeps track of the latest attacks, such as e-security company Sophos (www.sophos.com/security). US-based intrusion detection Web site DShield has reported that the 'survival time' for an unpatched computer (a computer that has security software that has not been equipped with the latest updates called *patches*) after connecting it to the Internet was only 16 minutes. That means such a computer only has 16 minutes before someone tries to attack it. If that doesn't scare you into updating your security software, we don't know what will.

Using Public Keys to Provide Security

The conversations Greg overhears as he drives his pre-teen daughters and their friends to events leave no doubt in his mind that different segments of society use code words that only their members can understand. Even computers use encoding and decoding to protect information they exchange on the Internet. The schemes used online are far more complex and subtle than the slang used by kids, however. This section describes the security method that is used most widely on the Internet, and the one you're likely to use yourself: Secure Sockets Layer (SSL) encryption.

The keys to public-key/ private-key encryption

Terms like *SSL* and *encryption* may make you want to reach for the remote, but don't be too quick to switch channels. SSL is making it safer to do business online and boosting the trust of potential customers. And anything that makes shoppers more likely to spend money online is something you need to know about.

The term *encryption* refers to the process of encoding data, especially sensitive data, such as credit-card numbers. Information is encrypted by means of complex mathematical formulas called *algorithms*. Such a formula may transform a simple-looking bit of information into a huge block of seemingly incomprehensible numbers, letters, and characters. Only someone who has the right formula, called a *key,* which is itself a complex mass of encoded data, can decode the gobbledygook.

Here's a very simple example. Suppose that your credit-card number is 12345, and you encode it by using an encryption formula into something like the following: 1aFgHx2O3gX4gLu5cy.

The algorithm that generated this encrypted information may say something like: 'Take the first number, multiply it by some numeral, and then add some letters to it. Then take the second number, divide it by x, and add y characters to the result', and so on. (In reality, the formulas are far more complex than this example, which is why you usually have to pay a licence fee to use them. But you get the general idea.) Someone who has the same formula can run it in reverse, so to speak, in order to decrypt the encoded number and obtain the original number, 12345.

In practice, the encoded numbers that are generated by encryption routines and transmitted on the Internet are very large. They vary in size depending on the relative strength (or uncrackability) of the security method being used. Some methods generate keys that consist of 128 bits of data; a *data bit* is a single unit of digital information. These formulas are called *128-bit keys*.

Encryption is the cornerstone of security on the Internet. The most widely used security schemes, such as the Secure Sockets Layer protocol (SSL), the Secure Electronic Transactions protocol (SET), and Pretty Good Privacy (PGP), all use some form of encryption.

Getting a certificate without going to school

On the Internet, how do you know that people are who they say they are when all you have to go on is a URL or an e-mail address? The solution in the online world is to obtain a personal certificate that you can send to Web site visitors or append to your e-mail messages.

How certificates work

A *certificate,* which is also sometimes called a Digital ID, is an electronic document issued by a certification authority (CA). The certificate contains the owner's personal information as well as a public key that can be exchanged with others online. The public key is generated by the owner's private key, which the owner obtains during the process of applying for the certificate.

In issuing the certificate, the CA takes responsibility for saying that the owner of the document is the same as the person actually identified on the certificate. Although the public key helps establish the owner's identity, certificates do require you to put a level of trust in the agency that issues it.

A certificate helps both you and your customers. It assures your customers that you're the person you say you are, plus it protects your e-mail communications by enabling you to encrypt them.

Obtaining a certificate from VeriSign

Considering how important a role certificates play in online security, it's remarkably easy to obtain one. You do so by applying and paying a licensing fee to a CA. One of the most popular CAs is VeriSign, Inc. (`www.verisign.co.uk`), which lets you apply for a range of SSL certificates that range in price from £259 for a basic one-year licence, to several thousands of pounds for more complicated packages.

Book II

Setting Up Your Web Site

A VeriSign Secure Site certificate, which you can use to authenticate yourself in e-mail, news, and other interactions on the Net, costs £259 plus VAT per year, but you can get a better deal signing up for longer terms, and you can try out a free certificate for secure e-mail IDs for 60 days. Follow these steps to obtain your Digital ID:

1. **Go to the VeriSign, Inc. Digital IDs for Secure E-Mail page at** www. verisign.co.uk/products-services/security-services/pki/ pki-security/email-digital-id/index.html.

2. **Click the Buy Now button whether you're certain you want an ID or you only want the trial version.**

   The Digital ID Enrollment page appears.

3. **Click Buy Now near the bottom of the page.**

   A page may appear (if you don't have JavaScript support) that asks you to identify the Web browser you use most often, and that you want to associate with the Digital ID. Click the browser you want. An application form for a Digital ID appears.

4. **Complete the application form.**

   The application process is pretty simple. The form asks for your personal information and a challenge phrase that you can use in case anyone is trying to impersonate you. It also requires you to accept a license agreement. (You don't need to enter credit-card information if you select the 60-day trial option.)

5. **Click the Accept button at the bottom of the screen.**

   A dialog box appears asking you to confirm your e-mail address. After you confirm by clicking OK, a dialog box appears asking you to choose a password. When you enter a password and click OK, VeriSign uses your password to generate a private key for you. The private key is an essential ingredient in public-key/private-key technology.

6. **Click OK to have your browser generate your private key.**

   A page appears asking you to check your e-mail for further instructions. In a few minutes, you receive a message that contains a Digital ID PIN.

7. **In your e-mail program, open the new message from VeriSign Customer Support Department.**

8. **Use your mouse to highlight the PIN and then choose Edit⇨Copy to copy the PIN.**

9. **Go to the URL for Digital ID Services that's included in the e-mail message and paste your PIN in the text box next to Enter The Digital ID Personal Identification Number (PIN).**

10. **Click Submit.**

The certificate is generated, and the Digital IDF Installation and Registration Page appears.

11. **Click the Install button.**

The ID from VeriSign downloads, and you're now able to view it with your browser. Figure 5-2 shows Greg's certificate for Netscape Navigator. (Copying this ID, or anyone else's, is pointless because this is only your public key; the public key is always submitted with your private key, which is secret.)

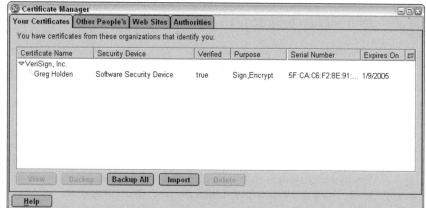

Figure 5-2:
A personal certificate assures individuals or Web sites of your identity.

After you have your Digital ID, what do you do with it? For one thing, you can use it to verify your identity to sites that accept certificate submissions. Some sites that require members to log in use secure servers that give you the option of submitting your certificate rather than entering the usual username and password to identify yourself. You can also attach your Digital ID to your e-mail messages to prove that your message is indeed coming from you. See your e-mail program's Help files for more specific instructions.

You can't encrypt or digitally sign messages on any computer other than the one to which your certificates are issued. If you're using a different computer than the one you used when you obtained your certificates, you must contact your certificate issuer and obtain a new certificate for the computer you're now using. Or, if your browser allows transfers, you can export your certificate to the new computer.

Keeping Other Noses Out of Your Business

Encryption isn't just for big businesses. Individuals who want to maintain their privacy, even while navigating the wilds of the Internet, can install special software or modify their existing e-mail programs in order to encode their online communications. You may not need to use software like this, but if you deal in sensitive data, then it's a must.

The TechWorld Web site (`www.techworld.com/security/features/index.cfm?featureid=993`) presents some good tips and strategies for personal protection on the Internet.

Encryption software for the rest of us

PGP (Pretty Good Privacy), a popular encryption program, has been around about as long as the Web itself. PGP lets you protect the privacy of your e-mail messages and file attachments by encrypting them so that only those with the proper authority can decipher the information. You can also digitally sign the messages and files you exchange, which assures the recipient that the messages come from you and that the information has not been tampered with. You can even encrypt files on your own computer.

PGP (`www.pgp.com/products/desktop/index.html`) is a personal encryption program. PGP offers a range of *plug-ins,* applications that work with other programs to provide added functionality. You can integrate the program with popular e-mail programs such as Microsoft Outlook (although Netscape Messenger is notably absent from the list of supported applications).

In order to use PGP Personal Privacy, the first step is to obtain and install the program. For a price list or more information about the 30-day free trial, go to the Web site at `www.pgp.com`. After you install the program, you can use it to generate your own private-key/public-key pair. After you create a key pair, you can begin exchanging encrypted e-mail messages with other PGP users. To do so, you need to obtain a copy of their public keys, and they need a copy of your public key. Because public keys are just blocks of text, trading keys with someone is really quite easy. You can include your public key in an e-mail message, copy it to a file, or post it on a public-key server where anyone can get a copy at any time.

After you have a copy of someone's public key, you can add it to your *public keyring,* which is a file on your own computer. Then you can begin to exchange encrypted and signed messages with that individual. If you're using an e-mail application supported by the PGP plug-ins, you can encrypt and sign your messages by selecting the appropriate options from your application's toolbar. If your e-mail program doesn't have a plug-in, you can copy your e-mail message to your computer's Clipboard and encrypt it there by using PGP built-in functions. See the PGP User's Guide files for more specific instructions.

Encrypting e-mail messages

You can use your existing software to encrypt your mail messages rather than have to install a separate program such as PGP. In the following sections, we describe the steps involved in setting up the e-mail programs that come with the biggest browser package, Microsoft Internet Explorer, to encrypt your messages.

If you use Outlook, Microsoft's e-mail program that you get as standard with the computer's Office suite, you can use your Digital ID to do the following:

- **Send a digital signature:** You can digitally shrink-wrap your e-mail message by using your certificate in order to assure the recipient that the message is really from you.

- **Encrypt your message:** You can digitally encode a message to ensure that only the intended party can read it.

To better understand the technical details of how you can keep your e-mail communications secure, read the Digital ID User Guide, which you can access at www.verisign.com/stellent/groups/public/documents/guides/005326.pdf.

After you have a digital ID, in order to actually make use of it, you need to follow these steps in Internet Explorer:

1. **After you obtain your own Digital ID, the first step is to associate it with your e-mail account by choosing Tools⇨Accounts.**

   The Internet Accounts dialog box appears.

2. **Select your e-mail account and click Properties.**

   The Properties dialog box for your e-mail account appears.

3. **Click the Security tab to bring it to the front.**

4. **Click the Select button in the Signing Certificate section; then when the Select Default Account Digital ID dialog box appears, select your Digital ID.**

Book II

Setting Up Your Web Site

5. Click OK to close the Select Default Account Digital ID dialog box; then click OK to close the Properties dialog box and click Close to close the Internet Accounts dialog box.

You return to the main Outlook window.

6. To send a digitally signed e-mail message to someone, click Create Message.

The New Message dialog box appears.

7. Click either or both of the security buttons at the extreme right of the toolbar, as shown in Figure 5-3.

The Sign button enables you to add your Digital ID. The Encrypt button lets you encrypt your message.

Figure 5-3:
When you click the Sign and Encrypt buttons, your message goes out encrypted and with your certificate attached.

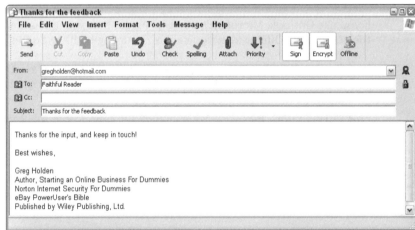

8. Finish writing your message and then click the Send button.

Your encrypted or digitally signed message is sent on its way.

The preceding steps show you how to digitally sign or encrypt an individual message. You have to follow these steps every time you want to sign or encrypt a message. On the other hand, by checking one or more of the options (Encrypt Contents and Attachments for All Outgoing Messages and Digitally Sign All Outgoing Messages) on the Security tab of the Options dialog box, you activate Outlook Express's built-in security features for *all* your outgoing messages. (You can still 'turn off' the digital signature or encryption for an individual message by deselecting the Sign or Encrypt buttons in the toolbar of the New Message dialog box.)

Picking passwords that are hard to guess

You put a lot of effort into picking the names of your kids and pets, and now you get to choose passwords. But the point of creating a password is to make it difficult for thieves to figure out what it is. That is true whether you're protecting your own computer, downloading software, subscribing to an online publication, or applying for a certificate (as we explain earlier in this chapter).

One method for choosing a password is to take a familiar phrase and then use the first letter of each word to form the basis of a password. For example, the old phrase 'Every Good Boy Deserves Fruit' would be EGBDF. Then, mix uppercase and lowercase, add punctuation, and you wind up with eGb[d]f. If you *really* want to make a password that's hard to crack, add some numerals as well, such as the last two digits of the year you were born: eGb[d]f48.

Whatever you do, follow these tips for effective password etiquette:

> ✔ **Don't use passwords that are in a dictionary:** It takes time but not much effort for hackers to run a program that tries every word in an online dictionary as your password. So if it's in the dictionary, they will eventually discover it.
>
> ✔ **Don't use the same password at more than one site:** It's a pain to remember more than one password, not to mention keeping track of which goes with what. Plus, you tend to accumulate lots of different passwords after you've been online for a while. But if you use the same password for each purpose and your password to one site on the Internet is compromised, all your password-protected accounts are in jeopardy.
>
> ✔ **Use at least six characters:** The more letters in your password, the more difficult you make the life of the code-crackers.

When it comes to passwords, duplication is not only boring but also dangerous. It's especially important not to reuse the same password that you enter to connect to your account on a commercial service such as AOL, Pipex, or Tiscali as a password to an Internet site. If a hacker discovers your password on the Internet site, that person can use it to connect to your AOL or Compu-Serve account, too – and you'll have to pay for the time they spend online.

A mouthful of protection with authentication

Authentication is a fun word to try to say quickly ten times in a row, and it's also another common security technique used on the Web. This measure

Book II

Setting Up Your Web Site

simply involves assigning approved users an official username and password that they must enter before gaining access to a protected network, computer, or directory.

Most Web servers allow you to set up areas of your Web site to be protected by username and password. Not all Web hosts allow this, however, because it requires setting up and maintaining a special password file and storing the file in a special location on the computer that holds the Web server software. If you need to make some content on your business site (such as sensitive financial information) available only to registered users, talk to your Web host to see whether setting up a password-protected area is possible.

Book III
Getting Known E-asily

'Shh — he's searching.'

In this book . . .

If you've set up your online business, you need to know your market and draw customers into your virtual shop. Having a good head for marketing and PR helps, as does the ability to research who's buying (and selling) what – and we point you in the right direction in this book. Getting up to speed with search engines and the Internet in general is just as important, and again, we cover what you need to know here.

Here are the contents of Book III at a glance:

Chapter 1

Marketing Your Wares

· ·

In This Chapter:

▶ Understanding the marketing mix and how to use it

▶ Deciding the advertising message

▶ Choosing the media

▶ Reviewing selling options

▶ Appreciating the legal implications

· ·

*E*ntering the market involves deciding on what mix of marketing ingredients to use. In cooking, the same ingredients used in different ways can result in very different products and the same is true in business. In business, the 'ingredients' are product (or service), price, place, and promotion. A change in the way these elements are put together can produce an offering tailored to meet the needs of a specific market. For example, a hardback book is barely more expensive to produce than a paperback. However with a bit of clever publicity, bringing them out a few weeks before the paperback edition and a hefty price hike, an air of exclusivity can be created which satisfies a particular group of customers.

Making Up the Marketing Mix

The key to successful promotion lies in knowing exactly what you want people to do. A few elements can make or break the successful marketing of your business. The elements you need to consider in the marketing mix are:

> ✔ The *product or service* is what people use, but what they buy are the underlying benefits it confers on them. For example, cameras, SLR or digital, lens, even film are not the end products that customers want; they are looking for good pictures.

✔ *Pricing* strategies can range from charging what the market will bear, right through to *marginal cost* (just enough to cover direct costs and a small contribution to overheads). While it is important to know your costs, this is only one element in the pricing decision. You also have to take account of the marketplace, your competition, and your product position (for example, if you offer a luxury item, your place in the market is different than someone who sells necessities).

✔ Place is a general title to cover everything from where you locate to how you get your product or service to market. Poor distribution often explains sluggish sales growth. If your type of product gets to market through several channels but you only use one of them, then no amount of price changes or extra promotion will make much difference.

Defining Your Product Parameters

To be successful in the marketplace, you need to have a clear picture of exactly what you want to do and for whom you're doing it. In other words, you need a vision and a mission.

To effectively market your product, you have to make decisions about factors such as product range and depth before you are ready to enter the market. Having decided to open a corner shop, for example, you still have to decide if you will focus on food only, or will you carry household items and perhaps newspapers and flowers too. You will also need to decide if you will carry more than one brand and size of each product.

If the key advantages of your corner shop are its location, opening hours, delivery service and friendly staff, all at competitive prices, then perhaps you don't need a wide or deep product range.

Using Advertising to Tell Your Story

The skill of advertising lies in reducing the global population to your target audience and reaching as many of them as you can at an economic cost. You first analyse the benefits or virtues of your product, isolate the features, and translate these into customer benefits. Who has a need for your product? Discover who your potential customers are.

Question all the time. Then set objectives for your campaign, decide on a budget, design the message, and pick the medium to reach your target audience, and determine how you're going to evaluate the success of your advertising.

When you understand the basics, which we go through in the following sections, you should be able to analyse advertisements better, to break them down, and avoid the all too common mistakes that are made every day.

Advertising by itself does not sell. It will not shift a bad product (more than once) or create new markets. Sales literature, order forms, a sales force, stocks, distributors, and a strategy must back it up.

Considering the customer's point of view

It is important to recognise that people buy a product or service for what it will do for them. Customers look for the benefits. As the seller, your mission is to answer the question 'What's in it for me?' from your potential customer's point of view.

Every time you compose a sales letter, write an advertisement, or plan a trade show, you must get to the heart of the matter. Why should customers purchase your wares? What benefit will it bring them?

All your marketing efforts need to be viewed from the prospect's point of view and not just your own. Once you know what you are selling and to whom, you can match the features of the product (or service) to the benefits the customer will get when they purchase. A *feature* is what a product has or is, and *benefits* are what the product does for the customer. Finally, include proof that these benefits can be delivered. Table 1-1 shows an analysis of features, benefits, and proofs.

Book III

Getting
Known
E-asily

Table 1-1	Listing Features and Benefits	
Feature	*Benefit*	*Proof*
We use a unique hardening process for our machine.	Our tools last longer and that saves you money.	We have a patent on the process; independent tests carried out by the Cambridge Institute of Technology show our product lasts longest.
Our shops stay open later than others in the area.	You get more choice when to shop.	Come and see.
Our computer system is fault tolerant using parallel processing.	You have no downtime for either defects or system expansion.	Our written specification guarantees this; come and talk to satisfied customers operating in your field.

You can use this format to examine the features, benefits, and proofs for your own products or services and use the information to devise your ads. Remember, the customer pays for the benefits and the seller for the features. So the benefit will provide the copy for most of your future advertising and promotional efforts.

Try this out for your business idea. Keep at it until you really have a good handle on what makes your customers tick. To make the process work you will need to talk to some real prospective customers in your target market.

Setting advertising objectives

There is no point in advertising your product or service unless it leads to the opportunity for a sale in a significant number of instances. Ask yourself what potential customers have to do to enable you to make these sales. Do you want them to visit your showroom, phone you, write to your office, return a card, or send an order in the post? Do you expect them to order now, or to remember you at some future date when they have a need for your services?

The more specifically you identify the response you want, the better you can tailor your promotional effort to achieve your objective, and the more clearly you can assess the effectiveness of your promotion.

The more general your advertising objective is – for example, to 'improve your image' or 'to keep your name in front of the public' – the more likely it is to be an ineffective way of spending your money.

Deciding the budget

Two methods are commonly used to calculate advertising budget numbers:

- ✔ **What can we afford?** This approach accepts that cash is usually a scarce commodity and advertising has to take its place alongside a range of competing demands.

- ✔ **Cost/benefit:** This approach comes into its own when you have clear and specific promotional goals. If you have spare capacity in your factory or want to sell more out of your shop, you can work out how much it will cost you to increase your production and sales, and how much you could benefit from those extra sales. You then figure out how much advertising money it takes to get you the extra business.

Suppose a £1,000 advertisement is expected to generate 100 enquiries for your product. If your experience tells you that on average 10 per cent of enquiries result in orders, and your profit margin is £200 per product, then you can expect an extra £2,000 profit. That benefit is much greater than the £1,000 cost of the advertisement, so it seems a worthwhile investment.

In practice, you should use all of these methods to decide how much to spend on promoting your products.

Defining the message

To define your message, you must look at your business and its products from the customer's standpoint and be able to answer the question, 'Why should I buy your product?' It is better to consider the answer in two stages:

1. **'Why should I buy your *product?*'**

    The answer is provided naturally by looking carefully at buying motives and the benefits customers get from the product.

2. **'Why should I buy *your* product?'**

    The only logical and satisfactory answer is: 'Because it is better and so it is different.'

    The difference can arise in two ways:

    1. You, the seller, are different. To achieve this, you establish a particular niche for your business.

    2. Your product is different. Each product should have a unique selling point, based on fact.

Your promotional message must be built around your product's strengths and must consist of facts about the company and about the product.

The stress here is on the word '*fact*' and although there may be many types of fact surrounding you and your products, your customers are only interested in two: the facts which influence their buying decisions, and the facts of how your business and its products stand out from the competition.

The assumption is that everyone buys for obvious, logical reasons only, but of course innumerable examples show that this is not so. Does a woman buy a new dress only when the old one is worn out? Do bosses have desks that are bigger than their subordinates' because they have more papers to put on them?

Choosing the media

Broadly, your advertising choices are media *above-the- line,* which is jargon for newspapers, TV, radio, and other broadcast media, and *below-the-line* activities such as distributing brochures, stationery letterhead, and the way you answer the phone. The printed word (newspapers and magazines) will probably take most of your above-the-line advertising budget. It is the accepted medium to reach the majority of customers. Most people read the newspaper, especially on Sunday, and there are magazines to cater for every imaginable interest from the parish magazine to the Sunday supplements.

You must advertise where your buyers and consumers are likely to see the message. Your market research tells you where your likely prospects lie. Before making your decision about which paper or journal to advertise in, you need to get readership and circulation numbers and the reader profile.

You can get this information directly from the journal or paper or from *BRAD* (British Rate and Data), www.brad.co.uk, which has a monthly classified directory of all UK and Republic of Ireland media. You should be able to access this through your local business library.

The approach to take when considering below-the-line advertising is to identify what business gurus call *moments of truth* – contact points between you, your product or service, and your customer. Those moments offer you a chance to shine and make a great impression. You can spot the difference at once when you get a really helpful person on the phone or serving you in a shop. The same is true of product literature that is actually helpful, a fairly rare event in itself.

Some of the most effective promotional ideas are the simplest, for example a business card with a map on the reverse side showing how to find you, or 'thank you cards', instead of letters, on which you can show your company's recently completed designs.

Choosing the frequency

The copy dates of some monthlies are two months before publication. This poses problems if you are waiting on a shipment or uncertain about a product change. Dailies or weeklies allow much prompter changes. The ultimate is probably radio, where messages can be slotted in on the same day. Yearbooks, diaries, and phone directories require long forward notice.

Providing opportunities to see

One claimed benefit of breakfast television is that it can get your message out before the shops open. Trade buyers are deluged with calendars, diaries, pen sets, and message pads in the hope that when the buyer is making a decision, the promotional materials are still close at hand and have an influence on the buyer's decision.

The more opportunities you give potential customers to see your name or your product, the greater the chance that they'll remember you. This is why direct mail letters usually involve more than one piece of literature. The theory is that each piece is looked at before being discarded. It may only be a brief scan but it gives the seller another chance to hook a customer. So rather than using different advertising messages, try getting the same or a similar message to one customer group several times.

Figuring your bang-for-the-buck ratio

Advertising should only be undertaken where the results can realistically be measured. Everything else is self-indulgent. The formula to keep in mind is:

Effectiveness = Total cost of the advertising activity concerned ÷ by the Results (in measurable units such as customers, new orders, or enquiries).

A glance at the advertising analysis below will show how one organisation tackled the problem.

Table 1-2 shows the advertising results for a small business course run in London. At first glance the Sunday paper produced the most enquiries. Although it cost the most, £340, the cost per enquiry was only slightly more than the other media used. But the objective of this advertising was not simply to create interest; it was intended to sell places on the course. In fact, only ten of the 75 enquiries were converted into orders – an advertising cost of £34 per head. On this basis the Sunday paper was between 2.5 and 3.5 times more expensive than any other medium.

Table 1-2		Measuring Advertising Effect			
Media Used	*Enquiries*	*Cost of Advertising*	*Cost per Enquiry*	*No. of Customers*	*Advertising Cost per Customer*
Sunday paper	75	£340	£4.50	10	£34
Daily paper	55	234	4.25	17	14
Posters	30	125	4.20	10	12
Local weekly paper	10	40	4.00	4	10
Personal recom-mendation*	20	N/A	N/A	19	N/A

Getting in the News

The surest way to get in the news is to write a press release. Better still write lots of them. To be successful, a press release needs to get attention immediately and be quick and easy to digest. Studying and copying the style of the particular journals (or other media) you want your press release to appear in can make publication more likely.

The introduction is the most vital part. You should ask yourself, 'Will it make the reader want to read on?' Avoid detail and sidetracks. The paragraphs should have bite and flow. Keep the sentences reasonably short. State the main point of the story early on. Follow these suggestions for a successful press release:

- Type the release on a sheet of A4 paper headed up 'Press Release' or 'Press Information'. Address it to the News Editor, News desk, or a named journalist.
- Use double spacing and wide margins to allow for editorial changes and printing instructions, respectively. Use one side of the paper only.
- Date the release and put a headline on to identify it.
- Tell your story in three paragraphs. The substance should come in the first one. The first paragraph must say who, what, why, when, and where, and succeeding paragraphs can fill in the detail. If space is short then the sub-editor will delete from the bottom and papers are always looking for fillers – short items that can be dropped into gaps. Even if the bulk of the story is cut, at least the main facts will get printed.
- Include at least one direct quotation or comment, always from a named individual and ideally from someone of standing or relevance.
- Keep it simple and write for the readership. The general public prefers images or descriptions to technical facts. For example a new car lock could be described as being able to keep out a professional thief for 30 minutes for a story in the general press. For the trade press the same story would be better supported by facts about the number of levers, codes, and so forth that are involved in beefing up the lock's security system.
- Finish with a contact for more information. Give phone numbers for work and home, as well as your e-mail and website addresses. This will help a journalist looking for more detail and by being available your story will be more attractive if a gap occurs suddenly.
- Submit the release before the paper or journal's deadline. All the media work to strict deadlines. Many local papers sold on a Friday are printed

on a Tuesday or Wednesday morning. A release that fails to make it by then will probably be ignored. The national dailies, of course, have more flexibility and often have several editions. At the other end of the scale, many colour supplements and monthly journals have a cut-off date six weeks in advance.

✔ Steer away from selling your firm and product, and write news. Anything else is advertising and will be discarded. You are not writing an advertisement, you are telling a story to interest the readers.

✔ A good picture, they say, is worth a thousand words. Certainly from a journalist's point of view it's worth half a page of text they don't have to write themselves.

Deciding who to contact

Remember that the target audience for your press release is the professional editor; it is he or she who decides to print. With UK editors receiving an average of 80–90 press releases per week, make sure that you are making your latest newsworthy item public, but make sure it is free of puffery and jargon.

Do your research to find not only the right newspapers or journals, but also the right journalists. Read their columns, or listen to or watch their programmes and become familiar with their style and approach to news stories. Hollis (www.hollis-pr.com) publish the details of all news contacts, listed by business area. Your goal is to write a press release that is so close to their own style that they have almost no additional work to do to make your news usable.

Book III

**Getting
Known
E-asily**

Following through

You will get better results by following up your press release with a quick phone call. Journalists get bogged down and distracted like everyone else, so don't be too surprised if your masterpiece sinks to the bottom of a pile of prospective stories before the day is out. That phone call, or even an e-mail if you can't get through, is often enough to keep up interest and get your story through the first sifting.

Once you start getting results you will want to keep it going. But even if you are not successful at first, don't be disappointed or disheartened. Keep plugging away. Try to find a story regularly for the local press and get to know your local journalists and editors. Always be truthful, helpful, and available. If they ring you and you are at a meeting, make sure you always ring back.

Some companies always seem to get a piece in the paper every week. The stories published are not always earth-shattering news, but the continuous drip of press coverage eventually makes an impact. For example, Virgin Air has been virtually created by successful press coverage. Few of the millions of words of copy written about Branson or Virgin have been paid for.

Selling and Salesmanship

Selling is at the heart of every business. Whatever kind of selling your business involves, from moving goods over a counter to negotiating complex contracts, you need to understand the whole selling process and be involved with every aspect of it.

Telling the difference between selling and marketing

Marketing involves the whole process of deciding what to sell, who to sell it to, and how. The theory is that a brilliant marketing strategy should all but eliminate the need for selling. After all, selling is mostly concerned with shoe-horning customers into products that they don't really want, isn't it? Absolutely not! Whilst it is true that the more effort you put into targeting the right product or service to the right market, the less arduous the selling process is, you still have a selling job to do.

The primary job of the sales operation is to act as a bridge or conduit between the product and the customer. Across that gulf flows information as well as products and services. Customers need to be told about your great new ideas and how your product or service will perform better than anything they have seen to date.

Most businesses need selling and marketing activities in equal measure to get their message across effectively and get goods and services into their markets.

Selling yourself

One of the most important operational issues to address is your personal selling style. If you've sold products or services before, you may have developed a successful selling style already. If not, you need to develop one that is appropriate for your customers and comfortable for you. Regardless of your experience, assessing your selling style will help define and reinforce your business goals.

Check you and your salespeople always see things from the customer's point of view. Review the sales style of your salespeople to see how they can be improved.

Consider if your selling style is consultative, where you win the customer over to your point of view, or hard, where you try forcing them to take your product or service.

In assessing your selling style, consider the following:

- Always have a specific objective for any selling activity, together with a fall back position. For example your aim may be to get an order but you would settle for the chance to tender for their business. If you don't have objectives there is a danger that much of your sales activity will be wasted on courtesy calls that never reach the asking-for-an-order stage.

- The right person to sell to is the one who makes the buying decision. You may have to start further down the chain, but you should always know whom you finally have to convince.

- Set up the situation so you can listen to the customer. You can best do this by asking open questions. When they have revealed what their needs really are, confirm them back to them.

- Explain your product or service in terms of the customer's needs and requirements.

- Deal with objections without hostility or irritation. Objections are a sign that the customer is interested enough in what you have to say to at least discuss your proposition. Once you have overcome their objections and established a broad body of agreement you can try to close the deal.

- Your approach to closing can be one of a number of ways. The *assumptive close* takes the tack that as you and the customer are so much in agreement an order is the next logical step. If the position is less clear you can go for the *balance sheet close,* which involves going through the pros and cons, arriving at a larger number of pros. So once again the most logical way forward is for the customer to order. If circumstance allow, you can use the *special situation* closing technique. This might be appropriate if a product is in scarce supply or on special offer for a limited period.

- If you are unsuccessful, start the selling process again using your fall back objective as the goal.

Outsourcing selling

Few small start-up firms can afford to hire their own sales force at the outset as it costs over £40,000 a year to keep a good salesperson on the road, including commission and expenses. Inevitably there is a period where no sales are coming in yet salary and expenses are being paid out. Plus, you run the very real risk of employing the wrong person.

A lower-cost and perhaps less risky sales route is via agents. Good agents should have existing contacts in your field, know buyers personally, and have detailed knowledge of your product's market. Unlike someone you recruit, a hired agent should be off to a flying start from day one.

The big thing is that agents are paid purely on commission: if they don't sell they don't earn. The commission amount varies but is rarely less than 7 per cent and 25 per cent is not unknown.

You can find an agent by advertising in your specialist trade press or the *Daily Telegraph*, and *Exchange and Mart*. You can also find agents' associations listed in trade directories. However the most reliable method is to approach outlets where you wish to sell. They know the honest, competent, and regular agents who call on them. Draw up a shortlist and invite those agents to apply.

When interviewing a potential sales agent, you should find out:

- ✔ What other companies and products they already sell. You want them to sell related but not competing products.
- ✔ What is their knowledge of the trade and geographical area covered? Sound them out for specific knowledge of your target market.
- ✔ Who are their contacts?
- ✔ What is their proven selling record? Find out who their biggest customers are and talk to them directly.
- ✔ Do they appear honest, reliable, and a fit person to represent your business? Take up references and talk to their customers.

It is a challenge to find professional representation so your product has to be first-class, growth prospects good, with plenty of promotional material and back-up support.

When you do find a person to represent your product, draw up an agreement to cover the main points including geographic area, commission rates, when payable, customers you will continue dealing with yourself, training and support given, prohibiting competing agencies, and periods of notice required to terminate. Also build in an initial trial period after which both parties can agree to part amicably.

Measuring results

Sales results can take time to appear. In the meantime you need to make sure you're doing the things that will eventually lead to successful sales. You should measure the following:

Activities

- ✔ Sales appointments made
- ✔ Sales calls made per day, per week, per month. Monitor trends, as last quarter's sales calls will give you a good feel for this quarter's sales results
- ✔ Quotations given

Results

- ✔ New accounts opened
- ✔ Old accounts lost
- ✔ Average order size

Pricing for Profit

Pricing is the biggest decision you have to make about your business and the one that has the biggest impact on company profitability. You need to keep pricing constantly under review.

To get a better appreciation of the factors that could have an influence on what you should charge, every business should keep these factors in mind.

Caring about business conditions

Obviously, the overall condition in the marketplace has a bearing on your pricing policy. In boom conditions, where products are so popular that they're virtually being rationed, the overall level of prices for some products could be expected to rise disproportionately. Conditions can vary so much from place to place as to have a major impact on pricing. For example, one business starter produced her beauty treatment price list based on prices near to her home in Surrey. However she planned to move to Cornwall to start her business, where prices were 50 per cent lower, reflecting lower rates of pay in the county. So whilst she got a boost by selling her Surrey home for much more than she paid for a house in Cornwall, that gain was offset by having to charge much lower prices for her services.

Seasonal factors can also contribute to changes in the general level of prices. A turkey, for example, costs less on the afternoon of Christmas Eve than it does at the start of Christmas week.

Working to your capacity

Your capacity to produce your product or service, bearing in mind market conditions, influences the price you set. Typically, a new venture has limited capacity at the start. A valid entry could be to price so high as to just fill your capacity, rather than so low as to swamp you.

Understanding consumer perceptions

A major consideration when setting your prices is the perception of the value of your product or service to the customers. Their opinion of value may have little or no relation to the cost, and they may be ignorant of the price charged by the competition, especially if your product or service is a new one.

Skimming versus Penetrating

The overall image that you want to portray in the marketplace influences the prices you charge. A high-quality image calls for higher pricing, naturally. However, within that pricing policy is the option of either a high price which will just *skim* the market by only being attractive to the small population of wealthier customers; or to go for a low price to *penetrate* the market, appealing to the mass of customers.

Skim pricing is often adopted with new products with little or no competition that are aimed at affluent buyers who are willing to pay more to be the trend-setters for a new product. Once the innovators have been creamed off the market, the price can be dropped to penetrate to lower layers of demand.

The danger with this strategy is that high prices attract the interest of new competitors. If you have a product that's easy to copy and impossible to patent, you may be better off setting the price low to discourage competitors and to spread your product throughout the market quickly.

Avoiding setting prices too low

The most frequent mistake made when setting a selling price for the first time is to pitch it too low. Either through failing to understand all the costs associated with making and marketing your product, or through yielding to the temptation to undercut the competition at the outset, you set your price so low that you risk killing your company.

Pondering Place and Distribution

Place is the fourth 'p' in the marketing mix. Place makes you review exactly how you get your products or service to your customers.

If you are a retailer, restaurateur, or garage proprietor, for example, then your customers come to you. Your physical location probably is the key to success. If your business is in the manufacturing field, you're more likely to go out and find customers. In this case, your channels of distribution are the vital link.

Even if you are already in business and plan to stay in the same location, it would do no harm to take this opportunity to review that decision. If you are looking for additional funds to expand your business, your location will undoubtedly be an area prospective financiers will want to explore.

Book III

Getting Known E-asily

Choosing a location

From your market research data you should be able to come up with a list of criteria that are important to your choice of location. Some of the factors you need to weigh up when deciding where to locate are:

- If you need skilled or specialist labour, is it readily available?
- Are the necessary back-up services, such as computer support, equipment repairs and maintenance, available?
- How readily available are raw materials, components, and other supplies?

✔ How does the cost of premises, rates, and utilities compare with other areas?

✔ How accessible is the site by road, rail, and air?

✔ Are there any changes in the pipeline, which might adversely affect trade? Examples include a new motorway by-passing the town, changes in transport services, and closure of a large factory.

✔ Are there competing businesses in the immediate neighbourhood? Will these have a beneficial or detrimental effect?

✔ Is the location conducive to the creation of a favourable market image? For instance, a high fashion designer may lack credibility trading from an area famous for its heavy industry and infamous for its dirt and pollution.

✔ Is the area generally regarded as low or high growth? Is the area pro-business?

✔ Can you and your key employees get to the area easily and quickly?

You may even have spotted a role model – a successful competitor, perhaps in another town, who appears to have got the location spot on. You can use their location criteria as a guide to developing your own.

Using these criteria you can quickly screen out most unsuitable areas. You may have to visit other locations several times, at different hours of the day and on different days of the week, before screening them out.

Selecting a distribution channel

Selecting a distribution channel involves researching methods and deciding on the best way to get your product to your customers. Distribution methods have their own language and customs. This section familiarises you with them.

Moving a product through a distribution channel calls for two sorts of selling activity. *Push* is the name given to selling your product in, for example, a shop. *Pull* is the effort that you carry out on the shop's behalf to help them sell your product out of that shop. Your advertising strategy or a merchandising activity may cause that pull. You need to know how much push and pull are needed for the channel you are considering. If you are not geared up to help the retailers to sell out your product, and they need that help, then this could be a poor channel.

The way in which you have to move your product to your end customers is an important factor to weigh up when choosing a channel. As well as such factors as the cost of carriage, you also have to decide about packaging materials. As a rough rule, the more stages in the distribution channel the more robust and expensive your packaging has to be.

Not all channels of distribution settle their bills promptly. Mail-order customers, for example, pay in advance, but retailers can take up to 90 days or more. You need to take account of this settlement period in your cash flow forecast.

If your customers don't come to you, then you have the following options in getting your product or service to them. Your business plan should explain which you have chosen and why.

- ✔ **Retail stores:** This general name covers the great range of outlets from the corner shop to Harrods. Some offer speciality goods such as hi-fi equipment, where the customer expects professional help from the staff. Others are mostly self-service, with customers making up their own minds on choice of product.

- ✔ **Wholesalers:** These organisations typically buy in bulk, store in warehouses and sell on in smaller quantities to retailers. The pattern of wholesalers' distribution has changed out of all recognition over the past two decades. It is still an extremely important channel where physical distribution, stock holding, finance, and breaking bulk are still profitable functions.

- ✔ **Cash & carry:** This slightly confusing route has replaced the traditional wholesaler as a source of supply for smaller retailers. In return for paying cash and picking up the goods yourself, the wholesaler shares part of their profit margin with you. The attraction for the wholesaler is improved cash flow and for the retailer a bigger margin and a wide product range. Hypermarkets and discount stores also fit somewhere between the manufacturer and the marketplace.

- ✔ **Internet and mail order:** This specialised technique provides a direct channel to the customer, and is an increasingly popular route for new small businesses.

- ✔ **Door-to-door selling:** Traditionally used by vacuum cleaner distributors and encyclopaedia companies, this is now used by insurance companies, cavity wall insulation firms, double-glazing firms, and others. Many use hard-sell techniques, giving door-to-door selling a bad name. However, Avon Cosmetics have managed to sell successfully door-to-door without attracting the stigma of unethical selling practices.

Book III

**Getting
Known
E-asily**

✔ **Party plan selling:** A variation on door-to-door selling, which is on the increase with new party plan ideas arriving from the USA. Agents enrolled by the company invite their friends to a get-together where the products are demonstrated and orders are invited. The agent gets a commission. Party plan has worked very well for Tupperware and other firms who sell this way.

✔ **Telephone selling:** This too can be a way of moving goods in one single step from maker to consumer. Few products can be sold easily in this way; however, repeat business is often secured via the telephone.

Consider these factors when choosing channels of distribution for your particular business:

✔ *Does it meet your customers' needs?* You have to find out how your customers expect their product or service to be delivered to them and if they need that particular route.

✔ *Will the product itself survive?* Fresh vegetables, for example, need to be moved quickly from where they are grown to where they are consumed.

✔ *Can you sell enough this way?* 'Enough' is how much you want to sell.

✔ *Is it compatible with your image?* If you are selling a luxury product, then door-to-door selling may spoil the impression you are trying to create in the rest of your marketing effort.

✔ *How do your competitors distribute?* If they have been around for a while and are obviously successful it is well worth looking at how your competitors distribute and using that knowledge to your advantage.

✔ *Is the channel cost-effective?* A small manufacturer may not find it cost-effective to supply retailers in Bristol because the direct 'drop' size, that is the load per order, is too small to be worthwhile.

✔ *Is the mark-up enough?* If your product cannot bear at least a 100 per cent mark-up, then it is unlikely that you will be able to sell it through department stores. Your distribution channel has to be able to make a profit from selling your product too.

Working from home

If you plan to work from home, have you checked that you are not prohibited from doing so by the house deeds, or whether your type of activity is likely to irritate the neighbours? This route into business is much in favour with sources of debt finance as it is seen to lower the risks during the vulnerable start-up period. Venture capitalists, on the other hand, would probably see it as a sign of 'thinking too small' and steer clear of the proposition. Nevertheless, working from home can make sound sense.

You will also have to consider if working from home suits you and your partner's domestic arrangements. For instance, if you have young children it may be difficult to explain to them that you are really at work, when everything looks much the same all the time.

If you are the type of person who needs the physical separation of work and home to give a structure to their lives, then working from home may not be right for you.

Looking at Legal Issues in Marketing

Nothing in business escapes the legal eye of the law and marketing is no exception. If anything, marketing is likely to produce more grey areas from a legal point of view than most others. You have patent and copyright issues to consider.

There are a number of vitally important aspects of your business that distinguish it from other similar firms operating in or near to your area of operations. Having invested time, energy, and money in acquiring some distinction you need to take steps to preserve any benefits accruing from those distinctions. Intellectual property, often known as IP, is the generic title that covers the area of law that allows people to own their creativity and innovation in the same way that they can own physical property. The owner of IP can control and be rewarded for its use, and this encourages further innovation and creativity.

The following three organisations can help direct you to most sources of help and advice across the entire intellectual property field. They also have helpful literature and explanatory leaflets and guidance notes on applying for intellectual property protection:

- ✔ UK Patent Office (www.patent.gov.uk)
- ✔ European Patent Office (www.european-patent-office.org)
- ✔ US Patent and Trade Mark Office (www.uspto.gov)

We cover the most common types of intellectual property in the following sections.

Naming your business

You are reasonably free to use your last name for the name of your business. The main consideration in choosing a business name, however, is its commercial usefulness. You will want one that will let people know as much as possible about what you do. It is therefore important to choose a name that will convey the right image and message.

Whichever business name you choose, it will have to be legally acceptable and abide by the rules of the Business Names Act 1985. Detailed information on this subject is available from the Business Names section at the Companies House website. Go to `www.companieshouse.gov.uk` and click on 'Guidance Booklets & FAQ' and then 'Business Names'.

Looking at logos

It is not mandatory to have a logo for your business, but it can build greater customer awareness. A logo could be a word, typeface, colour, or a shape. The McDonald's name is a logo because of its distinct and stylistic writing. Choose your logo carefully. It should be one that is easily recognisable, fairly simple in design and one that can be reproduced on everything associated with your business. As far as the law is concerned a logo is a form of trademark.

Registering a domain name

A domain name is your own web address, which you register so that your business will have the exclusive right to use. It identifies your business or organisation on the Internet, and it enables people to find you by directly entering your name into their browser address box. You can check whether your choice of name is available by using a free domain search service available at Web sites that register domain names such as `www.yourname.com`.

If your company name is registered as a trademark (see below), you may (as current case law develops) be able to prevent another business from using it as a domain name. Once you have decided on a selection of domain names, you can choose several different registration options:

- ✔ Use Nominet UK (`www.nic.uk`), which is the Registry for UK Internet domain names. Just as Companies House holds authoritative records for company names, Nominet maintains the database of UK registered Internet names. They charge £80 plus VAT for two years' registration.

- ✔ Most countries have a central registry to store these unique domain names. Two sites that maintain world directories of Internet domain registries are `www.internic.net` and `www.norid.no/domreg.html`, who between them cover pretty well every registration authority in the world.

In order to be eligible to register direct you must provide the Internet Protocol addresses of two named servers that are permanently connected to the Internet.

- ✔ Use Internet service providers (ISPs), which act as agents for their customers and will submit a domain name application for registration.

- ✔ Register online. Hundreds of websites now offer domain-name registration online; it's a good idea to search the Internet for these sites, as they often sell domain names as loss-leaders. Most of these providers also offer a search facility so you can see if your selected name has already been registered.

- ✔ Obtain free domain names along with free Web space by registering with an Internet community. These organisations offer you Web pages within their community space as well as a free domain name, but most communities only offer free domain names that have their own community domain tagged on the end – this can make your domain name rather long and hard to remember.

Once your domain name has been registered and paid for, you will receive a registration certificate, either directly or through your ISP. This is an important document as it confirms you as the legal registrant of a domain name. If any amendments need to be made at any point during the registration period, the registry and your ISP must be informed.

Protecting patents

The patent system in its current form was introduced over 100 years ago; although some type of protection has been around for about 350 years, as an incentive to get inventors to disclose their ideas to the general public and so promote technical advancement in general.

A patent can be regarded as a contract between an inventor and the state. The state agrees with the inventor that if she or he is prepared to publish details of their invention in a set form and if it appears that they have made a real advance, the state will then grant them a monopoly on their invention for 20 years: 'protection in return for disclosure'. The inventor uses the monopoly period to manufacture and sell the innovation; competitors can read the published specifications and glean ideas for their research, or they can approach the inventor and offer to help to develop the idea under licence.

The granting of a patent doesn't mean the proprietor is automatically free to make, use, or sell the invention themselves since to do so might involve infringing an earlier patent which has not yet expired. A patent really only allows the inventor to stop another person using the particular device which forms the subject of the patent. The state does not guarantee validity of a patent either, so it is not uncommon for patents to be challenged through the courts.

If you want to apply for a patent it is essential not to disclose your idea in non-confidential circumstances. If you do, your invention is already 'published' in the eyes of the law, and this could well invalidate your application. Ideally, the confidentiality of the disclosure you make should be written down in a confidentiality agreement and signed by the person to whom you are making the disclosure. This is particularly important if you are talking to a commercial contact or potential business colleague. The other way is to get your patent application on file before you start talking to anyone about your idea. You can talk to a Chartered Patent Agent in complete confidence as they work under strict rules of confidentiality.

There are two distinct stages in the patenting process:

- ✔ From filing an application up to publication of the patent
- ✔ From publication to grant of the patent

Two fees are payable for the first part of the process and a further fee for the second part. The Patent Office Search and Advisory Service will give some estimate of the costs associated with a specific investigation. They suggest, for example, that subject matter searches will cost upwards of £500, validity searches from £1000, and infringement searches from £1,500. And these are just the costs for the very start of the procedure.

The whole process takes some two and a half years. Relevant forms and details of how to patent are available free of charge from the Patent Office at www.patent.gov.uk. You can also write to them: The Patent Office, Concept House, Cardiff Road, Newport NP10 8QQ.

Registering a trademark

A *trademark* is the symbol by which the goods of a particular manufacturer or trader can be identified. It can be a word, a signature, a monogram, a picture, a logo, or a combination of these.

To qualify for registration the trademark must be distinctive, must not be deceptive and must not be capable of confusion with marks already registered. Excluded are national flags, royal crests, and insignia of the armed forces. A trademark can only apply to tangible goods, not services (although pressure is mounting for this to be changed).

The Trade Mark Act 1994 offers protection of great commercial value since, unlike other forms of protection, your sole rights to use the trademark continue indefinitely.

To register a trademark you or your agent should first conduct preliminary searches at the Trade Marks Branch of the Patent Office to check there are no conflicting marks already in existence. You then apply for registration on the official trademark form and pay a fee (currently £200). Your application is then advertised in the weekly *Trade Marks Journal* to allow any objections to be raised. If there are none, your trademark will be officially registered and you pay a further fee (currently £200).

Registration is initially for ten years. After this, it can be renewed for further periods of ten years at a time, with no upper time limit. It is mandatory to register a trademark.

If an unregistered trademark has been used for some time and could be construed as closely associated with the product by customers, it will have acquired a 'reputation' which will give it some protection legally, but registration makes it much simpler for the owner to have recourse against any person who infringes the mark.

Detailing your design

You can register the shape, design, or decorative features of a commercial product if it is new, original, never published before or – if already known – never before applied to the product you have in mind. Protection is intended to apply to industrial articles to be produced in quantities of more than 50. The Design Registry can be accessed at the Patent Office website www.patent.gov.uk.

Design registration only applies to features that appeal to the eye – not to the way the article functions.

To register a design, you should apply to the Design Registry and send a specimen or photograph of the design plus a registration fee (currently about £100).

There is no such thing as an all-embracing international registration for designs. If you want protection of your design outside the UK, you generally have to make separate applications for registration in each country in which you want protection.

You can handle the design registration yourself but it might be preferable to let a specialist do it for you.

Controlling a copyright

Copyright gives protection against the unlicensed copying of original artistic and creative works – articles, books, paintings, films, plays, songs, music, engineering drawings. To claim copyright the item in question should carry this symbol © with the author's name and date.

No other action is required to take out copyright. The Copyright service is accessed through the Patent Office website (www.patent.gov.uk).

Copyright does not last forever. The duration is dependant on the type of copyright involved and can be anything from 25 to 70 years after the creator's death.

Setting terms of trade

All business is governed by terms of trade, which are in turn affected by *contractual* relationships. Almost everything done in business, whether it is the supply of raw materials, the sale of goods and services, or the hire of a fax machine is executed under contract law. This is true whether the contract is in writing or whether it is verbal – or even merely implied.

Only contracts for the sale of land, hire-purchase, and some insurance contracts have to be in writing to be enforceable.

To make life even more complicated, a contract can be part written and part oral. So statements made at the time of signing a written contract can legally form part of that contract. For a contract to exist three events must take place:

- There must be an offer.
- There must be an acceptance.
- There must be a consideration – some form of payment.

When selling via the Internet or mail order the contract starts when the supplier 'posts' an acceptance letter, a confirmation, or the goods themselves – whichever comes first.

Under the Distance Selling Regulations brought into effect in October 2001, customers have seven working days after they have received the goods to change their minds and return them. They do not need a reason and can get a full refund.

Consumers must also be given:

- ✔ Information about the company they are dealing with, such as the business name, registered and trading addresses and directors
- ✔ Written confirmation of the order – by fax, letter, or e-mail
- ✔ A full refund if their goods do not arrive by the date agreed in the original order; if no date was agreed they must be delivered within 30 days
- ✔ Information about cancellation rights
- ✔ Protection against credit card fraud

Certain standards have to be met by law for the supply of goods and services. Over and above these you need your own terms and conditions if you are not to enter into 'contracts' you did not intend. You will need help to devise these terms. The following four basic propositions will govern your conditions:

- ✔ The conditions must be brought to the other party's attention before he or she makes the contract.
- ✔ The last terms and conditions specified before acceptance of an offer apply.
- ✔ If there is any ambiguity or uncertainty in the contract terms they will be interpreted against the person who inserted them.
- ✔ The terms may be interpreted as unreasonably unenforceable being in breach of various Acts of Parliament.

Book III

Getting Known E-asily

The Office of Fair Trading (www.oft.gov.uk) and the Trading Standards Institute (www.tradingstandards.gov.uk) and Trading Standards Service (www.tradingstandards.gov.uk) can provide useful information on most aspects of trading relationships.

Describing your goods

You can't make any claim you like for the performance of your goods or services. If you state or imply a certain standard of performance for what you are selling, your customers have a legally enforceable right to expect that to happen. So if you state your new slimming method will not only make people lose weight, but make them happier, richer, and more successful, then you had better deliver on all those promises.

The Trades Descriptions Acts and related legislation make it an offence for a trader to describe their goods falsely. The Acts cover everything from the declared mileage of second-hand cars to the country of manufacture of a pair of jeans.

The Trading Standards Service is operated at county level throughout the country to ensure trading laws are met. Contact your council by phone or via their website (www.tradingstandards.gov.uk).

Abiding by fair business rules

The whole way in which businesses and markets operate is the subject of keen government interest. It is not a good idea, for example, to gang up with others in your market to create a *cartel,* in which you all agree not to lower your prices, or to compete with each other too vigorously.

Any such action may be brought to the attention of the Office of Fair Trading (OFT). The OFT's (www.oft.gov.uk) job is to make markets work well for consumers. Markets work well when businesses are in open, fair, and vigorous competition with each other for the consumer's custom. As an independent organisation, the OFT have three main operational areas which make up three divisions – Competition Enforcement, Consumer Regulation Enforcement, Markets and Policies Initiatives.

The OFT's Consumer Regulation Enforcement department

- ✔ ensures that consumer legislation and regulations are properly enforced
- ✔ takes action against unfair traders
- ✔ encourages codes of practice and standards
- ✔ offers a range of information to help consumers understand their rights and make good choices
- ✔ liaises closely with other regulatory bodies that also have enforcement powers

Dealing with payment problems

Getting paid is not always as simple a process as sending out a bill and waiting for the cheque. Customers may dispute the bill, fairly or unfairly.

A businessperson can use the Small Claims Court to collect bills, to obtain a judgement for breach of contract, or to seek money for minor property damage claims – for example, suing someone who broke a fence around your property or parking area. The Small Claims Court offers you an opportunity to collect money that would otherwise be lost as it would be too expensive to sue in regular court. True, for very small cases, it's not always cost-effective, and occasionally you'll have problems collecting your judgement. But the Small Claims Court should still be part of the collection strategies of your business.

The Small Claims Court aims to provide a speedy, inexpensive resolution of disputes that involve relatively small amounts of money. The advantage of the Small Claims Court is that if you cannot afford a solicitor and you are not entitled to Legal Aid you can still bring your case to the court yourself. Even if you can afford a solicitor, their fees may be more than the amount you are claiming. If you do not manage to get your opponent to pay your costs then you will not be any better off.

The *jurisdictional limits* (the amount for which you can sue) in these courts are rising fairly quickly. In the UK if the amount of money claimed is under £5,000, it is likely to come under the jurisdiction of the Small Claims Court. However, if your claim is for personal injury it will only be heard in the Small Claims Court if the claim for the injury itself is not more than £1,000.

Before you start legal proceedings, investigate alternatives. If your case involves a written contract, check to see if the contract requires mediation or arbitration of disputes. If so, this may limit or cut off your right to go to any court, including the Small Claims Court. Second, consider other cost-effective options, such as free or low-cost publicly operated mediation programmes. If you're in a dispute with a customer, or perhaps another business, and you still have hopes of preserving some aspect of the relationship, mediation – even if not provided for in a contract – is often a better alternative than going to court. Any litigation tends to sour people's feelings.

Since January 2002 anyone claiming up to £100,000 can sue through the Internet at any time, day or night. If the claim is undefended, the money can be recovered without anyone having to go to court. The service, called Money Claim Online, can be reached at www.courtservice.gov.uk.

Book III

Getting Known E-asily

Chapter 2

Researching Your Customers, Competitors, and Industry

*W*hat makes your product or service better or worse than that of your competitors? That question, and more like it, can help you tighten up your strategy, make more accurate sales projections, and decide what to emphasise (visually or verbally) in your marketing communications. A little research can go a long way toward improving the effectiveness of your marketing.

One per cent of companies do 90 per cent of all market research. Big businesses hire research firms to do extensive customer surveys and to run discussion groups with customers. The marketers then sit down to 50-page reports filled with tables and charts before making any decisions. We don't recommend this expensive approach, which can lead to analysis paralysis – where those that can afford to spend more time pouring over the mountains of data they have generated than they do on actually acting on it.

Instead, in this chapter, we help you adopt an inquisitive approach by sharing relatively simple and efficient ways of learning about customers, competitors, and the environment. As a marketer, you need to challenge assumptions by asking the questions that lead to useful answers – something you can do on any budget. In the end, not only will you know what you need to know about your customers and competitors, but you'll also better understand your own business.

Why Research Matters – And What to Focus On

Many large companies do so much research, in part, to cover the marketer's you-know-what if the marketing campaign subsequently fails, and more than half of all market research expenditure really just builds the case for pursuing strategies the marketers planned to do anyway. These marketers use research in the same way a drunk uses a lamppost – for support rather than illumination. Other business people refuse to research anything at all because they know the answers already, or think they do. Gut instinct will only get them so far before the ideas, customers, or both run out.

Doing research to cover your derriere or to bolster your already-decided-upon plans is a waste of time and money spent doing endless surveys and focus groups. A *focus group* is a group of potential or actual customers who sit behind a one-way mirror discussing your product while a trained moderator guides their conversation and hidden video cameras immortalise their every gesture and phrase. Of course, you don't have to be so formal with your research techniques. You can always just ask your customers what they think of your product or service – it's not as impartial, but it may tell you everything you need to know without having to pay professional researchers.

So, what are good reasons to do research? Basically, if you can get a better idea or make a better decision after conducting market research, then research is worth your while. You should embrace research because it is the first step to making your company customer-orientated rather than product-orientated. In other words, asking what your customers want from your business is a better starting point than merely trying to sell them what you've already got – and makes for a more profitable business. If you can find out where your customers are, what they want, and how best to reach them, then you are on the right path to doing better business.

Research for better ideas

Information can stimulate the imagination, suggest fresh strategies, or help you recognise great business opportunities. So always keep one ear open for interesting, surprising, or inspiring facts. Don't spend much money on this kind of research. You don't need to buy in an expensive trendwatching service to keep a businesslike eye on new consumer developments that may affect your market. Instead, take subscriptions to a diverse range of publications and make a point of talking to people of all sorts, both in your industry and beyond it, to keep you in the flow of new ideas and facts. Also, ask other people for their ideas and interests.

Every marketer should carry an ideas notebook with them wherever they go and make a point of collecting a few contributions from people every day. This habit gets you asking salespeople, employees, customers, and complete strangers for their ideas and observations. You never know when a suggestion may prove valuable.

Research for better decisions

Do you have any situations that you want more information about before making a decision? Then take a moment to define the situation clearly and list the options you think are feasible. Choosing the most-effective advertising medium, making a more accurate sales projection, or working out what new services your customers want – these situations provide examples of important decisions that research can help you make.

Suppose, for example, that you want to choose between print ads in industry magazines and e-mail advertisements to purchased lists. Figure 2-1 shows what your notes may look like.

Research for your strengths and weaknesses

Perception is everything. What customers think of your product or service is ultimately what determines the success of your business, which is why you should make a habit of asking them, on a regular basis, what they love and what they hate about it.

So how do you find out what customers think? By asking customers to rank you on a list of descriptors for your business/product/service. The scale ranges from 1 to 10 (to get a good spread), with the following labels:

1	*2*	*3*	*4*	*5*	*6*	*7*	*8*	*9*	*10*
Very bad		Bad		Average		Good		Very good	

If you collect a rating of all the descriptive features of your product from customers, many of those ratings will prove quite ordinary. Consider the type of responses you'd get for a bank branch. The list of items to rate in a bank may include current accounts, savings accounts, speed of service, and friendliness of banking staff, along with many other things you'd need to put on the list in order to describe the bank, in detail. You're likely to discover that some items, like current accounts and saving accounts, get average ratings. The reason is that every bank offers those and, in general, handles such accounts in the same way. But a few of the features of a particular bank may be notably exceptional – for better or for worse.

Decision	Information Needs	Possible Sources	Findings
Choose between print ads in industry magazines and e-mail advertisements to purchased lists.	How many actual prospects can print ads reach?	Magazines' ad salespeople can tell us.	Three leading magazines in our industry reach 90 per cent of good customers, but half of these are not in our geographic region. May not be worth it?
	What are the comparable costs per prospect reached through these different methods?	Just need to get the budget numbers and number of people reached and divide available money by number of people.	E-mail is a third of the price in our market.
	Can we find out what the average response rates are for both magazine ads and e-mails?	Nobody is willing to tell us, or they don't know. May try calling a friend in a big ad agency; they may have done a study or something.	Friend says response rates vary wildly, and she thinks the most important thing is how relevant the customer finds the ad, not the medium used.
	Have any of our competitors switched from print to e-mail successfully?	Can probably get distributors to tell us this. Will call several and quiz them.	No, but some companies in similar industries have done this successfully.

Conclusions?

Seems like we'll spend less and be more targeted if we design special e-mails and send them only to prospects in our region. Don't buy magazine ad space for now; we can experiment with e-mail, instead. But we need to make sure the ads we send are relevant and seem important, or people just delete them without reading them.

Figure 2-1:
Analysing the information needs of a decision.

Bright spark

Here's a great example of discovering weaknesses through research and turning them into strengths. Comet, the chain of electrical stores, had been losing sales for several years to supermarkets and general retailers as they entered the market. It decided that some flashy destination stores would fix the problem and set about overhauling the layout, product ranges, and signage to differentiate them from Comet's new competitors.

The size and design of the stores was not the main solution to the problem, though. A simple

and, at £20,000, inexpensive research programme discovered that Comet's customers felt that its greatest weakness was the quality of its staff – a twofold problem as they also felt that the most important aspect of customer satisfaction was, you guessed it, the quality of the staff. Comet accepted the truth and acted on it by changing its criteria for customer satisfaction. Soon after, it achieved a record trading performance.

Notable negatives, such as long queues at lunchtime when people rush out to do their banking, stand out in customers' minds. They remember those lines and tell others about them. Long queues at lunchtime may lead customers to switch banks and drive away other potential customers through bad word of mouth. Similarly, notable customer service sticks in customers' minds, too. If that same branch has very friendly staff and express queues for more simple transactions during busy periods, this notable warmth and efficiency can build loyalty and encourage current customers to recruit new customers through word of mouth.

With this information, you know what things your customers think you do brilliantly and what features you need to do some work on. You can now improve on the worst-on-the-list features to make them average, at least, and emphasise the high-rated items by talking them up in marketing and investing even more in them to maximise their attractiveness.

Here are a few tips to keep in mind as you gather customer ratings:

- ✔ Draw a graph of all the features of your product, rated from negative to neutral to positive. A graph will give you a visual image of how your customers perceive your business's strengths and weaknesses. You'll find that most features cluster in the middle of the resulting bell curve, failing to differentiate you from the competition. A few features stick out on the left as notably negative, other features, hopefully, stand out on the right as notably positive.

- ✔ Offer customers a reward for filling in a survey sheet (that's how important survey sheets are). You can offer a free prize draw from the returned survey sheets, a reduction on current fees, or a discount on future products. Whichever option you choose, let your customers know that their views matter to you – that in itself can improve your customer service scores.

✔ If you want to get fancy, you can also ask some customers to rate the importance of each item on the list to them, personally. If you're lucky, your brilliant areas are important to them and your bad areas aren't.

Planning Your Research

Start research with a careful analysis of the decisions you must make. For example, say you're in charge of a two-year-old software product that small businesses use to manage their invoicing. As the product manager, what key decisions should you be making? The following are the most likely:

✔ Should we launch an upgrade or keep selling the current version?

✔ Is our current marketing plan sufficiently effective, or should we redesign it?

✔ Is the product positioned properly, or do we need to change its image?

So before you do any research, you need to think hard about those decisions. Specifically, you need to

✔ Decide what realistic options you have for each decision.

✔ Assess your level of uncertainty and risk for each decision.

Then, for any uncertain or risky decisions, you need to pose questions whose answers can help you reduce the risk and uncertainty. And now, with these questions in hand, you're ready to begin your research!

When you work through this thinking process, you often find that you don't actually need research. For example, maybe your boss has already decided to invest in an upgrade of the software product you manage, so researching the decision has no point. Right or wrong, you can't realistically change that decision. But some questions make it through the screening process and turn out to be good candidates for research. For these research points, you need to pose a series of questions that have the potential to reduce your decision-making uncertainty or to reveal new and exciting options for you as a decision-maker.

Take the question, 'Is the product positioned properly, or do we need to change its image?' To find out whether repositioning your product makes sense, you may ask how people currently perceive the product's quality and performance, how they view the product compared with the leading competitor's, and what the product's personality is. If you know the answers to all these questions, you're far better able to make a good decision.

You must start by defining your marketing decisions very carefully. Until you know what decisions you must make, market research has little point. See Figure 2-2 for a flowchart of the research process.

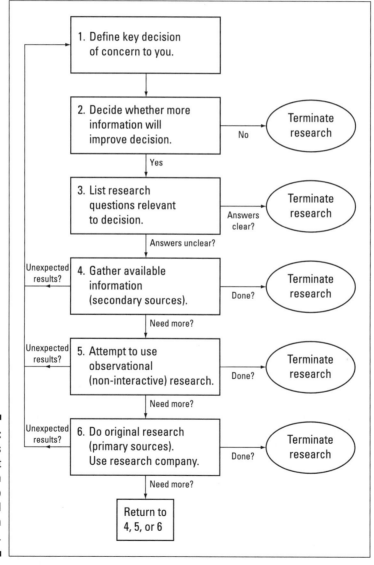

Book III

Getting Known E-asily

Figure 2-2:
Follow this market research process to avoid common errors.

Carrying Out Primary Research

Primary research gathers data from people by observing them to see how they behave or by asking them for verbal or written answers to questions. You can, and should, ask your customers all the time whether they are happy with the service they get from your company, but taking some time out to question your assumptions about how customers view your product or service can yield some of the most valuable insights.

Observing customers

Going 'back to the floor' has become something of a phenomenon of modern business, to the extent that the BBC made a popular TV series of the same name. The experiences of a senior manager who is thrown back into the thick of things can make hilarious viewing – but how and why did they become so disengaged from the basics of their business in the first place? Getting and staying close to your customers, as well as the front-line staff who deal with them every day, is one of the most valuable ways to spend your time.

Consumers are all around you – shopping for, buying, and using products. Observing consumers, and finding something new and of value from doing so, is not hard. And even *business-to-business marketers* (who sell to other businesses instead of end-consumers) can find plenty of evidence about their customers at a glance. The number and direction of a company's lorries on various roads can tell you where their business is heaviest and lightest, for example. Despite all the opportunities to observe, most marketers are guilty of Sherlock Holmes's accusation that 'You have not observed, and yet you have seen.' Observation is the most underrated of all research methods.

Find a way to observe one of your customers as she uses one of your products. Professional research firms can provide a location for customers to come and use your products, or can even put their people into the homes of willing customers. We want you to observe, not just watch. Bring along a pad and pencil, and take care to notice the little things. What does the customer do, in what order, and how long does she spend doing it? What does she say, if anything? Does she look happy? Frustrated? Disinterested? Does anything go wrong? Does anything go right – is she surprised with how well the product performs? Take detailed notes and then think about them. We guarantee that you end up gaining at least one insight into how to improve your product.

Asking questions

Survey research methods are the bread and butter of the market research industry, and for a good reason. You can often gain something of value just by asking people what they think. If your product makes customers happy, those customers come back. If not, adios. And because recruiting new customers costs on average ten times as much as retaining existing ones, you can't afford to lose any. You need to measure and set goals for customer satisfaction.

The survey methods do have their shortcomings. Customers don't always know what they think or how they behave – and even when they do, getting them to tell you can be quite costly. Nonetheless, every marketer finds good uses for survey research on occasion.

Measuring customer satisfaction

Try to design a customer satisfaction measure that portrays your company or product in a realistic light. You can measure customer satisfaction with survey questionnaires or with the rate of customer complaints; the best measures combine multiple sources of data into an overall index.

Your customer satisfaction has to be high, relative to both customer expectations and competitors' ratings, before it has much of an effect on customer retention rates. So make sure that you ask tough questions to find out whether you're below or above customers' current standards. To gauge customer satisfaction, ask your customers revealing questions, similar to the following list:

1. **Which company (or product) is the best at present?**

   (Give a long list with instructions to circle one, and give a final choice, labelled Other, where respondents can write in their own answer.)

2. **Rate [your product] compared with its competitors:**

   Far worse   Same   Far better

   1   2   3   4   5   6   7

3. **Rate [your product] compared with your expectations for it:**

   Far worse   Same   Far better

   1   2   3   4   5   6   7

You can get helpful customer responses by breaking down customer satisfaction into its contributing elements. (Focus groups or informal chats with customers can help you come up with your list of contributing elements.) For example, you can ask the following questions about a courier company:

1. **Rate Flash Deliveries compared with its competitors on speed of delivery:**

   Far worse   Same   Far better

   1   2   3   4   5   6   7

2. Rate Flash Deliveries compared with its competitors on reliability:

Far worse   Same   Far better

1   2   3   4   5   6   7

3. Rate Flash Deliveries compared with its competitors on ease of use:

Far worse   Same   Far better

1   2   3   4   5   6   7

4. Rate Flash Deliveries compared with its competitors on friendliness:

Far worse   Same   Far better

1   2   3   4   5   6   7

You can find useful guidelines on how to design a questionnaire on the Web site of the Market Research Society (`http://www.mrs.org.uk`), under Frequently Asked Questions. The site also includes advice on how to select a research agency and lists sources of free statistical and demographic information.

Customer satisfaction changes with each new interaction between customer and product. Keeping up with customer opinion is a never-ending race, and you must make sure that you're measuring where you stand relative to those shifting customer expectations and competitor performances.

Traps to avoid

As you conduct a customer survey, avoid these all-too-common traps which can render your research practically useless:

- ✔ **Make sure your survey (or surveyor, for that matter) doesn't fluff up customer satisfaction to conceal problems.** In bigger companies, we sometimes see people pressurising customers to give them good ratings because it helps their own prospects. We recently bought car insurance over the phone from an enthusiastic salesperson who unashamedly asked me to give her a high rating on a survey so that she could win the monthly customer service bonus – ten out of ten for effort, but probably not what the company had in mind when it set up the survey. Design your customer service measure to find areas of the business you can improve, which means asking questions that expose any weak spots. The more 'honest' your questions are, the more meaningful the responses will be.

- ✔ **Watch out for over-general questions or ratings.** Any measure based on a survey that asks customers to 'rate your overall satisfaction with our company on a 1-to-10 scale' isn't much use. What does an average score of 8.76 mean? This number seems high, but are customers satisfied? You didn't really ask customers this question – and even worse, you didn't ask them if they're more satisfied with you than they used to be or if they're less satisfied with competitors than with you. Ask a series of more specific questions, such as 'was it convenient and easy to do business with us?'

✔ **Don't lose sight of the end goal – customer satisfaction.** You may need to find out about a lot of other issues in order to design your marketing plan or diagnose a problem. None of what you find out matters, however, unless it boils down to increased customer satisfaction in the long run. Whatever else you decide to research, make sure you keep one eye on customer satisfaction: It's the ultimate test of whether your marketing is working!

Using the answers

When you have gathered the data, make sure that it gets put to good use, rather than becoming a pile of questionnaires gathering dust in the corner. So which parts of the information you have amassed should you include as an action point in your next marketing plan?

Even the most rudimentary piece of research can throw up a range of different, and sometimes contradictory, findings. One customer may think the most important thing is for you to lower your prices, another may be prepared to pay more for greater staff expertise. You probably can't achieve both of these goals at the same time. Here are a couple of strategies that can help you focus your response:

✔ **Your own instinct should allow you to sort the good research results from the bad.** This doesn't mean you should ignore what you don't want to hear, but it does mean you shouldn't unquestioningly react to everything the research tells you. When Sony asked people whether they would like a portable device so they could listen to music on the move, the company found there was no demand. They went ahead and launched the Walkman anyway, because they felt they had a great product innovation. You shouldn't believe the expression 'the customer is always right' but one that you can heed when doing any research is 'they don't know what they don't know'.

✔ **Concentrate on just one of the strengths and one of the weaknesses.** If you have a quality that's unique in your market in a meaningful way, then you need to exploit it to the full. If you have a real problem that may drive valuable customers away, it needs to be put right fast.

Book III

Getting Known E-asily

✔ **Pay attention to your most valuable customers.** You can't please all of the people all of the time, so don't try. One of the hidden benefits of observing and asking questions of customers is that it can help distinguish your most valuable customers from those you would be better off without (yes, they really do exist). By looking at survey responses, you will soon be able to spot ideas and customers that generate additional value, and those that simply want more for less. Surveys help you to establish priorities for your business that will keep profitable customers loyal.

The life cycle of any piece of research should last no longer than your next marketing plan – any longer and the market or competition will have moved anyway.

A Dozen Ideas for Low-Cost Research

You don't have to spend thousands of pounds researching ideas for a new ad campaign (or anything else). Instead, focus on ways of gaining insight or checking your assumptions using free and inexpensive research methods. But how can you do useful research without a lot of time, money, and staff to waste? This section shares a dozen ideas (plus an extra one for free) to get you off on the right foot.

Watching what your competitors do

When you compare your marketing approach to your competitors', you easily find out what customers like best. Make a list of the things that your competitors do differently to you. Does one of them price higher? Does another one give away free samples? Do some of them offer money-back guarantees? How and where do they advertise? Make a list of at least five points of difference. Now ask ten of your best customers to review this list and tell you what they prefer – your way or one of the alternatives. Keep a tally. And ask them why. You may find that all your customers vote in favour of doing something different to the way you do it now.

Creating a customer profile

Take photographs of people you think of as your typical customers. Post these pictures on a bulletin board and add any facts or information you can think of to create profiles of your 'virtual' customers. Whenever you aren't sure what to do about any marketing decision, you can sit down in front of the bulletin board and use it to help you tune into your customers and what they do and don't like. For example, make sure the art and wording you use in a letter or ad is appropriate to the customers on your board. Will these customers like it, or is the style wrong for them?

Entertaining customers to get their input

Invite good customers to a lunch or dinner, or hold a Customer Appreciation event. Entertaining your customers puts you in contact with them in a relaxed setting where they're happy to chat and share their views. Use these occasions to ask them for suggestions and reactions. Bounce a new product idea off of these customers or find out what features they'd most like to see improved. Your customers can provide an expert panel for your informal research, and you just have to provide the food!

Using e-mail for single-question surveys

If you market to businesses, you probably have e-mail addresses for many of your customers. Try e-mailing 20 or more of these customers for a quick opinion on a question. Result? Instant survey! If a clear majority of these customers say they prefer using a corporate credit card to being invoiced because the card is more convenient, well, you've just gained a useful research result that may help you revise your approach.

Watching people use your product

Be nosey. Find ways to observe people as they shop for and consume your product or service. What do they do? What do they like? What, if anything, goes wrong? What do they dislike? You can gain insight into what your consumers care about, how they feel, and what they like by observing them in action. Being a marketing voyeur provides you with a useful and interesting way to do research – at no charge. And if you're in a retail business, be (or ask someone else to be) a *secret shopper* by going in and acting like an ordinary customer to see how you're treated.

Establishing a trend report

E-mail salespeople, distributors, customer service staff, repair staff, or willing customers once a month, asking them for a quick list of any important trends they see in the market. You flatter people by letting them know that you value their opinion, and e-mail makes giving that opinion especially easy for them. A trend report gives you a quick indication of a change in buying patterns, a new competitive move or threat, and any other changes that your marketing may need to respond to. Print out and file these reports from the field and go back over them every now and then for a long-term view of the effectiveness of your marketing strategies, too.

Researching your strengths

Perhaps the most important element of any marketing plan or strategy is clearly recognising what makes you especially good and appealing to customers. To research the strengths that set you apart from the competition, find the simplest way to ask ten good customers this simple but powerful question: 'What is the best thing about our [fill in the name of your product or service], from your perspective?' (Or you can do the more detailed survey we describe in the 'Research for your strengths and weaknesses' section earlier in this chapter.)

The answers to this question usually focus on one or, at most, a few features or aspects of your business. Finding out how your customers identify your strengths proves a great help to your marketing strategy. After you know what you do best, you can focus on telling the story about that best whenever you advertise, do publicity, or communicate with your market in any way. Investing in your strengths (versus your competitors' strengths or your weaknesses) tends to grow your sales and profits most quickly and efficiently.

Analysing customer records

Most marketers fail to mine their own databases for all the useful information those databases may contain. A good way to tap into this free data (because you already own it!) is to study your own customers with the goal of identifying three common traits that make them different or special.

A computer shop Dan's a customer of went through their records and realised that its customers are

- ✔ More likely to be self-employed or entrepreneurs than the average person
- ✔ More sophisticated users of computers than most people
- ✔ Big spenders who care more about quality and service than the absolute cheapest price

This store revised its marketing goal to find more people who share these three qualities. What qualities do your customers have that make them special, and that would make a good profile for you to use in pursuing more customers like them?

Surveying your own customers

You can gather input from your own customers in a variety of easy ways because your customers interact with your employees or firm. You can put a stamped postcard in shipments, statements, product packages, or other communications with your customers. Include three or fewer simple, non-biased survey questions, such as, 'Are you satisfied with this purchase? no = 1 2 3 4 5 = yes.' Also leave a few lines for comments, in case the customers have something they want to tell you. You generally get low response rates with any such effort, but that's okay. If someone has something to tell you, they let you hear about it, particularly when it's negative. And even a 5 per cent response gives you a steady stream of input you wouldn't otherwise have.

Testing your marketing materials

Whether you're looking at a letter, Web page, press release, or ad, you can improve that material's effectiveness by asking for reviews from a few customers, distributors, or others with knowledge of your business. Do they like the material? Do they like it a lot? If the responses are only lukewarm, then you know you need to edit or improve the material before spending the money to publish and distribute it. Customer reviewers can tell you quickly whether you have real attention-getting wow-power in any marketing communication.

Big companies do elaborate, expensive tests of ads' readability and pulling power, but you can get a pretty good idea for much less money. Just ask a handful of people to review a new marketing material while it's still in draft form.

Interviewing defectors

You can find out far more from an angry customer than you can from ten happy ones. If you have a customer on the phone who wants to complain, then look on it as an opportunity, not a call to be avoided. If you can find out what went wrong and fix it, that customer may well become one of your greatest advocates.

You can easily overlook another gold mine – company records of past customers. Work out what types of customer defect, when, and why. If you can't pinpoint why a customer abandoned ship, try to make contact and ask them directly.

Tracking these lost customers down and getting them on the phone or setting up an appointment may prove difficult. Don't give up! Your lost customers hold the key to a valuable piece of information: What you do wrong that can drive customers away. Talk to enough of these lost customers and you may see a pattern emerge. Probably three-quarters of them left you for the same reason (which can be pricing, poor service, inconvenient hours, and so on – that's for you to find out).

Plug that hole and you lose fewer customers down it. And keeping those customers means you don't have to waste valuable marketing resources replacing them. You can keep the old customers and grow every time you add a new one.

Asking your kids

Seriously! Your children, or any kids on hand that you can get to think about your market for a few minutes, probably have a unique and more contemporary view than you. Ask them simple questions like 'What will the next big thing be in [name your product or service here]?' 'What's cool and what's not this year?' Kids know, and you don't. In any consumer marketing, you need to make sure that you're cool and your competitors aren't. Because kids lead the trends in modern society, why not ask them what those trends are? Even in business-to-business and industrial markets, kids and their sense of what's happening in society can be helpful – often giving you early indicators of shifts in demand that may have an impact all the way up the line, from consumers to the businesses that ultimately serve them.

Finding Free Data

Whatever aspect of marketing you are looking at there is further information available to you – and it won't cost you a penny. Some of that data can give you just what you need to get started on your research project. So before you buy a report or hire a research firm, dig around for some free (or at least cheap) stuff.

There is a world of free data out there, if you know where to look. Also keep in mind that free data generally falls into a category known as *secondary data* – meaning already collected or published by someone else – so you get it second hand. This data is not specific to your company and your competitors can easily access it, too.

Getting info off the Web

Throughout this book, we include numerous Web sites, as these are the quickest and easiest places to find free information. For instance, the Interactive Advertising Bureau (IAB) has more data on how many customers are connected to the Internet and who shop online than we can possibly include here. Look out for these Web site references, but more importantly remember that Internet search engines, such as Google!, make finding free data simple – and the more you use them, the easier it is to filter out all the sites you're not interested in.

Say you want to set up a Web site where customers can buy your products directly. You want to know how many people have access to the Internet in the UK and how many are prepared to use their credit card details to buy things. You may also want to find a Web site developer that can create a secure and fully transactional site for you. Already you have three questions that need answers and you haven't even started your search.

Go to the Google search engine (www.google.co.uk), type in the key words 'internet access', and then hit 'Search pages from the UK' – you'll get a list of 17 million sites, most of them trying to sell you something. You can narrow the information down by being more specific. The phrase 'online shoppers' will return 894,000 sites – better, but still too many. Type in 'online shoppers market size', however, and you get just 164,000 suggestions – even better. At the top of the list is that Interactive Advertising Bureau site we just mentioned, which has the answers to all three questions. A bit of practice is all you need to help you find relevant information on the Web quickly and easily.

Hooking up with a librarian

If you don't want to do the search yourself, you can get a professional to search for you, and it will hardly cost you a penny (well, maybe a few pounds). Libraries are an undervalued national treasure, and librarians are trained to archive information as well as know how to access it. Your local library is a good starting place, but you can also get a wealth of market information from university libraries and specialist business libraries.

You can find a lot of what you might need, including industry guides, through the British Library (www.bl.uk/welcome/business.html). You can make enquiries by phone: 020 7412 7454, or by e-mail: business-information@bl.uk.

Tapping into government resources

Often, the best source of free information is national and local government. Many governments collect copious data on economic activity, population size, and trends within their borders. In the UK, the Office of National Statistics (ONS) is the best general source of data on a wide range of demographic and economic topics.

We're always amazed at the sheer range and quantity of information available on the ONS site, and we're sure you will be too. Of course, we don't know whether you need to know the state of North Sea fish stocks, but if you do, then this is the right place! Described as the 'home of official UK statistics', you can access National Statistics Online at www.statistics.gov.uk.

A lot of the data on the UK population is based on the Census. Although the Census only takes place every ten years, you'll find it's very detailed and, usefully, you can break the data down by neighbourhood. The statistics on inflation and prices, consumer spending, business investment – in fact, anything financial – is more up to date, usually to the last full quarter.

Getting media data

If you're doing any advertising, ask the magazine, newspaper, Web site, or radio station you buy advertising from to give you information about their customer base – snippets about the people exposed to your ads. This information can help you make sure you reach an appropriate audience. You can also use the exposure numbers to calculate the effectiveness of your advertising.

If you've yet to decide where to advertise, or even in which media, then there are some useful media sites you can visit that will give you the numbers on how many and what kind of consumers each title or station will deliver. You can trust these sources, because in most cases they were set up and are supported by the media owners operating in that area to provide an independent verification of sales and audience profiles so that advertisers can see what they're getting – and hopefully buy more. That's why most of the data, for occasional users like you, is free.

The Audit Bureau of Circulations, or ABC as it's more commonly known (www.abc.org), has data on magazines, national and local newspapers, exhibition visitors, and Web sites. You can find out how many people are reading the title, where they live, and what type of consumers they are; for business-to-business magazines, you can find out what sector they work in and what their job titles are. Most of the different media have organisations that provide data like this: For TV it's BARB (www.barb.co.uk), for radio it's RAJAR (www.rajar.co.uk), for outdoor media such as posters it's POSTAR (www.postar.co.uk).

Chapter 3

Getting Net-Savvy

· ·

· ·

*T*he Internet is a relatively new phenomenon; only 30 years have elapsed since it was first invented and it was used for business for the first time in the early 1990s. Marketing is old – 'the second-oldest profession', as some of us would have it. Guess which topic is more misunderstood – the Internet or marketing?

The answer to that question is 'marketing'. Marketing can mean anything from pure public relations to all the stuff you do in running a company. We use a broad definition because we think marketing is vitally important.

Marketing, in our definition, is part of just about everything you do in creating a product. Identifying something that people might want to buy is a marketing activity, even if the person coming up with the idea is an engineer, salesperson, executive, or secretary. (A six-word description of how to get rich is: 'Find a need and fill it'. Doing so is the first step in marketing.)

So you've identified a need and want to fill it. Creating a specific definition of your product or service is also a marketing activity. Product development people might then take the ball and run with it for a while, creating a prototype of the product or service. But deciding when the product or service is acceptable and ready to sell is marketing, too.

The marketing department then sets the initial price and hands the whole thing to the sales department. Sales's job is to sell; marketing tracks the progress of sales and tweaks the product and price for maximum profit. Promotions, public relations, and packaging are also part of the marketing effort.

Marketing also influences areas that don't directly involve business. Politics has been revolutionised – for better or worse – by marketing-type practices. Job-hunting is increasingly understood to mean marketing yourself. Even non-profit organisations hire specialists to help them identify and reach target markets of donors and recipients of aid and services.

Companies vary widely in what areas they call 'marketing' and what they call product development, engineering, or something else, and that situation's fine with us. Our point is not to say that marketing should take over everything in a company, but to point out that marketing either determines or affects almost everything a company does. If you care about making something – anything – happen in this big, wide, wonderful world of ours, you care about marketing.

In this chapter, we introduce the Internet and how it fits the needs of marketers (which means just about all businesspeople). **Hint:** You've probably never thought of some aspects of the Internet the way we do, so be ready to discover something. We then justify the need for marketing on the Internet – so you can tell your boss why you're suddenly spending so much time surfing the Web – and show you how to find the market for your products or services online. We finish by telling you how to use digital marketing resources.

Marketing on the Internet

What is the Internet? Well, the Internet's a big mess – a mix of good and bad ideas, shaken, stirred, half-baked, and served buffet-style. More seriously, the Internet means many things to many people, but luckily we can give you a simple answer as to what it really is.

The Internet is simply an *inter-network* (which is where we get the word 'Internet' from); that is, a way to connect many smaller computer networks and computers with one another. The reason people call it *the* Internet, and not just *an* internet, is that the Internet is the one network that connects most of the computers on Earth, so it deserves to be recognised as one specific thing. What makes all this connecting possible is that the Internet has a set of unifying standards. Though doing so is simplistic, you can think of the Internet as just a whole load of wires that carry messages that are compatible with each other.

Each different type of content that goes over the Internet is called an Internet *service*; e-mail is one Internet service, and the Web is another. An Internet service meets agreed-on, public standards so that any computer on the Internet can access the particular service, using any of a variety of available software packages. These standards are based on *protocols*, each of which is like a language that the computers on the Internet speak when they want to transfer a particular kind of data. When people talk about the Internet today, they're not just talking about the underlying wiring; they're talking about the various Internet services and protocols that they use or have heard about.

One such Internet service is used to transfer any kind of file between computers. This service is known commonly as *FTP*, which stands for File Transfer Protocol. You can send text documents, computer programs, graphics, sound files – in fact, just about anything – with FTP. E-mail, which uses its own specific protocols, emerged as an early, text-only Internet service. The Web, another service with, again, its own protocol, became wildly popular by adding graphics to the mix. And Internet usage is growing even faster as people use small, wireless devices such as mobile phones and PDAs (Personal Digital Assistants) to communicate over the Internet. Expect to see more new Internet services, and lots of growth and change in existing ones, as the Web develops still further in the years to come.

Introducing the Web

The World Wide Web (or just *Web* for short) is the most talked-about online invention ever. Hyped beyond belief in the world press, and the force behind rags-to-riches stories like that of eBay, Amazon, and hundreds of other start-ups, the World Wide Web is one of the great business stories of all time.

Luckily, the hype does come with some real justification. As we explain in detail later in this chapter, the Web has billions of real users who collectively spend millions of hours a day surfing the Web around the world.

Using the Web is made possible by software programs called *Web browsers*, the runaway leader being Microsoft Internet Explorer – although others exist including Netscape Navigator, Firefox, and Safari.

From a marketer's point of view, the Web is best understood as a collection of shopping services, news sources, glossy company reports, and advertising collateral that can be accessed by a large and fast-growing group of unusually influential people. But the Web is a wild world. Side-by-side with the company and product information are college course materials, personal home pages known as blogs, that describe hobbies, children, and pets, political advertising, and anything else that you care to name. A glossy corporate home page is shown in Figure 3-1, and a personal home page is shown in Figure 3-2.

Book III

Getting Known E-asily

Figure 3-1:
The
corporate
look of the
Web.

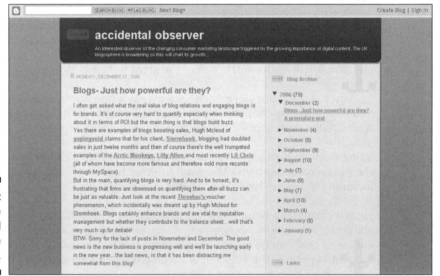

Figure 3-2:
The
personal
look of the
Web.

The Web is one of the best tools ever invented for marketing. Unlike television adverts, which force themselves on the viewer, Web sites are accessed only by users who *want* to see them – your message is reaching people who actually choose tosee it by logging onto your site or clicking on your advert. But to get people to stay with you, you need to make your site sticky – that is, interesting and relevant to the user so they 'stick around'.

Shouting above the noise on the Web is impossible. You can't get in people's faces on the Web the way you can with a television or radio commercial or even a print ad; people can click the Back buttons on their browsers to leave a site even faster than they can turn the page of a magazine or find the TV remote control hidden in the crevices of their sofas. The trick is to put up a competent, easy-to-use Web site and then help the people who want to find you do so.

The Internet has now begun to live up to its hype about being the most important communication tool in the world. Finding Web pages that use either audio or video features to spice up the experience of the user is increasingly common. However, this tactic isn't right for everyone – a rock anthem playing over the home page of your online flower delivery company may not send out the right image.

E-mail and mail lists:
Unsung online heroes

E-mail is one of the biggest reasons the Internet has become the success that it is today. The origins of the Internet are in the communication of information between different computers. A long time ago (during the 1980s), people had e-mail accounts with services, each with their own proprietary network and separate protocols. But people on each online service wanted to be able to send e-mail to friends and colleagues who used other services. To allow this interaction, the proprietary online services had to add *Internet gateways* (connections to the Internet) for e-mail to flow through from one person on one network to another person on another network. Businesses then connected their in-house e-mail systems to the Internet, and the Internet grew rapidly, setting the stage for the Web and other online resources.

Over the last ten years e-mail has evolved from a text-only format to one that is enriched with graphics, audio, and even video. *HTML mail* has now become the norm – although most companies will still offer their subscribers a text-only format. HTML mail is a message resembling a Web page, with graphics and formatted text, that can be viewed by most popular e-mail clients such as Microsoft Outlook, Yahoo! mail, and Hotmail. In both text and HTML forms, e-mail is still an important communications medium and a key part of online marketing.

Like real mail (or *snail mail* – the kind delivered by the Royal Mail), e-mail is a tempting channel for marketing. People have become used to getting advertising offers in their postal mail – though the disparaging terms *junk mail* or *spam* demonstrate what many people think of this kind of mailing. But e-mail, unlike much regular mail, feels very special to people; they seem to take their e-mail Inbox more personally than they do their postal mail. So when you're using e-mail for marketing to lots of people, proceed with caution, as we explain in detail in Chapters 5 and 6.

The most important things to remember when using e-mail for online marketing are two dos and a don't:

- ✔ **Do make sure that you and your company respond to all e-mail you receive.** We know managing your e-mail Inbox can be hard; and if you put an e-mail address on a popular Web site, you can easily get flooded with e-mail. But make sure that you don't ignore any contacts or prospective customers you bring in and that they receive quick and appropriate responses.

- ✔ **Do try to ensure that e-mail sent to people outside your company is positive and informative.** Every e-mail sent by anyone in your company is, at least in part, a marketing message.

- ✔ **Don't send unwanted e-mail, such as the mass e-mail *spam* that some companies send to prospective (that is, soon to be *ex*-prospective) customers.** Most recipients ignore spam e-mail; others respond aggressively, with angry notes or even *mail bombs*, automated mass mailings back to the sender that can choke the sender's mail system.

Most companies now have their own *mailing lists*, a set of e-mail addresses that have been collected or bought from third-party companies and represent people who are interested in receiving more information about specific companies, products, or services.

We describe the effective use of e-mail and creating, maintaining, and influencing a mail list in Chapters 5 and 6.

Online messageboards and forums: The threat and the promise

Thanks to the Internet, information can now be passed around the world at lightning speed. This speed of communication is a great thing for marketers as they can talk to a massive audience from just one PC, but it also comes with some very real dangers.

Traditional marketing in the offline world is usually a pretty safe one-way experience. The company wants to say something, so they tell the consumer about it. Any response from the consumer is usually on a one-to-one level with the company. Any problems or arguments that arise between company and consumer are also on a one-to-one basis – unless the consumer calls the BBC's *Watchdog* TV programme, for example.

Enter the Internet and chatrooms and forums. Chatrooms and forums are online meeting places for people who have similar interests and, as such, they can provide a source of potential customers. Interacting with people in this environment, though, can be very useful but also very dangerous.

Here's an example of how a forum destroyed the reputation of one product. Kryptonite, a US company, produces and markets supposedly super-strong bike locks. In 2004, on a fairly popular bike forum called bikeforums.net, a consumer posted an article saying that he could break into his lock using a cunning device – a biro – and did anyone else know about the flaw?

Within minutes the message thread had been viewed by thousands; in hours hundreds of thousands had seen it; and then videos were posted online showing the locks being picked using a pen.

Kryptonite remained unmoved by the growing furore and did not respond to the forum postings, despite being aware of the problem and being urged by consumers and other forums to post online and reassure people – or to give an explanation. The company took over a week to respond – initiating a product recall – but by this time the damage was done. The story was picked up by CNN and other major news channels and made the pages of newspapers such as the *New York Times*, as well as fuelling a lawsuit brought by aggrieved customers.

The irony behind the whole story is that not only could some of the flak have been deflected if the company had used online forums to address the problems, but also the story itself was old, having been first published in a British bicycle magazine in 1992 and on USENET, a messageboard operating in the 1990s, at the same time.

This story provides a perfect example of how the immediacy of the Internet can destroy a brand as it gives new power to the consumer and new currency to information.

Online advertising

Online advertising is the extreme case of digital marketing, in that online advertising is usually intended to produce an immediate and easily measurable result. In many ways, the Internet is the ideal medium for advertising, and in other ways, this medium's the worst place for ads.

A plethora of different kinds of online advertising exist, ranging from traditional Jpg or Gif banner ads, which are horizontal strips of advertising placed across the top or bottom of a Web page to full 'bells and whistles' all singing and dancing video- and audio-rich media ads that can take over a whole Web page.

Rich media ads have risen in popularity over the past few years as Internet connection speeds have increased and digital marketing has become more sophisticated. These ad formats can vary hugely but all have the same principle in that they are high-impact and attract the eye of the user more readily than standard banner ads. See companies such as Tangozebra (www.tangozebra.com) and Eyeblaster (www.eyeblaster.com) for examples.

Other forms of online advertising include sponsorships, search marketing – which allows companies to bid on keywords in search engines to display their ads above competitors on the results page – affiliate marketing and pretty much anything else you can dream up. Above all, the Internet is a versatile medium.

The good news is that the impact of Internet ads, unlike any other kinds of ads, can be easily measured by how many people click the ad. A typical *click-through rate* on an Internet ad – the percentage of people who click the ad – is less than 1 per cent. You can roughly measure the cost of an Internet ad campaign by taking the total cost of running the ads and dividing by the number of times that users clicked the ad, which yields the *cost per click*. Less than 1 per cent is still more than, say, response rates to direct marketing; proof of how powerful online advertising can be – if done properly.

Cost per click captures only the actions of users who are so highly motivated by the ad that they stop what they're doing and click an ad that will take them somewhere else on the Internet. Harder to measure is the impact on people who don't click, but later take some positive action because they've been influenced by your ad – just like newspaper, magazine, TV, radio, billboard, and just about every other kind of advertising. This additional effect of Internet ads, sometimes referred to as *branding* or *brand awareness*, is much harder to measure (although companies do exist who claim to be able to accurately do so).

As an Internet marketer, you need to decide whether to promote your own ads, called *house ads*, within your own site and whether to allow others' ads on your site. You also have to decide when and how to advertise your products and services on other people's sites – Chapter 5 is all about Internet advertising.

Wireless access

Strictly speaking, wireless access includes portable computers and even desktop computers that connect to the Internet without wires. But in common usage, wireless access refers to small-screen devices that can access the Internet, especially Palm handheld organisers and mobile phones with WAP (Wireless Access Protocol) and 3G capability.

What do these wireless devices have in common? Here's a brief list:

- **Small screens.** A Palm system displays roughly 15 lines of about 40 characters each, less than one-fourth the text of a small laptop screen. A typical WAP phone displays about 4 lines of 12 characters each, far less than a Palm system and a 3G phone, and although able to show video and audio it is also constrained by the size of the screen.

- **Varying connection speeds.** Most wireless devices used to have slow connections, but that isn't the case now. Investment in wireless networks from mobile phone companies and also the development of wireless 'hotspots' have led to ease of access and fast data transfer – although some devices do still experience problems. Even so, most people only want to read an e-mail on the go anyway.

- **High utility.** People tend to find their Palm devices and mobile phones indispensable, taking them everywhere they go and trying to find new uses for them. The excitement level is much like the early days of PCs, with people interrupting meetings to beam new software from one Palm to another or look up a stock quotation on a WAP phone.

- **Widespread use.** Mobile phones are far more common than PCs and spreading fast – the UK holds more mobile phones than people. Handheld devices are also selling quickly and can easily be deployed throughout a company. The huge popularity of the Blackberry e-mail device is just one example of this technology.

Book III

Getting Known E-asily

You may ask, like any good marketer, what can wireless devices do for you? For most marketing purposes, you probably don't need to do anything just yet. You need to consider whether you can usefully and profitably deliver needed information to customers who use wireless access. Being the first on your block to jump into wireless information access may not be cost effective, but not being ready to move when the time is right may be even more of a problem. Get the other elements of your digital marketing strategy in place; then consider extending your domain to the wireless world.

Finding Your Online Market

The online world has changed dramatically. By February 2006, over 10 million UK households were accessing the Internet via broadband, and most professional people in the UK have Internet access at work. (In general, the more purchasing power someone has, the more likely he or she is to be online.)

If you are doing marketing in the UK and you tell people that information they really want or need is available on your Web site, chances are that most of them can get to it if they want to. If you're selling goods and services to businesses, nearly all potential purchasers are likely to be online.

A few great sources for overall Internet data are OfCOM, – the communications regulator in the UK that can tell you the overall size of the market and other basic facts; IMRG, which can give you statistics on the amount of people shopping online and what they're buying; and organisations such as Jupiter Research and Forrester Research, which regularly carry out research into different market sectors. Some information is free, but the more detailed stuff will cost you. A very useful source of information for free is Alexa (www.alexa.com), an online service that gives you specific traffic information about Web sites such as reach, page views, and rank amongst other sites in its sector.

If you do your research properly you'll see that the online world is not the same as the offline world in the UK. In deciding how much time, energy, and money to spend on your digital marketing efforts, you really need to take some time to find out who's online and compare that to who you're trying to reach in your marketing efforts. Then you can size your online efforts to match your expected rewards.

Statistics are an attempt to capture a snapshot of current realities and can be accurate to within a few percentage points – or can be thoroughly biased, misrepresented, and misused. The statistics quoted here are the best freely available ones we could find. Projections are an attempt to *guesstimate* the future, and so are inherently unreliable unless you have Nostradamus on your team, or read tea leaves. We suggest that in your marketing planning for the online world, and indeed for all your marketing planning, you rely heavily on statistics and very lightly on projections.

People like to talk about how fast the online world is changing, but the results from many surveys of the online world are actually becoming increasingly consistent from one survey period to the next. Though the number of Internet users is growing rapidly, the characteristics of the user population – for example, the percentage of males versus females, types of professions represented, and so on – now change little in the six months between surveys. You can make decisions about your Internet presence today with relatively good confidence that the Internet population, though larger, will still look much the same by the time you implement your decisions.

Working in the Online World

You picked up this book to help yourself do effective marketing work online. In this chapter, we provide an overview to help you get a handle on the online world, what the pieces are that make it up, who's in it, and how to start matching your marketing goals to it. Here are some lessons to carry forward as you use the rest of this book:

- ✔ **You have to be online.** No, not everyone is online, but the people who are online are your customers. If you're not reaching them, you can be sure that your competitors are. You don't have to wrench your business up by the roots and replant it on the Internet; but if you ignore the online world, you do so at your peril.

- ✔ **Start with the Web.** The Web is the ruler of the online world. Start your online efforts by planning now to create a Web site if you don't have one or to regularly update your site if you do.

- ✔ **Use the power of the Internet to your advantage.** Search engines and search marketing, online advertising, e-mail advertising, blogs and communities, and many more channels can reach your consumers online. Use the information in this book to consider each route separately and decide how best to use it.

- ✔ **Take a moderate approach.** Online users want easy-to-navigate, fast-loading, up-to-date Web sites that look good on any device. They want product and reference information and don't want to work hard to get it. You don't have to bet your company on a big, fancy online presence; just be competent, accurate, informative, and up-to-date. The other chapters in this book show you how to create an effective digital marketing presence as quickly, easily, and cheaply as possible.

Chapter 4

Search Engines: What You Need to Know

. . . .

In This Chapter

▶ Analysing how search engines find your site

▶ Focusing on ways to improve your coverage on Google

▶ Adding keywords and registering your site with search engines

▶ Tracing referrals and visits to focus on the search services that count

. . . .

*1*f you can get your business mentioned in just the right place, customers will find you more easily. On the Web, search engines are the most important places to get yourself listed. One of the key requirements for any business is the ability to match up your products or services with potential customers and to ensure that your company shows up in lots of search results and that your site is near the top of the first page. You do have a measure of control over the quality of your placement in search results, and this chapter describes strategies for improving it.

Search engines have created a huge industry for themselves and the search engine optimisation businesses that feed off them. People around the world lodge billions of search enquiries every month, which lead to billions of results. You can see why it's easy for your Web site to get lost in the jumble of businesses who are vying for attention.

Understanding How Search Engines Find You

Have you ever wondered why some companies manage to find their way to the top of a page of search engine results – and occasionally pop up several times on the same page – while others get buried deep within pages and pages of Web site listings? In an ideal world, search engines would rank e-commerce sites by their design, functionality, and whether the businesses behind them give the best possible deals. But with so many millions of Web sites crowding the Internet, the job of processing searches and indexing Web site URLs and contents has to be automated. Because it's computerised, you can perform some magic with the way your Web pages are written that can help you improve your placement in a set of search results.

Your site doesn't necessarily need to appear right at the top of the first search results page. The important thing is to ensure that your site appears before that of your competition. You need to think like a searcher, which is probably easy because you probably do plenty of Web-based searches yourself. How do you find the Web sites you want? Two things are of paramount importance: keywords and links.

Keywords are key

A *keyword* is a word describing a subject that you enter in a search box in order to find information on a Web site or on the wider Internet. Suppose that you're trying to find a source for an herbal sleep aid called Nightol. You'd naturally enter the term *Nightol* in the search box on your search service of choice, click a button called Search, Search Now, Go, or something similar, and wait a few seconds for search results to be gathered.

When you send a keyword to a search service, you set a number of possible actions in motion. One thing that happens for sure is that the keyword is processed by a script on a Web server that is operated by the search service. The script makes a request (which is called, in computerspeak, a *query*) to a database file. The database contains contents culled from millions (even billions, depending on the service) of Web pages.

The database contents are gathered from two sources. In some cases, search services employ human editors who record selected contents of Web pages and write descriptions for those pages. But Web pages are so ubiquitous and changeable that most of the work is actually done by computer programs that automatically scour the Web. These programs don't record every word on every Web page. Some take words from the headings; others index the first 50 or 100 words on a Web site. Accordingly, when Dan did a search for Twix on Google.co.uk, the sites that were listed at the top of the first page of search results had two attributes:

- ✔ Some sites had the brand name Twix in the URL, such as `www.twix.com` or `en.wikipedia.org/wiki/Twix`.
- ✔ Other sites had the word Twix mentioned several times at the top of the home page.

A service called Wordtracker (`wordtracker.com`) does daily surveys of the keyword queries made to various search engines. It creates lists of what it finds to be the most popular search terms. It's not likely those terms apply to your own e-commerce Web site, of course. But if you want to maximise the number of visits to your site, or just make your site more prominent in a list of search results, you may do well to know what's trendy and write your text accordingly.

Adding your site's most important keyword to the URL is one solution to better search placement. But you can't always do this. When it comes to keywords, your job is to load your Web site's headings with as many words as you can find that are relevant to what you sell. You can do so by:

- ✔ Registering your site with one or more of the services (see the 'Going Gaga over Google' section, later in this chapter).

- ✔ Burying keywords in the `<META>` tag in the HTML for your home page so that they aren't visible to your visitors but appear to the spider programs that index Web pages (see the 'Adding keywords to your HTML' section, later in this chapter).

- ✔ Adding keywords to the headings and initial body text on your pages, as described in the 'Adding keywords to key pages' section, later in this chapter.

A keyword doesn't have to be a single word. You can also use a phrase containing two or more words. Think beyond single words to consider phrases people may enter when they're trying to find products or services you're offering.

Book III

Getting Known E-asily

Links help searchers connect to you

Keywords aren't the only things that point search services to Web sites. Services like Google keep track of the number of links that point to a site. The greater the number of links, the higher that site's ranking in a set of Google search listings. It's especially good if the URLs that form the links make use of your keywords.

Suppose that your ideal keywords are 'Dan's Shoe Shop'. The ideal URL would be `www.dansshoesshop.co.uk`, `www.dansshoeshop.com`, and so on. You can create the following HTML link to your e-commerce Web site on a personal Web page, or an eBay About Me page:

```
<a href='http://www.dansshoeshop.com'> Visit Dan's Shoe Shop
        </a>
```

Such a link would be doubly useful: A search service such as Google.co.uk would find your desired keywords ('Dan's Shoe Shop') in the visible, clickable link on your Web page, as well as in the HTML for the link.

Don't forget the human touch

We don't want to suggest that search engines work solely by means of computer programs that automatically scour Web pages and by paid advertisements. Computer programs are perceived to be the primary source, but the human factor still plays a role. Yahoo!, one of the oldest search engines around, originally compiled its directory of Web sites by means of real live employees. These days, its Web directory is hard to spot on Yahoo.co.uk. But editors still index sites and assign them to a category called New and Notable Sites, which includes sites that are especially cool in someone's opinion.

There's almost no way to make sure that a human editor indexes your Web site. The only thing you can do is to make your site as unique and content rich as possible, which helps your business not only show up in directories and search results but also drum up more paying customers for you, too.

Taking the initiative: Paying for ads

You can't get much better placement than right at the top of the first page of a set of search results, either at the top of the page or in a column on the right-hand side. It's even better if your site's name and URL are highlighted in a colour.

Unfortunately, the only way to get such preferred treatment is to pay for it. And that's just what a growing number of online businesses are doing – paying search engines to list their sites in a prominent location.

Knowing who supplies the search results

Another important thing to remember about search engines is that they often gather results from *other* search services. You may be surprised to find out that, if you do a search of the Web on AOL, your search results are primarily gathered from Google. That's because AOL has a contract from Google to supply such results. The same applies to thousands of major Web sites that have taken advantage of Google's powerful search capabilities (Myspace.com being another example). Not only that, but many search services are owned by parent search services.

Just what are the most popular search services in the world? A rundown appears in Table 4-1. The services are presented in rank order, beginning in the first row with Google, which is No. 1. Rankings were reported by Nielsen NetRatings in July 2006.

Table 4-1	Internet Search Services	
Search Service	**URL**	**Proportion of Searches**
Google	www.google.com	49.2%
Yahoo!	www.yahoo.com	23.8%
MSN Search	search.msn.com	9.6%
AOL Search	search.aol.com	6.3%
Ask.com	www.ask.com	2.6%
Others	none	8.5%

These search services are by no means the only ones around. Note that the 'other' search engines focus on Web sites and Internet resources in specific countries and account for 8.5 per cent of global searches. You can find more of them at www.searchenginewatch.com/links/article.php/2156121.

Going Gaga over Google

Book III

Getting Known E-asily

When it comes to search engines, Google is at the top of the heap. A few years ago, it was Yahoo! that was setting the pace, but Google's lightening quick searches and its comprehensive documenting of the Web has made it favourite.

Google is a runaway success thanks to its effectiveness. You're simply more likely to find something on Google, more quickly, than you are on its competitors. Any search engine placement strategy has to address Google first and foremost. But that doesn't mean you should ignore Google's competitors, such as Yahoo! and MSN.

Googling yourself

If you want to evaluate the quality of your search results placement on Google, you have to start by taking stock of where you currently stand. That's easily done: Just go to Google's UK home page (www.google.co.uk) and 'Google' yourself. (In other words, do a search for your own name or your business's name – a pastime that has also been called *egosurfing*.) See where your Web site turns up in the results and also make note of which other sites mention yours.

Next, click Advanced Search or go directly to `www.google.co.uk/advanced_search?hl=en`. Under the heading Page-Specific Search, enter the URL for your e-commerce site in the Links text box and then click Search. The results that appear in a few seconds consist of Web sites that link to yours. The list should suggest to you the kinds of sites you should approach to solicit links. It should also suggest the kinds of informational Web sites you may create for the purpose of steering business to your Web site. (See the 'Maximising links' section, later in this chapter, for a specific example.)

Playing Google's game to reach No. 1

Not long ago, some bloggers got together and decided to play a game called *Google bombing.* The game is simple: It consists of making links to a particular Web site in an attempt to get that site listed on Google. The more links the site has pointing to it, the higher that site appears in a set of search results. Of course, the links that are made all have to be connected with a particular keyword or phrase. In the game we're recalling, one phrase used was 'miserable failure'. The words 'miserable failure' were hyperlinks pointing to the Web site of the White House. The story went that if you went to Google, typed the words *miserable failure,* and clicked the I'm Feeling Lucky button, you would be taken to President Bush's biography on the White House Web site – this still worked at time of writing. (Incidentally, if you type those words and click Google Search rather than I'm Feeling Lucky, the No. 2 hit takes you to Jimmy Carter's biography on the White House Web site; and the No. 3 hit takes you to a story about search engine manipulation on the BBC News Web site and the No.4 hit brings up Michael Moore's Web site.) You can find out more about this interesting pastime on a Web site called The Word Spy (`www.wordspy.com/words/Googlebombing.asp`).

The Google game applies to your e-commerce Web site, too. Suppose that you sell yo-yos, and your Web site URL is `www.yoyoplay.com`. The game is to get as many other Web sites as possible to link to this URL. The terms that a visitor clicks to get to this URL can be anything: *Yo-Yos, Play Yo-Yos,* and so on. The more links you can make, the better your search results will be.

Leaving a Trail of Crumbs

In order to improve your site's search placement, you need to make it easy for searchers to find you. You leave a trail of digital crumbs. You add keywords to the HTML for your Web pages, and you make sure that your site is included in the databases of the most popular services.

Keep in mind that most Web surfers don't enter single words in search boxes. They tend to enter phrases. Combinations of keywords are extra effective. If you sell tools, don't just enter *tools* as a keyword. Enter keywords such as *tool box, power tool, tool caddy, pneumatic tool, electric tool,* and so on.

Adding keywords to your HTML

What keywords should you add to your site? Take an old-fashioned pencil and paper and write down all the words you can think of that are related to your site, your products, your services, or you – whatever you want to promote, in other words. You may also enlist the help of a printed thesaurus or the one supplied online at Dictionary.com (`www.dictionary.com`). Look up one term associated with your goods or services, and you're likely to find a number of similar terms.

After you have a set of keywords, you need to add them to the HTML for your Web pages. Keywords and Web site descriptions are contained within HTML commands that begin with <META>. If you type the commands by hand using a text editor, you need to locate the commands in between the <HEAD> and </HEAD> tags at the head of the document. They look like this:

```
<META NAME='description'>
<META NAME='keywords'>
```

Some Web page editors make this user friendly for you: You can type your information in specially designated boxes. Figure 4-1 shows Adobe Dreamweaver's commands, which are accessed by opening the Objects panel, clicking Keywords, and then typing the words in the Keywords dialog box.

You can also spy on your competitors' Web sites to see whether they have added any keywords to their Web pages by following these steps:

1. **Go to your competitor's home page and choose View↔Source if you're using Internet Explorer.**

   A new window opens with the page source supplied.

2. **Scroll through the code, looking for the <META> tags if they're present. (Press Ctrl+F, enter META, and click the Find button if you can't find them on your own.)**

   If the page's author used <META> tags to enter keywords, you'll see them on-screen.

3. **Make a note of the keywords supplied and see whether any may be applied to your own Web site.**

Keywords already present in HTML   Click here to add keywords

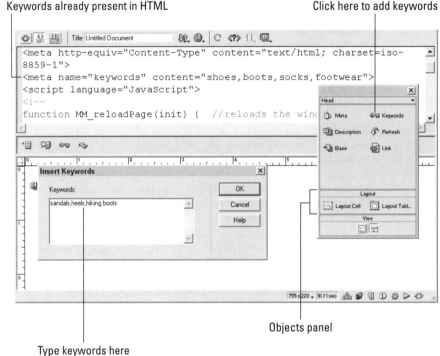

Figure 4-1:
Some Web
page editors
make it easy
to add
keywords
and descrip-
tions for
search
services
to find.

Objects panel

Type keywords here

Keywords, like Web page addresses, are frequently misspelled. Make sure that you type several variations on keywords that may be subject to typos: for example, **Aberdeen, Abberdeen, Aberdeene**, and so on. Don't worry about getting capitalisation just right, however; most searchers simply enter all lowercase characters and don't bother with capital letters at all.

Besides keywords, the <META> tag is also important for the Description command, which enables you to create a description of your Web site or Web page that search engines can index and use in search results. Some search services also scan the description for keywords, too, so make sure that you create a description at the same time you type your keywords in the <META> tags.

Registering your site with Google.co.uk

Google has a program that automatically indexes Web pages all over the Internet. The program actually has a name: Googlebot. However, you don't have to wait for Googlebot to find your site: You can fill out a simple form that adds your URL to the sites that are indexed by this program. Go to www. google.co.uk/addurl.html, enter your URL and a few comments about your site, and click the Add URL button. That's all there is to it. Expect to wait a few weeks for your site to appear among Google's search results if it doesn't appear there already.

Getting listed in the Yahoo! index

Yahoo! won't guarantee to list just any Web site, but don't fret, there are two ways to give yourself a fighting chance. One is building a vibrant and content rich Web site; the other is buying your way into its search pages.

For £60, Yahoo! sets you up with a pay-per-click search package. That means you pay Yahoo a small amount of money every time someone finds your Web pages through its search engine. To start with, this charge comes out of your initial £60 deposit; when that runs out, you can decide to top it up and continue to get your Web site listed prominently, or you can simply stop there. Follow this link for more information: searchmarketing.yahoo.com/en_GB/arp/srch.php?o=GB0176.

Search Engine Watch (searchenginewatch.com) is a great place to go for tips on how search engines and indexes work, and how to get listed on them. The site includes an article about one company's problems getting what it considers to be adequate Yahoo! Coverage.

What else can you do to get listed on Yahoo!? We have a three-step suggestion:

1. **Make your site interesting, quirky, or somehow attention grabbing.**

   You never know; you may just stand out from the sea of new Web sites and gain the attention of Yahoo's indexing software.

2. **Submit your Web site to the search engine.**

   a. **Go to www.yahoo.co.uk, and click the How To Suggest A Site link at the very bottom of the page.**

   The Yahoo! Submit Your Site page appears.

   b. **Click the Submit Your Site For Free button.**

   c. **Input your main domain name and the address of one other page you'd like people to go to.**

   d. **Press the Submit URL button.**

Book III

Getting
Known
E-asily

3. **Try a local Yahoo! index.**

   Yahoo! Local, like Google Local, aims to document all the useful bricks-and-mortar businesses around the UK. If you have a physical shop, you can do worse than getting listed with the search service. Go to `uk.local.yahoo.com` and click the Help link at the top right-hand corner of the page. You're asked to contact Yahoo! with your new business listing. Click the Contact Us link, and you're presented with a form to fill in. When you're finished, submit the form by simply clicking the Send button at the bottom of the page.

Getting listed with other search services

Search services can steer lots of business to a commercial Web site, based on how often the site appears in the list of Web pages that the user sees and how high the site appears in the list. Your goal is to maximise your site's chances of being found by the search service.

Some search services are part of the Overture network, but they still allow individuals to submit their sites for consideration. Here's a quick example that shows how to submit your site (for consideration) to one of the search engines that still gives you the do-it-yourself option:

1. **Connect to the Internet, start your Web browser, and go to AltaVista at** `uk.altavista.com`**.**

   The AltaVista home page appears.

2. **Click the Submit A Site link.**

   The AltaVista Submit A Site page appears.

3. **Click the Click Here link (under the heading Basic Submit).**

   The Yahoo! Search Sign In page appears. Confused? AltaVista gets its search results from Yahoo!. Therefore, you have to register Yahoo! in order to have people find you on AltaVista.

4. **Enter your Yahoo! ID and password. (If you don't have them yet, click the Sign Up Now link on the same page to obtain them.) Then click Sign In.**

   The Yahoo! Submit Your Site page appears.

5. **In the box labelled Enter the URL, type the URL for your site's home page and then click the Submit URL button.**

   Your page is added to the list of pages that Yahoo!'s 'crawler' program indexes. As the note on the Submit Your Site page says, you can expect the process to take several weeks.

Paying for search listings can pay off

Listing with search sites is growing more complex all the time. Many sites are owned by other sites. AltaVista is part of the Yahoo! Search Marketing network. You tell Yahoo! how much you'll pay if someone clicks your listing when it appears in a list of search results. The higher you bid, the better your ranking in the results. In exchange for the fees you pay to Yahoo!, your search listings appear in multiple search sites. The same system applies with Google.

Businesses on the Web can get obsessed with how high their sites appear on the list of search results pages. If a Web surfer enters the exact name of a site in the Excite search text box, for example, some people just can't understand why that site doesn't come back at the top – or even on the first page – of the list of returned sites. Of the millions of sites listed in a search service's database, the chances are good that at least one has the same name as yours (or something close to it) or that a page contains a combination of the same words that make up your organisation's name. Don't be overly concerned with hitting the top of the search-hit charts. Concentrate on creating a top-notch Web site and making sales.

Book III

Getting Known E-asily

Adding keywords to key pages

Earlier in this chapter (see 'Adding keywords to your HTML'), we show you how to add keywords to the HTML for your Web pages. Those keywords aren't ones that visitors normally see, unless they view the source code for your Web page. Other keywords can be added to parts of your Web page that are visible – parts of the page that those programs called *crawlers* or *spiders* scan and index:

- ✔ **The title:** Be sure to create a title for your page. The title appears in the title bar at the very top of the browser window. Many search engines index the contents of the title because it appears not only at the top of the browser window, but at the top of the HTML, too.

- ✔ **Headings:** Your Web page's headings should be specific about what you sell and what you do.

- ✔ **The first line of text:** Sometimes, search services index every word on every page, but others limit the amount of text they index. So the first lines may be indexed, while others are not. Get your message across quickly; pack your first sentences with nouns that list what you have for sale.

The best way to ensure that your site gets indexed is to pack it with useful content. We're talking about textual content: Search programs can't view photos, animations, or sounds. Make sure that your pages contain a significant amount of text as well as these other types of content.

Web sites that specialise in search-engine optimisation talk about something called *keyword density:* the number of keywords on your page, multiplied by the number of times each one is used. Keyword density is seen as a way to gain a good search engine ranking. In other words, if you sell shoes and you use ten different terms once, you won't get as good of a ranking compared to the use of six of seven words that appear twice, or a handful of well-chosen keywords used several times each.

Take the following passage taken from the home page of Startups.co.uk, which Dan used to be the editor of. It serves people who are considering starting a business, or those who have just taken the plunge. Notice how many times *business, start,* and *entrepreneur* are used. (The actual text is a lot longer, and the words are repeated several more times.)

Whether you are a budding entrepreneur ready to start a business for the first time or you are an established entrepreneur looking to do it a second time, we have all the news and information you need to get your business starting on the right foot.

Don't make your pages hard to index

Sometimes, the key to making things work is simply being certain that you aren't putting roadblocks in the way of success. The way you format Web pages can prevent search services from recording your text and the keywords you want your customers to enter. Avoid these obvious hindrances:

- ✔ **Your text begins too far down the page.** If you load the top of your page with images that can't be indexed, your text will be indexed that much slower, and your rankings will suffer.

- ✔ **Your pages are loaded with Java applets, animations, and other objects that can't be indexed.** Content that slows down the automatic indexing programs will reduce your rankings, too.

- ✔ **Your pages don't actually include the ideal keyword phrase you want your searchers to use.** If you have a business converting LP records to CDs, you want the phrase 'LP to CD' or 'convert LPs to CDs' somewhere on your home page and on other pages as well.

Every image on your Web page can potentially be assigned a textual label (also known as *ALT text* because the ALT element in HTML enables it to be used). The immediate purpose of the label is to tell visitors what the image depicts in case it cannot be displayed in the browser window. As a trick to produce more keyword density, you can assign keywords or keyword phrases to these names instead.

Maximising links

Along with keywords, hyperlinks are what search engines use to index a site and include it in a database. By controlling two types of links, you can provide search services with that much more information about the contents of your site:

- ✔ The hyperlinks contained in the bodies of your Web pages
- ✔ The links that point to your site from other locations around the Web

The section 'Links help searchers connect to you', earlier in this chapter, mentions the links in the bodies of your own Web pages. One of the most effective tricks for increasing the number of links that point to your online shop is to create several different Web sites, each of which points to that shop. That's just what Lars Hundley did with his main e-commerce site, Clean Air Gardening (www.cleanairgardening.com).

'Creating my own network of gardening sites that provide quality information helps me rise to the top of the search engines in many categories,' says Lars. 'People find the content sites sometimes and click through to Clean Air Gardening to buy related products.'

It's true: Do an Advanced Search on Google for sites that link to www.cleanairgardening.com, and you'll find links in the following locations. First, the ones that are run by Lars:

- ✔ Organic Pest Control (www.organicgardenpests.com)
- ✔ Guide to Using a Reel Mower (www.reelmowerguide.com)
- ✔ Organic Garden Tips (www.organicgardentips.com)
- ✔ CompostGuide.com (www.compostguide.com)
- ✔ Rain Barrel Guide (www.rainbarrelguide.com)

Book III

Getting Known E-asily

Next, just a sampling of the many sites that link to Clean Air Gardening and that aren't run by Lars:

- National Gardening Association (garden.garden.org)
- GardenToolGuide.com (www.gardentoolguide.com)
- Master Composter (www.mastercomposter.com)
- Organic Gardening (www.organicgardening.com)

For the sites that Lars doesn't run himself, he solicits links. 'I also exchange links with other high-ranking related sites, both in order to improve my rankings, and to provide quality links for my visitors. If you stick with quality links, you can never go wrong.'

Some companies may offer you *SEO in a box* – in other words, search engine optimising software. This software has its benefits but is probably not worth the money. If you're really serious about optimising your online visibility, try a consultancy like Oyster Web (www.oyster-web.co.uk). Either way, always make sure that you've exhausted all the free channels of search optimisation before you shell out any cash. A free online guide like the one at the following address is a good place to start: www.makemetop.co.uk/what_is_seo.

Monitoring Traffic: The Science of Webanalytics

How do you improve the number of times your site is found by search engines? One way is to analyse the traffic that comes to your site, a practice often called *Webanalytics*. When it comes to search engine placement, the type of research you need to perform is called *log file analysis,* which can tell you exactly what keywords already have been used to find your site. You can then combine those words into new keyword phrases, hopefully helping even more people find your site. You can get software that will do the analysis for you, or you can do it yourself:

- **Software options:** Some software options are specifically designed to help improve search engine optimisation. OptiLink (www.optilinksoftware.com/download.html) counts the number of keywords on a Web page. It analyses the links that point at the page and helps you analyse what the best keywords are, where they need to be located, and what specific text will make the links rank higher in Google's search results.

✔ **Do-it-yourself options:** The other, more labour-intensive way to analyse what drives visitors to your Web site is through analysis of log files. A *log file* is an electronic document that a Web server compiles as a record of every visit made to a Web page, image, or other object on a site. Most Web-hosting services let you look at the log file for your Web site. The log file gives you a rough idea of where your visitors are from and which resources on your Web site are the most visited. By focusing on particular types of log file data, you can evaluate how visitors find your site and which search services are doing the best job of directing visitors to you.

If you look at log file information in its raw text form, you're probably mystified by page after page of numbers and techie gibberish. Log files typically record information such as the IP address and the domain name of the computer that accesses a Web page. They don't tell you the name and address of the person using the machine at the time. They give you an idea of where the computer is located geographically, based on the suffix at the end of a domain name (such as .de for Germany or .fr for France). You'll probably need to make use of a log file analyser such as ClickTracks.com (www.clicktracks.com) or WebTrends (www.webtrends.co.uk), which present the data in a format that is easy to interpret.

When you're viewing log files, one important thing to track is *referrer reporting,* which gives you the site the visitor was viewing just before coming to yours. This report tells you what sites are directing visitors to yours. Make note of the search engines that appear most frequently; these are the ones you need to work on when it comes to improving your placement in sets of search results.

Book III

Getting Known E-asily

Chapter 5

Controlling the Message with Online Advertising

*I*f you want to make a die-hard, traditional marketer nervous, then suggest advertising on the Internet. For although print and broadcast advertising are well-developed advertising mediums, online advertising is still viewed as the Wild West. Even getting two online experts to agree on the same terminology can be a challenge.

Online advertising, however, allows you to maintain control of the marketing message, especially as the online advertiser's armoury is much more than just the humble banner ad. So keep these three key questions in mind when planning online advertising: What do you want to accomplish? What ad formats are appropriate? How do you know when the campaign has been a success?

Working Out Your Goals

Every campaign should begin with a clear set of goals. Two typical types of goal for Internet advertising are:

▶ **Building brand awareness:** Raising the visibility of your product or service for brand purposes, introducing a new item, and/or reinforcing your offline advertising efforts. Awareness is crucial in the selling process; many customers won't buy from you until they've heard of you a few times.

- ✔ **Acquisition:** Encouraging user action such as clicking the ad, visiting a Web site, purchasing an item, or filling out a survey. Acquisition is great because it is much easier to measure than awareness. Also, any acquisition-focused efforts will have some impact on brand awareness as well.

Be as detailed as possible when setting the goals for your campaign – but also be realistic. Do you want to increase orders on your Web site by 5 per cent? Boost recall of your company logo amongst your target audience? Increase the average add-on sale to your core product by £10 per order?

By being specific, you make measuring how well your campaign has done easier. By being realistic, you set achievable expectations and can more easily determine the appropriate amount to invest in an advertising campaign.

If you have trouble coming up with clearly defined, measurable goals, beware. You may have fallen into one of the two dangerous Internet advertising traps:

- ✔ **Me-too mentality:** Your competition or colleagues are doing it, so it seems as though you should too. As your (and our) mother said: 'If your friends all jumped off a building, would you too?'

- ✔ **One size does not fit all:** If you try to meet too many goals with one campaign you may end up meeting none of them at all, which is why you need to have your goals clearly defined.

The 'branding is advertising' trap

Advertising agencies will often approach companies and say, 'We can handle all your branding needs.' They can't. Branding isn't advertising alone and increasingly in the digital age, it goes far beyond traditional media and is much more about using the medium to engage the consumer.

Good advertising may be the outward reflection of a well-thought-out brand idea, but building a brand means building a customer's emotional connection to a product, service, or company. *Brand attributes* – what qualities make up a brand – are built by a combination of customer service, public relations, sales process, packaging, pricing, and the product or service itself. Advertising a logo or company name is not, by itself, 'branding', any more than buying a swimming costume is 'swimming'.

Online advertising should play an increasing role in your branding effort, but it shouldn't be the sum total of your branding effort. Online's main strength is to enhance and bolster your brand activity being run across other media.

Finding the Right Format

Now that you've decided what you want to accomplish, what are the most appropriate advertising formats to get you there? The most popular – and established – formats are banner ads, site sponsorship, e-mail newsletter ads, and search engine keywords.

Banner ads

Banner ads are the ubiquitous rectangular advertisements that run across the top or bottom of the most heavily trafficked Web pages. As one of the oldest forms of Internet advertising, banner ads are also one of the few with some standards. The Internet Advertising Bureau (www.iabuk.net) recognises a standard ad banner as 468 pixels wide by 60 pixels high, as shown in Figure 5-1. This space isn't much – filling only about 10 per cent of the screen area on a typical Web page – but provides enough for some text and graphics, often including simple animations. *Rich media* banner ads also exist that include HTML graphics. Generally recognised alternatives to horizontal, 468×60 banners are:

- Taller *vertical banners.*
- Smaller *buttons.*
- *Message plus units* (MPUs), which take the form of square adverts that usually occur in the middle of ordinary page content and involve text and graphics.
- *Overlays,* which are whole page ads, often animated, that take over the screen for a brief time.
- Full-screen *interstitials* – Web pages displayed before an expected content page. The user has to click somewhere on the screen to move on to the content.

Book III

**Getting
Known
E-asily**

Banners have fallen out of favour among some digital marketers because average *click-through rates* (CTR) – the percentage of users who actually click an ad – have dropped from 2 to 3 per cent a few years ago to 0.5 per cent or less now. However, average banner click-through rates aren't as important as several other factors:

- The *conversion rate* (the percentage of people who click through and take an action you're encouraging)
- How well a Web site your ads are on reaches your target audience (a better match usually means a better click-through rate)

✔ The quality of the ad graphics and copy (known as ad *creative*)

✔ The quality of the Web site the ad banner clicks through to (a bad or confusing destination Web site can destroy the conversion rate)

Also, banner ads that aren't clicked on still put your product name in front of a large number of people, much as TV and radio ads do. Debate continues between advertisers and online advertising networks as to how much this effect is worth. You need to work out for yourself whether this 'side effect' of banner advertising has value to you within a specific ad campaign.

Banner space can be purchased either from individual Web sites or more commonly through ad networks such as 24/7 Real Media, AdLINK, and ValueClick, which represent a number of sites.

Site sponsorships

Site sponsorships are a major step up from banner ads, in terms of commitment, and involve a brand sponsoring the content of the site.

Figure 5-1: The standard banner sizes (as prescribed by the IAB).

As sponsorships are not integrated into site editorial content, they're not standardised in terms of duration or level of presence. But expect to commit to a sponsorship from one month to a year at a flat rate and expect to pay a high price. Sponsorships are most effective when the site's editorial content (and/or target audience) and your product or service are closely aligned.

If you're new to online advertising, don't make sponsorship of a site your first foray into online ads. Sponsorship deals, from site to site, can be very different and can be a significant commitment in terms of contract length and budget. Starting with banner advertising is a better idea. Typically, sponsorship packages include a package of banner and other online ads. If you get your feet wet with banner advertising first, you'll see what works before you dive completely into sponsorship of a site.

E-mail lists

E-mail discussion lists and newsletters give you access to some of the most targeted audiences, because – unlike a Web site, which attracts all kinds of people – e-mail list readers identify themselves to the newsletter publisher when they opt in to receive information.

Advertising is either in the form of short text ads of four to eight lines each, or in the format of an HTML newsletter that allows graphic ads much like banners. The key mechanism for delivering customers to you is a link to your Web site in the ad (see Fig 5-2 for a typical HTML newsletter from `www.lastminute.com`).

Book III

Getting Known E-asily

Search engine keywords

Search engines like Google and Yahoo! auction keywords to the highest bidder, allowing you to target specific searches on the service. For example, if you sell football boots, you would want to buy the words 'football' and 'boots' to secure the best ranking. Keyword auctioning is now a multimillion pound industry but it doesn't stop companies from trying to bid for keywords – so being specific is crucial.

Keywords are sold on a click-through basis, but even if your ad is not clicked on, it can still deliver brand awareness.

Clinching the Deal

The three most important words to remember when buying online advertising are *clinching the deal*.

Figure 5-2:
A www.
last
minute.
com
newsletter.

Online inventory, more than in any other media, is elastic. You can only cram so many 30-second spots into an hour of TV, or column inches of advertising into a newspaper. But when owners of a Web site decide that they want more ad inventory, they can just make a Web page longer or add more Web pages – for significantly less cost than a print publication faces when printing and distributing more pages.

No hard and fast statistics exist on the amount of unsold ad inventory in the UK but according to the IAB, around 85–90 per cent of online ad spend goes to the top 20 sites such as Yahoo! and MSN. This situation means that a lot of unsold inventory exists on other sites, so Web site publishers try to maximise the value of this by joining ad networks such as 24/7 Real Media. Advertising on major sites or with niche players who have a very specific audience can be expensive, but ad networks will charge you anything down to about 50p for 1,000 banners on their network of sites. Even so, there will usually have to be a total bottom limit of about £500 for a campaign to make it worth their while.

A few words about words

To appear in the know in online advertising, you've got to speak the lingo (or, at least, realise that a language is being spoken). Some terms you'll come across include:

- ✔ **Cost Per Thousand (CPM):** The amount it costs to buy 1,000 ad impressions. CPMs can range from 50p for non-specialist inventory to upwards of £100 for highly targeted sites and e-mail newsletters, meaning that each respective impression costs 10p. CPM is the most common way to price online advertising. (Why 'M' for 'thousand'? 'M' is the equivalent Roman numeral.)

- ✔ **Cost Per Click (CPC):** What an advertiser pays the site or e-mail newsletter for every individual click on his or her ad. CPC is generally disliked by those selling the ads because they get paid only if the ad performs, and ad sellers (accurately) point out that CPC compensation is dependent on factors out of their control – the quality of the ad creative and of the Web site the ad clicks through to. But CPC is a good deal for you – the advertiser.

- ✔ **Impression:** One of the fuzziest words in the online advertising lexicon. When you're buying CPM, you're buying per 1,000 ad impressions. On the surface, it seems that the definition should be clear: An impression is counted when someone sees the ad, right? But how and when that count is made is the subject of significant advertising industry debate. Is it counted when the ad is requested from the server? Is it counted when the ad's completely delivered to the final pixel? As you may expect, media agencies like to count impressions when they're requested from the ad server (even if the viewer clicks away before the ad loads) and ad buyers like to count them when they're fully delivered. Make sure that you know what you're paying for – the difference between the two counting methods can be 10 to 20 per cent.

Never buy an ad based on *hits*. A hit is simply a request to a Web server for an element on a Web page. That request could be for a graphic, a text block, or a button and is a largely useless measure of the popularity of a Web site. Far better is to buy ads based on *page views* (the number of full pages that are actually served up by the site) or *unique visitors* (the number of individuals who come to a site). The site should be able to provide those statistics; ideally, the source of the numbers should be a neutral, third-party Web site measurement firm.

The purchase process

To prepare to buy an online advertising campaign, start at the Web site on which you're interested in placing ads. For an e-mail list, go to the list's home Web site or send an e-mail to the list moderator asking for advertiser information. Look or ask for a *media kit,* which contains current ad pricing on a *rate card,* with rates usually listed as cost per thousand (CPM) impressions, as shown in Figure 5-3. Then politely ignore it.

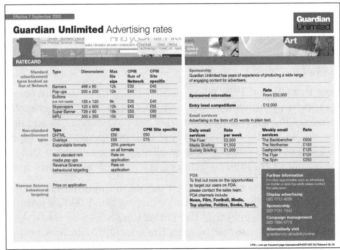

Figure 5-3:
A typical rate card.

Rate cards have become one of the most popular works of fiction published online. Rarely are significant campaigns ever bought based on rate card rates. But the key word is *significant,* as rate cards give you an indication of prices and a good starting point for bargaining.

Structuring an online campaign based on a hybrid payment model is also possible – balancing a lower CPM with a modest CPC of, say, 10p per click-through, for example. This model offers the publisher the carrot of higher revenues if the campaign is a success, but ensures you're not out of pocket if things go wrong. Alternatively, if you have a product, service, or Web site audience of interest to the site or e-mail list with which you want to advertise, you can structure some or all of the transaction as a *barter or contra* deal. But be careful: Generally, bartering occurs at the rate card price, so make sure to adjust the value of what you're bartering with to make sure you get value for money.

Bartering banners on your site

If you're looking to keep costs down, but still get some more exposure and traffic to your site, you can try bartering ad space on your site for advertising on others. Bartering is usually done through link or banner exchanges.

These bartering arrangements are very primitive but can be useful as a first step to online advertising. Beware, however: In return for space on your site you may get to place banners across the network, but the quality of banner that will be shown isn't guaranteed. Poor placement of your ad or a shoddy campaign can sometimes do more harm than good.

When to call in a professional

If you're uncomfortable negotiating media buying, you need advice on setting ad campaign goals, don't know what a realistic budget is, or don't know how to create effective ads, an agency can help. Interactive ad agencies have sprung up everywhere and this area's now big business. Agencies and individual ad consultants excel at:

- ✔ **Cutting the deal:** They've done this before and are likely to be on top of the shifting sands of what's currently 'standard' practice in a still non-standard industry.

- ✔ **Getting the best rates:** Agencies may already have placed ads with the sites you're targeting. Their existing relationship – and knowledge of how far to push – can be an asset.

- ✔ **Creating killer creative:** An ad campaign is no better than its worst creative – that is, graphics and ad copy – either on the ad or on the

Book III

Getting Known E-asily

destination Web page. Agencies either have in-house creative teams or can recommend freelancers.

✔ **Test, test, test:** A good agency knows how to rotate and test which ads get the best response, helping ensure that only ads that pull the best are the ones that are running.

If you're a small or medium-sized company, look for an agency of similar size. Odds are that you'll get more attention from the principals, and the cost structure will come without the large agency overhead. You can find interactive agencies through referrals on discussion groups, advertising e-mail lists, or from colleagues. Or simply find an online ad campaign you like and e-mail the advertiser about the agency it used.

Don't try online ad creative yourself, unless you already have experience doing it. The combination of skills – short, punchy copywriting, tiny yet effective graphic creation, and banner sizing and looping – are best left to people who do it for a living. A creative firm can also handle all the technical details of ads, such as knowing the maximum file size a site will allow, and acceptable colour palettes. Do understand what your goals and your advertising call to action are. But leave implementation to either a freelancer or an agency with experience in creating interactive ads so that your company looks good.

Still tempted to create your online ads yourself? You can find a number of freeware and shareware ad banner creation tools online. But remember that just as desktop publishing software was once credited with giving anyone the power to create incredibly ugly newsletters, many of the banner creation tools have done the same for interactive ads. So your ads will look basic and you will fail to stand out against your competition.

Measure by Measure

Ultimately, you'll want to know whether your ad campaign was a success. One simple and effective way to determine your success is to calculate the *Cost Per Action (CPA)*.

Say you buy 1 million ad impressions at £10 CPM. The ads had a click-through rate of 2 per cent and a subsequent conversion rate of, say, people filling out a form for more info, of 10 per cent. (You should have been tracking all these stats, or had your agency track them, throughout the campaign.)

1. **Calculate your CPA by taking the total cost of the ad campaign and dividing it by the number of customers who took the desired action.**

2. **Calculate the total cost of the campaign, by multiplying (1,000,000 impressions/1,000) by (£10 cost per thousand) for a total cost of £10,000.**

3. **Calculate how many people took direct action, by multiplying (1,000,000 impressions) by (0.02 click-through rate) by (0.10 conversion rate) to make a total of 2,000 total actions.** (Alternatively, you can track total actions directly on your Web site, if you feel that you can identify their source.)

4. **Calculate the final CPA.** Five pounds each in this example: £10,000 total cost divided by 2,000 desired actions.

With any luck, the value of each desired action was £5 or more. (If the desired action was to buy a £99 magazine subscription, you've done well; if it was to fill out a form for more information leading to a £4.50 purchase, you've overspent.)

CPA is most useful in determining the effectiveness of ad campaigns focused on generating a clear-cut action, such as completing a sale, filling out an online registration form, or attracting visitors to a Web page. However, measuring CPA to determine the effectiveness of your campaign does have flaws. Customers can easily see your ad, not click through, but return to your site later and complete the action – so remember to look at the total number of actions, as well as those that have come direct from your advertising, before deciding whether your campaign has been a success or not.

Using CPA to determine the effectiveness of an awareness-focused campaign isn't possible. These campaigns are much harder to measure, as TV adverts have been proving for years. For these campaigns, surveys on your Web site or pop-up window surveys on Web sites where you placed your ads may be more useful. An interactive agency may be able to help you with measuring the success of an awareness-orientated campaign using specifically designed tools.

No online ad campaign should be considered complete until you close the loop that begins with goals and ends with measurement.

Book III

Getting Known E-asily

Chapter 6

Spreading the Word with Internet PR

Despite the high-tech communications made possible by the Internet, one of the best ways to market a product online is through word of mouth and buzz marketing.

The primary marketing tactic for generating word-of-mouth buzz is *public relations* (PR), which is the ongoing management of a company's public image and how it's perceived by the wider public.

Whereas advertising gives you control over the message you want to convey, public relations gives you the unique power to influence. But unlike traditional PR, online PR provides a direct channel to your target audiences without always having to use the filter of the media.

In this chapter, we focus on how to understand and take advantage of the differences between Internet public relations and traditional PR. For a basic understanding of public relations in general, see *Marketing For Dummies,* by Craig Smith and Alexander Hiam (Wiley).

Whom Do You Want to Influence?

Public relations is primarily about relationships: Between your company and reporters and between the reporters and their audiences. And the first step in successful Internet PR is knowing which relationships you want to cultivate and which channels you're going to use to do that.

Targeting the right contacts

When you've targeted an audience for your product or service, you next need to determine the digital media these customers rely on for their information. Are they trade industry sites? Internet-only publications and trade magazine Web sites? Specific discussion groups or random blogs?

Next, work out who decides what editorial content goes into each of these media vehicles. Check publication Web site 'Contact Us' pages, and get the names of message board moderators and bloggers. Build a list of the key contacts you develop, or several lists if your products or services have multiple distinct audiences, particularly if they're niche products.

Finding the right Internet media contacts can require a fair amount of research. For Internet-only publications, check directories like those in the News & Media category of Yahoo!; for blogs search Technorati (www. technorati.com) or BritBlog (www.britblog.com); and for trade magazines, check out a directory like the bradgroup (www.intellagencia. com) or speak to contacts within your industry.

Make sure you set your sights on realistic coverage goals. If you're the manufacturer of hiking boots, odds are you won't be profiled in *Management Today* – unless your CEO is a celebrity. But you may be profiled in outdoor and adventure specialist publications and on their Web sites.

Keep in mind that print publications that cover your industry or appeal to your customers are more than likely to have Internet editions – and in many cases, those Internet versions have additional content not found in the offline version. For example, both FT.com (www.ft.com), the online version of the *Financial Times,* and media industry trade site MediaGuardian (www.media guardian.co.uk) feature significant amounts of content that you can't find in their print editions. These Web versions may have news desks that are separate from their print or broadcast counterparts, with a separate list of contacts.

Conversely, realise that some Web publications can't be influenced directly. Sites that rely on getting all their editorial content from sources outside the site itself have no editorial departments of their own to influence. In order to reach them, you have to know what their sources of editorial content are. These sources may be:

> ✔ **PR wire services:** For example, PR Newswire or BusinessWire
>
> ✔ **News wire services:** Such as Press Association or Reuters
>
> ✔ **Specialised content sites:** Including, say, ZDNet for tech news

Don't forget that your company's PR efforts may have more target audiences than the general marketing audiences for your products or services. Two common additional targets are analysts who follow your industry and the financial and investment press. Make a list for the online constituencies of each of these as well.

Using the right touch

After you develop a list of contacts, start your approach slowly. Indiscriminately blasting out a press release via e-mail to your new contact lists is probably the best way of alienating reporters and analysts – because you're creating spam! When researching editorial contacts, pay attention to how the contacts like to be approached – e-mail, telephone, fax, or not at all. Respect these wishes. Check if these contacts are happy to receive attachments; lots of journalists aren't and will just delete all e-mails with attachments. Having your well-crafted release deleted the minute it enters an inbox is the last thing you want to happen.

If you're not sure of the best approach, ask. Most reporters don't mind a very brief (one- or two-sentence) e-mail in which you introduce yourself, confirm that they cover what you think they do, and enquire as to how they would prefer to be contacted in future.

Fee-based Internet resources exist for finding editorial contacts and their preferences. Two of the best known are Gorkana (`www.gorkana.com`), shown in Figure 6-1, and MediaDisk (`www.romeike.com/mediadisk`).

The best place to start, though, is on the Web sites of publications that you already know reach your target audiences. No substitute exists for first-hand research and relationship building.

Make sure you're aware of the media outlet's news cycle. Sites with print monthly, weekly, and daily counterparts have different deadline structures, as do broadcast media and Web-only news sites. Not every Web site is updated daily; the ones that are can be pretty hungry for new comments and breaking news, so plan accordingly.

Book III

Getting Known E-asily

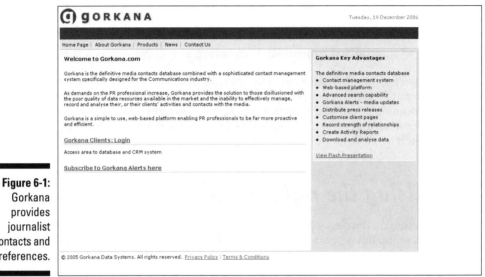

Figure 6-1:
Gorkana
provides
journalist
contacts and
preferences.

Planning an Internet PR Campaign

When you know whom you want to influence, you're ready to determine what you want to tell them.

As with any marketing tactic, your Internet public relations effort has to start with a plan. Effective public relations is not just about grinding out reams of press releases. Good public relations is about getting the right messages to the right audiences – which may be conveyed by press releases or by other means.

This PR rule is even more true of Internet PR because of the speed at which a message can travel and be posted on news Web sites, public relations Web sites, in blogs, and in discussion groups, sometimes with biting commentary.

In creating your Internet PR plan, determine what messages are important to your company and interesting to the press, how often you want to convey those messages, and whether you have the time and expertise to do it all yourself.

Messages are key

Before communicating with the press, ask yourself: What are your three key messages? In press communications you may be tempted to spew every tiny detail about your company. But face facts: Reporters, like anyone else, are busy people. Think about a unique aspect of your product or service that makes a difference to your target audience. Are you the fastest, the cheapest, the first? And why should anyone care? Consider the classic feature/benefit split.

Then take those messages and simplify, simplify, simplify. Unlike in advertising, in PR you can't influence how the message will be interpreted and filtered. The simpler and cleaner the messages, the more likely they'll be to survive the media grinder. Realise that your message, no matter how pretty, will be reworded and possibly re-interpreted. So, the message should be 'the first widget that gets computer screens squeaky clean', and not 'the first robust, scalable technology platform that utilises industry standard architecture to polish monitor surfaces to 98.6 per cent of their factory-manufactured tolerance'.

After you identify your key messages, repeat them in all your communications. And communicate only three messages, maximum. Anything else will get lost in translation because reporters have only so much space and time.

Excuse me, did you say something?

Your key messages are constants that permeate your news communications. But in order to make news, you can't just repeat your messages; you have to have a *news hook* – information that is likely to arouse a journalist's interest. And nowhere is that more important than on the Internet, where timeliness is crucial.

Typical times to contact the press – online or off – are when significant company news exists in the eyes of your target audiences. Such news includes new strategic relationships, new products, executive-level personnel changes, and so on.

But you can't leave news to chance, because you want your company and products to appear in the news regularly. Your PR plan should indicate how often, on average, you want to contact each news media target audience (see the 'Whom Do You Want to Influence?' section, earlier in this chapter) with company news.

Book III

**Getting
Known
E-asily**

Having a plan doesn't mean that you must slavishly stick to this schedule, but it gives you something to shoot for in terms of resources and budgeting: 'Contact industry analysts each quarter by e-mail', or 'Pitch key editors on a feature story every six months', or 'Distribute company press release every three weeks' may be targets.

Using Internet marketing means that you can have many more meaningful, casual contacts with members of the news media by using e-mail. You can politely e-mail a reporter who does an industry round-up (and didn't include your company) with a brief introduction, for example. The key to any of these casual contacts is to keep them brief.

PR agency or not?

You can do an awful lot of PR work yourself. But in some instances, hiring an outside public relations agency, PR freelancer, or marketing consultant to handle your PR makes sense. You can use outside help:

- ✔ To assist with messaging and planning when you can't get enough objective distance from your own products and services
- ✔ To ensure rapid turnaround of incoming press enquiries by e-mail or telephone; same day is a must, with a one-hour response the ideal
- ✔ To develop press lists from databases of contacts they have built from previous work or from specialised databases to which they have access
- ✔ To leverage their existing relationships with members of the press and knowledge of how media outlets like to be approached
- ✔ To write releases and other press materials, both online and offline, if you don't have the ability or time to do it well yourself

Do you need one of the many new agencies that 'specialise' in Internet PR? Probably not. As with everything from books to news, the Internet has rapidly become just another distribution channel and medium for press information. As more reporters have gone online, the PR professionals have followed.

But if all you get when you mention blogs, e-mail newsletters, communities, and forums are blank looks, go elsewhere.

Getting Your Release Distributed

Although PR is much more than just distributing press releases, the press release is still the primary communications medium. And putting it on paper has rapidly diminished in impact and importance as reporters have turned to the Internet for research.

Ready for release

When writing your press release, keep the following Internet-inspired changes in mind:

- ✔ **Keep it short.** The equivalent of a page to page-and-a-half of printed text is more than enough. Take into account that your release may be posted, verbatim, on blogs and message boards. Brevity is the basis of good online communication.

- ✔ **Provide links to more information.** These can be links to a news area on your Web site for background too detailed for a press release or for downloading high-resolution product photographs and company logos.

- ✔ **Include URLs and e-mail addresses for your company.** The *boilerplate* at the end of the release should include where you're located, your URL, and a brief description of the firm. Don't forget press contact info – telephone numbers, e-mail addresses, and a physical address. If you expect the release to be controversial or of wide interest, include the mobile number or even home phone number of the primary PR contact for your company.

Don't include anything in your press release that can't be reproduced as plain text – no special characters such as the trademark symbol (use '(TM)' in plain text instead), and no embedded graphics or HTML tags. Any non-text elements can get garbled in transmission and mess up your whole message. If something doesn't work in plain text e-mail, it shouldn't be in your press release.

Putting it on the wire

To get the release to reporters, you can (and should) maintain an in-house press e-mail distribution list. But press-release distribution services, or PR wire services, will broadly circulate your release to reporters and editors. Most such services charge a fee, which can range from fifty to several hundred pounds, depending on factors such as the PR wire service you've chosen, desired geographic reach, and press-release length. Following are examples of the different types of PR wire services:

- ✔ **BusinessWire** (www.businesswire.com) and **PR Newswire** (www.prnewswire.com), as shown in Figure 6-2, are the two mainstays of traditional PR wire services. They are routinely scanned by major on- and offline news organisations as well as industry analysts for story leads, and they charge based on which of their targeted topic and geographic media lists you select.

- ✔ **Sourcewire** (www.sourcewire.com) is a technology newswire, which is used by some of the UK's biggest tech companies and is also accessed by staff and freelance journalists.

Figure 6-2:
PR
Newswire
both
distributes
and displays
press
releases.

BusinessWire, PR Newswire, and other major PR wire services feed their press releases raw to hundreds of other Web sites that then reproduce them verbatim – and these releases are also available for viewing on the originating PR wire service site. Distribution points include such large sites as Yahoo! and MSN, and online syndicators like `newsnow.co.uk`. When you write your press release, keep this direct audience in mind: They could be customers reading about you in your own words. But the primary audience is still the analysts, reporters, and editors you hope to influence.

Tracking Your Release

Measuring public relations impact is hard enough in the offline world; on the Internet, the task is reminiscent of the phrase, 'Things are never so bad that they can't get worse'. Whereas print and broadcast made it at least possible to count column inches and placement (where in a newscast or magazine a story was slotted), few accepted parallels exist online.

However, if you can't easily measure your PR impact, you can at least monitor it. As in most things marketing, two methods are available: Do it yourself or pay someone else.

Stupid PR tricks

Do you want to know how to make a journalist into an enemy without any thought or effort? Don't put any thought or effort into your PR. You can irritate journalists in several ways with lazy PR moves unique to the Internet:

✔ **Blindly add journalists to e-mail press release distribution lists without asking.** This tactic is especially annoying if a journalist makes a one-time request or asks to receive limited information – for example, about a trade show in which your company is exhibiting – and you add him or her to your permanent PR distribution.

✔ **Include a press release as an attachment to an e-mail message.** Not only may you wrongly be assuming that the journalist has the right software handy to read the attachment (questionable if he or she is on the road and reading e-mail from a Web interface) but also quite a few journalists simply bin any attachments because they can harbour viruses – yes, even innocent-seeming Microsoft Word documents can contain them.

✔ **Attach graphics or full press kits to an e-mail message.** You may have a high-speed connection and not notice the transmission time, but not everyone does; journalists can be working from home with a narrowband connection. Plus, any attachment carries the threat of a virus.

✔ **Go on and on.** If you can't catch a journalist's attention in the first paragraph, you've lost him or her. No one likes to wade through paragraph after paragraph of self-congratulatory prose to see whether you'll ever make your point.

Many more 'don'ts' exist, but these are among the most universally despised.

Book III

Getting Known E-asily

Monitoring PR on your own is as simple as visiting specialised search engines that track news sources, using a content aggregator service such as www.bloglines.com or www.newsgator.com and/or setting up *clipping services* on a variety of sites.

Using these methods, you can track not only your own news coverage but also that of your competitors – providing a nice, fast tool for gauging comparative coverage and analysing your competition. Here is a list of services you should consider trying out:

✔ **Content aggregators:** A buzzword of the new Web movement, Web 2.0, content aggregators constantly check your favourite sites for updates and then feed you those updates through your browser. The best known are probably Bloglines (www.bloglines.com) and Newsgator (www.newsgator.com).

✔ **Clipping services:** These are available on a number of sites, including Google Alert, which can be customised based on your subject or companies of interest, and is available either free or by subscription, with farther options or enhancements. Other subscription alert services are available from the financial press, including the *Financial Times,* which offers an alert service through www.ft.com.

These services clip incoming news items and press releases for phrases, keywords, or categories of interest, and many alert you of a successful result by e-mail – although these are becoming less useful online with the advent of content aggregators.

✔ **PR wire services:** BusinessWire and PR Newswire both sell customised electronic feeds of their press releases, sliced by industry category or keyword, to non-journalists.

A press release of yours posted by others on a blog or message board gives you a great opportunity to see how that online community reacts to the news.

If you can afford it, you can use even more powerful publication search engines such as Dow Jones and Reuters' Factiva (www.factiva.com) and Lexis-Nexis (www.lexis-nexis.com). But you'll pay for the privilege – on some databases, for both the news story you retrieve and the initial search to find it.

Book IV
Keeping Business Ticking Over

'There's been a mistake here — we ordered
12 <u>tins</u> not 12 tons of salmon from
fishathome.co.uk.'

In this book . . .

Staying in business is the name of the game in this book. Here we give you the tools to keep on top of your finances, stay on the right side of the legal line, and make the most of the available accounting tools. What's more, we offer advice on running your business effectively, and look at ways of assessing and improving it.

Here are the contents of Book IV at a glance:

Chapter 1: Operating Effectively

Chapter 2: Controlling Your Books, Your Records, and Your Money

Chapter 3: Counting Your Sales

Chapter 4: Monitoring and Improving Your Business

Chapter 5: Making It All Legal

Chapter 6: Online Business Accounting Tools

Chapter 1

Operating Effectively

*A*lthough you have decided to go into business, it doesn't necessarily mean that you have to make your own product, or carry out every aspect of a business yourself. It might be the best use of your time to outsource the most time-consuming and least valuable aspect of your business. For example, we bet you can't get a package from Milton Keynes to Penzance in under 24 hours and see change of a twenty pound note! But a delivery service could.

Whether you buy in most of what you sell, or just some components and assemble them yourself, you will have to choose between the dozens if not hundreds of suppliers in the market. Price alone is rarely a good enough guide to which supplier to choose. If they can't deliver on time, price is irrelevant.

You will have to face risks in your business, not all of which you will either want to or be able to shoulder yourself. For these you will have to make choices about insurance types and levels. Even as a director some of those company risks will fall on you and the consequences of getting it wrong can be serious, even catastrophic.

Fortunately you don't have to face all these decisions alone. There are plenty of advisers out there to help. This chapter looks at these risks and decisions and helps you to choose someone to help you through the minefield.

Taking the Make-or-Buy Decision

If your business involves making or constructing products then you should address the issue of whether to make the product yourself, or buy it either ready to sell, or as components for assembly.

Making it yourself, pros and cons

If you decide to make the whole of your product, or at least a major part of it, yourself, you will need to decide exactly what plant and equipment you need and how many pieces you can produce at what rate. Then you need to consider such factors as: what engineering support, if any, will you need? How will you monitor and control quality?

Put down a rough sketch of the layout of your manufacturing unit, showing the overall size of facility needed, the positioning of equipment, and the path of materials and finished goods.

The great advantage of manufacturing your product yourself is that you have control over every aspect of the business and its products. You can, in theory at least, step up production to meet extra demand, make minor modifications to a product to meet a customer's particular needs and have the resources in-house to develop prototypes of new products to respond to changing market conditions.

However, some possible disadvantages of making products yourself in a start-up business are:

- ✔ The large outlay of money needed from day one
- ✔ The deflection of management time, mostly your own, to looking inwards at processes rather than outwards at the marketplace
- ✔ Established manufacturers may be better and cheaper than you are at various elements of the production process – after all they've been at it longer than you and have the benefit of being further up the learning curve and further down the cost curve than any start-up could realistically expect to be

Outsourcing, the pros and cons

Outsourcing, contracting out the production of your product, has become a buzz-word in our economy. There are thousand s of articles and hundreds of books written on it and you can attend countless seminars on the subject. An Internet search on 'outsourcing' will bring up more links that you could ever hope to handle.

One way to set the boundaries for outsourcing is to decide what you are good at then outsource everything else. In other words focus your company on your core competency, and stick to the knitting. That logic is sound in theory, and to a certain degree in practice, but like everything else you can take it too far. The key is to understand your business and its goals and decide how outsourcing can help you attain them.

There are some things that are central to your business that you should probably not outsource at the outset. You need to keep an eye (your eye!) on them until you have them fully under control. These include cash flow management and most aspects of customer relations. Later on you may consider, for example, outsourcing collecting cash from customers to an invoice discounter or factoring service (which we talk about in Book II), who may have better processes in place to handle larger volumes of invoices than you could afford.

Some tasks make sense to outsource initially and bring in-house later. If you plan to offer a product service that you're not expert at, it makes sense to contract out the core function, at least until you gain confidence and expertise. For example, if you plan to start an upmarket soup kitchen but aren't very experienced at making soup, you could turn to an established soup chef to cook for you. The outside expert will charge you a premium, but for that you get significant value: the contractor understands your requirements, produces the product and delivers to your site with little risk to you. If the quality is wrong, send it back. If you need more product, order it. You don't have to wait for your new equipment to arrive before you can step up production. You may find hidden benefits.

Reasons to outsource

Whether you want access to world-class expertise, increased staffing flexibility, a more predictable cost structure, or the ability to focus on your core business, *outsourcing* offers many strategic advantages.

- ✔ **Meeting unexpected deadlines:** It is often difficult and costly to ramp up your staffing to respond quickly to new technologies, or business needs. Sometimes, it's simply impossible – especially when you're trying to balance your resources to cover numerous other conflicting priorities at the same time. Buying in resources allows you to meet deadlines.

- ✔ **Access to expertise:** The rapid obsolescence of technology and skills is an accepted fact of life, in almost every sphere of business. It can be almost impossible for a small firm, especially in the start-up phase, to attract and retain a team with the latest expertise. It is easier for larger established firms to attract and retain a team with the latest expertise and for you to hire that expertise as needed.

- ✔ **Greater scalability:** It just isn't cost-effective to have production resources on hand from the outset to meet possible future demand. By outsourcing to one or more suppliers you can have, in effect, any level of output you want, all at a variable cost, rather than a fixed cost.

- ✔ **More predictable costs:** While outside suppliers and manufacturers can sometimes provide products and services at a lower cost than doing it yourself, the main financial reason for choosing an outsourcing solution is to make costs more predictable and establish a smoother cash flow.

✔ **Free-up your time:** Turning over non-core functions and self-contained projects that require specific, cutting-edge expertise lets you and your team focus on strategic development and core business functions to ensure that you are contributing real value to your enterprise.

✔ **Economies of scale:** An outsource supplier has multiple clients with similar needs, and can often leverage this to your advantage when negotiating price and service agreements with equipment, software and raw material providers, and so forth. The outsourcer's range of experience often allows for a more efficient use of equipment for added cost savings.

Reasons to hesitate before outsourcing

While there are many benefits to outsourcing, there are inherent risks involved as well. Many of these risks can be reduced via a well-structured contract with clearly defined responsibilities and expectations, but sometimes a function is simply not a good candidate for outsourcing. The following are some considerations to examine before going for outsourcing:

✔ **Rapidly changing requirements:** If you anticipate frequent changes to your products, processes, and volumes, cost and communication issues may make handling the process yourself more efficient, especially if you need to respond quickly to user needs or want to maintain direct control over the problem resolution.

✔ **In-house expertise:** If best-in-class knowledge is required to stay in business, as in for example the bio-technology markets, then it may be essential for you to acquire and retain key operations staff from the outset. Expensive though it will be, this is a market-entry cost. On the positive side these costs also act as a barrier, keeping other new small firms off your patch.

✔ **Confidentiality of data:** This is a fundamental concern for any business, and is an obvious and essential part of your relationship with an outsourcing partner. Basic contractual provisions, including copyright and non-disclosure agreements, should be established to protect corporate secrets, confidential information, and intellectual property. If the activity to be outsourced is such that the confidentiality of your critical data cannot be ensured, the task is probably not a good candidate for outsourcing.

Making the decision

Whether to make it yourself or to buy in from outside is rarely a cut and dried decision that you can make using a spreadsheet. You always have questions. Can I trust them to keep our trade secrets? Will they be as reliable as they claim? Will they put their prices up once they have us in the bag? There are no easy answers to any of these questions, you just have to weigh up the pros and cons yourself.

Setting quality standards

Quality may well be, like beauty, in the eye of the beholder, but you would be wise to set clear standards that you expect every aspect of your end product, or for that matter service, to conform to. This is true whether you make in-house or outsource.

A number of well-regarded quality standards may help you monitor and control your quality. The BS EN ISO 9000 series are perhaps the best-known standards. They can ensure that your operating procedure delivers a consistent and acceptable standard of products or services. If you are supplying to large firms they may insist on your meeting one of these quality standards, or on auditing your premises to satisfy themselves. The British Standards Institute (www.bsi.global.com) can provide details of these standards.

A number of commercial organisations provide user-friendly guidelines and systems to help you reach the necessary standard. Searching the Web using keywords such as 'Quality Standards' or 'Measurement' will bring you some useful sites.

Choosing a Supplier

Selecting the wrong supplier for your business can be a stressful and expensive experience. This section offers some pointers on how to find a supplier and make sure your supplier can meet your business needs.

Look for value in the service a supplier offers rather than just the price you pay. The key questions you should ask about any prospective supplier to your business are:

- ✔ Do they offer a guaranteed level of service?

- ✔ Do they have a strong business track record and evidence of financial stability? Check out their accounts at Companies House (www.companies house.co.uk).

- ✔ Do they have clients in your business sector and local area?

- ✔ Can they provide you with client references and impartial evidence of their quality? You should check out references to make sure they are reliable and can meet deadlines.

- ✔ Can they meet rushed deliveries in case of emergency?

- ✔ What level of after-sales support do they provide?

Book IV

Keeping Business Ticking Over

✔ Do they provide you with value for money when compared to competitor services?

✔ Do you think you will enjoy working with them? If so the relationship will be more productive.

Thomas's Register (www.thomasregister.com), Kelly's (www.kelly.co.uk), and Kompass (www.kompass.com) between them have details on over 1.6 million UK companies and hundreds of thousands of US and Canadian manufacturers, covering 23 million key products and 744,000 trade and brand names. If someone makes it, you will find their details in one of these directories.

Some free search facilities are available online and your local business library will have hard copies and may even have Internet access to all the key data you could ever need on suppliers.

Evaluating trading terms

Buying is the mirror image of selling. Remember that as you negotiate with suppliers, who are essentially selling their services. Even if they have no deliberate intention to mislead, you may be left thinking that a supplier will be doing things that they are not committed to in any way. The moral of that story is to get it in writing.

The starting point in establishing trading terms is to make sure the supplier can actually do what you want and what they claim to be able to do. This involves checking them out and taking up references.

The next crunch point is price. As a small business you may feel you are fairly short on buying power. Whilst there is some truth in that, there is always room for negotiation. All suppliers want more customers and there is always a time when they want them badly enough to shift on price.

If you do your research by contacting several suppliers so you have a good idea of the price parameters before you talk seriously to any supplier set yourself a target discount price, and start negotiating 10 per cent or so below that. In any negotiation you may well have to give ground, so if you start at your target price, you will end up paying more.

The supplier's opening claim is likely to be that they never negotiate on price. Don't be deterred. There are lots of ways to get your costs down without changing the headline price. Some examples are:

- ✔ Allowing a certain percentage of free product, along the line of the free bottle of wine with every half case, can nudge the price down by 15 per cent.

- ✔ Agreeing to hold stock in their warehouse that will save you renting your own warehouse.

- ✔ Extending an extra 30 days' credit eases your cash flow and may be the difference between growing your young business and standing still.

You need to examine all the contract terms, such as delivery, payment terms, risk, and ownership (the point at which title to the goods passes from the maker to you), warranties and guarantees, termination, arbitration rules if you fall out, and the governing law in the case of dealings with overseas suppliers.

Building a relationship

To ensure that problems you have with your suppliers are handled effectively, you need to build relationships with them. That means talking to them and keeping them informed of your plans and intentions. If you're planning a sales drive, new price list, or some other similar activity, let the suppliers know so they can anticipate the possible impact on them. Keeping them informed does not commit you to buying extra product, or indeed any product beyond that contracted for, but it does make your suppliers feel part of the value chain between you and your customers. By involving them you are indirectly encouraging them to commit to helping you meet your goals.

Many business people pay too much for the goods or services they purchase, which shows up as lower gross margin and poorer performance than the competition. Many of these people don't raise the issue with their supplier but instead start looking elsewhere for an alternative source. Don't make their mistake. More often than not, your supplier would rather discuss the terms of your arrangement than lose your business. In many cases, you both end up with a better deal than before.

Three other tips for building good long-term relationships:

- ✔ Pay your bills on time.

- ✔ Ask for favours only when you really need them.

- ✔ Treat your supplier's representatives and agents with courtesy and respect; they are the front line and will convey their experiences of dealing with you to their bosses.

The Chartered Institute of Purchasing and Supply (www.cips.org) administers education and qualifications in the field of purchasing and supply chain management.

Book IV

Keeping Business Ticking Over

Buying online

Buying online has a range of important benefits for a small firm. Big companies have buying departments whose job is to find the best suppliers in the world with the most competitive prices and trading terms. A small firm can achieve much the same at a fraction of the cost. By buying online, a small firm can lower costs, save scarce management time, get supplies just in time hence speeding up cash flow and reducing stock space, along with a range of other benefits.

The range of goods and services that can be bought online is vast and getting larger. As well as office supplies you can buy computer equipment, software, motor vehicles, machine tools, vending equipment, insurance, hotel accommodation, airline tickets, business education, building materials, tractors, work clothing, and cleaning equipment online, to name but a few.

You can use several methods to buy business supplies online. We explain the most useful methods in the following sections.

Joining an e-buying group

Various names are given to online buying groups, including trading hubs, e-marketplaces, online communities, aggregators, and cost reducers.

Buying in this way allows you to collect information from potential vendors quickly and easily. These online markets gather multiple suppliers in one place so you can comparison shop without leaving your office or picking up the phone. For example, if you need to buy toner cartridges for your office laser printer, you can go to an online marketplace and search the catalogues of multiple office supplies vendors, buying from the one that offers the best deal. You can also do this for bigger ticket items such as office furniture or photocopiers. No more calling a handful of potential suppliers, sitting through sales presentations, and negotiating prices. You save time for more valuable business activities and get a better rate through comparison shopping.

Going in for auctions

Online auctions are another way to buy supplies online. Their advantage is that you pay only as much as you're willing to pay. The disadvantage is you may have to wait for the right deal to come up.

Auctions are a great way to significantly reduce the funds you need to purchase items on your business *wish list* – items you want now or will need eventually but that aren't a current necessity.

Bartering online

You can avoid using hard cash by taking advantage of online barter exchanges. These e-exchanges let you trade your company's products and services for those of other businesses. You can swap ad space for accounting services, consulting for computers. For start-ups or cash-strapped companies, barter can be an effective way to get products or services you might otherwise be unable to afford.

Minimising Risk and Assessing Liability

As the saying goes, no pain, no gain. Some of the pain is routine and can be allowed for in the normal course of events. Employees come and go, suppliers have to be paid, premises have to be moved in and out of. But some events are less easy to predict and can have serious if not disastrous consequences for your business. What happens if the warehouse burns down or your pizzas send a few customers to hospital?

You can't be expected to know such things will happen ahead of time, but you can be reasonably sure that *something* will happen *sometime.* The laws of probability point to it and the law of averages give you a basis for estimating your chances. You have to be prepared to deal with the unexpected, which is what this section helps you do.

Insurance forms a guarantee against loss. You must weigh up to what extent your business assets are exposed to risk and what effect such events could have on the business if they occurred.

One very simple way to assess risk is to get an insurance quote to cover the risk. Insuring against an earthquake in London will be very cheap, but the same cover in Istanbul will be a significant sum.

Insurance is an overhead, producing no benefit until a calamity occurs. It is therefore a commercial decision as to how much to carry, and whilst it is a temptation to minimise cover, you should resist it. You must carry some cover, either by employment law, or as an obligation imposed by a mortgager.

Establish your insurance needs by discussing your business plans with an insurance broker. Make sure you know exactly what insurance you are buying; and, as insurance is a competitive business, get at least three quotations before making up your mind.

The Association of British Insurers (ABI) (www.abi.org.uk) and the British Insurance Association (BIBA) (www.biba.org.uk) can put you in touch with a qualified insurance expert.

Book IV

Keeping Business Ticking Over

Protecting your employees

You must carry at least £2 million of liability insurance to meet your legal lia-bilities for death or bodily injury incurred by an employee during the course of business. In practice, this cover is usually unlimited, with the premiums directly related to your wage bill.

Employer's liability covers only those accidents in which the employer is held to be legally responsible. You may want to extend this cover to any acci-dent to an employee whilst on your business, whosoever is at fault. You may also have to cover your own financial security, particularly if the business depends on your being fit.

Covering yourself when an employee sues

The advent of the no-win, no-fee legal support is encouraging more individu-als to feel confident enough to take on companies both big and small, and often in circumstances where their chances of success are not immediately obvious.

The growing burden of employment legislation facing small firms is forcing more and more businesses to take out legal expense insurance as the risk for being prosecuted for breaking the law rises.

But it is not only the risk that is rising. The consequences are spiralling upwards too. The ceiling for unfair dismissal awards has risen from £12,000 to £50,000 as one example of the burden of new employment laws. In 2001 there was a 40 per cent rise in payouts for discrimination claims, for example, and employment tribunals awarded £3.53million for sex, race, and disability claims.

The remedy for the small firm without its own human resources department to keep it operating clearly within legal boundaries and a legal department to fend of any legal threats, is to take out legal expense insurance.

Firms that sign up for this type of insurance can not only expect any fines and awards to be paid, but their costs associated with defending themselves against allegations will also be met. In many cases, whether the employer wins or loses, they will pay their own legal costs, which makes insurance cover especially attractive. For the small employer, who often takes on the task of handling disputes with employees himself, this is a great benefit, saving not only time but lifting the concerns and anxieties that inevitably accompany litigation.

Protecting assets

Obviously, you need to insure your business premises, plant, and equipment. However, you can choose a couple of ways to do that:

- ✔ **Reinstatement** provides for full replacement cost
- ✔ **Indemnity** meets only the current market value of your asset, which means taking depreciation off first

You have to consider related costs and coverage, as well. For example, who pays for removing debris? Who pays the architect to design the structure if you have to rebuild? Who reimburses employees for any damaged or destroyed personal effects? And potentially the most expensive of all, who covers the cost of making sure that a replacement building meets current, possibly more stringent and more expensive, standards? These factors are covered in the small print of your insurance policy, so if they matter to you check them out.

Also from raw materials through to finished goods, stock is as exposed as your buildings and plant in the event of hazards such as fire and theft. Theft from commercial property runs to hundreds of millions of pounds per annum.

Once in business you can expect threats from within and without. A *fidelity guarantee*, the name given to this particular type of insurance, can be taken to protect you from fraud or dishonesty on the part of key employees. Normal theft cover can be taken to protect your business premises and its contents.

Covering loss of profits

Meeting the replacement costs of buildings, plant, equipment, and stock does not compensate you for the loss of business and profit arising out of a fire or other disaster. Your overheads, employees' wages, and so on may have to continue during the period of interruption. You may incur expenses such as getting subcontracted work done. Insurance for *consequential loss,* as this type of insurance is known, is intended to restore your business's finances to the position they were in before the interruption occurred.

Goods in transit

Until your goods reach your customer and he accepts them, they are still at your risk. You may need to protect yourself from loss or damage in transit.

Book IV

Keeping Business Ticking Over

One newly-established business, planning to expand its activities economically, sought and found a specialist supplier of second-hand reconditioned woodworking machinery – lathes, turners, band saws and so on. After inspecting the machinery in Yorkshire they arranged for it to be transported by the vendor under his own goods in transit insurance cover to their factory in the West Country. While a particularly heavy piece was being unloaded, it fell from the transporter on to the ground immediately outside their factory, and was damaged beyond repair. Their own insurance only covered machinery inside their workshop, the vendor's only while the goods were on the transporter. The gap in between was an insurance 'no man's land', where neither party had cover.

Protecting yourself

Anyone who puts a substantial amount of money into your business – the bank or a venture capitalist, for example – may require you to have *key man insurance*. This type of insurance provides a substantial cash cushion in the event of your death or incapacity – you being the key man (even if you're a woman) on whom the business's success depends.

Key man insurance is particularly important in small and new firms where one person is disproportionately vital in the early stages. Partners may also consider this a prudent protection.

Warranting goods and services

As well as your own specifications confirming how your products or service will perform, you may have legal obligations put on you under the *Consumer Protection Act*, which sets out safety rules and prohibits the sale of unsafe goods and the *Sale of Goods Acts* that govern your contractual relationship with your customer. In addition the common law rules of negligence also apply to business dealings.

If you're a principal in a partnership with unlimited liability, it would be quite possible to be personally bankrupted in a lawsuit concerning product liability. Even if the business was carried out through a limited company, although the directors may escape personal bankruptcy, the company would not. If you believe the risks associated with your product are real, then you need to consider taking out product liability insurance.

If your business involves foodstuffs, you must also pay close attention to the stringent hygiene regulations that now encompass all food manufacture, preparation, and handling. The defence of 'due diligence' will only hold water if thorough examination and identification of all the hazard points has taken place. Trading Standards and Environmental Health Officers are there to help and advise in a free consultative capacity.

Obligations are placed on producers or importers of certain types of goods under both the Consumer Protection Act 1987 and the Sale of Goods Act 1979. Importers can be sued for defects, they cannot disclaim liability simply because they have not been involved in manufacture.

Other liabilities you should consider taking insurance cover are:

✔ Public Liability: Legal liability to pay damages consequent upon bodily injury, illness, or disease contracted by any other person, other than employees, or loss of or damage to their property caused by the insured.

✔ Professional Indemnity: Professional indemnity provides protection against any action by clients who believe they received bad or negligent services, and incurred a loss as a result. Most professional bodies have professional indemnity cover – in some cases it is compulsory. Anyone who supplies advice or services such as consultancy should consider professional indemnity.

The main points of liability law in the UK are:

✔ Do not make claims like 'So simple a child could understand.' You are laying yourself wide open to rebuttal.

✔ Instructions should be crystal clear both on the packet and on the article if possible.

✔ Textiles must carry fibre content, labelling, and washing instructions.

✔ Because the Acts cover the European Union, if you are exporting to another country in the Union you must double-check translations. It is now possible, for example, for a German person to sue you as manufacturer in a German court for goods exported to Germany that have a product defect.

✔ You must keep records for ten years and be ready to institute a product recall operation if necessary.

Dissecting Directors

If you decide to trade as a limited liability company then you will in all probability have to become a director of the business. You may be the only director, or you may be one of several, but as well as the status you have responsibilities too.

Some of a director's duties, responsibilities, and potential liabilities are:

Book IV

Keeping Business Ticking Over

✔ To act in good faith in the interests of the company; this includes carrying out duties diligently and honestly

✔ Not to carry on the business of the company with intent to defraud creditors or for any fraudulent purpose

✔ Not knowingly to allow the company to trade while insolvent ('wrongful trading'); directors who do so may have to pay for the debts incurred by the company while insolvent

✔ Not to deceive shareholders

✔ To have a regard for the interests of employees in general

✔ To comply with the requirements of the Companies Acts, such as providing what is needed in accounting records or filing accounts

In the UK alone over 1,500 directors are disqualified each year from being directors, so can no longer legally manage and control their own business. The reasons for their disqualification range from fraud to the more innocuous wrongful trading, which means carrying on doing business whilst the business is insolvent. This latter area is more difficult to recognise by a director before the event, but you need to be aware of the danger signs and remedies.

In practice, a director's general responsibilities are much the same as those for a sole trader or partner. By forming a company you can separate your own assets from the business assets (in theory at any rate, unless personal guarantees have been extracted). However, a director also has to cope with more technical and detailed requirements; for example, sending in your accounts to Companies House. More onerous than just signing them, a director is expected and required in law to understand the significance of the balance sheet and profit and loss account and the key performance ratios.

Directors' risks can be insured using Directors Insurance, covering negligent performance of duties and breach of the Companies Acts – particularly the Insolvency Act, which can hold directors personally liable to a company's creditors. The cost of the insurance is borne by the company as the directors are acting on its behalf.

The most dangerous areas of a director's responsibilities are ones that could get you disqualified. In summary the areas to avoid at all costs are:

✔ Trading whilst insolvent, which occurs when your liabilities exceed your assets. At this point the shareholders' equity in the business has effectively ceased to exist, which puts directors personally at risk. Directors owe a duty of care to creditors – not shareholders. If you find yourself even approaching this area you need the prompt advice of an insolvency practitioner. Directors who act properly will not be penalised, and will live to fight another day.

  ✔ Wrongful trading can apply if, after a company goes into insolvent liqui-
  dation, the liquidator believes that the directors ought to have concluded earlier that the company had no realistic chance of survival. In
  these circumstances the courts can make directors personally liable for
  the company's debts.

  ✔ Fraudulent trading is rather more serious than wrongful trading. Here
  the proposition is that the director(s) were knowingly party to fraud
  on their creditors. The full shelter of Limited Liability can be removed in
  these circumstances.

Former directors of insolvent companies can be banned from holding office
as a company director for periods of up to 15 years. Fraud, fraudulent trading, wrongful trading, or a failure to comply with company law may result in
disqualification.

Undischarged bankrupts cannot act as a director or take part, directly or
indirectly, in the management of a company unless they obtain the permission of the court.

Breaches of a disqualification order can lead to imprisonment and/or fines.
Also you can be made personally liable for the debts and liabilities of any
company in which you are involved. If you're disqualified you can't issue
your orders through others, having them act as a director in your place.
Doing so puts them at personal risk also.

A register of disqualified directors is available for free access on the
Companies House Web site (www.companieshouse.co.uk).

Finding and Choosing Business Advisers

You need lots of help to get started in business and even more when you are
successful. Here are some tips on dealing with some of the key people you
are almost bound to need at some stage. There are dozens of others including: tax consultants, advertising and public relations consultants, technology
and IT advisers, and the like. The rules and tips in the following sections
should steer you through dealing with most situations involving choosing
and using outside advisers.

Book IV

**Keeping
Business
Ticking
Over**

Tallying up an accountant

Keeping your financial affairs in good order is the key to staying legal and
winning any disputes. A good accountant inside or outside the firm can keep

you on track. A bad accountant is in the ideal position to defraud you at worst, or derail you through negligence or incompetence. What attributes should you look for and how can you find the right accountant for your business? The key steps to choosing a good accountant are:

- ✔ Check they are members of one of the recognised accounting bodies such as the Chartered Institute of Management Accountants (www.cima global.com) or the Institute of Chartered Accountants in England and Wales (www.icaew.co.uk).

- ✔ Have a clear idea of what services you require. You need to consider how complete your bookkeeping records are likely to be, whether you need the VAT return done, budgets and cash flow forecasts prepared and updated, as well as an audit.

- ✔ Clarify the charges scale at the outset. It may well make more sense to spend a bit more on bookkeeping, both staff and systems, rather than leaving it all to a much higher charging qualified accountant.

- ✔ Use personal recommendations from respected fellow businesspeople. There is nothing like hearing from a fellow consumer of a product or service. Pay rather less attention to the recommendation of bankers, government agencies, family and friends, without totally ignoring their advice.

- ✔ Take references from the accountant's clients as well as from the person who recommended them. It could just be a lucky event that they get on. They may even be related!

- ✔ Find out what back-up they have for both systems and people. The tax authorities will not be very sympathetic whatever the reason for lateness. It would be doubly annoying to be fined for someone else's tardiness.

- ✔ See at least three accountants before making your choice, making sure they deal with companies your size and a bit bigger. Not so much bigger as to have no relevant advice and help to offer, but big enough for you to have some room for growth without having to change accountants too quickly.

- ✔ Find out whom else the accountant acts for. You don't want them to be so busy they can't service your needs properly, or to be working for potential competitors.

- ✔ Make the appointment for a trial period only, and set a specific task to see how they get on.

- ✔ Give them the latest accounts of your business and ask them for their comments based on their analysis of the figures. You will quickly see if they have grasped the basics of your financial position.

Investing in a bank

You may wonder why choosing a bank is listed in this section covering choosing business advisers. Well the answer, crazy as it may seem, is that your banker is almost invariably the first person you turn to when the chips are down. It's not so surprising when you think about it. After all most big business problems turn on money and bankers are the people who turn the money on.

Get the wrong bank and you could lose more than your overdraft. You may lose the chance to acquire a free, or at least nearly free, business adviser.

These are the top ten questions to ask before taking on a bank manager:

- ✔ How quickly can you make decisions about lending? Anything longer than ten days is too long.

- ✔ What rate of interest will you charge? Two or three per cent above the Bank of England base rate is fairly normal. Above four per cent is on the high side.

- ✔ What factors do you take into consideration in arriving at that rate? If the bank proposes a high rate of interest, say four per cent above Bank of England base rate or higher, then you need to know why. It may be that all the bank is asking for is some further security for their loan, which you might think worth giving in return for a lower interest rate.

- ✔ What other charges will there be? For example will you be charged for every transaction in and out of the account and if so how much?

- ✔ Do you visit your clients and get to know their business? If the bank doesn't visit its hard to see how they will ever get to really understand your business.

- ✔ Under what circumstances would you want personal guarantees? When the bank is feeling exposed to greater risk than it wants to take it will ask you to shoulder some of that risk personally. Under the terms of a bank's loan to your business they may state that their lending should not exceed a certain sum. You need to be clear what that sum is.

- ✔ What help and advisory services do you have that could be useful to me? Banks often provide advice on export trade, currency dealing, insurance and a range of other related services.

- ✔ What is unique about your banking services that would make me want to use your rather than any other bank? This factor rather depends on what you consider to be valuable. A bank that delivers all its service on the Internet may be attractive to one person and anathema and turnoff to another.

Book IV

Keeping Business Ticking Over

✔ How long will it be before my present manager moves on? If managers are routinely moved every few years then it's hard to see any value in forming personal relationships.

✔ Are there any situations when you would ask for repayment of a loan to be made early? A bank may insist that if you break any major condition of the loan, such as the overdraft limit or repayment schedule, the whole loan is repayable. You need to find out if this is so, and what sum will cause this to happen.

Choosing a lawyer

Lawyers or solicitors are people you hope never to have to use and when you do need one you need them yesterday. Even if you don't appoint a company lawyer, you may well need one for basic stuff if you are forming a company or setting up a partnership agreement. Follow the same rules as you would for choosing an accountant (refer to the earlier 'Tallying up an accountant' section).

The fact is that, in business, you know that one day you will need a lawyer. The complexity of commercial life means that, sooner or later, you will find yourself either initiating or defending legal action. It may be a contract dispute with a customer or supplier, or perhaps the lease on your premises turns out to give you far fewer rights than you hoped. A former employee might claim you fired them without reason. Or the Health and Safety Inspector finds some aspect of your machinery or working practices less than satisfactory.

The range of possibilities is extensive, and when things do go wrong, the time and money required to put them right can be an unexpected and unwelcome drain on your cash. By doing things right from the start, you can avoid at least some of the most common disputes and cope more easily with catastrophes.

In addition to ensuring that contracts are correctly drawn up, that leases are free from nasty surprises, and that the right health and safety procedures are followed, a solicitor can also advise on choosing the best structure for your company, on protecting your intellectual property, and on how to go about raising money.

It makes sense to either see your solicitor before your problems arise, and find out what they can do for you or, at the very least, make yourself conversant with the relevant laws. Taking timely action on legal issues may help you gain an advantage over competitors and will almost certainly save you money in the long run.

Finding a Lawyer For Your Business

Lawyers For Your Business (www.lfyb.law society.org.uk) represents some 1,400 firms of solicitors in England and Wales, which have come together to help ensure that all businesses, and especially the smaller owner-managed ones, get access to sound legal advice whenever they need it. LFYB is administered by the Law Society, and backed by Business in the Community, the Federation of Small Business, and the Forum of Private Business.

To remove the risk of incurring unexpectedly high legal costs, all Lawyers For Your Business members offer a free consultation, lasting at least half-an-hour, to diagnose your legal problem and any need for action, with full information, in advance, on the likely costs of proceeding.

The Law Society (www.lawsociety.org.uk) will send you a list of Lawyers For Your Business members in your area, and a voucher for a free consultation.

Simply choose one of the firms in the list and arrange an appointment, mentioning Lawyers For Your Business and the voucher.

If you are going to see a lawyer, it is always best to be well prepared. Have all the facts to hand and know what you want help with.

Considering management consultants

If you are facing a new major problem you have no expertise in, particularly a problem you don't expect to experience again, then hiring a consultant is an option worth considering. For example if you are moving premises, changing your computer or accounting system, starting to do business overseas, or designing an employee share ownership scheme, it may well make sense to get the help of someone who has covered that area several times before and who is an expert in the field.

The time taken for a consultant to carry out most tasks a small business might require is likely to be between a fortnight and three months. Anything much longer will be too expensive for most small firms and anything much shorter is unlikely to have much of an impact on the business. That's not to say they will be working continuously on your project for that time. After an initial meeting a consultant may do much of the work off site and in chunks of time. Costs vary dependant on both the skill of the consultant and the topic covered. A tax consultant, for example can cost upwards of £450 an hour, whilst a training consultant might cost the same sum for a day.

Book IV

Keeping Business Ticking Over

Take on a consultant using much the same procedures as you would a key employee (see Book V). Take time to brief them thoroughly. Don't expect to just dump the problem on their doorstep and walk away. Set the consultant a small measurable part of the task first and see how they perform. Never give them a long-term contract or an open book commitment.

Remember you can't delegate decision-making. You can only delegate the analysis of problems and the presentation of options. In the end you have to choose which way to go. Don't let consultants implement decisions on their own. The line responsibility between yourself and your staff needs to be preserved. If they see someone else giving orders it will undermine the chain of command. If the consultant's solution is so complex it needs their expertise to implement, you have the wrong solution.

The Institute of Management Consultants (www.imc.co.uk) list the 10 golden rules for choosing a consultant. You will also find that your local Business Link will have a national register of approved (and insured) specialist consultants for most business needs.

Chapter 2

Controlling Your Books, Your Records, and Your Money

*E*very business takes in cash in some form or another: Notes and coins, cheques, and credit card and electronic payments are all eventually deposited as cash into the business's accounts. Before you take in that first penny, your initial concern must be controlling that cash and making sure that none of it walks out the door improperly.

Finding the right level of cash control, while at the same time allowing your employees the flexibility to sell your products or services and provide ongoing customer service, can be a monumental task. If you don't have enough controls, you risk theft or embezzlement. Yet if you have too many controls, employees may miss sales or anger customers.

In this chapter, we explain the basic protections you need to put in place to be sure that all cash coming into or going out of your business is clearly documented and controlled. We also review the type of paperwork you need to document the use of cash and other business assets. Finally, we tell you how to organise your staff to control the flow of your assets properly and insure yourself against possible misappropriation of those assets.

Putting Controls on Your Business's Cash

Think about how careful you are with your personal cash. You find various ways to protect the cash you carry around, you dole it out carefully to your family members, and you may even hide cash in a safe place in the house just in case you need it for unexpected purposes.

You're very protective of your cash when you're the only one who handles it, but consider the vulnerability of your business cash. After all, you aren't the only one handling that cash. You have some employees encountering incoming cash at cash registers, others opening the mail and finding cheques for orders to purchase products or pay bills, as well as cheques from other sources. And don't forget that employees may need petty cash to pay for mail sent COD (Cash on Delivery), or to pay for other unexpected, low-cost needs.

If you watch over every transaction in which cash enters your business, you have no time to do the things you need to do to grow your business. When the business is small, you can sign all cheques and maintain control of cash going out, but as soon as the business grows, you just may not have the time.

The good news is that just putting in place the proper controls for your cash can help protect it. Cash flows through your business in four key ways:

✔ Deposits and payments into and out of your current accounts

✔ Deposits and payments into and out of your savings accounts

✔ Petty cash funds in critical locations where quick access to cash may be needed

✔ Transactions made in your cash registers

The following sections cover some key controls for each of these cash flow points.

Current accounts

Almost every penny that comes into your business flows through your business's current account (at least that *should* happen). Whether the cash is collected at your cash registers, payments received in the mail, cash used to fill the cash registers or petty cash accounts, payments sent out to pay business obligations, or any other cash need, this cash enters and exits your current account. Thus, your current account is your main tool for protecting your cash flow.

Choosing the right bank

Finding the right bank to help you set up your current account and the controls that limit access to that account is crucial. When evaluating your banking options, ask yourself the following questions:

- ✔ Does this bank have a branch conveniently located for my business?
- ✔ Does this bank operate at times when I need it most?
- ✔ Does this bank offer secure ways to deposit cash even when the bank is closed?

   Most banks have secure drop boxes for cash so you can deposit receipts as quickly as possible at the end of the business day rather than secure the cash overnight yourself.

Visit local bank branches yourself, and check out the type of business services each bank offers. Pay particular attention to

- ✔ The type of personal attention you receive
- ✔ How questions are handled
- ✔ What type of charges may be tacked on for personalised attention

Some banks require business account holders to call a centralised line for assistance rather than depend on local branches. Most banks charge if you use a cashier rather than an ATM (automatic teller machine). Other banks charge for every transaction, whether a deposit, withdrawal, or cheque. Many banks have charges that differ for business accounts. If you plan to accept credit cards, compare the services offered for that as well.

The general rule is that banks charge businesses for everything they do. However, they charge less for tasks that can be automated and thus involve less manual effort. So, you save money when you use electronic payment and receipt processes. In other words, pay your suppliers electronically and get your customers to pay you the same way, and you reduce your banking costs.

Deciding on types of cheques

After you choose your bank, you need to consider what type of cheques you want to use in your business. For example, you need different cheques depending upon whether you handwrite each cheque or print cheques from your computerised accounting system.

Writing cheques manually

If you plan to write your cheques, you're most likely to use a business cheque book, which in its simplest form is exactly the same as a personal cheque

Book IV

Keeping Business Ticking Over

book, with a counter foil (or cheque stub) on the left and a cheque on the right. This arrangement provides the best control for manual cheques because each cheque and counter foil is numbered. When you write a cheque, you fill out the counter foil with details such as the date, the cheque's recipient, and the purpose of the cheque. The counter foil also has a space to keep a running total of your balance in the account.

Printing computer-generated cheques

If you plan to print cheques from your computerised accounting system, you need to order cheques that match that system's programming. Each computer software program has a unique template for printing cheques. Figure 2-1 shows a common layout for business cheques that a computerised accounting system prints out. The key information is exactly what you expect to see on any cheque – payee details, date, and amount in both words and numbers.

Figure 2-1:
Businesses that choose to print their cheques using their computerised accounting systems usually order them with their business name already printed on the cheque. This particular cheque is compatible with Sage Line 50.

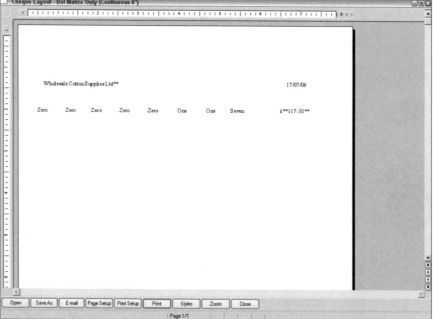

You can also set up your computer accounting system to print out the precise details you'd expect to find on a manual cheque – the current date, name of the recipient, and the value of the cheque. Unlike a manually-prepared cheque, you don't have a counter foil to fill in, which is not a problem because your computerised accounting system records this information for you: It keeps an internal record of all cheques issued. If you need to check that you issued a cheque correctly, you can always run a report or make an on-screen enquiry on your computerised accounting system.

Initially, when the business is small, you can sign each cheque and keep control of the outflow of money. But as the business grows, you may find that you need to delegate cheque-signing responsibilities to someone else, especially if you travel frequently. Many small business owners set up cheque-signing procedures that allow one or two of their staff to sign cheques up to a designated amount, such as £5,000. Any cheques above that designated amount require the owner's signature, or the signature of an employee and a second designated person, such as an officer of the business.

Making deposits in the current account

Of course, you aren't just withdrawing from your business's current account (that would be a big problem). You also need to deposit money into that account, and you want to be sure that your paying in slips contain all the necessary detail as well as documentation to back up the deposit information. Most banks provide printed paying in slips with all the necessary detail to be sure that the money is deposited into the appropriate account, together with who wrote each cheque, the value, and the date received.

A good practice is to record cheques immediately as part of a daily morning routine. Enter the details onto the paying in slip and update your computerised or manual accounting system at the same time. Make sure that you pay in any money received before 3:30 p.m. on the same day, to ensure that your bank account gets credit that day rather than the next. (We talk more about controls for incoming cash in the 'Dividing staff responsibilities' section, later in this chapter.) If you get both personal and business cheques sent to the same address, instruct the person opening the mail about how to differentiate the types of cheques and how each type of cheque needs to be handled to best protect your incoming cash, whether for business or personal purposes.

You may think that making bank deposits is as easy as 1-2-3, but when it comes to business deposits and multiple cheques, things get a bit more complicated. To make deposits to your business's current account properly, follow these steps:

Book IV

Keeping Business Ticking Over

1. **Record on the paying in slip the full details of all cheques being deposited as well as the total cash being deposited. Also make a note of how many cheques you're paying into the bank on that paying in slip.**

2. **Record the details regarding the source of the deposited cash before you make the deposit; file everything in your daily bank folder.**

   (We talk more about filing in the section 'Keeping the Right Paperwork', later in this chapter.)

3. **Make sure that the cashier at the bank stamps the paying in slip as confirmation that the bank has received all the cheques and cash.**

   If you're paying in cheques via the ATM then treat it exactly as if you were paying in via the cashier. Still prepare your own paying slip and make sure that you pick up the receipt that the ATM gives you. This does not ensure that things will not go wrong but it will ensure you have a paper trail if they do.

Savings accounts

Some businesses find that they have more cash than they need to meet their immediate plans. Rather than keep that extra cash in a non-interest bearing account, many businesses open a savings account to store the extra cash.

If you're a small business owner with few employees, you probably control the flow of money into and out of your savings account yourself. As you grow and find that you need to delegate the responsibility for the business's savings, ensure that you think carefully about who gets access and how you can document the flow of funds into and out of the savings account. Treat a savings account like a current account and use paying in slips to record deposits and cheque book stubs to record payments.

Petty cash accounts

Every business needs cash on almost a weekly basis. Businesses need to keep some cash on hand, called *petty cash,* for unexpected expenses such as money to pay for letters and packages delivered COD, money to buy a few emergency stamps to get the mail out, or money for some office supplies needed before the next delivery.

You certainly don't want to have a lot of cash sitting around in the office, but try to keep £50 to £100 in a petty cash box. If you subsequently find that you're faced with more or less cash expenses than you expected, you can always adjust the amount kept in petty cash accordingly.

No matter how much you keep in petty cash, make sure that you set up a good control system that requires anyone who uses the cash to write a petty cash voucher specifying how much was used and why. Also ask that a cash receipt, for example from the shop or post office, is attached to the voucher in order to justify the cash withdrawal whenever possible. In most cases, a member of staff buys something for the business and then gets reimbursed for that expense. If the expense is small enough, you can reimburse through the petty cash fund. If the expense is more than a few pounds, ask the person to fill out an expense account form and get reimbursed by cheque. Petty cash is usually used for minor expenses of £10 or less.

The best way to control petty cash is to pick one person in the office to manage the use of all petty cash. Before giving that person more cash, he or she should be able to prove the absence of cash used and why it was used.

Poor control of the petty cash box can lead to small but significant losses of cash. Quite often you can find it difficult or impossible to identify or prove who took the cash. The best solution is to make it slightly more difficult for employees to obtain petty cash, than having a free-for-all system. A locked box in cupboard works very well.

For the ultimate control of cash, use the imprest system in which a fixed amount is drawn from the bank and paid into petty cash (the float). After that, cash is issued only against a petty cash voucher. This system means that, at any point, cash, or cash plus vouchers, should be equal to the total of the petty cash float. At the end of the week (or month) the vouchers are removed and the cash made up to the original amount.

Cash registers

Have you ever gone into a business and tried to pay with a large note only to find out that the cashier has no change? This frustrating experience happens in many businesses, especially those that don't carefully monitor the money in their cash registers. Most businesses empty cash registers each night and put any cash not being deposited in the bank that night into a safe. However, many businesses instruct their cashiers to deposit their cash in a business safe periodically throughout the day and get a paper voucher to show the cash deposited. These daytime deposits minimise the cash held in case the store is the victim of a robbery.

All these types of controls are necessary parts of modern business operations, but they can have consequences that make customers angry. Most customers just walk out the door and don't come back when they can't buy what they want using the notes they have on hand.

At the beginning of the day, cashiers usually start out with a set amount of cash in the register. As they collect money and give out change, the register records the transactions. At the end of the day, the cashier must count out the amount of change left in the register, run a copy of all transactions that passed through that register, and total the cash collected. Then the cashier must prove that the amount of cash remaining in that register totals the amount of cash the register started with plus the amount of cash collected during the day. After the cashier balances the register, the person in charge of cash deposits (usually the shop manager or someone on the accounting or bookkeeping staff) takes all the cash out, except the amount needed for the next day, and deposits it in the bank. (We talk more about separation of staff duties in the section 'Dividing staff responsibilities', later in this chapter.)

In addition to having the proper amount of cash in the register necessary to give customers the change they need, you also must make sure that your cashiers are giving the right amount of change and actually recording all sales on their cash registers. Keeping an eye on cashier activities is good business practice in any case, but you can also protect against cash theft by your employees in this way. Three ways exist in which cashiers can pocket some extra cash:

- ✔ **They don't record the sale in the cash register and instead pocket the cash.** The best deterrent to this type of theft is supervision. You can decrease the likelihood of theft through unrecorded sales by printing up sales tickets that the cashier must use to enter a sale in the cash register and open the cash drawer. If cash register transactions don't match sales receipts, the cashier must show a voided transaction for the missing ticket, or explain why the cash drawer was opened without a ticket.

- ✔ **They don't provide a sales receipt and instead pocket the cash.** In this scenario the cashier neglects to give a sales receipt to one customer in the queue. The cashier gives the next customer the unused sales receipt but doesn't actually record the second transaction in the cash register. Instead, he or she just pockets the cash. In the business's books, the second sale never took place. The customer whose sale wasn't recorded has a valid receipt though it may not match exactly what was bought. Therefore, the customer is unlikely to notice any problem unless something needs to be returned later. Your best defence against this type of deception is to post a sign reminding all customers that they must get a receipt for all purchases and that the receipt is required to get a refund or exchange. Providing numbered sales receipts that include a duplicate copy can also help prevent this problem; cashiers need to produce the duplicates at the end of the day when proving the amount of cash flow that passed through their registers.

In addition to protection from theft by cashiers, the printed sales receipt system can be used to monitor shoplifters and prevent them from getting money for merchandise they never bought. For example, suppose a shoplifter takes a blouse out of a store, as well as some blank sales receipts. The next day the shoplifter comes back with the blouse and one of the stolen sales receipts filled out as though the blouse had actually been purchased the day before. You can spot the fraud because that sales receipt is part of a numbered batch of sales receipts that you've already identified as missing or stolen. You can quickly identify that the customer never paid for the merchandise and call the police.

✔ **They record a false credit voucher and keep the cash for themselves.** In this case the cashier writes up a credit voucher for a nonexistent customer and then pockets the cash refund. Most shops use a numbered credit voucher system to control this problem, so each credit can be carefully monitored with some detail that proves its connection to a previous customer purchase, such as a sales receipt. Customers are often asked to provide an address and telephone number before receiving a refund. Although this may not put off the determined fraudster, the opportunist thief is likely to be deterred. Also, shops usually require that a manager review the reason for the credit voucher, whether a return or exchange, and approve the transaction before cash or credit is given. When the bookkeeper records the sales return in the books, the number for the credit voucher is recorded with the transaction so that the detail about that credit voucher is easy to find if a question is raised later about the transaction.

Even if cashiers don't deliberately pocket cash, they can inadvertently give the wrong change. If you run a retail outlet, training and supervising your cashiers is a critical task that you must handle yourself or hand over to a trusted employee.

Keeping the Right Paperwork

When handling cash, you can see that a lot of paper changes hands, whether from the cash register, deposits into your current accounts, or petty cash withdrawals. Therefore, careful documentation is paramount to control the movement of cash into and out of your business properly. And don't forget about organisation; you need to be able to find that documentation if questions about cash flow arise later.

Monitoring cash flow isn't the only reason why you need to keep loads of paperwork. In order to do your taxes and write off business expenses, you need receipts for those expenses. You also need details about the money you pay to employees, and tax and National Insurance contributions collected for your employees, in order to file the proper reports with HM Revenue & Customs. Setting up a good filing system and knowing what to keep and for how long is very important for any small businessperson.

Creating a filing system

To get started setting up your filing system, you need the following supplies:

- **Filing cabinets:** Pretty self-explanatory – you can't have a filing system with nothing to keep the files in.

- **File folders:** Set up separate files for each of your suppliers, employees, and customers who buy on credit, as well as files for backup information on each of your transactions. Many bookkeepers file transaction information using the date the transaction was added to their journal. If the transaction relates to a customer, supplier, or employee, they add a duplicate copy of the transaction to the individual files as well.

  Even if you have a computerised accounting system, you need to file paperwork related to the transactions you enter into your computer system. You still need to maintain employee, supplier, and customer files in hard copy just in case something goes wrong – for example, if your computer system crashes, you need the originals to restore the data. Back up your computerised accounting system's data regularly to minimise the effects of such a crisis. Daily backups are best; one week is the longest you should ever go without a backup.

- **Ring binders:** These binders are great for things like your Chart of Accounts, your Nominal Ledger and your system of journals (see Paul Barrow and Lita Epstein's *Bookkeeping For Dummies*, published by Wiley, for more details on these) because you add to these documents regularly and the binders make adding additional pages easy. Make sure that you number the pages as you add them to the binder, so you can quickly spot a missing page. How many binders you need depends on how many financial transactions you have each accounting period. You can keep everything in one binder, or you may want to set up a binder for the Chart of Accounts and Nominal Ledger and then a separate binder for each of your active journals. The decision is based on what makes your job easier.

✔ **Expandable files:** These files are the best way to keep track of current supplier activity and any bills that may be due. Make sure that you have

- **An alphabetical file:** Use this file to track all your outstanding purchase orders by supplier. After you fill the order, you can file all details about that order in the supplier's individual file in case questions about the order arise later.

- **A 12-month file:** Use this file to keep track of bills that you need to pay. Simply place the bill in the slot for the month payment is due. Many businesses also use a 30-day expandable file. At the beginning of the month, the bills are placed in the 30-day expandable file based on the dates that they need to be paid. This approach provides a quick and organised visual reminder for bills that are due.

If you're using a computerised accounting system, you don't need the expandable files because your accounting system can remind you when bills are due (as long as you add the information to the system when the bill arrives).

✔ **Blank computer disks or other storage media:** Use these to backup your computerised system on a weekly or, better yet, daily basis. Keep the backup discs in a fire safe or somewhere unaffected if a fire destroys the business. (A fire safe is the best way to keep critical financial data safe, and is therefore a must for any business.)

Working out what to keep and for how long

As you can probably imagine, the pile of paperwork you need to hold on to can get very large very quickly. As they see their files getting thicker and thicker, most businesspeople wonder what they can toss, what they really need to keep, and how long they need to keep it.

Generally, keep most transaction-related paperwork for as long as HM Revenue & Customs can come and audit your books. For most types of audits, that means six years. But if you fail to file your tax return or file it fraudulently (and we hope this doesn't apply to you), HM Revenue & Customs may question you at any time, because no time limitations exist in these cases.

HM Revenue & Customs isn't the only reason to keep records around for longer than one year. You may need proof-of-purchase information for your insurance company if an asset is lost, stolen, or destroyed by fire or other accident. Also, you need to hang on to information regarding any business

Book IV

Keeping Business Ticking Over

loan until paid off, just in case the bank questions how much you paid. After the loan's paid off, ensure that you keep proof of payment indefinitely in case a question about the loan ever arises. Information about property and other asset holdings needs to be kept around for as long as you hold the asset and for at least six years after the asset is sold. You're legally required to keep information about employees for at least three years after the employee leaves.

Keep the current year's files easily accessible in a designated filing area and keep the most recent past year's files in accessible filing cabinets if you have room. Box up records when they hit the two-year-old mark, and put them in storage. Make sure that you date your boxed records with information about what they are, when they were put into storage, and when you can destroy them. Many people forget that last detail, and boxes pile up until total desperation sets in and no more room is left. Then someone must take the time to sort through the boxes and figure out what needs to be kept and what can be destroyed – not a fun job.

It is a legal requirement to keep information about all transactions for six years. After that, make a list of things you want to hold on to longer for other reasons, such as asset holdings and loan information. Check with your lawyer and accountant to get their recommendations on what to keep and for how long.

Protecting Your Business Against Internal Fraud

Many businesspeople start their operations by carefully hiring people they can trust, thinking: 'We're a family – they'd never steal from me.'

Often a business owner finds out too late that even the most loyal employee may steal from the business if the opportunity arises and the temptation becomes too great – or if the employee gets caught up in a serious personal financial dilemma and needs fast cash. In this section, we talk about the steps you can take to prevent people stealing from your business.

Facing the reality of financial fraud

The four basic types of financial fraud are

✔ **Embezzlement,** which is the illegal use of funds by a person who controls those funds. For example, a bookkeeper may use business money for his or her own personal needs. Many times, embezzlement stories don't appear in the newspapers because businesspeople are so embarrassed that they choose to keep the affair quiet. They usually settle privately with the embezzler rather than face public scrutiny.

✔ **Internal theft,** which is the stealing of business assets by employees, such as taking office supplies or products the business sells without paying for them. Internal theft is often the culprit behind stock shrinkage.

✔ **Payoffs and kickbacks,** which are situations in which employees accept cash or other benefits in exchange for access to the business, often creating a scenario where the business that the employee works for pays more for the goods or products than necessary. That extra money finds its way into the pocket of the employee who helped facilitate the access. For example, say Business A wants to sell its products to Business B. An employee in Business B helps Business A get in the door. Business A prices its product a bit higher and gives the employee of Business B the extra profit in the form of a kickback for helping it out. A payoff is paid before the sale is made, essentially saying 'please'. A kickback is paid after the sale is made, essentially saying 'thank you'. In reality, payoffs and kickbacks are a form of bribery, but few businesses report or litigate this problem (although employees are fired when deals are uncovered).

✔ **Skimming,** which occurs when employees take money from receipts and don't record the revenue on the books.

Although any of these financial crimes can happen in a small business, the one that hits small businesses the hardest is embezzlement. This crime happens most frequently when one person has access or control over most of the business's financial activities. For example, a single bookkeeper may write cheques, make deposits, and balance the monthly bank statement – talk about having your fingers in a very big till.

Dividing staff responsibilities

Your primary protection against financial crime is properly separating staff responsibilities when the flow of business cash is involved. Basically, never have one person handling more than one of the following tasks:

✔ **Bookkeeping:** Involves reviewing and entering all transactions into the business's books. The bookkeeper makes sure that transactions are accurate, valid, appropriate, and have the proper authorisation. For example, if a transaction requires paying a supplier, the bookkeeper makes sure that the charges are accurate and someone with proper authority has approved the payment. The bookkeeper can review documentation of cash receipts and the overnight deposits taken to the bank, but shouldn't actually make the deposit. Also, if the bookkeeper is responsible for handling payments from external parties, such as customers or suppliers, he or she shouldn't enter those transactions in the books.

✔ **Authorisation:** Involves being the manager or managers delegated to authorise expenditures for their departments. You may decide that transactions over a certain amount must have two or more authorisations before cheques can be sent to pay a bill. Spell out authorisation levels clearly and make sure that everyone follows them, even the owner or managing director of the business. (Remember, as owner, you set the tone for how the rest of the office operates; when you take shortcuts, you set a bad example and undermine the system you put in place.)

✔ **Money-handling:** Involves direct contact with incoming cash or revenue, whether cheque, credit card, or credit transactions, as well as outgoing cash flow. The person who handles money directly, such as a cashier, shouldn't also prepare and make bank deposits. Likewise, the person writing cheques to pay business bills shouldn't be authorised to sign those cheques; to be safe, have one person prepare the cheques based on authorised documentation, and a second person sign those cheques, after reviewing the authorised documentation.

When setting up your cash-handling systems, try to think like an embezzler to figure out how someone can take advantage of a system.

✔ **Financial report preparation and analysis:** Involves the actual preparation of the financial reports and any analysis of those reports. Someone who's not involved in the day-to-day entering of transactions in the books needs to prepare the financial reports. For most small businesses, the bookkeeper turns over the raw reports from the computerised accounting system to an outside accountant who reviews the materials and prepares the financial reports. In addition, the accountant does a financial analysis of the business activity results for the previous accounting period.

We realise that you may be just starting up a small business and therefore not have enough staff to separate all these duties. Until you do have that capability, make sure that you stay heavily involved in the inflow and outflow of cash in your business. The following tips tell you how:

✔ **Periodically (once a month) open your business's bank statements, and keep a close watch on the transactions.** Someone else can be given the responsibility of reconciling the statement, but you still need to keep an eye on the transactions listed.

✔ **Periodically look at your business cheque book counterfoils to ensure that no cheques are missing.** A bookkeeper who knows that you periodically check the books is less likely to find an opportunity for theft or embezzlement. If you find that a cheque or page of cheques is missing, act quickly to find out if the cheques were used legitimately. If you can't find the answer, call your bank and put a stop on the missing cheque numbers.

✔ **Periodically observe your cashiers and managers handling cash to make sure that they're following the rules you've established.** This practice is known as *management by walking around* – the more often you're out there, the less likely you are to be a victim of employee theft and fraud.

Insuring Your Cash through Employee Bonding

If you have employees who handle a lot of cash, insuring your business against theft is an absolute must. This insurance, known as *employee bonding,* is often offered as an extension to an existing business insurance policy, and helps to protect you against theft and reduce your risk of loss.

If you carry a bond on your cash handlers, you're covered for losses sustained by any employee who's bonded. You also have coverage when an employee's act causes losses to a client of your business. For example, when you're a financial consultant and your bookkeeper embezzles a client's cash, you're protected for the loss.

A *fidelity bond* is a type of insurance that you can buy through the company that handles your business insurance policies. It is a stand alone policy, unlike employee bonding. The cost varies greatly depending on the type of business you operate and the amount of cash or other assets that are handled by the employees you want to bond. If an employee steals from you or one of your customers, the insurance covers the loss.

Employers also bond employees who may be in a position to steal something other than cash. For example, a cleaning service may bond its workers in case a worker steals something from one of its customers. If a customer reports something missing, the insurance company that bonded the employee covers the loss. Without a bond, an employer must pay back the customer for any loss.

Chapter 3

Counting Your Sales

. . . .

In This Chapter

▶ Taking in cash

▶ Discovering the ins and outs of credit

▶ Managing discounts for best results

▶ Staying on top of returns and allowances

▶ Monitoring payments due

▶ Dealing with bad debt

. . . .

*E*very business loves to take in money, and this means that you, the book-keeper, have lots to do to ensure that sales are properly recorded in the books. In addition to recording the sales themselves, you must monitor customer accounts, discounts offered to customers, and customer returns and allowances.

If the business sells products on credit, you have to monitor customer accounts carefully in Accounts Receivable, including monitoring whether customers pay on time and alerting the sales team when customers are behind on their bills and future purchases on credit need to be declined. Some customers never pay, and in that case, you must adjust the books to reflect non-payment as a bad debt.

This chapter reviews the basic responsibilities of a business's bookkeeping and accounting staff for tracking sales, making adjustments to those sales, monitoring customer accounts, and alerting management to slow-paying customers.

Collecting on Cash Sales

Most businesses collect some form of cash as payment for the goods or services they sell. Cash receipts include more than just notes and coins; cheques and credit and debit card payments are also considered cash sales for book-keeping purposes. In fact, with electronic transaction processing (when a customer's credit or debit card is swiped through a machine), a deposit is usually made to the business's bank account the same day (sometimes within seconds of the transaction, depending on the type of system the business sets up with the bank).

The only type of payment that doesn't fall under the umbrella of a cash payment is purchases made on credit. And by *credit,* we mean credit your business offers to customers directly rather than through a third party, such as a bank credit card or loan. We talk more about this type of sale in the section 'Selling on Credit', later in this chapter.

Discovering the value of sales receipts

Modern businesses generate sales receipts in one of three ways: by the cash register, by the credit or debit card machine, or by hand (written out by the salesperson). Whichever of these three methods you choose to handle your sales transactions, the sales receipt serves two purposes:

- ✔ Gives the customer proof that the item was purchased on a particular day at a particular price in your shop in case he or she needs to exchange or return the merchandise.

- ✔ Gives the shop a receipt that can be used at a later time to enter the transaction into the business's books. At the end of the day, the receipts are also used to cash up the cash register and ensure that the cashier has taken in the right amount of cash based on the sales made. (In Chapter 7, we talk more about how to use cash receipts as an internal control tool to manage your cash.)

You're familiar with cash receipts, no doubt, but just to show you how much useable information can be generated for the bookkeeper on a sales receipt, Figure 3-1 shows a sample receipt from a bakery.

Receipts contain a wealth of information that can be collected for your business's accounting system. A look at a receipt tells you the amount of cash collected, the type of products sold, the quantity of products sold, and how much Value Added Tax (VAT) was collected. In the example used in Figure 3-1 there is no VAT chargeable as food products are currently exempt from VAT.

Unless your business uses some type of computerised system that integrates the point of sale (usually the cash register) with the business's accounting system, sales information is collected throughout the day by the cash register and printed out in a summary form at the end of the day. At that point, you enter the details of the sales day in the books.

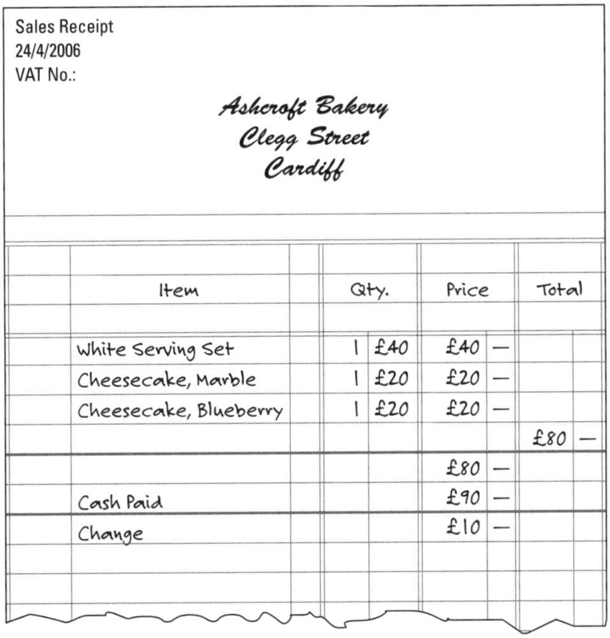

```
Sales Receipt
24/4/2006
VAT No.:
                        Ashcroft Bakery
                          Clegg Street
                            Cardiff
```

Item	Qty.	Price	Total
White Serving Set	1 £40	£40 —	
Cheesecake, Marble	1 £20	£20 —	
Cheesecake, Blueberry	1 £20	£20 —	
			£80 —
		£80 —	
Cash Paid		£90 —	
Change		£10 —	

Figure 3-1:
A sales
receipt from
Ashcroft
Bakery.

If you don't use a computerised system to monitor stock, you use the data collected by the cash register to simply enter into the books the cash received, total sales, and VAT collected. Although you're likely to have many more sales and much higher numbers at the end of the day, the entry in the Cash Receipts journal for the receipt appears as follows:

	Debit	*Credit*
Bank Account	£80.00	
Sales		£80.00

Cash receipts for 25 April 2006

In this example entry, Bank Account is an Asset account shown on the balance sheet, and its value increases with the debit. The Sales account is a revenue account on the profit and loss statement, and its balance increases with a Credit, showing additional revenue (for more information on these accounting basics, check out Paul Barrow and Lita Epstein's *Bookkeeping For Dummies*, published by Wiley). The VAT Collected account is a Liability account that appears on the balance sheet, and its balance increases with this transaction.

Businesses pay VAT to HM Revenue & Customs monthly or quarterly depending on rules set by HM Revenue & Customs. Therefore, your business must hold the money owed in a Liability account so you're certain you can pay the VAT collected from customers when due.

Recording cash transactions in the books

If you're using a computerised accounting system, you can enter more detail from the day's receipts and record stock sold as well. Most of the computerised accounting systems include the ability to record the sale of stock. Figure 3-2 shows you the Sage Line 50 sales receipts form that you can use to input data from each day's sales.

In addition to the information included in the Cash Receipts journal, note that Sage Line 50 also collects information about the items sold in each transaction. Sage Line 50 then automatically updates stock information, reducing the amount of stock on hand when necessary. If the sales receipt in Figure 3-2 is for an individual customer, you enter his or her name and address in the A/C field. At the bottom of the receipt, the Print tab takes you to a further menu where you have the option to print or e-mail the receipt. You can print the receipt and give it to the customer or, for a phone or Internet order, e-mail it to the customer. Using this option, payment can be made by any method such as cheque, electronic payment, or credit or debit card. (For an additional fee, Sage Line 50 allows you to process credit card receipts.)

If your business accepts credit cards, expect sales revenue to be reduced by the fees paid to credit card companies. Usually, you face monthly fees as well as fees per transaction; however, each business sets up individual arrangements with its bank regarding these fees. Sales volume impacts how much you pay in fees, so when researching bank services, ensure that you compare credit card transaction fees to find a good deal.

Selling on Credit

Many businesses decide to sell to customers on credit, meaning credit the business offers and not through a bank or credit card provider. This approach offers more flexibility in the type of terms you can offer your customers, and you don't have to pay bank fees. However, credit involves more work for you, the bookkeeper, and the risk of a customer not paying what he or she owes.

When you accept a customer's bank-issued credit card for a sale and the customer doesn't pay the bill, you get your money; the bank is responsible for collecting from the customer, taking the loss if he or she doesn't pay. This doesn't apply when you decide to offer credit to your customers directly. If a customer doesn't pay, your business takes the loss.

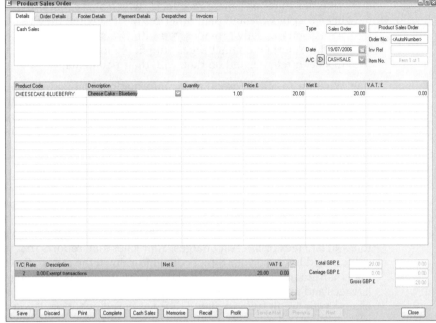

Figure 3-2:
Example of
a sales
receipt
in Sage
Line 50.

Deciding whether to offer credit

The decision to set up your own credit system depends on what your competition is doing. For example, if you run an office supply store and all other office supply stores allow credit to make it easier for their customers to get supplies, you probably need to offer credit to stay competitive.

You need to set up some ground rules when you want to allow your customers to buy on credit. For personal customers you have to decide

- ✔ How to check a customer's credit history
- ✔ What the customer's income level needs to be for credit to be approved
- ✔ How long to give the customer to pay the bill before charging interest or late fees

If you want to allow your trade or business customers to buy on credit, you need to set ground rules for them as well. The decisions you need to make include

- ✔ Whether to deal only with established businesses. You may set an outer limit to businesses that have been trading for at least two years.

Book IV

**Keeping
Business
Ticking
Over**

✔ Whether to require *trade references,* which show that the business has been responsible and paid other businesses when they've taken credit. A customer usually provides you with two suppliers that offered them credit. You then contact those suppliers directly to see if the customer has been reliable and on time with their payments.

✔ Whether to obtain credit rating information. You may decide to use a third party credit checking agency to provide a credit report on the business applying for credit. This report suggests a maximum credit limit and whether the business pays on time. Of course a fee is charged for this service, but using it may help you avoid making a terrible mistake. A similar service is available for individuals.

The harder you make getting credit and the stricter you make the bill-paying rules, the less chance you have of a taking a loss. However, you may lose customers to a competitor with lighter credit rules. For example, you may require a minimum income level of £50,000 and make customers pay in 30 days to avoid late fees or interest charges. Your sales staff reports that these rules are too rigid because your direct competitor down the street allows credit on a minimum income level of £30,000 and gives customers 60 days to pay before late fees and interest charges. Now you have to decide whether you want to change your credit rules to match those of the competition. If you do lower your credit standards to match your competitor, however, you may end up with more customers who can't pay on time (or at all) because you've qualified customers for credit at lower income levels and given them more time to pay. If you do loosen your qualification criteria and bill-paying requirements, monitor your customer accounts carefully to ensure that they're not falling behind.

The key risk you face is selling products for which you're never paid. For example, if you allow customers 30 days to pay and cut them off from buying goods when their accounts fall more than 30 days behind, the most you can lose is the amount purchased over a two-month period (60 days). But if you give customers more leniency, allowing them 60 days to pay and cutting them off after payment is 30 days late, you're faced with three months (90 days) of purchases for which you may never be paid.

Recording credit sales in the books

When sales are made on credit, you have to enter specific information into the accounting system. In addition to inputting information regarding cash receipts (see 'Collecting on Cash Sales', earlier in this chapter), you update the customer accounts to make sure that each customer is billed and the money is collected. You debit the Accounts Receivable account, an Asset account shown on the balance sheet, which shows money due from customers.

Here's how a journal entry of a sale made on credit looks:

	Debit	**Credit**
Accounts Receivable	£80.00	
Sales		£80.00

Cash receipts for 25 April 2006

In addition to making this journal entry, you enter the information into the customer's account so that accurate statements can be sent out at the end of the month. When the customer pays the bill, you update the individual customer's record to show that payment has been received and enter the following into the bookkeeping records:

	Debit	**Credit**
Accounts Receivable	£80.00	
Sales		£80.00

Payment from Mrs Jolly on invoice 5

If you're using Sage Line 50, you enter purchases on credit using an invoice form like the one in Figure 3-3. Most of the information on the invoice form is similar to the sales receipt form (see 'Collecting on Cash Sales', earlier in this chapter), but the invoice form also has space to enter a different address for shipping (the Delivery Address field) and includes payment terms (the Settlement Terms field).

Sage Line 50 uses the information on the invoice form to update the following accounts:

- ✔ Accounts Receivable
- ✔ Stock
- ✔ Customer's account
- ✔ Value Added Tax account

Based on this data, when the time comes to bill the customer at the end of the month, with a little prompting from you, Sage Line 50 generates statements for all customers with outstanding invoices. You can easily generate statements for specific customers or all customers on the books. Figure 3-4 shows a statement for Mrs Jolly.

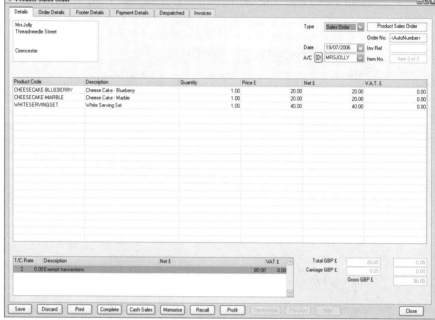

Figure 3-3:
Sage Line
50 sales
invoice for
purchases
made on
credit.

When you receive payment from a customer, here's what happens:

1. **You enter the customer's name on the customer receipts form (shown in Figure 3-5).**

2. **Sage Line 50 automatically lists all outstanding invoices.**

3. **You enter how much the customer is paying in total.**

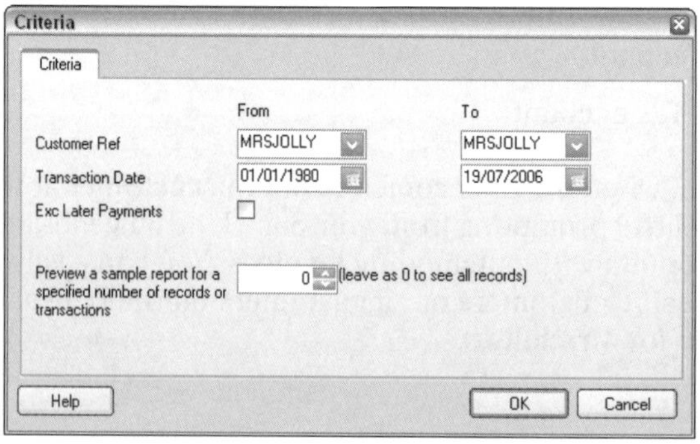

Figure 3-4:
Generating
state-
ments for
customers
using Sage
Line 50.

4. **You select the invoice or invoices paid.**

5. **Sage Line 50 updates the Accounts Receivable account, the Cash account, and the customer's individual account to show that payment has been received.**

If your customer is paying a lot of outstanding invoices, Sage Line 50 has two very clever options that may save you some time. The first option, Pay in Full, marks every invoice as paid if the customer is settling up in full. The other option, Wizard, matches the payment to the outstanding invoices by starting with the oldest until it matches up the exact amount of the payment.

If your business uses a point of sale program integrated into the computerised accounting system, recording credit transactions is even easier for you. Sales details feed into the system as each sale is made, so you don't have to enter the detail at the end of day. These point of sale programs save a lot of time, but they can get very expensive.

Even if customers don't buy on credit, point of sale programs provide businesses with an incredible amount of information about their customers and what they like to buy. This data can be used in the future for direct marketing and special sales to increase the likelihood of return business.

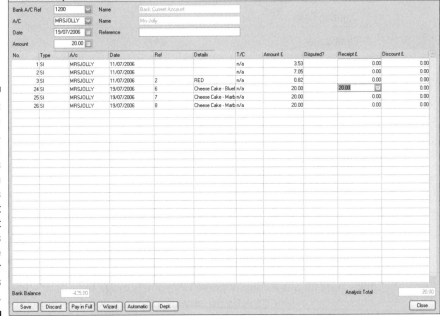

Figure 3-5:
In Sage Line 50, recording payments from customers who bought on credit starts with the customer receipts form.

Book IV

Keeping
Business
Ticking
Over

Cashing Up the Cash Register

To ensure that cashiers don't pocket a business's cash, at the end of each day, cashiers must *cash up* (show that they have the right amount of cash in the register based on the sales transactions during the day) the amount of cash, cheques, and credit sales they took in during the day.

This process of cashing up a cash register actually starts at the end of the previous day, when cashier John Smith and his manager agree on the amount of cash left in John's register drawer. Cash sitting in cash registers or cash drawers is recorded as part of the Cash on Hand account.

When John comes to work the next morning, he starts out with the amount of cash left in the drawer. At the end of the business day, he or his manager runs a summary of activity on the cash register for the day to produce a report of the total sales taken in by the cashier. John counts the amount of cash in his register as well as totals for the cheques, credit card receipts, and credit account sales. He then completes a cash-out form that looks something like this:

Cash Register: John Smith	**25/4/2006**	
Receipts	*Sales*	*Total*
Opening Cash	£100	
Cash Sales	£400	
Credit Card Sales	£800	
Credit Account Sales	£200	
Total Sales		£1,400
Sales on Credit		£1,000
Cash Received		£400
Total Cash in Register		£500

A manager reviews John Smith's cash register summary (produced by the actual register) and compares it to the cash-out form. If John's ending cash (the amount of cash remaining in the register) doesn't match the cash-out form, he and the manager try to pinpoint the mistake. If they can't find a mistake, they fill out a cash-overage or cash-shortage form. Some businesses charge the cashier directly for any shortages, whereas others take the position that the cashier's fired after a certain number of shortages of a certain amount (say, three shortages of more than £10).

The manager decides how much cash to leave in the cash drawer or register for the next day and deposits the remainder. She carries out this task for each of her cashiers and then deposits all the cash and cheques from the day in a night deposit box at the bank. She sends a report with details of the deposit to the bookkeeper so that the data appears in the accounting system. The bookkeeper enters the data on the Sales Receipts form (refer to Figure 3-2) if a computerised accounting system is being used, or into the Cash Receipts journal if the books are being kept manually.

Monitoring Sales Discounts

Most business offer discounts at some point in time to generate more sales. Discounts are usually in the form of a sale with 10 per cent, 20 per cent, or even more off purchases.

When you offer discounts to customers, monitor your sales discounts in a separate account so you can keep an eye on how much you discount sales in each month. If you find you're losing more and more money to discounting, look closely at your pricing structure and competition to find out why you're having to lower your prices frequently to make sales. You can monitor discount information very easily by using the data found on a standard sales register receipt. Figure 3-6 shows a bakery receipt that includes sales discount details.

Sales Receipt
25/4/2005
VAT No.:

Ashcroft Bakery
Clegg Street
Cardiff

Item	Qty.	Price	Total
White Serving Set	1	£40 —	£40 —
Cheesecake, Marble	1	£20 —	£20 —
Cheesecake, Blueberry	1	£20 —	£20 —
			£80 —
Sales Discount @ 10%		(8.00) —	
			£72 —
Cash Paid		£80 —	
Change		£8 —	

Figure 3-6: A sales receipt from Ashcroft Bakery showing sales discount.

From this example, you can see clearly that the business takes in less cash when discounts are offered. When recording the sale in the Cash Receipts journal, you record the discount as a debit. This debit increases the Sales Discount account, which is subtracted from the Sales account to calculate the Net Sales. Here's what the bakery's entry for this particular sale looks like in the Cash Receipts journal:

	Debit	*Credit*
Bank Account	£72.00	
Sales Discounts	£8.00	
Sales		£80.00

Cash receipts for 25 April 2006

If you use a computerised accounting system, add the sales discount as a line item on the sales receipt or invoice, and the system automatically adjusts the sales figures and updates your Sales Discount account.

Recording Sales Returns and Allowances

Most businesses deal with *sales returns* on a regular basis. Customers regularly return purchased items because the item is defective, they change their minds, or for any other reason. Instituting a no-return policy is guaranteed to produce very unhappy customers: Ensure that you allow sales returns to maintain good customer relations.

Accepting sales returns can be a complicated process. Usually, a business posts a set of rules for returns that may include:

- Returns allowed only within 30 days of purchase.
- You must have a receipt to return an item.
- When you return an item without a receipt, you can receive only a credit note.

You can set up whatever rules you want for returns. For internal control purposes, the key to returns is monitoring how your staff handles them. In most cases, ensure that a manager's approval is required on returns. Also, make sure that your staff pays close attention to how the customer originally paid for the item being returned. You certainly don't want to give a customer cash when they took credit – you're just handing over your money! After a return's approved, the cashier returns the amount paid by cash or credit card. Customers who bought the items on credit don't get any money back, because they didn't pay anything but expected to be billed later. Instead, a form is filled out so that the amount of the original purchase can be subtracted from the customer's credit account.

Sales allowances (sales incentive programmes) are becoming more popular with businesses. Sales allowances are most often in the form of a gift card. A sold gift card is actually a liability for the business because the business has received cash, but no merchandise has gone out. For that reason, gift card sales are entered in a Gift Card Liability account. When a customer makes a purchase at a later date using the gift card, the Gift Card Liability account is reduced by the purchase amount. Monitoring the Gift Card Liability account allows businesses to keep track of how much is yet to be sold without receiving additional cash.

You use the information collected by the cashier who handled the return to input the sales return data into the books. For example, a customer returns a £40 item that was purchased with cash. You record the cash refund in the Cash Receipts Journal like this:

	Debit	Credit
Sales Returns and Allowances	£40.00	
Value Added Tax @ 17.5%	£7.00	
Bank Account		£47.00

To record return of purchase, 30/4/2006

If the item was bought with a discount, you list the discount as well and adjust the price to show that discount.

In this journal entry:

- ✔ The Sales Returns and Allowances account increases. This account normally carries a debit balance and is subtracted from Sales when preparing the profit and loss statement, thereby reducing revenue received from customers.

- ✔ The debit to the Value Added Tax account reduces the amount in that account because Value Added Tax is no longer due on the purchase.

- ✔ The credit to the Bank Account reduces the amount of cash in that account.

Monitoring Accounts Receivable

Making sure that customers pay their bills is a crucial responsibility of the bookkeeper. Before sending out the monthly bills, prepare an *Aged Debtor Report* that lists all customers who owe money to the business and the age of each debt. If you keep the books manually, you collect the necessary information from each customer account. If you keep the books in a computerised accounting system, you can generate this report automatically. Either way, your Aged Debtor Report looks similar to this example report from a bakery:

Aged Debtor Report – as of 1 May 2006				
Customer	*Current*	*31– 60 Days*	*61–90 Days*	*>90 Days*
S. Smith	£84.32	£46.15		
J. Smith			£65.78	
H. Harris	£89.54			
M. Man				£125.35
Totals	**£173.86**	**£46.15**	**£65.78**	**£125.35**

The Aged Debtor Report quickly tells you which customers are behind in their bills. In this example, customers are put on stop when their payments are more than 60 days late, so J. Smith and M. Man aren't able to buy on credit until their bills are paid in full.

Give a copy of your Aged Debtor Report to the sales manager so he or she can alert staff to problem customers. The sale manager can also arrange for the appropriate collections procedures. Each business sets up its own specific collections process, usually starting with a phone call, followed by letters, and possibly legal action, if necessary.

Accepting Your Losses

You may encounter a situation in which a customer never pays your business, even after an aggressive collections process. In this case, you have no choice but to write off the purchase as a *bad debt* and accept the loss.

Most businesses review their Aged Debtor Reports every 6 to 12 months and decide which accounts need to be written off as bad debt. Accounts written off are recorded in a Nominal Ledger account called *Bad Debt.* The Bad Debt account appears as an Expense account on the profit and loss statement. When you write off a customer's account as bad debt, the Bad Debt account increases, and the Accounts Receivable account decreases.

To give you an idea of how you write off an account, assume that one of your customers never pays £105.75 due. Here's what your journal entry looks like for this debt:

	Debit	*Credit*
Bad Debt	£105.75	
Accounts Receivable		£105.75

In a computerised accounting system, you enter the information using a customer payment form and allocate the amount due to the Bad Debt Expense account.

If the bad debt included Value Added Tax (VAT), you have suffered a double loss because you've paid over the VAT to HM Revenue & Customs, even though you never received it. Fortunately, you can reclaim this VAT when you do your next VAT return.

Book IV

Keeping Business Ticking Over

Chapter 4

Monitoring and Improving Your Business

In This Chapter
▶ Obtaining a better Web address for your online shop
▶ Upgrading your Web server to handle more traffic
▶ Reorganising your e-commerce site to improve usability
▶ Managing your sales stock: Sourcing, replenishing inventory, and fulfilling orders

*O*ne of the many advantages of doing business online is the ease with which you can shift your shop's focus. With a bricks-and-mortar outlet, changing the business's name, address, or physical appearance can be labour-intensive and expensive. On the Web, however, you can rebuild your shop's *front door* (your home page) in a matter of minutes, while, in theory, you can revamp your sales catalogue in under an hour.

Because it's relatively easy to make changes to your Web site, you have no excuse for not making regular improvements and updates to what you're offering. Giving the shop an overhaul doesn't just mean changing the colours or the layout on your Web site, which is the part of your operation that customers notice. It also means jazzing up back-office functions that customers don't see, such as inventory management, invoices, labels, packing, and shipping. This chapter examines different ways to test, check, and revise your Web site based on its current performance so that you can boost your revenue and increase sales as well as make your Web site more usable.

Bolstering Your Infrastructure

Every business has its foundations – some elements that give it a presence in the marketplace or in the place where it is physically located. For a traditional, bricks-and-mortar business, this foundation may be an address or phone number, or the building in which the merchandise is presented and the employees work. That's how the post office gets mail to the business, and how the customers find the stuff you want to sell.

For an online business, your infrastructure is made up of the domain name that forms your Web address, and the Web server that presents your Web site files – which, in turn, present the merchandise you have for sale. Your server makes your site available, and your URL gives your customers a way to find you: Together, they're the equivalent of your high street address and the physical space you rent. Over time, you may have to change your domain name – say, if customers complain that your site is too hard to find or your URL is too long. You may also need to find a new Web server in order to keep your business running efficiently if any of the following occur:

- ✔ Your pages slow down.
- ✔ Customers complain that your forms don't work.
- ✔ You run out of storage space on your server, and your host wants to charge you armfuls of cash for more space.

Other regular upgrades need to be made to your domain and/or your Web server, as described in the following sections.

Renewing your domain name

You have a choice of two different types of domain names: One that is relatively short (for example, mynewebusiness.co.uk) and one that is long-winded and difficult to recall off the top of your head (myinternetprovider.co.uk/ ~mynewebusiness). Even though the first type of domain name is obviously preferable, many individuals who are creating their first Web sites start with the longer one. They get a certain amount of Web server space along with their monthly access account from their Internet Service Provider. Their natural inclination is to use the directory space they're given (which has a long URL like the latter example) just to get the site started.

Does this sound like you? There's nothing wrong with doing things the easiest way possible when you're a beginner, but be aware that your businesses will evolve as it grows. Before long, you'll need to find a domain name that more accurately fits your business or is easier to remember.

Making your own name a domain

Even if you don't make it active right away, it's a good idea to lock up a name to give you the option of using it in the future. For example, creating a personal Web site may well still be on your to-do list. But, if your name is Joe Bloggs, you may want to purchase the domain name joebloggs.co.uk for future use. If you don't, you may eventually have to deal with cyber squatters – the scourge of domain name buyers.

Cyber squatters are businesses that make money by buying up lots of domain names, knowing that at some point in the future, someone will want the domain name enough to buy it at a premium price. If your ideal domain name is owned by a cyber squatter or by another business, you may have to come up with a variation on your original name. When Greg was looking for domain names, for example, he was unable to buy `Holden.com` because a car manufacturer in Australia was already using it. However, he was lucky enough to find `gregholden.com` and snapped it up straight away – even though, at the time, he didn't have a home page of his own. You should be doing the same for your own name or your business's name right now.

Deciding which top-level domain name to use

Where does a business like yours get the easy-to-remember addresses you need? You purchase them from one of the approved domain name registrars. A *registrar* is a business that has been designated as having the responsibility for keeping track of the names registered in one of the top-level domains. Originally, there were six domains, but as `.com`, `.co.uk`, and others became crowded, alternatives were eventually approved. The list of available domains is growing all the time, but the originals are still the most recognisable, so ideally you should try for a `.com`, `.co.uk`, `.net`, or `.info`. The total list of domains is bewildering, so we include a scaled down version in Table 4-1.

A *top-level domain* (TLD) is one of the primary categories into which addresses on the Internet are divided. It's the part of a domain name that comes after the dot, such as `com` in `.com`. A *domain name* includes the part that comes before the dot, such as `wiley` in `wiley.co.uk`. A fully qualified domain name includes the host name – for example, `www.wiley.com` or `infozoo.co.uk`.

Table 4-1	Top-Level Domain Names		
Domain Name	**Primary Use**	**In Original Six Domains?**	**Good for Online Businesses?**
`.biz`	Businesses	No	Yes
`.com`	Companies or individuals involved in commerce	Yes	Yes
`.co.uk`	Same as above, but for business located in the UK	No	Yes
`.gov.uk`	Government agencies	Yes	No

(continued)

Table 4-1 *(continued)*

Domain Name	Primary Use	In Original Six Domains?	Good for Online Businesses?
.info	Sites that provide information about you, your ideas, or your organisation	No	Yes
.name	Any individual	No	No
.net	Network providers	Yes	Potentially
.org	Not-for-profit organisations	Yes	No
.pro	Licensed professionals	No	Potentially

Some of the newer domain names, of course, haven't really taken off. They were created in order to provide alternatives for organisations that couldn't find names in the original domains. In reality, it has forced big companies and other organisations to keep buying up domain names to prevent others from trading on their good name.

A perfect example of why this is necessary occurred when Pricewaterhouse-Coopers, an accountancy firm, changed the name of its consulting arm to Monday. To spread the word, it bought the domain name www.introducing monday.com. It didn't buy the co.uk equivalent, however, which was promptly snapped up by a group of tricksters with too much time on their hands. They created a Web site mocking the new name, a fact which helped to destroy the rebrand.

Having said that, one or two of the newer domains have gathered popularity. In particular, the .info name has taken off. According to its registry service, Afilias (www.afilias.info), it is the sixth largest domain on the Internet, with around half a million sites. Because virtually every business needs to put information about itself online, the .info domain is a good alternative if your first-choice domains aren't available.

Certain domains are 'restricted' only to particular types of individuals or organisations. For example, .gov.uk is restricted to government-funded groups, while .org.uk is restricted to noncommercial organisations, such as lobbies, trade unions, and so on. In actual practice, businesses don't observe such restrictions very strictly. The .net domain, which was originally intended for network service providers such as ISPs and Web hosts, is commonly used by businesses that can't find their ideal name in the .com or .co.uk domains, for example. You aren't limited to one domain, either.

Registering domain names related to yours

Even if you already have a domain name, it makes sense to pay a nominal fee to lock up a related name. That way, other businesses or cyber squatters can't attempt to register a domain that's like yours and possibly steal some of your visits. For example, Dan owns www.infozoo.co.uk, but he doesn't own www.infozoo.com. To go about registering such a domain, follow these steps:

1. **Start up your Web browser and go to a recognised domain name provider, such as Nominet, Easyspace, Ukreg, or 123-reg.**

   The home page for your choice opens.

2. **All domain name providers allow you to check whether your domain name is available, so type the name in the space provided and click Go.**

   In most cases, you see a screen saying 'Yes it's available' or 'No it's not'.

   If the domain name isn't available, the provider should offer alternative TLDs. If not, simply search again.

   If your domain is available, then snap it up as quickly as possible! Providers accept switch and credit cards, and domains vary in price from around £8 to around £25, depending on whether they're national (.co.uk) or international (.com).

Most organisations that sell domain names also offer servicing such as hosting and design. If you're just starting out and are keen to get going with your Web site then give it some thought, if not ignore these.

Nominet may be the best-known registrar, but it's not the least expensive. You'll save money by shopping around for domain name registrars. A simple search using the phrase 'domain names' can turn up hundred of options.

Finding a new Web server

You should always consider the option of finding a new Web host if you aren't happy with the one you have. Chances are you're on a server that shares space with lots of other individuals and Web sites. If some of the organisations that share space on your server start streaming audio or video or experience heavy traffic, the performance of your Web site will likely suffer. You may even experience Web site downtime, too. In either case, you should arrange with your hosting service to find a better Web server to house your site or find another host altogether.

One upgrade you may consider is renting a *dedicated computer* – a computer on which yours is the only Web site. This option is far more expensive than a shared hosting account, but after you've developed a customer base and have the resources, it may be worth it. Also consider the following factors that you may find with another host:

- ✔ **File transfer capability:** The amount of data, in gigabytes, megabytes, or kilobytes, of information that you're allowed to transfer each month before you're charged an additional fee. Successful e-commerce sites can quickly pile up thousands of page views per month, and if you go over your limit, you can get a shock when your bill arrives.

- ✔ **Marketing services:** Some Web hosting services help you advertise your online business. For example, Easyspace (www.easyspace.com) offers business directory listings and search engine optimisation to improve your business's marketing reach.

- ✔ **Technical support:** When you're just starting an online business, you'll probably have questions you just can't answer or problems you can't solve on your own. Therefore, you should choose a host that can provide you with round-the-clock tech support.

Another option you have open to you, if you have a broadband Internet connection (and you should!), is setting up your own Web server. This option gives you total control over the management of your Web site. That sounds really nice, but keep in mind that it also means that if something goes wrong, it's your responsibility to get things up and running again. If you're ambitious and technically able, you should consider the popular (not to mention free) Web server program Apache (www.apache.org).

Setting up and running a Web site in this way is not for beginners. If your kids unplug or crash the computer on which your Web site is running, your business goes offline, which can cost you money. If your computer runs slowly or doesn't have enough memory, your site's performance may suffer. It's generally best for beginners to leave the hosting to professionals. Web hosts have the ability to purchase and maintain the best hardware available and have technicians on call to solve problems round the clock. If you leave the hosting to someone else, you have more time to focus on essentials such as building inventory, maintaining the content on your site, and providing good customer service.

Performing Basic Web Housekeeping

To be better prepared to maintain and improve your Web site, you should visit it yourself on a regular basis. In fact, you should be the first one to view your pages when they go online; after that, you need to revisit as often as you can to make sure that your photos display correctly and that your links take you where you want them to go. Other helpful tips are described in the following sections.

All Web browsers are not created equally in the way that they handle colours, fonts, and other Web page elements. Be sure to visit your site by using different browsers in order to confirm that things work the way you want in all cases. At the very least, check your site with Microsoft Internet Explorer and Netscape Navigator; you may also want to use a popular alternative browser called Firefox (www.mozilla.com).

Making sure that your site is organised

One of the basic principles of e-commerce is that products must be easy to find. The way you organise your Web site defines whether customers find your products easily or get caught up in an impromptu game of hide and seek. The people who make a living writing about and designing Web sites call this *usability*. As long as the Web has existed, experts have been studying what makes a Web site usable. Most agree on the following essential characteristics:

- ✔ **Keep it logical.** Create an organised path through your site that leads to your shopping trolley and checkout area.

- ✔ **Keep it simple.** Each one of your Web pages should do one thing and one thing only.

- ✔ **Keep it searchable.** Shoppers who are in a hurry want to jump past all your sales categories, enter a product name in a search box, and go straight to a page of search results which satisfy their enquiry. Give them the chance to do it.

- ✔ **Keep it navigable.** The best Web sites offer plenty of points at which users can return to the home page, check out, or navigate back to a broad category.

You can add a search box to your site and have your pages indexed by a service such as FreeFind (www.freefind.com), which is free if you consent to display ads in your search results, or as little as £3 a month for ad-free results.

Make sure that your site has a logical page flow. How many Web pages do your customers have to click through before making their purchases? The general rule 'the fewer the better' applies. Your goal is to lead shoppers into your site and then encourage them to search through your sales catalogue.

Adding navigational links

Another reason to review your e-commerce Web site is to evaluate the number of navigational buttons or other links you give your visitors. The most common options are a row of buttons or links across the top of the page and a column along the left side of the page. These spots are the most obvious places to put such links, but by no means the only types of navigational aids you can add. Your goal should be to provide three types of links when the customer is viewing a sales item:

✔ Links that make it easy to 'back out' of the category the customer is in by following links to the previous level

✔ A link to your site's home page

✔ Links to other parts of your site so that the shopper doesn't need to return to the home page continually when they want to explore new parts of your site

Amazon.co.uk, shown in Figure 4-1, shows a range of useful links that appear on a catalogue page. Along the top, the shopper sees a row of buttons leading to different areas within the site; in the middle of the page, links appear to related items and to other categories within the site.

Figure 4-1: Highly visible links show the customer exactly what's on offer.

Ensuring that your site is searchable

The single most useful type of navigational aid is a *search box* – a text box into which visitors enter keywords to search your catalogue by product name or number. Here again, you have different options for adding such a box to your site:

- ✔ **The hard way:** You create a Web page with a text box. You write a script that will process the data submitted by visitors. The server that hosts your site needs to be able to process such scripts. Usually, this requirement means it has to have the programming language present.

   For example, if a script is written in the programming language Perl, the host needs to have Perl running on the server. Not all hosts allow the execution of scripts on their servers, however; check with yours to make sure.

- ✔ **The less hard way:** You create a Web page with a text box, but you borrow a script so that you don't have to write your own. You can use the popular Simple Search form at Matt's Script Archive (www.scriptarchive.com).

- ✔ **The Microsoft way:** Most Web hosts allow the use of a set of programs called the FrontPage Server Extensions. If you have FrontPage, you can use it to create your own searchable site index.

- ✔ **The easy way:** You sign up with a service that indexes your site – in other words, scours your Web pages and records their contents – and provides you with a search box that you can add to your site.

- ✔ **The alternative way:** You get your Web site designed and built for you by a professional company, at a cost. In your brief to them, you stipulate that you'd like users to search through your products. They'll do the rest for you.

Because the 'easy way' is the one that doesn't require any programming and is easiest for beginners, we describe it in more detail. Services that make other people's Web sites searchable usually provide two options. One is free, but the results that appear when someone searches your site have advertisements displayed as well. The other isn't free, but the search results *are* ad-free. These days, shoppers are so accustomed to seeing ads displayed all over the Web that they probably won't be put off if some appear in your search results. So we wouldn't be reluctant to choose the free search option if it is available.

Book IV

Keeping Business Ticking Over

Picosearch makes it easy to place a search box on a Web site, either on a free, ad-supported basis or on a monthly subscription basis. Go to the site's home page at www.picosearch.com and follow these steps to use the free service:

1. **Type your site's URL and your e-mail address in the boxes supplied, and click Submit.**

   The Site Search New Account Setup page appears.

2. **Type your name and a password in the boxes supplied.**

3. **Type the URLs for the pages you want to serve as entry points to your site.**

4. **Adjust the options for indexing and *spidering* (the amount of searching that can be done).**

   If you're in doubt about which options to choose, just leave the defaults for now; you can change them later.

5. **Scroll to the bottom of the New Account Setup page, select the check box that says you agree to the terms of the Picosearch licence, and click OK, Build My FREE Search Engine!**

   A page appears informing you that your Web site is being indexed. You'll also receive at least two e-mails from Picosearch. You need to click a link in the first e-mail in order to complete the registration for your free account. (The second tells you that your site is being indexed.) A third e-mail (which can take up to 24 hours to arrive) tells you the indexing is done.

6. **Click the link supplied in the first message from Picosearch; when the Select A Plan page appears, click Subscribe next to Free Plan.**

   A page appears informing you that your registration is complete and reminding you to view another e-mail message. This message instructs you on how to add the all-important search box to your Web page.

7. **Open the message and copy the code for your search box by dragging the mouse pointer across all the following and pressing Ctrl+C:**

   ```
   <!-- Begin Picosearch Code -->
   [code follows]
   <!-- End Picosearch Code -->
   ```

8. **Open the code for your Web page in a Web page editor or a text editor such as Notepad. Position the text cursor at the spot where you want the search box to appear and then press Ctrl+V to paste the copied code.**

   The text is added to your Web page code.

9. **Save your Web page code and upload the new Web page to your Web server.**

After you've uploaded your page, open it in your Web browser to view the box. Greg's Web site search box is shown in Figure 4-2.

Do a search on your page to see how the service works. As you can see from Figure 4-3, ads are included in a search of Greg's Web site. But because Greg searched for the term *eBay,* the ads are at least related to the topic – in other words, the ads are keyword-based.

Figure 4-2:
Free site
search
services
index your
Web site
contents
and provide
you with a
searchable
text box.

A search of your Web site is only as effective as the most recent index of your pages and their contents. If you revamp or improve your Web site (as you should periodically), you need to have your site re-indexed by your search service. Picosearch allows its customers to re-index their site manually at any time – in other words, you go to the Picosearch Web site and request that your site be re-indexed. But if you pay a monthly fee for Picosearch instead of using the free version, you can schedule automatic re-indexing so that you don't have to worry about requesting a new survey of your site on your own.

Whenever you sign up for 'free' services and submit an e-mail address, you are liable to receive unsolicited commercial e-mail (that is, *spam*) at that address. One solution is to not use your primary e-mail address for such registrations. Instead, set up an address specifically for this purpose and then cancel it when it becomes overrun by too much spam.

Taking your site for a test run

After you've enhanced your Web site with navigational aids, search boxes, and other changes, you need to visit it yourself to make sure that everything

Book IV

**Keeping
Business
Ticking
Over**

works the way you want. You not only need to make sure that your site creates a good visual impression, but also watch out for any problems you have to undo, such as:

- ✔ Background colours that are too similar to the colour of your body text and that make it hard to read

- ✔ Images that aren't cropped closely enough, which makes them bigger in file size than they need to be (which, in turn, makes them appear on screen too slowly)

- ✔ Pages that are overcrowded, with insufficient room between columns or between images and text

- ✔ Errors in spelling or grammar

- ✔ Type that's too small and can't be read easily by older viewers

- ✔ Copyright notices or 'This site was last updated on . . .' messages that are old and out of date

- ✔ Factual statements that are no longer accurate

It makes sense to perform such evaluations when you change your site. But you should test things whenever you move files from your computer to your Web server. In order to know how to best make improvements, it is important to continue to test and make evaluations.

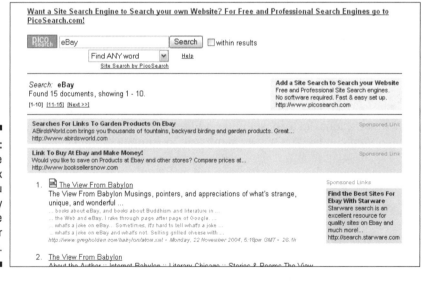

Figure 4-3:
A free search box requires you to display Google-type ads in your results.

If you want an entertaining rundown of bad Web design features to avoid on your own site, visit Web Pages That Suck (www.webpagesthatsuck.com). Author Vincent Flanders includes a feature called Mystery Meat Navigation that shows how *not* to guide visitors through your Web site.

Managing Goods and Services

Shoppers on the Web are continually in search of The New: the next new product, the latest price reduction, the latest must-know information and up-to-the-minute headlines. As a provider of content, whether in the form of words or images or products for sale, your job is to manage that content to keep it fresh and available. You also need to replenish stock as it's purchased, handle returns, and deal with shipping options.

Sourcing goods

Sourcing is a fancy term for buying items at a really low price so that you can sell them for a profit. For a small business just starting out on the Internet, sourcing isn't an easy prospect. Lots of online businesses advertise themselves as wholesale sellers. Many say they will *drop-ship* their merchandise – in other words, ship what's purchased directly from their wholesale facility so that you never actually have to handle them and may never see them.

Sound too good to be true? In some cases, it is, and you should always exercise a healthy dose of caution when you're looking for wholesale suppliers. The eBay sellers we've talked to who have faithful, reliable wholesalers guard the identities of those suppliers jealously. They usually find such suppliers only by word of mouth: Rather than answering an ad or visiting a Web site, they ask someone who knows someone who . . . you get the idea.

If you aren't in the business of selling goods or services that you manufacture yourself, you need to find a steady stream of merchandise that you can sell online. Your goal is to find a wholesaler who can supply you with good-quality items at rock-bottom prices; you can mark up the prices and make a profit while keeping the prices low enough to make them attractive. Generally, the best wholesale items are small objects that can be packed and shipped inexpensively. On eBay, things like cheap watches, t-shirts, jewellery, and other small gift items are commonly sold by PowerSellers, along with the occasional antique or collectible. Here are a few general rules for finding items you can sell:

> ✔ **Try them out yourself.** Purchase a few items yourself to start with or ask the wholesaler for samples. (Resist any attempts by the wholesaler to sell you, say 10,000 items at a supposedly dirt-cheap price straight off

the bat.) Take a few of the items for a test drive. It's easier to convince others to buy what you like yourself.

✔ **Try to sell many small, low-priced items rather than a few large ones.** Instead of computers or printers, consider selling computer memory chips or printer ink cartridges, for example.

✔ **Ask for references.** Talk to businesspeople who have already worked with the supplier. Ask how reliable the supplier is and whether the prices are prone to fluctuate.

When looking for merchandise to sell, try to build on your own hobbies and interests. If you collect model cars, try to develop a sideline selling parts, paints, and components online. You'll find the process more enjoyable when you're dealing in things you love and know well.

Handling returns

Your returns policy depends on the venue where you make your sales. If you sell primarily on eBay, you should accept returns, if only because many of the most experienced and successful sellers do, too. That doesn't mean you need to accept every single item that is returned. Most businesses place restrictions on when they will receive a return and send a refund. The items must be returned within 30 days; the packages must be unopened; the merchandise must not be damaged; and so on.

Adding shipping rates

As part of creating a usable e-commerce catalogue, you need to provide customers with shipping costs for your merchandise. Shipping rates can be difficult to calculate. They depend on your own geographic location as well as the location where you're planning to ship. If you are a small-scale operation and you process each transaction manually, you may want to ship everything a standard way (for example, via Royal Mail). Then you can keep a copy of your shipper's charges with you and calculate each package's shipping cost individually.

Maintaining inventory

Shoppers on the Web want things to happen instantly. If they discover that you've run out of an item they want, they're likely to switch to another online business instead of waiting for you to restock your shop. With that in mind, obey the basic principle of planning to be successful: Instead of ordering the bare minimum of this or that item, make sure that you have enough to spare. In other words, too much inventory initially is better than running out early.

Rely on software or management services to help you keep track of what you have. If you feel at ease working with databases, record your initial inventory in an Excel spreadsheet from Microsoft. This step forces you to record each sale manually in the database so that you know how many items are left. You can connect your sales catalogue to your database by using a program such as ColdFusion from Macromedia. Such a program can update the database on the fly as sales are made. But you may need to hire someone with Web programming experience to set the system up for you and make sure it actually works.

If you sign up with a sales management provider like Marketworks (`www.market works.com/uk`), inventory is tracked for you automatically. Marketworks is popular with eBay.co.uk auction sellers, but there's no reason why you can't establish an account with back-end functions such as payment, invoices, and inventory management for any online business. Whether you do the work yourself or hire an outside service, you have to be able to answer basic questions such as

- **When should you reorder?** Points in your business cycle at which you automatically reorder supplies (when you get down to two or three items left, for example).

- **How many do you have in stock right now?** You need to forecast not only for everyday demand but also in case a product gets hot or the holiday season brings about a dramatic increase in orders. Know when stuff will be in demand (sunglasses in summer, for example) and buy accordingly.

An e-commerce hosting service may also be able to help you with questions that go beyond the basics, such as the past purchasing history of customers. Knowing what customers have purchased in the past means you can suggest additional items your customers may want. But in the early stages, make sure that you have a small cushion of additional inventory – you don't want demand to outstrip supply early on – that may dent your reputation just when you're trying to establish a good one!

Book IV

Keeping Business Ticking Over

Chapter 5

Making It All Legal

● ●

In This Chapter

▶ Using trademarks to protect your company's identity

▶ Paying licence fees

▶ Avoiding copyright infringement

▶ Deciding whether to incorporate

▶ Keeping on the right side of the law

● ●

*A*s the field of e-commerce becomes more competitive, e-patents, e-trade-marks, and other means of legal protection multiply correspondingly. The courts are increasingly being called upon to resolve smaller e-squabbles and, literally, lay down the e-law.

For example, when Google purchased the video-sharing Web site YouTube for $1.65 billion, it was forced to pull large numbers of video files from its archive. Why? Because users were uploading all sorts of copyrighted material that they had no licence to broadcast. Now, some commentators think that YouTube is less valuable, because, for example, you can no longer get sneak previews of up-and-coming films unless it has been okayed by the film companies themselves.

In an earlier example, in April 2002, the popular search service Overture sued another popular search service, Google, for allegedly stealing its patented system of presenting search results based on bids placed by advertisers and Web sites.

In 2003, the US WIPO Arbitration and Mediation Center was confronted with 1,100 domain name disputes – an average of 3 per day. Many of these were filed by large corporations seeking to gain control over domain names that were allegedly being held by small business cybersquatters. In summer 2004, Microsoft settled a lawsuit it had filed in US district court by paying $20 million to stop a company called Lindows.com from infringing on its trademarked name Windows.

As a new business owner, you need to remember that ignorance is not an excuse. This area may well make you nervous because you lack experience in business law and you don't have lots of money with which to hire lawyers and accountants. You don't want to be discovering for the first time about copyright or the concept of intellectual property when you're in the midst of a dispute. In this chapter, we give you a snapshot of legal issues that you can't afford to ignore. Hopefully, this information can help you head off trouble before it occurs.

Thinking about Trade Names and Trademarks

A *trade name* is the name by which a business is known in the marketplace. A trade name can also be *trademarked,* which means that a business has taken the extra step of registering its trade name so that others can't use it. At the same time, it's important to realise that a trade name can be a trademark even though it hasn't been registered as such. Specifically, a trademark is a word, phrase, symbol, or design that identifies and distinguishes the source of your goods or services. Big corporations protect their trade names and trademarks jealously, and sometimes court battles erupt over who can legally use a name.

Although you're unlikely to ever get involved in a trademark battle yourself, and you may never trademark a name, you need to be careful which trade name you pick and how you use it. Choose a name that's easy to remember so that people can associate it with your company and return to you often when they're looking for the products or services that you provide. Also, as part of taking your new business seriously and planning for success, you may want to protect your right to use your name by registering the trademark, which is a relatively easy and inexpensive process.

Take the example of SoOrganic, a Web Site run by managing director Samantha Burlton, which sells organic and ethically sourced food, clothes, toys, and household products. Do a Google.co.uk search for her Web site, and you'll see her described as the 'real' SoOrganic. Why? Because Sainsbury's supermarket chain has launched a line of organic foods by the same name. They currently sit No. 1 and 2 on the Google search ranking, so you can see why some conflict may occur!

You can trademark any visual element that accompanies a particular tangible product or line of goods, which serves to identify and distinguish it from products sold by other sources. In other words, a trademark is not necessarily just for your business's trade name. In fact, you can trademark letters, words, names, phrases, slogans, numbers, colours, symbols, designs, or shapes. For example, take a look at the cover of the book you're reading right now. Look closely and see how many (tm) or ® symbols you see. The same trademarked items are shown at the Dummies Web site, as you can see in Figure 5-1. Even though the *For Dummies* heading doesn't bear a symbol, it's a trademark – believe us.

For most small businesses, the problem with trademarks is not so much protecting your own as it is stepping on someone else's. Research the name you want to use to make sure that you don't run into trouble. A good place to start is by checking out Companies House's Web site (`www.companieshouse.co.uk`), which is the definite list of businesses operating (and recently folded) in the UK. It'll tell you what company names are currently taken, and which you can use – you can also register your own business name through the site, at a cost of £20.

Determining whether a trademark is up for grabs

To avoid getting sued for trademark infringement and having to change your trade name or even pay damages if you lose, you should conduct a trademark search before you settle on a trade name. The goal of a trademark search is to discover any potential conflicts between your trade name and someone else's. Ideally, you conduct the search before you actually use your trade name or register for an official trademark.

Figure 5-1:
You don't have to use special symbols to designate logos or phrases on your Web site, but you may want to.

We spoke to David Adler of the law firm David M. Adler, Esq. & Associates (www.ecommerceattorney.com). Based in Chicago, in the United States, Adler knows a thing or two about copyright law. (Far more cases of infringement are contested in the United States every year than in the UK.) He says, 'If you don't have a registered trademark, your trade name becomes very difficult to protect. It's a good idea to do a basic search on the Internet. But keep in mind that just because you don't find a name on the Internet doesn't mean it doesn't exist. Follow that up with a trademark search. You don't want to spend all the money required to develop a brand name only to find that it isn't yours.'

Far and away the best method of searching for patent information is to do a search online, or simply call or write to the Patent Office (www.patent.gov.uk). The Patent Office has all the information you could possibly need about how to avoid infringing other people's copyrighted material and how to protect your own. You can also check out one of the helpful online business magazines, such as www.realbusiness.co.uk or www.startups.co.uk, for more information and examples of how people and businesses have protected themselves in practice.

Cyberspace goes beyond national boundaries. A trademark search in your own country may not be enough. Most industrialised countries, including the United Kingdom, have signed international treaties that enable trademark owners in one country to enforce their rights against infringement by individuals in another country. Conducting an international trademark search is difficult to do yourself, so you may want to pay someone do the searching for you.

The consequences of failing to conduct a reasonably thorough trademark search can be severe. In part, the consequences depend on how widely you distribute the protected item – and on the Internet, you can distribute it worldwide. If you attempt to use a trademark that has been registered by someone else, you could go to court and be prevented from using the trademark again. You may even be liable for damages and solicitor's fees. So it's best to be careful.

Protecting your trade name

The legal standard is that you get the rights to your trade name when you begin using it. You get the right to exclude others from using it when you register your trademark with the Patent Office. But when you apply to register a trademark, you record the date of its first use. Effectively, then, the day you start using a name is when you actually obtain the rights to use it for trade.

After researching your trade name against existing trademarks, you can file an application with the Patent and Trademark Office online by following these steps:

1. **Connect to the Net, start up your browser, and go to the Patent Office home page (**www.patent.gov.uk**), shown in Figure 5-2.**

2. **Click on Trade marks and then, on the Trade marks page, click the link entitled How To Apply.**

   Read this section thoroughly; it gives you all your options when applying for protection.

3. **If you think applying online is the best way forward, click Making Your Application Online.**

   Again read this section thoroughly; it tells you how to avoid making mistakes that may delay your application.

4. **At the bottom of the page click the link Electronic Trade Mark Application Form.**

   Fill the form in as prompted and click the Send button. If you need any further guidance, simply scroll to the bottom of the page and click the Help Filling In This Form link.

Figure 5-2:
You can quickly apply for your own registered trademark online by using this site.

Book IV

Keeping
Business
Ticking
Over

Be prepared for a lengthy approval process after you file your application. Trademark registration can take months, and it's not uncommon to have an application returned. Sometimes, an applicant receives a correspondence that either rejects part of the application or raises a question about it. If you receive such a letter, don't panic. You need to go to a lawyer who specialises in or is familiar with trademark law and who can help you respond to the correspondence. In the meantime, you can still operate your business with your trade name.

Costs vary (from £50 to £200) depending on what *class* of trademark you want to apply for. It's too complicated to go into here – but you can get all the information you need by logging on to www.patent.gov.uk, clicking Trade Marks, and checking out the Costs and Timeline section.

Trademarks are listed in a searchable register called GB esp@cenet (accessible through www.patent.gov.uk), last for ten years, and are renewable. You don't have to use the (tm) or ® symbol when you publish your trademark, but doing so impresses upon people how seriously you take your business and its identity.

Ensuring that your domain name stays yours

The practice of choosing a domain name for an online business is related to the concept of trade names and trademarks. By now, with cybersquatters and other businesspeople snapping up domain names since 1994 or so, it's unlikely that your ideal name is available in the popular .com or .co.uk domain. It's also likely that another business has a domain name very similar to yours or to the name of your business. There are two common problems:

✔ Someone else has already taken the domain name related to the name of your existing business.

✔ The domain name you choose is close to one that already exists or to another company with a similar name. (Check out the Microsoft Windows/Lindows.com dispute detailed at the beginning of this chapter.)

If the domain name that you think is perfect for your online business is already taken, you have options. You can contact the owner of the domain name and offer to buy it. Alternatively, you can choose a domain name with another suffix. If a .com name isn't available, try the old standby alternatives, .co.uk (which, in theory at least, is for nonprofit organisations) and .net (which is for network providers).

You can also choose one of the new Top-Level Domains (TLDs), a new set of domain name suffixes that have been made available, which include the following:

- ✔ `.biz` for businesses
- ✔ `.info` for 'information' or general use
- ✔ `.name` for personal names
- ✔ `.tv` for Web site audio and video feeds
- ✔ `.eu` for Web sites aimed at European Union countries

You can find out more about the new TLDs at the nominet Web site (`www.nominet.org.uk`), the official register of UK Web domains, and in Chapter 4 of this Book.

You can always get around the fact that your perfect domain name isn't available by changing the name slightly. Rather than `treesurgeon.com`, you can choose `tree-surgeon.com` or `treesurgery.com`. But be careful, lest you violate someone else's trademark and get into a dispute with the holder of the other domain name.

Practising Safe Copyright

What's the difference between a trademark and a copyright? Trademarks are covered by trademark law and are distinctive words, symbols, slogans, or other things that serve to identify products or services in the marketplace. *Copyright,* on the other hand, refers to the creator's ownership of creative works, such as writing, art, software, video, or cinema (but not names, titles, or short phrases). Copyright also provides the owner with redress in case someone copies the works without the owner's permission. Copyright is a legal device that enables the creator of a work the right to control how the work is to be used.

Although copyright protects the way ideas, systems, and processes are embodied in the book, record, photo, or whatever, it doesn't protect the idea, system, or process itself. In other words, if William Shakespeare were writing Romeo and Juliet today, his exact words would be copyrighted, but the general ideas he expressed would not be.

Even if nobody ever called you a nerd, as a businessperson who produces goods and services of economic value, you may be the owner of intellectual property. *Intellectual property* refers to works of authorship as well as certain inventions. Because intellectual property may be owned, bought, and sold just like other types of property, it's important that you know something about the copyright laws governing intellectual property. Having this information maximises the value of your products and keeps you from throwing away potentially valuable assets or finding yourself at the wrong end of an expensive lawsuit.

Copyright you can count on

Everything you see on the Net is copyrighted, whether a copyright notice actually appears. Copyright exists from the moment a work is fixed in a tangible medium, including a Web page. For example, plenty of art is available for the taking on the Web, but look before you grab. Unless an image on the Web is specified as being copyright free, you'll be violating copyright law if you take it. HTML tags themselves aren't copyrighted, but the content of the HTML-formatted page is. General techniques for designing Web pages aren't copyrighted, but certain elements (such as logos) are.

Keep in mind that it's okay to use a work for criticism, comment, news reporting, teaching, scholarship, or research. That comes under the *fair use* limitation. (See the nearby sidebar 'Fair use . . . and how not to abuse it' for more information.) However, we still contend that it's best to get permission or cite your source in these cases, just to be safe.

Making copyright work for you

A copyright – which protects original works of authorship – costs nothing, applies automatically, and lasts more than 50 years. When you affix a copyright notice to your newsletter or Web site, you make your readers think twice about unauthorised copying and put them on notice that you take copyright seriously. Check out Dan's Web site at www.infozoo.co.uk and notice the copyright notice subtly included at the bottom of the every page.

Creating a good copyright notice

Even though any work you do is automatically protected by copyright, having some sort of notice expresses your copyright authority in a more official way. Copyright notices identify the author of a given work (such as writing or software) and then spell out the terms by which that author grants others the right (or the licence) to copy that work to their computer and read it (or use it). The usual copyright notice is pretty simple and takes this form:

```
Copyright 2007 [Your Name] All rights reserved
```

Fair use . . . and how not to abuse it

Copyright law doesn't cover everything. According to Business Link (`www.businesslink.gov.uk`), the government group that gives advice to businesses, you can make *limited use* of copyrighted material without the author's permission in the following circumstances:

✔ For use as teaching material

✔ For criticising and reviewing

✔ For news reporting

✔ When it applies to court proceedings

Fair use, as this is sometimes referred to as, has some big grey areas that can be traps for people who provide information on the Internet. Don't fall into one of these traps. Shooting off a quick e-mail asking someone for permission to reproduce his or her work isn't difficult. Chances are that person will be flattered and will let you make a copy as long as you give him or her credit on your site. Fair use is entirely dependent on the unique circumstances of each individual case, and this is an area where, if you have any questions, you should consult a solicitor.

You don't have to use the © symbol, but it does make your notice look more official. In order to create a copyright symbol that appears on a Web page, you have to enter a special series of characters in the HTML source code for your page. For example, Web browsers translate the characters `&copy;` as the copyright symbol, which is displayed as © in the Web browser window. Most Web page creation tools provide menu options for inserting special symbols such as this one.

Copyright notices can also be more informal, and a personal message can have extra impact. On its 100% Design conference Web site (`www.100percent design.co.uk`), Reed Exhibitions includes both the usual copyright notice plus a very detailed message about how others can use its design elements (`www.100percentdesign.co.uk/page.cfm/Link=2/t=m`).

Protecting with digital watermarks

In traditional offset printing, a *watermark* is a faint image embedded in stationery or other paper. The watermark usually bears the name of the paper manufacturer, but it can also identify an organisation for whom the stationery was made.

Watermarking has its equivalent in the online world. Graphic artists sometimes use a technique called *digital watermarking* to protect images they create. This process involves adding copyright or other information about the image's owner to the digital image file. The information added may or may not be visible. (Some images have copyright information added, not visible in the body of the Web page but in the image file itself.) Other images, such as the one shown in Figure 5-3, have a watermark pasted right into the visible area, which makes it difficult for others to copy and reuse them.

Digimarc (www.digimarc.com), which functions as a plug-in application with the popular graphics tools Adobe Photoshop (www.adobe.com) and Paint Shop Pro 7 (www.corel.com), is one of the most widely used watermarking tools.

Doing the paperwork on your copyright

There is no official copyright registrar in the UK, because copyright is automatic, but a number of unofficial companies will log your claim to a copyright for you. That step will help if you ever have the misfortune of falling into a dispute with another party, but you should think very carefully before handing over your hard-earned cash. You can guard copyrighted material for a much lower cost in several other ways.

The most common method is to send material to yourself via recorded delivery, and not open the package when you receive it. That gives a clear date before which the material must have been created. When it comes to digital information, designs, logos, and so on, you can protect your copyright by printing screen grabs of your work and following the process from there.

Figure 5-3: If your products are particularly precious, such as unique works of art, assert your copyright over them on your Web site.

Understanding Legal Basics

The UK prides itself on the ease with which you can start a business. If you know what you're doing, it can take just a couple of days compared to weeks and months elsewhere in the world. That's not to say you can just set up shop and start trading, however. To start with, restrictions regulate the selling of certain types of products, such as food and agricultural products, and your own software, as well as running businesses where you are responsible for the well-being of others (say, if you ran a paintball business, where you teach your customers how to use the guns, you oversee games, or where you may need to use basic first aid).

You must also register your business with Her Majesty's Revenue and Customs (HMRC), an organisation which takes a close interest in any money you make from the business. If your business is successful, you soon have to register for Value Added Tax (VAT). But even at the very beginning, you have to register yourself as self-employed for tax purposes – even if your business is part-time or you have a nine-to-five job, too. It means you have to start filling in your own self-assessment tax forms annually and must declare your earnings each year.

So, you need accounting software to keep track of your finances and a business bank account that is separate from your current account. These elements, along with any special qualifications you may require to start your business, are essential. They're as important as your product, promotional material, and informing the tax authorities; all are required before you start a business.

Business Link, part of the Department for Trade and Industry, is a service dedicated to helping businesses get off the ground. In our opinion, the best thing about Business Link is its Web site (www.businesslink.gov.uk), which has a huge budget and numerous staff dedicated to keeping track of the evolving rules and regulations about starting up, as well as a whole range of hints, tips, and straight-talking advice on how you can give yourself the best chance of success.

We can't cover every small legal detail applying to every type of business here, but the Business Link Web site does, plus it offers links to industry specific organisations that can help you further. Our advice is to read all the information relevant to you as thoroughly as possible and check out links to organisations that cover your sector well before you start your own business venture. Remember: Forewarned is forearmed!

Book IV

Keeping
Business
Ticking
Over

Your Business in the Eyes of the Law

It's true that no two businesses are alike, but you have the option of picking not only your product, marketing material, and Web design, but also the legal form that your business takes. You have a number of options from which to choose, and the choice can affect the amount of taxes you pay and your liability in case of loss. The following sections describe your alternatives.

If you're looking for more information, Colin Barrow explores the legal and financial aspects of launching and operating a small business in *Starting a Business For Dummies* and *Bookkeeping For Dummies* (both by Wiley).

Sole trader

If you're a *sole trader,* you're the only boss. You make all the decisions, and you get all the benefits. On the other hand, you take all the risk, too. This setup is the simplest and least expensive type of business because you can run it yourself. You don't need an accountant or lawyer to help you form the business, and you don't have to answer to partners or stockholders, either. To become a trader, you just have to declare yourself as such with Her Majesty's Revenue and Customs (www.hmrc.gov.uk).

Partnership

In a *partnership,* you share the risk and profit with at least one other person. Ideally, your partners bring skills to the endeavour that complement your own contributions. One obvious advantage to a partnership is that you can discuss decisions and problems with your partners. All partners are held personally liable for losses. The rate of taxes that each partner pays is based on his or her percentage of income from the partnership.

If you decide to strike up a partnership with someone, drawing up a *partnership agreement* is a good idea. Although you aren't legally required to do so, such an agreement clearly spells out the duration of the partnership and the responsibilities of each person involved. In the absence of such an agreement, the division of liabilities and assets is considered to be equal, regardless of how much more effort one person has put into the business than the other.

Statutory business entity

A *statutory business entity* is a business whose form is created by statute, such as a corporation or a limited liability company. If sole traders and partnerships are so simple to start up and operate, why would you consider incorporating? After all, you almost certainly need a lawyer to help you incorporate. Besides that, you may undergo a type of *double taxation:* If your corporation earns profits, those profits are taxed at the corporate rate, and any shareholders have to pay income tax, too.

Despite these downsides, you may want to consider incorporation for the following reasons:

- ✔ If you have employees, you can deduct any health and disability insurance premiums that you pay.
- ✔ You can raise money by offering stock for sale.
- ✔ Transferring ownership from one shareholder to another is easier.
- ✔ The company's principals are shielded from liability in case of lawsuits.

Limited company

The main difference between a limited liability company and a partnership is that the liabilities of the business are not passed on to the owners. You are only liable for any debt you incurred (say, if the founders jointly took out a loan), but you don't have liability for the company's taxes. Similarly to a partnership, some form of written agreement is essential here. Overseen by an impartial witness (preferably a lawyer), the operating agreement shows who holds what position in the business, what roles they perform, and how much of the business they own for tax purposes.

A limited liability company gets taxed twice, once for income and once for profits. The owners work out how much tax they have to pay and then submit a self-assessment form to HM Revenue & Customs.

Corporation

When you think of a corporation, your head may be filled with multibillion pound making entities like BP, Nike, and Coca-Cola. This is fair enough, but it doesn't reflect the whole picture. (For starters, only very few corporations make profits in the billions!) In terms of structure, all corporations are alike: They have their own names, bank accounts, and taxes to file. They are legal entities (much like people are) that are created for the sole purpose of doing business. Because of this legal status, they are the biggest and most complex form of business you will come across, and the vast majority of startups don't have to worry about becoming incorporated for some time yet (if at all).

Corporations pay corporation tax (duh!); how much you pay depends on

- ✔ How much profit you make
- ✔ Whether you keep that profit to yourself or invest it straight back into developing the business

Book IV

Keeping Business Ticking Over

Top whack corporation tax is 30 per cent of earnings, or *profits*. That applies to profits of more than £1.5 million (wowza!), but the government offers taper relief so that smaller profits are taxed proportionately. Corporation tax is precisely nought if you make less than ten grand and plough the whole lot into the business.

Because our venerable Chancellor keeps tinkering with the tax system, in order to close loopholes and get his hands on all your lovely wonga, there's an ongoing debate whether it's better to incorporate your business or not. The truth is, incorporation depends on your personal circumstances, type of business, profits, and plans for the future. Ask an accountant what he or she thinks before you take action. Try an online business forum, such as the one on RealBusiness.co.uk (www.realbusiness.co.uk), and see whether anyone's prepared to give you some free advice.

Keeping Out of Legal Trouble

A big part of keeping your online business legal is steering clear of so-called business opportunities that can turn into big problems. In the following list, we highlight some areas to watch out for.

- ✔ **Get it in writing!** Perhaps the most important way to avoid legal trouble is to get all your agreements in writing. (Notice how lawyers always do that?) Even if the parties involved type and sign a simple one-page sheet describing what is to be done and what is to be paid, that's far better than a verbal agreement. It's also better than an e-mail message – an e-mail doesn't enable signatures, and a single message doesn't clearly point out that both parties have actually agreed to something. A qualified lawyer can help you prepare contracts that you can send to both suppliers and customers who engage your services.

  The other important things to get in writing are *policy statements:* statements that spell out how a customer is to use your goods or services, or statements as to how you manage your customers' personal information. Such statements build trust among your clientele. But remember that when you publish a policy statement on your Web site, you need to actually follow what it prescribes; you can be sued if you violate it.

- ✔ **Ever thought of health and safety?** It may come as a surprise, but as soon as you set up and register your online business, you must create a safe and risk free environment for your employees (even if the only employee is you!). It sounds silly, but the Health & Safety Executive is taking no chances – it's ultimately responsible for the welfare of British workers and is charged with keeping accidents and illnesses down. Follow this link to the HSE Web site (`www.hse.gov.uk/businesses.htm`) for the lowdown on your responsibilities.

✓ **Remember the red tape or form-filing.** A lot is made in the UK about red tape (for example, the various regulations defining what you can and can't do). Businesspeople tell Dan that it's not the rules themselves, or even the taxes, that are the main problem; it's the reams of forms that you have to fill in to show you've complied. Take Dan's pals who run a husband-and-wife window-cleaning company, number of employees: two. They recently had to fill in a form describing the demographic makeup of their business. In other words they had to declare that their business was 50 per cent men (the husband) and 50 per cent female (the wife), that the business was exclusively made up of British people, and that all the staff were in their 40s.

Of course, in a business of two people, you'd be forgiven for employing only 40-something Brits, but that doesn't apply to larger businesses. You can scoff at these documents, but (unfortunately) you still have to fill them in and return them to the authorities.

✓ **Adult content is risky business.** Be careful if you provide so-called adult content. There's no doubt about it: Cyberspace is full of X-rated sites, many of which do make money. (Porn is one of the Net's most successful industries!) But this area is risky.

If you do sell adult items online, consider working with a blocking company, such as CyberPatrol (`www.cyberpatrol.com`) or Net Nanny (`www.netnanny.com/home/home.asp`), which can prevent minors from visiting your site. Always put up a front page warning users that entering the site will expose them to adult content, and in general do all you can to protect youngsters – you have been warned.

✓ **What you don't know about acceptable use policies can hurt you.** Be aware of acceptable use policies set up by agencies that control what goes out online. Usually, the company that hosts your Web site has a set of acceptable use guidelines spelling out what kind of material you can and can't publish. For example, AOL has its own policies for its members who create home pages using its platform.

Another important kind of acceptable use policy that you need to know about is the acceptable use policy issued by your Internet service provider. The most common restriction is one against *spamming* (sending unsolicited bulk mailings). Not following your Web host's or your ISP's guidelines can get you kicked off the Internet, so make sure that you're aware of any restrictions by reading the guidelines posted on your ISP's or Web host's site.

Book IV

**Keeping
Business
Ticking
Over**

Chapter 6

Online Business Accounting Tools

Some people have a gift for keeping track of expenses, recording financial information, and performing other fiscal functions. Unfortunately, we, and many of you, do not have these rare skills. Yet we know (and you should know) the value of accounting procedures, especially those that relate to an online business.

Without having at least some minimal records of your day-to-day operations, you won't have any way – other than the proverbial gut feeling – of knowing whether your business is truly successful. Besides that, banks and the taxman don't put much stock in gut feelings. When the time comes to ask for a loan or to pay taxes, you'll regret not having water-tight records close at hand.

In this chapter, we introduce you to simple, straightforward ways to handle your online business's financial information – and all businesspeople know that accurate record keeping is essential when revenues dwindle and expenses must be reduced. In this chapter, you discover the most important accounting practices and find out about software that can help you tackle the essential fiscal tasks that you need to undertake to keep your new business viable. (For more information on these topics, also see *Bookkeeping For Dummies,* Wiley.)

ABCs: Accounting Basics for Commerce

We can summarise the most important accounting practices for your online business as follows:

   ✔ **Deciding what type of business you're going to be:** Are you going to be a sole trader, partnership, limited business, or corporation? (See more about determining a legal form for your business in Chapter 5 in this Book.)

✔ **Establishing good record-keeping practices:** Record expenses and income in ways that will help you at tax time.

✔ **Obtaining financing when you need it:** Although getting started in business online doesn't cost a lot, you may want to expand someday, or borrow money to buy stock, and good accounting can help you do it.

There's nothing sexy about accounting (unless, of course, you're married to an accountant; in that case, you have a financial expert at hand and can skip this chapter anyway!). Then again, there's nothing enjoyable about unexpected cash shortages or other problems that can result from bad record keeping.

Good accounting is the key to order and good management for your business. How else can you know how you're doing? Yet many new businesspeople are intimidated by the numbers game. Use the tool at hand – your computer – to help you overcome your fear: Start keeping those books!

Choosing an accounting method

Accepting that you have to keep track of your business's accounting is only half the battle; next, you need to decide how to do it. The point at which you make note of each transaction in your books and the period of time over which you record the data make a difference not only to your accountant but also to agencies such as HM Revenue & Customs (HMRC). Even if you hire someone to keep the books for you, you need to know what options are open to you.

Consult the HMRC Web site (www.hmrc.gov.uk) and check out the section on Businesses & Corporations. It's got a whole host of information telling you how and when accounting procedures come into play. You may also want to check out the Chartered Institute of Taxation (www.tax.org.uk) or an accountancy firm like TaxAssist Accountants (www.taxassist.co.uk).

Cash-basis versus accrual-basis accounting

Don't be intimidated by the terms in this section: They're simply two methods of totalling up income and expenses. Exactly where and how you do the recording is up to you. You can take a piece of paper, divide it into two columns labelled *Income* and *Expenses,* and do it that way. (We describe some more high-tech tools later in this chapter.) These methods are just two standard ways of deciding when to report them:

✔ **Cash-basis accounting:** You report income when you actually receive it and write off expenses when you pay them. This is the easy way to report income and expenses, and probably the way most new small businesses do it.

✔ **Accrual-basis accounting:** This method is more complicated than the cash-basis method, but if your online business maintains an inventory, you must use the accrual method. You report income when you actually receive the payment; you write down expenses *when services are rendered* (even though you may not have made the cash payment yet). For example, if a payment is due on December 1, but you send the cheque out on December 8, you record the bill as being paid on December 1, when the payment was originally due.

Accrual-basis accounting creates a more accurate picture of a business's financial situation. If a business is experiencing cash flow problems and is extending payments on some of its bills, cash-basis accounting provides an unduly rosy financial picture, whereas the accrual-basis method would be more accurate.

Choosing an accounting period

The other choice you need to make when it comes to deciding how to keep your books is the accounting period you're going to use. Here, again, you have two choices:

✔ **Calendar year:** The calendar year ends on December 31. This is the period with which you're probably most familiar and the one most small or home-based businesses choose because it's the easiest to work with.

✔ **Fiscal year:** In this case, the business picks a date other than December 31 to function as the end of the fiscal year. Many large organisations pick a date that coincides with the end of their business cycle. Some pick March 31 as the end, others June 30, and still others September 30.

If you use the fiscal-year method of accounting, you must file your tax return three and a half months after the end of the fiscal year. If the fiscal year ends on June 30, for example, you must file by October 15.

Book IV

Keeping Business Ticking Over

Knowing what records to keep

When you run your own business, it pays to be meticulous about recording everything that pertains to your commercial activities. The more you understand what you have to record, the more accurate your records will be – and the more deductions you can take, too. Go to the office supply retailer and get a financial record book (or *journal*), which is set up with columns for income and expenses.

Tracking income

Receiving cheques, bank transfers, and credit-card payments for your goods or services is the fun part of doing business, and so income is probably the kind of data that you'll be happiest about recording.

You need to keep track of your company's income (or, as it is sometimes called, your *gross receipts*) carefully. Not all the income your business receives is taxable. What you receive as a result of sales (your *revenue*) is taxable, but loans that you receive aren't. Be sure to separate the two and pay tax only on the sales income. But keep good records: If you can't accurately report the source of income that you didn't pay taxes on, the HRMC will label it *unreported income,* and you'll have to pay taxes, and possibly fines, on it.

Just how should you record your revenue? For each item, write down a brief, informal statement. This statement is a personal record that you may make on a slip of paper or even on the back of a cancelled cheque. Be sure to include the following information:

- ✔ Amount received
- ✔ Type of payment (credit card, electronic cash, or cheque)
- ✔ Date of the transaction
- ✔ Name of client or customer
- ✔ Goods or services you provided in exchange for the payment

Collect all your cheque stubs and revenue statements in a folder labelled *Income* so that you can find them easily at tax time.

Assessing your assets

Assets are resources that your business owns, such as your office and computer equipment. *Equity* refers to your remaining assets after you pay your creditors.

Any equipment you have that contributes to your business activities constitutes your assets. Equipment that has a life span of more than a year is expected to help you generate income over its useful life; therefore, you must spread out (or, in other words, *expense*) the original cost of the equipment over its life span. Expensing the cost of an asset over the period of its useful life is called *depreciation.* In order to depreciate an item, you estimate how many years you're going to use it and then divide the original cost by the number of years. The result is the amount that you report in any given year. For example, if you purchase a computer that costs £900 and you expect to use it in your business for three years, you expense £300 of the cost each year.

You need to keep records of your assets that include the following information:

✔ Name, model number, and description

✔ Purchase date

✔ Purchase price, including fees

✔ Date the item went into service

✔ Amount of time the item is put to personal (as opposed to business) use

File these records in a safe location along with your other tax-related information.

Recording payments

Even a lone entrepreneur doesn't work in a vacuum. An online business owner needs to pay a Web host, an ISP, and possibly Web page designers and other consultants. If you take on partners or employees, things get more complicated. But in general, you need to record all payments in detail as well.

Your accountant is likely to bring up the question of how you pay the people who work for you. You have two options: You can treat them either as full- or part-time employees or as independent contractors. HMRC uses a stringent series of guidelines to determine who is a contractor and who is a full-time employee. Check out the following link, which describes the legal difference between contractors and employees: `www.yourpeoplemanager.com/YUgHntBoivVsHw.html`.

Hiring independent contractors rather than salaried workers is far simpler for you: You don't have to pay benefits to independent contractors, for one thing, plus you don't have to schedule their holidays, pension payments, or life insurance policies. Just be sure to get invoices from any independent contractor who works for you. If you have full-time employees whom you pay an hourly wage or annual salary, things get more complicated, and you had best consult an accountant to help you set up the salary payments.

Listing expenses

Get a big folder and use it to hold any receipts, contracts, cancelled cheques, credit-card statements, or invoices that represent expenses. It's also a great idea to maintain a record of expenses that includes the following information:

✔ Date the expense occurred

✔ Name of the person or company that received payment from you

✔ Type of expense incurred (equipment, utilities, supplies, and so on)

Recalling exactly what some receipts are for is often difficult a year or even just a month after the fact. Be sure to jot down a quick note on all cancelled cheques and copies of receipts to remind you of what the expense involved.

Understanding the Ps and Qs of P&Ls

You're likely to hear the term *profit-and-loss statement* (also called a P&L) thrown around when discussing your online business with financial people. A P&L is a report that measures the operation of a business over a given period of time, such as a week, a month, or a year. The person who prepares the P&L (either you or your accountant) adds up your business revenues and subtracts the operating expenses. What's left are either the profits or the losses.

Most of the accounting programs listed later in this chapter include some way of presenting profit and loss statements and enable you to customise the statements to fit your needs.

Accounting Software for Your Business

The well-known commercial accounting packages, such as Microsoft Money, QuickBooks, and Sage, let you prepare statements and reports and even tie into a tax preparation system. Stick with these programs if you like setting up systems such as databases on your computer. Otherwise, go for a simpler method and hire an accountant to help you.

Whatever program you choose, make sure that you're able to keep accurate books and set up privacy and backup schemes that prevent your kids from zapping your business records.

If your business is a relatively simple one – say, if you're a sole trader – you can record expenses and income on a spreadsheet or by hand and add them up at tax time. Then input them into a HMRC tax return. Alternatively, you can record your entries and turn them over to a tax advisor who can prepare a profit and loss statement and tell you the balance due on your tax payment.

If you're looking to save a few quid and want an extra-simple accounting program that you can set up right now, look no further than Microsoft's own Excel spreadsheet software, which comes with standard Microsoft Office package. It can help you tot up your earnings and deduct tax, but you'll need some practice to get it right.

Turbo Cash 7 (www.turbocashuk.com), is a step up from a spreadsheet, but so simple that even financially impaired people like us can pick it up quickly.

Turbo Cash is *open source* (meaning anyone can use it under the terms of the General Public Licence) and is designed to enable people with no prior accounting experience to keep track of income and expenses. Go to the Web site to see how it stands up against more established players like QuickBooks and Sage.

Another popular, basic, and cheap accounting tool is Owl Simple Business Accounting. The following steps illustrate how easy it is to start keeping books with SBA. These instructions assume that you have downloaded and installed the software from the Owl Software Web site (`www.owlsoftware.com/sba.htm`).

1. **Choose Start⇨All Programs⇨OWL Business Apps⇨SB Accounting 2.**

   The main Owl Simple Business Accounting window appears, as shown in Figure 6-1.

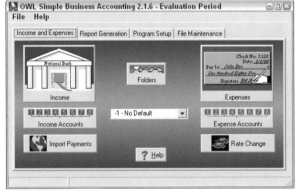

Figure 6-1: SBA uses folders to contain income and expense data that you report.

The program comes with a set of sample data already entered to help you get accustomed to its features. Choose Help⇨Help to open the SBA User's Guide help files. Click the topic Getting Started if you want an overview of how the program operates.

2. **Click the Program Setup tab to bring it to the front and than make any custom changes you may want:**

   • If you want to operate in a fiscal year different from the pre-entered January 1, enter the number for the new month that you want to set as the beginning of your fiscal year.

   • If you want your on-screen and printed reports to be in a different font than the pre-selected one (MS Sans Serif), click the Report Font button, choose the font you want, and then click OK to close the Font dialog box. Times New Roman is usually a good choice because it's relatively compact.

3. Click the File Maintenance tab to bring it to the front and then click the Erase Data button. When asked whether you want to erase expense data or other information, click OK.

This step erases the sample data that was pre-entered to show you how the program works.

4. Select the Income and Expenses tab to bring it to the front and then click the Folders button to create folders for your business data.

The PickFol dialog box appears, as shown in Figure 6-2. This dialog box lists any folders that have been created.

Figure 6-2:
Use this dialog box to add, delete, or edit folders that hold your business data.

5. Click New.

The Folder Definition dialog box appears.

6. Enter a new name in the Description box and click Save.

A Confirm dialog box appears, asking whether you want to add another folder.

7. If you do, click Yes and repeat Step 6; when you're done, click No.

The Folder Definition dialog box closes, and you return to the PickFol dialog box, where your renamed folder or folders appear.

You may want to create separate folders for your personal or business finances, for example. After your folders are set up, you can record data as the following steps describe.

8. Click Exit.

The PickFol dialog box closes and you return to the main OWL Simple Business Accounting window.

9. **Select the Income and Expenses tab to bring it to the front and then click either the Income Accounts or Expense Accounts button to create an Income or Expense Account.**

   The Select Account dialog box appears.

10. **Click New.**

    The Account Definition dialog box appears.

11. **Enter a name for the account in the Description dialog box and then click Save.**

    A dialog box appears, asking whether you want to create another account.

12. **If you do, click Yes and repeat Step 11; when you're done, click No.**

    The Select Account dialog box appears, listing the items you just created.

13. **Click Exit.**

    You return to the main OWL Simple Business Accounting window.

14. **When you've created Income and Expense Accounts, click either the Income button or the Expense button, depending on the type of data you want to enter.**

    Depending on the button you clicked, the Select Income or Select Expense dialog box appears.

15. **Click New to enter a new item.**

    A dialog box named either Income or Expense appears, depending on the button you selected in Step 14.

16. **Enter the amount and description in the appropriate fields and click Save.**

    The Confirm dialog box appears, asking you to confirm that you either want to add or delete a record.

17. **Click No.**

    You return to the Income or Expense dialog box, where you can make more entries.

18. **When you finish, click Save.**

    You return to the Select Item dialog box, where you can review your changes.

19. **Click Exit.**

    You return to the Income and Expenses options.

20. **When you're all finished, choose File⇨Exit to exit the program until your next accounting session.**

After entering some data, you can select the Report Generation tab, run each of the reports provided by SBA, and examine the output. When running the reports, be sure to select a reporting period within the current calendar year.

The Taxman Cometh: Concerns for Small Business

After you make it through the startup phase of your business, it's time to be concerned with taxes. Here, too, a little preparation up front can save you lots of headaches down the road. But as a hard-working entrepreneur, time is your biggest obstacle.

Successive surveys reveal that a large number of entrepreneurs leave filing their taxes until the last minute. A few return their tax returns late and incur fines from HM Revenue and Customs. Planning is really important for taxes. In fact, HMRC rules state that businesses must keep records appropriate to their trade or business for several years after the transactions are made. HMRC has the right to view these records if it wants to audit your business's (or your personal) tax return. If your records aren't to HMRC's satisfaction, the penalties can be serious.

Should you charge VAT?

Here's one of the most frequently asked questions we receive from readers: Should I charge sales tax for what I sell online? The short answer is that, as always, it depends. VAT is a tax that applies to the transfer of goods and services. You have to register for VAT when your turnover reaches £61,000 per year, but you can register before your business gets to this stage.

Once you've registered, you must charge varying levels of VAT, depending on what you sell. You must also keep records of what you charge for what products or services. This is called your *output tax*. There's a comprehensive guide to VAT on the HMRC Web site. Follow these steps to find it.

1. **Log on to** www.hmrc.gov.uk.

    Look toward the top right-hand corner of the home page and locate the VAT link under Businesses & Corporations. Clicking the link takes you to the VAT home page.

2. **Locate the navigation panel on the left-hand side.**

    This features click-throughs to online forms, rates, and codes, but also Information & Guides. Click this link.

3. **Click Introduction To VAT and scroll down to the What Is VATable link.**

   This step brings up a guide to the various rates of VAT (including the zero rate), what you can charge (and be charged) VAT on, and where to go for more information.

It's a good idea to familiarise yourself with this and other guides on the Web site, because they help shed light on seemingly complex issues. Bookmark this section and refer back to it when you need to.

Remembering other business taxes

There's a whole range of taxes that you have to consider, if not always pay. As your business grows, the number and complexity of taxes you must deal with grows, too. That's why businesses often start up using accountancy software, then hire a part-time bookkeeper, then a full-time accountant, and then eventually an accounts department and outsourced consultants.

To start with, however, you just need to think about taxable income. Anything you make money from is taxable in theory, but the authorities don't get interested until your making a few thousand pounds a year (which, of course, you must make to survive). That's where income or corporation tax comes in, depending on the business model you choose to adopt. (See Chapter 5 for more on the types of businesses you can start.)

Another area that adds to tax considerations is the business costs you incur, many of which are tax deductible. Then there's business rates, or council tax, the level of which depends on the size and location of your premises, as well as staff pay – it's down to you to organise their income tax and national insurance contributions.

Happily, this confusing sounding series of taxes is nicely summarised on Business Link's Web site (www.businesslink.gov.uk), where you can find accessible information on what you have to pay and what you don't.

Deducing your business deductions

One of the benefits of starting a new business, even if the business isn't profitable in the beginning, is the opportunity to take business deductions and reduce your tax payments. Always keep receipts from any purchases or expenses associated with your business activities. Make sure that you're taking all the deductions for which you're eligible.

For example, if you work at home (and we're assuming that, as an entrepreneur, you do), set aside some space for a home office. This space isn't just a territorial thing. It can result in some nifty business deductions, too.

Say that you have your office in your spare bedroom. Paint the room, and you can claim money back on the paint you use. The same applies to equipment and furniture. Again, Business Link's Web site (www.businesslink.gov.uk) has a full rundown of what you can claim tax-back against. To find it, click the following link path from the site's home page: Taxes⇨Returns and Payroll⇨ Business Expenses⇨Business Expenses and Dispensations.

Book V
Handling Customers and Staff

'Come now, Mr Scrimfold, aren't you a little too old to ask your parents to help you with your contract of employment?'

In this book . . .

This book helps you to keep staff contented and customers happy. Without these, your business is going to struggle! We look at ways of finding the best employees . . . and how to keep them once they've joined you! We also look at your customer base and help you decide how to draw in and keep your customers, from allowing customer interaction and offering an easy-to-use Web site, to anticipating your online customers' purchasing needs and offering them great service across the Internet.

Here are the contents of Book V at a glance:

Chapter 1

Employing People

In This Chapter

▶ Finding the best employees for your business

▶ Finding motivations and rewards

▶ Keeping on the right side of employment law

*U*nless you intend working on your own, you will be involved in employing and motivating others to do what you want them to do. Even if you don't employ people full-time, or if you outsource some portion of your work to others, you will have to choose who to give those tasks to, how to get the best out of them, and how to reward their achievements.

Profiling Great Employees

Firstly you may need to change your attitude to the whole hiring process. Most entrepreneurs dislike hiring employees and do it as little as possible and fit it around their other 'more important' tasks.

Finding good staff is *the* number one job for the boss. You need good people to delegate to. The current team needs a stream of new people who do not need to be carried and who can bring fresh and innovative ideas with them to stimulate everyone on to greater things.

Recruitment has to become a routine task, like selling or monitoring cash flow, that you do every day. Furthermore you need a budget to carry out the recruitment and selection task, just as you need a budget for equipment and rent. If you don't have a recruitment budget, you shouldn't be surprised if a task for which no money is budgeted goes wrong.

Deciding on full- or part-timers

One important decision you need to make before you can start your search for staff is whether you need to hire a full-time person. There are some very good reasons why you may not. If, for example, the demand for your products is highly seasonal and has major peaks and troughs it may make no sense to keep people on during slack periods. This could be the case if you were selling heating oil, where you might expect to peak in the autumn and tail off in the late spring because of variations in the weather. Other examples of seasonal fluctuations are increased sales of garden furniture and barbeques in summer and toys and luxury items before Christmas.

Using part-timers can open up whole new markets of job applicants, sometimes of a higher quality than you might expect on the general job market. Highly skilled and experienced retired workers, or mothers who have given up successful careers to have a family, can be tempted back into temporary or part-time work. It can sometimes make sense to have two part-time staff sharing the one job, each working part-time. This tactic can also be used to retain key staff that want to leave full-time employment. This makes for continuity in the work, allows people to fit in work around their personal circumstances, and brings to the business talents that might have been lost if full-time work had been insisted upon.

Part-time work is more prevalent than many people think. Up to a third of all those in employment in some countries are working part-time and most of those are working in small firms whose flexibility in this area can often be a key strength over larger firms when it comes to recruiting and retaining employees.

You can find part-time staff using the same methods as for full-time employees, which we discuss in the next sections. If you are looking for people to work anti-social hours, or to do just a few hours' work at short notice to meet sudden peaks, then the chances are you will have to recruit close to your work. In such a situation you may get the best results by circulating a leaflet that sets out your requirements. Target housing estates close to your premises or on good transport routes that operate at the times you want people to start and finish work. Make your leaflet stand out as lots of junk mail goes through most people's doors today. Have a key benefit that will grab people's attention, then give the basic details of the work, hours, pay, and who to contact.

Recruiting and selecting

To make sure that you get great people into your business, follow the tips in these sections.

Review your business goals

The starting point for any recruitment activity is a review of your short- and medium-term business goals. If you have recently updated your business plan, then your goals will be fresh in your mind. If not, then you need to do so. For example if you plan to sell, service, and dispatch software via your website, then the people needed will be quite different from those required if you plan dispatching physical products.

Define the job(s)

You need to set out the scope and responsibilities of the job before you start recruiting. The job description should include the measurable outcomes that you expect, as well as a description of the tasks. So for a salesperson you need to spell out what the sales target is, how many calls should be made, what the customer retention target is, and so on.

Too many small firms don't get round to preparing the job description until the person is in place, or worse still they don't have job descriptions at all. The argument advanced is that, as jobs in the small business world have a short shelf-life because the company is growing and changing all the time, why bother?

Profile the person

Flesh out your idea of the sort of person who could do the job well. If you are looking for a salesperson, then communication skills and appearance are important factors to consider, as might their personal circumstance, which may have to allow them to stay away from home frequently.

As well as qualifications and experience, keep in mind their team skills and that all too rare attribute, business savvy.

Advertise the job

You can fill positions from inside your company or outside it. Don't overlook your existing staff. You may be able to promote from within, even if you have to provide some additional training. Also your staff, suppliers, or other business contacts may know of someone in their network who might be suitable.

Press advertising is still a popular external source of new staff. The Internet is now exploding onto the recruitment market. But despite the hype only a few percentage of jobs are actually filled from advertisements on the Internet.

The type of vacancy will determine the medium. The Internet might be right for design engineers, but a leaflet drop on a housing estate would be better when looking for shift workers.

Advertising for recruitment is subject to legal restrictions that vary from country to country. The laws most likely to apply are those of libel, and those relating to discrimination on the grounds of gender, race, or age. Avoid sexist language and the words 'he' or 'she' and select your words carefully to avoid stipulating characteristics that exclude potential applicants of a specific sex or race or in a particular age range. If in doubt consult your Advertising Standards Authority or take legal advice. Most restrictions apply to newspapers, magazines, radio, and television; however, you would be wise to include the Internet on that list.

Advertising is intended to give you a reasonable choice of applicants. If you get it right you should end up with enough applicants to have a choice to make.

Make your selection

Firstly screen out the people who don't meet your specifications. Phone them if you need to clarify something, for example to establish whether they have experience of a particular software package. Then interview your shortlist perhaps using a test where possible. There are many self-administered tests, custom-designed for different types of work – we talk about tests in the upcoming 'Testing to find the best' section.

Let the applicants meet others in the business. This will give them a better feel for the company and you can get a second opinion on them. When Apple was developing the Macintosh the entire Mac team was involved in every new appointment. Applicants spent a day with the team, and only when the team decided a person was suitable did they let them in on the project.

Ideally, you end up with at least three people who you would be happy to appoint. Offer the job to the best candidate, keeping the others in reserve. You must have a reserve in case your first choice lets you down, accepts but then changes their mind, or quits or is fired after a week or two.

Always take up references, preferably on the phone. Don't take 'testimonials' at face value.

Make the new employee welcome

Having got the right people to join you, make sure they become productive quickly and stay for a long time. The best way to do this is to have a comprehensive induction process showing them where everything is and the way things are done in your business. Keep them posted of developments, put them on the memo/e-mail list. Set them short-term objectives and monitor performance weekly, perhaps even daily at first, giving praise or help as required. Invite them to social events as appropriate.

Testing to find the best

What are known as the classic trio of selection methods, application forms, interviews and references, can be supplemented by other tools which can improve your chances of getting the right candidate for most of the jobs you may want to fill. These tools are often clustered under the general heading of psychometric tests, although most of the tests themselves have less to do with psychology than with basic aptitude.

Tests are particularly useful for those in small firms as they can provide a much needed and valuable external view on candidates, which big firms have already in their human resources departments. Tests can also be applied quickly and without using many scarce internal resources.

Used correctly and fairly and in the right situations, tests can objectively measure skills (such as word processing or software proficiency), assess acquired knowledge and qualifications, and determine aptitude for certain jobs. But although tests are popular and becoming more reliable, they are neither certain to get selection decisions right nor are they risk-free.

There are dozens of commercial test publishers producing over 3,000 different tests. You can locate the appropriate test for your business through the British Psychological Society (www.bps.org.uk) or the Chartered Institute of Personnel and Development (www.cipd.co.uk).

Exploring Sources

You don't have to do everything involved in recruiting employees yourself. You can find a recruitment consultant or use a government Job Centre to do much of the hard work for you. In fact they may even be better at this than you will be, as they recruit and select every day of the week. Research suggests that Recruitment Consultants, for example, are twice as successful at filling vacancies than are entrepreneurs on their own.

You could consider taking the job in question out of your business and pay someone else to do it. See the section 'Outsourcing jobs' for more on this.

Outsourcing jobs

Almost every part of the work you do can probably be bought in. Web sites can be designed and hosted, and technology can be rented. There are e-wholesalers and packers and Internet-only delivery groups. Customer services can be handled by third-party call centres, and online banks compete with traditional banks to offer online payment processing. Almost every other aspect of business from accounting and recruitment, to payroll and human resource services can be outsourced, often via the Internet itself.

So you need to be very sure that you need to do everything yourself or with your own employees all the time. Clearly, if you can buy something in cheaper than you can do it yourself then it makes sense to do so. You might also consider outsourcing in areas that may not be cheaper but could save scarce cash or unnecessary upheaval. For example if your premises will fit six people and no more, it may make sense to outsource packaging and despatch to a fulfilment house and use the space saved to fit in more salespeople, or any other high skilled high value-adding job. The alternative of moving to larger premises will mean disruption and a higher fixed cost, which you may not feel ready for yet.

Using agencies

There may well be occasions when you feel that either you are unable or unwilling to do the job of recruiting yourself. In such circumstances you may find it useful to use a recruitment agency. Their costs may sound high, but when you reckon up the internal costs you may find they are not that expensive. Doing the recruiting yourself could take several days of your time and that of others in your firm. If you are working on your own or with just one or two others, this may be too great a distraction from other key tasks.

Costs that are deferred or reduced by the use of an outside recruitment agency include:

✔ The salaries and benefits of those involved in the recruitment process in your firm, including your own

✔ The cost of advertisements, trade shows, phone time and so on incurred via alternative methods

✔ The cost of the work that is not getting done while those doing the recruitment are busy on the search

✔ Associated costs of staff due to travel, food, lodging, and entertainment expenses

✔ Costs associated with developing sources to look for prospective employees

✔ Office expenses such as telephone time and expenses, mailings, and postage

✔ The time/effort involved in keeping track of applicants, reviewing CVs, checking references, dealing with unqualified applicants, interviewing qualified ones

✔ The cost of revealing your hiring needs and strategies to competitors

✔ The cost of getting it wrong. On average recruitment consultants are more likely to succeed than you are. After all, they recruit people every day; they are more likely to find a suitable candidate and one who stays in the job.

Choosing a recruitment consultant

Fundamentally there are two types of recruitment agency, contingency agencies and retained agencies, and they charge you in different ways.

A contingency agency charges a fee only when they find a suitable candidate for the position, whereas a retained agency asks for payment of their fees up-front, and will not provide a refund even if they fail to fill the position. For this reason, retained agencies are normally only used to find very skilled individuals within higher salary bands (perhaps £40,000 or more), whereas a contingency agency will find candidates for a range of positions – analysts, bookkeepers, consultants. You could use several contingency agencies at a time to find a candidate, because there is no risk of losing money.

All finding fees are based on the first year's annual salary, which consists of the income guaranteed to the applicant by the employer, including shift allowances and bonuses. It is hard to say precisely what commission rate you will be charged by a recruitment agency, because this information is related to the position you wish to fill. For example, the finding fee for a software engineer is likely to be higher than the one for a secretary. Specialist qualifications such as a degree, number of years of experience, and language skills, for example, are also taken into consideration.

Finding fees are generally 18–20 per cent of the first year's annual salary, although in some sectors this is significantly higher.

Fees are always open to discussion as this is a highly competitive marketplace, so you should try and negotiate the percentage you want to pay for a candidate.

Using Job Centre Plus

Job Centre Plus is the government-run employment services, which have professionally run offices with a growing number of SME (Small and Medium Enterprises) specialist staff. Typically these employment services are run out of 1,000 Job Centres based in towns where job-seekers are likely to live. At any one time they have 400,000 job-seekers on their database.

Their services are particularly helpful to small firms with little experience of recruiting as they offer a wide range of free help and advice on most matters concerned with employing people as well as signposting to other related services.

The Job Centre Plus range of services includes everything you would expect of a recruitment consultant. But unlike other recruitment agencies, many of their services are free and in any event will cost less than using any other external recruiter.

Screening over the Internet

The fastest growing route to new job applicants is via the Internet itself. The number of websites offering employment opportunities has exploded in recent years. The advantages of Internet recruitment to both candidates and clients are obvious. Internet recruitment offers fast, immediate, and cheap service compared to more traditional methods of recruitment. However, a number of Internet recruitment sites have established formidable reputations in Europe and the US. These include:

- ✔ *Futurestep* (`www.futurestep.com`), which covers all job functions and industry sectors.

- ✔ *LeadersOnline* (`www.leadersonline.com`) is becoming one of the leading Internet recruitment sites, aided by the fact that is focused towards technology professionals and handles recruitment between a salary range of £50,000 to £100,000.

- ✔ *monster.co.uk* (`www.monster.co.uk`) attracts approximately 100,000 visits per month and contains over one million CVs. Vacancies cover every industry sector and regional area.

Another option is to have a job-listing section on your own Web site. This is absolutely free, however you are certain to be trawling in a very small pool. This may not matter if the right sort of people are already visiting your site. At least they will know something about your products and services before they apply.

Motivating and Rewarding Employees

Management is the art and science of getting people to do what you want them to do, because *they* want to do it. This is easier said than done.

Most entrepreneurs believe that their employees work for money and their key staff work for more money. Pay them enough and they'll jump through any hoop. This view is not borne out by most of the research, which ranks pay as third or even fourth in the reasons why people come to work.

If it isn't necessarily money, why do people work where they do? I help provide some of the answers in the following sections.

The practice of management

In this section, we give you some practical tools you can use to get the very best out of your employees.

The starting point in getting people to give of their best is to assess them as individuals and to recognise their specific needs and motivations. These differences are in part influenced by age, gender, or job. They are also affected by an individual's personality. You need to tailor your actions to each person to get the best results.

My best advice is: Get to know everyone. This may sound insane in a small firm and after all you almost certainly recruited them all in the first place. By observing and listening to your employees you can build a picture of them that will help you motivate them by making them feel special.

- ✔ Show an interest in people's work. This is nothing to do with monitoring performance and more to do with managing by walking about, and seeing everyone, and talking with them as often as possible.

 If you employ less than five people you need to spend some time with each of them every day, up to ten people every week. After that, you should have managers doing much the same thing, but you still need to get around as often as possible.

 There is a famous management story, known as the Hawthorne Experiment, which demonstrates the power of this approach as a motivator. A manager was trying to improve output in a manufacturing unit so he called in some consultants to see what could be done. First they tried altering the lighting to make it easier for employees to see what they were doing. Output rose immediately. Then they gave them control of the speed of the production line and output rose again. Next they rearranged the flow of work, after discussions with the work team, and output improved again. The consultants, despite much deliberation, could see no logical link between their actions and the employees' improved work output. In the end they concluded that what really made the difference was that for the first time in years someone showed an interest in what they were doing and how they could improve their lot.

- ✔ Promote from within when you can. Too often people look outside for every new appointment. That is more or less saying that people you currently employ are not up to the task. There will be occasions where you have to bring someone in with new skills and special abilities. But if you can promote from within everyone can be a winner. When one employee gets a promotion others see career prospects perhaps they hadn't seen before, and you have someone you know and trust in a key job. Your newly promoted employee can help train someone up to take his or her former job, thereby saving you training time, also.

- ✔ Give title promotions in lieu of job promotions. A worker you don't want to lose may crave a certain position that you know he or she would fail in. Make the employee's benefits and status the same as for the desired position and add a new title to show that you value the employee and his or her work.

A likely situation is with a great salesperson. If they are ambitious as well as a brilliant salesperson they will want to become sales manager, which is an important step on their career ladder and demonstrates to their spouse, partner, and peers, as well as to themselves that they are doing a good job. Unfortunately most great salespeople make lousy managers. If you promote them the chances are you'll lose a good salesperson and have to fire them for being a useless manager in a few months' time. So keep them motivated by giving them the same package you would a sales manager, the same level of car, salary and other employment conditions, and promote them to a new title, sales executive or key account manager, for example. After all if they are selling so much they must be making good money for the business. They have the status and the cash and you keep a great salesperson doing what they do best, selling.

This can be a strategy in a small firm to create career progression for more people than might otherwise be possible.

✔ **Give praise as often as you can.** The rule is simple: Minimise your reaction to bad results and maximise your appreciation of good results. Autocratic employers continually criticise and complain, finding only poor performance wherever they look. Criticism reinforces poor behaviour. Everyone wants to be recognised and strangely enough people often prefer to be shouted at than ignored. So if doing things wrong is the only way to get noticed that's what may well happen.

You can always leaven out criticism with some favourable comment. For example if an employee is making some progress, but is short of being satisfactory, saying something like, 'This is certainly an improvement, but we still have a way to go. Let's spend a little time together and I'll see if we can't get to the bottom of what is holding you back', might produce a better level of motivation than just shouting out your criticism.

✔ **Create a no-blame culture.** Everything in business is a risk. If it were not there would be no chance of making a profit. It's the uncertainty around all business processes that creates that opportunity to make money. Not many bookmakers would be prepared to take a bet on a horse race after it had happened and the winner had been announced.

To a greater or lesser extent, you delegate some of the responsibility for taking risks on to your employees. But how should you react when the inevitable happens and things go wrong, as they will in some cases. If you jump up and down with rage, then no one will ever take a risk again. They'll leave all the decisions to you and you'll become even more overworked. Good people will get highly de-motivated and leave. If you take a sympathetic and constructive attitude to failure you will motivate and encourage employees to try again.

You need to make clear that tolerance of mistakes has its limits and repetition of the same mistake will not receive an equally tolerant reaction.

✔ **Reduce de-motivation.** In fact, very often the problem is not so much that of motivating people, but of avoiding de-motivating them! If you can keep off the backs of employees, it is quite possible that they will motivate themselves. After all, most of us want the same things: a sense of achievement or challenge, recognition of our efforts, an interesting and varied job, opportunities for responsibility, advancement, and job growth. But in a small firm the potential for de-motivation is high. Workloads invariably peak and there is never any slack in the systems of a small firm. Inevitably some employees will feel overloaded, neglected, or just plain hard done by. It may not reach the stage where people will complain, or start taking time off sick, but having de-motivated people around can create an unhealthy climate for everyone else.

So you need to look out for any negative behaviour and find out the cause. A 'couldn't care less attitude', lack of enthusiasm, or any signs of aggression can be useful indicators that all is not well. You need to counter de-motivators with a burst of motivators such as recognition and advancement, which cause satisfaction.

✔ Motivate off-site employees. Part-time workers, telecommuters, and key subcontractors, who either do much of their work off-site or who are not around all of the time, have to be built into your motivational plans too.

Dealing with difficult or de-motivated employees

Difficult or de-motivated people need prompt and effective managing. Dissatisfaction can spread quickly and lower motivation levels in others. The first step is to identify the causes of the problem. The causes may be to do with the employee or with the job itself. The problem may be brought about by illness, stress, or a personality clash between people working together.

Whatever the cause, the initiative for re-motivating them has to come from you. However the only reason for going through this effort is because either that employee has delivered satisfactory results in the past or you believe they have the potential to do so, if you can just find the key.

A good starting point is to recognise some basic truths about difficult or de-motivated people.

✔ Difficult people are not always out to take advantage of you or others. It is possible to pull them into a partnership if you can find the right shared goals. These have to be exciting, realistic, attainable, and important to them as well as the business.

✔ Difficult people can change. Dramatic changes in behaviour are possible and even the most intransigent employee can be won over. Very often it's just the approach taken to the problem that limits a difficult person's desire to change. If, for example, an employee consistently comes in late, you could start by warning them, then shouting at them, and finally you could threaten them with disciplinary action. It may even have to come to that. But how would events turn out if you started by giving the business reasons why turning up on time is important, with some examples of how being late affects their performance and ultimately limits their options for advancement.

✔ Difficult people can't be ignored. Unfortunately employees who set their own standards of behaviour well below the standard you expect of others do have a bad influence, especially on new employees. You can hardly demand punctuality of some people and not of others. Nor can you adopt the philosophy that if you leave them long enough they will really step out of line and then you can fire them. As the boss you have to manage all those who you employ and motivate them to perform.

Keeping motivation all in the family

Over 80 per cent of small businesses are family businesses in which one or more family members work in the organisation. Family businesses have both strengths and weaknesses when it comes to motivation. By being aware of them you can exploit the former to do your best to overcome the latter to give your business a better chance of prospering.

The factors that motivate or de-motivate family members can be different than those affecting non-family members.

The overwhelming strength of the family business is the different atmosphere and feel that a family concern has. A sense of belonging and common purpose more often than not leads to good motivation and performance. Another advantage is that the family firm has greater flexibility, since the unity of management and shareholders provides the opportunity to make quick decisions and to implement rapid change if necessary. On the downside, there are several weaknesses. Although these are not unique to family businesses, family firms are particularly prone to them. These are the main ones:

✔ Unwillingness to change has been identified as the single most common cause of low motivation in family firms. Family firms often do things the way they've always done them just because that's the way they've always done them. This can lead to stagnation in the marketplace and failing confidence in investors. Resistance to change is exacerbated by diminishing vitality, as founders grow old.

✔ Family goals and commercial goals come into conflict. Unlike other businesses, family firms have additional objectives to their financial performance targets, for example: building family reputation and status in the community; providing employment for the family; protecting family wealth; ensuring independence; a dynastic wish to pass on a position, in addition to wealth, to the next generation. However, superimposing these family values on the business can lead to difficulties. For example nepotism may lead to employment of family members beyond their competence, or a salary above their worth. This can lead to discontent and be de-motivational for non-family members.

✔ Facing conflict between growth and ownership. Families prefer majority ownership of a small company to minority holdings in a big company where they are answerable to outside shareholders. Basically a dilemma that all family managers face is one of either growing the company, keeping purely commercial goals in mind at whatever risk to family control, or to subordinating the firm's welfare to family constraints. This affects all areas of the business, from recruitment through to management.

✔ Impact of and career prospects of non-family employees may be limited. At management level family pride will sometimes not allow a situation where its members are subordinate to an outsider – even if the outsider is a better person for the job. Also, reliance on family management to the exclusion of input from outsiders may starve a growing firm of new ideas. A family firm may become inward looking, insensitive to the message of the marketplace, unreceptive to outside ideas, and unwilling to recruit competent outside managers. None of these are factors likely to be motivational to others in the business.

These are problems a family firm must address if all the effort put into motivating employees is not to be seen as a cynical deception. It would certainly be helpful to have a clear statement of family policy on the employment of family members, succession, and on ownership. Then non- family members can either buy in or not join in the first place.

Rewarding achievements

Whilst people often come to work for a set number of hours each week, it is what they do during that time that matters most to the organisation. Different types of work have different measurable outcomes. Those outcomes have to be identified and a scale arrived at showing the base rate of pay and payment above that base for achieving objectives. Different types of 'payment by results' schemes are in common use in different types of firm and the conditions that most favour these types of pay need to be carefully examined to make sure you pick the right mix of goals and rewards.

Ground rules in matching pay to performance:

✔ Make the rules clear so everyone knows how the reward system will work.

✔ Make the goals specific and if possible quantifiable.

✔ Make the reward visible so everyone knows what each person or team gets.

✔ Make it matter. The reward has to be worthwhile and commensurate with the effort involved.

✔ Make it fair, so people believe their reward is correctly calculated.

✔ Make it realistic because if the target is set too high no one will try to achieve it.

✔ Make it happen quickly.

The following sections address specific reward systems.

Paying a commission

This is perhaps the easiest reward system, but it really only works for those directly involved in selling. A *commission* is a payment based in some way on the value of sales secured by the individual or team concerned.

You have to make sure that the order is actually delivered or executed before any commission is paid and you may even want to make sure the customer has paid up. However, as with all rewards, you must keep the time-scale between doing the work and getting the reward as short as practicably possible, otherwise people will have forgotten what the money is for.

It makes sense to base the commission on your gross profit rather than sales turnover; otherwise you could end up rewarding salespeople for generating unprofitable business.

Awarding bonuses

A *bonus* is a reward for successful performance, usually paid in a lump sum related as closely as possible to the results obtained by an individual, team, or the business as a whole. In general, bonuses are tied to results so that it's less obvious how an individual contributed directly to the result achieved. For example a company bonus may be paid out if the firm achieves a certain level of output. Keeping everyone informed as to how the firm is performing towards achieving that goal may well be motivational, but the exact role say a cleaner or office-worker has in helping attain that goal is not easy to assess – not as easy as it is to calculate a salesperson's commission, say.

Bonuses can be paid out periodically or as a one-off payment for a specific achievement.

Sharing profits

Profit sharing involves giving a specific share of the company's profit to the firm's employees. The share of the profits can be different for different jobs, length of service, or seniority.

This type of reward has the great merit of focusing everyone's attention on the firm's primary economic goal – to make money. It is quite possible that one or more employees can be performing well, but others drag down the overall performance. The theory is that the performing staff puts pressure on the others to come up to the mark.

If profits go up, people get more; but it can go the other way too, which can be less attractive. Also, profit targets can be missed for reasons outside of the employees' direct control. If you are dependent on customers or supplies from overseas, for example, and the exchange rate moves against you, profits, and hence profit-related pay, can dip sharply. However unfair this may seem to a receptionist who has been hoping for extra cash to pay for a holiday, this is the hard reality of business. If you think your employees are adult enough to take that fact on board, then this can be a useful way to reward staff.

Sharing ownership

Share option schemes give employees the chance to share in the increase in value of a company's shares as it grows and prospers.

The attraction of turning employees into shareholders is that it gives them a long-term stake in the business and hopefully will make them look beyond short-term issues and ensure their long-term loyalty. Of course, there can be unwelcome side effects if the value of the business goes down rather than up.

Giving skill and competence awards

You can give a skill or competence award when an employee reaches a certain level of ability. These awards are not directly tied to an output such as improved performance, but you must believe that raising the skill or competence in question will ultimately lead to better business results.

The award itself could be cash, gift certificates, extra days of holiday, a trip to a show or sports event, or whatever else your employees might appreciate. Bottles of wine always seem to be well received!

Compensating Your Employees

Finding and motivating employees is one part of the employment equation. The other is recompensing them for their efforts and achievements either by way of pay, or by some other benefit that is at least as appealing to each individual employee.

Setting payment levels

It's certainly true that people don't come to work just for money. But they certainly won't come if you don't pay them and they won't stay and be motivated to give of their best if you don't give them the right pay. But how much is the right amount? Get it too low and your ability to attract and retain productive and reliable people capable of growing as your business grows is impaired. But pay too much and your overheads rise so much you become uncompetitive. That is a real danger for small firms where the wages bill often represents the largest single business expense.

These ground rules are not very complicated but they are important:

- ✔ Only pay what you can afford. There is no point in sinking the company with a wage bill that it can't meet.

- ✔ Make sure pay is fair and equitable and is seen as such by everyone.

- ✔ Make sure people know how pay scales are arrived at.

- ✔ See that pay scales for different jobs reflect the relative importance of the job and the skills required.

- ✔ Ensure your pay scales are in line with the law on minimum wage requirements. Since April 1999 a *statutory minimum wage* is in effect in the UK. The amount is governed by the age of the employee and whether an employee is undergoing training. The hourly rate changes over time, so you need to keep abreast of the latest rates. (www.jobcentreplus.gov.uk has information on current rules in this area).

- ✔ Ensure your pay scales are competitive with those of other employers in your region or industry.

Big companies go in for a process known as 'job evaluation'. This involves looking at each job and evaluating it against a range of factors such as complexity, qualifications, skills, experience required, any dangers or hazards involved, and the value of the contribution to your business. Creating and maintaining a structure like this is a full-time job in itself. It is certainly not something a small business should undertake lightly.

You can get most of the advantages of having a job evaluation system by finding out the going rate for key jobs in other people's businesses. The going rate is the pay rate that normally applies to a particular job in a particular geographic area. Inevitably not all jobs are identical and certain aspects involve differences in employment conditions that inevitably affect the going rate. For example, working hours, employment conditions, security of tenure, pension rights, and so forth vary from firm to firm. You need to have a procedure in place to routinely monitor local going rates and a system to correct for variations in employment conditions between your firm and other similar firms.

The consequence of being too far out of line with the going rate is that staff turnover will rise. As long as the businesses you look at are reasonably similar and the jobs much the same you will end up with a defendable, credible, and acceptable pay structure, which should only take you a couple of hours' work twice or at most three times a year.

Ways to find out the going rate for a job include:

- ✔ Read articles on pay, job advertisements on the Internet, in the local papers and the relevant trade journals. You may have to correct some pay rates to allow for variations. For example, pay rates for similar jobs are often much higher in or near major cities than they are in rural areas.

- ✔ Talk to your Chamber of Commerce or Trade Association, some of whom publish salary surveys, and to other local employers and business owners in your network.

- ✔ Contact employment agencies including those run by government agencies. They are usually a bit ahead of the rest of the market in terms of pay information. Other employers only know what they are paying their present staff. Recruitment agencies know what you will have to pay to get your next employee.

Deciding arbitrarily the pay rates of people who work for you may appear to be one of the perks of working for yourself. But inconsistent pay rates will quickly upset people and staff will jump ship at the first opportunity.

Creating a menu of benefits

A *benefit* is defined as any form of compensation that is not part of an employee's basic pay and that isn't tied directly to their performance in those jobs. These non-salary benefits such as pension, working conditions, and company policy can also play a part in keeping people on side.

A wide range of other perks ranging from being allowed to wear casual dress (almost essential) to onsite childcare is on offer to employees in organisations. Personal development training, company product discounts, flexible hours, telecommuting, and fitness facilities are all benefits that people can expect in certain jobs today.

Some benefits have become pretty well obligatory. For example, since October 2001, small firms in the UK that employ more than five people are obliged to provide their employees with a pension. These companies have to contend with choosing an appropriate scheme, setting up the logistics for collecting contributions, and communicating their decisions to their employees.

Interestingly enough, the approach recommended by the UK government to how small firms should handle pensions may form the model to inspire them to introduce a wide range of other benefits.

Staying on the Right Side of the Law

A business operates within a legal framework, the elements of which the owner-manager must be aware. The areas I cover in the following sections summarise only a few of the key legal issues. Different types of business may have to pay regard to different legal issues and employment law itself is dynamic and subject to revision and change.

The Advisory, Conciliation and Arbitration Service (ACAS) (www.acas.org.uk) and The British Safety Council (www.britishsafetycouncil.org) are useful organisations who can help with aspects of employment issues, and Emplaw (www.emplaw.co.uk) is a Web site covering basic British employment law information and will direct you to a lawyer in your area who specialises in the aspect of employment law you are concerned with.

Keeping employment records

You need to keep records about employees both individually and collectively. When you only employ one or two people this may seem like a bureaucratic chore. You may even feel that you can remember all the important details about your employees without keeping copious records. However the particulars on even a few employees are too much data to carry in your head, especially alongside all the other things you have to remember. The record system can be a manual one, it can be computerised or, as is the case in most small firms, a mix of the two. The great strength of computerised records lies in the ease with which collective data on employees past and present can be produced. This can throw up trends, which may help in recognising problems and setting them in proper context. For example the collective employee data will show average absenteeism and lateness statistics, which you can then use as a comparison during an individual's appraisal.

Some of the data you need to keep is a legal requirement, such as information on accidents. Some of the information will be invaluable in any dispute with an employee, for example in a case of unfair dismissal. All of the information makes the process of employing people run more smoothly.

Individual employee information should include:

- ✔ The application form
- ✔ Interview record and the results of any selection tests used
- ✔ Job history, including details of promotions and assignments
- ✔ Current and past job descriptions
- ✔ Current pay and bonus details and a record of the amount and date of any changes
- ✔ Details of skills and competences
- ✔ Education and training records with details of courses attended
- ✔ Details of performance assessments and appraisals
- ✔ Absence, lateness, accident, medical and disciplinary records, together with details of any formal warnings and suspensions
- ✔ Holiday entitlement
- ✔ Pension contribution data
- ✔ Termination record giving date, details of exit interview, and suitability for re-engagement
- ✔ Copies of any correspondence between you and the employee

Collective information should include:

- ✔ Numbers, grades, and job titles
- ✔ Absenteeism, staff turnover, and lateness statistics
- ✔ Accident rates
- ✔ Age and length of service records
- ✔ Wage and salary structures
- ✔ Employee costs
- ✔ Overtime statistics showing hours worked and costs
- ✔ Records of grievances and disputes

✔ Training records showing how many person days have been devoted to training and how much that has cost

✔ Gender, ethnic, and disability profiles

Employees have three basic rights over the information an employer keeps in their employment records:

✔ To be able to obtain access to one's own personal data

✔ To be able to claim damages for losses caused by the use of inaccurate data or the unauthorised use of data, or by the loss or destruction of data

✔ To apply to the courts if necessary for rectification or erasure of inaccurate data

This means that an employee is entitled to gain access to his or her personal data at reasonable intervals and without undue delay or expense. It is a legal requirement that this request be put in writing, although you may choose not to insist on this and you must provide the information within 40 days of the request.

Preparing contracts of employment

Employees have to be given a written statement of a defined list of terms and conditions of their employment within two months of starting working for you.

The list of terms which go into a job description include the following:

✔ The employee's full name

✔ When the employee started working for you

✔ How and how much your employee is paid

✔ Whether pay is weekly or monthly

✔ The hours you expect them to work

✔ The number of days holiday they are allowed, including public holidays and how that holiday is accumulated

✔ The employee's job title or a brief description of his or her work

✔ Where you expect the employee to work and what conditions will apply if you expect them to work elsewhere

✔ You need to state if you intend the employment to be permanent or, if it is for a fixed term, when it will start and finish

✔ Details of who the employee will be managed by and who they can talk to if they have any dispute with that person

✔ Any terms and conditions relating to sickness or injury, including any provision for sick pay

✔ Any terms and conditions relating to pensions and pension schemes

✔ Any disciplinary rules applicable to the employee

✔ The period of notice required, which increases with length of service; a legal minimum of one week's notice per year of service is required up to a maximum of 12 weeks (this may be overridden by express terms in the contract)

The job description forms the cornerstone of the contract of employment that exists between employer and employee. However the contract is rarely a single document and may not even be completely documented. A contract comes into existence as soon as someone accepts an offer of paid employment, even if both offer and acceptance are only oral. In practice the most important contractual document may be the letter offering a person the job, together with the salary and other basic employment conditions.

The contract consists of four types of condition:

✔ **Express terms:** Terms specifically agreed to between employer and employee, whether in writing or not.

✔ **Implied terms:** Terms considered to be so obvious that they don't need spelling out. These include such matters as the employee complying with reasonable instructions and taking care of business property and equipment. For the employer these can include taking reasonable care of the employee and paying them for work done.

✔ **Incorporated terms:** Terms from outside sources, most commonly from trade union agreements, that are included in the contract.

✔ **Statutory terms:** These include any work requirements laid down by law – safety regulations, for example.

Working legal hours

Whilst the owner of a business may be content to work all hours, since 1999 the law has strictly governed the amount of time employees can be asked to put in. The Working Time Regulations, as they are known, apply to any staff over the minimum school-leaving age. This includes temporary workers, home workers, and people working for you overseas. The regulations are summarised in the following points:

- Staff cannot be forced to work more than 48 hours a week. However, an employee may work over those hours if he or she agrees to it by signing an opt-out agreement.

- You cannot force an employee to sign an opt-out agreement from any aspect of the regulations.

- Working time includes travelling when it is part of the job, working lunches and job-related training.

- For night workers, there is a limit of an average of eight hours' work in 24. They are also entitled to receive a free health assessment.

- All workers are entitled to 11 hours rest a day, a day off each week, and an in-work rest break of at least 20 minutes if the working day is longer than six hours.

- If a worker misses some rest, he or she is entitled to *compensatory rest,* which is another period of rest the same time as the part of the period of rest missed.

- Full-time staff are entitled to four weeks' paid holiday a year after a 13-week qualification period. However, they do not have the right to choose when to take leave. It must be agreed with the employer.

As an employer, you must keep records that show you comply with the working-time limits and that you have given night workers the opportunity for a health assessment.

Granting leave

As an employer, occasions are bound to arise when you will be obliged, to give your staff time off work other than their usual holidays or when they are unwell. You may not have to pay them when these occasions occur, but you do have to respect their right to be absent.

Protecting maternity and paternity rights

All pregnant employees have rights in four main areas. These include the right to reasonable time off to have antenatal care; the right not to be unfairly dismissed; the right to maternity leave; and the right to return to work. There are many conditions and exceptions so you need to examine each case carefully to see how to proceed.

Parental leave applies to men and women alike who have been employed for more than one year and have responsibility for a child as a biological, foster, adoptive, or step parent.

The minimum period of parental leave that can be taken in one go is one week (unless the child is entitled to disability living allowance) and the maximum is four weeks.

Recognising emergency leave

Employees have the right to reasonable unpaid leave where their *dependants* – spouses, children, parents, and other people living in an employee's house (except lodgers), and others who might rely on an employee in emergencies, such as elderly neighbours – are affected by:

- ✔ Illness, injury, assault, or childbirth
- ✔ Breakdown in childcare/other care arrangements
- ✔ The consequences of a death
- ✔ A serious incident at school or during school hours

To take this leave, your employee should give notice as soon as reasonably practicable giving the reason for, and likely duration of, absence. 'Reasonable' time off is not defined but, usually, one or two days should suffice.

Avoiding discrimination

By and large business owners can employ whomever they want to employ. However when setting the criteria for a particular job or promotion it is usually illegal to discriminate on the grounds of sex, race, marital status, or union membership. If you employ more than 15 people, then disabled employees have the right not to be discriminated against in either the recruitment process or when they are employed.

Whether you can impose age limits on job applicants or on your employees is debatable. You may find that by imposing an age limit you are indirectly discriminating against women, for example, who have had time off work to have children.

New regulations designed to prevent part-time employees from being treated less favourably than comparable full-time employees – that is someone doing broadly similar work and with a similar level of skills and qualifications – are coming into force in the UK. Business owners will have to ensure part-time employees receive equal sick pay and maternity pay (on a pro rata basis), equal hourly rates of pay, and equal access to pension schemes. Employers will also be obliged to ensure that part-time employees have equal access to training opportunities and that part-time employees are not treated less favourably than full-timers in a redundancy situation. The Emplaw website (www.emplaw.co.uk) has a free area covering the current regulations on UK Employment Law and also details on how you can find a lawyer in your area who specialises in the aspect of employment law you are concerned with.

Discrimination starts right from when vacancies are advertised – you cannot include such phrases as 'no women' or 'no men', or 'no blacks' or 'no whites'. It extends to the pay, training, and promotion of those who work for you.

It is also illegal to victimise by treating unfairly someone who has complained about being discriminated against. Sexual harassment is also a form of discrimination defined as the 'unwanted conduct of a sexual nature or other conduct based on sex affecting the dignity of men and women at work'. This can include unwelcome physical, verbal, or non-verbal conduct. Finally it is unfair to include in your reason for dismissing an employee that they are a member of a particular minority group protected by law.

To avoid discriminating in your employment you need to ensure that all your policies and procedures meet the following criteria:

- ✔ They are applied equally to all who work for you irrespective of sex, race, and so forth

- ✔ They don't limit the proportion of one group who comply compared with another

- ✔ They don't disadvantage an individual

- ✔ They can be objectively justified. For example there is no case to argue when being a man or woman is a genuine occupational qualification – for example, for the purpose of a particular photographic modelling assignment or an acting role. The same is true when you have a part-time vacancy so have no need of a full-time employee.

To make sure you are not discriminating at work follow this six-point checklist:

- ✔ Ensure your business has an equal opportunities policy

- ✔ Train staff in equal opportunities

- ✔ Keep records of interviews showing why candidates were rejected

✔ Ensure complaints are taken seriously, fully investigated, and addressed if needed

✔ Conduct staff surveys to help determine where discrimination may exist within your business

✔ Examine the payroll – pay should reflect an employee's job title, not their gender

Keeping the work environment safe

You have to provide a reasonably safe and healthy environment for your employees, visitors, and members of the general public who may be affected by what you do. This applies to both the premises you work from and the work itself. An inspector has the right to enter your premises to examine it and enforce legal requirements if your standards fall short in any way.

Once you have employees you must take some or all of the following measures dependent on the number of people you employ. However a prudent employer should take all these measures whether or not required by law. Doing so sets the standard of behaviour that is common in the very best firms.

✔ Inform the organisation responsible for health and safety at work for your business of where you are and what you do. For most small businesses this is the Environmental Health Department of your local authority (contact details may be found in your local telephone directory). The Health and Safety Executive website has a section devoted to Small Firms, covering both regulations and advice on making your work environment safer (their Web site is www.hse.gov.uk).

✔ Get employer's liability insurance to cover you for any physical injury or disease your employees may get as a result of their work. The amount of coverage must be at least £2 million and the insurance certificate must be displayed at all your places of work.

You, as an employer, can in turn expect your employees:

✔ To take reasonable care of their own health, safety at work, and of other persons who may be affected by their acts or omissions.

✔ To co-operate with the employer in ensuring that the requirements imposed by the relevant statutory provisions are complied with.

Chapter 2

Inspiring Employees to Better Performance

The question of how to motivate employees has loomed large over managers ever since management was first invented. Most of management comes down to mastering skills and techniques for motivating people – to make them better, more productive employees who love their jobs more than anything else in the world. Well, perhaps not quite that much; but you do want them to turn up and be as happy, effective, and productive as possible.

You have two ways to motivate employees – rewards and punishments. If employees do what you want them to do, reward them with incentives that they desire – awards, recognition, important titles, money, and so on. We often call these *positive consequences*. Alternatively, if employees don't do what you want, punish them with what they don't desire – warnings, reprimands, demotions, firings, and so on – often known as *negative consequences*. By nature, employees are drawn towards positive consequences and shy away from negative consequences.

Increasingly, however, with today's employees, to be an effective manager you have to work harder at providing a greater number of positive consequences on an ongoing basis when employees perform well (they expect it). And you have to be *much* more selective as to when and how you use negative consequences. It is much harder to fire people than in previous times, and wrongful and unfair dismissals get you into trouble with the law.

This chapter deals with the positive side of employee motivation – positive consequences, especially recognition and rewards. Besides, 100 years of research in behavioural science and continuing extensive studies at all of the world's major business schools show that you have a much greater impact on getting the performance you want from your employees when you use positive consequences rather than negative ones.

We aren't saying that negative consequences don't have a place; sometimes you have no choice but to punish, reprimand, or even dismiss employees. However, first give your employees the benefit of the doubt that they do want to do a good job and acknowledge them when they do so. Make every effort to use positive recognition, praise, and rewards to encourage the behaviours you seek, and catch people doing things right. If you do this, your employees are more motivated to want to excel in their jobs, performance and morale improve, and your company is considered a much better place to work.

By leading with positive reinforcements, not only can you inspire your employees to do what you want, but you can also develop happier, more productive employees in the process – and that combination is tough to beat.

The Greatest Management Principle in the World

We're about to let you in on the Greatest Management Principle in the World. This simple rule can save you countless hours of frustration and extra work, and it can save your company many thousands or perhaps even millions of pounds. Sounds pretty awe inspiring, doesn't it? Are you ready? Okay, the statement is:

You get what you reward.

Don't let the seeming simplicity of the statement fool you – read on to explore it.

Recognition isn't as simple as it looks

You may think that you're rewarding your employees to do what you want them to do, but are you really?

Consider the following example. You have two employees: Employee A is incredibly talented and Employee B is a marginal performer. You give similar assignments to both employees. Employee A completes the assignment before the due date and hands it in with no errors. Because Employee A is already done, you give her two additional assignments. Meanwhile, Employee

B is not only late, but when she finally hands in the report you requested, it is full of errors. Because you're now under a time crunch, you accept Employee B's report and then correct it yourself.

What's wrong with this picture? Who's actually being rewarded: Employee A or Employee B?

If you answered Employee B, you're right. This employee has discovered that submitting work that is substandard and late is okay. Furthermore, she also sees that you personally fix it. That's quite a nice reward for an employee who clearly doesn't deserve one. (Another way to put it is that Employee B certainly has you well trained!)

On the other hand, by giving Employee A more work for being a diligent, outstanding worker, you're actually punishing her. Even though you may think nothing of assigning more work to Employee A, she knows the score. When Employee A sees that all she gets for being an outstanding performer is more work (while you let Employee B get away with doing less work), she's not going to like it one little bit. And if you end up giving both employees basically the same pay rise (and don't think that they won't find out), you make the problem even worse. You lose Employee A, either literally, as she takes another job, or in spirit, as she stops working so hard.

If you let the situation continue, all your top performers eventually realise that doing their best work is not in their best interest. As a result, they leave their position to find an organisation that values their contribution, or they simply sit back and forget about doing their best work. Why bother? No one (that means you, the manager) seems to care anyway.

Biscuit motivation

Giving everyone the same incentive – the same salary increase, equal recognition, or even equal amounts of your time – we call *biscuit motivation*. Although this treatment may initially sound fair, it isn't.

Nothing is as unfair at work as the equal treatment of unequal performers. You need to assess the performance of everyone. You then make clear to each person why they have received rewards and bonuses, or why they have not. These rewards must be evenly and honestly distributed. And if everyone meets the standards demanded, then reward them all as you have promised.

If people are not performing up to standard, then take the particular individuals aside and tell them why. Tell them what they need to do to make the grade, and how they can go about it. This is a much better way of going about things than letting people go about things without your active involvement and interest. You want everyone working as well as possible, and your job is to sort out those who aren't up to scratch.

Don't forget the Greatest Management Principle in the World – you get what you reward.

Before you set up a system to reward your employees, make sure that you know exactly what behaviours you want to reward and then align the rewards with those behaviours.

After you put your employee reward system in place, check periodically to see that the system is getting the results that you want. Check with those you're trying to motivate and see if the programme is still working. If it isn't, change it!

Discovering What Employees Want

In today's tight, stressful, changing times, what things are most important to employees? Bob conducted a survey of about 1,500 employees from across seven industries to answer that question. We list the top ten items that employees said were most important, along with some thoughts on how you can better provide each of these elements to your own employees:

- **A learning activity (No. 1) and choice of assignment (No. 9):** Today's employees most value opportunities in which they gain skills that can enhance their worth and marketability in their current job as well as future positions. Discover what your employees want to find out, how they want to grow and develop, and where they want to be in five years. Give them opportunities as they arise and the ability to choose work assignments whenever possible. When you give employees the choice, more often than not they rise to meet or exceed your expectations.

- **Flexible working hours (No. 2) and time off from work (No. 7):** Today's employees value their time – and their time off. Be sensitive to their needs outside work, whether these needs involve family or friends, charity or church, education or hobbies. Provide flexibility whenever you can so that employees can meet their obligations. Time off may range from an occasional afternoon to attend a child's play at school or the ability to start the workday an hour early so the employee can leave an hour early. By allowing work to fit best with an employee's life schedule, you increase the chances that they're motivated to work harder while they are at work, and do their best to make their schedule work. And from a managerial standpoint, as long as the job gets done, what difference does it matter what hours someone works? And in any case, employees now have a legal right to request flexible working hours, and you have a legal obligation to consider their request.

✔ **Personal praise – verbal (No. 3), public (No. 8), or written (No. 10):** Although you can thank someone in 10 to 15 seconds, most employees report that they're never thanked for the job they do – especially not by their manager. Systematically start to thank your employees when they do good work, in person, in the hallway, in a group meeting, on voice-mail, in a written thank-you note, on e-mail, or at the end of each day at work. Better yet, go out of your way to act on and share and amplify good news when it occurs – even if it means interrupting someone to thank her for a great job she's done. By taking the time to say you noticed and appreciate her efforts, you help those efforts – and results – to continue. And bring her efforts to your manager's attention – this reinforces your own integrity, as well as making sure that full credit goes where it's due.

✔ **Increased autonomy (No. 5) and authority (No. 4) in their job:** The ultimate form of recognition for many employees is to have increased autonomy and authority to get their job done, including the ability to spend or allocate resources, make decisions, or manage others. Greater autonomy and authority says, 'I trust you to act in the best interests of the company, to do so independently and without approval of myself or others.' Increased autonomy and authority should be awarded to employees as a form of recognition itself for the past results they achieved. Autonomy and authority are privileges, not rights, which should be granted to those employees who have most earned them, based on past performance, and not based on tenure or seniority.

✔ **Time with their manager (No. 6):** In today's fast-paced world of work in which everyone is expected to get more done faster, personal time with your manager is in itself also a form of recognition. As managers are busier, taking time with employees is even more important. The action says, 'Of all the things I have to do, one of the most important is to take time to be with you, the person or people I most depend on for us to be successful.' Especially for younger employees, time spent with a manager is a valued form of validation and inspiration, as well as serving a practical purpose of learning and communication, answering questions, discussing possibilities, or just listening to an employee's ideas, concerns, and opinions.

By the way, you may wonder where money ranked in importance in this survey. A 'cash reward' ranked thirteenth in importance to employees. (We say more about the topic of money as a motivator later in this chapter.) Everyone needs money to live, but work today involves more than what anyone gets paid.

Employees report that the most important aspects at work today are primarily the intangible aspects of the job that any manager can easily provide – if she makes it a priority to do so. Now we're going to tell you a big secret. This secret is the key to motivating your employees. You don't need to attend an all-day seminar or join the management-video-of-the-week club to discover this secret: We are letting you in on it right here and right now at no extra charge:

Ask your employees what they want.

This statement may sound silly, but you can take a lot of the guesswork out of your job by simply being clear about what your employees most value in their jobs. It may be one or more of the items mentioned earlier in this section, or it may be something entirely different. The simplest way to find out how to motivate your employees is to ask them. Often managers assume that their employees want only money. These same managers are surprised when their employees tell them that other things – such as being recognised for doing a good job, being allowed greater autonomy in decision making, or having a more flexible work schedule – may be much more motivating than cash. Regardless of what preferences your employees have, you're much better off knowing those preferences explicitly rather than guessing or ignoring them. So:

- **Plan to provide employees with more of what they value.** Look for opportunities to recognise employees for having done good work and act on those opportunities as they arise, realising that what motivates some employees doesn't motivate others.

- **Stick with it over time.** Motivation is a moving target and you need to constantly be looking to meet your employees' needs in order to keep them motivated to help you meet your needs.

Consider the following as you begin setting the stage for your efforts:

1. **Create a supportive environment for your employees by first finding out what they most value.**

2. **Design ways to implement recognition to thank and acknowledge employees when they do good work.**

3. **Be prepared to make changes to your plan, based on what works and what doesn't.**

Creating a supportive environment

The new business realities of the present day bring a need to find different ways to motivate employees. Motivation is no longer an absolute, my-way-or-the-highway proposition. The incredible acceleration of change in business and technology today is coupled with greatly expanded global competitive forces. With these forces pressing in from all sides, managers can have difficulty keeping up with what employees need to do, much less figure out what to tell them to do. In fact, a growing trend is for managers to manage individuals who are doing work that the managers themselves have never done. (Fortunately, given a little time and a little trust, most employees can work out what needs to be done by themselves.)

Inspiring managers must embrace these changing business forces and management trends. Instead of using the power of their position to motivate workers, managers must use the power of their ideas. Instead of using threats and intimidation to get things done, managers must create environments that support their employees and allow creativity to flourish.

Book V

Handling
Customers
and Staff

You, as a manager, can create a supportive workplace in the following ways:

  ✔ **Build and maintain trust and respect.** Employees whose managers trust and respect them are motivated to perform at their best. By including employees in the decision-making process, today's managers get better ideas (that are easier to implement) and, at the same time, they improve employees' morale, loyalty, and commitment.

  ✔ **Removing the barriers of getting to work.** If you ask your employees what are the biggest hurdles they face in coming to work, you get a huge range of answers – rush-hour traffic, getting the kids to school, having to use public transport, and so on. By allowing them to choose their hours of work, you give them the opportunity to work around these barriers. You are also entitled to expect that, having chosen their hours of work, they then show up and do a good job. You cannot do this for every eventuality, and crises always happen. However, as long as the employee is prepared to give you a reasonable and regular pattern of hours, you should at least consider being flexible.

  ✔ **Open the channels of communication.** The ability of all your employees to communicate openly and honestly with one another is critical to the ultimate success of your organisation and plays a major role in employee motivation. Today, quick and efficient communication of information throughout your organisation can be what differentiates you from your competition. Encourage your employees to speak up, to make suggestions, and to break down the organisational barriers – the rampant departmentalisation, turf protection, and similar roadblocks – that separate them from one another, where and whenever they find them.

  ✔ **Make your employees feel safe.** Are your employees as comfortable telling you the bad news as they are telling you the good news? If the answer is no, you haven't created a safe environment for your employees. Everyone makes mistakes; people discover valuable lessons from their mistakes. If you want employees who are motivated, make it safe for them to take chances and to let you know the bad along with the good. And use mistakes and errors as opportunities for growth and development; never ever punish mistakes and errors except those generated as the result of negligence or incompetence.

  ✔ **Develop your greatest asset – your employees.** By meeting your employees' needs, you also achieve your organisation's needs. Challenge your employees to improve their skills and knowledge and provide them with the support and training that they need to do so. Concentrate on the positive progress they make and recognise and reward such success whenever possible.

Having a good game plan

Motivated employees don't happen by accident. You must have a plan to reinforce the behaviour you want. In general, employees are more strongly motivated by the potential to earn rewards than they are by the fear of punishment. Clearly, a well thought out and planned motivation, incentive, and rewards system is important to creating a committed, effective workforce. Here are some simple guidelines for setting up a system of low-cost rewards in your organisation:

- ✔ **Link rewards to organisational goals.** To be effective, rewards need to reinforce the behaviour that leads to achieving an organisation's goals. Use rewards to increase the frequency of desired behaviour and decrease the frequency of undesired behaviour.

- ✔ **Define parameters and mechanics.** After you identify the behaviours you want to reinforce, develop the specifics of your reward system. Create rules that are clear and easily understood by all employees. Make sure that goals are attainable and that all employees have a chance to obtain rewards, whatever their job and occupation.

- ✔ **Obtain commitment and support.** Of course, communicate your new rewards programme to your employees. Many organisations publicise their programmes at group meetings. They present the programmes as positive and fun activities that benefit both the employees and the company. To get the best results, plan and implement your rewards programme with your employees' direct involvement.

- ✔ **Monitor effectiveness.** Is your rewards system getting the results you want? If not, take another look at the behaviours you want to reinforce and make sure that your rewards are closely linked to the behaviours. Even the most successful reward programmes tend to lose their effectiveness over time as employees begin to take them for granted. Keep your programme fresh by discontinuing rewards that have lost their lustre and bringing in new ones from time to time.

Deciding What to Reward

Most organisations and managers reward the wrong things, if they reward their employees at all. This tendency has led to a crisis of epic proportions in the traditional system of incentives and motivation in business. For example:

- ✔ A major London commodity market gave bonuses of 6 per cent of salary to outstanding employees; and it gave bonuses of 3 per cent of salary to everyone else. Average and adequate performers were therefore receiving exactly the same reward except for the extra three per cent of salary delivered to top performers.

✔ A top professional footballer on many thousands of pounds a week joined one of the very top football clubs, only to find himself playing in the reserve team at exactly the time when he was trying to develop his career and reputation through playing regularly. He was therefore receiving a very good reward, but not the one that he wanted.

✔ A council employee rated 'exceptional' was told by her manager that she had to be downgraded to 'average' because the County Council Social Services Department had no money to pay her bonus.

If workers aren't being rewarded for doing outstanding work, what are they being rewarded for? As we point out in the 'Biscuit motivation' section earlier in the chapter, organisations often reward employees just for showing up for work.

For an incentive programme to have meaningful and lasting effects, it must be contingent; that is, it must focus on performance – nothing less and nothing more.

'But wait a second,' you may say, 'that isn't fair to the employees who aren't as talented as my top performers.' If that's what you think, we can straighten out that particular misunderstanding right now. Everyone, regardless of how smart, talented, or productive they are, has the potential to be a top performer.

Suppose that Employee A produces 100 widgets an hour and stays at that level of performance day in and day out. On the other hand, Employee B produces 75 widgets an hour but improves output to 85 widgets an hour. Who should you reward? Employee B! This example embodies what you want to reward: The efforts that your employees make to improve their performance, not just to maintain a certain level (no matter how good that level is).

The following are examples of *performance-based measures* that any manager must recognise and reward. Consider what measures you should be monitoring, measuring, and rewarding in your organisation. Don't forget, just showing up for work doesn't count.

✔ Defects decrease from 25 per 1,000 to 10 per 1,000.

✔ Annual sales increase by 20 per cent.

✔ The department records system is reorganised and colour-coded to make filing and retrieval more efficient.

✔ Administrative expenses are held to 90 per cent of the authorised budget.

✔ The organisation's mail is distributed in 1 hour instead of 1½ hours.

Some managers break incentives into two categories – 'results measures', where measures are linked to the bottom line, and 'process measures', where the link to the bottom line isn't as clear. You need to recognise achievement in both categories.

Starting with the Positive

You're more likely to lead your employees to great results by focusing on their positive accomplishments rather than by finding fault with and punishing their negative outcomes. Despite this fact, many managers' primary mode of operation is correcting their employees' mistakes instead of complimenting their successes.

In a recent study, 58 per cent of employees reported that they seldom received a personal 'thank you' from their manager for doing a good job even though they ranked such recognition as their most motivating incentive. They ranked a written thank you for doing a good job as motivating incentive No. 2, while 76 per cent said that they seldom received thanks from their managers. Perhaps these statistics show why a lack of praise and recognition is one of the leading reasons people leave their jobs.

Years of psychological research clearly show that positive reinforcement works better than negative reinforcement for several reasons. Without getting too technical, the reasons are that positive reinforcement:

✔ Increases the frequency of the desired behaviour

✔ Creates good feelings within employees

On the other hand, negative reinforcement may decrease the frequency of undesired behaviour, but doesn't necessarily result in the expression of desired behaviour. Instead of being motivated to do better, employees who receive only criticism from their managers eventually come to avoid their managers whenever possible. Furthermore, negative reinforcement (particularly when manifested in ways that degrade employees and their sense of self-worth) can create tremendously bad feelings in employees. And employees who are unhappy with their employers have a much more difficult time doing a good job than the employees who are happy with their employers.

The following ideas can help you seek out the positive in your employees and reinforce the behaviours you want:

✔ **Have high expectations for your employees' abilities.** If you believe that your employees can be outstanding, soon they believe it, too. When Peter was growing up, his parents rarely needed to punish him when he did something wrong. He needed only the words 'we know that you can do better' to get him back on course.

✔ **Recognise that your employees are doing their best.** If a shortfall in performance occurs, then support and encourage; punishing people for things that they cannot do in any case has little point.

✔ **Give your employees the benefit of the doubt.** Do you really think that your employees want to do a bad job? No one wants to do a bad job; so your job is to work out everything you can do to help employees do a good job. Additional training, encouragement, and support should be among your first choices – not reprimands and punishment.

✔ **Catch your employees doing things right.** Most employees do a good job in most of their work, so instead of constantly catching your employees doing things wrong, catch them doing things right. Not only can you reinforce the behaviours that you want, but you can also make your employees feel good about working for you and for your organisation.

Making a Big Deal about Something Little

Okay, here's a question for you: Should you reward your employees for their little day-to-day successes, or should you save up rewards for when they accomplish something really major? The answer to this question lies in the way that most people get their work done on a daily basis.

The simple fact is that for most people in business, work is not a string of dazzling successes that come one after another without fail. Instead, the majority of work consists of routine, daily activities; employees perform most of these duties quietly and with little fanfare. A manager's typical workday, for example, may consist of an hour or two reading memos and e-mail messages, listening to voice-mail messages, and talking to other people on the phone. The manager spends another couple of hours in meetings and perhaps another hour in one-on-one discussions with staff members and colleagues, much of which involves dealing with problems as they occur. With additional time spent on preparing reports or filling out forms, the manager actually devotes precious little time to decision making – the activity that has the greatest impact on an organisation.

For a line worker, this dearth of opportunities for dazzling success is even more pronounced. If the employee's job is assembling lawnmower engines all day (and she does a good, steady job), when does she have an opportunity to be outstanding in the eyes of her supervisor?

We've taken the long way around to say that major accomplishments are usually few and far between, regardless of your place in the organisational chart. Work is a series of small accomplishments that eventually add up to big ones. If you wait to reward your employees for their big successes, you may be waiting a long time.

Therefore, reward your employees for their small successes as well as for their big successes. You may set a lofty goal for your employees to achieve – one that stretches their abilities and tests their resolve – but remember that praising your employees' progress towards the goal is perhaps even more important than praising them when they finally reach it.

Money and Motivation

You may think that money is the ultimate incentive for your employees. After all, who isn't excited when they receive a cash bonus or pay rise? *As visions of riches beyond her wildest dreams danced through her head, she pledged her eternal devotion to the firm.* The problem is that money really isn't the top motivator for employees – at least not in the way that most managers think. And it can be a huge demotivator if you manage it badly.

Compensating with wages and salaries

Money is clearly important to your employees. They need money to pay bills, buy food and clothes, put petrol in their cars, and afford the other necessities of life.

Most employees consider the money they receive to be a fair exchange for the work they put in. Payment for work carried out is a legal right. Recognition, on the other hand, is a gift. Using recognition, however, helps you get the best effort from each employee.

Realising when incentives become entitlements

In particular, employees who receive annual bonuses and other periodic, money-based rewards quickly come to consider them part of their basic pay. The problem arises when achieving bonuses and incentives is easy or straightforward. Productivity and output begin to flatten out; and the incentive effect of the payments themselves begins to diminish. People work on the basis that the incentives and bonuses are forthcoming anyway.

Incentives work best when they're related to direct goals or targets and short-term performance. In particular, incentives do not make a bad or boring job more interesting – they make it more bearable, and that only in the short term.

So the issue becomes again: What are you rewarding? You need to work out what the goals and priorities are, what rewards people expect for achieving them, and the best way of delivering these rewards. Consolidating incentives into standard pay and reward packages simply puts up the payroll costs without any tangible returns.

The ineffectiveness of money as a motivator for employees is a good news/bad news kind of thing. We start with the bad news first. Many managers have thrown lots of money into cash-reward programmes, and for the most part these programmes really didn't have the positive effect on motivation that the managers expected. Although we don't want to say that you waste your money on these programmes, you can use it more effectively.

Now you get the good news: Because you know that money is not the most effective motivation tool, you can focus on using tools that are more effective – and the best forms of recognition cost little or no money!

Working out what motivates your staff

If you're a busy manager, cash rewards are convenient because you simply fill out a single request to take care of all your motivation for the year. By contrast, the manager-initiated, based-on-performance stuff seems like a lot of work. To be frank, running an effective rewards programme does take more work on your part than running a simple but ineffective one. But as we show you, the best rewards can be quite simple. After you get the hang of using them, you can easily integrate them into your daily routine. Doing so is part of managing today.

To achieve the best results:

- ✔ Concentrate on what the employees need, want, and expect. The only way to be absolutely sure is to ask them.
- ✔ Concentrate rewards on the things you really want done. And keep in mind that what gets rewarded gets done.

Don't save up recognition for special occasions only – and don't just use them with the top performers. You need to recognise every employee when they do good work in their job. Your employees are doing good things – things that you want them to do – every day. Catch them doing something right and recognise their successes regularly and often.

The following incentives are simple to execute, take little time, and are the most motivating for employees:

- ✔ Personal or written congratulations from you for a job well done
- ✔ Public recognition, given visibly by you for good job performance

✔ Morale-building meetings to celebrate successes

✔ Time off or flexibility in one's working hours

✔ Asking employees their opinions and involving them in decision making

Realising that you hold the key to your employees' motivation

In our experience, most managers believe that their employees determine how motivated they choose to be. Managers tend to think that some employees naturally have good attitudes, that others naturally have bad attitudes, and that managers can't do much to change these attitudes. 'If only we could unleash the same passion and energy people have for their families and hobbies,' these managers think, 'then we could really get something done around here.'

As convenient as blaming your employees for their bad attitudes may be, looking in a mirror may be a more honest approach. Managers need to:

✔ Recognise their employees for doing a good job

✔ Provide a pleasant and supportive working environment

✔ Create a sense of joint mission and teamwork in the organisation

✔ Treat their employees as equals

✔ Avoid favouritism

✔ Make time to listen when employees need to talk

For the most part, you determine how motivated (and demotivated) your employees are. Managers create a motivating environment that makes it easier for employees to be motivated. When the time comes, recognise and reward them fairly and equitably for the work they do well.

When you give out rewards, keep in mind that employees don't want handouts, and they hate favouritism. Provide rewards for the performance that helps you be mutually successful. Don't give recognition when none is warranted. Don't give it just to be nice, or with the hope that people will like you better. Doing so not only cheapens the value of the incentive with the employee who received it, but makes you lose credibility in the eyes of your other employees. Trust and credibility are two of the most important qualities that you can build in your relationship with your employees; if you lose these qualities, you risk losing the employee.

Chapter 3

Harnessing the Power of Technology

*L*ike everything else in life, technology has its good and bad points. With computers, for example, managers and workers alike have more ways to waste time than ever before. When all you could do with a keyboard was type, you couldn't get any manager anywhere near one – they used to have secretaries to do that kind of stuff. Now, call it a computer, add e-mail and the Internet, and you can't get managers away from it. Some research shows that managers spend up to five hours of their working day on the computer; and when you add the average of three hours a day in meetings, this does not leave very much time for the real work to be done. And do you really need to spend half an hour typing, editing, spellchecking, and colour printing a gorgeous, 64-shades-of-grey memo when a handwritten note or quick phone call works just as well? You may automatically assume that your employees are more productive simply because they have computers at their fingertips, but are you (and your organisation) really getting the most out of this innovative and expensive technology?

So in this chapter, we explain how to harness *information technology* – technology used to create, store, exchange, and use information in its various forms. We examine the technology edge, and consider how technology can help or hinder an organisation. We look at how technology can improve efficiency and productivity, and how to get the most out of technology. Finally, we describe how to create a technology plan.

Using Technology to Your Advantage

You can easily get the impression that information technology is taking over the world. Certainly, computers and telecommunications technology are ever more important. CEOs, top and senior managers all use computers and mobile phones exactly the same as everyone else, because they too (some would say above all) need to be able to be instantly flexible and responsive when required. Overall, information technology can give you and your business tremendous advantages and, as a manager, you must capitalise on them – before your competition does.

Information and telecommunications technology are only as good as the people who use them. So whatever technology you implement, make sure that your staff know and understand how they're supposed to use their equipment; and especially, make sure that they understand where the boundaries lie – what they are *not* allowed to use the technology for (such as booking holidays in the firm's time, and downloading from controversial or obscene Web sites).

First, understand the technology and what it can do for you, your organisation, and your staff. You need to take the decision whether you are going to let technology use you, or use it yourself for more effective, productive, and high-quality work.

The following sections outline four basic considerations for putting modern technology to work for you.

Know your business

Before you can design and implement an effective information technology strategy for your business, you have to completely understand how your business works – what work is done, who's doing it, and what resources they need to get their work done.

One way to know your business is to approach it as an outsider. Pretend you're a customer and look at how your company's people and systems handle you. Do the same with your competitors to see how their people and systems handle you. Compare the differences and the similarities to determine how you can improve your own organisation as a result of what you've discovered.

Create a technology-competitive advantage

Few managers understand how technology can become a competitive advantage for their businesses. Although they may have vague notions of potential efficiency gains or increased productivity, they're clueless when dealing with specifics.

Information technology can create real and dramatic competitive advantages over other businesses in your markets, specifically by:

- ✔ Using the Internet as a marketing tool, as a part of your corporate and institutional presentation and image building. The Internet can enhance and develop the image and presentation that you want for all of your marketing activities, as well as being a vehicle for sales.

- ✔ Make sure that the messages you put out on the Internet are the same or complementary to those put out elsewhere.

- ✔ Using the Internet as an additional marketing, sales, customer, and client liaison vehicle.

- ✔ Using the Internet to discover potential (and we stress *potential*) staff, suppliers, customers, and product and service outlets.

- ✔ Linking everyone in the company with each other, and with key suppliers, distributors, outlets, customers, and clients.

- ✔ Providing up-to-the-minute information on pricing, products, and services.

Any Web site that you develop must be kept up to date. If it is to be fully effective and complementary to the full range of your business activities, you must have it checked once a week; some organisations do this once a day, and the best have staff dedicated to changing the Web site as soon as anything occurs that requires a change.

Develop a plan

If you're serious about using information technology to full advantage, you must have a plan for its implementation. You can find details about creating a technology plan later in this chapter (see the section 'Planning and Implementation'), but the following are several points to remember in the planning process:

✔ **Don't buy technology just because it's the latest and greatest thing.** Everybody loves gadgets – and everybody loves the latest gadget above all. However, just because an item is new doesn't mean that it's right for your business. Be sure that whatever technology you include in your plan makes sense for your business.

✔ **Plan for the right period of time.** Different kinds of businesses require different *planning horizons*, the time periods covered by their plans. If you're in a highly volatile market – wireless communications, for example – then your planning horizon may be only six months or so ahead. If you're in a stable market – say, a grocery chain – your planning horizon may extend three to five years into the future.

✔ **Make the planning process a team effort.** You're not the only one who's going to be affected by all this new technology that you bring into your company. Keep customers and suppliers informed of any changes that affect them; and above all, involve your staff – they are the people, after all, who are going to be using the new technology.

✔ **Weigh up the costs of upgrading your old system versus moving to a new system.** Every system eventually comes to the end of its useful life. So you have to choose whether to patch up what you have or replace it altogether. And you need to approach that decision from the point of view of how long the system is likely to remain useful into the future, whether you're patching it up or replacing it.

Get some help

If you're a fan of technology and expert in it, that's great – but beware! Don't get drawn down the line of being blinded by technology for its own sake; always keep in mind the use to which you are going to put it, and how people less expert and enthusiastic than you are going to use it. Involve everyone, and if necessary, engage a technician or technology consultant to advise on the process. If you do bring in a consultant, again make sure that you involve the staff affected in making the changes.

Evaluating the Benefits and Drawbacks of Technology

Think for a moment about the incredible progress of information technology just in your lifetime. Can you believe that three decades ago, the personal computer had yet to be introduced commercially? Word processing used to mean a typewriter and a lot of correction fluid or sheets of messy carbon paper, but computers have revolutionised the way in which business people can manipulate text, graphics, and other elements in their reports and other documents. Mobile phones, fax machines, the Internet, and other business technology essentials are all fairly recent innovations.

So how can technology help your business? Information technology can have a positive impact in two very important ways:

✔ **By automating processes:** Not too many years ago, most business processes were manual. For example, your organisation's accounting and payroll departments most likely did their calculations entirely by hand, using only calculators to assist them. What used to take hours, days, or weeks can now be accomplished in minutes. Other commonly automated processes are stock tracking, customer service, call analysis, and purchasing.

✔ **By automating personal management functions:** Managers now need to have their diaries and personal planners on computer for ready access. While this doesn't replace wallcharts (which are essential for everyone to see in public anyway), managers do increasingly need to have their own personal data with them at all times. Managers are additionally finding that they can use their own computers to keep track of projects, get product and service performance data for themselves, contact employees by e-mail and mobile phone, and surf the Internet for data that they need to know.

Before you run off and automate or upgrade everything, keep this piece of information in mind: If your present system is inefficient or ineffective, simply upgrading the existing system won't necessarily make your system perform any better. In fact, upgrading it can make your system perform worse than the manual version. Whatever you do, review and evaluate all processes in detail. Cut out any unnecessary steps as you go along, and make sure that your system is designed for the future and not the past. And if that sounds a time-consuming process, it is time well spent.

Just as information technology can help a business, it can also hinder it. Here are a few examples of the negative side of information technology:

✔ Widespread worker abuse of Internet access has reduced worker productivity by 10 to 15 per cent. Forrester Research, an American think tank, estimates that 20 per cent of employee time on the Internet at work doesn't involve their jobs; other studies in the United Kingdom by the Chartered Management Institute, put the figure as high as 30 per cent of time.

✔ Hackers have sent periodic waves of computer viruses and malicious attacks through the business world, leaving billions of pounds of damage and lost productivity in their wake.

✔ E-mail messages can be unclear and confusing, forcing workers to waste time clarifying the intention or covering themselves in case of problems.

✔ Employees are forced to wade through an ever-growing quantity of spam and junk e-mail messages.

✔ The slick, animated, and sound-laden computer-based full-colour presentations so common today often tend to drown out the message you're trying to get across. People lose sight of what they are supposed to absorb, do, or act on as the result of the presentation.

So you have to take the bad with the good with information technology. But don't take the bad lying down. You know the problems and difficulties – so recognise them at the outset, and take active steps to prevent them occurring. You can do this by:

✔ **Staying abreast of the latest information technology innovations and news.** Although you don't need to become an expert on how to install a network server or configure your voice-mail system, you do need to become conversant in the technology behind your business systems.

✔ **Hiring experts.** Although you must have a general knowledge of information technology, plan to hire experts to advise you on the specifics. Always seek expert advice in the design and implementation of critical information technology-based systems.

✔ **Managing by walking around.** Make a habit of dropping in on employees, wherever they're located, and observe how they use your organisation's information technology. Ask them for their opinions and suggestions for improvement. Research and implement changes as soon as you discover a need.

One point is certain: Everyone is lumbered with the present state of technology, and the great speed at which it develops. You therefore have to know and understand what technology can do for you; and also to become quickly aware of what any new innovations or inventions can do for you.

Improving Efficiency and Productivity

In recent years, British industry has shifted from primary manufacturing and engineering activities to domination by the service sector. The service sector – whether public services, commerce, financial services, leisure, travel, tourism, or retail – depends on the speed and quality of information and data processing to maintain, secure, and develop competitive advantage.

The idea that businesspeople who manage information best have a competitive advantage in the marketplace seems obvious enough. The sooner you receive information, the sooner you can act on it. The more effectively you handle information, the easier you can access that information when and where you need it. The more efficiently and effectively you deal with information, the fewer expenses you incur for managing and maintaining your information.

Managers often cite the preceding reasons, and others like them, as justification for spending obscenely huge amounts of corporate resources to buy computers, install e-mail and voice-mail systems, and train employees to use them. Unfortunately, for years researchers found no evidence to prove that office automation resulted in measurable productivity gains. This led many to label the phenomenon the 'productivity paradox', meaning that technology that is supposed to make a job easier, quicker, to a higher standard, and with fewer errors actually results in fewer results delivered, less quickly. The problem is now that work is done at the speed at which the machine goes, rather than at the speed at which the individual works.

The key to effective planning and implementation of information technology systems is knowing and understanding what they are supposed to do for you. You also need to know and understand the full environment and context in which they are to be implemented, and, above all, the results that they are to deliver for you. For example:

✔ Ryanair and easyJet have transformed the entire air travel sector of Western and Central Europe. They cut out the costs of employing travel agents to make bookings, requiring people to book online or, at a high premium, through their own call centres. However, the online booking facility is not an end in itself, it is underpinned by the major cost and price advantages that each of the companies delivers, relative to the competition and alternatives from European flag-carrier airlines. And when Michael O'Leary, the CEO of Ryanair, was asked whether by getting customers to book online he was eliminating those who did not have computer access, he simply replied: 'We are the largest volume carrier in Europe; and we carry more passengers than British Airways.'

✔ Honda UK at Swindon has a fully automated supply-side process. As parts are removed from the shelves to go on to the production lines, they are automatically deducted from the stock levels; and when the stock level reaches a particular point, a request to suppliers is automatically generated. The supply side contract means that suppliers must dispatch within two hours, and Honda must receive their requirements within four hours.

Other companies have taken an enlightened view of 'the technology in its environment' to great effect. For example:

✔ Semco, a Brazilian manufacturing company and global iconic organisation, cancelled one computerised accounting and billing system because it did the job more slowly than clerks working with calculators.

✔ Mobile communications retailer Carphone Warehouse forbids its staff to send e-mails to each other unless, and until, they have first talked face to face, or unless the particular member of staff is not on the premises for some reason. This is because the company takes the view that far more gets done far more quickly when people talk to each other, than when they write to each other.

So merely installing computers and other information technology does not automatically lead to gains in employee efficiency or product and service performance. As a manager, you must take the time to analyse and evaluate the environment in which the work has to be done. To be fully effective, the technology must integrate fully with the aims and objectives of the business, the ways in which it delivers products and services, and the capabilities and qualities of the staff doing the work.

Getting the Most Out of Information Technology

The personal computer shifted the power of computing away from huge mainframes and onto the desks of individual users. Now, computer networks are bringing about a new revolution in business. Although the personal computer is a self-sufficient island of information, when you link these islands together in a network, individual computers have the added benefit of sharing with every computer on the network. So you have a huge potential to tap into. Nevertheless, make sure that you concentrate especially on the following:

- ✔ **Networks improve communication:** Computer networks allow anyone in an organisation who is connected to the network to communicate with anyone else quickly and easily. With the click of a button, you can send messages to individuals or groups of employees. You can send replies just as easily. Furthermore, employees on computer networks can access financial, marketing, and product information needed to do their jobs from throughout the organisation.

- ✔ **Networks save time and money:** In business, time is money. The faster you can get something done, the more tasks you can complete during the course of your business day. E-mail allows you to create messages, memos, and other internal communications, to attach work files, and then to transmit them instantaneously to as many colleagues as you want. And these colleagues can be located across the room or around the world – and they all get the same message at the same time.

- ✔ **Networks improve understanding of markets, products and services:** Information communicated via computer networks is timely, direct, and standardised. Everyone gets the same message and so everyone can have the same understanding of the company's vision and values; and especially of its products, services, and markets, and the ways in which these are performing. All staff therefore ought to have a much clearer understanding than was previously possible of just how products and services are delivered, and what the markets need, want, and demand.

✔ **Networks improve and underpin staff cohesion:** Because everybody has the same access to information, and receives the same messages in an unfiltered way, there is a much greater potential for mutual cohesion and commitment, provided that networks are used to support the organisation's core values and staff management practices. However, problems always occur if you deliver different messages to different groups of staff – and this information and these differences will become very much more apparent more quickly as the result of the presence of information technology, simply because so many people have access to so much more information. Be very careful to set yourself high standards and transparency in your approach.

So your first step towards getting the most out of information technology is to commit yourself to concentrating on each of these areas. Of course, additional functional requirements exist for everyone connected. However, using networks to underpin culture, values, product and service knowledge, and staff awareness reinforces the very foundations of the organisation.

Planning and Implementation

When it comes to the fast-changing area of technology, having a *technology plan* – a plan for acquiring and deploying information technology – is a must. Many businesses buy bits and pieces of computer hardware, software, and other technology without considering the technology that they already have in place, and without looking very far into the future. Then, when they try to hook everything together, they're surprised that their thrown-together system doesn't work.

Managers who take the time to develop and implement a technology plan don't have this problem, and aren't forced to spend far more money and time fixing systems problems. Follow these steps for a smooth process:

1. **Create the plan.** As manager, you have the vision and purpose – what the technology is supposed to deliver, how, when, where, and to whom. However, in order to give this vision life, you have to be able to present it in ways that your colleagues and staff can understand, so get them involved. Without doubt, they will be able to see potential that you have not thought of; and they will also be able to see any glitches or problems; it is they, after all, who are going to be implementing and using the technology in the pursuit of your grand vision.

2. **Screen and select suppliers.** Go out yourself to actual and potential suppliers. Once you have debated your requirements with your staff and created a technology plan, take the plan with you. Show potential suppliers what you want, and ask them if they can deliver it. And if they say 'No, we cannot deliver this; but we can deliver something that is much better', listen to them, evaluate their response, and take the issue back

to your organisation for debate with your colleagues – or else walk away. If a supplier says 'No, we cannot deliver this; we will deliver what we always deliver regardless of customer requirements' – then just walk away.

3. **Implement the plan.** So everyone has agreed the technology plan and you have chosen your supplier. Now comes the tricky part – implementation. Be in absolutely no doubt that glitches, delays, overruns, and teething troubles are going to occur – everyone has these, and you're no different. At the implementation phase build in as much slack and leeway as necessary to allow for these problems to arise and for you to resolve them.

4. **Monitor performance.** And so finally your system is up and running. Congratulations all round! However, this is crunch time to determine whether the system is really going to deliver what you planned. Keep in mind that, especially in the early stages, glitches and teething troubles with the system are going to happen. So make sure that you have a tight and high-quality service level agreement with your supplier, committing it to coming in and fixing any problems as soon as they arise or become apparent. Make sure that your supplier has staff who are fully trained in your system; if not, then call the supplier to account for this. And if (hypothetically of course!) the system does not deliver what you and your colleagues expected, then you have a serious problem, but one that you have to face; otherwise you find yourself in the position of all the large corporations and public service bodies that have tried to make the unworkable work.

'Everything takes twice as long as you think, and costs twice as much.' While this is never an excuse for organisational slackness or waste of resources, it does underpin the point that nothing ever goes completely according to schedule.

Technology is a strategic expense; and all organisations and managers need to see technology projects as investments on which there are demonstrable and quantifiable returns. Make sure that whatever you do is guided by the business, product, service, and market drivers of the organisation, and the goals, results, and targets that the organisation expects you to deliver as a manager. Use this as your guiding principle when planning and implementing technology projects, and you get much less wrong than those who do not take the time and trouble to prepare fully.

Chapter 4

Attracting and Keeping Customers

· ·

In This Chapter

▶ Creating compelling content through links and hooks

▶ Promoting your business by providing objective, useful information

▶ Making less do more through concise, well-organised content

▶ Writing friendly, objective prose that sells your products and services

▶ Inviting customer interaction with forms, e-mail, and more

· ·

A s writers, we know only too well the challenge of staring at a totally white piece of paper or a blank computer screen. It's at times like these that Greg remembers his teacher telling him to 'let it flow' and worry about editing after he'd let his creative juices flow. That's good advice up to a point, especially for something like a Web log (blog). But when it comes to a business Web site, you have to get it just right before you invite people to have a look. You need to present the *right* content in the *right* way to make prospective clients and customers want to explore your site the first time and then return down the road.

One of our primary points in this chapter is that you need to express your main message on your business site up front. We do the same by explaining what we consider to be general content rules for an online business. You should

✔ Remember that people who are online get bored quickly

✔ Make it easy for visitors to find out who you are and what you have to offer

✔ Be friendly and informal in tone, concise in length, and clear in your material's structure

✔ Develop the all-important one-to-one-relationship with customers and clients by inviting dialogue and interaction, both with you and with others who share the same interests

In other words, you need to be straightforward about who you are and where you're coming from on your business site. This chapter is obviously about writing for the Web. But the idea is not to be satisfied with generating just any old text. The goal is to craft exciting, well-organised, and easily digestible information. What follows is how to put these objectives into action.

Including Features That Attract Customers

Half the battle with developing content for a business Web site is knowing what shoppers want and determining strategies for giving it to them. Identifying your target audience helps you devise a message that will make each potential customer think you're speaking directly to him or her. But you also should keep in mind some general concepts that can help you market successfully to all ages, both genders, and every socioeconomic group.

Studies of how people absorb the information on a Web page indicate that people don't really read the contents from top to bottom (or left to right, for that matter) in a linear way. In fact, most Web surfers don't *read* in the traditional sense at all. Instead, they browse so quickly that you'd think they're on a timer. They 'skip through pages' by clicking link after link. As more Internet users connect with broadband technologies, such as DSL and cable, they can absorb complex graphics and multimedia. On average, people stay on each Web page for just a few seconds, unless they find something that really grabs them. Next time you're online for half an hour or so, press the Back button and check out the Web pages you've visited; you'll be amazed at how many you've browsed.

In addition, lots of users are beginning to use palm devices, pocket PCs, Web-enabled cell phones, and even Internet-ready automobiles to get online. These new devices only add to the 'can't hang about' Web surfing trend. Because your prospective customers don't necessarily have tons of computing power or hours' worth of time to explore your site, the best rule is to keep it simple.

People who are looking for things on the Web are often in a state of hurried distraction. Think about a television watcher browsing during a commercial or a harried parent stealing a few moments on the computer while the baby naps, or even, dare we say, while at work when they're supposed to be concentrating on other things. Imagine this person surfing with one hand on a mouse, the other dipping tortillas into salsa. This person – your average customer – isn't in the mood to listen as you tell your fondest hopes and dreams for success, which started with selling sweets in the playground. Here's what this shopper is probably thinking:

> 'What's this? Why does this page take so long to load? And I paid good money to get a quick broadband! I swear, sometimes I wish the Web didn't have any graphics. Here, I'll click this. No, wait! I'll click that. Oh, no, now the baby is crying again.

> Look, I don't have time to read all this. My show is about to come back on, and I still need to go to the bathroom.'

The following sections describe some ways to attract the attention of the distracted and get them to scroll down exactly where you want them to go.

Don't be shy about what you have to say

Don't keep people in suspense about what your business does. People in general, and Web users in particular, want to know what it does and why. Make it hard for them to find out, and they'll be off without giving your business a second thought. Answer the golden questions, on the other hand, and you're well on your way to retaining them:

- Who are you, anyway?
- All right, so what are you selling?
- Well, then, why do I want to buy it?
- Why should I choose your site to investigate rather than all the others out there?

A survey by BizRate (www.bizrate.co.uk) revealed that around three in ten consumers abandon online shopping trolleys (or fail to buy the goods they have selected online) without making a purchase.

Web surfers are opportunists and, in many cases, aren't particularly loyal. Many discover new sites as they trawl randomly through the Web. If they find something easier and quicker, they'll move on. When it comes to Web pages, it pays to put the most important components first: who you are, what you do, and how you stand out from any competing sites. If you can, illustrate these points without using words – make the product completely self-explanatory (think Google) or brilliantly designed so that people naturally want to find out more.

If you have a long list of items to sell, you probably can't fit everything you have to offer right on the first page of your site. Even if you could, you wouldn't want to: As in a television newscast, it's better to prioritise the contents of your site so that the *breaking stories,* or the best contents, appear at the top, and the rest of what's in your catalogue is arranged in order of importance.

Think long and hard before you use features that may scare people away instead of wowing them. We're talking about those *splash pages* that contain only a logo or short greeting and then reload automatically and take the visitor to the main body of a site. We also don't recommend loading up your home page with Flash animations or Java applets that take your prospective customers' browsers precious seconds to load.

Encourage visitors to click, click, click!

Imagine multitasking Web surfers arriving at your Web site with only a fraction of their attention engaged. Make the links easy to read and in obvious locations. Having a row of links at the top of your home page, each of which points the visitor to an important area of your site, is always a good idea (see Figure 4-1). Such links give visitors an idea of what your site contains in a single glance and immediately encourage viewers to click a primary subsection of your site and explore further. By placing an interactive table of contents right up front, you direct surfers right to the material they are looking for.

Figure 4-1: Notice how real business.co. uk uses lots of clearly labelled buttons to draw users' attention.

The links can go at or near the top of the page on either the left or right side. The Dummies.com home page, shown in Figure 4-2, has a few links just above the top banner, but also sports links down *both* the left and right sides.

Figure 4-2:
Putting at
least five or
six links
near the top
of your
home page
is clearly a
good idea!

If you want to be ranked highly by search engines (and who doesn't?), you have another good reason to place your site's main topics near the top of the page in a series of links. Some search services index the first 50 or so words on a Web page. If you can get lots of important keywords included in that index, the chances are better that your site will be ranked highly in a list of links returned by the service in response to a search.

Use the following steps to create links to local files on your Web site by using Netscape Composer, the free Web page editor that comes with the Netscape Communicator Web browser. The steps assume that you've started up the program and that the Web page you want to edit is already open.

1. **Select the text or image on your Web page that you want to serve as the jumping-off point for the link.**

    If you select a word or phrase, the text is highlighted in black. If you select an image, a black box appears around the image.

2. **Choose Insert⇨Link or press Ctrl+L.**

    The Link Properties dialog box appears, as shown in Figure 4-3.

Figure 4-3:
If you keep all your related Web pages in the same directory, you have to enter only a simple filename as the link destination.

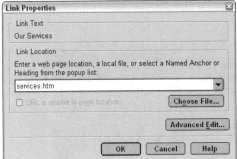

3. **In the box beneath Link Location, enter the name of the file you want to link to if you know the filename.**

   If the page you want to link to is in the same directory as the page that contains the jumping-off point, you need to enter only the name of the Web page. If the page is in another directory, you need to enter a path relative to the Web page that contains the link (or click the Choose File button, locate the file in the Open HTML File dialog box, and click the Open button).

4. **Click OK.**

   The Link Properties dialog box closes, and you return to the Composer window. If you made a textual link, the selected text is underlined and in a different colour. If you made an image link, a box appears around the image.

Presenting the reader with links up front doesn't just help your search engine rankings, it also indicates that your site is content rich and worthy of a thorough look.

Tell us a little about yourself

One thing you need to state clearly as soon as possible on your Web site is who you are and what you do, or what people can get out of using your Web site. Technorati, the blog search engine, encapsulates what it does in a very slick way:

   Who's saying what. Right now.

Can you identify your primary goal in a single sentence? If not, try to boil down your goals to two or three sentences at the most. Whatever you do, make your mission statement more specific and customer oriented than simply saying, 'Out to make lots of money!' Tell prospects what you can do for them; the fact that you have three kids in college and need to make money to pay their tuition isn't really their concern. Dan's mission statement on Infozoo.co.uk is 'Get known. Know more', which is meant to sum up his Web site's service of helping small businesses 'get known' and their customers 'know more' about some great services on offer.

Add a search box

One of the most effective kinds of content you can add to your site is a search box. A *search box* is a simple text-entry field that lets a visitor enter a word or phrase. By clicking a button labelled Go, Search, or something of the sort, the search term or terms are sent to the site, where a script checks an index of the site's contents for any files that contain the terms. The script then causes a list of documents that contain the search terms to appear in the visitor's browser window.

A search box invites visitors to interact instantly with your Web site. If you can find a Web host that will help you set up a search box, you don't have to mess around with computer scripts and indexing tools. (See the section, 'Make your site searchable', later in this chapter, for more information.)

Search boxes are commonly found on commercial Web sites. You usually see them at the top of the home page, right near the links to the major sections of the site. The Dummies.com page, shown in Figure 4-4, includes a search box in the upper right corner of the page.

Figure 4-4:
Many surfers prefer using a search box to clicking links.

Although Greg's always looking for freelance writing jobs, even he has to admit that you don't really need to hire a professional to make a Web site compelling. You're not writing an essay, a term paper, or a book here. Rather, you need to observe only a couple of simple rules:

- Provide lots of links and hooks that readers can scan.
- Keep everything concise!

The key word to remember is *short.* Keep sentences brief and snappy. Limit paragraphs to one or two sentences in length. You may also want to limit each Web page to no more than one or two screens in length so that viewers don't have to scroll down too far to find what they want – even if they're on a laptop or smaller Internet appliance.

Making your content scannable

When you're writing something on paper, whether it's a letter to your Mum or your shopping list, contents have to be readable. Contents on your Web site, on the other hand, have to be scannable. This principle has to do with the way people absorb information online. Eyes that are staring at a computer screen for many minutes or many hours tend to jump around a Web page, looking for an interesting bit of information on which to rest. In this section, we suggest ways to attract those tired eyes and guide them toward the products or services you want to provide.

We're borrowing the term *scannable* from John Morkes and Jakob Nielsen of Sun Microsystems, who use it in their article 'Concise, Scannable, and Objective: How to Write for the Web' (www.useit.com/papers/webwriting/writing.html). We're including a link to this article (which was written eons ago in Web terms, but still holds true) in the Internet Directory on this book's Web site, along with other tips on enriching the content of your Web pages. See the section of the Directory called 'Developing Compelling Content' for more information.

Point the way with headings

One hard-to-miss Web page element that's designed to grab the attention of your readers' eyes is a heading. Every Web page needs to contain headings that direct the reader's attention to its most important contents. This book provides a good example. The chapter title (we hope) piques your interest first. Then the section headings and subheadings direct you to more details on the topics you want to read about.

Most graphics designers we've worked with label their heads with letters of the alphabet: 'A', 'B', 'C', and so on. In a similar fashion, most Web page editing tools designate top-level headings with the style Heading 1. Beneath this heading, you place one or more Heading 2 headings. Beneath each of those, you may have Heading 3 and, beneath those, Heading 4. (Headings 5 and 6 are too small to be useful, in our opinion.) The arrangement may look like the following.

```
Miss Cookie's Delectable Cooking School (Heading 1)
  Kitchen Equipment You Can't Live Without (Heading 2)
  The Story of a Calorie Counter Gone Wrong (Heading 2)
  Programmes of Culinary Study (Heading 2)
  Registration (Heading 3)
  Course Schedule (Heading 3)
```

You can energise virtually any heading by telling your audience something specific about your business. Instead of 'Ida's Antique Shop', for example, say something like 'Ida's Antique Shop: The Perfect Destination for the Collector and the Crafter'. Instead of simply writing a heading like 'Stan Thompson, Pet Grooming', say something specific, such as 'Stan Thompson: We Groom Your Pet at Our Place or Yours'.

Become an expert list maker

Lists are simple and effective ways to break up text and make your Web content easier to digest. They're easy to create and easy for your customer to view and absorb. For example, suppose that you import your own decorations, and you want to offer certain varieties at a discount during various seasons. Rather than bury the items you're offering within an easily overlooked paragraph, why not divide your list into subgroups of sale items so that visitors will find what they want without being distracted?

The following example shows how easy lists are to implement if you use Adobe Dreamweaver, a popular Web page creation tool that you can test for yourself for a 30-day trial period by downloading the program from the Macromedia Web site (www.adobe.com/uk/products/dreamweaver). You have your Web page document open in Dreamweaver, and you're at that point in the page where you want to insert a list. Just do the following:

1. **Type a heading for your list and then select the entire heading.**

   For example, you may type and then select the words *This Month's Specials*.

2. **Choose Text⇨Paragraph Format.**

   A list of paragraph styles appears as a submenu next to the Paragraph Format submenu.

3. **Click a heading style, such as Heading 3, to select it from the list of styles.**

   Your text is now formatted as a heading.

4. **Click anywhere in the Dreamweaver window to deselect the heading you just formatted.**

5. **Press Enter to move to a new line.**

6. **Type the first item of your list, press Enter, and then type the second item on the next line.**

   Repeat until you've entered all the items of your list.

7. **Select all the items of your list (but not the heading).**

8. **Choose Text⇨List⇨Unordered List.**

   A bullet appears next to each list item, and the items appear closer together on-screen so that they look more like a list. That's all there is to it! Figure 4-5 shows the result.

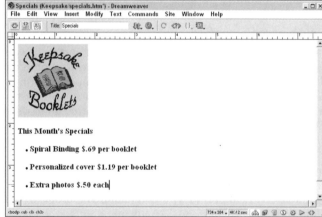

Figure 4-5: A bulleted list is an easy way to direct customers' attention to special promotions or sale items.

Most Web editors let you vary the appearance of the bullet that appears next to a bulleted list item. For example, you can make it a hollow circle rather than a solid black dot, or you can choose a rectangle rather than a circle.

Lead your readers on with links

We mean for you to interpret your headings literally, not figuratively. In other words, we're not suggesting that you make promises on which you can't deliver. Rather, you should do anything you can to lead your visitors to your site and then get them to stay long enough to explore individual pages. You can accomplish this goal with a single hyperlinked word that leads to another page on your site:

More . . .

We see this word all the time on Web pages that present a lot of content. At the bottom of a list of their products and services, businesses place that word in bold type: **More . . .** and we're always interested in finding out what more they could possibly have to offer me.

Magazines use the same approach. On their covers you'll find taglines that refer you to the kinds of stories that you'll find inside. You can do the same kind of thing on your Web pages. For example, which of the following links is more likely to get a response?

Next

Next: Paragon's Success Stories

Whenever possible, tell your visitors what they can expect to encounter as a benefit when they click a link. Give them a tease – and then a big pay-off for responding.

Enhance your text with well-placed images

You can add two kinds of images to a Web page: an *inline image,* which appears in the body of your page along with your text, or an *external image,* which is a separate file that visitors access by clicking a link. The link may take the form of highlighted text or a small version of the image called a *thumbnail.*

The basic HTML tag that inserts an image in your document takes the following form:

```
<IMG SRC="URL">
```

This tag tells your browser to display an image (<IMG>) here. "URL" gives the location of the image file that serves as the source (SRC) for this image. Whenever possible, you should also include WIDTH and HEIGHT attributes (as follows) because they help speed up graphics display for many browsers:

```
<IMG HEIGHT=51 WIDTH=48 SRC="target.gif">
```

Most Web page editors add the WIDTH and HEIGHT attributes automatically when you insert an image. Typically, here's what happens:

1. **You click the location in the Web page where you want the image to appear.**

2. **Then you click an Image toolbar button or choose Insert➪Image to display an image selection dialog box.**

3. **Next you enter the name of the image you want to add and click OK.**

   The image is added to your Web page.

A well-placed image points the way to text that you want people to read immediately. Think about where your own eyes go when you first connect to a Web page. Most likely, you first look at any images on the page; then you look at the headings; and finally, you settle on text to read. If you can place an image next to a heading, you virtually ensure that viewers will read the heading.

Freebies: Everyone's favourite

No matter how much money you have in the bank, you're bound to respond to a really good deal. If you want sure-fire attention, use one of the following words in the headings on your online business site's home page:

- ✔ Free
- ✔ New
- ✔ Act (as in Act Now!)
- ✔ Sale
- ✔ Discount
- ✔ Win (although this word can sound like a scam if used in the wrong context)

Contests and sweepstakes

The word *free* and the phrase *Enter Our Contest* can give you a big bang for your buck when it comes to a business Web page. In fact, few things are as likely to get viewers to click into a site as the promise of getting something for nothing.

Giveaways have a number of hidden benefits, too: Everyone who enters sends you personal information that you can use to compile a mailing list or prepare marketing statistics. Giveaways get people involved with your site, and they invite return visits – especially if you hold contests for several weeks at a time.

Of course, in order to hold a giveaway, you need to have something to *give away*. If you make baskets or sell backpacks, you can designate one of your sale items as the prize. If you can't afford to give something away, offer a big (perhaps 50 per cent) discount.

You can organise either a sweepstakes or a contest. In our definition, a *sweepstake* chooses its winner by random selection; a *contest* requires participants to compete in some way. The most effective contests on the Internet tend to be simple. If you hold one, consider including a Rules Web page that explains who is eligible, who selects the winner, and any rules of participation.

Be aware of the laws and regulations that cover sweepstakes and contests. Such laws often restrict illegal lotteries, as well as the promotion of alcoholic drinks, cigarettes, drugs, or weapons. Telemarketing is sometimes prohibited in connection with a contest. Following are some other points to consider:

✔ Unless you're sure that it's legal to allow Web surfers from other countries to participate, you're safest limiting your contest to UK residents only.

✔ On the contest rules page, be sure to clearly state the starting and ending dates for receiving entries. These dates protect you if someone claims they entered the competition on time, but didn't.

✔ Don't change the ending date of your contest, even if you receive far fewer entries than you had hoped for.

✔ Define the rules of the contest clearly. Include exactly what the prize is, how many you'll give away, and when you'll announce the winner.

If you do hold a contest, announce it at the top of your Web page and hint at the prizes people can win. Use bold and big type to attract the attention of your visitors.

Expert tips and insider information

Giveaways aren't just for businesspeople in retail or wholesale salespeople who have merchandise they can offer as prizes in a contest. If your work involves professional services, you can give away something just as valuable: your knowledge. Publish a simple newsletter that you e-mail to subscribers on a periodic basis. Or answer questions by e-mail. Some Web page designers (particularly college students who are just starting out) work for next to nothing initially, until they build a client base and can charge a higher rate for their services.

Make your site searchable

Search boxes let visitors instantly scan the site's entire contents for a word or phrase. They put visitors in control right away and get them to interact with your site. They're popular for some very good reasons.

We recommend some sort of search utility for e-commerce sites. However, adding a search box to your site doesn't make much sense if you have only five to ten pages of content. Add search capability only if you have enough content to warrant searching. If your site has a sales catalogue driven by a database, it makes more sense to let your customers use the database search tool instead of adding one of the site search tools that we describe in this section.

The problem is that search boxes usually require someone with knowledge of computer programming to create or implement a program called a CGI script to do the searching. Someone also has to compile an index of the documents on the Web site so that the script can search the documents. An application such as ColdFusion can do it, but it's not a program for beginners.

You can get around having to write CGI scripts to add search capabilities to your site. Choose one of these options:

- ✔ **Let your Web host do the work:** Some hosting services will do the indexing and creation of the search utility as part of their services.

- ✔ **Use a free site search service:** The server that does the indexing of your Web pages and holds the index doesn't need to be the server that hosts your site. A number of services will make your site searchable for free. In exchange, you display advertisements or logos in the search results you return to your visitors.

- ✔ **Pay for a search service:** If you don't want to display ads on your search results pages, pay a monthly fee to have a company index your pages and let users conduct searches. FreeFind (www.freefind.com) has some economy packages, a free version that forces you to view ads, and a professional version priced at £10 per month for a site of 1,000 pages or less. SiteMiner (siteminer.mycomputer.com) charges just over £10 per month for up to 1,500 pages, but lets you customise your search box and re-index your site whenever you add new content.

Judy Vorfeld went beyond having a simple Search This Site text box on her Office Support Services Web site. She has one at `www.ossweb.com/search.html`, which makes use of Google's search engine. But as you can see in Figure 4-6, she also provides a separate sitemap page that provides a list of links to her site's most important contents.

Figure 4-6: A Search This Site text box or sitemap page lets visitors instantly match their interests with what you have to offer.

 You say you're up to making your site searchable, and you shudder at the prospect of either writing your own computer script or finding and editing someone else's script to index your site's contents and actually do the searching? Then head over to Atomz (`www.atomz.com`) and check out the hosted application Atomz Search. If your site contains 500 pages or less, you can also add a search box to your Web page that lets visitors search your site. Other organisations that offer similar services include:

- PicoSearch (`www.picosearch.com`)
- Webinator (`www.thunderstone.com/texis/site/pages/webinator.html`)

Writing Unforgettable Text

Quite often, business writing on the Web differs from the dry, linear report writing one is called upon to compose (or worse yet, read) in the corporate world. So you have the chance to express the real you: You're online, where sites that are funny, authors who have a personality, and content that's quirky are most read.

Striking the right tone

When your friends describe you to someone who has never met you, what do they say first? Maybe it's your fashion sense or your collection of salt and pepper shakers. Your business also has a personality, and the more striking you make its description on your Web page, the better. Use the tone of your text to define what makes your business unique and what distinguishes it from your competition.

Getting a little help from your friends

Blowing your own trumpet is a fine technique to use in some situations, but you shouldn't go overboard with promotional prose that beats readers over the head. Web readers are looking for objective information they can evaluate for themselves. An independent review of your site or your products carries far more weight than your own ravings about how great your site is. Sure, you know your products and services are great, but you'll be more convincing if your offerings can sell themselves, or you can identify third parties to endorse them.

What's that you say? *Wired* magazine hasn't called to do an in-depth interview profiling your entrepreneurial skills? Yahoo! hasn't graced you with the coveted glasses icon (indicating, in the estimation of Yahoo!'s Web site reviewers, a cool site worthy of special attention) on one of its long index pages? Take a hint from what we and our colleagues do when we're writing computer books such as the one you're reading now: We fire up our e-mail and dash off messages to anyone who may want to endorse our books: our mentors, our friends, and people we admire in the industry.

 People should endorse your business because they like it, not simply because you asked for an endorsement. If they have problems with your business setup, they can be a great source of objective advice on how to improve it. Then, after you make the improvements, they're more likely than ever to endorse it.

Satisfied customers are another source of endorsements. Approach your customers and ask whether they're willing to provide a quote about how you helped them. If you don't yet have satisfied customers, ask one or two people to try your products or services for free and then, if they're happy with your wares, ask permission to use their comments on your site. Your goal is to get a pithy, positive quote that you can put on your home page or on a page specifically devoted to quotes from your clients.

Don't be afraid to knock on the doors of celebrities, too. Send e-mail to an online reporter or someone prominent in your field and ask for an endorsement. People love to give their opinions and see their names in print. You just may be pleasantly surprised at how ready they are to help you.

Sharing your expertise

Few things build credibility and ensure return visits like a Web site that presents inside tips and goodies you can't get anywhere else. The more you can make your visitors feel that they're going to find something on your site that is rare or unique, the more success you'll have.

Tell what you know. Give people information about your field that they may not have. Point them to all sorts of different places with links.

Inviting Comments from Customers

Quick, inexpensive, and *personal:* These are three of the most important advantages that the Web has over traditional printed catalogues. The first two are obvious pluses. You don't have to wait for your online catalogue to get printed and distributed. On the Web, your contents are published and available to your customers right away. Putting a catalogue on the Web eliminates (or, if publishing a catalogue on the Web allows you to reduce your print run, dramatically reduces) the cost of printing, which can result in big savings for you.

But the fact that online catalogues can be more personal than the printed variety is perhaps the biggest advantage of all. The personal touch comes from the Web's potential for *interactivity.* Getting your customers to click links makes them actively involved with your catalogue.

Getting positive e-mail feedback

Playing hide and seek is fun when you're amusing your baby niece, but it's not a good way to build a solid base of customers. In fact, providing a way for your customers to interact with you so that they can reach you quickly may be the most important part of your Web site.

Add a simple *mailto* link like this:

Questions? Comments? Send e-mail to info@mycompany.com

A mailto link gets its name from the HTML command that programmers use to create it. When visitors click the e-mail address, their e-mail program opens a new e-mail message window with your e-mail address already entered. That way, they have only to enter a subject line, type the message, and click Send to send you their thoughts.

Most Web page creation programs make it easy to create a mailto link. For example, if you use Dreamweaver, follow these steps:

1. **Launch and open the Web page to which you want to add your e-mail link.**

2. **Position your mouse arrow and click at the spot on the page where you want the address to appear.**

   The convention is to put your e-mail address at or near the bottom of a Web page. A vertical blinking cursor appears at the location where you want to insert the address.

3. **Choose Insert⇨Email Link.**

   The Insert Email Link dialog box appears.

4. **In the Text box, type the text that you want to appear on your Web page.**

   You don't have to type your e-mail address; you can also type *Webmaster, Customer Service,* or your own name.

5. **In the EMail box, type your e-mail address.**

6. **Click OK.**

   The Insert Email Link dialog box closes, and you return to the Dreamweaver Document window, where your e-mail link appears in blue and is underlined to signify that it is a clickable link.

Other editors work similarly but don't give you a menu command called Email Link. For example, in World Wide Web Weaver, a shareware program for the Macintosh, you choose Tags⇨Mail. A dialog box called Mail Editor appears. Enter your e-mail address and the text you want to appear as the highlighted link, and then click OK to add the mailto link to your page.

The drawback to publishing your e-mail address directly on your Web page is that you're virtually certain to get unsolicited e-mail messages (commonly called *spam*) sent to that address. Hiding your e-mail address behind generic link text (such as 'Webmaster') may help reduce your chances of attracting spam.

Creating Web page forms that aren't off-putting

You don't have to do much Web surfing before you become intimately acquainted with how Web page forms work, at least from the standpoint of someone who has to fill them out in order to sign up for Web hosting or to download software.

When it comes to creating your own Web site, however, you become conscious of how useful forms are as a means of gathering essential marketing information about your customers. They give your visitors a place to sound off, ask questions, and generally get involved with your online business.

Be clear and use common sense when creating your order form. Here are some general guidelines on how to organise your form and what you need to include:

- ✔ **Make it easy on the customer:** Whenever possible, add pull-down menus with pre-entered options to your *form fields* (text boxes that visitors use to enter information). That way, users don't have to wonder about things such as the level of detail you expect them to include in their address.

- ✔ **Validate the information:** You can use a programming language called JavaScript to ensure that users enter information correctly, that all fields are completely filled out, and so on. You may have to hire someone to add the appropriate code to the order form, but it's worth it to save you from having to call customers to verify or correct information that they missed or submitted incorrectly.

- ✔ **Provide a help number:** Give people a number to call if they have questions or want to check on an order.

- ✔ **Return an acknowledgment:** Let customers know that you have received their order and will be shipping the merchandise immediately or contacting them if more information is needed.

As usual, good Web page authoring and editing programs make it a cinch to create the text boxes, check boxes, buttons, and other parts of a form that the user fills out. The other part of a form, the computer script that receives the data and processes it so that you can read and use the information, is not as simple. See Chapter 6 for details.

Not so long ago, you had to write or edit a scary CGI script in order to set up forms processing on your Web site. But an alternative recently turned up that makes the process of creating a working Web page form accessible to nonprogrammers. Web businesses, such as BOCC E-forms (www.bocc.co.uk/products) and FormMail.To (www.formmail.to), can lead you through the process of setting up a form and provide you with the CGI script that receives the data and forwards it to you.

Providing a guest book

The basic idea of a guestbook is not all that new and exciting. You have probably gone to plenty of special events where they ask you to sign in and write a little something about the guests of honour, the place where the party is being held, or the occasion marked by the event you're attending. But a guestbook on your Web site can add a whole other dimension to your business, making your customers feel that they're part of a thriving community. When you provide a guestbook or comments page on one of your business's Web pages, your clients and other visitors can check out who else has been there and what others think about the site.

If you set out to create your own Web page guestbook from scratch, you'd have to create a form, write a script (fairly complicated code that tells a computer what to do), test the code, and so on. Thankfully, an easier way to add a guestbook is available: You simply register with a special Web business that provides free guestbooks to users. One such organisation, Smart Guestbook (www.smartgb.com), offers a guestbook service that is free to use and doesn't come with pop-ups or similarly annoying advertising.

To sign up, you just have to fill in a few details, such as your Web site's domain name, a title for your guestbook, and your business type. Then all you do is click Create Guestbook and presto!

Another useful service, which is only marketed in the United States – but you can use over here – is Html Gear run by Lycos (htmlgear.lycos.com/specs/guest.html). Again, if you register with Html Gear's service, you can have your own guestbook right away with no fuss. (Actually, Html Gear's guestbook program resides on one of its Web servers; you just add the text-entry portion to your own page.) Here's how to do it:

1. **Connect to the Internet, start up your Web browser, and go to**
   `htmlgear.lycos.com/specs/guest.html`.

2. **Scroll down the page and click the Get This Gear! link.**

   You go to the Network Membership page.

3. **Click the Sign Me Up! button and follow the instructions on subsequent pages to register for the guestbook and other software on the Html Gear site.**

   The program asks you to provide your own personal information, choose a name and password for your guestbook, enter the URL of the Web page on which you want the guestbook to appear, and provide keywords that describe your page.

   After you register, a page entitled Gear Manager appears.

4. **Click Add Gear and then click Get Gear, which is next to Guest Gear.**

   After a few seconds, a page called Create Guest Gear appears. This page contains a form that you need to complete in order to create the guest-book *text-entry fields* (the text boxes and other items that visitors use to submit information to you) to your Web page.

5. **Fill out the Create Guest Gear form.**

   The form lets you name your guestbook and customise how you want visitors to interact with you. For example, you can configure the guest-book to send you an e-mail notification whenever someone posts a message.

6. **When you're done filling out the form, click Save & Create.**

   The Get Code page appears. A box contains the code you need to copy and add to the HTML for your Web page.

7. **Position your mouse arrow at the beginning of the code (just before the first line, which looks like this: `<!-- \/ GuestGEAR Code by htmlgear.com \/ ->`), press and hold down your mouse button, and scroll across the code to the last line, which reads: `<!-- /\ End GuestGEAR Code /\ -->`.**

   The code is highlighted to show that it's been selected.

8. **Choose Edit⇨Copy to copy the selected code to your computer's Clipboard.**

9. **Launch your Web editor, if it isn't running already, and open the Web page you want to edit in your Web editor window.**

   If you're working in a program (such as Dreamweaver or HotDog Pro) that shows the HTML for a Web page while you edit it, you can move on to Step 10. If, on the other hand, your editor hides the HTML from you, you have to use your editor's menu options to view the HTML source for your page. The exact menu command varies from program to program. Usually, though, the option is contained in the View menu. In FrontPage, for example, you click the HTML tab at the bottom of the window. The HTML for the Web page you want to edit then appears.

10. **Scroll down and click the spot on the page where you want to paste the HTML code for the guestbook.**

    How do you know where this spot is? Well, you have to add the code in the BODY section of a Web page. This is the part of the page that is contained between two HTML tags, `<BODY>` and `</BODY>`. You can't go wrong with pasting the code just before the `</BODY>` tag – or just before your return e-mail address or any other material you want to keep at the bottom of the page. The following example indicates the proper place-ment for the guestbook code:

```
<HTML>
<HEAD>
<TITLE>Sign My Guestbook</TITLE>
</HEAD>
<BODY>
The body of your Web page goes here; this is the part
        that appears on the Web.
Paste your guestbook code here!
</BODY>
</HTML>
```

11. Choose Edit⇨Paste.

The guestbook code is added to your page.

12. Close your Web editor's HTML window.

Exactly how you do so varies depending on the program. If you have a separate HTML window open, click the close box (X) in the upper-right corner of the HTML window, if you are working in a Windows environment. (If you're working on a Mac, close the window by clicking the close box in the upper-left corner of the window that displays the HTML.)

The HTML code disappears, and you return to your Web editor's main window.

13. Choose File⇨Save to save your changes.

14. Preview your work in your Web browser window.

The steps involved in previewing also vary from editor to editor. Some editors have a Preview toolbar button that you click to view your page in a Web browser. Otherwise, launch your Web browser to preview your page as follows:

- If you use Netscape Navigator, choose File⇨Open Page, click the name of the file you just saved in the Open Page dialog box, and then click Open to open the page.

- If you use Internet Explorer, choose File⇨Open, click the name of the file you just saved in the Open dialog box, and then click Open to open the page.

The page opens in your Web browser, with a new Guestbook button added to it, as shown in Figure 4-7.

Figure 4-7:
Add a
guestbook
link to your
Web page.

Now, when visitors to your Web page click the Sign My Guestbook link, they go to a page that has a form they can fill out. Clicking the View My Guestbook link enables visitors to view the messages that other visitors have entered into your guestbook.

The problem with adding a link to a service that resides on another Web site is that it makes your Web pages load more slowly. First, your visitor's browser loads the text on your page. Then it loads the images from top to bottom. Besides this, it has to make a link to the Html Gear site in order to load the guestbook. If you decide to add a guestbook, images, or other elements that reside on another Web site, be sure to test your page and make sure that you're satisfied with how long the contents take to appear. Also make sure to use the 'Moderation' feature that enables you to screen postings to your guestbook. That way, you can delete obscene, unfair, or libellous postings before they go online.

Chit-chatting that counts

You've accomplished a lot by the time you've put your business online. Hopefully, you're already seeing the fruits of your labour in the form of e-mail enquiries and orders for your products or services.

That's all good, but this is no time to rest on your laurels. After visitors start coming to your site, the next step is to retain those visitors. A good way to do so is by building a sense of community by posting a bulletin-board-type discussion area.

A *discussion area* takes the form of back-and-forth messages on topics of mutual interest. Each person can read previously posted messages and either respond or start a new topic of discussion. For an example of a discussion area that's tied to an online business, visit the Australian Fishing (www.ausfish.com.au) discussion areas, one of which is shown in Figure 4-8.

The talk doesn't have to be about your own particular niche in your business field. In fact, the discussion will be more lively if your visitors can discuss concerns about your area of business in general, whether it's flower arranging, boat sales, tax preparation, clock repair, computers, or whatever.

How, exactly, do you start a discussion area? The first step is to install a special computer script on the computer that hosts your Web site. (Again, discussing this prospect with your Web hosting service beforehand is essential.) When visitors come to your site, their Web browsers access the script, enabling them to enter comments and read other messages.

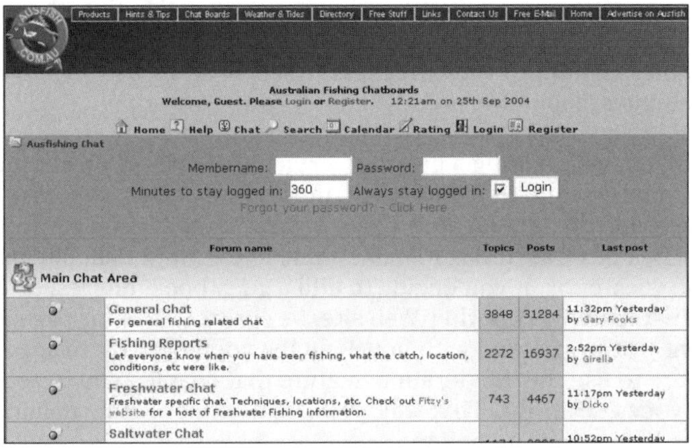

Figure 4-8:
A discussion
area
stimulates
interest and
interaction
among like-
minded
customers.

Here are some specific ways to prepare a discussion area for your site:

✔ Install Microsoft FrontPage, which includes the scripts you need to start a discussion group. You can't download a trial version, but you can get the 2003 version for around £120 on Amazon.

`www.microsoft.com/uk/office/frontpage/howtobuy/default.mspx`

✔ Copy a bulletin board or discussion-group script from either of these sites:

- Extropia.com (`www.extropia.com/applications.html`)
- Matt's Script Archive (`www.worldwidemart.com/scripts`)

✔ Start your own forum on a service such as HyperNews, by Daniel LaLiberte, or install the HyperNews program yourself (`www.hypernews.org/HyperNews/get/hypernews.html`)

Chapter 5

Accepting Payments

. . . .

In This Chapter

▶ Anticipating your online customers' purchasing needs

▶ Applying for credit-card merchant status

▶ Finding shortcuts to processing credit-card data

▶ Providing shoppers with electronic purchasing systems

▶ Delivering your products and services

. . . .

Starting up a new business and getting it online is exciting, but believe us, the real excitement occurs when you get paid for what you do. Nothing boosts your confidence and tells you that your hard work is paying off like receiving the proverbial cheque in the post.

The immediacy and interactivity of selling and promoting yourself online applies to receiving payments, too. You can get paid with just a few mouse clicks and some important data entered on your customer's keyboard. But completing an electronic commerce (*e-commerce,* for short) transaction isn't the same as getting paid in a traditional retail store. The customer can't personally hand you cash or a cheque. Or, if a credit card is involved, you can't verify the user's identity through a signature or photo ID.

In order to get paid promptly and reliably online, you have to go through some extra steps to make the customer feel secure – not to mention protect yourself, too. Successful e-commerce is about setting up the right atmosphere for making purchases, providing options for payment, and keeping sensitive information private. It's also about making sure that the goods get to the customer safely and on time. In this chapter, we describe ways in which you can implement these essential online business strategies.

Sealing the Deal: The Options

As anyone who sells online knows, the point at which payment is transferred is one of the most eagerly awaited stages of the transaction. It's also one of the stages that's likely to produce the most anxiety. Customers and merchants who are used to dealing with one another face to face and who are accustomed to personally handing over identification and credit cards suddenly feel lost. On the Web, they can't see the person they're dealing with.

For some customers, paying for something purchased over the Internet is still fraught with uncertainty, even though security is improving. For merchants like you, it can still be nerve-wracking; you want to make sure that cheques don't bounce and purchases aren't being made with stolen credit cards.

Your goal, in giving your customers the ability to provide payments online, should be to accomplish the following:

- **Give the customer options.** Online shoppers like to feel that they have some degree of control. Give them a choice of payment alternatives: phone, cheque, and credit/debit cards are the main ones.

- **Keep their credit-card numbers secure.** Pay an extra fee to your Web host in order to have your customers submit their credit-card numbers or other personal information to a secure server – a server that uses Secure Sockets Layer (SSL) encryption to render it unreadable if stolen.

- **Make payment convenient.** Shoppers on the Web are in a hurry. Give them the Web page forms and the phone numbers they need so that they can complete a purchase in a matter of seconds.

Though the goals are the same, the options are different if you sell on eBay.co.uk or on a Web site other than eBay's (see Book VI). If you sell on eBay.co.uk, either through an auction or an eBay shop, you can take advantage of eBay's fraud protection measures: a feedback system that rewards honesty and penalises dishonesty; fraud insurance; investigations staff; and the threat of suspension. These safeguards mean that it's feasible to accept cash and personal cheques or money orders from buyers. If you don't receive the cash, you don't ship. If you receive cheques, you can wait until they clear before you ship.

 On the Web, you don't have a feedback system or an investigations squad to ferret out dishonest buyers. You can accept cheques or money orders, but credit or debit cards are the safest and quickest option, and accordingly, they're what buyers expect. It's up to you to verify the buyer's identity as best you can in order to minimise fraud.

Enabling Credit-Card Purchases

Having the ability to accept and process credit-card transactions makes it especially easy for your customers to follow the impulse to buy something from you. You stand to generate a lot more sales than you would otherwise.

But although credit cards are easy for shoppers to use, they make *your* life as an online merchant more complicated. We don't want to discourage you from becoming credit-card ready by any means, but you need to be aware of the steps (and the expenses) involved, many of which may not occur to you when you're just starting out. For example, you may not be aware of one or more of the following:

- **Merchant accounts:** You have to apply and be approved for a special bank account called a *merchant account* in order for a bank to process the credit-card orders that you receive. If you work through a traditional bank, approval can take days or weeks. However, a number of online merchant account businesses are providing hot competition, which includes streamlining the application process.

- **Setup fees:** Fees can be high but they vary widely, and it pays to shop around. Some banks charge a merchant setup fee (up to a couple of hundred pounds). On the other hand, some online companies such as Smart Merchant (www.smartmerchant.co.uk) charge no setup fee, while others, like Nochex (www.nochex.com), charge only a nominal fee of £50.

- **Usage rates:** All banks and merchant account companies (PayPal included) charge a *usage fee.* Typically, this fee ranges from 1 to 4 per cent of each transaction. Plus, you may have to pay a monthly premium charge to the bank. Nochex asks for £50 upfront and then charges you 2.9 per cent plus 20p per transaction. However, if you sell regularly, you pay no monthly fee, and the charges come down.

For more advice about online payment software services, check out the following bCentral link: www.bcentral.co.uk/business-technology/your-company-website/online-payment-services.mspx.

You must watch out for credit-card fraud, where criminals use stolen numbers to make purchases. You, the merchant – not the issuing bank – end up being liable for most of the fictitious transactions. To combat this crime, before completing any transaction, verify that the shipping address supplied by the purchaser is the same (or at least in the same vicinity) as the billing address. If you're in doubt, you can phone the purchaser for verification – it's a courtesy to the customer as well as a means of protection for you. (See the later section, 'Verifying credit-card data'.)

Setting up a merchant account

The good news is that getting merchant status is relatively easy, as banks have come to accept the notion that businesses don't have to have an actual, physical shop front in order to be successful. Getting a merchant account approved, however, still takes time, and, of course, you have to pay for the privilege. Banks look more favourably on companies that have been in business for several years and have a proven track record, but they see the benefits of taking on newbies, too. When Dan was setting up www.InfoZoo.co.uk, he received letter after letter from his bank offering more services and enquiring when the first transactions would be made.

Traditional banks are reliable and experienced, and you can count on them being around for a while. The new Web-based companies that specialise in giving online businesses merchant account status welcome new businesses and give you wider options and cost savings, but they're new; their services may not be as reliable, and their future is less certain.

You can find more information about institutions that provide merchant accounts for online businesses at the following site: www.merchantaccount forum.com.

The list of merchant account providers is growing so long that knowing which company to choose is difficult. We recommend visiting Business Link's Web site (www.businesslink.gov.uk), which provides you with a good overview of what's required to obtain a merchant account.

MyTexasMusic.com, a family-run business, uses a Web-based merchant account company called GoEmerchant.com (www.goemerchant.com) to set up and process its credit-card transactions. This company offers a shopping trolley and credit-card and debit-card processing to businesses that accept payments online. MyTexasMusic.com chose to use GoEmerchant after an extensive search because it found that the company would help provide reliable processing, while protecting the business from customers who purchased items fraudulently.

One advantage of using one of the payment options set up by VeriSign Payment Services (www.verisign.com/products/payment.html) is that the system (which originated with a company called CyberCash) was well known and well regarded before VeriSign acquired it. We describe the widely used electronic payment company in the section 'Exploring Online Payment Systems', later in this chapter.

In general, your chances of obtaining merchant status are enhanced if you apply to a bank that welcomes Internet businesses, and if you can provide good business records proving that you're a viable, moneymaking concern.

Be sure to ask about the monthly rate that the bank charges for Internet-based transactions before you apply. Compare the rate for online transactions to the rate for conventional 'card-swipe' purchases. Most banks and credit-card processing companies charge 1 to 2 extra percentage points for online sales.

Do you use an accounting program such as QuickBooks or MYOB Accounting? The manufacturers of these programs enable their users to become credit-card merchants through their Web sites. See the 'Accounting Software' section of this book's online Internet Directory for more information.

Finding a secure server

A *secure server* is a server that uses some form of encryption, such as Secure Sockets Layer, which we describe in Book II, to protect data that you receive over the Internet. Customers know that they've entered a secure area when the security key or lock icon at the bottom of the browser window is locked shut.

If you plan to receive credit-card payments, you definitely want to find a Web-hosting service that will protect the area of your online business that serves as the online store. In literal terms, you need secure server software protecting the directory on your site that is to receive customer-sent forms. Watertight security should be a given by now, but it's always good to make sure that your customers will be protected. Ask your host (or hosts you're considering) whether any extra charges apply.

Verifying credit-card data

Unfortunately, people are out there who try to use credit-card numbers that don't belong to them. The anonymity of the Web and the ability to shop anywhere in the world, combined with the ability to place orders immediately, can facilitate fraudulent orders, just as it can benefit legitimate ones.

Protecting yourself against credit-card fraud is essential. Always check the billing address against the shipping address. If the two addresses are thousands of miles apart, contact the purchaser by phone to verify that the transaction is legit. Even if it is, the purchaser will appreciate your taking the time to verify the transaction.

You can use software to help check addresses. Here are three programs that perform this service:

- ✔ CapScan (www.capscan.com/products.htm)
- ✔ Worldpay (support.worldpay.com/fraud/body.html)
- ✔ QAS, part of credit reporting company Experian (www.qas.co.uk/products)

Processing your orders

You can hire a company to automatically process credit-card orders for you. These companies compare the shipping and billing addresses to help make sure that the purchaser is the person who actually owns the card and not someone trying to use a stolen credit-card number. If everything checks out, they transmit the data directly to the bank.

Loads of different companies offer a range of payment-processing packages. Do a search on Google.co.uk for 'online payment processing' and get in contact with a few of the organisations that take your fancy. Dan recommends PayPal for ease of use and Protx for its low cost options. See the upcoming section on shopping trolley software for more information.

Automatic credit-card processing works so fast that your customer's credit card can be charged immediately, whether or not you have an item in stock. If a client receives a bill and is still waiting for an item that is on back order, the person can get very unhappy. For this reason, some business owners choose not to use them.

Exploring Online Payment Systems

A number of organisations have devised ways to make e-commerce secure and convenient for shoppers and merchants alike. These alternatives fall into one of three general categories:

- ✔ Organisations that help you complete credit-card purchases (for example, VeriSign Payment Services).
- ✔ Escrow services that hold your money for you in an account until shipment is received and then pay you, providing security for both you and your customers.

✔ Organisations that provide alternatives to transmitting sensitive information from one computer to another. A number of attempts to create 'virtual money' have failed. However, companies like Electracash (www.electracash.com) let customers make payments by directly debiting their cheque accounts.

In order to use one of these systems, you or your Web host has to set up special software on the computer that actually stores your Web site files. This computer is where the transactions take place. The following sections provide general instructions on how to get started with setting up each of the most popular electronic payment systems.

To work smoothly, some electronic payment systems require you to set up programming languages such as Perl, C/C++, or Visual Basic on your site. You also have to work with techy documents called *configuration files*. This is definitely an area where paying a consultant to get your business set up saves time and headaches and gets your new transaction feature online more efficiently than if you tackle it yourself. VeriSign, for example, provides support in setting up systems for its merchants; you can find an affiliate to help you or call the company directly. Visit the VeriSign Payment Processing page (www.verisign.com/products/payment.html) for links and phone numbers.

Which payment system is right for you? That depends on what you want to sell online. If you're providing articles, reports, music, or other content that you want people to pay a nominal fee to access, consider a micropayment system. The important things are to provide customers with several options for submitting payment and to make the process as easy as possible for them.

Shopping trolley software

When you go to the supermarket or another retail outlet, you pick goodies off the shelves and put them in a shopping trolley. When you go to the cash till to pay for what you've selected, you empty the trolley and present your goods to the cashier.

Shopping trolley software performs the same functions on an e-commerce site. Such software sets up a system that allows online shoppers to select items displayed for sale. The selections are held in a virtual shopping trolley that 'remembers' what the shopper has selected before checking out.

Shopping trolley programs are pretty technical for nonprogrammers to set up, but if you're ambitious and want to try it, you can download and install a free program called PerlShop (www.perlshop.org). Signing up with a Web host that provides you with shopping trolley software as part of its services, however, is far easier than tackling this task yourself.

Reach for your wallet!

One of the terms commonly thrown around in the jargon of e-commerce is *wallet*. A wallet is software that, like a real wallet that you keep in your bag or pocket, stores available cash and other records. You reach into the cyberwallet and withdraw virtual cash instead of submitting a credit-card number.

Wallets looked promising a few years ago, but they have never really taken off. The idea is that a cybershopper who uses wallet software, such as Microsoft .NET Passport (www.passport.com), is able to pay for items online in a matter of seconds, without having to transfer credit-card data. What's more, some wallets can even 'remember' previous purchases you have made and suggest further purchases.

The problem with wallets is that shoppers just aren't comfortable with them. Credit cards are quick and convenient, and they've proven to be secure enough for most consumers. Consumers who are committed to using Microsoft's services can use .NET Passport, which offers a 'single sign-in' to register or make purchases on sites that support this technology. It also enables consumers to create a wallet that stores their billing and shipping information. (Credit-card numbers are stored in an offline database when users sign up for a .NET Passport.) Customers can then make purchases at participating sites with the proverbial single mouse click. In order for your online business Web site to support .NET Passport, you need to download and install the .NET Passport Software Development Kit (SDK) on the server that runs your Web site. You may need help in deploying this platform; a list of consultants, as well as a link to the SDK, is included on the .NET Passport home page.

A shopping trolley is often described as an essential part of many e-commerce Web sites, and Web hosts usually boast about including a trolley along with their other businesses services. But the fact is that you don't *have* to use a shopping trolley on your site. Some shoppers are put off by them and are just as likely to abandon a purchase than follow through by submitting payment. Plenty of other e-businesses have users phone or fax in an order or fill out an online form instead.

PayPal

PayPal was one of the first online businesses to hit on the clever idea of giving business owners a way to accept credit- and debit-card payments from customers without having to apply for a merchant account, download software, apply for online payment processing, or some combination of these steps.

PayPal is essentially an *escrow service:* It functions as a sort of financial middleman, debiting buyers' accounts and crediting the accounts of sellers – and, along the way, exacting a fee for its services, which it charges to the merchant receiving the payment. The accounts involved can be credit-card accounts, checking accounts, or accounts held at PayPal into which members

Book V

Handling
Customers
and Staff

directly deposit funds. In other words, the person making the payment sets up an account with PayPal by identifying which account (credit card or debit card, for example) a payment is to be taken from. The merchant also has a PayPal account and has identified which debit- or credit-card account is to receive payments. PayPal handles the virtual 'card swipe' and verification of customer information; the customer can pay with a credit card without the merchant having to set up a merchant account.

PayPal is best known as a way to pay for items purchased on eBay. eBay, in fact, owns PayPal. But the service is regularly used to process payments both on and off the auction site. If you want to sell items (including through your Web site), you sign up for a PayPal Business or Premier account. You get a PayPal button that you add to your auction listing or sales Web page. The customer clicks the button to transfer the payment from his or her PayPal account to yours, and you're charged a transaction fee.

Setting up a PayPal account is free. Here's how you can set up a PayPal Business account:

1. **Go to the PayPal home page (**www.paypal.co.uk**) and click the Sign Up Now button.**

   You go to the PayPal Account Sign Up page.

2. **Click the button next to Business Account, choose your country of residence, and click Continue.**

   The Business Account Sign Up page appears.

3. **Follow the instructions on the registration form page and set up your account with PayPal.**

   After you've filled out the registration forms, you receive an e-mail message with a link that takes you back to the PayPal Web site to confirm your e-mail address.

4. **Click the link contained in the e-mail message.**

   You go to the PayPal – Password page.

5. **Enter your password (the one you created during the registration process) in the Password box and then click the Confirm button.**

   You go to the PayPal – My Account page.

6. **Click the Merchant Tools tab at the top of the My Account page.**

   If you want to create a shopping trolley, click the Shopping Cart link. For the purposes of this exercise, click Buy Now Buttons.

7. **Provide some information about the item you're selling:**

   • Enter a brief description of your sales item in the Item Name/Service box.

   • Enter an item number in the Item ID/Number Box.

- Enter the price in the Price Of Item/Service box.
- Choose a button that shoppers can click to make the purchase. (You can choose either the PayPal logo button or a button that you've already created.)

8. **When you're done, click the Create Button Now button.**

   You go to the PayPal – Web Accept page shown in Figure 5-1.

9. **Copy the code in the For Web Pages box and paste it onto the Web page that holds your sales item.**

   That's all there is to it.

The nice thing about using PayPal is that the system enables you to accept payments through your Web site without having to obtain a merchant account. It does put a burden on your customers to become PayPal users, but chances are those who buy or sell on eBay already have one. The thing to remember is that both you and your customers place a high level of trust in PayPal to handle your money. If there is a problem with fraud, PayPal will investigate it – hopefully. Some former PayPal users detest PayPal due to what they describe as a lack of responsiveness, and they describe their unhappiness in great detail on sites like `www.paypalsucks.com`. You should be aware of such complaints in order to have the full picture about PayPal and anticipate problems before they arise.

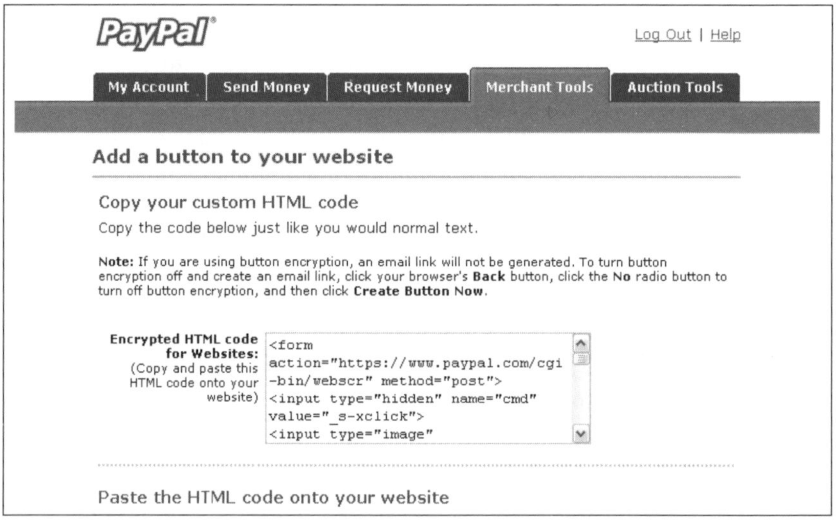

Figure 5-1:
Copy this code to your sales catalogue Web page to enable other PayPal users to transfer purchase money to your account.

PayPal   Log Out | Help

My Account | Send Money | Request Money | Merchant Tools | Auction Tools

Add a button to your website

Copy your custom HTML code
Copy the code below just like you would normal text.

Note: If you are using button encryption, an email link will not be generated. To turn button encryption off and create an email link, click your browser's **Back** button, click the **No** radio button to turn off button encryption, and then click **Create Button Now.**

Encrypted HTML code for Websites: (Copy and paste this HTML code onto your website)
```
<form action="https://www.paypal.com/cgi-bin/webscr" method="post">
<input type="hidden" name="cmd" value="_s-xclick">
<input type="image"
```

Paste the HTML code onto your website

Actinic

Actinic is a British multi-award winning payment software, which can help you build a payment platform for any type of business, but it specialises in small and medium-sized enterprises. Actinic's range of services is too broad to cover here, so why not just to its Web site at www.actinic.co.uk?

Micropayments

Micropayments are very small units of currency that are exchanged by merchants and customers. The amounts involved may range from a fraction of a penny to a few pounds. Such small payments enable sites to provide content for sale on a per-click basis. In order to read articles, listen to music files, or view video clips online, some sites require micropayments in a special form of electronic cash that goes by names such as *scrip* or *eCash*.

Micropayments seemed like a good idea in theory, but they've never caught on with most consumers. On the other hand, they've never totally disappeared, either. The business that proved conclusively that consumers are willing to pay small amounts of money to purchase creative content online is none other than the computer manufacturer Apple, which revolutionised e-commerce with its iPod music player and its iTunes music marketplace. Every day, users pay 99p to download a song and add it to their iPod selections. But they make such payments with their credit cards, using real pounds and pence.

In other words, iTunes payments aren't true micropayments. The micropayment system is supposed to work like this:

1. **As a vendor, you authorise a broker such as BitPass** (www.bitpass.com) **to sell content to your customers by using its payment system.**

   Typically, BitPass content is creative: cartoons, audiobooks, craft projects, and music. If a customer goes to your site and wants to purchase articles or other content, the customer has to follow a few steps.

2. **The customer first purchases a prepaid card that contains a certain amount of virtual money at face value from the broker.**

   (The purchase is made through PayPal, interestingly.)

3. **The broker then pays you, the merchant, the purchase of virtual money that the customer made, minus a service fee.**

4. **The customer is then free to make purchases from your site by clicking items that have been assigned a certain value.**

5. **The micropayment service's software causes the money to be automatically subtracted from the user's supply of scrip.**

   No credit-card numbers are exchanged in these micropayment transactions.

Fulfilling Your Online Orders

Being on the Internet can help when it comes to the final step in the e-commerce dance: order fulfilment. *Fulfilment* refers to what happens after a sale is made. Typical fulfilment tasks include the following:

- ✔ Packing up the merchandise
- ✔ Shipping the merchandise
- ✔ Solving delivery problems or answering questions about orders that haven't reached their destinations
- ✔ Sending out bills
- ✔ Following up to see whether the customer is satisfied

Order fulfilment may seem like the least exciting part of running a business, online or otherwise. But from your customer's point of view, it's the most important business activity of all. The following sections suggest how you can use your presence online to help reduce any anxiety your customers may feel about receiving what they ordered.

The back-end (or, to use the Microsoft term, BackOffice) part of your online business is where order fulfilment comes in. If you have a database in which you record customer orders, link it to your Web site so that your customers can track orders. Adobe Dreamweaver or ColdFusion can help with this process. (The most recent version, Dreamweaver 8, contains built-in commands that let you link to a ColdFusion database.)

Provide links to shipping services

One advantage of being online is that you can help customers track packages after shipment. The Parcelforce online order-tracking feature, shown in Figure 5-2, gets thousands of requests each day. If you use Parcelforce, provide a link to its online tracking page at www.parcelforce.com/portal/pw/track?catId=7500082.

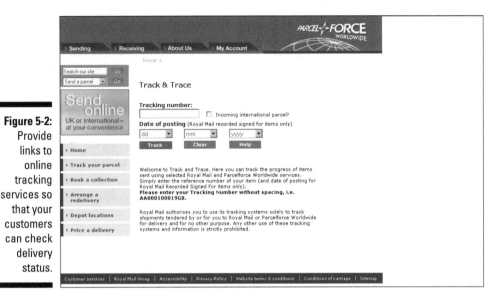

Figure 5-2:
Provide links to online tracking services so that your customers can check delivery status.

The other shipping services have also created their own online tracking systems. You can link to these sites, too:

✔ United Parcel Service (www.ups.com/gb)

✔ Royal Mail (www.royalmail.co.uk)

✔ DHL (www.dhl.co.uk)

Present shipping options clearly

In order fulfilment, as in receiving payment, it pays to present your clients with as many options as possible and to explain the options in detail. Because you're online, you can provide your customers with as much shipping information as they can stand. Web surfers are knowledge hounds – they can never get enough data, whether it's related to shipping or other parts of your business.

When it comes to shipping, be sure to describe the options, the cost of each, and how long each takes. (See the sidebar 'Keeping back-office functions personal', earlier in this chapter, for some good tips on when to require signatures and how to present shipping information by e-mail rather than on the Web.) Here are more specific suggestions:

- ✓ **Compare shipping costs.** Don't settle for a shipping provider until you've done the rounds and assessed who is the most reliable for the least cost.

- ✓ **Make sure that you can track.** Pick a service that lets you track your package's shipping status.

- ✓ **Be able to confirm receipt.** A confirmation helps everyone's peace of mind.

Many online shops present shipping alternatives in the form of a table or bulleted list of options. (*Tables,* as you probably know, are Web page design elements that let you arrange content in rows and columns, making them easier to read; refer to Chapter 5 for more on adding tables to your site.) You don't have to look very far to find an example; just visit the John Wiley & Sons Web site (www.wiley.com) and order a book from its online store. When you're ready to pay for your items and provide a shipping address, you see the bulleted list shown in Figure 5-3.

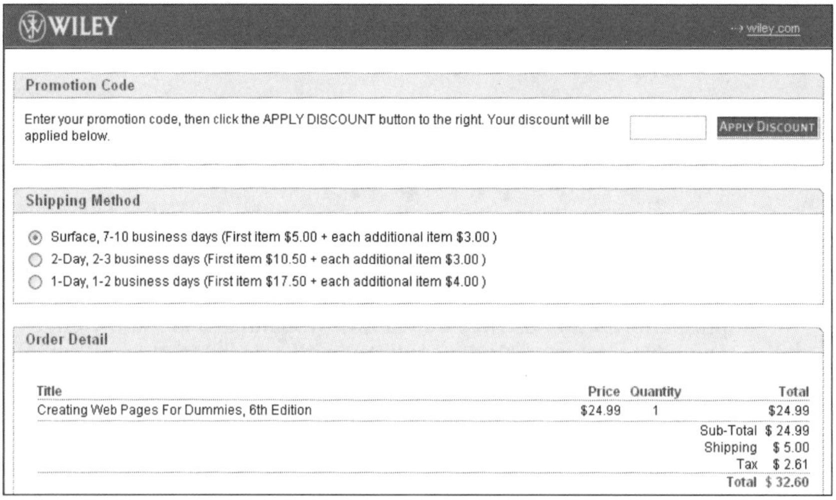

Figure 5-3:
Tables help
shoppers
calculate
costs, keep
track of
purchases,
and choose
shipping
options.

WILEY ·→ wiley.com

Promotion Code

Enter your promotion code, then click the APPLY DISCOUNT button to the right. Your discount will be applied below.　　　　　APPLY DISCOUNT

Shipping Method

◉ Surface, 7-10 business days (First item $5.00 + each additional item $3.00)
○ 2-Day, 2-3 business days (First item $10.50 + each additional item $3.00)
○ 1-Day, 1-2 business days (First item $17.50 + each additional item $4.00)

Order Detail

Title	Price	Quantity	Total
Creating Web Pages For Dummies, 6th Edition	$24.99	1	$24.99
		Sub-Total	$ 24.99
		Shipping	$ 5.00
		Tax	$ 2.61
		Total	$ 32.60

Chapter 6

Service with a Virtual Smile

*I*t's only human nature: Customers often wait until the last minute to request a gift or other item for a specific occasion, and that leads to an emergency for you. It may not seem fair, but a delay in responding to your customers can lead to lost business. These days, everything seems to be instant, from your porridge to your Internet connection. We take it for granted that shops no longer close on a Sunday and that they'll be open late into the evening for our convenience. Many shoppers still like to spend hours milling around the shopping centre, browsing and lunching at their leisure. But chances are that your customer is coming to you in the first place to save time as well as money. And they expect to get what they want – and fast.

Customer service is one area in which small, entrepreneurial businesses can outshine brick-and-mortar chain shops – and even larger online competitors. It doesn't matter whether you're competing in the areas of e-trading, e-music, or e-tail sales of any sort. Tools such as e-mail and interactive forms, coupled with the fact that an online commerce site can provide information on a 24/7 basis, give you a powerful advantage when it comes to retaining customers and building loyalty.

What constitutes good online customer service, particularly for a new business that has only one or two employees? Whether your customers are broadband or dialup, you need to deal with them one at a time and connect one to one. But being responsive and available is only part of the picture. This chapter presents ways to succeed with the other essential components: providing information, communicating effectively, and enabling your clientele to talk back to you online.

The Best Customer Is an Informed Customer

In a manner of speaking, satisfaction is all about managing people's expectations. If you give your customers what they're expecting or even a little bit more, they'll be happy. But how do you go about setting their level of expectation in the first place? Communication is the key. The more information you can provide up front, the fewer phone queries or complaints you'll receive later. Printed pamphlets and brochures have traditionally described products and services at length. But online is now the way to go.

Say that you're talking about a 1,000-word description of your new company and your products and/or services. If that text were formatted to fit on a 4-x-9-inch foldout brochure, the contents would cover several panels and cost an arm and a leg to print enough copies to make it worthwhile.

On the other hand, if those same 1,000 words were arranged on a few Web pages and put online, they'd probably be no more than 5K to 10K in size, so they wouldn't slow your site at all and would cost next to nothing. The same applies if you distribute your content to a number of subscribers in the form of an e-mail newsletter. In either case, you need pay only a little to publish the information.

And online publishing has the advantage of easier updating. When you add new products or services or even when you want a different approach, it takes only a little time and effort to change the contents or the look.

Why FAQs are frequently used

It may not be the most elegant of concepts, but it has worked for an infinite number of online businesspeople and it will work for you. A set of *frequently asked questions* (FAQs) is a familiar feature on many online business sites – so familiar, in fact, that Web surfers expect to find a FAQ page on every business site.

Even the format of FAQ pages is pretty similar from site to site, and this predictability is itself an asset. FAQ pages are generally presented in Q-and-A format, with topics appearing in the form of questions that have literally been asked by other customers or that have been made up to resemble real questions. Each question has a brief answer that provides essential information about the business.

But just because we're continually touting communication doesn't mean we want you to bore your potential customers with endless words that don't apply to their interests. To keep your FAQ page from getting too long, we recommend that you list all the questions at the top of the page. This way, by clicking a hyperlinked item in the list, the reader jumps to the spot down the page where you present the question that relates to them and its answer in detail.

Book V

Handling Customers and Staff

Just having a FAQ page isn't enough. Make sure that yours is easy to use and comprehensive. Clarity and accessibility are both essential factors in successful Web sites, and your FAQ section should reflect these qualities. Check out the blueyonder user group Internet FAQs for some guidelines: `www.by-users.co.uk/faqs/nontechfaq/internet/index.html`.

Sure, you can compose a FAQ page off the top of your head, but sometimes getting a different perspective helps. Invite visitors, customers, friends, and family to come up with questions about your business. You may want to include questions on some of the following topics:

- ✔ **Contact information:** If I need to reach you in a hurry by mail, fax, or phone, how do I do that? Are you available only at certain hours?

- ✔ **Instructions:** What if I need more detailed instructions on how to use your products or services? Where can I find them?

- ✔ **Service:** What do I do if the merchandise doesn't work for some reason or breaks? Do you have a returns policy?

- ✔ **Value Added Tax (VAT):** Is VAT added to the cost I see on-screen?

- ✔ **Shipping:** What are my shipping options?

You don't have to use the term FAQ, either. The retailer Lands' End, which does just about everything right in terms of e-commerce, uses the term Fact Sheet for its list of questions and answers. Go to the Lands' End home page (`www.landsend.co.uk`) and click the About Us link to see how Lands' End presents the same type of material.

Writing an online newsletter

You may define yourself as an online businessperson, not a newsletter editor. But sharing information with customers and potential customers through an e-mail newsletter is a great way to build credibility for yourself and your business.

For added customer service (not to mention a touch of self-promotion), consider producing a regular publication, say once a fortnight or once a month, that you send out to a mailing list. Your mailing list would begin with customers and prospective customers who visit your Web site and indicate that they want to subscribe.

An e-mail newsletter doesn't happen by magic, but it can provide your business with long-term benefits that include:

✔ **Customer tracking:** You can add subscribers' e-mail addresses to a mailing list that you can use for other marketing purposes, such as promoting special sales items for return customers.

✔ **Low-bandwidth:** An e-mail newsletter doesn't require much memory. It's great for businesspeople who get their e-mail on the road via laptops, palm devices, or appliances that are designed specifically for sending and receiving e-mail.

✔ **Timeliness:** You can get breaking news into your electronic newsletter much faster than you can put it in print.

The fun part is to name your newsletter and assemble content that you want to include. Then follow these steps to get your publication up and running:

1. **Create your newsletter by typing the contents in plain-text (ASCII) format.**

   Optionally, you can also provide an HTML-formatted version. You can then include headings and graphics that appear in e-mail programs that support HTML e-mail messages.

   If you use a plain-text newsletter, format it by using capital letters; rules that consist of a row of equal signs, hyphens, or asterisks; or blank spaces to align elements.

2. **Save your file with the proper filename extension: `.txt` for the text version and `.htm` or `.html` if you send an HTML version.**

3. **Attach the file to an e-mail message by using your e-mail program's method of sending attachments.**

4. **Address your file to the recipients.**

   If you have lots of subscribers (many newsletters have hundreds or thousands), save their addresses in a mailing list. Use your e-mail program's address book function to do this.

5. **Send your newsletter.**

TIP

It's a good idea to consider when your newsletter will be best received by your customers. As a business journalist specialising in Web publications, Dan has sent innumerable newsletters in his time. He found that small businesses are most receptive (more of them opened their newsletters) on a Thursday afternoon. If you're a fashion retailer, for example, trying sending yours on a Friday, when most people will be at their work desks but will also be winding down for the weekend!

Managing a mailing list can be time consuming. You have to keep track of people who want to subscribe or unsubscribe, as well as those who ask for more information. You can save time and trouble by hiring a company such as ListCast (www.listcast.com) to do the day-to-day list management for you.

Mixing bricks and clicks

If you operate a bricks-and-mortar business as well as a Web-based business, you have additional opportunities to get feedback from your shoppers. Take advantage of the fact that you meet customers personally on a regular basis and ask them for opinions and suggestions that can help you operate a more effective Web site, too.

When your customers are in the checkout line (the real one with the cash till, not your online shopping trolley), ask them to fill out a questionnaire about your Web site. Consider asking questions like the following:

✔ Have you visited this shop's Web site? Are you familiar with it?

✔ Would you visit the Web site more often if you knew there were products or content there that you couldn't find in our physical location?

✔ Can you suggest some types of merchandise, or special sales, you'd like to see on the Web site?

Including your Web site's URL on all the printed literature in your shop is a good idea. The feedback system works both ways, of course: You can ask online customers for suggestions of how to run your bricks-and-mortar shop better, and what types of merchandise they'd like to see on your real as opposed to your 'virtual' shelves.

Helping Customers Reach You

Greg's the type of person who has an ex-directory home phone number. But being anonymous is not the way to go when you're running an online business. (He uses a different number for business calls, by the way.) Of course, you don't have to promise to be available 24/7 to your customers in the flesh. But they need to believe that they'll get attention no matter what time of day or night. When you're online, contact information can take several forms. Be sure to include

- ✔ Your snail mail address
- ✔ Your e-mail address(es)
- ✔ Your phone and fax numbers, and a free (0800) number (if you have one)

Most Web hosting services (such as the types of hosts that we describe in Chapter 3) give you more than one e-mail inbox as part of your account. So it may be helpful to set up more than one e-mail address. One address can be for people to communicate with you personally, and the other can be where people go for general information. You can also set up e-mail addresses that respond to messages by automatically sending a text file in response. (See the 'Setting up autoresponders' section, later in this chapter.)

Even though you probably won't meet many of your customers in person, you need to provide them with a human connection. Keep your site as personal and friendly as possible. A contact page is a good place to provide some brief biographical information about the people visitors can contact, namely you and any employees or partners in your company.

Not putting your contact information on a separate Web page has some advantages, of course. Doing so makes your patrons have to wait a few seconds to access it. If your contact data is simple and your Web site consists only of a few pages, by all means put it right on your home page.

Going upscale with your e-mail

These days, nearly everyone we know, including our respective parents, has an e-mail account. But when you're an online businessperson, you need to know more about the features of e-mail than just how to share a joke or exchange a recipe. The more you discover about the finer technical points of e-mail, the better you're able to meet the needs of your clients. The following sections suggest ways to go beyond simply sending and receiving e-mail messages, and utilise e-mail for business publishing and marketing.

Setting up autoresponders

An *autoresponder,* which also goes by the name *mailbot,* is software that you can set up to send automatic replies to requests for information about a product or service, or to respond to people subscribing to an e-mail publication or service.

You can provide automatic responses either through your own e-mail program or through your Web host's e-mail service. If you use a Web host to provide automatic responses, you can usually purchase an extra e-mail address that can be configured to return a text file (such as a form letter) to the sender.

Look for a Web host that provides you with one or more autoresponders along with your account. Typically, your host assigns you an e-mail address that takes the form info@mycompany.co.uk. In this case, someone at your hosting service configures the account so that when a visitor to your site sends a message to info@yourcompany.com, a file of your choice, such as a simple text document that contains background information about you and your services, automatically goes out to the sender as a reply.

Greg's own Web host and ISP, XO Communications, lets Greg create and edit an autoresponse message for each of his e-mail accounts. First, he logs on to his host's gateway, which is the service it provides customers for changing their e-mail settings. He clicks the link Edit E-mail Settings to go to the page called E-mail Settings shown in Figure 6-1. He checks the Auto Respond box to turn the feature on and then clicks Edit Autoresponse Message to set up his autoresponse text.

Figure 6-1: Many Web hosts and ISPs enable users to create their own auto-response messages.

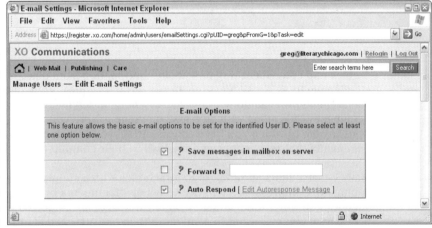

If the service that hosts your Web site does not provide this service free, you can always do it through your basic Outlook e-mail software, which comes with Microsoft Office packages. Read the walkthrough at this address to find out exactly how it's done: www.pcanswers.co.uk/tips/default. asp?pagetypeid=2&articleid=28816&subsectionid=616.

Noting by quoting

Responding to a series of questions is easy when you use *quoting* – a feature that lets you copy quotes from a message to which you're replying. Quoting, which is available in almost all e-mail programs, is particularly useful for responding to a mailing list or newsgroup message because it indicates the specific topic being discussed.

How do you tell the difference between the quoted material and the body of the new e-mail message? The common convention is to put a greater-than (>) character in the left margin, next to each line of the quoted material.

When you tell your e-mail software to quote the original message before you type your reply, it generally quotes the entire message. To save space, you can *snip* (delete) out the part that isn't relevant. However, if you do so, it's polite to type the word ‹snip› to show that you've cut something out. A quoted message looks something like this:

```
Mary Agnes McDougal wrote:
>I wonder if I could get some info on <snip>
>those sterling silver widgets you have for sale . . .
Hi Mary Agnes,
Thank you for your interest in our premium collector's line
of widgets. You can place an order online or call our toll-
free number, 0800-WIDGETS.
```

Attaching files

A quick and convenient way to transmit information from place to place is to attach a file to an e-mail message. In fact, attaching files is one of the most useful things you can do with e-mail. *Attaching,* which means that you send a document or file along with an e-mail message, allows you to include material from any file to which you have access. Attached files appear as separate documents that recipients can download to their computers.

Many e-mail clients allow users to attach files with a simple button or other command. Compressing a lengthy series of attachments by using software such as StuffIt or WinZip conserves bandwidth. Using compression is also a necessity if you ever want to send more than one attached file to someone whose e-mail account doesn't accept multiple attachments.

Creating a signature file that sells

One of the easiest and most useful tools for marketing on the Internet is called a signature file, or a sig file. A *signature file* is a text blurb that your system automatically appends to the bottom of your e-mail messages and newsgroup postings. You want your signature file to tell the readers of your message something about you and your business; you can include information such as your company name and how to contact you.

Creating a signature file takes only a little more time than putting your John Hancock on the dotted line. First, you create the signature file itself, as we describe in these steps:

1. **Open a text-editing program.**

   This example uses Notepad, which comes built in with Windows. If you're a Macintosh user, you can use SimpleText. With either program, a new blank document opens on-screen.

2. **Press and hold down the hyphen (–) or equal sign (=) key to create a dividing line that will separate your signature from the body of your message.**

   Depending on which symbol you use, a series of hyphens or equal signs forms a broken line. Don't make this line too long, or it will run onto another line, which doesn't look good; 30 to 40 characters is a safe measure.

3. **Type the information about yourself that you want to appear in the signature, pressing Enter after each line.**

   Include such information as your name, job title, company name, e-mail address, and Web site URL. A three- or four-line signature is the typical length.

   If you're feeling ambitious at this point, you can press the spacebar to arrange your text in two columns. Greg's agent (who's an online entrepreneur himself) does this with his own signature file, as shown in Figure 6-2.

Figure 6-2:
A signature file often uses divider lines and can be arranged in columns to occupy less space on-screen.

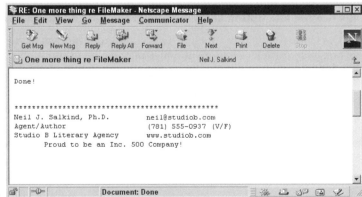

Always include the URL to your business Web site in your signature file and be sure to include it on its own line. Why? Most e-mail programs will recognise the URL as a Web page by its prefix (`http://www.`) and suffix (`.com`, `.co.uk`, and so on). When your reader opens your message, the e-mail program displays the URL as a clickable hyperlink that, when clicked, opens your Web page in a Web browser window.

4. **Choose File⇨Save.**

   A dialog box appears, enabling you to name the file and save it in a folder on your hard drive.

5. **Enter a name for your file that ends in the filename extension `.txt`.**

   This extension identifies your file as a plain text document.

6. **Click the Save button.**

   Your text file is saved on your computer's hard drive.

Now that you've created a plain-text version of your electronic signature, the next step is to identify that file to the computer programs that you use to send and receive e-mail and newsgroup messages. Doing so enables the programs to make the signature file automatically appear at the bottom of your messages. The procedure for attaching a signature file varies from program to program; the following steps show you how to do this by using Microsoft Outlook Express 6:

1. **Start Outlook Express and choose Tools⇨Options.**

   The Options dialog box opens.

2. **Click the Signatures tab.**

3. **Click New.**

   The options in the Signatures and Edit Signature sections of the Signatures tab are highlighted.

4. **Click the File button at the bottom of the tab and then click Browse.**

   The Open dialog box appears. This standard Windows navigation dialog box lets you select folders and files on your computer.

5. **Locate the signature file that you created in the previous set of steps by selecting a drive or folder from the Look In drop-down list. When you locate the file, click the filename and then click the Open button.**

   The Signature File dialog box closes, and you return to the Options dialog box. The path leading to the selected file is listed in the box next to File.

6. **Click the Add Signatures to All Outgoing Messages check box and then click OK.**

   The Options dialog box closes, and you return to Outlook Express. Your signature file is now automatically added to your messages.

To test your new signature file, choose File➪New➪Mail Message from the Outlook Express menu bar. A new message composition window opens. Your signature file should appear in the body of the message composition window. You can compose a message by clicking before the signature and starting to type.

Creating forms that aren't formidable

In the old days, people who heard 'here's a form to fill out' usually started to groan. Who likes to stare at a form to apply for a job or for financial aid or, even worse, to figure out how much you owe in taxes? But as an online businessperson, forms can be your best friends because they give customers a means to provide you with feedback as well as essential marketing information. Using forms, you can find out where customers live, how old they are, and so on. Customers can also use forms to sound off and ask questions.

Forms can be really handy from the perspective of the customer as well. The speed of the Internet enables them to dash off information right away. They can then pretty much immediately receive a response from you that's tailored to their needs and interests.

Forms consist of two parts, only one of which is visible on a Web page:

- ✔ The visible part includes the text-entry fields, buttons, and check boxes that an author creates with HTML commands.

- ✔ The part of the form that you don't see is a computer script that resides on the server that receives the page.

The script, which is typically written in a language such as Perl, AppleScript, or C++, processes the form data that a reader submits to a server and presents that data in a format that the owner or operator of the Web site can read and use.

Getting the data to you

What exactly happens when customers connect to a page on your site that contains a form? First, they fill out the text-entry fields, radio buttons, and other areas you have set up. When they finish, they click a button, often marked Submit, in order to transmit, or *post,* the data from the remote computer to your Web site.

A computer script called a Common Gateway Interface (CGI) program receives the data submitted to your site and processes it so that you can read it. The CGI may cause the data to be e-mailed to you, or it may present the data in a text file in an easy-to-read format.

Optionally, you can also create a CGI program that prompts your server to send users to a Web page that acknowledges that you have received the information and thanks them for their feedback. It's a nice touch that your customers are sure to appreciate.

Writing the scripts that process form data is definitely in the field of webmasters or computer programmers and is far beyond the scope of this book. But you don't have to hire someone to write the scripts: You can use a Web page program (such as Microsoft FrontPage or Adobe Dreamweaver) that not only helps you create a form but also provides you with scripts that process the data for you. (If you use forms created with FrontPage, your Web host must have a set of software called FrontPage Server Extensions installed. Call your host or search the host's online Help files to see whether the extensions are present.)

Some clever businesspeople have created some really useful Web content by providing a way for nonprogrammers such as you and us to create forms online. Appropriately enough, you connect to the server's Web site and fill out a form provided by the service in order to create your form. The form has a built-in CGI that processes the data and e-mails it to you. See the 'Free Forms Online' section of the Internet Directory (on this book's Web site) to find some free form creation and processing services.

Using FrontPage to create a form

You can use the Form Page Wizard that comes with Microsoft FrontPage to create both parts of forms: the data-entry parts (such as text boxes and check boxes), as well as the behind-the-scenes scripts, called *WebBots,* that process form data. Creating your own form gives you more control over how it looks and a greater degree of independence than if you use a ready-made forms service.

The first step in setting up a Web page form is determining what information you want to receive from someone who fills out the form. Your Web page creation tool then gives you options for ways to ask for the information you want. Start FrontPage and choose Insert⇨Form, and a submenu appears with many options. The most commonly used options are the following:

✔ **Textbox:** Creates a single-line box where someone can type text.

✔ **Text Area:** Creates a scrolling text box.

✔ **File Upload:** Lets the user send you a text file.

✔ **Checkbox:** Creates a check box.

✔ **Option Button:** Creates an option button, sometimes called a radio button.

✔ **Drop-Down Box:** Lets you create a drop-down list.

✔ **Picture:** Lets you add a graphic image to a form.

Figure 6-3 shows the most common form fields as they appear in a Web page form that you're creating.

When you choose Insert⇨Form, FrontPage inserts a dashed, marquee-style box in your document to signify that you're working on Web page form fields rather than normal Web page text.

Forms submenu

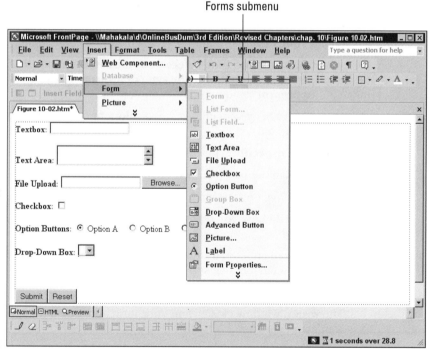

Figure 6-3:
FrontPage
provides
you with
menu
options for
creating
form
elements.

The Form Page Wizard is a great way to set up a simple form that asks for information from visitors to your Web site. It lets you concentrate on the type of data you want to collect rather than on the buttons and boxes needed to gather it. We show you how to create such a form in the following steps. (These steps are for FrontPage 2002; version 2003 requires similar steps, but provides you with more options.)

1. **Choose Start⇨Programs⇨Microsoft FrontPage.**

   FrontPage starts and a blank window appears.

2. **Choose File⇨New⇨Page Or Web.**

   The New Page or Web task pane appears.

3. **Click Page Templates.**

   The Page Templates dialog box appears.

4. **Double-click Form Page Wizard.**

   The first page of the Form Page Wizard appears. (You can click Finish at any time to see your form and begin editing it.)

5. **Click Next.**

6. **Follow the instructions presented in succeeding steps of the wizard to create your form.**

   a. **Click Add and then select from the set of options that the wizard presents you with for the type of information you want the form to present.**

      This data may include account information, ordering information, and so on.

   b. **Select specific types of information you want to solicit.**

   c. **Choose the way you want the information to be presented.**

      You have options such as a bulleted list, numbered list, and so on.

   d. **Identify how you want the user-submitted information to be saved.**

      You can choose to save information as a text file, a Web page, or with a custom CGI script if you have one.

7. **Click Finish.**

   The wizard window closes, and your form appears in the FrontPage window.

When you finish, be sure to add your own description of the form and any special instructions at the top of the Web page. Also add your copyright and contact information at the bottom of the page. Follow the pattern you've set on other pages on your site. You can edit the form by using the Forms submenu options if you want to.

 Be sure to change the background of the form page from the boring default grey that the wizard provides to a more compelling colour. See Book II for more specific instructions on changing the background of Web pages you create.

Making Customers Feel That They Belong

In the old days, people went to the market often, sometimes on a daily basis. The shopkeeper was likely to have set aside items for their consideration based on individual tastes and needs. More likely than not, the business transaction followed a discussion of families, politics, and other village gossip.

Good customer service can make your customers feel like members of a community that frequent a family bakery – the community of satisfied individuals who regularly use your goods and services. In the following sections, we describe some ways to make your customers feel like members of a group, club, or other organisation who return to your site on a regular basis and interact with a community of individuals with similar interests.

Putting the 'person' into personal service

How often does an employee personally greet you as you walk through the door of a shop? On the Web as well as in real life, people like a prompt and personal response. Your challenge is to provide someone on your Web site who's available to provide live customer support.

Some Web sites do provide live support so that people can e-mail a question to someone in real-time (or close to real-time) Internet technologies, such as chat and message boards. The online auction giant eBay.co.uk has a New Users Board, for example, where beginners can post questions for eBay support staff, who post answers in response.

An even more immediate sort of customer support is provided by *chat,* in which individuals type messages to one another over the Internet in real time. One way to add chat to your site is to start a Yahoo! group, which we describe later in this chapter.

LivePerson (www.liveperson.com) provides a simpler alternative that allows small businesses to provide chat-based support. LivePerson is software that enables you to see who is connected to your site at any one time and instantly lets you chat with them, just as if you're greeting them at the front door of a bricks-and-mortar shop.

LivePerson works like this: You install the LivePerson Pro software on your own computer (not the server that runs your site). With LivePerson, you or your assistants can lead the customer through the process of making a purchase. For example, you may help show customers what individual sale items look like by sending them an image file to view with their Web browsers. You can try LivePerson Pro for free for 30 days and then pay around £50 per month thereafter.

Not letting an ocean be a business barrier

You're probably familiar with terms such as *global village* and *international marketplace.* But how do you extend your reach into the huge overseas markets where e-commerce is just beginning to come into its own? Making sure that products are easily and objectively described with words as well as clear images and diagrams, where necessary, is becoming increasingly important. There are other ways to effectively overcome language and cultural barriers, some of which are common sense while others are less obvious.

Keep in mind the fact that shoppers in many developing nations still prefer to shop with their five senses. So that foreign customers never have a question on how to proceed, providing them with implicit descriptions of the shopping process is essential. You should make information on ordering, payment, execution, and support available at every step.

Customer support in Asia is, in many ways, a different creature than in the West. While personalisation still remains critical, language and translation gives an e-commerce site a different feel. You may have to replace a Western site that works well by looking clean and well organised with the more chaotic blitz of characters and options that's often found more compelling by Eastern markets. In Asia, Web sites tend to place more emphasis on colour and interactivity. Many e-commerce destinations choose to dump all possible options on the front page, instead of presenting them in an orderly, sequential flow.

Having a discussion area can enhance your site

Can we talk? Even Greg's pet birds like to communicate by words as well as squawks. A small business can turn its individual customers into a cohesive group by starting its own discussion group on the Internet. Discussion groups work particularly well if you're promoting a particular type of product or if you and your customers are involved in a provocative or even controversial area of interest.

The three kinds of discussion groups are

- ✔ **A local group:** Some universities create discussion areas exclusively for their students. Other large companies set aside groups, sometimes called *intranets,* that are restricted to their employees. Outsiders can't gain access because the groups aren't on the Internet but rather are on a local server within the organisation.

- ✔ **A Usenet newsgroup:** Individuals are allowed to create an Internet-wide discussion group in the `alt` or `biz` categories of Usenet without having to go through the time-consuming application and approval process needed to create other newsgroups.

- ✔ **A Web-based discussion group:** Microsoft FrontPage includes easy-to-use wizards that enable you to create a discussion area on your business Web site. Users can access the area from their Web browsers without having to use special discussion-group software. Or, if you don't have FrontPage, you can start a Yahoo! group, which we describe in the section named (surprise!) 'Starting a Yahoo! group'.

Of these three alternatives, the first isn't appropriate for your business purposes. The following sections focus on the last two types of groups.

In addition to newsgroups, many large corporations host interactive chats moderated by experts on subjects related to their areas of business. But small businesses can also hold chats, most easily by setting up a chat room on a site that hosts chat-based discussions. But the hot way to build goodwill and establish new connections with customers and interested parties is an interactive Web-based diary called a *blog* (short for Web log).

Starting an alt discussion group

Usenet is a system of communication on the Internet that enables individual computer users to participate in group discussions about topics of mutual interest. Internet newsgroups have what's referred to as a hierarchical structure. Most groups belong to one of seven main categories: `comp`, `misc`, `news`, `rec`, `sci`, `soc`, and `talk`. The name of the category appears at the beginning of the group's name, such as `rec.food.drink.coffee`. In this section, we discuss the `alt` category, which is just about as popular as the seven we just mentioned and which enables individuals – like you – to establish their own newsgroups.

In our opinion, the `biz` discussion groups aren't taken seriously because they are widely populated by unscrupulous people promoting get-rich-quick schemes and egomaniacs who love the sound of their own voices. The `alt` groups, although they can certainly address some wild and crazy topics, are at least as well known and often address serious topics. Plus, the process of setting up an `alt` group is well documented.

The prefix `alt` didn't originally stand for *alternative,* although it has come to mean that. The term was an abbreviation for Anarchists, Lunatics, and Terrorists, which wasn't so politically incorrect back in those days. Now, `alt` is a catchall category in which anyone can start a group, if others show interest in the creator's proposal.

The first step to creating your own `alt` discussion group is to point your Web browser to Google Groups (`groups.google.com`) or launch your browser's newsgroup software. To start the Outlook Express newsgroup software, click the plus sign next to the name of the newsgroup software in the program's Folders pane (both options assume you've already configured Outlook Express to connect to your ISP's newsgroup server) and access the group called `alt.config.newgroups`. This area contains general instructions on starting your own Usenet newsgroup. Also look in `news.answers` for the message 'How to Start a New Usenet Newsgroup'.

To find out how to start a group in the `alt` category, go to Google (`www.google.com`), click Groups, and search for the message 'How to Start an Alt Newsgroup'.) Follow the instructions contained in this message to set up your own discussion group. Basically, the process involves the following steps:

1. **You write a brief proposal describing the purpose of the group you want to create and including an e-mail message where people can respond with comments.**

   The proposal also contains the name of your group in the correct form (`alt.groupname.moreinfo.moreinfo`). Try to keep the group name short and official looking if it's for business purposes.

2. You submit the proposal to the newsgroup `alt.config`.

3. You gather feedback to your proposal by e-mail.

4. You send a special message called a *control message* to the news server that gives you access to Usenet.

   The exact form of the message varies from server to server, so you need to consult with your ISP on how to compose the message correctly.

5. Wait a while (a few days or weeks) as news administrators (the people who operate news servers at ISPs around the world) decide whether to adopt your request and add your group to their list of newsgroups.

Before you try to start your own group, look through the Big Seven categories (`comp`, `misc`, `news`, `rec`, `sci`, `soc`, and `talk`) to make sure that someone else isn't already covering your topic.

Starting a Yahoo! group

When the Internet was still fresh and new, Usenet was almost the only game in town. These days, the Web is pretty much (along with e-mail) the most popular way to communicate and share information. That's why starting a discussion group on the Web makes perfect sense. A Web-based discussion group is somewhat less intimidating than others because it doesn't require a participant to use newsgroup software.

Yahoo! groups are absolutely free to set up. The service exists only on the `.com` version of Yahoo! and not the `.co.uk` one as yet, but then that's the great thing about the Internet: It's not confined by national borders. (To find out how to set up a group, just go to the FAQ page, `help.yahoo.com/help/us/groups/index.html` and click the How Do I Start a Group? link.) They not only enable users to exchange messages, but they can also communicate in real time by using chat. And as the list operator, you can send out e-mail newsletters and other messages to your participants, too.

Simply operating an online shop isn't enough. You need to present yourself as an authority in a particular area that is of interest. The discussion group needs to concern itself primarily with that topic and give participants a chance to exchange views and tips on the topic. If people have questions about your shop, they can always e-mail you directly – they don't need a discussion group to do that.

Creating a Web discussion area with FrontPage

The reason that Microsoft FrontPage is such a popular tool for creating Web sites is that it enables you to create Web page content that you would otherwise need complicated scripts to tackle. One example is the program's Discussion Group Wizard, which lets you create Web pages on which your members (as opposed to customers, remember?) can exchange messages and carry on a series of back-and-forth responses (called *threads*) on different topics. Newcomers to the group can also view articles that are arranged by a table of contents and accessible by a searchable index.

Follow these steps to set up your own discussion group with Microsoft FrontPage:

1. **Start FrontPage by choosing Start⇨All Programs⇨Microsoft FrontPage.**

   The FrontPage window opens.

   You can create a new discussion *web* (that is, a group of interlinked documents that together comprise a Web site) of Web pages by using one of the built-in wizards that comes with FrontPage.

2. **To use the FrontPage Discussion Group Wizard, choose File⇨New⇨Page Or Web.**

   The New Page Or Web task pane appears.

3. **Click Web Site Templates.**

   The Web Site Templates dialog box appears.

4. **Select Discussion Web Wizard and then click OK.**

   A dialog box appears, stating that the new discussion web is being created. Then the first of a series of Discussion Web Wizard dialog boxes appears.

5. **Click Next.**

   The second dialog box lets you specify the features you want for your discussion web. If this is the first time you've created a group, leave all the options checked.

6. **Click Next.**

   A dialog box appears that lets you specify a title and folder for the new discussion web. Enter a title in the box beneath Enter a descriptive title for this discussion. You can change the default folder name _disc1 if you want.

7. **Click Next.**

   The dialog box that appears lets you choose one of three options for the structure of your discussion:

   - Select Subject, Comments if you expect visitors to discuss only a single topic.
   - Select Subject, Category, Comments if you expect to conduct discussions on more than one topic.
   - Select Subject, Product, Comments if you want to invite discussions about products you produce and/or sell.

   After you select one of these options, the next Discussion Web Wizard dialog box appears. Go through this and the subsequent dialog boxes, answering the questions they present you with in order to determine what kind of discussion group you're going to have. At any time, as you go through the series of Discussion Web Wizard pages, you can click the Finish button to complete the process.

8. **When you're finished, the preset pages for your discussion web appear in the FrontPage Explorer main window.**

The middle column of the FrontPage window shows the arrangement of the discussion documents. The right side of the window is a visual map that shows how the discussion group is arranged and how the pages are linked to each other.

When you set up a discussion area with FrontPage, you have the option of designing your pages as a *frameset,* or a set of Web pages that has been subdivided into separate frames. To find out more about frames, see Book II.

Editing the discussion pages

After you use the Discussion Group Wizard to create your pages, the next step is to edit the pages so that they have the content you want. With your newly created pages displayed in the FrontPage window, you can start editing by double-clicking the icon for a page (such as the Welcome page, which has a filename such as `disc_welc.htm`) in your discussion web. Whatever page you double-click opens in the right column of the FrontPage window.

For example, you may add a few sentences to the beginning of the Welcome page that you have just created in order to tell participants more about the purpose and scope of the discussion group. You can add text by clicking anywhere on the page and typing.

To edit more pages in your discussion group, choose File⇨Open. The Open File dialog box appears with a list of all the documents that make up your discussion group. You can double-click a file's name in order to edit it. When you finish editing files, choose File⇨Save to save your work.

To see how your discussion pages look, use the FrontPage Preview feature. Choose File⇨Preview In Browser, and the page you've been editing appears in your browser window.

Posting your discussion area

The final step is to transfer your discussion web of pages from your own computer to your Web host's site on the Internet. Many Web-hosting services support one-step file transfers with Microsoft FrontPage. If you plan to use FrontPage often, we recommend locating a host that offers this support. (If your host doesn't support such transfers, you need to use an FTP program such as Fetch or WS_FTP to transfer your files.)

With one-step file transfers, you simply connect to the Internet, choose File⇨Publish Web from the FrontPage menu bar, and enter the URL of your directory on your host's Web server where your Web pages are published. Click OK, and your files are immediately transferred.

Book VI
Using eBay.co.uk

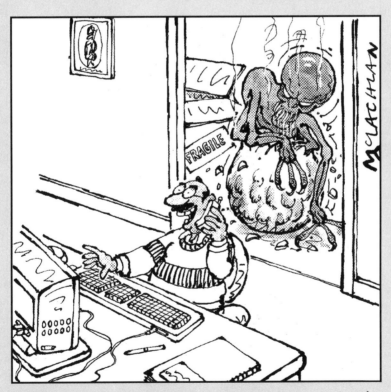

'Well, I've just received through eBay my hunk of so-called rock from Mars, and I must admit it's the weirdest piece of rock I've ever seen.'

In this book . . .

*e*Bay.co.uk offers everyone with an Internet connection the chance to become an online entrepreneur by selling and auctioning goods. With this in mind, we've decided to dedicate this whole book to using eBay.co.uk. Starting by looking at the advantages of using eBay, we then talk you through launching your business on eBay, running an eBay shop, and making your auctions as appealing as possible. We wrap things up by considering your options for organising, keeping track of, and shipping all of those items you're selling.

Here are the contents of Book VI at a glance:

Chapter 1

Why eBay Is a Great Place to Buy and Sell

*e*Bay has emerged as *the* marketplace for the twenty-first century. The founders had a very clever idea back in 1995, and a decade later the world is obsessed with shopping and selling online. eBay is a safe and fun place to shop for everything from collectables to clothing, all from the comfort of your home.

eBay is now also a marketplace for new merchandise. It's no longer just the destination for obscure collectables and old china patterns. These days you can buy new and useful items, such as alarm systems, fancy electric toothbrushes, designer clothing, cars, homes, villas in Portugal – more or less anything you can think of.

Have a look around your house. Nice toaster. Unusual clock. Natty microwave. Not to mention all the other fab stuff you own. All these household appliances and collectables are lovely to own, but when was the last time your toaster turned a profit? When you connect to eBay, your PC or Mac magically turns into a money-machine. Just visit eBay and marvel at all the items that are just a few mouse clicks away from being bought and sold.

In this chapter, we tell you what eBay is and how it works. eBay is the perfect alternative to spending hours wandering through antique shops or car boot sales looking for the perfect thingamyjig. It can also be your personal shopper for presents and day-to-day items. Not only can you buy and sell stuff in the privacy of your home, but you can also meet people who share your interests. The people who use the eBay site are a friendly crowd, and soon you'll be buying, selling, swapping stories, and trading advice with the best of them.

What Is eBay, and How Does It Work?

The Internet is spawning all kinds of new businesses (known as *e-commerce* to City types), and eBay is one of its few superstars. The reason is simple: It's the place where buyers and sellers can meet, do business, share stories and tips, and have a laugh.

eBay *doesn't* sell a thing. Instead, the site does what all good hosts do: It creates a comfy environment that brings people with common interests together. You can think of eBay as you think of the person who set you up on your last blind date – except the results are often a lot better. Your matchmaking friend doesn't perform a marriage ceremony but does get you in the same room with your potential soul mate. eBay puts buyers and sellers in a virtual shop and lets them conduct their business safely within the rules that eBay has established.

All you need to do to join eBay is fill in a few online forms and click. Congratulations – you're a member, with no big fees or secret handshakes. After you register, you can buy and sell anything that falls within the eBay rules and regulations. (Jane Hoskyn and Marsha Collier's *eBay.co.uk For Dummies* eases you through the registration process.)

The eBay home page, shown in Figure 1-1, is your first step to finding all the smart things you can see and do at eBay. You can conduct searches, find out what's happening, and get an instant link to the My eBay page, which helps you keep track of every auction item you have up for sale or are bidding on. You can read more about the eBay home page and find out more about My eBay in Jane Hoskyn and Marsha Collier's *eBay.co.uk For Dummies*.

Argh! What happened? The eBay home page on your computer looks nothing like the one in Figure 1-1? Don't rub your eyes – even squinting hard won't help: eBay has a different version of the home page for those who have never registered on eBay. Even if *you* have never registered, someone else who uses the computer may have done. Have a look at Figure 1-2 and see if it's a closer match.

Figure 1-1:
The eBay
home page,
your starting
point for
bargains
and for
making
some
serious
cash.

Book VI

**Using
eBay.co.uk**

Figure 1-2:
The eBay
home page
for new
users.

All About Auctions

The value of an item is determined by how much someone is willing to spend to buy it. That's what makes auctions exciting. eBay offers several kinds of auctions, but for the most part, they all work the same way. An *auction* is a unique sales event where the exact value of the item for sale is not known. As a result, there's an element of surprise involved – not only for the bidder (who may end up with a tasty bargain) but also for the seller (who may end up making a killing). Here's how an auction works from the perspective of a seller and a bidder:

- **Seller:** A seller pays a fee, fills in an online form, and sets up the auction, listing the *minimum bid* he or she is willing to accept for the item. Think of an auctioneer at Sotheby's saying, 'The bidding for this diamond neck-lace starts at £5,000.' You might *want* to bid £4,000, but the bid won't be accepted. Sellers can also set a *reserve price* – sort of a financial safety net that protects them from losing money on the deal. We explain how these things work later in this section.

- **Bidder:** Bidders in auctions battle it out over a period of time (the mini-mum is one day, but most eBay auctions last a week or 10 days) until one comes out victorious. Usually, the highest bidder wins. The tricky thing about taking part in an auction (and the most exciting part) is that no one knows the final price an item goes for until the last second of the auction.

eBay auctions

Unlike 'traditional' live auctions that end with the familiar phrase 'Going, going, gone!' eBay auctions are controlled by the clock. The seller pays a fee and lists the item on the site for a pre-determined length of time; the highest bidder when the clock runs out takes home the prize.

Reserve-price auctions

Unlike a minimum bid, which is required in any eBay auction, a *reserve price* protects sellers from having to sell an item for less than the minimum amount they want for it. You may be surprised to see a 1968 Jaguar XKE sports car up for auction on eBay with a minimum bid of only a pound. It's a fair bet that the seller has put a reserve price on this car to protect himself from losing money. The reserve price allows sellers to set lower minimum bids, and lower minimum bids attract bidders. Unfortunately, if a seller makes the reserve price too high and no one has met it by the end of the auction, no one wins.

eBay charges a fee for sellers to run these auctions. Nobody (except the seller and the eBay computer system) knows what the reserve price is until the auction is over, but you can tell from the auction page whether you're dealing with a reserve-price auction. Reserve-price auctions are in the listings alongside the other items, so you have to click and open an auction to find out whether it has a reserve. If bids have been made on an item, a message also appears on the page saying whether the reserve price has been met.

Private (shhh-it's-a-secret) auctions

Some sellers choose to hold private auctions because they know that some bidders may be embarrassed to be seen bidding on a pair of kinky boots in front of the rest of the eBay community. Others may go the private route because they are selling very valuable items and don't want to disclose their bidder's financial status.

Private auctions are run like the typical timed auctions except that each bidder's identity is kept secret. At the end of the auction, eBay provides contact info to the seller and to the high bidder, and that's it.

You can send e-mail questions to the seller in a private auction, but you can't check out your competition because the auction item page shows the current bid price but not the high bidder's User ID.

Multiple Item (Dutch) auctions

Multiple Item – *Dutch* – auctions have nothing to do with clogs, Edam cheese, or halving the bill on a date. A *Multiple Item auction* allows a seller to put multiple, identical items up for sale. Instead of holding 100 separate auctions for 100 pairs of clogs, for example, a seller can sell them all in one listing. As a buyer, you can elect to bid for 1, 3, or all 100 pairs. But unless you're running an alternative Euro-boutique (or know a giant centipede who needs all those clogs), you probably want to bid on just one pair.

A Multiple Item auction can't be conducted as a private auction.

Buying It Now at eBay

You don't have to bid in an auction on eBay to buy something. If there's something you want to buy – if it's something you *must* have and you don't want to wait for an auction to end – there's a good chance that you can find one on eBay to buy immediately. Of course, using Buy It Now (*BIN* in eBay speak) doesn't have the thrill of an auction, but buying an item for a fraction of the retail price without leaving your chair or waiting for an auction to end has its own warm and fuzzy kind of excitement. If you seek this kind of instant gratification on eBay, look for the Buy It Now icon in the lists of items for sale. You can also visit the eBay shops, where you'll find loads of Buy It Now items lined up for the taking.

eBay Shops

Visiting eBay Shops is as easy as clicking the eBay Shops link from the home page. Thousands of eBay sellers have set up shops, with much of the merchandise available to Buy It Now. Here you can buy anything from socks to jewellery to sports memorabilia – or even a kitchen sink!

Sellers who open an eBay shop have to meet a certain level of experience on eBay, and when you buy from eBay Shops, you're protected by the same fraud protection policy that you are covered with in eBay auctions. Figure 1-3 shows the eBay Shops home page.

Figure 1-3: From the eBay Shops home page, you can find almost anything without having to wait for an auction to end.

So You Want to Sell Stuff

If you're a seller, creating an auction page at eBay is as simple as filling in an online form. You type in the name of your item and a short description, add a crisp digital picture, set your price, and *voilà* – it's up for auction. (Alright, it's a tad more involved than that – but not much.) eBay charges a small fee (£0.15 to £2.00) for the privilege. When you list your item, millions of people (eBay has more than 147 million registered users) from all over the world can have a gander at it and place bids. With a bit of luck, a bidding war may break out and drive the bids up high enough for you to turn in a nice profit. After the auction, you deal directly with the buyer, who sends you the payment either through a payment service such as PayPal or through the post. Then you send them the item. Abracadabra – you just turned your item (unwanted clutter, perhaps) into cash.

Book VI

Using eBay.co.uk

So You Want to Buy Stuff?

If you're a collector or you just like to shop for bargains, you can browse 24 hours a day through the items up for auction in eBay's thousands of categories, which range from Antiques to Wholesale lots. Find the item you want, do some research on what you're buying and who's selling it, place your bid, and keep an eye on it until the auction closes.

When you see an item you like, you can set up a bidding strategy and let the games begin. You can bid as many times as you want on an item, and you can bid on as many auctions as you want. Just keep in mind that each bid is a binding contract, and you'll be required to pay if you win.

Research for Fun and Profit

eBay's powerful search engine allows you to browse through countless *categories* of items up for sale. As a buyer, you can do lots of comparison shopping for that special something you just can't live without, or just browse around until something catches your eye. If you're a seller, the search engine allows you to keep your eye on the competition and get an idea of how popular your item is. That way, you can set a competitive price.

The search engine also lets you find out what other people are bidding on. From there, you can read up on their *feedback ratings* (eBay's ingenious reputation system) to get a sense of what other customers thought of their service – *before* you deal with them.

eBay's Role in the Action

Throughout the auction process, eBay's computers keep tabs on what's going on. When the auction or sale is over, eBay takes a small percentage of the final selling price and sends an e-mail to the seller and buyer. At this point, eBay's job is more or less over, and it steps aside.

Most of the time, everything works fine, everybody's happy, and eBay never has to step back in. But if you happen to run into a spot of bother, eBay can help you settle the problem, whether you're the buyer or the seller.

eBay regulates members with a detailed system of checks and balances known as *feedback*. The idea is that the eBay community polices itself. eBay is more than happy to jump in when dodgy dealings comes to light, but the people who do most to keep eBay safe are the buyers and sellers themselves, the people who have a common stake in doing business fairly and squarely. Every time you sell something or win an auction, eBay members have a chance to leave a comment about you. You should do the same for them. If they're happy, the feedback is positive; otherwise, the feedback is negative. Either way, your feedback sticks to you like glue.

Building a great reputation with positive feedback ensures a long and profitable eBay career. Negative feedback, like multiple convictions, is a real turnoff for most people and can make it hard for you to do future business on eBay.

If your feedback rating sinks to a –4 (minus 4), eBay suspends your buying and selling privileges.

Features and Fun Stuff

So eBay is all about making money? Not exactly. The people at eBay aren't joking when they call it a community – a place where people with similar interests can compare notes, argue, buy and sell, and meet each other. Yes, people have got married after meeting on eBay. (Wonder if they set up a wedding list on eBay?)

Getting in the community spirit

eBay has dozens of specific discussion boards and groups whose topics range from advertising to wildlife (no, you can't sell wildlife on eBay – but you can talk about it until your typing fingers hurt). So if you have no idea what that old Esso petrol station sign you found in your granddad's garden shed is worth, just post a message on the Community Question & Answer board. Somewhere out there is an expert with an answer for you. Your biggest problem is deciding whether to keep the sign or put it up for auction. Those are good problems to have!

One of the most useful places to hang around when you first start trading on eBay is the New to eBay help board. The people on this board won't slam you for asking basic questions, and they're always happy to help or at least lend an ear.

eBay's Safety Centre

The Safety Centre is eBay's one-stop resource for information and services about keeping eBay safe – and for advice on what to do if things go wrong. Sometimes, despite your best efforts to be a good eBay user, buyers or sellers don't keep their word. In a small proportion of cases, unscrupulous chancers sometimes do invade the site and try to scam people. You may buy an item that isn't as it was described, or the winner of your auction doesn't send the payment. Sometimes even honest members get into disputes. The Safety Centre is an excellent resource for when you need questions answered or you need a professional to come in and settle an out-of-hand situation.

Extra Gadgets You May Want

As you get into the swing of buying and selling on eBay, you grow more comfortable with all the technical hoops you have to jump through to make the eBay magic happen. Once you're at that point, you may be ready to invest in a few extra gizmos, such as digital cameras and scanners that can make all the difference to your auction listings – and your profit margins.

Chapter 2

Using eBay.co.uk to Launch Your Business

. . . .

In This Chapter

▶ Getting serious about your business

▶ Making decisions about what to sell

▶ Having what it takes to make a living online

▶ Running an efficient auction

. . . .

*Y*ou've decided to get serious about your sales on eBay.co.uk, so now you have to decide how much time you have to devote to your eBay business. We talk about all kinds of eBay businesses in this book. Even though you're not quitting your day job and selling on eBay full time (yet!), we still think you're serious. A large portion of sellers, even eBay PowerSellers (those who gross more than £750 a month in sales), work on eBay only part time.

eBay sellers come from all walks of life. A good number of stay-at-home mums are out there selling on eBay. And so many retirees are finding eBay a great place to supplement their income that we wouldn't be surprised if the Pensions Service creates a special eBay arm for them. If you're pulled out of your normal work routine and faced with a new lifestyle, you can easily make the transition to selling on eBay.

In this chapter, we talk about planning just how much time you can devote to your eBay business – and how to budget that time. We also talk here about working out what to sell. eBay businesses don't grow overnight, but with dedication and persistence, you may just form your own online empire.

Getting Down to Business

Before launching any business, including an eBay.co.uk business, you need to set your priorities. And to be successful at that business, you must apply some clear level of discipline.

We won't bore you with the now-legendary story of how Pierre Omidyar started eBay to help fulfil his girlfriend's Pez dispenser habit, blah, blah, blah. We *will* tell you that he started AuctionWeb with a laptop, a regular Internet Service Provider (ISP), and an old school desk. Omidyar and his friend Jeff Skoll (a Stanford MBA) ran the 24-hours-a-day, 7-days-a-week AuctionWeb all by themselves. When we began using the service, we had a lot of questions and we always got prompt, friendly answers to our e-mails. When the site started attracting more traffic, Pierre's ISP began to complain about all the traffic and raised his monthly fees. To cover the higher costs, Pierre and Jeff began charging 25 cents to list an auction. Pierre was so busy running the site that the envelopes full of cheques began to pile up – he didn't even have time to open the post.

When Pierre and Jeff incorporated eBay AuctionWeb in 1996, they were each drawing a salary of $25,000. Their first office consisted of one room, and they had one part-time employee to handle the payments. Pierre and Jeff started small and grew.

Choosing eBay.co.uk as a part-time money maker

A part-time eBay.co.uk business can be very profitable. We stress repeatedly in this book that the more time and energy you spend on your eBay business, the more money you can make, but for now we move on to the lowest possible level of time that you should devote to your business.

Maybe you enjoy finding miscellaneous items to sell on eBay. You can find these items somehow in your day-to-day life. Suppose that you can spend at least a few hours (maybe three) a day on eBay. Now you must include the time you take to write up your auctions. If you're not selling only one type of item, allow about 15 minutes to write your auction, take your picture or scan your image, and, of course, upload it to eBay.co.uk or a photo-hosting site.

How much time it takes to perform these tasks varies from person to person and improves according to your level of expertise. Every task in your eBay auction business takes time, however, and you must budget for that time. See the sidebar 'Some handy eBay.co.uk time-saving tips' for pointers.

Only you can decide how much time you want to spend researching going rates for items on eBay.co.uk and deciding which day or time your item will sell for the highest price. You can take great photos and write brilliant descriptions, but cashmere cardigans don't sell for as much in the heat of summer as they do in winter. Doing your research can take up a good deal of time when you're selling a varied group of items.

Some handy eBay.co.uk time-saving tips

Stuck for time? Following are some features that you're sure to find useful and handy:

✔ **HTML templates:** In Chapter 5, we give you some tips on finding basic HTML format templates for attractive auctions. These templates cut your auction design time to a few minutes. Most experienced eBay sellers use preset templates to speed up the task of listing auctions, and this should be your goal.

✔ **Turbo Lister program:** When you want to list a lot of auctions at once, use the eBay Turbo Lister program– it enables you to put together and upload ten auctions in just 15 minutes.

✔ **Re-listing (or Sell Similar) feature:** When you sell the same item time after time, you can use Turbo Lister (it archives your old listings so you can repeat them) or the handy eBay re-listing or Sell Similar features. When your auction ends on eBay, links pop up offering to re-list your listing or to Sell Similar. If you want to run a different auction with a similar HTML format to the one that just ended, simply select the Sell Similar option and cut and paste the new title and description into the Sell Your Item page of your new listing.

✔ **Auction management software:** See the 'Software you can use' section in this chapter.

Consider also how much time shopping for your merchandise takes. You may have to travel to dealers, go to auctions, or spend time online discovering new ways to find your auction merchandise. Many sellers set aside a full day each week for this undertaking. Your merchandise is what makes you money, so don't skimp on the time you spend identifying products. The time you spend on resourcing your products comes back to you in higher profits.

Here's a list of various activities that you must perform when doing business on eBay.co.uk:

✔ Photograph the item.

✔ Clean up and resize the images in a photo editor (if necessary).

✔ Upload the images to eBay Picture Services when you list or before listing to your ISP or third-party hosting service.

✔ Weigh the item and determine the shipping cost.

✔ Choose an auction title with keywords.

✔ Write a concise and creative description.

- ✔ List the auction on eBay.co.uk.
- ✔ Answer bidder questions.
- ✔ Send end-of-auction e-mails.
- ✔ Carry out banking.
- ✔ Perform bookkeeping.
- ✔ Pack the item safely and securely.
- ✔ Address the label and affix postage.
- ✔ Go to the post office.

Time yourself to see how long you take to accomplish each of these tasks. The time varies when you list multiple items, so think of the figures that you come up with as your *baseline,* a minimum amount of time that you must set aside for these tasks. Use this information to help you decide how many hours per month you need to devote to running your part-time eBay business.

Jumping in with both feet: Making eBay.co.uk a full-time job

The tasks required for your eBay business can be time consuming. But careful planning and scheduling can turn your business into a money-spinning empire.

The best way to go full time on eBay is to first run your business part time for a while to iron out the wrinkles. After you become comfortable with eBay.co.uk as a business, you're ready to make the transition to full-time seller. The minimum gross monthly sales for a Bronze-level PowerSeller is £750. If you plan your time efficiently, you can easily attain this goal.

Running a full-time business on eBay is the perfect option for working parents who prefer staying at home with their children, retirees looking for something to do, or those who'd just rather do something else than work for their boss.

See Figure 2-1 for an example of the eBay.co.uk home page, the first stop for most buyers on eBay.co.uk. Note how eBay makes an effort to reflect some sort of promotion to better market the items you put up for sale.

Figure 2-1:
The
eBay.co.uk
home page,
where it all
starts!

Deciding What to Sell

What should I sell? That is *the* million-dollar question! In your quest for merchandise, you're bound to hear about soft goods and hard goods. *Soft*, or non-durable, goods are generally textile products, such as clothing, fabrics, and bedding. *Hard* goods are computer equipment, homewares, and anything else that's basically non-disposable.

Following are just a few points to consider when you're deciding what to sell:

✔ **Shipping costs:** Some differences exist between shipping hard and soft goods. Soft goods can fold up and be packed in standard box sizes or (better yet) in bubble wrap or jiffy bags for much lower shipping costs. Most hard goods come in their own boxes, which may or may not be individually shippable. You also need to use Styrofoam peanuts or bubble cushioning or double package items in oddly sized boxes.

✔ **Other shipping considerations:** Do you want to handle large boxes and deal with the hassles of shipping them?

✔ **Possible storage problems:** Do you have the room to store enough merchandise to keep you going? Soft goods can take up considerably less space than hard goods.

You don't always have to buy your items in bulk to make money on eBay. The first things you sell may be items you find in your garage or loft. To find out about some other fun ways to acquire goods to sell, check out the next section.

Turning your hobby into a business

Admit it, you've got a hobby; everyone does! Did you collect stamps or coins as a kid? Play with Barbie dolls? Maybe your hobby is cars? Did you inherit a load of antiques? Been collecting figurines for a few years? eBay.co.uk has a market for almost anything.

You can't possibly be an expert on everything. You need to keep up-to-date on the market for your items, and following more than four or five basic item groups may divert your attention from selling.

Selling within a particular category or two can be a good idea for repeat business. Should you decide to major in miscellany and sell anything and everything, you may not realise the highest possible prices for your items. If you have a source that permits you to buy items at dirt-cheap pricing, however, you may not mind selling at a lower price.

Collectibles: Big business on eBay

The story goes that Pierre Omidyar started eBay with the idea to trade collectible Pez dispensers (actually, the first item ever sold on eBay was a broken laser pointer). eBay.co.uk now lists countless categories of collectibles (see Figure 2-2), and those categories are divided into many times more categories, sub-categories, and sub-sub-categories. Almost anything that you'd want to collect is here, from advertising memorabilia to Girl Scout badges to Zippo lighters!

If you have a collection of your own, eBay.co.uk is a great way to find rare items. Because your collection is something dear to your heart and you've studied it on and off for years, you can probably call yourself an expert. Bingo – you're an expert at something! Hone your skills to find things in your area of expertise at discount prices (you're liking this more and more, aren't you?) and then sell them on eBay for a profit. Start small and start with something you know.

If there's one thing you know, it's fashion!

Are you one of those people who just knows how to put together a great outfit? Do you find bargains at charity shops but people think you've spent hundreds on your garb? Do you know where to get hold of end-of-line designer gear? Looks like you've found your market (see Figure 2-3).

Figure 2-2:
The
eBay.co.uk
Collectibles
hub with
links to
categories.

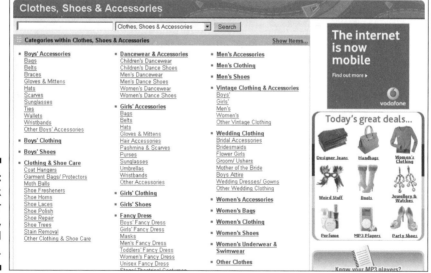

Figure 2-3:
eBay.co.uk
area for
clothing,
shoes, and
accessories.

Buy as many of those stylish designer dresses as you can, and set them up on the mannequin you've bought to model your fashions for eBay photos. Within a week, you just may be doubling your money – 'cause sweetie-darling, who knows fashion better than you?

If a ball, a wheel, or competition is involved – it's for you

Many men like to watch sport, play sport, and look good while they're doing it – opening up venues for a profitable empire on eBay.co.uk. We don't want to leave out all the women out there who excel and participate in many sports. Women may have even more discriminating needs for their sporting endeavours! Your golf game may stink – but you do make a point to at least look good when you go out there, with respectable equipment and a fabulous outfit.

eBay.co.uk has an amazing market for football, rugby and tennis equipment – and that's the tip of the iceberg. The last time we looked, golf items totalled almost 20,000 listings! What a bonanza! New stuff, used stuff – it's all selling on eBay (see Figure 2-4). All this selling is enough to put your local pro shop out of business – or perhaps put *you* in business.

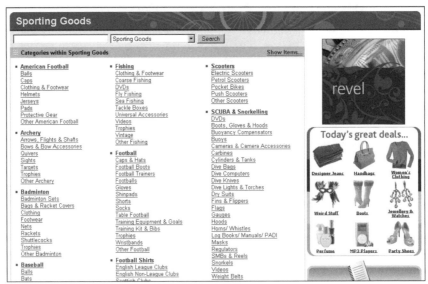

Figure 2-4: Sporting goods on eBay.co.uk.

Including the whole family in the business

Sometimes just the idea of a part-time business can throw you into a tizzy. Don't you have enough to do already? School, work, football practice, kids glued to the TV – you may sometimes feel as if you've no time for family time. However, the importance of family time is what brought us to eBay in the first place. We were working long hours in our own businesses, and at the end of the day, when the kids wanted to go shopping, perhaps for some Hello Kitty toys or a Barbie doll, we were often just too tired.

One of us, Marsha, has a great story:

I'd heard about AuctionWeb from a friend and had bought some things online for my own collections. (Okay, you got me; I collected Star Trek stuff – call me geek with a capital *G*.) I'd also browsed around the site and found some popular toys selling for reasonable prices. So one evening I introduced my daughter to eBay, and life has never been the same. We'd go to toy shops together immediately they opened on Saturday morning, so we'd get first dibs on shipments of the hottest, newest toys. My daughter headed for dolls, and I'd go to the action figures. After buying several items, we'd go home, and post them for sale on eBay. We made money, yes, but the best part was our toy runs – they will always remain a special memory.

My daughter has since graduated from university (she majored in business and marketing – must have been inspired by our eBay enterprise) but she still phones home when she finds a hot CD or a closing-down sale. My daughter and I still purchase and list items together. The family that eBays together . . . always does.

This short trip down memory lane has a point: A family business can succeed, and everyone can enjoy it. An adult can be in charge of the financing and the packing while a youngster can look up postcodes on the Internet and put pins in a 4' x 5' map showing every town that we bought or sold from. Children can learn some excellent lessons in marketing, advertising, and geography, all in one go.

Toys, books, and music

Having children in your home brings you closer to the latest trends than you can ever imagine. We remember sitting in a café a couple of years ago watching some dads and their sons pouring over notebooks full of Pokémon cards. (Actually, the kids were off playing somewhere, and the dads were coveting the cards.)

And what about Star Wars? Star Trek? Men in Black? Can you say action figures? (If boys have them, they're not dolls – they're action figures.) If you have access to the latest and greatest toys, buy them up and sell them to those who can't find them in their neck of the woods.

Is your home one of those where books pile up all over the place? If your children have outgrown educational books (even university textbooks), they can be turned into a profit. Remember that not every book is a classic that needs to be part of your library forever. Let another family get the pleasure of sharing children's tales!

If anything piles up faster than books, it's CDs, videos, and DVDs. Somehow the old lambada or macarena music doesn't hold the magic it once did and those pre-school videos drive you insane. You can get rid of your own items and find plenty of stock at car boot sales – buy them cheap and make a couple of quid.

Selling children's clothes

Last time we looked there were more than 42,000 baby clothes auctions in progress – and the bidding was hot and heavy. For stay-at-home parents, selling baby and children's clothing is a great way to pick up extra income.

If you've had a baby, you know all too well that friends and relatives shower new mums with lots of cute outfits. If you're lucky, your baby gets to wear one or two of these outfits (maybe only for a special picture) before outgrowing them. These adorable clothes can earn you a profit on eBay.co.uk. Many parents, with children a few steps behind yours, are looking for bargain clothing on eBay – a profitable hand-me-down community. As your children grow up (and out of their old clothes), earn some money while helping out another parent.

Bringing your business to eBay.co.uk

Do you already have a business? eBay.co.uk isn't only a marketplace where you're able to unload slow or out-of-season merchandise. You can also set up your shop on eBay (see Figure 2-5). An eBay shop allows you to list a fixed-price item at a reduced fee and keep the item online until it sells. When you run your regular auctions for special items, they have a link to your shop, thereby drawing in new shoppers to see your merchandise.

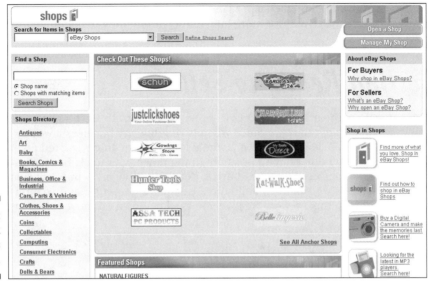

Figure 2-5: eBay.co.uk shops central.

Here are a few ways you can expand your current business with eBay.co.uk:

- ✔ **Opening a second shop on eBay.co.uk:** How many people run shops that sell every item, every time? If you're a retailer, you've probably made a buying mistake. Maybe the item that *isn't* selling in your shop *is* selling like hotcakes in similar shops elsewhere in the country. eBay gives you the tools to sell those extra items to make room for more of what sells at your home base.

  Perhaps you just need to raise some cash quickly. eBay has tens of thousands of categories in which you can sell regular stock or speciality items.

- ✔ **Selling by mail order:** If you've been selling by mail order, what's been holding you back from selling on eBay? Listing your item on eBay is much cheaper than running an ad in any publication. Plus, on eBay, you get built-in buyers from every walk of life. If your item sells through mail order, it will sell through eBay.

- ✔ **Licensed estate agents:** Plenty of land, houses, and flats are selling on eBay.co.uk right now. List your properties online so that you can draw from a nationwide audience and get more action.

You won't find a cheaper landlord than eBay. Jump over to Chapter 4 if you really can't wait for more information about how to set up your eBay shop.

Getting Ready to Sell

We've heard many sellers-to-be say they want to start a business on eBay so that they can relax. Since when is running any business a way to relax? Granted, you don't need a whole lot of money to get started on eBay.co.uk and you don't have a boss breathing down your neck. But to run a successful eBay business, you need drive, determination, and your conscience to guide you, as well as a few solid tools, such as a computer and an Internet connection. In this section, we give you the low-down on these things and more.

Computer hardware

First, you need a computer. In our basic assumptions about you (see this book's Introduction), we think that you have one and know how to use it. Your computer doesn't have to be the latest, fastest, and best available – but it does help if it has a good deal of memory to process your Web browsing and image touch-ups. One of our eBay selling computers is an antique Pentium 3, an absolute dinosaur next to my new 4.3GHz model. But combined with a speedy Internet connection, my little machine enables me to run many eBay auctions easily.

Hard drives are getting cheaper by the minute and the bigger your hard drive, the more space you have to store images for your auctions. (Individual pictures shouldn't take up much space because each should max at 50K.) A warning: The bigger your hard drive, the more chance for making a mess of it by losing files. When you get started, set up a sensible filing system by using folders and sub-directories.

Check out Chapter 5 for details of the other stuff you may need, such as a scanner and a digital camera.

Connecting to the Internet

If you've been on eBay for any length of time, you know that your Internet connection turns into an appendage of your body. If your connection is down or you can't log on due to a power cut, you can't function and instead flounder around, babbling to yourself. We understand because we've been there. If you're selling in earnest, pull the plug on your dial-up connection unless you have no choice.

Before investing in any broadband connection, visit `www.broadband checker.co.uk` (see Figure 2-6) and check out details of ISPs in your area. Alternatively, `www.broadband.co.uk` allows you to compare and contrast the connections available. You can also find a broadband beginners' guide at http://www.broadband.co.uk/guide.jsp, in case you're not sure about the ins and outs of high-speed Internet connections.

Dial-up connections

If you must use a dial-up connection, avail yourself of the many free trials that different Internet Service Providers (ISPs) offer to see which one gives your computer the fastest connection. After you find the fastest, be sure that the connection is reliable and has at least a 99 per cent uptime rate – otherwise you could be in for frustrating delays.

Most of the UK still logs on to the Internet with a dial-up connection, so what can be so wrong? Yet, this type of connection is painfully slow. An auction with lots of images can take minutes to load. The average eBay user wants to browse many auctions and doesn't wait while your images load; he or she just goes to the next auction.

To make the best use of your time when running your auctions and conducting research, you need to blast through the Internet – answering e-mails, loading images, and conducting your business without waiting around for snail-pace connections. Common quibbles from dial-up users are that transfer speeds are too slow and that their telephone lines are tied up during a session, so they can't even use the phone! Although a modem is supposed to link up at 56K, the highest connection we've ever experienced on a dial-up was 44K – much too slow!

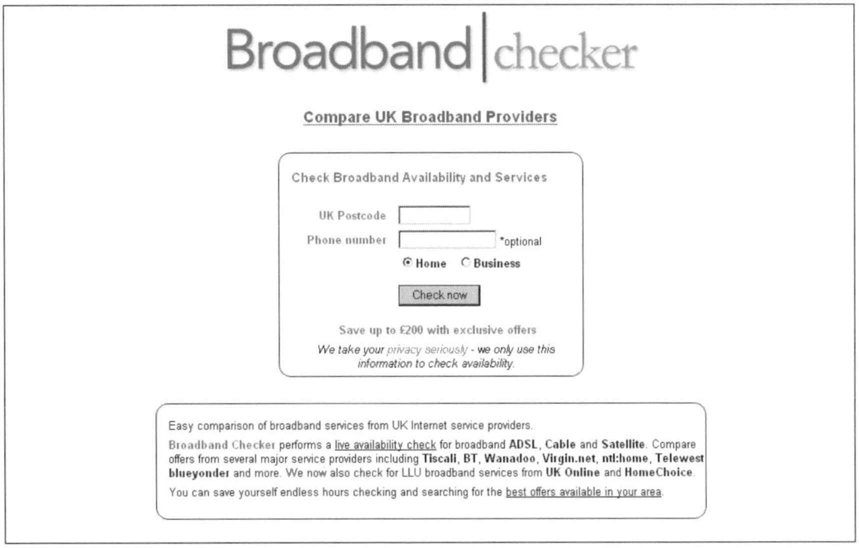

Book VI

Using eBay.co.uk

Figure 2-6:
The search page on www. broadband checker. co.uk.

Broadband | checker

Compare UK Broadband Providers

Check Broadband Availability and Services

UK Postcode [   ]

Phone number [   ] *optional

◉ Home   ○ Business

[Check now]

Save up to £200 with exclusive offers

We take your privacy seriously - we only use this information to check availability.

Easy comparison of broadband services from UK Internet service providers.

Broadband Checker performs a live availability check for broadband **ADSL**, **Cable** and **Satellite**. Compare offers from several major service providers including **Tiscali**, **BT**, **Wanadoo**, **Virgin.net**, **ntl:home**, **Telewest blueyonder** and more. We now also check for LLU broadband services from **UK Online** and **HomeChoice**.

You can save yourself endless hours checking and searching for the best offers available in your area.

DSL

A confusing number of Digital Subscriber Line (DSL) flavours (ASDL, IDSL, SDSL, and more) are available nowadays, ranging from reasonably priced to out of sight. DSL, when it works as advertised, is fast and reliable. A DSL line depends on the reliability of your telephone service: Crackling or unreliable phone lines can be a barrier to using it.

The main problem with a DSL connection is that your home or office needs to be within a certain distance from your local exchange. This distance is usually several thousand feet and shouldn't be a problem for most people, but it might be worth checking with your chosen ISP if you live in a more remote area. The service runs from about £10 a month, but it usually costs more, especially if you get DSL through a *booster* that boosts the signal to a location farther away than the minimum 18,000-foot border.

If you can get it, true DSL service can give you a connection as fast as 1.5MB per second download. (IDSL is only 144K.)

We had DSL for about a year and was initially blown away by the speed. Unfortunately, every time it rained our service went out. We had to call time after time to get a service call. Sadly, this is a well-known drawback of DSL. Your local telephone company (Telco in DSL-speak) owns your home or office phone lines. Because DSL goes over POTS (plain old telephone service), your DSL provider has to negotiate connection problems with the people at your telephone company. As you can guess, one company often blames the other for your problems.

A friend of ours tried to get around this issue by getting DSL from the local phone company, which sounded great to us. Unfortunately, this arrangement turned out to be not so great because local phone companies tend to form companies to handle high-speed connections. So even though the two companies are technically the same, the two still argue about who's responsible for your problems. Broadband with this much difficulty can be too much trouble.

Digital cable

Eureka, we think we've found the mother lode of connections: cable. If you can get cable television, you can probably get a blazingly fast cable Internet connection. Your cable company is probably replacing old cable lines with newfangled digital fibre optic lines. These new lines carry a crisp digital TV signal and an Internet connection as well. (These fancy new lines have plenty of room to carry even more stuff, and hot new services are being introduced all the time.)

Digital cable Internet connections are generally fast and reliable – you can download data at 1844 kilobauds per second. Compare that speed to the old-fashioned baud rate of dial-up (remember the old 300 baud modems?). And, the service is usually very reliable. Digital cable usually comes as a package with Internet, a phone line, and multi-channel digital TV, so prices vary and it's worth browsing for deals that suit your particular needs.

As far as the myth about more users on the line degrading the speed, a cable connection is more than capable of a 10Mbps transfer – that's already about 10 times faster than DSL. A lot of degrading would be necessary to noticeably slow down your connection. (Your computer still has to load the browser.)

Choosing your eBay.co.uk user ID

'What's in a name?' On eBay, there's a whole lot in your name! When you choose your eBay user ID, it becomes your name – your identity – to all those who transact with you online. These people don't know who you are; they know you only by the name they read in the seller's or bidder's spot.

Ever wonder why you don't see many banks named Joe and Fred's Savings and Investments? Even if Joe is the president and Fred is the chairman of the board, the casual attitude portrayed by their given names doesn't instil much confidence in the stability of the bank. Joe and Fred might be a better name for a plumbing supply company – or a great name for blokes who sell plumbing tools on eBay! Joe and Fred strike us as the kind of friendly, trustworthy fellas who might know something about plumbing.

Does your retail business have a name? If you don't have your own business (yet), have you always known what you'd call it if you did? Your opportunity to set up your business can start with a good, solid respectable sounding business name. If you don't like respectable (it's too staid for you), go for trendy. Who knew what a Napster was? Or a Kelkoo? Or a Bubblefast, which is a popular shipping supplier among eBay users in the US.

Are you selling flamingo-themed items? How about pink flamingos for your selling identity? Be creative; *you* know what name best describes your product.

Stay away from negative sounding names. If you really can't think up a good user ID, using your own name is fine.

eBay.co.uk protects and does not reveal your e-mail address. If another user wants to contact you, he or she can do so by clicking your user ID. The e-mail is sent to you through eBay's e-mail system.

Finding your eBay.co.uk feedback

The number that eBay lists next to your name is your feedback rating; see Figure 2-7 for a sample rating. Anyone on the Internet has only to click this number to know how you do business on eBay – and what other eBay users think of you. At the top of every user's feedback page is an excellent snapshot of all your eBay transactions for the past six months.

Figure 2-7:
Sample
eBay
feedback
rating.

If you're really serious about this business thing, and your feedback rating isn't as high as you'd like it to be, go online and buy some stuff. Even though eBay.co.uk now distinguishes between Buyer and Seller feedback, the numbers still grow. Feedback should always be posted for both buyers and sellers. Every positive feedback increases your rating by +1; a negative decreases it by –1. To get a high rating, rack up those positives.

Making Your Auctions Run More Smoothly

In this section, we discuss a few more niceties you need to round out your eBay.co.uk home base. The following tools are important, but you must decide which ones you'll use. Some people prefer a totally automated office while others like to do things the old-fashioned way. One of our favourite eBay PowerSellers works with file folders, a hand-written ledger book, and hand-written labels. If pen and paper make you happy, do it your way. We're going to suggest a few options that ease the pain of paperwork.

Software you can use

Software is now available to accomplish just about anything. An all-encompassing software package exists that can help you with your auction, right? Well, maybe. Whether you use it depends on how much you want your software to do and how much of your business you want to fully control. In this section, we describe some software examples that you may find useful.

Auction management

Auction management software can be a very good thing. This software can automate tasks and make your record keeping easy. You can keep track of inventory, launch auctions, and print labels using one program. Unfortunately, most of these programs can be daunting when you first look at them (and even when you take a second look).

You have choices to make regarding the software: How much are you willing to spend, and do you want to keep your inventory and information online? Maintaining your listing information online enables you to run your business from anywhere; you just log on and see your inventory. Online management software is tempting and professional, and may be worth your time and money.

A good many sellers prefer to keep their auction information on their own computers. This method is convenient and allows sellers to add a closer, more personal touch to their auctions and correspondence. Some people say that keeping information local, on their own computer, is more suited to the small-time seller, but we think it's a matter of preference.

HTML software

You may want to try some basic HTML software to practise your ad layouts. We tell you where to find some templates in Chapter 5, but you'll want to preview your auctions before you launch them.

You can use a full-blown Web page software package, such as FrontPage, to check out how your auction will look, or you may want to keep things simple. We use software called CuteHTML because it's about as simple as it gets.

Spreadsheets and bookkeeping

Many sellers keep their information in a simple spreadsheet program such as Excel. The program has all the functionality you need to handle inventory management and sales info.

For bookkeeping, we use QuickBooks. This program is straightforward, but only if you have a basic knowledge of accounting. QuickBooks also integrates with spreadsheets.

Collecting the cash

Credit cards are the way to go for the bulk of your auctions. Often, credit cards make the difference between a sale and no sale. People are getting savvy (and more comfortable) about using their credit cards online because they're becoming better informed about the security of online transactions and certain guarantees against fraud. So although you may truly love money orders, you need to take credit cards as well. In this section, we discuss another decision you need to make: Do you want your own private merchant account or would you rather run your credit card sales through an online payment service? For more about these options, read on.

Online payment services

Until you hit the big time, you may want to go with the services of an online payment service such as the eBay-owned PayPal. PayPal offers excellent services, and their rates are on a sliding scale, according to your monthly cash volume. Online payment services accept credit cards for you; they charge you a small fee and process the transaction with the credit card company. The auction payment is deposited in an account for you. Unless your sales go into tens of thousands of pounds a month, an online payment service can be more economical than your own merchant account.

Your own merchant account

As you may or may not know (depending on the amount of spam in your e-mail), thousands of merchant credit card brokers guarantee that they can set you up so that you can take credit cards yourself. These people are merely middlemen. You have to pay for the brokers' services and it is wise to keep in mind that some of these brokers are dependable businesses while others are nothing more than hustlers. If you have decent credit, you don't need these people: Go straight to your bank!

Your bank knows your financial standing and credit worthiness better than anybody. Your bank is, therefore, the best place to start to get your own *merchant account* – an account in which your business accepts credit cards directly from your buyers. You pay a small percentage to the bank, but it's considerably less than you pay to an online payment service. Some banks don't offer merchant accounts for Internet transactions because ultimately the bank is responsible for the merchandise related to the account if you fail to deliver the goods. Remember that your credit history and time with the bank play a part in whether or not you can get a merchant account.

The costs involved in opening a merchant account can vary, but you need at least £200 to get started.

Nine banks currently offer Internet merchant accounts. You need to set up an Internet merchant account even if you already have an account for face-to-face transactions. On top of the £200-ish sign-up fee, expect to pay additional day-to-day charges based on either a fixed fee or a percentage of your sales. For example, credit card payments often attract a commission fee, while fixed fees often apply to debit card transactions.

Home base: Your Web site

eBay.co.uk offers you a free page – the About Me page – that's the most important link to your business on eBay. The About Me page is part of your eBay.co.uk shop if you have one. You can insert a link on your About Me page that takes bidders to your auctions. You can link also to your own Web site from the About Me page!

If you don't have your own Web site, we recommend that you get one, especially if you're serious about running an eBay business.

You can keep your complete inventory of items on your Web site and list them as auctions or in your eBay.co.uk shop as their selling season comes around. No listing or final value fee is due when you have repeat customers on your Web site.

Setting up your shop

Office and storage space are a must if you plan to get big. Many a business was started at the kitchen table (that's how Pierre started eBay), but to be serious with a business, you must draw definite lines between your home life and your online ventures. Concentrating when you have a lot of noise in the background is difficult, so when we say draw a line, we mean a physical line as well as an environmental one.

Your dedicated office

You must first separate the family from the hub of your business. Many eBay sellers use a spare bedroom As time progresses and your business grows, you may have to move, maybe into your garage. Remember, you'll need electricity and phone lines, lighting and furniture. And don't forget storage space for your saleable items.

One PowerSeller that we know moved all the junk out of his cellar and set up shop there. He now has three computers and employs his wife and a part-time *lister* (who put his auctions up on eBay) to run the show. This guy's cellar office is networked and is as professional as any office.

Your eBay room

If you're able to set up an office, your storage space should be ensured for a while. For a real business, a cupboard just won't do. Seclude your stuff from your pets and family by moving it into another room and get shelving to organise your merchandise and admin properly. We talk more about organising your business in Chapter 6.

Chapter 3

Running a Business on eBay.co.uk

*H*ere's a quick quiz: Throughout the ups and downs of e-commerce in the 1990s and early 2000s, what marketplace has remained strong and continued to grow at a steady rate? As you probably know already, it's eBay – we say you probably know this piece of trivia because chances are you've already bought or sold some things yourself on the world's most popular auction site (or maybe this chapter's title gave you a hint).

There's a difference, though, between selling occasionally in order to make a few extra quid and doing what thousands have already done: selling on eBay.co.uk as a means of self-employment. eBay itself has estimated that as many as 450,000 individuals across the world run a business on the auction site full time. Countless others do it on a permanent part-time basis to earn a little sideline cash. Whatever the reason, you can't overlook eBay.co.uk as a way to get a first business off the ground. With eBay, you don't necessarily have to create a Web site, develop your own shopping trolley, or become a credit-card merchant: The auction site itself handles each of those essential tasks for you. But that doesn't mean that developing your own eBay business is easy. It takes hard work and a commitment, combined with the important business strategies described in this chapter. For a more in-depth assessment of starting and running a business on eBay.co.uk, check out Dan's book *Starting a Business on eBay.co.uk For Dummies* (by Wiley, 2006).

Running a business on eBay.co.uk doesn't necessarily mean that you depend on eBay as the sole source of your income. You may sell on eBay.co.uk part-time for some supplementary income each month. This chapter assumes that you want to sell regularly on eBay and build up a system for successful sales that can provide you with extra money, bill-paying money, or 'fun money'.

Understanding eBay.co.uk Auctions

In any contest, you have to know the ground rules. Anyone who has held a garage sale knows the ground rules for making a person-to-person sale. But eBay.co.uk strives to be different, and not just because auctions are the primary format – a rare way of selling in the UK, especially online. eBay.co.uk gives its members many different ways to sell, and each sales format has its own set of rules and procedures. It pays to know something about the different sales so that you can choose the right format for the item you have.

This section assumes that you have some basic knowledge of eBay.co.uk and that you have at least shopped for a few items and possibly won some auctions.

When it comes to putting items up for sale, eBay gets more complicated. You've got the following sales options:

- ✔ **Standard auctions:** This is the most basic eBay auction. You put an item up for sale, and you specify a starting bid (usually a low amount because you want to generate interest in your item). If you don't have a reserve price; the highest bidder at the end of the sale wins (if there is a highest bidder). Standard auctions and other auctions on eBay can last one, three, five, seven, or ten days. The ending time is precise: If you list something at 10:09 a.m. on a Sunday and you choose a seven-day format, the sale then ends at 10:09 a.m. the following Sunday.

- ✔ **Reserve auctions:** A *reserve price* is a price you specify as a minimum in order for a purchase to be successful. Any bids placed on the item being offered must be met or exceeded; otherwise, the sale will end without the seller being obligated to sell the item. You know if a reserve price is present by the message `Reserve Not Yet Met` next to the current high bid. When a bid is received that exceeds the reserve, this message changes to `Reserve Met`. The reserve price is concealed until the reserve is met.

- ✔ **Multiple-item auctions:** This type of sale, also known as a Dutch auction, is used by sellers who want to sell more than one identical item at the same time. The seller specifies a starting bid and the number of items available; bidders can bid on one or more items. But the question of who wins can be confusing. The bidders who win are the ones who have placed the lowest successful bid that is still above the minimum price, based on the number of items being offered. For example, suppose six items are offered, and ten bidders place bids. One bidder bids £20 for two items. Another bids £24 for one. Three others bid £18, two others bid £14, and three bid £10. The winners are the ones who bid £24, £20, and £18, respectively. The others lose out because only six items are available.

- ✔ **Fixed-price Buy It Now sales:** A Buy It Now price is a fixed price that the seller specifies. Fixed prices are used in all eBay.co.uk shops: The seller specifies that you can purchase the item for, say, £10.99; you click the Buy It Now button, agree to pay £10.99 plus shipping, and you instantly win the item.

- ✔ **Mixed auction/fixed price sales:** Buy It Now (BIN) prices can be offered in conjunction with standard or reserve auctions. In other words, even though bidders are placing bids on the item, if someone agrees to pay the fixed price, the item is immediately sold, and the sale ends. If a BIN price is offered in conjunction with a standard auction, the BIN price is available until the first bid is placed; then the BIN price disappears. If a BIN price is offered in conjunction with a reserve auction, the BIN price is available until the reserve price is met. After the BIN price disappears, the item is available to the highest bidder.

Book VI

Using eBay.co.uk

Those are the basic types of sales. You can also sell cars on eBay.co.uk Motors or even your home (check out `home-garden.listings.ebay.co.uk`). By knowing how eBay.co.uk sales work and following the rules competently, you'll gradually develop a good reputation on the auction site.

How you sell is important, but the question of exactly *what* you should sell is one you should resolve well before you start your eBay.co.uk business, just like in any business. Sell something you love, something you don't mind spending hours shopping for, photographing, describing, and eventually packing up and shipping. Sell something that has a niche market of enthusiastic collectors or other customers. More importantly, sell something that *isn't already there* or that there's clearly a lot of demand for. Do some research on eBay.co.uk to make sure that a thousand people aren't already peddling the same things you hope to make available.

Building a Good Reputation

In order to run a business on eBay.co.uk, you need to have a steady flow of repeat customers. Customer loyalty comes primarily from the trust that is produced by developing a good reputation. eBay.co.uk's feedback system is the best indicator of how trustworthy and responsive a seller is because past performance is a good indication of the kind of service a customer can expect in the future. Along with deciding what you want to sell and whether you want to sell on eBay.co.uk on a part- or full-time basis, you need to have the development of a good reputation as one of your primary goals.

Feedback, feedback, feedback!

eBay's success is due in large measure to the network of trust it has established among its millions of members. The feedback system, in which members leave positive, negative, or neutral comments for the people with whom they have conducted (or tried to conduct) transactions, is the foundation for that trust. The system rewards users who accumulate significant numbers of positive feedback comments and penalises those who have low or negative feedback numbers. By taking advantage of the feedback system, you can realise the highest possible profit on your online sales and help get your online business off the ground.

There probably aren't any scientific studies of how feedback numbers affect sales, but we've heard anecdotally from sellers that their sales figures increase when their feedback levels hit a certain number. The number varies, but it appears to be in the hundreds – perhaps 300 or so. The inference is that prospective buyers place more trust in sellers who have higher feedback numbers because they have more experience and are presumably more trustworthy. Those who have PowerSeller status, denoted by the PowerSeller icon, are even more trustworthy. (See the 'Striving for PowerSeller status' section, later in this chapter.)

Developing a schedule

One thing that can boost your reputation above all else on eBay.co.uk is timeliness. If you respond to e-mail enquiries within a few hours, or at most a day or two, and if you can ship out merchandise quickly, you're virtually guaranteed to have satisfied customers who leave you positive feedback. The way to achieve timely response is to observe a work schedule.

It's tedious and time consuming to take and retake photos, edit those photos, get sales descriptions online, and do the packing and shipping that's required at the end of a sale. The only way to come up with a sufficient number of sales every week is to come up with a system. And a big part of coming up with a system is developing a weekly schedule that spells out when you need to do all your eBaying. Table 3-1 displays a possible schedule.

Table 3-1	eBay Business Schedule	
Day of Week	*First Activity*	*Second Activity (optional)*
Sunday	Get seven-day sales online	Send end-of-sale notices
Monday	Packing	E-mails
Tuesday	Shipping	E-mails
Wednesday	Plan garage sales	Take photos
Thursday	Go to garage sales	Prepare descriptions
Friday	More sales	Prepare descriptions
Saturday	Respond to buyer enquiries	Get some sales online

You'll notice that something is conspicuously missing from this proposed schedule: a day of rest. You can certainly work in such a day on Sunday (or whatever day you prefer). If you sell on eBay.co.uk part time, you can probably take much of the weekend off. But most full-time sellers (and full-time self-employed people in general) will tell you that it's difficult to find a day off, especially when it's so important to respond to customer e-mails within a day or two of their receipt. You don't have to do everything all by yourself, however. You can hire full- or part-time help, which can free up time for family responsibilities.

Creating an About Me page

One of the best ways to build your reputation on eBay.co.uk is to create a Web page that eBay makes available to each of its members free of charge called About Me. Your About Me page should talk about who you are, why you collect or sell what you do, and why you're a reputable seller. You can also talk about an eBay shop, if you have one, and provide links to your current auction sales. It takes only a few minutes to create an About Me page (not much longer than filling out the Sell Your Item form to get a sale online, in fact). If you want to include a photo, you should take a digital image and edit it in an image-editing program, such as Paint Shop Pro or Photoshop, just as you would any other image. But a photo isn't absolutely necessary. Kimberly King, the eBay seller profiled later in this chapter, has a simple About Me page (see Figure 3-1).

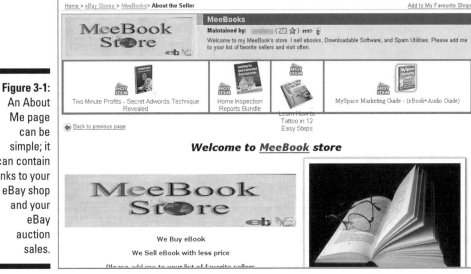

Figure 3-1:
An About
Me page
can be
simple; it
can contain
links to your
eBay shop
and your
eBay
auction
sales.

When you've decided what you want to say on your page, you need to save a digital photo if you want to include one. Then follow these steps:

1. **Click My eBay on the navigation bar at the top of virtually any eBay.co.uk page.**

   A login page appears.

2. **Type your User ID and password and click Sign In Securely.**

   The My eBay page appears.

3. **Click Personal Information under the My Account heading in the links on the left-hand side of the page.**

   The My eBay Account: Personal Information page appears.

4. **Scroll down to the About Me link and click Edit.**

   The About Me page appears.

5. **Look toward the bottom of the page and click Create Your Page.**

   The Choose Page Creation Option page appears.

6. **Leave the Use Our Easy Step-By-Step Process option selected and click Continue.**

   The About Me: Enter Page Content page appears.

7. **As indicated on the page, type a heading and text for your page. Label your photo and enter the URL for the photo in the Link to Your Picture text box. You can also type links to favourite pages and your own Web page if you have one. When you're done, click Continue.**

   The Preview and Submit page appears, as shown in Figure 3-2.

8. **Choose one of three possible layouts for your page and preview your page content in the bottom half of the page. When you're finished, click Submit.**

   Your page goes online.

Like any Web page, you can change your About Me page at any time by following the preceding steps.

 Another way to build a good reputation as a seller is to participate actively in eBay's discussion boards. Pay special attention to boards that pertain to the type of merchandise you buy and sell. Responding to questions from new users and offering advice based on your experience can boost your standing within the user community.

About Me: Preview and Submit

1. Choose Page Creation Option   2. Enter Page Content   ③ **Preview and Submit**

Select a page layout from the three shown here (Layout A is shown below).

⊙ Layout "A"   ○ Layout "B"   ○ Layout "C"

Once you've chosen a layout that you like, click the **Submit** button below.

Note: If you don't have JavaScript enabled on your computer, you'll still be able to choose any of these layouts. However, you won't be able to preview your selection below.

‹ Back   Submit ›

Preview - Here's what your page will look like.

| About Me: ███ (35 ☆) | LAYOUT A |

███ **Stuff**

This page will be used to advertise the stuff that I'm looking to sell.

Figure 3-2: Take a few minutes to proofread your About Me page before you post it online.

Preparing Sales Descriptions That Sell

How do you actually go about selling on eBay.co.uk? The aim is similar to other forms of e-commerce: You select merchandise, take photos, type descriptions, and put the descriptions online in a catalogue.

But there are some critical differences as well. You don't have to specify a fixed price on eBay.co.uk; you can set a starting bid and see how much the market will bear. All sales descriptions are not created equal, however. Many sellers would argue that clear, sharp photos are the most important part of a description and that, if you show the item in its best light, it will practically sell itself. We're of the opinion that a good heading and descriptions that include critical keywords are just as important as good photos. The art of creating descriptions is best discovered by inspecting other people's sales listings; the essentials are described in the following sections.

Details, details

The primary way of getting your sales online is eBay.co.uk's Sell Your Item form. You can access this form at any time by clicking Sell on the eBay navigation bar, which appears at the top of just about any page on the eBay.co.uk Web site. The Sell Your Item form is easy to use, so we don't take you through every little option. In this section, however, we do point out a few features you may overlook and that can help you get more attention for your sales.

The Sell Your Item form is by no means the only way to get eBay sales online. Many full- or part-time businesspeople use special software that allows them to upload multiple images at once or schedule multiple sales so they all start and end at the same time. The auction services Andale (uk.andale.com) and MarketWorks (www.marketworks-uk.co.uk/ebay-auction-software.asp) offer eBay.co.uk auction listing tools. In addition, eBay offers two programs you may find helpful:

- ✔ **Turbo Lister** (pages.ebay.co.uk/turbo_lister/index.html), which is free, provides sellers with design templates that they can use to add graphic interest to their sales descriptions.

- ✔ **Selling Manager** (pages.ebay.co.uk/selling_manager/index.html), a monthly subscription service, is sales and management software. It provides you with convenient lists that let you track what you have up for sale, which sales have ended, which items have been purchased, and what tasks you have yet to do – for example, sending e-mails to winning bidders or relisting items that didn't sell the first time.

Choosing a second category

One of the first things you do in the Sell Your Item form is to choose a sales category in which to list your item. We recommend using the search box at the top of the All Categories page. Enter a keyword and click Search. You're presented with some auctions and a detailed list of sales categories on the left hand side of the page. The best thing about the list is that it is ranked in order of the ones that are most likely to sell items matching your desired keywords. The categories near the top of the list are the ones to choose.

We also recommend paying an extra few pence or so (when you choose a second category, your listing fee is doubled) and listing the item in a second category – especially if the second category has a ranking that's almost as high as the first.

Book VI

Using eBay.co.uk

Focusing on your auction heading

The heading of an eBay sales description is the set of six or seven words that appears in a set of search results or in a set of listings in a category. In other words, it's the set of words that a potential customer initially sees when he or she is deciding whether to investigate a sale and possibly bid on it. Keep your heading short and specific. Include dates, colours, or model numbers if applicable. Try to pick one word that may attract a buyer, such as Rare, Hard-to-Find, Mint, New, or something similar.

Choosing a good ending time for your sale

With eBay sales, it's not the starting time that counts but the ending time that makes a difference. The more attention you can get at the end of a sale, the more likely you are to make a profit. Most sales get attention on weekends, when the majority of shoppers aren't working. The optimal time, in fact, is to have the sale end some time on a Saturday or Sunday afternoon.

Of course, bidders can come from all over the world, and what's early afternoon on a Sunday morning in London is the middle of the night in Australia. But don't worry too much about such distinctions: Pick an ending time that's convenient for eBay.co.uk shoppers in your own country to be present – not in the middle of a workday, but on the weekend.

To keep delivery costs down, you can specify that you'll only accept bids from people within the UK. Don't worry about getting your item seen by everybody in the world; this country alone has more than enough people!

Adding keywords

When you prepare an auction description, you don't have to make it overly lengthy. It's not the length that counts; it's the number of keywords you include. A *keyword* is a word or phrase that describes the item you have for sale and that prospective buyers are likely to enter in their eBay searches. If your description contains a keyword that someone enters, your sale will show up in search results. And just showing up in the search results is half the battle: If a buyer can find your item, he or she can then follow through with its purchase.

The more keywords you can add to your description, the more frequently that sale will be found by searchers. It's to your advantage, then, to think of all the terms that someone would use when looking for your item and add as many of those keywords to the heading and to the body of the description as you can. If you're selling an electric drill, for example, use keywords such as *cordless, electric, drill, Black & Decker,* or anything else a likely buyer may enter.

Upgrading your listings

Near the end of the Sell Your Item form, you get the option to specify whether you want to upgrade your listings. *Upgrade,* in this case, means adding graphic highlights that are intended to help your listing stand out from those around it, either in search results or on category pages. You can choose from the options shown in Table 3-2.

Table 3-2	Listing Upgrades	
Upgrade	*Description*	*Cost*
Highlight	A coloured strip is drawn across the auction title.	£2.50
Bold	The auction title is formatted in bold type.	75p
Gallery	A thumbnail image appears next to auction title.	15p
Gallery Featured Plus!	A Gallery image appears in a 'Featured Items' area at the top of Gallery pages.	£9.95
Home Page Featured	Your auction title is listed randomly along with other sales on eBay's home page.	£49.95

Of these, the single most cost-effective upgrade, in our opinion, is the Gallery thumbnail image, which costs only 15p and draws more attention to your sales listing – especially when you consider that most other listings around yours also have Gallery images. The Home Page may be expensive, but it gives you a chance of having your sale on eBay's home page and guarantees exposure for your sale on featured areas. Reserve this upgrade for big money sales, like a car or expensive furniture.

In eBay's early days, if you wanted a sale to end at a particular time (say, 7 p.m. on a Sunday, when lots of bidders are online), you had to physically be present to create the description at a certain time. For example, if you wanted such a sale to last seven days, you had to list it at precisely 7 p.m. the preceding Sunday. Now, you don't have to be physically present exactly a week, five days, three days, or one day before you want your sale to end: You can specify an ending time when you fill out the Sell Your Item form.

Although it's free to register for an account on eBay.co.uk and free to fill out the Sell Your Item form, eBay charges you an Insertion Fee when you actually put an item up for sale. The Insertion Fee is based on the starting price of the auction. The fee is only 15p for a starting bid of 99p or less, which explains why many starting bids are less than £1. A Final Value Fee is also charged at the end of the auction, and it depends on the sale price. On a sale of £25, the Final Value Fee is 5.25 per cent of the final amount; at £700 it's 5.25 per cent of the initial £29.99, plus 3.25 per cent of the £30–£599, plus 1.75 per cent of remaining value. Complicated? Certainly! Luckily, eBay calculates it all for you. For a detailed explanation of the formula used to calculate fees, see `pages.ebay.co.uk/help/sell/fees.html`.

Book VI

Using eBay.co.uk

Include clear images

No matter how well written your auction's headings and description, all your work can quickly be undone by digital images that are dark, blurry, or slow to load because they're too large in either physical or file size. The same principles that you use when capturing digital images for your e-commerce Web site apply to images on eBay.co.uk:

- ✔ Make sure that you have clear, even lighting (consider taking your photos outdoors).
- ✔ Use your camera's auto-focus setting.
- ✔ Crop your images so that they focus on the merchandise being sold.
- ✔ Keep the file size small by adjusting the resolution with your digital camera or your image editing software.

Some aspects to posting images along with auction descriptions are unique to eBay:

- ✔ **Image hosting:** If you run a business on eBay.co.uk and have dozens, or even hundreds, of sales items online at any one time, you can potentially have hundreds of image files to upload and store on a server. If you use eBay Picture Services as your photo host, the first image for each sale is free. Each subsequent image costs 12p. It's worth your while to find an economical photo hosting service, such as FileHigh (`www.filehigh.com`) or Auctionpix (`www.auctionpix.co.uk`).

✔ **Close-ups:** If what you're selling has important details such as brand names, dates, and maker's marks, you need to have a camera that has *macro capability* – that is, the ability to get clear close-ups. Virtually all digital cameras have a macro setting, but it can be tricky to hold the camera still enough to get a clear image (you may need to mount the camera on a tripod). If you use a conventional film (not recommended) camera, you'll need to invest in a macro lens.

✔ **Multiple images:** You'll never hear an eBay shopper complaining that you included too many images with your auction listings. As long as you have the time and patience and an affordable image host, you can include five, six, or more views of your item (for big, complex objects such as cars and motorbikes, multiple images are especially important).

Be sure to crop and adjust the brightness and contrast of your images after you take them, using a program such as Paint Shop Pro by Jasc (`www.jasc.com`) or Adobe Photoshop Elements by Adobe Systems (`www.adobe.com`).

If you want to find out more about creating sales descriptions (and practically every aspect of buying or selling on eBay.co.uk, for that matter), take a look at Dan's book, *Starting a Business on eBay.co.uk For Dummies* (Wiley).

Be flexible with payment options

It may seem like payments are the most nerve-wracking part of a transaction on eBay.co.uk. They have been, in the past, but as time goes on, eBay provides more safeguards for its customers. That doesn't mean you won't run into the occasional bidder who doesn't respond after winning your auction, or whose cheque bounces. But as a seller, you have plenty of protections: If someone doesn't respond, you can relist your item; if someone's cheque bounces, you don't lose out on your sales item because you held on to it during the process of the cheque clearing process.

As an eBay.co.uk seller, you should accept the basic forms of payment. A PayPal account covers most of your customers, but some will want to pay by cheque, card, or a standard bank transfer. You can enable your customers to pay with a credit card, either by using your merchant credit-card account if you have one, or by using one of a handful of popular electronic payment services, which include eBay's own PayPal (`www.paypal.com`), Protx (`www.protx.com`), or WorldPay (`www.worldpay.com`). In the case of PayPal, you're charged a nominal fee (1.4 to 3.4 per cent of the amount plus a 20p fee) when a buyer transfers money electronically to your account.

You should generally not accept other forms of payment from buyers. Occasionally, a buyer insists on sending you cash in an envelope; you should insist, in turn, that the buyer sends a money order instead.

Providing Good Customer Service

When you make the decision to sell on eBay.co.uk on a regular basis, you need to develop a good reputation. Earlier in this chapter, we outline ways that you can do that. But one of the best ways to achieve this goal – providing a high level of customer service to your buyers – is an issue that warrants a separate discussion. The single best way to do *that* is to be responsive to e-mail enquiries of all sorts. Good customer service means checking your e-mail a few times a day and spending lots of time responding to your customers' questions. If you take days to get back to someone who asks you about the colour or the condition of an item you have for sale, it may just be too late for that person to bid. And slow response to a high bidder or buyer after the sale can make the buyer nervous and result in 'neutral' feedback – not a complaint about fraud or dishonesty, but a note about below-par service. Such feedback is considered as bad as a negative comment on eBay.co.uk.

Book VI

Using eBay.co.uk

Setting terms of sale

One aspect of good customer service is getting back to people quickly and communicating clearly and with courtesy. When you receive enquiries, you should always thank prospective customers for approaching you and considering the sale; even if they don't end up placing bids, you'll have spread goodwill, which hopefully you'll get back.

Another way to be good to your customers is to be clear about how you plan to ship your merchandise and how much it will cost. When you fill out the Sell Your Item form (which we discuss in the earlier section, 'Details, details'), you can specify either an *actual shipping cost* (a cost based on weight and the buyer's residence) or a *flat shipping fee* (a shipping fee you charge for all your items).

The moment you specify a shipping charge in the Sell Your Item form, you set eBay's automated Checkout system in motion. The Checkout system enables buyers to calculate their own shipping charges. The advantage to you, as the seller, is that you don't need to send your buyers a message stating how much they need to pay you.

Packing and shipping safely

One of the aspects of selling on eBay that is often overlooked (not by *buyers*) is the practice of packing and shipping. After sending payment for something, buyers often wait on tenterhooks, expecting to receive their items while dreading the prospect of an unresponsive seller who neglects to ship what has been purchased.

Besides the danger of fraud, there's the danger that the item you send will be damaged in transit. Be sure to use sturdy boxes when you ship and to adequately cushion your merchandise within those boxes. We've received boxes from sellers who stuffed the insides with bubble wrap and newspaper, and we were happy for the trouble. If you're shipping something particularly fragile, consider double-boxing it: Put it in a box, place the box in a larger one, and put cushioning material between the two. Your customers will be pleased to receive the merchandise undamaged, and you'll get good feedback as a result.

Place a thank-you note, business card, or even a small gift inside the box with your shipment. It will remind buyers that you're a trustworthy seller and let them know how to get in touch with you in the future.

Moving from Auctioneer to eBay.co.uk Businessperson

Few eBay.co.uk sellers start out proclaiming, 'I'm going to be a PowerSeller, and I'm going to sell full-time on eBay for a living!' Rather, they typically start out on a whim. They find an object lying around in a box, in the loft, or on a shelf, and they wonder: Will anyone pay money for this? Other sellers are existing businesses who join eBay.co.uk to earn some extra cash, many of whom soon realise it's not just a supplement but an essential component of their business.

For example, take Nick Talley, who runs the phenomenally popular eBay.co.uk shop iPosters. He gave up his courier business after 16 years because of rising bills and set up a Web site called `www.pop-culture.biz`.

Like many people he thought eBay.co.uk would provide a useful second source of income, but 25,000 sales later, Nick is pulling in some very useful profits. Nick says, 'Good old-fashioned customer service, as well as in-demand products and a well-designed site, are the most essential components of any online business. But on eBay.co.uk, which brings together so many sellers in one place, this matters more than ever.'

Opening an eBay.co.uk shop

An *eBay.co.uk Shop* is a Web site within eBay's own voluminous Web empire. It's a place where sellers can post items for sale at fixed prices. The great advantage of having a shop is that it enables a seller to keep merchandise available for purchase for 30, 60, 90, or even an unlimited number of days at a time. It gives customers another way to buy from you, and it can significantly increase your sales, too. eBay itself, at a recent eBay Live event, made the claim that eBay shops brought about a 25 per cent increase in overall sales.

eBay.co.uk's own Education section is well worth a look. It describes how you can set up your shop, make it look good, sell effectively, and get it picked up by major search engines.

For more on getting your shop noticed, check out the following link: `pages.ebay.co.uk/education/SEO/SEO-eBay-Store/index.html`.

Striving for PowerSeller status

PowerSellers are eBay.co.uk's elite. Those members who have the coveted icon next to their names feel justifiably proud of their accomplishments. They have met the stringent requirements for PowerSellers, which emphasise consistent sales, a high and regular number of completed sales, and excellent customer service. Moving from occasional seller to PowerSeller is a substantial change. Requirements include:

- ✔ At least 100 unique feedback results – 98 per cent of which are positive

- ✔ A minimum of £750 of average gross monthly sales for three consecutive months

- ✔ A good standing record – achieved by complying with eBay Listing Policies

- ✔ A current account – achieved by contacting bidders within three business days and upholding the eBay Community Values

In return for the hard work required to meet these standards, PowerSellers do get a number of benefits in addition to the icon. These include priority e-mail support, free banner ads, a special discussion board just for PowerSellers, and invitations to eBay events. They also have the opportunity to become featured PowerSellers in the introductory section for eBayers who want to upgrade.

The PowerSeller programme isn't just something you apply for. eBay.co.uk reviews your sales statistics and invites you to join the programme when you have met the requirements. You can find out more about the requirements and benefits of the PowerSeller programme at `pages.ebay.co.uk/services/buyandsell/powerseller/benefits.html`.

Finding lots of merchandise to sell

Moving up to PowerSeller status means an ongoing commitment to conducting a large number of sales, responding quickly to customers, and shipping efficiently. It also means finding a steady and reliable stream of merchandise to sell. When you need to get 50 or more items up for sale each week, car boot sales quickly become impractical for all but the most dedicated. Many PowerSellers manage to find sufficient stock by heading to antiques fairs, garage sales, and car bootathons in teams, showing up in the pre-dawn hours and waiting in line, and then buying as many things as they can grab. Others find a wholesale supplier who can provide them with low-cost items, such as figurines, coffee, or holiday decorations, in bulk.

Finding a wholesale supplier

All the PowerSellers we've spoken to in recent years have assured us that it's not easy to find a reputable, reliable wholesaler. They urge other sellers to do their homework by getting references and talking to satisfied customers. Many wholesalers are primarily interested in taking sellers' money and not providing good service, they say. Often, finding wholesalers is a matter of word of mouth: You ask someone who knows someone, and so on. Kimberly King (the seller we profile in the 'PowerSeller keeps sales going with a little help from her friends' sidebar) used connections left over from her former management position at an herbal tea company to find a supplier.

'You're not going to find someone on eBay who is going to tell you their whole-saler,' she cautions. 'They're too valuable. My advice is to make sure to call and check out references; do everything you can to find out everything about a company. Some force you to make an initial order of maybe £500 minimum up front, knowing when you see the product you'll never order it again.'

Chapter 4

Opening a Shop, Virtually

· ·

In This Chapter

▶ Figuring out the lure of the online shop

▶ Choosing a name

▶ Setting up and managing your eBay.co.uk shop

▶ Selling your stuff

▶ Closing your sales

· ·

*I*f you're doing well selling your items on eBay.co.uk auctions, why open a shop? Have you used the eBay Buy It Now feature in one of your listings? Did this enticement work? In an eBay shop, all items are set at a fixed price and online until cancelled (or listed at least 30 days), so the shop is rather like a giant collection of Buy It Now featured items. Get the idea?

When you're opening a shop, you have just three main rules to remember and apply: Location, location, location. If you were opening a bricks-and-mortar shop, you could open it on the high street, in a shopping centre, or even somewhere out of town. You'd decide in what location your shop would do best; that goes for an online shop as well. Loads of locations exist for an online shop, including online shopping centres (when you can find them) and sites such as Amazon, Yahoo!, and, of course, eBay.

You have to pay rent for your online shop, but opening and running an online shop isn't nearly as expensive as a shop in the real world (where you also have to pay electrical bills, maintenance bills, and more). Plus, the ratio of rent to sales makes an online shop a much easier financial decision, and your exposure can be huge.

In this chapter, we show you step-by-step how to get business booming by opening your own eBay shop.

Online Shops Galore

Amazon, Yahoo!, and eBay make up the big three of online shops – they're the top locations and get the most visitors. According to US-based Web site tracker comScore Media Metrix, in April 2004 these sites garnered an astounding number of *unique* visitors (that counts *all* of one person's visits to the sites just *once* a month):

- Yahoo!: 113,190,000 (it's a search engine; we must hit it ten times a day – but we rarely visit the auctions)
- eBay: 60,016,000
- Amazon: 39,083,000 (it sells books, CDs, DVDs, and lots of other merchandise)

No doubt feeling competition from Yahoo! and Amazon, eBay decided to open its doors to sellers who wanted to open their own shops. The fixed price shops were a normal progression for eBay in its quest to continue as the world's marketplace. And eBay Shops make sense: They're a benefit to all current eBay sellers and open doors to new shoppers who don't want to deal with auctions.

eBay.co.uk is an online shop that specialises in selling *your* stuff, not *theirs*. This shop doesn't stock merchandise, and it isn't in competition with you. In addition to its staggering number of visitors, eBay offers you the most reasonable shop rent. To see what we mean, check out the sample rents in Table 4-1.

Table 4-1	Online Starter Shop Monthly Costs	
	eBay	*Amazon Marketplace (Pro-Merchant)*
Basic rent	From £6 per month	£28.75 per month
Listing fee	£0.05	none
High final value fee	From 5.25% of item value	17.25% of value (8.05% for electrical items)

For more information on current rankings, go to the Hitwise Web site at `www.hitwise.co.uk` and search for *eBay*. This site keeps a monthly scorecard of unique visitors to the UK's top Internet sites. Have a look at the comScore site now and then to see where the online industry is going.

We don't think you need a rocket scientist to convince you that having a space in eBay Shops (see Figure 4-1) is a better bargain than setting up shop anywhere else. We know the shops aren't based on auctions, but Buy It Now items are as easy to handle as auctions. To review prices and rules before opening your shop, go to

`pages.ebay.co.uk/help/sell/storefees.html`

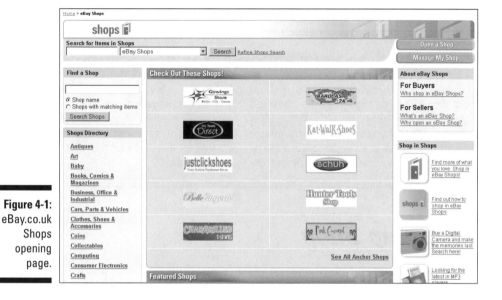

Book VI

Using eBay.co.uk

Figure 4-1: eBay.co.uk Shops opening page.

Choosing Your eBay.co.uk Shop Name

You are taking the plunge and opening an eBay.co.uk shop. Do you have an eBay user ID? Have you thought of a good name for your shop? Your shop name doesn't have to match your eBay user ID, but they're more recognisable if they relate to each other. You can use your company name, your business name, or a name that describes your business. We recommend that you use the same name for your eBay shop that you plan to use in all your online businesses. By doing so, you begin to create an identity (or as the pros call it, a *brand*) that customers will come to recognise and trust.

Your online eBay shop shouldn't replace your Web site; it should be an extension of it. When people buy stuff at your eBay shop, take the opportunity to also make them customers of your Web site through your shop's About the Seller page (which is also your About Me page on eBay). Bargain!

Minding your underscores and hyphens

If you want to use your eBay.co.uk user ID for your shop name, you can – unless it contains a hyphen (-) or an underscore (_). While eBay recommends that you break up words in your user ID with a dash or an underscore, that's no good for an eBay shop name. Without the underscore, your user ID may translate into a user ID that someone else has already taken, which means you can't use it. Also, your user ID may not be an appropriate name for a shop. If so, find a name instead that suits your merchandise to a T.

Setting up Shop

To get down to business, go to the eBay Shops hub and click the <u>Open a Shop</u> link in the upper –right-hand corner of the screen (refer to Figure 4-1). Doing so takes you to the Seller's starting point of eBay Shops, as shown in Figure 4-2.

Before you click that link to open your shop, ask yourself two questions:

- ✔ **Can I make a serious commitment to my eBay shop?** A shop is a commitment and it won't work for you unless you work for it. You need the merchandise to fill your shop and the discipline to continue listing shop and auction items. Your shop is a daily, monthly, and yearly obligation. When you go on holiday, you need someone else to ship your items or your customers may go elsewhere. You can close your shop for a holiday, but eBay.co.uk reserves your shop name for only 30 days. After that time, you have to come up with a new name (and your competition may have taken over your famous shop name).

- ✔ **Will I work for my eBay shop even when I don't feel like it?** You need to be prepared for the times when you're ill or just don't feel like shipping, but orders are waiting to be shipped. You have to do the work anyway; it's all part of the commitment.

eBay.co.uk gives you the venue, but making your mercantile efforts a success is in your hands. If you can handle these two responsibilities, read on!

If you're serious and ready to move on, click the <u>Open Your eBay Shop</u> link on the left-hand side of the page (refer to Figure 4-2). Because you're always signed in on your home computer, you're escorted to a page reminding you that eBay shops fall under the same User Agreement that you agreed to when you began selling on eBay. Click the Continue button to access the Open Your Shop pages (see Figure 4-3).

Figure 4-2:
The Open
Your eBay
Shop
welcome
page.

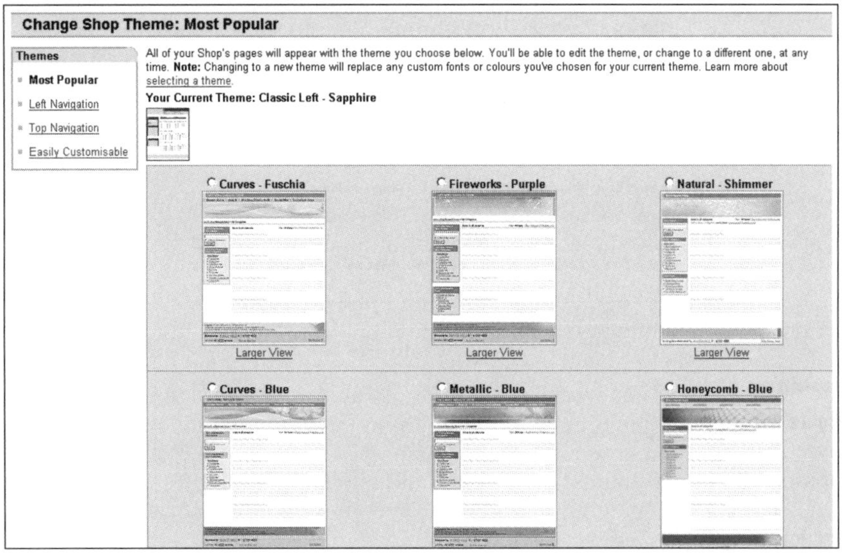

Figure 4-3:
Select your
shop theme.

You need to make a few decisions to create a good shop. So before building your shop, read the following sections.

1. Choose a colour theme.

EBay.co.uk provides some elegant colour and graphics themes. You can change the colour scheme or layout later, so until you have time to go berserk and design a custom masterpiece, choose one of the 14 clearly organised layouts, either pre-designed or with easily customisable themes. Don't select something overly bright and vibrant – a colour scheme that's easy on the eyes is more conducive to a comfortable selling environment.

You have the option of selecting a shop theme that doesn't require you to insert a custom logo or banner but we highly recommend against it. You need to establish a unifying brand for your online business.

2. Click Continue.

3. Type your new shop's name (see Figure 4-4).

Your eBay shop name can't exceed 35 characters. Before you type your chosen name, double-check that you aren't infringing on anyone's copyrights or trademarks. You also can't use any permutation of eBay trademarks in your shop's name.

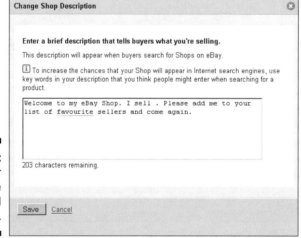

Figure 4-4: Type your shop's name and description.

Within the figure:

Change Shop Description

Enter a brief description that tells buyers what you're selling.

This description will appear when buyers search for Shops on eBay.

To increase the chances that your Shop will appear in Internet search engines, use key words in your description that you think people might enter when searching for a product.

Welcome to my eBay Shop. I sell . Please add me to your list of favourite sellers and come again.

203 characters remaining.

Save   Cancel

4. **Type a short description of your shop.**

   When we say short, we mean *short*. The paragraph you're reading now is 270 characters, and you have only *300* characters to give a whiz-bang, electric description of your shop and merchandise. You can't use HTML coding to jazz up the description, and you can't use links. Just write the facts please, plus a little bit of dazzle.

   This description is hugely important. When people search eBay.co.uk shops and descriptions, the keyword information you put here is referenced. Also, if the shop header contains your description (as in the Classic style themes), search engines such as Google and Yahoo! look in this description for the keywords to classify and list your shop.

 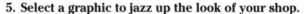

   Write your copy ahead of time in Word. Then, still in Word, highlight the text and choose Tools⇨Word Count. Word gives you the word count of the highlighted text. Check the character count with spaces, to be sure your text fits.

5. **Select a graphic to jazz up the look of your shop.**

   You can use one of eBay's clip-art style banners or create a custom 310 x 90 pixel size one. If you use one of eBay's graphics, you must promise (hand on heart) that you won't keep it there for long. (See the text after this set of steps for info on designing your own graphics – or hiring someone to do it for you.)

6. **Click Continue.**

   At this point, your eBay shop looks something like what you see in Figure 4-5. You are about to open an eBay shopfront (drum roll, please).

7. **Sign up for the basic shop (£6.00 a month), and click the Start My Subscription Now button.**

   Your shop is now LIVE on the Internet with nothing up for sale – yet.

8. **Click the supplied link to customise your shop further.**

You decide in which category your shop is listed on the eBay Shops home page. eBay.co.uk checks the items as you list them in the standard eBay category format. For example, if you have six books listed in the Books: Fiction and Non-fiction category and five items in the Cameras & Photo category, you'll be in the listings for both of those categories. Your custom shop categories (read on) will be used to classify items only in your shop.

Book VI

Using eBay.co.uk

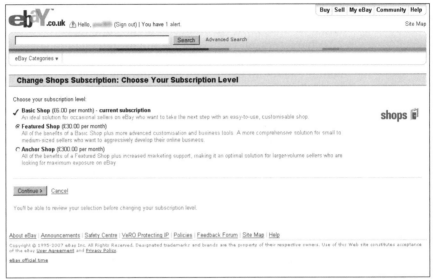

Figure 4-5:
Verify your
choices and
become a
shop owner.

If you use one of eBay's prefab graphics, people buying things at your eBay shop will know that you aren't serious enough about your business to design a simple and basic logo. We've had many years of experience in advertising and marketing, and we must tell you that a custom look beats clip art any day. Your shop is special – put forth the effort to make it shine.

If you have a graphics program, design a graphic with your shop's name. Start with something simple; you can always change your design later when you have more time. Save the image as a GIF or a JPG, and upload it to the site where you host your images (your own Web site, your ISP, or a hosting service).

Many talented graphic artists make their living selling custom Web graphics on eBay.co.uk. If you aren't comfortable designing, search eBay for *web banner* or *banner design*. Graphic banners on eBay sell for about £10 to £20 – certainly worth the price in the time you'll save.

Improving Your Offering

You can customise your shop at any time by clicking links in the Shop Design area of the Manage My Shop box, which is at the bottom of your shop's page and in the upper right-hand corner of the eBay Shop's hub page. The page shown in Figure 4-6 appears, with headings describing important tasks for your shop.

Shop design and marketing

In the Shop Design and Marketing list, you can perform the major tasks required for your store:

✔ **Display Settings:** You can go to Display Settings (the shop set-up area) to change the name of your shop or the theme of your pages. You can also change the way your items are displayed: gallery view (as in Figure 4-7) or list view (as in Figure 4-8). Neither view is inherently better, but we like the gallery view because it shows the thumbnails of your items.

Book VI

Using eBay.co.uk

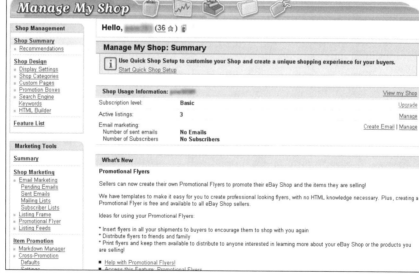

Figure 4-6: You can perform all the necessary tasks for running a shop here.

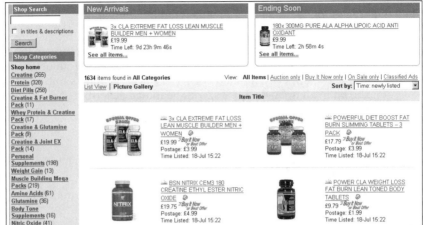

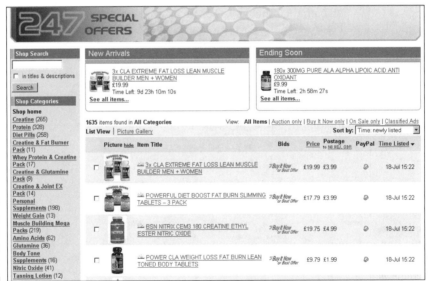

You can also select the order in which your items will sort, for example Highest priced first, Lowest priced first, Items ending first, or Newly listed first. Choosing Ending first as your sort is a good idea, so that buyers can get the chance to swoop in on items closing soon.

✔ **Custom pages:** Most successful eBay sellers have a shop policies page – Figure 4-9 shows you an example. When you set up a policies page, eBay.co.uk supplies you with a choice of layouts. Go to Custom Pages and click the <u>Create New Page</u> link to see the template that you want to use, as shown in Figure 4-10. Don't freak out if you don't know HTML, eBay helps you out with an easy-to-use HTML generator.

Following are some important policies to include:

- Indicate to what locations you ship.

- State your customer service and return policy. Fill in the information regarding how you handle refunds, exchanges, and so on. Also include whatever additional shop information you think is pertinent.

Book VI

Using eBay.co.uk

Figure 4-9: Example eBay.co.uk shop policies page.

Shop Search	Specialisation		Unique, chic and sexy items listed daily. All items are brand new.
☐ in titles & descriptions	**Terms and Conditions** Payment and postage terms may vary on individual items.	Payment methods	Pay Pal VISA 🔲🔲🔲🔲 Banker's Draft/Postal Order, Personal Cheque WE DO NOT CHARGE EXTRA FOR PAYPAL.
Search			We are happy to combine postage on multiple wins within 7 days, all payments must be received within 7 days. Combined postage is calculated using the highest priced postage first. Please make cheques payable to Blue Banana (on-line) Limited.
Shop Categories			
Shop home Tops up to 8 (94) Tops size 10 (291) Tops size 12 (254) Tops size 14 (114) Tops size 16 (31) Tops size 18 + (53) Dress up to 8 (36) Dress size 10 (179) Dress size 12 (144) Dress size 14 (118) Dress size 16 (67) Dress size 18 + (20) Skirt/Trouser/Jeans upto 8 (24) Skirt/Trouser/Jeans size 10 (23) Skirt/Trouser/Jeans size 12 (20) Skirt/Trouser/Jeans 14+ (13) Jackets/Coats (38) Footwear (54) Accessories (2)		Shop ship-to locations	WORLDWIDE:- UK: All items are sent Recorded Delivery (provides insurance to the value of £34). If you do not require this, please deduct 50p from P&P. Alternatively, if you require insurance greater than £34 then please take the Special Delivery option. Overseas: PayPal only. All items are sent via Airsure (provides insurance). If you do not require this, please deduct £4.00 from P&P. Please be aware that that you may be charged an import tax on goods purchased outside of your country.
		Postage & packaging	Buyer Pays Shipping.
		Customer service & return policy	We are happy to refund (excluding postage) if an item is unsuitable when notified within 7 days of receipt of the item. The returning item must be dispatched within 3 days of informing us that a refund is required. The garment must be unworn and all tags intact and it is important that your eBay user ID is enclosed with the item. Any queries, then please contact us!100% satisfaction guaranteed!!
Shop Pages » Shop Policies	**Additional Shop Information**		If you have any questions or need further information then please contact us....We are always happy to help!

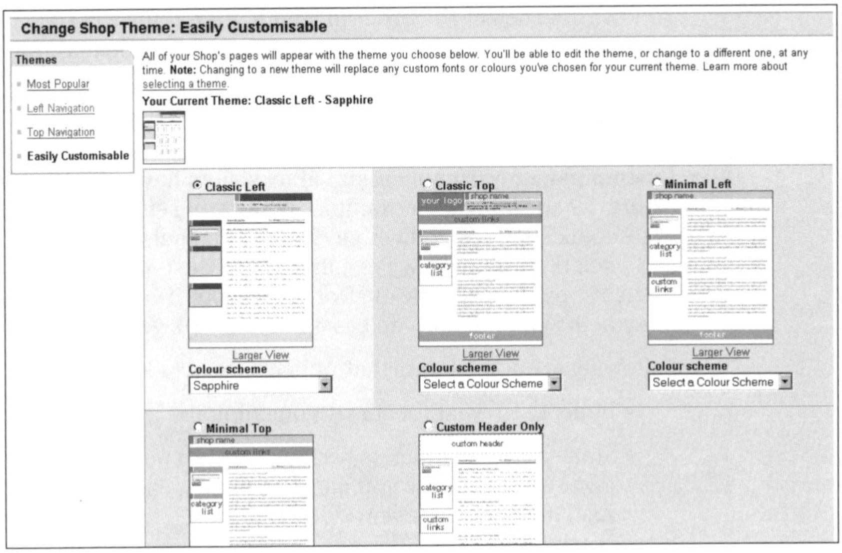

Figure 4-10:
eBay Shop
page
customising
templates.

You can also set up a custom home page for your shop, but doing so is not a popular option. Letting your visitors go straight to the page listing what you're selling is a better idea, don't you think?

✔ **Custom categories:** You really make your shop your own here. You may name up to 19 custom categories that relate to the items you sell for your shop.

✔ **Custom listing header:** The custom listing header display is one of the best tools you can use to bring people into your shop – so use it! Click the link and select the option to show your custom listing header on all your eBay auctions and fixed-price sales. Doing so encourages shoppers to visit your eBay shop when they browse your eBay listings.

When customising, include your shop logo as well as a shop search box. In Figure 4-11, you can see how the shop header looks at the top of an eBay listing.

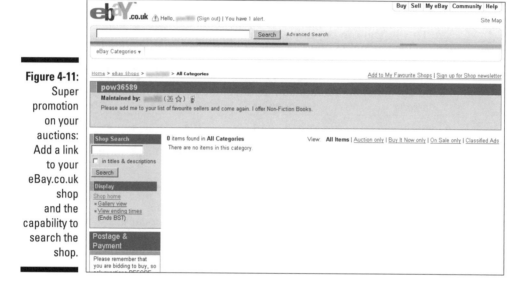

Book VI

Using eBay.co.uk

Figure 4-11:
Super
promotion
on your
auctions:
Add a link
to your
eBay.co.uk
shop
and the
capability to
search the
shop.

Managing your items

We assume you've listed items on eBay.co.uk, so we won't bore you
with a tutorial on how to list your items here. Following are the main
differences between listing an item in your shop and listing an auction
on eBay.co.uk:

- ✔ You have to assign your item to one of the prescribed shop categories
  that you designated while setting up your shop. If your new item falls
  into a category that you haven't defined, you can always go back to
  your shop and add a category (as many as 19) or put it in the eBay-
  generated Other Items category.

- ✔ You don't place a minimum bid or a reserve price on your shop
  items because everything you list in your eBay shop is a Buy It
  Now item.

✔ Listings in an eBay shop can be put up for sale for 30 or 90 days, or GTC (Good 'Til Cancelled). The listing fees are shown in Table 4-2. Finally, you can buy something for 5p!

Table 4-2	Shop Inventory Insertion (Listing) Fees		
Duration	*Insertion Fee*	*Surcharge*	*Total*
30 days	£0.05	N/A	£0.05
90 days	£0.05	£0.10	£0.15
Good 'Til Cancelled	£0.05 / 30 days	N/A	£0.05 / 30 days

The items you list in your eBay.co.uk shop *will not* appear in the regular eBay site title search. Your items *will* be seen if one of your buyers does a Seller or Shops search from the eBay.co.uk search page, which is why you pay only 5p per listing for 30 days. You *must* put a link in your auctions to your eBay shop (see the next section) – and tell the auction browsers that you have more stuff for them that they 'can't find in a regular eBay search'.

Promotions

eBay.co.uk has added some excellent ways to promote your shop. As an eBay shop owner, you have access to promotional tools that other sellers can't use. The most valuable of these tools is cross promotions – using it is free, too! The cross-promotion box appears after a buyer places a bid on or purchases an item from an eBay seller.

The beauty of having a shop is that the cross-promotion box appears *twice*: once with your regular listings and again with a different assortment of items (if you want), after someone buys an item. Best of all you get to select which items are shown with your individual auctions.

Figure 4-12 shows you a cross-promotion box that appears when someone views an auction.

You can set up the promotions so that they default to show other items from related shop categories, or you can go in and set them up yourself for individual auctions. Again, every listing has two sets of options: one for when a user views your listings, and the other for when someone bids or wins your item.

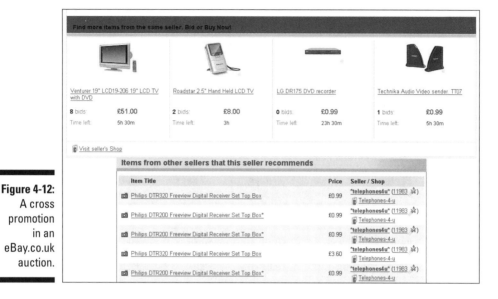

Find more items from the same seller. Bid or Buy Now!

Venturer 19" LCD19-206 19" LCD TV with DVD	Roadstar 2.5" Hand Held LCD TV	LG DR175 DVD recorder	Technika Audio Video sender TT07
8 bids £51.00	**2** bids £8.00	**0** bids £0.99	**1** bids £0.99
Time left: 5h 30m	Time left: 3h	Time left: 23h 30m	Time left: 5h 30m

Visit seller's Shop

Items from other sellers that this seller recommends

Item Title	Price	Seller / Shop
Philips DTR320 Freeview Digital Receiver Set Top Box	£0.99	"telephones4u" (11983) ☆ Telephones-4-u
Philips DTR200 Freeview Digital Receiver Set Top Box*	£0.99	"telephones4u" (11983) ☆ Telephones-4-u
Philips DTR200 Freeview Digital Receiver Set Top Box*	£0.99	"telephones4u" (11983) ☆ Telephones-4-u
Philips DTR320 Freeview Digital Receiver Set Top Box	£3.60	"telephones4u" (11983) ☆ Telephones-4-u
Philips DTR200 Freeview Digital Receiver Set Top Box*	£0.99	"telephones4u" (11983) ☆ Telephones-4-u

Figure 4-12:
A cross
promotion
in an
eBay.co.uk
auction.

Marketing Your Wares

eBay.co.uk has more tempting options that you can use to spruce up your shop items. These options work exactly like the ones eBay offers for your auctions. When choosing whether to use these options, remember that your eBay shop items only appear when someone searches in the eBay shops. eBay shop items don't appear in a regular eBay search, so the Gallery option may be the most beneficial option at this time. Check out Table 5-3 for a run-down of optional feature fees.

Table 4-3	eBay Optional Shop Features		
eBay Picture Services Fees			
Feature	**30 days**	**90 days**	**Good 'Til Cancelled (recurring 30-day listing)**
First picture	Free	Free	Free
Each additional picture	£0.12	£0.12	£0.12/30 days

(continued)

Table 4-3 *(continued)*

Feature	30 days	90 days	Good 'Til Cancelled (recurring 30-day listing)
Supersize image	£0.60	£0.60	£0.60/30 days
Picture Show	£0.15	£0.30	£0.15/30 days
Picture Pack	£0.90	£0.90	£0.90/30 days

Listing Upgrade Fees

Feature	30 days	90 days	Good 'Til Cancelled (recurring 30-day listing)
Gallery	£0.05	£0.05	£0.05/30 days
Item subtitle	£0.35	£0.35	£0.35/30 days
Listing designer	£0.07	£0.07	£0.07/30 days
Bold	£0.05	£1.50	£0.05/30 days
Highlight	£2.50	£2.50	£2.50/30 days
Featured in search	£9.95	£14.95	£9.95/30 days
Scheduled Listings	£0.06	£0.06	£0.06/30 days

eBay.co.uk Shops versus Auctions

From the buyer's point of view, shopping at an eBay.co.uk shop is different to winning an auction. eBay shops feature fixed-price sales; the buyer gets the merchandise as soon as you can ship it (instead of waiting for the auction to run its course). Even though your auctions show up on your shop's home page, all regular listings in your eBay shop are Buy It Now items.

When a buyer makes a purchase from your eBay shop, this is what happens:

1. **The buyer clicks the Buy It Now button on the listing page.** The Review Payments page appears, where the buyer can review the purchase. This page contains the shipping amount that you specified when you listed the item.

2. **The buyer provides shipping information (required).** When eBay notifies you that a sale has been made, you have all the information you need. You don't have to scurry around looking for the return address on the envelope when the payment arrives.

3. **The buyer reviews the transaction and then clicks the Confirm button.** The information about the sale is e-mailed to you, and the buyer receives confirmation of the sale.

Your eBay shop can be an essential back-up to your auctions. You can use your shop to sell out-of-season items, accessories for the items you sell actively, and even consignment items between re-listings. Considering the price of an eBay shop, you only need to make a few sales per month to pay for it – and when your sales start to build, your efforts will be greatly rewarded!

Chapter 5

Jazzing Up Your Auctions

. . . .

In This Chapter

▶ Writing a great description

▶ Setting up a photo studio

▶ Shooting great pics

▶ Scanning your items

▶ Sprucing up your photos with imaging software

▶ Hosting your pics

▶ Finding HTML templates

. . . .

Rule number 1: A good photograph and a concisely written description are the goal for all your auctions. If you're trying to fetch the highest possible bid for an item, keep your auction listings simple and professional: No dancing clowns (unless you're selling clowns), no overdone graphics, and no difficult-to-read typefaces. Less is more.

In this chapter, you find out how to write eye-catching descriptions and improve the visual elements of your auction listings.

Writing Winning Text

When you write descriptions for your auctions, describe your items clearly and completely. Mention everything about the object, including flaws or damage. When you're honest up front, you'll have a happy bidder. Remember to include your terms of sale and specify what type of payments and credit cards you accept. Include your shipping charges, too. Following is a checklist of things to mention:

✔ Size, style, colour (garment measurements are also valuable because sizes aren't always universal)

✔ Condition (new, new with tags, used, gently used, well-worn)

✔ Manufacturer's name

✔ Year of manufacture (if important)

✔ Fabric or material (if important)

✔ Any damage to the item

✔ Special features

✔ That you've stored it in a clean, dry place (if you have)

After you list all the facts, get excited and add a little flowery text in your description. Think infomercial! Think Shopping Channel! The descriptions used by these media make things sound so good that you absolutely *must* have whatever item they're selling. You can use the same technique, if you take the time.

Setting Up Your eBay.co.uk Photo Studio

Taking pictures? No problem! You have a digital camera, and you know how to use it. Just snap away and upload that picture, right? Sorry, but no. A good way and a bad way exist to take photos for eBay.co.uk and, believe it or not, the professional way isn't necessarily the most expensive way.

We recommend that you set up a mini photo studio for taking your eBay auction pictures. That way, you don't have to clean off your kitchen counter every time you want to take pictures.

If you must use the kitchen counter or a desktop, use an inexpensive photo stage, which you can find on – where else – eBay.co.uk.

You need several basic things in your photo studio; the extras you may require are based on the type of merchandise you're selling. An eBay *generalist*, someone who will sell almost anything online – like us! – should have quite a few extras for taking quality photos. Check out a portion of a home photo studio in Figure 5-1.

What you find in this section may be more than you thought you'd need to take good pictures. But your photographs can help sell your merchandise, so take this part of your business seriously. Of course, if you sell only one type of item, you don't need such a varied selection of stuff, just the basic photo set-up. Spend only as much on photographic equipment as is prudent at the time – you can add to it as you go along. Also, check www.coolebaytools.com for more ideas.

eBay Seller's Photo Lighting Kit

Tired of your auctions having fuzzy pictures? The answer is to use this professional photo light kit, designed for online images. It consists of two 10" reflectors with zinc die-cast stand adapters. Each reflector has an integrated ceramic socket for bulbs as high as 250 watts, with wood handling knobs. Two 6 foot all metal adjustable stands complete the kit. The kit comes with a short image tutorial by the author of "eBay for Dummies".

Bid with confidence and win this set at close to wholesale price as it is selling with NO RESERVE! Winning bidder to pay shipping & handling of $9, and must submit payment within a week of winning the auction. Credit cards are accepted through Billpoint and PayPal. Good luck!

GOOD LUCK, HAPPY BIDDING!

Click below to...
View my other auctions - Win more than one and $AVE on shipping!

Figure 5-1: An eBay photo set-up, featuring here in an eBay.co.uk auction.

Digital camera

Digital cameras are mysterious things. You may read about *mega pixels* (a million pixels) and think that more is supposed to be better, but that doesn't apply to eBay.co.uk applications or to Web images. Mega pixels measure the image resolution that the camera is capable of recording. For online use, all you need from a camera is 640 x 480 pixels (or at most 800 x 600) because computer monitors are incapable of taking advantage of more pixels. If you use a higher resolution picture, all you do is produce a pixel-bloated picture that takes a looooong time to load online.

You don't need a million pixels, but you do need the following:

- **Quality lens:** If you wear glasses we're sure you can tell the difference between a good lens and a cheap one. Really cheap cameras have plastic lenses, and the quality of the resulting pictures is accordingly lousy. Your camera is your work horse, so buy one from a company known for making quality products.

- **Removable media:** Taking the camera to your computer and using cables and extra software to download pictures to your hard drive is annoying. Removable media eliminates this annoyance. The most popular are Smart

Media cards (black wafer-thin cards), Compact Flash cards (in a plastic shell), and Sony Media Sticks; all are no larger than a matchbook. Insert these cards into your computer, if your computer has ports for them, or you can get an adapter that connects to your computer through a USB or parallel port. You can get either device on eBay.co.uk for about £20.

Some cameras (specifically the Sony Mavica FD series) use a regular 3½-inch floppy disc as a convenient storage method. These cameras are hugely popular with eBay sellers for just that reason.

✔ **Tripod and tripod mount:** Have you ever had a camera hanging around your neck while you're trying to repackage some eBay merchandise that you've just photographed? Or perhaps you've set down the camera for a minute and then can't find it? Avoid this hassle by using a tripod to hold your camera. Tripods also help you avoid blurry pictures from shaking hands. To use a tripod, you need a *tripod mount*, the little screw hole that you see in the bottom of some cameras. In the following section, we give you some tips on finding the right tripod.

✔ **Macro setting capability or threading for a lens adapter:** If you need to photograph coins, jewellery, or small detailed items, these tools will come in handy. A camera's macro setting enables you to get in really close to items while keeping them in focus. A threaded lens mount enables you to add different types of lenses to the camera for super macro focus or other uses.

✔ **Autofocus and zoom:** These options just make life easier when you want to take pictures. The ability to zoom in and keep things in focus should be standard features.

We bet you can find a camera that fits your needs right now on eBay.co.uk for less than £100. Remember that many digital camera users buy the newest camera available and sell their older, low-megapixel cameras on eBay for a pittance. Many professional camera shops also sell used equipment.

Other studio equipment

Certain endeavours seem to be open pits that you throw money into. You can avoid having your eBay.co.uk photo studio become one of these pits – if you follow our advice.

Tripod

A tripod is an extendable aluminium stand that holds your camera. Look for one that has a quick release so that if you want to take the camera off the tripod for a close-up, you don't have to unscrew it from the base and then screw it back on for the next picture.

The legs of the tripod should extend to your desired height, should lock in place with clamp-type locks, and should have a crank-style geared centre column so that you can raise your camera up and down for different shots. Most tripods also have a panning head for shooting from different angles. You can purchase a tripod from a camera shop or on eBay.co.uk for as little as £15.

Power supplies

Digital cameras can blast through batteries faster than chocolate through a five year old. A reliable power supply is a must and you can accomplish this in a couple of ways:

- ✔ **Rechargeable batteries:** Many specialists on eBay.co.uk sell rechargeable batteries and chargers. Pick up quality Ni-MH (nickel metal hydride) batteries because this kind, unlike Ni-Cad (nickel cadmium) batteries, has no memory effect. That means you don't have to totally discharge them.

- ✔ **CR-V3 lithium ion batteries:** This is a new kind of battery that takes the place of two standard AA batteries. Lithium batteries are the longest lasting and lightest batteries available, but they're also expensive. Then some smart guy figured out a way to put two batteries into one unit, thus considerably cutting the price. This new battery can average 650 photos before you have to change it. The CR-V3 is available also in a rechargeable form, thereby extending the life even further (and reducing your battery budget significantly).

If your eBay.co.uk photo studio includes a camera on a tripod (and it should), you can use a good, old-fashioned AC adapter (you know, the one that plugs into the wall).

Lighting

Trying to take good pictures of your merchandise can be frustrating. If you don't have enough light and use the camera's flash, the image may appear washed out. If you take the item outside, the sun may cast a shadow.

We've seen some eBay.co.uk sellers use a flash and instruct their children to shine a torch on the item as they photograph it from different angles – all the while hoping that the colour isn't wiped out. The autofocus feature on most digital cameras doesn't work well in low light.

After consulting specialists in the photo business to solve the digital camera lighting problem, we put together an inexpensive studio lighting set for online auction photography. Check out `www.coolebaytools.com` for information on how to obtain this package (refer also to Figure 5-1 to see the lighting set in use in a home photo studio).

Professional studio lights can be expensive, but you may be able to find a set for around £80. (You need at least two lights, one for either side of the item, to eliminate shadows.) Search eBay.co.uk for used studio lighting; we're sure you can find good deals.

Cloud Dome

If you're going to attempt to photograph a lot of jewellery, collectable coins, or other metallic items, you'll become frustrated at the quality of your pictures. Metallic objects seem to pick up random colour from any kind of light you shine on them for picture taking. Gold jewellery photographs with a silver tone and silver looks gold-ish!

After conferring with lots of eBay.co.uk photo gurus, we were told the secret of getting crisp, clear, close-up pictures: use a Cloud Dome. This device stabilises your camera (just as if you were using a tripod) and filters out all unwanted colour tones, resulting in image colours that actually look like your item.

The Cloud Dome is a large plastic bowl that you mount your camera on. You take pictures through the dome. The translucent white plastic diffuses the light so that your item is lit evenly from all sides, eliminating glare and bad shadows. Check out the manufacturer's Web site at `www.clouddome.co.uk` to see some amazing before and after pictures.

The Cloud Dome also manages to get the best images from gems – you can actually capture the light in the facets! Pearls, too, will show their lustre. Several eBay.co.uk members sell the Cloud Dome; we highly recommend it!

Props

To take good photos, you need some props. Although you may think it strange that a line item in your accounting program reads 'Props', they do qualify as a business expense. (Okay, you can put it under photography expense; *props* just sounds so Hollywood!)

How often have you seen some clothing on eBay.co.uk from a quality manufacturer, but you just couldn't bring yourself to bid more than £5 because it looked like it had been dragged behind a car and then hung on a hanger before it was photographed? Can you see how the fabric hangs on a body? Of course not. Take a look at Figure 5-2; that dress looks simply fantastic, darling!

Mannequin

If you're selling clothing, photograph it on a mannequin. If you don't want to dive right in and buy a mannequin, at least get a body form to wear the outfit. Just search eBay.co.uk for *mannequin* to find hundreds of hollow forms selling for less than £20. If you sell children's clothing, get a child's mannequin form as well; and the same goes for men's clothes. Alternatively, find a friend to model the clothes. No excuse justifies hanger-displayed merchandise in your auctions.

Diane Von Furstenberg BRAND NEW with tags!

100% Silk Jersey dress
Fits Size 6 or 8

This lovely silk number is THE sexiest dress! It's by hot designer Diane Von Furstenberg (who is featured in the new issue of Vogue). It's a fabulous silk jersey spaghetti strap dress, with a sexy cowl neckline. The original price of the dress is $220, and it can be yours for the highest bid. Draping beautifully on the body, it's got a sexy below the knee length and a very flattering cut.

Bid with confidence and bid whatever you feel this great dress is worth to you as it is selling with NO RESERVE! Winning bidder to pay shipping & handling of $5.25, and must submit payment within a week of winning the auction. Credit cards are accepted through Billpoint and PayPal.

GOOD LUCK, HAPPY BIDDING!

Click below to...
View my other auctions - Win more than one and $AVE on shipping!

Figure 5-2: Midge, the mannequin, modelling one of our eBay.co.uk successes.

Our mannequin has a great body and everything she wears sells at a profit. Many shops upgrade their mannequins every few years or so. If you know people who work at a clothes shop, ask when they plan to sell their old mannequins; you may be able to pick one up at a reasonable price.

Steamer

Clothing is fairly crumpled when it comes out of a shipping box. An item may also get crumpled lying around, waiting for you to photograph it and sell it on eBay.co.uk. If the clothing isn't new but is clean, run it through your dryer with Dryel (a home dry-cleaning product from the US) to take out any musty smells. Old, musty-smelling clothes can certainly sour a potentially happy customer. You can find Dryel on eBay.co.uk – surprise, surprise!

The clothes you want to sell may be crumpled, but ironing is a bind (and may damage the fabric), so do what retail professionals do: Use steamers to take the wrinkles out of freshly unpacked clothing. Get the type of steamer that you use while the article of clothing is hanging up, so you can just run the steamer up and down and get the wrinkles out. The gold standard of steamers is the Jiffy Steamer: It holds a large bottle of water (distilled only), rolls on the floor, and steams from a hose wand. Some models of Jiffy Steamer sell on eBay.co.uk for under £75. Until you're ready to make an investment that big, at least get a small handheld version that removes wrinkles; search eBay for *(garment,clothes) steamer* to find some deals.

Display stands, risers, and more

Jewellery does not photograph well on most people's hands and actually looks a lot better when you display it on a stand (see Figure 5-3) or a velvet pad. If you're selling a necklace, display it on a necklace stand, not on a person. We bought our display stands from a manufacturer but had to wait several months to receive them. Apparently, this type of quality display stand is made to order, so we recommend searching for them on eBay.co.uk (you'll get them sooner).

Ralph Lauren Signed Silver 16' Necklace

This stunning, brand new designer necklace is just the right length, 16" – and adjustable for smaller necks. Signed on reverse of stirrup goldtone plate *(see photo below)*, also signed on the silver toggle. Your chance to get this retail $48 necklace for a fraction of the cost! The perfect gift for you or a friend.

Bid with confidence and bid whatever you feel this item is worth to you, as it is selling with *NO RESERVE*! I pack all my items carefully. Winning bidder to pay shipping & handling of $3, and must submit payment within a week of winning the auction. I will accept credit cards through BillPoint and PayPal - Good Luck, Happy Bidding!

Figure 5-3: An eBay. co.uk listing featuring a professional jewellery display.

Risers can be almost anything that you use to prop up your item to make it more attractive in a picture. Put riser pieces that aren't attractive under the cloth that you use as a background. (You can find risers on eBay.co.uk.)

You wouldn't believe what the back of some professional photo set-ups look like. Photographers and photo stylists think resourcefully when it comes to making the merchandise look good – from the front of the picture, anyway! We've seen the most creative things used to prop up items for photography:

✔ **Bottles of mercury:** Mercury is a heavy liquid metal. A photographer we once worked with used little bottles of this stuff to prop up small boxes and other items in a picture. But mercury is a poison, so we suggest you do the same with small bottles (prescription bottles work well) filled with sand.

✔ **Beeswax and clay:** To set up photos for catalogues, we've seen photographers prop up fine jewellery and collectable porcelain with beeswax (the kind you can get from the orthodontist works great) or clay. Beeswax is a neutral colour and doesn't usually show up in the photo. However, you must dispose of beeswax often because it picks up dirt from your hands and fuzz from fabric.

✔ **Museum Gel and Quake Hold:** These two products are invaluable when you want to hold a small object at an unnatural angle for a photograph. (These products are like beeswax and clay, but cleaner.) Museums use these putty-like products to securely keep breakables in one place – even during an earthquake!

✔ **un-du:** un-du is a clear liquid that removes sticky residue from almost anything. If your item has sticker residue on it, the mess is bound to show up in the picture. Squirt on a little un-du and use its patented scraper to remove the goo and bring back the shine. Although this is sold in the US, you can get hold of un-du (and QuakeHold) through sellers on ebay.com – expect to pay more for shipping!

✔ **Metal clamps and duct tape:** These multipurpose items are used in many photo shoots in some of the strangest places. Your mannequin may be a few sizes too small for the dress you want to photograph. How do you fix that problem? Don't pad the mannequin; simply fold over the dress in the back and clamp the excess material with a metal clamp, or use a small piece of duct tape to hold the fabric taut.

Keep a collection of risers and propping materials in your photo area so they're always close at hand.

Backgrounds for your images

Backgrounds come in many shapes and sizes. You can use paper, fabric, or one of the portable photo stages for smallish items.

In professional photo-talk, *seamless* is a large roll of 3-foot (and wider) paper that comes in various colours and is suspended and draped behind the model and over the floor. (Ever wonder why you never see the floor and wall come together in professional photos?) Photographers also drape the seamless over tabletop shots. Some people use fabrics such as muslin instead of seamless.

We keep satin and velvet on hand. (Clean black velvet with sticky tape before you use it in a picture – lint appears huge in photos.) Use neutral fabrics (such as white, light grey, natural, and black) for photographing your merchandise so that the colour of the fabric doesn't clash with or distract from your items.

The Cloud Dome people have also invented a great photo stage, which is portable (easy to store), non-breakable, simple to clean, and inexpensive. This stage is sold on eBay.co.uk and is pictured in Figure 5-4.

Figure 5-4:
Cloud
Dome's
photo stage
(bottle not
included!).

Taking Good Pictures

If you have a small home photo studio set-up (see the preceding section) with a quality camera, a tripod, props, and lights, you're well on your way to taking some quality shots for your auctions. A few things to remember:

- ✓ **Zoom in on your item:** Don't leave a load of extraneous background in your pictures. Crop extra background in your photo-editing program (see the 'Image-Editing Software' section, a bit later in this chapter) before you upload the images to your image-hosting service.

- ✓ **Watch out for distracting backgrounds:** If you don't have a studio table-top, or if the item is something that won't fit on a table, try to make the background of the photo as simple as possible. If you're shooting the picture outside, shoot away from chairs, tables, hoses – you get the idea. If you're shooting in your home, move the laundry basket out of the picture.

One of our favourite eBay pictures featured a piece of fine silver taken by the husband of the woman selling the piece on eBay.co.uk. Silver and reflective items are hard to photograph because they pick up everything in the room in their reflection. In her description, the woman explained that the man reflected in the silver coffeepot was her husband and not part of the final deal. She handled that very well!

✔ **Be sure the items are clean:** Cellophane on boxes can get scruffy look-ing, clothing can get linty, and all merchandise can get dirt smudges. Not only do your items photograph better if they're clean, they sell better, too.

Clean plastic or cellophane with WD-40 (no kidding); this product takes off any sticker residue and icky smudges. un-du is the best adhesive remover for paper, cardboard, clothing, and more, plus it comes with a handy plastic scraper. Also keep an art rubber around to clean off small dirt smudges on paper items. Any cleaning solution can help your items, but use these chemicals with care so that you don't destroy the item while cleaning it.

✔ **Check the camera's focus:** Just because a camera has an autofocus fea-ture doesn't mean that pictures automatically come out crisp and clear. Low light, high moisture, and other things can contribute to a blurred image. Double-check the picture before you use it.

Book VI

Using eBay.co.uk

Using a Scanner

Scanners have come a long way in the past few years. This once expensive item can now be purchased new for a little more than £50. If you sell books, autographs, stamps, or documents, a scanner may be all you need to shoot your images for eBay.co.uk.

When shopping for a scanner, don't pay too much attention to the resolution. As with digital cameras, images for the Internet (JPEGs) needn't be any higher than 72 ppi (pixels per inch). Any quality scanner can get that resolution these days. Quality makes a difference in the manufacture of the scanner, so stick with brand names.

Use a *flatbed* scanner, on which you lay out your items and scan away. You can use an HP OfficeJet, which is not only a scanner but also a printer and reducing/enlarging colour copier – most even come with a fax! These nifty flatbed units are available brand new on eBay.co.uk for around £150.

A few tips on scanning images for eBay.co.uk:

✔ If you're taking traditionally processed photographs and scanning them on a scanner, print them on glossy paper because they scan much better than those with a matt finish.

✔ You can scan 3-D items, such as a doll, on your flatbed scanner and get some respectable-looking images. To eliminate harsh shadows, lay a black or white t-shirt over the doll or her box so that it completely covers the glass. This way you have a clean background and you get good light reflection from the scanner's light.

✔ If an item is too big for your scanner's glass, simply scan the item in pieces, and then reassemble it to a single image in your photo-editing program (see the following section).

✔ Boxed items are a natural for a flatbed scanner. Just set them on top of the glass, and scan away. You can crop the shadowed background with your photo-editing software (see the following section).

Image-Editing Software

Lose the idea that the software that comes with your scanner is good enough. That software may be just fine for some uses, but the kind of control that you need is only available in *real* image-editing software, not a mere e-mail picture generator.

We've always been happy using Photoshop. However, this program is large, expensive, and a bit of an overkill for eBay.co.uk images. Recently we started using Paint Shop Pro by Jasc software (now part of Corel), a robust professional program at a fraction of the price of Photoshop. Paint Shop Pro is also one of the easiest-to-learn programs on the market. We've seen new packages of Paint Shop Pro 8.1 sell for as low as £13.99 (if you're a good shopper, we know you *can* find these deals). Hint: Look for sellers putting *Paint Shop* as one word (*Paintshop*) in the title.

Paint Shop Pro offers features that enable you to make a good picture out of a bad one. This program also has a brilliant export-to-Web feature that compresses the images so that they hold their quality while becoming smaller. Images compressed in this fashion download a lot faster for dial-up customers. You can also touch up your family photos in this easy-to-use program.

Don't forget that you are working with images not only for eBay items but also for your Web site. The Corel Web site (`www.corel.co.uk/servlet/Satellite?pagename=Corel3Uk/Downloads/Trials`) offers free trial downloads.

A Home for Your Images

You need a professional and safe place to store your pictures for eBay.co.uk. If your images don't appear when someone clicks your auction, or if your images take too long to load, a user may click off your auction and go to the next one. If you have more than one option, test each with a few pictures because you want the most reliable one.

If you use auction management software, you may not need an FTP program to upload your images. Most complete management programs integrate their own FTP program as part of the package and may also include image storage space on their server.

 Always put your eBay.co.uk images in a separate directory – not in an active part of your Web site. You may think that using your business Web site is a good place to store your images, but it isn't. If you want to keep track of your site statistics, such as the number of visitors, hits, and the like, hosting your own images will ruin the data. A call for one of your eBay images counts as a hit on your site, and you never get accurate Web site stats.

Free ISP space

Most ISPs (Internet Service Providers) give you at least 5MB of storage space for your personal home page. Although not appropriate for your final business site, this 5MB space is a perfect place to host your pictures. Everyone has an ISP, and all ISPs give you space. You may have to use an FTP program to upload to your Web space, or your ISP may supply its own uploader. Go to the home pages for your ISP (the member area), and check out what it offers.

Auction management sites

If you're using one of the auction management Web sites that we discuss in Chapter 9, you're covered for most of your back office tasks. These Web sites supply enough Web space to hold all your eBay.co.uk images. They also have a convenient one-click upload from your hard drive.

eBay.co.uk Picture Services

You can also use eBay.co.uk Picture Services to host your photos for eBay, but the quality of your photos is better if you host them directly from a site. Really clear pictures on Picture Services are few and far between. Picture Services reformats your photo to fit in a layout 400 pixels wide by 300 pixels tall and then compresses the file for quick viewing. This process can destroy the quality of your carefully photographed images if you haven't saved them in a compatible size. You're running a business, so be businesslike and use the method that presents your photos in their best light.

TIP

To get the free top-of-page image that you see on many auctions, you must use eBay Picture Services. We suggest that you use eBay Picture Services for your primary image and also use secondary images of your items hosted elsewhere. If one of the picture servers goes down, at least your listing will have pictures. The first picture is free; all you have to do is click the box on the Sell Your Item page's Picture Services area, next to Add picture. This picture will also be the default picture for use as your all-important gallery image.

eBay.co.uk offers two versions of Picture Services. The basic version (see Figure 5-5) allows you to upload eBay-ready images as they appear on your computer.

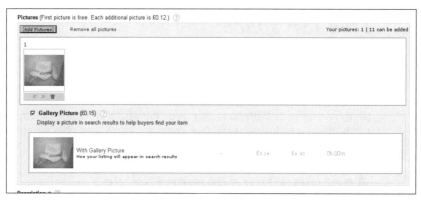

Figure 5-5:
The basic
Picture
Services
photo-
hosting
page.

If you want to rotate or crop the picture, you need the enhanced picture service. Click the Upgrade link, and a screen similar to Figure 5-6 appears. It's worth noting that you must be using Internet Explorer to get access to the enhanced picture service. It doesn't work with the Firefox browser.

To upload your pictures using the enhanced version, follow these steps:

1. **Click the Add Picture button, which appears in the picture frame.**

   A browsing window appears.

2. **Locate the directory that holds your eBay images on your computer.**

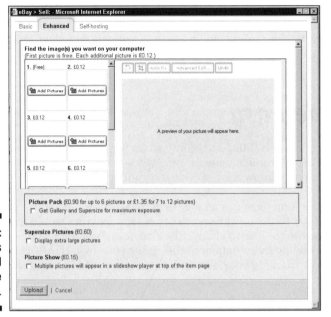

Figure 5-6:
eBay.co.uk's
Enhanced
Picture
Services.

3. **Click the image in the browsing window.**

   The image name appears in the filename box.

4. **Click the Open box.**

   The selected image appears in the picture frame.

5. **To rotate the image, click the circular arrow (at the upper left of the main image box).**

6. **To crop the image:**

   a. **Click the crop box in the right corner of the larger image.**

      Two squares appear at opposite corners of your main image.

   b. **Click the frame on the outside of your image, and move the bar until the offensive area is cropped out.**

      You can crop like this from the sides, top, and bottom of the picture.

Sometimes Picture Services shrinks your image to a too-small size, but you can't do much about it. Just be sure to reload the image each time you re-list the item; otherwise, the gallery image may just get smaller and smaller. eBay continues to improve Picture Services, so don't give up on it. Use Picture Services for the free image, and be sure to upload secondary images from an outside site.

HTML Made Easy

Our small grasp of HTML gets us only so far. We usually use a program such as CuteHTML to produce code for our Web site or eBay.co.uk listings. Luckily, you don't have to know a lot of code to produce eBay auctions.

The Sell Your Item form has an excellent, basic HTML generator that has a toolbar similar to the one in a word processor. As you can see in Figure 5-7, you can use the toolbar to change the size, font, or colour of the text. You can also insert coding by switching to the 'Enter your own HTML' view of the description to include your own hosted images in the listing description.

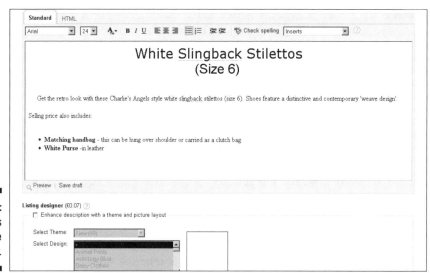

Figure 5-7: eBay.co.uk's HTML code generator.

For a quick and easy HTML fix, go to

```
www.coolebaytools.com
```

Then go to the Tolls area and click <u>Cool free ad tool</u>. You get a quick HTML generator; feel free to use it as often as you like. You incur no charge. You can select border colours and include an image in your description area – nothing fancy, mind you, just nice clean HTML. You type your information as indicated and select colours. When you finish, click the View Ad button. On the next page, you see HTML code for your auction description that you can cut and paste into the auction description area of the Sell Your Item page.

Book VI

Using eBay.co.uk

Chapter 6

Building an eBay.co.uk Back Office

*T*he more items you sell, the more confusing things can get. As you build your eBay.co.uk business, the little side table you use for storing eBay merchandise isn't going to work. You must think industrial. Even part-time sellers can benefit by adding a few professional touches to their business areas.

In this chapter, we emphasise the importance of setting up and organising your back office. We cover everything from stacking your stock to keeping inventory to choosing packing materials and online postage services. Organisation is your byword. Dive right in. The sooner you read this chapter, the sooner you can build your eBay back office and get down to business.

The Warehouse: Organising Your Space

Whether you plan to sell large or small items, you need space for storing them. As you make savvy purchases, maintaining an item's mint condition is one of your greatest challenges. Organised storage in itself is an art, so in this section we cover the details of what you need to safeguard your precious stock.

Shelving your profits

Before you stock the shelves, it helps to have some! You also need a place to put the shelves: Your garage, a spare room, or somewhere else. You have a choice between three basic kinds of shelves:

- **Plastic:** If you're just starting out, you can always go to the local DIY shop to buy inexpensive plastic shelves. They're light and cheap – and they'll buckle in time.

- **Wooden:** When you think about cheap wooden furniture, one shop springs to mind: Ikea. It's got loads of different styles with a starting price of less than £1 – you can't argue with that when you're starting up on a budget!

- **Steel:** If you want to get your storage right first time, buy steel shelving. The most versatile steel shelving is the wire kind (versus solid-steel shelves), which is lighter and allows air to circulate around your items. Steel wire shelving assembles easily. The shelving comes with levelling feet and 4-inch casters, so should you need to move a shelf unit, you can. Installing casters is up to you. You can combine steel wire shelving units to create a full wall of shelves. Each shelf safely holds as much as 250kgs of merchandise.

  Search eBay.co.uk for **shelving** to find sellers offering this kind of industrial shelving. The main problem with ordering this product online is that the shipping usually costs more than the shelving.

Box 'em or bag 'em?

Packing your items for storage can be a challenge. Pick up some plastic bags in different sizes. Sandwich bags are perfect for storing smaller items, for example. When items are stored in plastic, they can't pick up any smells or become musty before you sell them. The plastic also protects the items from rubbing against each other and causing possible damage. If you package your merchandise one item to a bag, you can then just lift one off the shelf and put it directly into a shipping box when the auction is over.

Your bags of items have to go into boxes for storage on the shelves. Clear plastic storage boxes are great for bulky items. These big plastic containers are usually 26 inches deep, so before you buy them make sure they'll fit on your shelving comfortably and that you'll have easy access to your items. Using cardboard office-type file storage boxes from an office supply shop is another option. These cardboard boxes are 10 x 12 x 16 inches, which is a nice size for storing medium-size products; they're also the most economical choice. The downside is that you can't see through cardboard boxes, so if your label falls off, you have to take the box off the shelf and open it to check its contents. Smaller see-through plastic boxes with various compartments, such as the kind sold in DIY shops as toolboxes, work great for storing very small items.

When using large plastic bins, tape a pad of Post-it notes on the end of the box so you can quickly identify the contents. You *can* use regular sticky labels, but changing them leaves large amounts of paper residue over time, and your storage ends up looking sloppy and unprofessional.

Inventory: Keeping Track of What You Have and Where You Keep It

Savvy eBay.co.uk sellers have different methods of handling inventory. They use everything from spiral-bound notebooks to sophisticated software programs. Although computerised inventory tracking can simplify this task, starting with a plain ol' handwritten ledger is fine, too. Choose whichever method works best for you, but keep in mind that as your eBay business grows, a software program that tracks inventory for you may become necessary.

Most of these inventory systems wouldn't work for a company with a warehouse full of stock but will work nicely in an eBay sales environment. Many sellers tape sheets of paper to their boxes to identify them by number, and use that as a reference to a simple Excel spreadsheet for selling purposes. Excel spreadsheets are perfect for keeping track of your auctions as well, but if you're using a management service or software, you don't need both for physical inventory. After you're running a full-time business, however, you have to keep the tax inspectors happy with pounds and pence accounting of your inventory, so keep your inventory records in a standardised program such as QuickBooks.

You may also want to use Excel spreadsheets for your downloaded PayPal statements, to hold information waiting to transfer to your bookkeeping program.

Plan in advance where you want to put everything. Organise your items by theme, type, or size. If you organise before planning, you may end up with organised chaos.

The Shipping Department: Packin' It Up

In this section, we look at some of the essentials for a complete, smooth-running shipping department, such as cleaning supplies and packing materials. The *handling fee* portion of your shipping charges pays for these kinds of items. Don't run low on these items and pay attention to how you store them – they must be kept in a clean environment.

Packaging clean up

Be sure the items you send out are in tip-top shape. A few everyday chemicals can gild the lily, for example:

- **WD-40:** The decades-old lubricant works very well at getting price stickers off plastic and glass without damaging the product. The plastic on a toy box may begin to look nasty, even when stored in a clean environment. A quick wipe with a paper towel with a dash of WD-40 will make the plastic shine like new. WD-40 also works incredibly well for untangling jewellery chains and shining up metallic objects.

- **Goo Gone (available from US eBay sellers):** Goo Gone works miracles in cleaning up gooey sticker residue from non-porous items.

- **un-du (available from US eBay sellers):** This amazing liquid easily removes stickers from cardboard, plastic, fabrics, and more without causing damage. un-du comes packaged with a patented mini-scraper top that can be used in any of your sticker cleaning projects. If you can't find un-du, check out www.coolebaytools.com for places to purchase it. You can also use lighter fluid (which is, of course, considerably more dangerous and may damage your item).

Packing materials

To ensure that your items arrive at their destinations in one piece, keep the following on hand at all times:

- **Bubble wrap:** A clean, puffy product that comes in rolls, bubble wrap is available in several sizes. Depending on your product, you may have to carry two sizes of bubble wrap to properly protect the goods. Bubble wrap can be expensive, but check out vendors at eBay.co.uk; you'll find quite a lot of them (and possibly a deal).

✔ **Styrofoam packing beads:** Polystyrene beads (or peanuts) protect just about everything you ship. Storing them is the tricky part. One of the most ingenious storage solutions we've seen is putting the beads into big plastic rubbish bags, and then hanging these bags on cup hooks (available at the hardware shop) around the walls in a garage. When packing with peanuts, be sure that you place the item carefully and use enough peanuts to fill the box *completely*; leaving any airspace defeats the point of using the peanuts in the first place.

✔ **Plastic bags:** Buy plastic bags in bulk to save money. Buy various sizes and use them for both shipping and storing. Even large kitchen rubbish bags are good for wrapping up posters and large items; the plastic protects the item from inclement weather by waterproofing it.

✔ **Two or three-inch shipping tape:** You need clear tape to place over address labels to protect them from scrapes and rain. Don't risk a lost package for want of a few inches of tape. See the following section on boxes for more information.

✔ **Padded envelopes:** If you send items that fit nicely into these bubble wrap-lined envelopes, use them. This type of envelope – with paper on the outside and bubble wrap on the inside – is perfect for mailing small items or clothing using first class mail. Jiffy bags are available in quantity (an economical choice) and don't take up much storage space.

Book VI

Using eBay.co.uk

Packaging – the heart of the matter

Depending on the size of the item you sell, you can purchase boxes in bulk at reliable sources. Try to purchase from a manufacturer that specialises in B2B (business to business) sales. Some box companies specialise in selling to the occasional box user – knowing the size that you need enables you to bulk buy.

The Post Room: Sendin' It Out

In this section, we give you the low-down on the main Internet postage vendor: Royal Mail.

Printing labels on your printer is convenient until you start sending out a dozen packages at a time, then cutting the paper and taping the label gets a bit too time consuming. Do yourself a favour and get a label printer. Yes, these printers can be expensive, but you can find some great deals on eBay.co.uk. A label printer can save you countless hours.

Royal Mail has an online postage service called SmartStamp that enables you to print postage directly from your computer while online. To register online and download their software, go to the Royal Mail Web site at

`www.royalmail.com`

and click the SmartStamp link.

Here are some features of the SmartStamp service:

- ✔ You can print postage directly onto envelopes or labels.
- ✔ You can personalise your mail with a company logo.
- ✔ No minimum mailing amount is required, so a small time eBayer can benefit as much as a multi-national company.
- ✔ You can even add your own company strapline or promotional message.

With SmartStamp you pay a monthly or annual subscription plus whatever you shell out in postage costs. At time of writing, Royal Mail offers the service for £4.99 a month or £49.99 a year.

Book VII

Understanding Web 2.0

'My friends on the dock helped me
with the slogan.'

In this book . . .

Web 2.0 offers online businesses a whole new way of interacting with customers. We cover the advantages of using e-tools, blogging, live chat, and plenty more, and focus on how this can help you sell more goods to more people. We also look at mastering the various technologies available through Web 2.0.

Here are the contents of Book VII at a glance:

Chapter 1

Profiting from New Business Tools

. . . .

In This Chapter

▶ Taking advantage of round-the-clock availability and new communications

▶ Identifying new products and services

▶ Marketing through your Web site

▶ Creating your own business blog

▶ Making sure that your online business promotes community spirit

. . . .

*W*hen you open shop on the Internet, you don't just begin to operate in isolation. The whole point of the Web is the fact that it's a community. It's the same for businesses as it is for individuals. Whether you like it or not, you're not alone. You have access to thousands, even millions, of other businesses that are in the same situation you are – or that went through the same kinds of uncertainties you're encountering before they achieved success.

Advantages of Doing Business Online

The fact that you're online means that you enjoy advantages over businesses operating solely in the bricks-and-mortar marketplace. E-mail, blogging, and the Internet in general give you much better access to your customers – and there's no equivalent in the offline world. You also have access to services such as search engines that can help you find suppliers and do business research and marketing. This chapter provides you with a user friendly overview of the many new opportunities available to you when you start an online business, including tools, services, and opportunities for partnering so that you can advertise your new business in ways that help you succeed without breaking your budget.

Sometimes, a big step toward success is simply being aware of all the opportunities available to you. The worst reason you can have for going online is simply that 'everybody's doing it'. Instead of focusing on one way of advertising or selling, take stock of all the aspects of online business that you can exploit. Then when you create your Web site, select a payment option, or set up security measures, you'll do things right the first time around. The next few sections describe some advantages you need to make part of your business plan.

Operating 24/7

One of the first reasons why entrepreneurs flock to the Web is the ability to do business around the clock with customers all over the world. It still applies today: It may be 2 a.m. in the UK, but someone can still be making a purchase in Rome, Los Angeles, or Sydney from your Web site or eBay shop.

If you're just starting out and you're trying to reach the widest possible audience of consumers for your goods or services, be sure they're

- ✓ **Small:** That means they're easy to pack and easy to ship.

- ✓ **Something that people need and can use worldwide:** DVDs, CDs, computer products, action figures, and sports memorabilia appeal to many.

- ✓ **Something that people can't find in their local area:** Many sites resell gourmet foodstuffs that can't easily be found overseas, for example.

Make sure that you appeal to a small, niche segment of individuals around the world. It's better to do one thing extremely well than lots of things badly. That applies to all businesses, from the smallest start-ups to the biggest multinationals. Keeping your business lean and mean improves your chances of success.

If you do sell DVDs online, be aware that DVD players are required to include codes that prevent the playback of DVDs in geographical regions where movies haven't been released to video as yet. A disc purchased in one country may not play on a player purchased in another country. You need to pay attention to the codes assigned to the DVDs you sell so that your customers will actually be able to play them.

Communicating with etools

Nothing beats e-mail, in our opinion, for reaching customers in a timely and friendly way. We know all about the immediacy of talking to people over the phone, the sophistication of desktop alerts, and the benefits of print advertising. But phone calls can be intrusive, alerts are expensive, and mag ads only work for certain types of business. As you can probably testify as a consumer, most people are wary of anyone who wants to market to them with an out-of-the-blue phone call that interrupts their day. E-mail messages can come in at any time of the day or night, but they don't interrupt what customers are doing. And if customers have already made a purchase from your company, they may welcome a follow-up contact by e-mail, especially because they can respond to you at their own convenience. Not only that, but you can include links to products and services in e-mails that could tempt customers into further purchases. You can announce new product ranges, special offers, even an entirely new business.

One of the most popular online communications systems, instant messaging (IM), is useful for keeping in touch with business partners and colleagues. But be very wary of using it to approach current or potential customers. Consumers are used to dropping everything to answer instant messages from friends. When they discover that it's a marketing message, they're not going to be happy – it's the online equivalent of taking a telesales call when you're enjoying a nice bath.

Besides e-mail newsletters, what kinds of communications strategies work with online shoppers? The following sections give a few suggestions.

Giving away a free sample

Greg was in the grocery shop the other day, looking at a hunk of luxury cheese that costs a pretty penny, wishing he could open up the package and taste-test it before handing over big bucks. The concept of the 'free sample' is one that everyone loves – especially Web surfers. Newspapers like the *Financial Times* and *The Independent* do it by making the first few paragraphs of archived articles available online; if you want to read the rest, you're asked to pay a pound, or a similar nominal fee. Amazon.co.uk makes brief excerpts of selected CD tracks available on its Web site so that shoppers can listen to the music before deciding whether or not to buy the CD.

On the Internet, software producers have been giving away free samples for many years in the form of computer *shareware:* software program that users can download and use for a specified period of time. After the time period expires, the consumers are asked (or required, if the program ceases to function) to pay a shareware fee if they want to keep the program. A tiny Texas company called id Software started giving away a stripped-down computer game on the Internet back in 1993, in the hope of getting users hooked on it so that they would pay for the full-featured version. The plan worked, and since then, more than 100,000 customers have paid as much as $40 (£22) for a full copy of the game, which is called Doom. id Software has gone on to create and sell many other popular games since.

Giving out discounts

One reason shoppers turn to the Internet is to save money. Thanks to sites such as PriceRunner (www.pricerunner.co.uk), Kelkoo (www.kelkoo.co.uk), and Moneysupermarket.com (www.moneysupermarket.com), which allow you to compare prices on various Web sites for books, holidays, electrical equipment, or whatever you like, shoppers expect some sort of discount from the Internet. They love it if you offer special Internet-only prices on your Web site or give them money off or 'promotional' offers.

Giving customers the chance to talk back

Another great thing about the Internet is that it gives customers the chance to get involved in the design and manufacturer of products. They can create their own clothing ranges, sportswear, or even artwork and have it sent to them by post. Adidas is a famous example of a brand that people like to customise to their own tastes. Through the Web site, you can book an appointment at their Harrods-based shop, where you're measured up, given a choice of colour and design combinations, and even have your feet tested to see what combination of cushioning and support you need.

A number of forward-looking companies are building their reputations by letting customers voice opinions and make suggestions online. The shoe and sporting apparel manufacturer Nike isn't exactly a small business, but it's taken a leading position in building community among its customers. Every week, a live chat session is held for Nike customers. Discussion boards are also available; the site (www.nikechat.com) boasts more than 33,000 registered members and a total of 3.5 million messages posted.

Chat doesn't make sense unless you have a solid user base of at least several hundred regular users who feel passionately about your goods and services and are dedicated enough to want to type real-time messages to one another and to you. However, discussion groups are practical, even for small businesses; you can set them up with a discussion area through Microsoft FrontPage or on Yahoo! (uk.groups.yahoo.com).

Taking advantage of micropayments' rebirth

Credit-card payments make the Web a viable place for e-commerce. But the cost of the typical credit-card transaction makes payments of less than £1 pointless. The popular payment service PayPal (www.paypal.co.uk) charges 3.4 per cent plus a 20p fee for each sale, which makes it impractical for content providers to sell something for, say, 30p. Such small transactions are known as *micropayments*.

In the early dotcom days, the term micropayment was thrown around quite a bit, both by writers and by companies hoping that they could induce Web surfers to pay small amounts of money for bits of online content. Many of those companies failed to find success and disappeared, in part because the process of setting up micropayments was cumbersome and highly technical.

Today, micropayment systems are attempting a comeback. A large percentage of Web surfers have high-speed broadband connections and are used to paying for content online. A system called BitPass brings small payments to more than 100 Web sites. There's much more content online, including articles, music clips, and cartoons, that could only be sold for small amounts of money. If your business involves text, music, art, or other kinds of content, you may be able to make a few pence for your work by using one of the following payment services:

- ✔ **BT Click&Buy:** Thousands of businesses around the world use BT's micropayments service (`www.clickandbuy.com`). It allows payments from as little as 50p to hundreds of pounds, whilst giving customers the option of being charged through their phone bill. Your customers get a 24/7 helpline and the reassurance that they're using a reputable company. But charges are fairly steep at just under 10 per cent commission plus a one-off set up fee and a small monthly charge.

- ✔ **mENABLE:** This Mobile Enable solution (`www.m-enable.com/content`) is a pretty natty bit of kit. It allows Web sites to charge for access, using micropayments over SMS, WAP, phone, credit card, or bank debit. The company has won awards for its secure service and has a big range of payment options, which you can tailor to your business's needs.

- ✔ **SpaceCoin:** This company (`www.spacecoin.com`) is based in Sweden but operates all over the world. It offers plenty of payment options, including its quick set-up Plug and Play Shop and shopping trolley software.

- ✔ **TechnaPay:** These guys (`www.tecknapay.com`) are WorldPay-accredited resellers who specialise in products complementing WorldPay's payment platform. On top of the usual stuff, they offer payment page design for £149, shopping trolley functionality, and even £50 cashback when you sign up to their service.

If you can link your Web site, eBay shop, or other venues to your offerings on these micropayment sites, you begin to achieve synergy: Your various sales sites point to one another and build attention for your overall sales efforts.

Book VII

Under-standing Web 2.0

Auctioning off your professional services

There's nothing new about making a living selling your design, consultation, or other professional services. But the Internet provides you with new and innovative ways to get the word out about what you do. Along with having your own Web site in which you describe your experience, provide samples of your work, and make references to clients you've helped, you can find new clients by auctioning off your services in what's known as a *reverse auction*. In a reverse auction, the provider of goods or services doesn't initiate a transaction – rather, the customer does.

The UK government is a big fan of reverse auctions as a way of getting the best price for contracts. For example, say the Department for Culture, Media and Sport needs a new stationery supplier. It advertises the contract in the form of a tender and invites bids; the lowest bid (from a reputable supplier) wins the deal. Even the Ministry of Defence is involved. Check out `www.contracts.mod.uk` if you don't believe us!

Elance Online, a reverse auction site based in the United States, enables professional contractors to offer their services and bid on jobs. (Go to `www.elance.com` and click Elance Online.) The site is ideal if you don't offer bits of content, such as stories or articles, but usually charge by the hour or by the job for your services. In this case, the customer is typically a company that needs design, writing, construction, or technical work. The company posts a description of the job on the Elance site. Essentially, it's a Request for Bids or Request for Proposals: Freelancers who have already registered with the site then make bids on the job. The company can then choose the lowest bid or choose another company based on its qualifications.

Exploring New Products and Services You Can Sell

The choices you make when you first get started in e-commerce have an impact on the success with which you target your customers. One of the main choices is determining what you plan to sell online. Because you've made the decision to sell on the Internet, chances are good that you're a technology-savvy businessperson. You're open to new technologies and new ways of selling. The 21st century has seen an explosion in products and services that were unheard of just a decade or so ago. If you can take advantages of one of these opportunities, you increase your potential customer base.

Music files and other creative work

Today's online customers are quite sophisticated about shopping online. You can make your music or audio clips available online from your Web site. The easiest option is to use your computer or a digital recorder to make the recording and save the file in `.wav` (Waveform Audio Format), MP3, `.ram` (RealAudio), or `.wma` (Windows Media Audio). Chances are excellent that your visitors have one or more media players that can process and play at least one of these types of files.

One of the biggest online music stories of the last few years is, of course, the music marketplace Napster (`www.napster.co.uk`). It started as an illegal site for sharing music cheaply, by bypassing licensing laws. After a clampdown a few years back, Napster went legit and is no less successful for that move. Groups routinely provide links to their albums on the Napster music site, where you can download each track separately for less than a pound each, and albums for around eight quid. Even if you're just starting out in the biz, you can digitise your audio files and post them online so that others can download them in the same way.

Groceries and other household services

Small, easily shipped merchandise like golf balls or tools are undeniably well suited to online sales. But your online business doesn't need to be restricted to such items. Even perishable items like foodstuffs can be, and frequently are, purchased online. Initially, the field attracted *pure plays* – companies that devoted their sales activities solely to the Internet. They failed to compete with bricks-and-mortar shops.

The good news is that traditional bricks-and-mortar grocery shops are finding success by selling their products on the Web as a way of supplementing their traditional in-store offering. The Web site for Wiltshire Farm Foods (www.wiltshirefarmfoods.com), shown in Figure 1-1, gives its customers the convenience of 'meals on wheels' delivered to their door – but with an emphasis on quality. Elderly customers who aren't able to visit one of its outlets around the UK can buy tasty meals online and have them delivered.

Figure 1-1:
Regional
grocers
and food
producers
are widen-
ing their
customer
bases
thanks to
the Web.

Book VII

**Under-
standing
Web 2.0**

Big supermarkets such as Sainsbury's (`www.sainsburys.co.uk`) and Waitrose (`www.ocado.co.uk`), who spend millions of pounds promoting, maintaining, and selling through their Web sites, have conducted numerous studies into what makes people buy food online. Generally, people buy groceries this way for three main reasons:

- ✔ Cost savings
- ✔ Convenience
- ✔ Greater product variety

If you're able to offer food items that consumers can't find elsewhere, and at a competitive price, you should consider selling food online. People hate navigating multi-storey car parks and waiting in long queues at the checkout. People who live alone and who have difficulty getting out (such as the elderly or sick) naturally turn to buying their groceries online.

Are you interested in reaching online grocery shoppers online? The Food Standards Agency has a useful Web site (`www.eatwell.gov.uk/keepingfoodsafe/shoppingforfood/onlinemailorder`) detailing the standards of quality, packaging, and delivery you have to achieve.

Customers have plenty of rights in this area; for example you have to make descriptions of your products full and accurate, and you must send a confirmation e-mail once your customer has ordered food. Non-food sellers also have to provide a 'cooling off period' of seven days, during which customers are allowed to change their minds and cancel orders. Also check out Food First (`www.foodfirst.co.uk`) for details and inspiration about the food industry.

M-commerce

The needs and habits of consumers drive what sells best online. These days, consumers are going online in many more ways than just sitting at a computer – that is, they're branching out from e-commerce to *m-commerce* (mobile commerce). Consumers are using their mobile phones, PDAs, and pocket computers to connect to cyberspace. Retailers are hungry to reach these new mediums any way they can; here are just three examples:

- ✔ Receiving an unsolicited text trying to sell you something is just as annoying as e-mail spam. So, what kinds of selling *do* work online? Here's an example: When Greg first got his spiffy new Web-enabled mobile phone, he thought it would be fun to get some gimmicks for the kids (at least, he told them the gimmicks were for them; they were for him, too). He went online and downloaded a ring tone that was available on his phone, and he later purchased a game that could be played on his phone as well. Companies like Jamster (`www.jamster.co.uk`) have made millions selling ringtones, mobile wallpaper, and games.

✔ With new and more powerful phones available, retailers have adapted and expanded what they sell through mobile technologies. On Dan's PDA, he surfs the Internet almost as easily as on his laptop. He can check out bargains at eBay.co.uk and shop online at Amazon.co.uk.

✔ M-commerce group Reporo (`www.reporo.co.uk`) has been going for a few years now. It lets you download Java-based software, which you can use to shop via your e-mail. Reporo has teamed up with a host of retailers, including Boots, Dominos Pizza, CD Wow, Firebox.com, and Game.

Companies selling software so that you can sell to mobile users are cropping up all over the place. One of the bigger ones, Bango (`www.bango.com`), has partnered with big mobile companies such as Vodafone, Orange, Telefonica, and O2 and can process micropayments through phone bills, premium SMS (text messages), and PayPal.

Adding Online Content and Commentary

Plenty of traditional publications have discovered that they can supplement home delivery and newsstand sales by providing some parts of their content online on a subscription-only basis. Typically, some content is available for free, while other stories are designated as *premium content,* made available only to subscribers who have paid to subscribe to the site and who can enter a valid username and password.

Book VII

Under-standing Web 2.0

The online versions of the *Economist* (`www.economist.com`) and *The Spectator* (`www.spectator.co.uk`) both have premium content that is available only to paying subscribers. However, more and more magazines are starting to offer extra content for free, reasoning that they'll make more money through advertising on a free Web site than through subscriptions on a paid-for model. For example, as we were writing this book, *The Guardian* had just announced that more of its content would be accessible for no charge.

Blogging to build your brand

People have been speaking their minds for fun and profit for as long as there have been media to broadcast their words. Think about famous orators like Socrates, Lenin, and Martin Luther King. What would they have done in the age of the Internet? They would have started their own blogs, that's what!

A *weblog* (*blog* for short) is a type of online journal or diary that can be frequently updated. Blogs can be about anything in particular or nothing at all: You can blog about your daily activities or travels and let your family and friends know what you've been up to lately, or you can get your views and opinions out in the world and develop a community of like-minded readers.

Many blogs consist of commentary by individuals who gather news items or cool Web pages and make them available to their friends (or strangers who happen upon their blogs). This vision, in fact, was the original idea behind blogs, and the concept followed by many of the most popular ones: highlighting little-known Web sites or articles or shops in the media that readers are too busy to visit, and providing alternative views and commentary about those Web sites, news stories, or other current events.

Is it really possible to make a living by blogging? It's certainly possible to supplement one's income this way. Andrew Sullivan, who writes Daily Dish (`www.andrewsullivan.com`) in the United States, one of the most popular blogs around, reported on his site that he was getting as many as 300,000 visitors each day in the days leading up to the presidential election of 2004, when dedicated readers like Greg were flocking to politically oriented blogs to get opinion and analysis. After the election, visits went down, but they still hit 100,000 a day. And Sullivan could proclaim in his blog that ad revenue from an advertising service that specialises in blogs, Blogads (`www.blogads.com`), was making it possible for him to continue.

Of course, the best bloggers are good writers and have special knowledge that is in demand. If you plan to make money through blogging, it's absolutely essential that you have something to say. People aren't going to flock to a site that talks about daily life in a boring way.

One of the most popular blogs around is by former Microsoft whiz kid Robert Scoble (`scobleizer.wordpress.com`). For many years, 'the Scobleizer' was as much a public face of Microsoft as Bill Gates, and his insights into technological developments fascinated many. The same could be said for Seth Goden (`sethgodin.typepad.com`) who talks about marketing strategies in an inventive and engaging way. His blog is read by most people in marketing who want to sharpen up their skills.

Finding your niche

Blogging, like anything on the Web, works when you identify a niche group and target that group by providing those people with content that they're likely to want. The challenge is finding something to say and putting time and energy into saying it on a regular basis. Although Greg has set up his own blog at `www.gregholden.com`, he finds it difficult to devote the time and commitment for daily contributions.

Yet, the most successful blogs seem to be ones that are created by people who are used to writing something every day, such as journalists. Dan writes a news blog on his Web site (`www.realbusiness.co.uk`); it's easy to find time when you're paid to do it! Academic faculty members who are published and well regarded in their fields also run popular blogs. Even CEOs are getting into it, although their position of responsibility makes their writing uncontroversial and therefore usually pretty boring.

What do you feel strongly about? What do you know well? Is there something you would love to communicate and discuss every day? If so, that's what you should use to organise your blog. A blog can be about anything you like – and we mean anything. A prime example: the Appliance Blog, in which an appliance repairman in Springfield, Oregon, provides a daily diary of his service calls and repairs. Along the way, he provides links to the Web sites of major appliance manufacturers as well as a forum where you can ask questions about your own appliance problems. The repairman's blog isn't a place where you can find out what he had for breakfast or what he thinks about world peace; it's focused solely on what he knows, and it's a useful resource for anyone who is having a problem with an appliance.

Starting a blog

How, exactly, do you start a blog? Most people sign up for an account with an online service that streamlines the process. Some of the best known are

- ✔ Blogger (`www.blogger.com`)
- ✔ Brit Journal (`www.brit-journal.com`)
- ✔ WordPress (`wordpress.org`)
- ✔ Typepad (`www.typepad.com`)

Book VII

Understanding Web 2.0

Before the year 2000, you had to be a programmer to figure out how to create a blog on your Web page. But a number of online services are available online to streamline the process for nonprogrammers. Blogger (`www.blogger.com`) lets you create your own blog for free, so it's a good place to start. Google owns Blogger, so the site enables you to participate in Google's AdWords program (see Chapter 13) as well, so you may gain some revenue from your blog. As with any Web-based content, you should do some planning and write down notes, such as

- ✔ A name for your blog
- ✔ What you want to talk about
- ✔ Some ideas for your first few blog entries

Then follow these steps:

1. **Start up your Web browser, go to the Blogger home page (`www.blogger.com`), and click Create Your Blog Now.**

   The Create Blogger Account page appears.

2. **Fill out the form with a username, password, and e-mail address; read the terms of service; select the Acceptance of Terms check box; and click Continue.**

   The Name Your Blog page appears.

3. **Come up with a short name for your blog; add that blog to the URL supplied and click Continue.**

   For example, if your blog is called ToolTime, your URL should be `tooltime.blogspot.com`.

   The Choose A Template page appears.

4. **Click the button beneath the graphic design (or template) you want to use and then click Continue.**

   A page appears with a light bulb icon and the notice Creating Your Blog. After a few seconds, a page appears with the notice Your Blog Has Been Created!

5. **Click Start Posting.**

   A page appears in which you type a title for your first posting and then type the posting itself (see Figure 1-2).

6. **Click the Publish Post button at the bottom of the page.**

   Your blog post is published online. That's all there is to it!

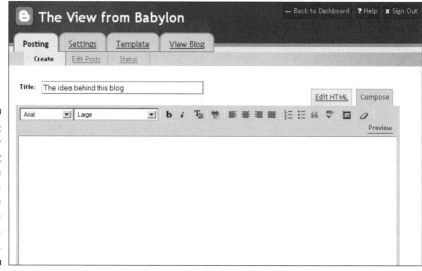

Figure 1-2: Blogger makes it easy to create a blog for free and give it a graphic design.

Building an audience

Blogs that are odd, quirky, based on dramatic human-interest situations such as wartime journals, or that are politically oriented tend to be the most successful. That said, here are some ways to build up an audience for your blog:

- **Writing for other bloggers:** Your first audience will probably consist of family or friends, or other bloggers who live in the same geographic area or write about the same subjects you do. Contact those bloggers and ask them to exchange links with your blog; ask your other readers to spread the word about your blog, too.

- **Sprinkling keywords and categories:** Blogs are like other Web pages: Although their contents change frequently, search engines index them. The more keywords you include in your postings and the greater the range of subjects you cover, the more likely you are to have your blog turn up in a set of search results.

- **Posting consistently:** When readers latch on to a blog they like, they visit it frequently. You need to post something – anything – on a daily basis, or at least several times a week.

- **Syndicating your blog:** One way of spreading the word about your blog is providing a 'feed' of its latest contents, such as the headings of posts and the dates of the latest posts. This summary is automatically prepared in XML (eXtensible Markup Language) by most blogging tools. You make the feed of your blog available on its home page; sites that aggregate (in other words, collect) the feeds from many of their favorite blogs can collect them and quickly know when the blogs have been updated.

 If you can make a living at blogging or at least end up with some fun money at the end of each month, more power to you. But don't go into blogging with that attitude, or you'll lose interest right away. Look at a blog as another tool in your online business arsenal – another way of getting your message before the public, another place where you can steer visitors to your Web site or your shop on eBay or Yahoo!. It makes sense to treat your blog as a venue where you talk about what you like to buy and sell online and to strike up ongoing conversations among your customers and clients. In other words, you don't generate income with a blog by selling directly to the public. You try to build up a number of loyal readers and attract advertising revenue – or simply attract more customers to your Web site.

Book VII

Under-standing Web 2.0

Building a Community

Studies consistently show that people who spend large amounts of time in community venues such as discussion forums end up spending money on the same Web site. (eBay is the perfect example.) It's a *value proposition,* but you can't attach a specific dollar value to it.

Community building on commercial Web sites doesn't necessarily involve discussion boards or chat rooms. Anything you can do to get your customers communicating with one another will do it. On Amazon.com, a kind of community feel is created by the book reviews written by individual readers, and Top 10 book lists let visitors share their views.

Partnerships

The notion of online community cuts both ways: It's not only for consumers who visit Web sites and join communities, but for businesspeople like you, too. Some of the liveliest and most popular online communities are eBay groups – discussion forums started by eBay members themselves. And among those, some of the most popular are the ones in which sellers share tips and advice about boosting their online incomes, finding merchandise to sell, identifying mystery items, and so on.

Don't forget that even though you may run a business by yourself from your home, you're not really alone. If you need some encouragement, join a discussion group, or consult the tips and resources in the Small Business Associations section of this book's Online Directory.

Market research

Given the sheer number of consumers who are on the Web, it stands to reason that you can find out a lot about those individuals by going online. If you don't have any awareness of who your potential customers are and what they want, you may never get them to pull out their credit cards. You can do your own market research by going online to find your customers, listen to their views in chat rooms and on discussion forums, and do some market research. Approach consumers who already buy the types of products or services that you want to sell.

Consult the Guerrilla Marketing books (gmarketing.com) for insights into different ways to reach your target consumers.

The other aspect of market research that is perfectly executed with a Web browser is research into your own online competitors – businesses that already do what you hope to do. It can be discouraging, at first, to discover companies that have already cleared the trail that you hoped to blaze. The chances of doing something absolutely unique on the Web are small, but use the discovery as an educational opportunity to find out whether a market exists for your product and a way to sell it that differs from existing competitors. Take note of features displayed by your competitors' Web sites, such as the following:

✔ **Selling:** How does the Web site do its selling? Does it sell only in one location, or does its Web site supplement eBay.co.uk or Amazon.co.uk sales or a brick-and-mortar business? Does the site make suggestions about related items that a consumer may want (a practice known as up-selling)?

✔ **Design:** How does the site look? Is it well put together? What makes it attractive and does it draw you in? It's not the same to ask, Is it pretty? Many ugly Web sites are also virtual gold mines.

✔ **Organisation:** How is the Web site organised? Is it easy to find specific products or information about them? How many navigational aids (navigation bars, drop-down menu lists, site maps, and the like) are provided?

✔ **Depth:** How many levels of information are included on the Web site? The more information is offered on the site, the *stickier* (more able to hold a visitor's attention) the site becomes. Try to imagine how your customers will react to the content on your Web site; are they encouraged to plough on, uncovering new content, or better yet click through to buy some of your stuff?

In your review of the competition's Web presentation, make a list of features that you can emulate as well as features you can improve on. Your goal should not be to copy the site, but to discover your own unique niche and identify customers whose needs may not be addressed by the other venue.

Don't you wish you could install a hidden microphone to eavesdrop on your customers as they surf the Web? You can do some eavesdropping, but on a different part of the Internet – namely, Usenet. *Usenet,* the part of the Internet that consists of thousands of newsgroups, is separate from the Web but can be accessed from the Web through sites such as `www.usenet.org.uk`. You can 'listen in' on newsgroup discussions by finding groups that fit your type of commerce and then *lurking* – that is, reading the messages without responding to them. After acquainting yourself with the group's concerns, you can post your own newsgroup messages and begin to determine your customers' concerns more directly. Keep in mind, though, that it's important to avoid overt advertising for your business in a newsgroup, which can provoke an angry response from the group's membership.

Book VII

Under-standing Web 2.0

Web 2.0 – What on Earth Does That Mean?

The phrase *Web 2.0* doesn't just mean the second generation of the Internet, although faster connections and greater bandwidth underpins it. In essence, Web 2.0 refers to the ability to collaborate and share information online, in a way that we weren't capable of doing just a few years ago.

Web 1.0 was all one-way traffic. A webmaster would stick something on a site, and you'd either read it or buy it. Now, users are demanding greater involvement in their Web experiences. They don't just want to look at Web sites, they want to help build them! Web sites like MySpace (www.myspace.com), Bebo (www.bebo.co.uk), Digger (www.digger.com), YouTube (www.youtube.com), and hundreds of others all rely on contributions from people like you and us to survive.

It all derives from people's desire to talk about themselves, or to put it another way, to be famous and respected. If you can offer this service to them in an innovative way, then you're bound to build traffic quickly. The great thing about Web 2.0 is that other people populate the site, so you need fewer resources to get the thing going. Bebo, for example, is rumoured to be worth more than £100 million, yet it employs just 12 staff members.

Web sites like Friends Reunited (www.friendsreunited.com) started the craze, by allowing people to write about themselves and seek out old pals. Other sites, such as Startups (www.startups.co.uk), set up forums so that users (in this case, startup businesses) could ask questions and chat about their experiences.

Wikis (Web sites that allow anyone to add their content), *social bookmarking* (the act of bookmarking your favourite Web sites for other like-minded people to share), *podcasting* (downloading audio files), and *vodcasting* (the same but for visual files) have developed from this trend. Now sites from the BBC to Google and Amazon use these cool tools.

The most famous example of a Wiki is Wikipedia.com, which has 5 million pages of content contributed by the public. The Web site is an encyclopaedia of people's knowledge, and despite the fact that anyone can edit it, it's almost totally accurate.

Pod and vodcasting are expensive and certainly don't suit all businesses. A few companies offer to film or tape things for you and convert the information into a downloadable file for your Web site, but it can cost hundreds of pounds a time.

If you want to learn more about what Web 2.0 really means, check out this short essay by Internet expert Tim O'Reilly. It's a nice comprehensive overview of what you need to know:

www.oreillynet.com/pub/a/oreilly/tim/news/2005/09/30/what-is-web-20.html

Chapter 2

The Emergence of Web 2.0

*W*eb 2.0 is the name digital specialists are using to categorise the second boom in the popularity and usage of the Internet – both for consumers and big business.

When the first dotcom bubble burst in early 2000, pessimism abounded about the long-term future of both the Internet and the impact it was having on our lives. Big business became anti-Web and a lot of the big dotcom projects were either mothballed, went bust, or were left to carry on with very little financial backing. A few notable exceptions existed, such as Amazon and eBay, which, having built up flourishing businesses, were able to ride the storm. The big companies had their fingers badly burnt – some watched £100 million valuations turn into £1 valuations overnight – and lost interest in the Web. Consumers, however, had well and truly caught the Web bug and carried on not only using it, but using it more and more. With the advent of broadband, consumer take-up of the Internet has exploded, with most of the country now 'wired', and accessing the Web at least once a day, at work or at home. Web 2.0 is intended to signify this constant reliance on the Internet and the fact that thanks to broadband, the Web's now a much more useful and engaging place.

Grasping the Basics of Web 2.0

The early phases of Internet development – retrospectively named Web 1.0 – were all about its 'wow' factor: Web 2.0 is all about its 'lifestyle' factor as the Web becomes a vital part of all of our lives. Our explanation of Web 2.0 concerns the lifestyle angle anyway but as with all things Internet-related, what it actually means is a topic of hot debate, one which you can follow on the Web site of the company that claims to have been the first to use the term: www.oreillynet.com/pub/a/oreilly/tim/news/2005/09/30/what-is-web-20.html.

Undoubtedly, the advent of Web 2.0, in 2005, led to a reawakening of interest in the Web from big business. Digital is 'cool' again and companies now demand to know how to use the Web to best connect with their customers.

Perhaps the best example of the world's biggest companies once again investing heavily in the Web as they try and play catch up is the case of MySpace, which we cover in more detail in the 'Understanding the MySpace Generation' section, later in this chapter.

Originally set up as a chat room for college kids in the US to communicate with each other, MySpace (see Figure 2-1) has become a global phenomenon and has created a whole new buzz phrase – *social networking*. MySpace's rise to global fame was cemented when Rupert Murdoch's News Corporation bought it in 2005 for £318 million. In the UK alone, it has over 3.5 million users.

MySpace's formula for success was very simple: Build an easy-to-use site, which its users could personalise and in which they could add their own areas; launch it with a *viral* and buzz marketing campaign – depending on users to pass on the marketing material by e-mail – and then encourage all its users to tell all their friends about it, thus building one of the world's biggest virtual communities.

Figure 2-1:
The MySpace homepage is a gateway to a vast virtual community.

Web 2.0 has three key factors relating to how people use the Internet: community, communication, and content:

- **Community:** The community aspect of Web 2.0 is all about using the Web to manage your social and professional networks and expressing your likes and dislikes via Web sites – just as hundreds of thousands of people are doing with MySpace.

- **Communication:** People have been using the Internet to communicate since the very early days of the Web, but now broadband is enabling more advanced communication and participation through video messaging via Instant Messenger and telephone calls over the Internet with services such as Skype.

- **Content:** Again, content is not new to the Web but now a number of content-based services exist that encourage the individual to self-publish. Numerous video sharing sites are available, such as www.youtube.com. These sites have sought to harness user-generated content by asking people to send in videos of themselves doing funny – and some not so funny – things, which other people then send on in their thousands.

Web publishing tools are also launching en-masse to help even the least technology-literate person not only write content for the Web but even build their own Web log – or *blog*. Blogging has opened up Web publishing to the masses.

Book VII

Under-standing Web 2.0

Understanding Blogging

Blogging is a way of recording thoughts, collecting links, and sharing ideas with other people via a very simple Web site. In effect, blogs are online journals for individuals or organisations and currently a blogging craze is sweeping the world, with millions of people writing blogs on a daily basis. In April 2006, more than 35 million blogs existed around the world, with a new one being launched every second according to the blogging search engine, technorati (www.technorati.com).

According to blogger.com, which is owned by Google,

> *A blog is a personal diary. A daily pulpit. A collaborative space. A political soapbox. A breaking-news outlet. A collection of links. Your own private thoughts. Memos to the world.*

Blogging is now massively popular in the UK, providing some of the best-known political blogs, such as Guido Fawkes at 5thnovember.blogspot.com, or the daily musings of a Saville Row Taylor, www.englishcut.com. Everyone's blogging, from David Cameron to London Underground tube drivers.

As blogging is often done on an anonymous basis, it has become a whistle-blower's paradise and an easy source of stories for journalists, who are turning to the *blogosphere* – as the blogging world is known – in droves.

Blogs can also turn their authors into mini-celebrities. Guido Fawkes – although remaining anonymous – is now a journalists' and politicians' daily must-read.

Getting started in the blogosphere

Blogging is very simple and after you get started, you can update your blog as often as you like. Bear in mind, though, that if you want people to keep coming back to look at your blog you need to keep it up to date, interesting, and relevant. Boring blogs are a turn-off.

Lots of blogging tools exist to help you get started but perhaps the best-known are Blogger.com, Wordpress, and Typepad. As Blogger is perhaps the best-known, we use this tool as the example (see Figure 2-2). If you want to use another tool though, just do a quick search on Google and you'll be presented with a multitude of options.

Figure 2-2:
The Blogger homepage provides an easy guide to publishing your blog online.

Not all blogging tools are free. Blogger is, but others aren't and will charge you a monthly or annual subscription. Because moving your blog from one tool to another isn't easy, make your decision carefully.

Getting started with Blogger is a simple three-step process:

1. **Type in** www.blogger.com **to your browser and click on the button 'Create your blog now'.** Page one will ask you to choose a user name, a password, to give your e-mail address, and to accept its terms of service.

2. **Click 'Next' and you'll be asked to give a name to your blog – for example, 'Accidental Observer'.** Choose the Web address (for example, accidentalobserver.blogspot.com).

3. **Click 'Next' for the last time and choose your template.** You have lots of different colours, or *skins* as they're known, to choose from. After you choose your template you're ready to blog and have become the world's latest blogger!

To actually write a post, you need to access your *dashboard,* which includes basic word editing tools and also gives you the ability to upload images into your blog. From there you just type what you want and then click 'Publish' to make it go live. The beauty of blogs is that you can make them as simple or as complicated as you like and can add pictures, video, and music all at the touch of a button. Hundreds of thousands of people use Blogger to publish blogs, so if you want any tips or hints use the message boards and help sections to get going.

Getting your blog seen

With so many blogs being launched, taking some basic steps to ensure that people can find yours is important. Firstly, make sure that what you're writing about is likely to be interesting to someone out there. Your content can range from gardening tips to disclosing complicated scientific formulae. The key to a successful blog is that someone somewhere wants to read it. Secondly, when asked by Blogger during the set-up, make sure that your blog is visible to Google and other search engines. Finally, and perhaps most importantly, to keep people coming back and to attract new visitors, keep updating your site. And don't be afraid to self-promote your blog to your friends or colleagues or by advertising it at the bottom of your e-mail or by linking to it from a Web site – if you already have one. Just taking some basic steps like these means you'll have traffic from day one. But as with all things, if you leave the blog and don't update it, people won't come and check it out.

Book VII

Under-standing Web 2.0

Maintaining a company blog

Blogging mania isn't limited to individuals. A number of the biggest companies in the UK are now using blogs to communicate with their customers – with varying degrees of success – including Guinness, Honda, and BT. These blogs are known as corporate blogs. The Guinness blog (`www.guinnessblog.co.uk`) is perhaps the most engaging of these because the content's written by the black stuff's marketing team and gives Guinness fans a behind-the-scenes look into how the blog is produced and how the adverts are made. As more and more companies are starting to view blogging as a crucial communications tool, you need to follow a few guidelines to ensure that your company gets the most out of blogging.

- ✔ Be open and honest. Hiding the truth on the Internet is impossible and if you try and mislead consumers via your blog you'll get heavily criticised, or *flamed* as the experience is known in blogland.

- ✔ Keep your blog up to date, relevant, and interesting.

- ✔ Be clear what the aims of your blog are from the outset and stick to them.

- ✔ Do let bloggers comment on what you write and make sure that you don't overreact if and when they post anything negative about your company.

- ✔ If negative posts do appear, react in a balanced, open, and honest way. Blogs are a very useful way of 'getting your point of view across'.

- ✔ Avoid 'corporate speak'.

- ✔ Don't try and sell to your customers. Blogs should be about commentary and observations, not product details or hard sell.

- ✔ Make sure that only one or two people are blogging on behalf of the company otherwise the content becomes confused and inconsistent.

Bloggers hate being sold to, and react badly to companies that try and do that – especially by subversive means. See the sidebar 'When it all goes Bang' for an example of how such subversive blogging can backfire.

Mastering Podcasting

Unless you've been living on a different planet recently then you'll have heard of *podcasting*. Podcasting is a way of subscribing to and receiving popular content such as radio shows from the Internet and then either playing them on your computer or on your iPod. Like blogging, podcasting is becoming a craze and is hugely popular amongst Net-savvy teenagers.

Podcasting is being mentioned everywhere, and is fast establishing itself as the best way of getting either audio or visual content from the Web.

Comedian Ricky Gervais's podcast has been downloaded more than 5 million times and is the most popular one in the UK. Other popular podcasts include those made by Radio 1 DJs like Chris Moyles and Scott Mills and the Baddiel and Skinner podcast during the World Cup in Germany in 2006.

If you download podcasts and a subscription option is offered, take it – your computer will then automatically check for updates and download the latest podcasts if you're already subscribed.

Podcast files on a computer are exactly the same as digital music files, normally MP3 format, and can be transferred and played on most players. Video podcasts are also starting to be introduced by companies such as Apple, which has just launched a film download service.

Podcasting is not quite as simple as blogging and does require some level of expertise if you want to use it. Some companies now offer their AGM or annual results via podcasts online, but the main use for the medium continues to be entertainment.

If you want to get involved in podcasting, check out this site, which gives you some tips on how to get started: `podcasts.yahoo.com/publish`.

Networking with the MySpace Generation

If you have teenage kids then you probably know about MySpace – the Web site that has revolutionised the way people (children and students in particular) use the Internet. MySpace is made up of millions of profiles crafted by individuals to tell the rest of the world about themselves. Some profiles are very basic while others have obviously taken hours to design. MySpace is so big that a whole new cottage industry has sprung up giving MySpace users the tools to redesign and build their own profiles. Just do a quick search on Google and you'll see how many Web sites are selling MySpace materials. MySpace has also become a unique marketing tool for unsigned bands, with one band in particular, The Arctic Monkeys, famous for having used it to get people to listen to their music and talk about them.

No chapter on Web 2.0 is complete without a look at MySpace, as not only has it had a major impact on how people use the Internet but it has also helped to develop a whole new type of Web site – a social network – of which hundreds are launching all the time. The MySpace generation are typically aged between about 12 and 24. They're spending less time watching TV and a lot more time surfing the Internet and sites like MySpace. A recent UK government survey found that over 70 per cent of this age group visit and use social networks, while a third are bloggers or run their own message boards.

MySpace is actually a whole new group of Web sites, which young people regularly visit and share with their mates. If you want to develop digital marketing, you need to know about these sites. They include www.youtube.com, detailed earlier in this chapter; www.bebo.com, another social network, which is competing with www.myspace.com but has more of a UK audience because you have to sign up based on what school you go to; www.flickr.com, where you can host and share photos; and http://del.icio.us/, which enables you to store all your favourite bits of Web content and access them from any computer or device. All these sites have the basic Web 2.0 principles at their heart – community, communication, and content – and are fast becoming some of the most popular Web sites in the world.

From a marketing perspective, knowing how to take advantage of the Web 2.0 opportunity is very difficult and some companies are doing it better than others.

A lot of companies are looking at how to build communities for their customers – again, some more successfully than others.

The marketing advantages for tapping into a community are pretty clear. You get a ready made, extremely active audience who are aged primarily between 16 and 24 – that dream age group for all marketers. In theory, you can use communities like MySpace to build your own branded environments letting the site's users come and see what you have to offer through your community. But the reality is very different. Only brands that have a right to be in the community (for example, music acts or films) can really make community work because let's be honest, as a consumer you are much more likely to go to the Web site of your favourite band than you are to a soap powder community! However, advertisers can and do add value, normally where they offer members of the community something they can't get elsewhere (for example, behind-the-scenes clips of the film or interviews with the band). This sort of added-value marketing is becoming increasingly popular and is known as *engagement marketing*.

Content is another area that brands are looking to exploit through the creation of their own films or viral clips – video clips that can be forwarded to friends for their amusement, which are then distributed through Web sites such as YouTube (www.youtube.com).

Nike has been particularly successful using this tactic, distributing clips of some of the footballers it backs, including Ronaldinho, across the video-sharing sites. These have then been accessed by hundreds of thousands of people.

If you want to take advantage of the change in how people are using the Internet, talking to the experts before trying to launch your own community or viral is worthwhile. Anything which is hastily done can reflect badly on your brand and can even annoy your customers. So, if you have one, speak to your digital agency and ask them what they think the opportunities are; if you don't have an agency, speak to a digital consultant who knows what works online and what doesn't.

Book VII

Under-standing Web 2.0

Index

• P •

• **Q** •

FOR

DUMMIES

Do Anything. Just Add Dummies

UK editions

PROPERTY

Buying and Selling a Home
978-0-7645-7027-8

Renting Out Your Property
978-0-470-02921-3

Buying a Property in Eastern Europe
978-0-7645-7047-6

PERSONAL FINANCE

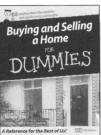

Investing
978-0-7645-7023-0

Personal Finance & Investing
978-0-470-51510-5

Bookkeeping
978-0-470-05815-2

BUSINESS

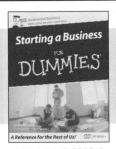

Starting a Business
978-0-7645-7018-6

Marketing
978-0-7645-7056-8

Business Plans
978-0-7645-7026-1

Answering Tough Interview Questions For Dummies
(978-0-470-01903-0)

Arthritis For Dummies
(978-0-470-02582-6)

Being the Best Man For Dummies
(978-0-470-02657-1)

British History For Dummies
(978-0-470-03536-8)

Building Self-Confidence For Dummies
(978-0-470-01669-5)

Buying a Home on a Budget For Dummies
(978-0-7645-7035-3)

Children's Health For Dummies
(978-0-470-02735-6)

Cognitive Behavioural Therapy For Dummies
(978-0-470-01838-5)

Cricket For Dummies
(978-0-470-03454-5)

CVs For Dummies
(978-0-7645-7017-9)

Detox For Dummies
(978-0-470-01908-5)

Diabetes For Dummies
(978-0-470-05810-7)

Divorce For Dummies
(978-0-7645-7030-8)

DJing For Dummies
(978-0-470-03275-6)

eBay.co.uk For Dummies
(978-0-7645-7059-9)

English Grammar For Dummies
(978-0-470-05752-0)

Gardening For Dummies
(978-0-470-01843-9)

Genealogy Online For Dummies
(978-0-7645-7061-2)

Green Living For Dummies
(978-0-470-06038-4)

Hypnotherapy For Dummies
(978-0-470-01930-6)

Life Coaching For Dummies
(978-0-470-03135-3)

Neuro-linguistic Programming For Dummies
(978-0-7645-7028-5)

Nutrition For Dummies
(978-0-7645-7058-2)

Parenting For Dummies
(978-0-470-02714-1)

Pregnancy For Dummies
(978-0-7645-7042-1)

Rugby Union For Dummies
(978-0-470-03537-5)

Self Build and Renovation For Dummies
(978-0-470-02586-4)

Starting a Business on eBay.co.uk For Dummies
(978-0-470-02666-3)

Starting and Running an Online Business For Dummies
(978-0-470-05768-1)

The GL Diet For Dummies
(978-0-470-02753-0)

The Romans For Dummies
(978-0-470-03077-6)

Thyroid For Dummies
(978-0-470-03172-8)

UK Law and Your Rights For Dummies
(978-0-470-02796-7)

Writing a Novel and Getting Published For Dummies
(978-0-470-05910-4)

FOR DUMMIES®

Do Anything. Just Add Dummies

HOBBIES

Poker
978-0-7645-5232-8

Sewing
978-0-7645-6847-3

Drawing
978-0-7645-5476-6

Also available:

Art For Dummies
(978-0-7645-5104-8)

Aromatherapy For Dummies
(978-0-7645-5171-0)

Bridge For Dummies
(978-0-471-92426-5)

Card Games For Dummies
(978-0-7645-9910-1)

Chess For Dummies
(978-0-7645-8404-6)

Improving Your Memory
For Dummies
(978-0-7645-5435-3)

Massage For Dummies
(978-0-7645-5172-7)

Meditation For Dummies
(978-0-471-77774-8)

Photography For Dummies
(978-0-7645-4116-2)

Quilting For Dummies
(978-0-7645-9799-2)

EDUCATION

Cooking Basics
978-0-7645-7206-7

The Koran
978-0-7645-5581-7

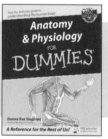

Anatomy & Physiology
978-0-7645-5422-3

Also available:

Algebra For Dummies
(978-0-7645-5325-7)

Algebra II For Dummies
(978-0-471-77581-2)

Astronomy For Dummies
(978-0-7645-8465-7)

Buddhism For Dummies
(978-0-7645-5359-2)

Calculus For Dummies
(978-0-7645-2498-1)

Forensics For Dummies
(978-0-7645-5580-0)

Islam For Dummies
(978-0-7645-5503-9)

Philosophy For Dummies
(978-0-7645-5153-6)

Religion For Dummies
(978-0-7645-5264-9)

Trigonometry For Dummies
(978-0-7645-6903-6)

PETS

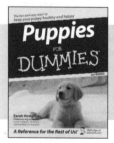

Puppies
978-0-470-03717-1

Dog Training
978-0-7645-8418-3

Cats
978-0-7645-5275-5

Also available:

Labrador Retrievers
For Dummies
(978-0-7645-5281-6)

Aquariums For Dummies
(978-0-7645-5156-7)

Birds For Dummies
(978-0-7645-5139-0)

Dogs For Dummies
(978-0-7645-5274-8)

Ferrets For Dummies
(978-0-7645-5259-5)

Golden Retrievers
For Dummies
(978-0-7645-5267-0)

Horses For Dummies
(978-0-7645-9797-8)

Jack Russell Terriers
For Dummies
(978-0-7645-5268-7)

Puppies Raising & Training
Diary For Dummies
(978-0-7645-0876-9)

Available wherever books are sold. For more information or to order direct go to www.wiley.com or call 0800 243407 (Non UK call +44 1243 843296)

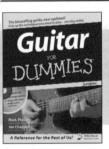

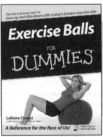

FOR

DUMMIES®

Helping you expand your horizons and achieve your potential

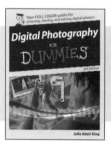